U0636219

国家社科基金
GUOJIA SHEKE JIJIN HOUQI ZIZHU XIANGMU
后期资助项目

袁同礼年谱长编

Yuan Tongli: A Chronicle

三

雷　强　撰

中華書局
ZHONGHUA BOOK COMPANY

一九四一年　四十七岁

一月初

先生由重庆出发飞抵香港，将奉令赴美。〔《中华图书馆协会会报》第 15 卷第 3-4 合期，1941 年 2 月，页 11、15〕

按：行前，先生命平馆将馆藏部分西文期刊移送重庆寄存南开大学经济研究所（求精中学），并在此设驻渝办事处。昆明所存重要书籍疏散到北郊桃源村，并请胡英回馆服务，暂代行馆务。

先生致信王伯祥，请其撰写抗战爆发后上海出版界概况，并请拣选开明书店出版的精品用以携带至美国展示、宣传。〔《王伯祥日记》第 17 册，页 33、26〕

按：此信由钱存训代转，于 17 日送达，王伯祥当日即覆。本月 12 日，钱存训赴开明书店，将先生赴美计划告知，并拣选出版品，王伯祥选定《新元史》《师石山房丛书》。

先生致信平馆驻沪办事处，请派人至开明书店，商洽出版《国学论文索引五编》。

按：22 日，陈贯吾往开明书店与王伯祥洽询。〔《王伯祥日记》第 17 册，页 42〕

一月四日

先生致信 Charles C. Williamson，告知即将访美，并请其赐赠哥伦比亚大学图书馆年度报告。

January 4, 1941

Dear Dr. Williamson:

During my last trip to the United States the new library of Columbia University, then under construction, was perhaps the most impressive structure in the academic world which has lingered in my mind all these years. For several times I have been hoping to take a short trip to America in order to be able to visit my Alma Mater which has been a source of encouragement and inspiration to my work in China. Since I have been tied up with various duties in China, I have been obliged to postpone my trip until this year.

I am glad to inform you that I expect to visit the United States shortly on a cultural mission, so I am looking forward with keen pleasure to seeing you as well as all the members of my Alma Mater. I shall arrive sometime in March and shall remain in the States for half a year.

As I have not seen your report ending June 30th, 1940, will you kindly send me a copy care of Miss Sophia Han, 1716 Hunnewell Street, Honolulu, T. H.

With sincere greetings of the Season and with my best personal regards to you and Miss Sanderson,

Yours sincerely,

T. L. Yuan

Director

〔平馆(冯平山图书馆转)英文信纸。Columbia University Library, New York State Library School Collection, Series 2 Student Records, Box 65, Folder Yuan, T. L.〕

按:Miss Sophia Han 应指韩权华(1903—1985),曾在北京大学、女子师范大学读书,后赴美留学,经杨步伟推荐前往檀香山教书。① 此件为打字稿,落款处为先生签名,于2月11日送达。

一月八日　香港

晚,许地山、周俟松夫妇在罗便臣道面壁斋设宴,柳亚子、马鉴、冼玉清、陈君葆、叶恭绰、先生和陈寅恪、唐筼夫妇受邀与席。〔《传记文学》第88卷第5期,页103〕

鲍曼致电先生,告中国纪念堂内部所需装饰物的最大尺寸。

UNIVERSITY WELCOMES MISSION OFFERS HOSPITALITY AND

① 参见 Ch'en Shou-yi Papers, Box 1, Folder 3, Item 10.

SCIENTIFIC CONTACTS ROOM NEEDS ANTIQUE WALL HANGING ANY DOMINANT COLOR EXCEPT RED ALSO ANTIQUE LACQUER CABINET OR CHEST MAXIMUM DIMENSIONS HEIGHT TWO FEET SIX INCHES LENGTH SIX FEET

BOWMAN

〔University of Pittsburgh Library, John Gabbert Bowman, Administrative Files, Box 2 Folder 13, Chinese Material〕

按:该件为录副,有铅笔标注。

一月九日

下午六时,先生以平馆馆长身份在香港电台广播中作演讲,主题为"三年来我国科学家之贡献"。〔《大公报》(香港),1941 年 1 月 10 日,第 6 版〕

一月十日

先生致信鲍曼,告知访美计划略作推迟并请其寄送中国纪念堂内部照片。

January 10, 1941

Dear Chancellor:

I thank you very sincerely for your telegram of January 8th.

I have postponed my trip until the end of February so there is plenty of time for you to communicate with me before my departure from Hongkong.

Among other things, I would like to have a photograph showing the interior of the China Memorial Room in the Cathedral of Learning, so that it would give me some idea of the contents as well as your arrangement.

I hope to receive the photograph as soon as you are able to send it.

With kindest regards,

Yours sincerely,

T. L. Yuan

Director

〔平馆(冯平山图书馆转)英文信纸。University of Pittsburgh Library, John Gabbert Bowman, Administrative Files, Box 2 Folder 13, Chinese Material〕

按:此件为打字稿,落款处为先生签名,以航空信方式寄送。

一月十三日

Marshall C. Balfour 覆函先生，告知已为先生预订船位，并谈其最近行程计划。

January 13, 1941

Dear Mr. Yuan:

Your letter of January 9 and two of the 10th, arrived today. As requested, I have gotten in touch with the American Express, Manila, and they advise that they are holding a First-class reservation for you on the S. S. KLIPFONTEIN, but will substitute Tourist-class, if a place becomes available. This ship is now late returning from the West Coast, and it is not unlikely that its departure will be later then February 24.

My present plans are to leave Manila on the S. S. PRESIDENT COOLIDGE February 19, due Hong Kong on the 21st. I am booked for the C. N. A. C. early morning of the 22nd to Chungking. If the COOLIDGE should be delayed, I will either fly on the 27th from Hong Kong, or plan an earlier arrival in Hong Kong by Clipper. Although the connection may be close and time limited, I assume that it will be sufficient for such consultations as we may have. On the other hand, it appears that we might miss each other, so I am hopeful that you can plan your arrival in Manila before the 19th, unless the known schedule of the S. S. KLIPFONTEIN is such that you can await me in Hong Kong. I will pass on any news which I obtain, and trust that you will keep me informed of your plans.

Although the remark is probably unnecessary, I assume that your travel to the U. S. is not concerned with our grant to the National Library. To avoid misunderstanding, I merely observe my lack of authorization to deal with such a question, which would require consultation with New York.

I have noted your arrangements with the Chinese Red Cross regarding transportation. Shipment of the Medical literature has been ordered by cable and we will use R. J. Holmes, Lashio, as an agent, pending your final arrangements. Such material will probably not reach Lashio before your service is ready to handle it. I will expect to hear again regarding the order and arrangements for Kweiyang, following your further steps with Dr. C. U. Lee.

Very truly yours,

M. C. Balfour

〔Rockefeller Foundation. Series 601: China; Subseries 601.R: China-Humanities and Arts. Vol. Box 47. Folder 390〕

按:Lashio 即缅甸腊戌;Dr. C. U. Lee 即李宗恩(Chung-un Lee, 1894-1962),江苏武进人,热带病学医学家及医学教育家,1947年担任北平协和医学院院长。

一月十八日

中午十二时,北京大学旅港同学会假大道中华人行九楼大华饭店举行理事会议并聚餐。陈友琴、黄铁铮为主,先生、陈寅恪为客。〔《大公报》(香港),1941年1月18日,第6版〕

按:此次宴请极有可能是欢送先生赴美宣传、陈寅恪赴英讲学。

一月二十日

先生撰写 A Tentative Memorandum, Re The Sino-American Cultural Exchange。〔台北胡适纪念馆,档案编号 HS-JDSHSE-0486-013〕

一月二十一日

先生致信史蒂文斯,告知自己即将前往美国为两国文化事业交流服务,将特别携带中国自九世纪至十九世纪的印刷品、抗战以来的科学出版物赴美展出。

January 21, 1941

Dear Stevens:

In spite of my long silence, you have been constantly in my thoughts. As I am coming to the States very soon, I am looking forward with keen pleasure to seeing you as well as other officials of your Foundation.

In 1934 and again in 1936 I recommended two applicants for fellowships in library service. Since then, I have refrained from doing so, partly because of the interruptions caused by the war and partly because of the fact that qualified men were either not easily available or could not be spared. As China is now engaged in economic and cultural reconstruction, we are in urgent need of your Foundation in the training of personnel in library service as well as in museum work.

Owing to the over-emphasis on the training of engineers and practical men by the Chinese government, there has been an utter neglect of trained personnel in the field of humanities. It is therefore natural that all of us who are engaged in cultural work are counting upon you for further assistance.

One of the objects of my trip is to endeavor to facilitate cultural interchange and dissemination between our two countries by organizing a Sino-American Cultural Exchange whose business would be to ensure the speedy transmission not only of printed matter between libraries, but also cultural material between museums. At a time when the whole world is engaged in armament and national defense, I doubt whether this is an opportune moment to present such a proposal to the American public. However, I shall prepare a short memorandum which I hope to submit to you very shortly.

I hope to be able to attend the annual conferences of the American Library Association and the American Association of Museums in order to meet my old friends and colleagues interested in the promotion of Sino-American cultural relations.

I am bringing with me 100 specimen copies of Chinese printing showing the development of printing art in China from the 9th to the 19th century. I shall also bring over a number of scientific publications issued in China since the war. I hope to arrange an exhibition of these specimens in order to show the American public what we have been doing in the midst of an armed invasion.

Among other things I should like very much to make a survey of Chinese materials available for research in American institutions, so I hope to be able to visit all centres of Chinese studies. I shall be very grateful to you if your office could inform them of my forthcoming visit and if possible, prepare a tentative itinerary for me. You can get in touch with me through my cousin Miss Sophia Han care of the Oriental Institute, University of Hawaii, as I expect to arrive at Honolulu after March 9th.

Looking forward to seeing you and with my very best personal regards,

Yours sincerely,

T. L. Yuan

Director

〔平馆（冯平山图书馆转）英文信纸。Rockefeller Foundation. Series 601: China; Subseries 601.R: China-Humanities and Arts. Vol. Box 47. Folder 390〕

按：100 specimen copies of Chinese printing 即后来由美国使领馆寄出的两箱善本书。此件为打字稿，落款处为先生签名。

先生致信 Marshall C. Balfour，告知自己预计二月十七日前往马尼拉。〔Rockefeller Foundation. Series 601: China; Subseries 601.R: China-Humanities and Arts. Vol. Box 47. Folder 390〕

一月二十三日

先生致信陈立夫，禀告平馆南迁善本书运美困难和后续计划，并谈赴美工作设想，请教育部给予"考察文化事业"名义，以利开展活动。

立夫部长尊鉴：

上月离渝来港，适钧座赴蓉，未能一望颜色。曾将移运存书困难情形及赴美计划托一樵次长代为转达，谅荷鉴察。存书以美方不肯负责代运，迁延至今。除遵嘱陆续化整为零外，拟俟卡尔大使抵港与之商洽、另筹办法，一俟稍有头绪再行奉闻。关于抵美后之工作，部中曾嘱多为青年学者觅得出国研究机会，并代征集图书、仪器及收音机等，自当勉力为之。此外，拟获得美方之援助，组织一中美文化交换，先从小规模入手，逐渐扩充，奉上节略草案一件，尚希时赐指示，俾有遵循。如能由部中予以考察文化事业名义，则接洽一切较为便利，是否有当，并恳尊裁为感。在出国以前,馆务均已布置妥切,并拟调王重民君返国代为主持馆务,一俟职馆委员会予以同意外,自当另行呈报。先此,敬候道祺。

职袁同礼谨上

一月廿三日

顾、余次长同此致意。

香港通讯处:香港冯平山图书馆转交。

〔台北"国家发展委员会档案管理局",〈国际文化合作——美国〉,档号 A309000000E/0030/640.66/0001〕

按:该信附 3 页备忘录,题为 A Tentative Memorandum, The Sino-American Cultural Exchange,似于 2 月 4 日送达教育部。先生赴美计划彻底落空后,教育部于 7 月改派郭任远赴美接洽中美文化合作事宜。

先生致信平馆委员会委员,请中基会补助购书款并拟与美国大学图书馆交换书籍办法。

径启者,查本馆经费向由中华教育文化基金董事会按期拨付。自庚款停付以来,该会重要经费来源因之断绝,更无力拨付美金,以致本馆购西文书报之款不得不另外设法。而年来物价狂涨异于寻常,该会每年所拨之各项经费均感不敷分配,故三载以还,无论中文书、西文书、印刷费、经常费均赖罗氏基金会之补助,馆务始能勉强维持。此项补助费将于本年六月期满,在未申请之前不得不略事联络,以期继续。兹拟请假壹年赴美接洽,用特将拟进行各事分列如左:

一、代青年学者觅得出国研究之旅费及奖学金。

二、代教育部募集图书、仪器及收音机等。

以上系教育部委托之件。

三、代本馆筹募经费尤注意出版费及西文购书费。

四、组织中美文化交换协助国内各大学附英文节略。

根据本馆与美国学术界之已往关系,以上各项计划似不难实现。又念十载以来,日本在美国各大学中所用文化宣传之费为数不赀。而我国仅知向人索书请款,始终一毫不拔,此次孔院长虽拨给国币壹万元,嘱购书籍分赠各大学,但数目甚微,深感不敷分配。查本馆年来受赠之书，其价值已逾美金数万元。亟应仿效日人之办法，赠送书籍以资交换，尤应高瞻远瞩，俾将来更可得大量之援助。兹拟办法两条，敬希采纳：

一、选美国各大学赠本馆书籍最多者，每处赠予价值国币叁千元之新书作为第一次之交换，并注意地域之分配，如东部为 Columbia、Harvard、Yale、Princeton，中部为 Chicago、Michigan，西部为 California、Hawaii，俾能普及而受效本馆西文购书费按国币拨付，则在中国市场购买新书籍以换取西文书报，似为极合理之办法。

二、同礼到美考察后，如发现有新中心点愿与本馆大量交换书籍者，拟即通知会计拨款购书用作交换，但每处以不超过国币叁千元，而总额又不超过本馆预算为限。在请假赴美公干期内，拟调王重民君返国代为主持馆务，王君在青年学者中为最有希望之人，与馆中又有长久之历史，必能胜任逾快。又同礼鉴于本馆经费之困难，在出国期中拟不支领薪水，惟赴美旅费拟请酌予补助美金六百元，此款既不便在罗氏基金补助费内拨付，应请本馆存款内另行设法，俾能早日成行。敢布区区，即希鉴核示复为荷。此上

国立北平图书馆委员会

袁同礼谨启

一月二十三日

〔《胡适遗稿及秘藏书信》第 31 册，页 625－626〕

按：英文节略应即同日致陈立夫信中的 A Tentative Memorandum, The Sino-American Cultural Exchange。傅斯年、蒋梦麟等人均收到此信及其附上的英文节略，后者将此件以航空信方式转寄胡适，略晚于 3 月 22 日送达。[1]

一月二十五日

Marshall C. Balfour 覆函先生，告知将在马尼拉等候先生，并介绍菲律宾大学校长。

January 25, 1941

Dear Mr. Yuan,

---

① 台北胡适纪念馆，档案编号 HS-JDSHSC-1635-003，该件华盛顿收讫的邮戳时间为 3 月 22 日。

From your letter of January 21, I have noted with satisfaction that you expect to arrive in Manila on the PRESIDENT COOLIDGE about February 17. I will be on the look-out for you and if I do not see you at the pier, you will find that our office is just a few steps from the landing.

I know Dr. Gonzales, President of the U. of the Philippines, quite well. I will inform him of your coming and will be glad to provide the introduction.

I am forwarding your letter to Mr. Stevens as requested, having noted the various points of interest. I am sure that Mr. Stevens will be keenly interested in its contents.

Very truly yours,

M. C. Balfour

〔Rockefeller Foundation. Series 601: China; Subseries 601.R: China-Humanities and Arts. Vol. Box 47. Folder 390〕

按:此件为录副。

一月二十七日

鲍曼覆函先生,寄上中国纪念室照片及描述文字,并询问先生抵达匹兹堡时间及随行人员数量。

January 27, 1941

Dear Dr. Yuan:

I have your kind note of January 10. Enclosed herewith I am sending you a picture of the China Memorial Room and some description of the room which was used in the program at the time of the dedication. We have a more complete description in preparation.

It gives me pleasure to ask that you and the members of your mission be my guests while you are in Pittsburgh. I should like to arrange for your care, either at the University Club or at the Schenley Hotel. At your convenience, please let me know the time of your arrival and the number to be in the party.

It will give me real pleasure to see you again. In the meantime, here are all best wishes to you.

Faithfully yours,

〔University of Pittsburgh Library, John Gabbert Bowman, Administrative Files, Box 2 Folder 13, Chinese Material〕

按:此件为录副。

二月二日

先生访颜惠庆,谈夫人袁慧熙的病情。〔《颜惠庆日记》第3卷,页315〕

二月三日

先生致信王重民,告知将由美国使领馆寄送展览古籍一百种至华盛顿,并谈代理馆长、职务安排等。

有三吾弟如晤:

连接十三日、十九日、廿一日航函,承函告各节,至以为感。所提议各件,深表赞同,兹已一一照办。致胡先生函随函奉上,请交子明兄一阅,即代付邮是盼。Jameson 如能来华,最佳。馆长处亦寄一函装在吴函内,表示欢迎。此外,曾选善本书样本100种,由美领代寄华京,以备展览之用。兄出国后,馆长一职遵尊意请中基会之秘书林伯遵君代理,予吾弟以秘书长或编辑部主任名义代拆代行,并函孙先生请其汇上美金三百元,供尊夫人及小孩之旅费(不必向他人言),至吾弟旅费仍请恒君设法,如能与 Jameson 同来尤佳,则旅费可由胡先生设法也。惟孙君近来对于兄之请款单,每不照办,寄尊处旅费之请款单如仍不理,俟到美后再设法可也。匆匆,顺颂旅安。

同礼

二月三日

林君来电不肯就,故仍盼大驾早日返国。

〔中国书店·海淀,四册〕

按:Jameson 应指翟孟生,时在国会图书馆服务。2月6日,“善本书样本100种”分装两箱,由美国驻沪领事 Frank P. Lockhart(1881-1949)直寄华盛顿国会图书馆,翌日该批古籍随 S. S. President Monroe 离沪。[①]

① National Archives, RG 59 General Records of the Department of State, Decimal File, 1940-44, Box 5865。另,此两箱书籍由钱存训交予美国驻沪使领馆,本拟请该处先寄送香港再转运美国,Frank Lockhart 则建议由该处直寄华盛顿,费用由平馆承担。

二月初

先生致信云南省政府,请汇寄该省建设资料、图表照片等。大意如下:

> 留滇两载,备承款待,现奉令赴美,从事文化宣传,极愿将滇省在抗战中之建设事业,为有系统之介绍,俾彼邦人士对我神圣抗战益增同情与援助。请将建设资料、图表照片以及说明书检寄全份。

〔《中央日报》(昆明),1941年2月8日,第4版〕

按:接到该信后,省政府即饬各局将有关文件检出并寄送先生。

二月八日

先生致电美国国会图书馆,欢迎恒慕义前往上海协助转运平馆善本并告自己将推迟赴美。

> APPRECIATE SINCERELY YOUR EFFORTS RELEASING BOOKS SHANGHAI. WELCOME DR. HUMMEL'S VISIT. POSTPONING MY TRIP TEMPORARILY. APPRECIATE INFORMATION DATE ARRIVAL.
>
> YUAN

〔台北胡适纪念馆,档案编号 HS-JDSHSE-0237-004〕

按:恒慕义收到此电后,于2月11日致信胡适,表示如果需要愿意亲赴上海协助平馆将存沪善本运美,另王重民的儿子因病住院。

先生致信 Bernardus Becquart,感谢震旦博物馆给予的支持,但因平馆经费极其困难无法给予实际性回馈。

February 8, 1941

Dear Monsieur Becquart:

I beg to acknowledge with many thanks the receipt of your letter of January 23rd. Owing to my illness I am sorry that I have not been able to write you earlier.

I am sorry to hear that Father Piel has not been enjoying good health. Whenever you write to him, kindly convey my best wishes for his early recovery.

It is most kind of you to continue to give us a space for the storing of our books. Your scholarly collaboration in according us all the facilities is greatly appreciated. I am asking Mr. Clarence L. Senn, our honorary

Treasurer, to call on you and to make a contribution to your museum as an expression of our gratitude.

Unfortunately, this Library, working under immense difficulties, is also facing financial embarrassment; otherwise, we would be very pleased to give more support to your worthy cause.

May I take this opportunity of thanking you once more for your assistance rendered to us in the past. We shall look forward to continued collaboration between our two institutions.

With kindest regards,

Yours sincerely,

T. L. Yuan

Director

〔平馆(昆明)英文信纸。上海市档案馆,档案编号 Q244-1-499〕

按:Bernardus Becquart(1910-?)法国耶稣会士,中文名白纳多,1928 年入会,1935 年来华,先在献县天主堂服务,1939 年至 1941 年至上海神学院进修,并协助郑璧尔管理震旦大学博物馆。此件为打字稿,落款处为先生签名。

二月十日

先生致信傅斯年,谈赴美计划并挽留傅斯年继续担任平馆委员会副主席之职。〔《傅斯年遗札》,页 1153-1155〕

按:1 月 6 日,傅斯年分别致信中基会、平馆委员会,辞去其在平馆委员会所担任的所有职务。蒋梦麟、孙洪芬、周诒春、任鸿隽等平馆委员均覆函傅斯年表示挽留,后傅斯年又分别致信仍然坚辞。

先生致信史蒂文斯,寄上以中美文化交换为题的备忘录,并告自己因候恒慕义来华护送平馆存沪善本书运美,故将访美时间略作推迟。

Hongkong

February 10, 1941

Dear Dr. Stevens:

With reference to my letter of January 21st forwarded to you through the courtesy of Dr. Balfour, I beg to submit herewith a memorandum regarding the proposed Sino-American Cultural Exchange. In view of your interest in the promotion of cultural understanding with the Far East, I hope this memorandum will receive your valuable support.

It was my original plan to submit the memorandum to your Foundation on my arrival in the States. It was also my intention to talk over details with Mr. Chi Meng, the director of the China Institute in America, but since I am now postponing my trip temporarily, I am sending the memorandum to you by airmail through the office of Dr. Balfour.

Among the details to be worked out, I should like to make this provision: That the bureau in China should have on its staff at least one American who is acquainted with cultural conditions in the United States. There are many advantages in having an American on the staff in China besides that of imparting information, as we would like to have no official interference in the carrying out of our plans.

In order to make the proposed Cultural Exchange a success, we must be well prepared in China not only in the careful selection of books, films and specimens of cultural objects, but also in their prompt transportation and delivery. I have asked Professor George Yeh, formerly professor of English literature in the National Tsing-Hua University to devote his time in making the preliminary arrangements, so that as soon as a grant is made, we shall be able to render an efficient service.

You have probably been informed that the collection of our rare books now kept in Shanghai will be transferred to Washington not only for safe custody, but also for the purpose of micro-filming. In view of the international tension in the Pacific, the sooner these books can be released, the better.

As Dr. Hummel will be coming out to China for this purpose, I have been obliged to postpone my trip in order to meet him here in Hongkong. When my sailing schedule is more definite, I shall write to you again.

With kindest regards,

Yours sincerely,

T. L. Yuan

〔Rockefeller Foundation. Series 601: China; Subseries 601.R: China-Humanities and Arts. Vol. Box 47. Folder 390〕

按:此为抄件。

二月十一日

先生致信 Marshall C. Balfour,推荐陈梦家赴美研究。〔Rockefeller Foundation. Series 601: China; Subseries 601.R: China-Humanities and Arts. Vol. Box 47. Folder 390〕

二月十二日

Charles C. Williamson 覆函先生,请先生告知抵达纽约时间,期待见面。

February 12, 1941

Dear Mr. Yuan:

Your letter of January 4th brings us good news indeed. We are delighted to welcome you to these shores, and I know your presence here will bring great pleasure to your many friends. Please let us know as soon as possible approximately when you will be reaching New York and how long you expect to be with us. I hope you will be in New York during much of your six months' visit.

Miss Sanderson joins me in assuring you of our highest personal regards.

Sincerely yours

Dean

P. S. My report for the year ending June 30, 1940, is due from the press at any moment, and I will see that a copy is forwarded to you.

〔Columbia University Library, New York State Library School Collection, Series 2 Student Records, Box 65, Folder Yuan, T. L.〕

按:此函寄送韩权华,由其转寄先生,该件为录副。

二月十七日

李耀南致函先生,报告平馆上海办事处经费开支情况。

谨将本馆上海部分现支各费，开列如左：

（一）馆员薪俸及津贴，每月共肆百肆拾伍元。右馆员三人，计钱存训月薪壹百叁拾元，陈贯吾、李耀南月薪各壹百贰拾元。三人津贴，每月各贰拾伍元，均系二年前所规定。

（二）馆役工资及津贴，每月共叁拾伍元。右馆役一名，工资贰拾元，津贴拾伍元。

（三）文具费，每月贰拾伍元。

（四）邮费，每月贰拾伍元。

（五）杂费，每月叁拾元。右杂费一项，通常所用每月不过十余元，间有运书及开书箱时，每次用至四五十元不等，此为每月平均之数。

（六）房租每月壹百元。右房租一项，在今年二月起租，适价高涨，仅租一小间，暂时试用。如将来房价低落，或再行觅房另租。

（七）各处茶役、节赏，每节伍拾元。右节赏一项，每年分三节，每节赏震旦博物院茶役拾余元，赏中国科学社茶役贰拾余元，连同其他共五十元。三节百五十元。

以上（一）项至（六）项，每月共陆百陆拾元，连同节赏一项，全年共捌千零柒拾元。除房租一项，暂由《季刊》项下开支外（因房间用处以办理《季刊》事宜为名），余均由经常费支出。

李耀南呈

三十年二月十七日

〔《北京图书馆馆史资料汇编（1909-1949）》，页730-731〕

按：此件为底稿。

傅斯年覆函先生，告不再担任平馆委员会任何职务。

守和吾兄左右：

自李庄返，奉读手书，知贵体复原，至慰。此次纠纷，弟不能加入漩涡，故只有辞去委员之一法。其理由前致委员会书业已言之，不赘述。弟已认为摆脱，文件奉还，以后乞勿再寄也。专此，敬颂旅安。

弟斯年谨复

二月十七日

〔《傅斯年遗札》，页1154-1155〕

按:随函寄还数份文件,包括1月23日致平馆委员会函(抄件)、先生致胡适英文信,2月10日先生致傅斯年信、先生致蒋梦麟信(抄件)等。

二月十八日

Marshall C. Balfour 覆函先生,告知陈梦家的免疫记录已转给史蒂文斯,并告平馆账户余额,询问是否调整平馆资助款拨付的幅度,其抵达香港后会与先生面谈。

February 18, 1941

Dear Mr. Yuan:

I am acknowledging receipt of your letter of February 11. As requested, the Record of Immunization for Mr. Chen Meng-Chia has been forwarded on to Mr. David H. Stevens in New York.

Your financial report for October-December 1940 is also acknowledged. This has been examined and seems to be in order. We note that you had a balance of US $ 1,619.51 at the end of December, and in January, we forwarded you a further US $ 2,000. We are due to make you another remittance of US $ 2,000 the early part of April, and in view of the large balance you now have in hand, possibly you would like to revise your scale of payments for the ensuing year.

I have noted that your proposed trip to the United States has had to be postponed, owing to unforeseen circumstances, and that you will not now be visiting Manila. I am therefore expecting to see you in Hong Kong, and will get in touch with you shortly after my arrival there.

No letters have yet been received for you at this office, but in case any arrive, your instructions to forward them on to your Hong Kong address until further notice, has been noted.

Very truly yours,

M. C. Balfour

〔Rockefeller Foundation. Series 601: China; Subseries 601.R: China-Humanities and Arts. Vol. Box 47. Folder 390〕

按:此件为录副。

二月中旬

先生致信王伯祥，请将开明书店选取的送美陈列之书送钱存训处，由后者代寄。〔《王伯祥日记》第17册，页99〕

按：21日，钱存训将该信转送到王伯祥处。

二月二十五日

王伯祥覆函先生，附上抗战后上海出版界概况，并商洽由开明书店代售平馆书刊事。〔《王伯祥日记》第17册，页107、108、407〕

按：其中，王伯祥告知开明书店选送书籍已送交钱存训处。7月18日，钱存训告知王伯祥，先生赴美之计取消，《新元史》《师石山房丛书》两书可取回。

二月底

教育部令先生赴美考察。

按：该令应为高教第49号，只存缮稿，时间为2月25日，并未标注发出时间，似与陈立夫26日覆函一并寄出，陈函大意如下，

守和吾兄大鉴：

接奉一月廿三日惠书，敬悉种切。吾兄此次赴美，望顺便考察美国图书馆事业及社会教育设施，已由部另备正式文件附奉。过美时并请便中留意国内青年学者有无出国研究之机会，随时示知为盼。代征集图书、仪器等，至纫公感。考察名义，部中自可照办。至于中美文化交换计划，业经拜读，至佩硕筹。惟目前以绌于经费，似宜暂缓施行。专此奉覆，顺颂时绥。

弟陈〇〇敬启

〔台北"国家发展委员会档案管理局"，〈国际文化合作——美国〉，档号A309000000E/0030/640.66/0001〕

二月二十八日

王重民由旧金山抵达香港，访先生，商平馆存沪善本运美事。〔《胡适来往书信选》中，页775〕

是年春

先生致信福建省教育厅，请拣选出版物、图片、照片等，拟携带赴美时作宣传之用。〔《闽南新报》（漳州），1941年3月17日，第2版〕

三月四日

先生与王重民离港赴上海，查看平馆存沪善本书现状及古籍装箱运美事宜。〔《胡适来往书信选》中，页775〕

按：2月21日，郑振铎致信张咏霓，提及"袁守和不日或将来沪。此人妒忌心极重。公开言：要破坏刘家事；不能不防之，且更不能不早日解决也！盖此人成事不足，败事有余。人心险恶，殊可叹也！"3月7日，再致信张咏霓，告"袁守和等已到沪（乞秘之），我辈可放下一桩心事矣。同来者有王某，欲来此，为美国国会图书馆购宋版书；见面时，当劝其为子孙多留些读书余地也！"①此种极不友善态度，似与其1939年秋割舍历年所藏戏曲珍本与平馆一事有关。1940年1月16日郑振铎与蒋复璁见面后，即为中央图书馆利益考虑，意欲与平馆争锋；1940年3月8日郑振铎从报纸上得知美国国会图书馆声称"中国珍贵图书，现正源源流入美国，举凡希世孤本，珍稿秘藏，文史遗著，品类毕备"，联想到王重民的到来，多有迁怒于先生。

三月十六日

先生访顾廷龙，告知自己将赴美，平馆馆务拟由王重民主持。〔《顾廷龙日记》，页146〕

三月十九日

顾廷龙访先生。〔《顾廷龙日记》，页146〕

三月二十日

先生致信史蒂文斯，递交拍摄留平善本书缩微胶片备忘录，并告其《图书季刊》英文本成本猛增。

Shanghai, March 20, 1941

Dear Dr. Stevens:

When Dr. Balfour was visiting Hong Kong on his way to the interior, I discussed with him about the urgent need of making film copies of our rare books still kept in Peiping. As we have no idea how long we could

① 陈福康整理《为国家保存文化——郑振铎抢救珍稀文献书信日记辑录》，北京：中华书局，2016年，页160、161。

hold on under Japanese occupation, it would be a blessing indeed if we could make the films as soon as we can.

As Mr. Augustine Li has returned, I am asking him to go back to Peiping and to supervise this work. I am enclosing herewith a memorandum setting forth the reasons for our request. I sincerely hope that this application will receive the favorable consideration from your Trustees.

With regard to the publishing of our *Quarterly Bulletin of Chinese Bibliography*, I wish to state that although we have been benefited by the present favorable rate of exchange, yet the cost of paper and printing has increased to such an extent that it has made the value of the Chinese dollar practically nil. This situation applies, of course, to all commodities that have been affected by the war and by the depreciation of local currency.

I shall return to Hong Kong early in April and I hope to write you more fully after my return.

Yours sincerely,

T. L. Yuan

Director

〔平馆(Occidental Book Fund)英文信纸。Rockefeller Foundation. Series 300 Latin America-Series 833 Lebanon; Subseries 601. Box 9. Folder 87〕

按:随信附 Memorandum re the Need of Additional Appropriation for Filming Rare Books at Peiping and for the Publication of the *Quarterly Bulletin of Chinese Bibliography* 两页。此件为打字稿,落款处为先生签名,于 4 月 8 日送达纽约洛克菲勒基金会总部。

三月二十三日

晚,顾廷龙设宴,先生、徐森玉、王重民、刘咸、浦江清受邀与席,叶景葵、潘博山、潘景郑作陪。〔《顾廷龙日记》,页 147-148〕

三月二十七日

下午,张凤举、李宗侗招宴,徐森玉、先生、郑振铎、张寿镛等人受邀与席。〔《为国家保存文化——郑振铎抢救珍稀文献书信日记辑录》,页 166〕

按:张凤举(1895—1986),字定璜,江西南昌人,早年赴日本留学获东京帝国大学文学士,历任北京大学、中法大学教授。

三月二十九日

先生访顾廷龙,告知将返香港。顾廷龙借机索取平馆所出期刊,先生表示已经航邮平馆(昆明)嘱寄送,并告刘承幹藏书已部分售与中央图书馆。〔《顾廷龙日记》,页149〕

按:似因访美事突生变故,先生颇多牢骚,另王重民未与先生一同返回香港,而是留在上海。4月9日《图书季刊》中文本送到,顾廷龙致信表示谢意。

三月

先生以中华图书馆协会理事长身份呈请教育部增加该会补助费,将此前的每月一百元提升至三百元。此外,先生呈请中央宣传部恢复补助。〔《中华图书馆协会会报》第15卷第5期,1941年4月,页8;《中华图书馆协会会报》第15卷第6期,1941年6月,页6〕

按:教育部并未批准该请,但中央宣传部指令,准自七月份起按月给予补助费一百元。

四月三日

先生抵达香港。〔中国书店·海淀,四册〕

四月五日

先生致信教育部总务司,呈上三千元美金之收据。

径复者,日昨奉到三月三十一日大函,并附美金汇票三千元一纸,业已如数收讫。兹奉上正式收据,即希查收为荷。此致

教育部总务司

袁同礼谨启

三十年四月五日

〔中国第二历史档案馆,教育部档案·全卷宗五,国立北平图书请拨员工学术研究补助费经常费有关文书,案卷号11616(1)〕

按:此款为平馆善本书运美费用。该件为先生亲笔并钤印。

四月七日

先生致信王重民,告知已与教育部通电但尚未得到回覆,并请转告钱存训购买旧书事。

有三吾弟：

濒行承厚赐，又蒙走送，至以为谢。三日到港，部款四号始行汇到，已汇罗君美金壹千伍百元，惟海关方面是否已接到部电，甚以为念。顷已电询，盼日内得覆。弟到港后即电催矣。

托舍亲袁女士交钱存训君国币壹万元，系教部指定专购中文旧书之款，请从速购买，所有发票及单据均写三月一号以前之日期，购书以有系统为要。中基会十七号开会，兄除提出增加预算案外，并请各董事考虑赔款停止后，本馆之基金问题。结果如何，容再奉闻。专此，顺询旅祺。

同礼顿首

四月七日

〔中国书店·海淀，四册〕

按："罗君"即 Frank P. Lockhart（1881－1949），美外交官，时任美驻沪总领事，以下 5 月 5 日、20 日、10 月 8 日、30 日各信中均提及此人；"舍亲袁女士"似为袁慧燕。

四月八日

先生访颜惠庆，告自己将于六月动身赴美，并谈与平馆委员会、孙洪芬之间的误会。〔《颜惠庆日记》第 3 卷，页 331〕

按：《颜惠庆日记》排印为"与申君发生了误会"，因其日记原为英文，此处应是错译了孙洪芬（Clarence L. Senn）的英文名。

四月十五、十六日

先生致信王重民，谈购买旧书及托运行李、旅费等事。

有三吾弟：

前接四日来函，欣悉购书工作业已开始，购书款想已由钱先生处取到矣。渝电既发出，想近日接洽运输必极忙碌，此事承鼎力协助，有功于文献匪浅，未识人与物能同时东渡否？前托带韩女士之皮箱，因内中有绣衣及皮衣，恐上岸时要上税，而足下款又不充裕，刻下国防时期，收件人又不能到船上或码头及海关来接，故拟请将下列各物抽出送交韩女士，其余者仍装箱内，将该箱连同钥匙送交福开森路 394 号刘宅，交袁慧燕女士收存，俟兄经过上海再行走取较为便利。现仍拟六月间经沪东渡，明日开委员会，结果如何再函告。又前请孙先生拨付旅费三百元,渠嘱先与罗氏基金会商洽后,再行办理,顷已函该会(在菲),将来必可寄华京留交也。余容再函,顺候旅安。

兄同礼顿首

四月十五

收到此信即来一覆音。

顷接本日来电,知丁电仍未到,焦灼万状,已再电陈顾去催矣。

十六晨

〔中国书店·海淀,四册〕

按:"韩女士"应指韩权华,"丁电"应指行政院电江海关华人主事丁贵堂(1891—1962)放行平馆运美善本书,"电陈"则指请陈立夫催促行政院。

四月十九日

上午,先生访翁文灏。〔《翁文灏日记》,页669〕

按:18日为中基会年会,19日为中基会执委会。

四月二十六日

先生致信 Marshall C. Balfour,请求洛克菲勒基金会支付王重民在美参观各图书馆的旅费。大意如下:

April 26, 1941

Thank you so much for your letter of April 4, enclosing a letter from Mr. Marshall, the contents of which have been noted. In view of the difficulty of transportation in Free China, I think it would not be a bad idea to give up temporarily the attempt to promote cultural interchange. All such efforts would be futile so long as the transportation problem is not solved.

My trip to the States has been postponed until June. During my absence from China, I have asked Mr. C. M. Wang who is now working in the Library of Congress to return to China and act for me. It is my desire that before returning Mr. Wang should be given an opportunity to visit some of the leading libraries in the States and learn the latest development of library methods and technique. For this reason, I hope it would be possible for us to pay him US $ 250 to $ 300 out of your grant as a partial payment for his travel expenses. Although it can be paid out under the heading of "development of library services", I should like to obtain your permission before asking our Treasurer to send him the check.

Our quarterly statement to your office was lost in an airmail between Shanghai and Kunming. I am asking our Treasurer to send me a duplicate copy which will be forwarded to you in due course.

〔Rockefeller Foundation. Series 601: China; Subseries 601.R: China-Humanities and Arts. Vol. Box 47. Folder 390〕

按:该信存抄录件。

四月二十七日

吴宓致函先生,请为张尔琼在港购物。〔《吴宓日记》第8册,页77〕

四月二十八日

Marshall C. Balfour 覆函先生,前请支付王重民旅费须等待洛克菲勒基金会总部的批复。

April 28, 1941

Dear Mr. Yuan,

I am forwarding an extract of your letter of April 26 to Mr. Marshall for his information and decision regarding the proposal to use some of year funds for Mr. C. M. Wang's travel in the States. I believe we should have New York's decision on the question, of which I will ask for a cabled reply, and since the Clipper leaves tomorrow, I think we may expect an answer within ten days to two weeks.

I observe that a copy of your last quarterly statement is being sent to us.

Very truly yours,

M. C. Balfour

〔Rockefeller Foundation. Series 601: China; Subseries 601.R: China-Humanities and Arts. Vol. Box 47. Folder 390〕

按:此件为录副。

四月

平馆向教育部呈文,为在滇馆员申请救济,具先生名并钤印。

查迩来滇省接壤安南昆明市空,时受敌机不断之轰炸,摧毁我城市、破坏我机关，以致后方人民屡受物质上之损失。兹有职馆馆员毛宗荫、岳梓木、袁克勤等于二月廿六日昆市被炸时，其家宅均遭毁坏，全部坍塌，损失情形颇为严重。查该员等月薪实支均在一百元以内，并携有眷属，当此百物昂贵，平时既感生活之困难，而又遭此意外之损失，情实可悯。兹据该员等分别填具空袭受损报告单各一纸前来，职审查属实，理合备文呈请大部俯赐鉴核准予救济，匪特该员等沾感无涯已也。谨呈

教育部部长陈

国立北平图书馆代理馆长袁同礼

〔中国第二历史档案馆，教育部档案·全卷宗5，国立北平图书馆请拨员工学术研究补助费经常费有关文书，案卷号11616(1)〕

按：教育部应于4月26日收到该呈文。是年6月中旬，毛宗荫、岳梓木、袁克勤分别领到救济费240、70、150元。

《中国博物馆协会会报》刊登先生的文章，题为《抗战期中我国博物馆之动态与前途》。〔《中国博物馆协会会报》复刊第1卷第1期，页2-4〕

按：先生文章大致分为四部分，分别为“文物之保存”“各博物馆西迁后工作之炽盛”“战时新博物馆之筹备与成立”“中国博物馆事业之前瞻”。[①] 中国博物馆协会会址为重庆海棠溪百子桥四号，编辑部则在澳门妈阁街十五号。

四五月间

先生介绍钱亚新赴蓝田国立师范学院任教，担任教育系讲师。〔谢欢著《钱亚新年谱》，上海：上海古籍出版社，2021年，页79-80〕

按：此时国立湖南大学人事更迭，相当数量的教员离职他就。7月9日，钱亚新偕家眷抵达蓝田镇，8月1日正式入职。

先生委托王重民将爱心杯带去美国并赠与美国图书馆协会。〔“A. L. A. News.” *Bulletin of the American Library Association*, vol. 35, no. 9, 1941, p. 524〕

按：该件礼物象征着中国图书馆界感激美国图书馆界无私的援助，本拟由裘开明携至美国图书馆协会波士顿会议，因故推迟，最终于7月10日送达美国图书馆协会总部。

---

① 文章除标题外，文中“博物馆”三字均以新造字“𬳿”代替，特此说明。

五月五日

上午,黄炎培至香港大学冯平山图书馆,访许地山,遇先生。〔《黄炎培日记》第7卷,页98、112、114〕

按:原文为"托抄廿四史篇目表遇袁守和(同礼)","托抄"一词似指复旦大学史地学系教授李晋芳托黄炎培抄《廿五史篇目表》。

先生致信王重民,附与丁贵堂信,请其与之接洽善本出关问题,并告采购中文旧籍注意事项。

有三吾弟:

接电知改期返美,俾能与存件同行,至慰。惟一再延缓,九月间能否返国,颇资疑虑。兹奉上致丁函已托此间税务司代寄,请托徐公再为切实接洽,得到后即访Basset,请其协助为要。罗君处曾汇去1500元,并有专函托其代觅舱位矣。稿费八百元本已交上海银行汇上,而汇费竟约六十元,嗣恐大驾东行赶不上,爰又撤回,银行索损失费五元。前电告在袁女士取795元,想已取到。购书费尚存数千元,兹致孙先生一函,请转交,并请继续采购。已购妥者,嘱李君写卡片或简单分类,以免以后再有重复。敝处不日迁移,以后函电均寄冯平山圕。如有必要当前来协助,如何之处望随时电示为盼。顺颂大安。

同礼顿首

五月五日

〔中国书店·海淀,四册〕

按:5月8日,王重民离沪返美。Basset似为Arthur Basset,时任American University Club(美国同学会)主席、American Advisory Committee for Civilian Relief in China主席①。

五月六日

Marshall C. Balfour致函先生,告知洛克菲勒基金会同意给予王重民旅费补助。

May 6, 1941

Dear Mr. Yuan,

This is to confirm my telegram to you of today in which you were

---

① *The North-China Desk Hong List*, 1939, p. 76; Marcia R. Ristaino, *The Jacquinot Safe Zone: wartime refugees in Shanghai*, 2008, p. 107.

notified that we have received a cable from Mr. Marshall, indicating approval of the payment from the current grant to the National Library of Peiping, of an amount for the travel expenses of Mr. C. M. Wang, as outlined in your letter of April 26.

Very truly yours,

M. C. Balfour.

〔Rockefeller Foundation. Series 601: China; Subseries 601.R: China-Humanities and Arts. Vol. Box 47. Folder 390〕

按:此件为录副。

五月七日

史蒂文斯覆函先生,告知洛克菲勒基金会不考虑额外资助平馆拍摄留在北平的古籍善本。

May 7, 1941

Dear Dr. Yuan:

The correspondence sent to the New York office of the Foundation during recent weeks has been acknowledged by Mr. Marshall, most recently in his cable of April 21. This reported the inability of the Foundation to assist in your projected plan of visit to the United States.

On other matters in earlier letters, I can now give the only possible answer under present conditions. It is that we could not recommend to the trustees of the Foundation entry upon plans for library development in China in the terms of your letter of March 20. The much larger proposal noted in earlier letter of Mr. Marshall and Dr. Balfour had to do with the proposed Sino-American Cultural Exchange. Under date of March 19, you sent a tentative budget on this plan. I regret that this is quite beyond possibility of consideration.

I am most gratified that Dr. Balfour was able to see you personally. His conversation gave you the assurance that your old friends are interested in the welfare of the institutions of China, whether or not it is in our power to deal with specific problems of today. I am happy that Mr. Augustine Li has returned safely. Please send word to him that I wish him well in his new work. Also, I should like it if you would give the same word to any other men previously aided by this division of the Foundation.

Very sincerely yours,

David H. Stevens

〔Rockefeller Foundation. Series 601: China; Subseries 601.R: China-Humanities and Arts. Box 47. Folder 390〕

按:该函寄送香港,并抄送给 Balfour、格雷夫斯二人。

五月十四日

先生致信王重民,告知善本运美因海关问题暂停并就此电请教育部与行政院沟通,并谈自己赴美访问计划等事。

有三吾弟:

存件运美以梅君之阻难,功亏一篑,但停运一节应由教部询明孔君意见,明令指示后吾人方能脱卸责任。发电教部已四日,尚无覆电。据目下情势看,海关既不负责,中央亦毫无办法也。前请孙君付尊处美金三百元(旅费),渠迟迟不办,将请款单压起。近接罗氏基金会复电,谓付尊处之三百元,该会完全同意,即将原电寄孙先生并请其如数汇至华京,想可照办。兄致罗氏基金会之函内称因拟赴美请吾弟代理,在返国以前应到各大城之图书馆参观,藉资学习等语,该会既允在其补助费内拨付,最好不让 Hummel 知之,一俟书目编完仍向他索一笔旅费,则贤伉俪之旅费问题即可解决,惟小孩似需付半票轮船须付,不知火车如何。敝意弟在返国以前,一人可到哈佛、哥伦比亚两地参观,所费亦甚有限。如能于九月间返国最佳,兄六月出国之事恐须作罢(因无旅费),教部之款势须退回国库,最大希望则为拨付本馆购买西文书,容接洽后再奉告。如无旅费,则须候明年中基会开会再说,但该会届时亦无美金可付旅费也。惟孙君之无理取闹及对于迁移善本书不负责任等等,便中可向胡先生一说。盖银钱在他手上,随时均可阻难,办事棘手之处亦须向他说明。在出国以前最好先得其谅解如能凑成旅费,则拟十月赴美,渠与孙私交最笃,故不易办。极盼台驾早日返国,可分一部分责任,届时行动或可自由,目下只有忍气吞声,一切为馆中着想而已。《燉煌叙录》是否全在大同书店,已函子刚,如能售出,该款可留交在沪代购各书，其发票想已交钱先生矣。余容再函，顺颂旅安。

同礼顿首

五月十四日

胡先生担任旅费而事无成，晤面时祈代达谢意。日内当再函谢，因候教部覆电。

印燉煌古写本事，据叶玉虎先生面告，谓英庚款在第一年度可补助壹万五千元，请将应印之书，先开一书目上次所开的多凭记忆，恐尚须修改，并写一说明。

许地山先生托将燉煌内关于道藏部分开示一书目，并盼便中为之，渠现正编一道藏书目也。

运美展览书箱两件，如已收到，请国会圕来函证明注明暂代收存。

〔中国书店·海淀，四册〕

按："梅君"即梅乐和（Frederick W. Maze，1871－1959），英国人，1891年来华，在舅父赫德的提携下加入清朝海关，1929年1月起任第4任中国海关总税务司。

先生致信史密斯森协会，告知收到十三箱寄送中华图书馆协会的书籍，并希望该协会今后将运往中华图书馆协会及平馆的交换品寄送上海，接收人为钱存训。

May 14, 1941

Dear Sirs:

I beg to inform you that your consignment of 13 boxes of books dispatched to this Association as mentioned in your letter of February 11 has recently been received. On behalf of this Association, I wish to convey to you once more our heartfelt thanks for your untiring efforts in forwarding us the books and journals which we need in replenishing our devastated libraries.

Ever since the closure of the Indo-China-Yunnan Railway, the difficulty of transportation to Free China becomes a serious one. Although the facilities along the Burma Road have been greatly improved, it is now exclusively used for transport of war materials.

As the shipping facilities have become quite normal at Shanghai, we should like to request you to ship your future consignments both for the

Library Association of China as well as for the National Library of Peiping to our Shanghai agent Mr. T. H. Tsien, Room 404, National City Bank Building, 45 Kiukiang Road, Shanghai. Mr. Tsien will attend to the work of distribution for this Association.

In the past it has been your practice to include in your consignment boxes or packages intended for the Lingnan University, Canton. Henceforth please ship them separately and send them directly to that University, c/o University of Hongkong, Hongkong.

Thanking you very much for your kind attention,

Yours sincerely,

T. L. Yuan

Chairman, Executive Board

〔中华图书馆协会(冯平山图书馆转)英文信纸。Smithsonian Institution Archives, Records, 1868-1988 (Record Unit 509), Box 1, Library Association of China, Hong Kong〕

按:此件为打字稿,落款处为先生签名,于6月16日送达。

五月十五日

先生致信詹森大使,告知平馆善本书运美计划受阻、个人访美计划亦推迟。

May 15, 1941

His Excellency Ambassador Nelson T. Johnson

c/o American Consulate General

Hongkong & Shanghai Bank Building

Hongkong

Dear Ambassador:

I am delighted to learn that you have arrived at Hongkong. I am looking forward to the pleasure of seeing you before you leave for Washington.

Owing to my extended stay in Shanghai, I regret that I have not been able to report to you earlier about the shipment of our rare books to Washington. While there, I was able to move them out of the French Concession and Mr. Lockhart promised to give us every possible assistance in arranging for their transportation.

Unfortunately the Inspector General of Customs viewed the matter in a different light. Although several instructions have been received from the Executive Yuan, he holds the opinion that it would not be advisable to make the shipment at the present time and the required Customs export permit was not issued. Unless such a permit is issued, there is nothing that the Consul General can do about making arrangements for the shipment.

My trip to the States has been delayed by the shipment of these books. Under the present circumstances, I am afraid that I have to postpone it indefinitely.

I shall pay my respects to you one of these days and I am looking forward to seeing you.

Yours faithfully,

T. L. Yuan

Director

〔平馆(冯平山图书馆转)英文信纸。Library of Congress, Nelson T. Johnson Papers〕

按:此件为打字稿,落款处为先生签名。

五月二十日

先生致信胡适,谈平馆善本运美受阻、平馆被教育部忽视、希望申请美援等事。

适之先生尊鉴:

关于运送沪上存件,想有三兄返美后业将经过情形为公陈述,兹不再赘。梅乐和君不肯发给出口放行证,确是好意。当即电部请示,奉陈部长来谕嘱仍继续接洽,并亲致梅氏一函,嘱予转寄。政府既具决心,则吾人今后必须改变方式方能启运。日前詹森大使来港,曾与之谈及此事。渠主张由平馆与国会图书馆订一契约,声明借用年限五年左右,再由国务院授权总领事,嘱其报关时作为美国财产,由其负责启运。今箱数既已减少,则罗君进行此事似不甚难。如公对此办法予以同意,即希就近与该馆接洽,并请代表本馆签署此项契约,一切统希钧酌为感。美国援华团体自成立联合组织后,声势较前浩大。据Luce谈,谓内中将有一笔钜款援助我国学术机关继续文化及研究之努力,未识将来如何支配?我公如能为平馆设法,尤所感谢。近教育部以八十余万美金分配国内各学术机关，西南联大及中央研究院均各得三万五千美金，中央图书馆亦得一万美金，平馆则分文未得。而中基会拨付之西文购书费近又由国币五万元减为二万五千元，中文购书费则仍为国币六千元，重要西文杂志均无法订购，普通书籍则更无法购买。凡此种种，事业上深受严重之打击昆明馆址被炸三次，而生活日昂，同人中十余日不知肉味者比比皆是，不得不希望美国方面能予若干之援助。今日之援华团体虽侧重于救济，但建设事业之实际需要似亦包括在内。如吾人迟迟不进，则又为教会大学捷足先登。我公对平馆事业素所关怀，尚希在可能范围内相机进行，翘企无已。专此申谢，敬候道祺。

后学同礼拜上

五月廿日，香港

〔台北胡适纪念馆，档案编号 HS-JDSHSC-1636-003〕

按："美国援华团体"即 United China Relief，1941 年 2 月 7 日由 Henry R. Luce（1898－1967）发起成立的援华联合会，总部设在纽约百老汇 1790 号，在全美 78 个城市设有地方劝募委员会；Luce 为美国报业大亨，生于中国山东登州一个美国传教士家庭，幼年在烟台内地会学校读书，1920 年毕业于耶鲁大学，《时代周刊》（*Time*）《财富》（*Fortune*）和《生活》（*Life*）杂志的创始人之一。

五月二十九日

先生致信吴俊升，恳请教育部从美金拨款中为平馆分润若干。

士选吾兄大鉴：

弟前奉部令护送善本书赴美，曾到沪接洽，以海关不予放行无法启运，美洲之行只得作罢。近孟麟先生见告谓部中近有八十余万美金分配各大学，联大方面曾得三万五千美金，中央研究院、中央图书馆亦各得一二万云云。想吾兄必参预此事，未识能否为敝馆设法分润若干。敢祈鼎力赞助，并请代向王司长说项弟尚未谋面，故不便冒然请求，公私均感。专此拜恳，静候道祺。

弟袁同礼顿首

五月廿九日

香港冯平山图书馆转

按：吴俊升时任教育部高教司司长，收到该信后，于 6 月 10 日向

陈立夫等人上一条陈。[①] 内容如下，

据北平图书馆袁馆长函请酌拨美金购置图书，拟照中央图书馆例，在制造及运输工具款项六万七千元项，酌拨二千元，是否可行，理合签请鉴核示遵。谨呈

部长、次长

俊升

三十年六月十日

〔中国第二历史档案馆，教育部档案·全宗号五，国立中央图书馆北平图书馆国立北平研究院等单位动支美借款购运图书仪器的有关文书，案卷号5468〕

六月三日

先生致信鲍曼，告知受行政院孔祥熙委托将赠送匹兹堡大学的礼物寄出，其中有教育部长陈立夫夫人的画作，自己则因为种种原因推迟前往美国。

June 3, 1941

Dear Chancellor:

Sometime ago I communicated to you the desire of the Chinese Government to present a suitable gift to the China Memorial Room in the Cathedral of Learning. Dr. H. H. Kung, the Acting Premier, has commissioned me to make the selection of the various items and it is his desire that I should present the gift to your University in person.

As I am now obliged to postpone my trip owing to unforeseen circumstances, I am arranging to pack the major part of the gift in one wooden case which will be shipped to you by freight. Some of the porcelains and bronzes will be brought over by a friend of mine and will be reforwarded to you from New York.

I enclose herewith a list of the gift from the Chinese Government. Dr. Kung hopes that it will form an appropriate addition to the China Memorial Room in your great University.

---

① 同日，陈立夫批示可行。

Mr. Chen Li-fu, the Minister of Education and an alumnus of your University, is also greatly interested in the China Memorial Room and has asked me to bring over two scrolls of Chinese painting, one is intended for the University, while the other painted by Madame Chen is presented to you personally. These two scrolls will be forwarded to you by the Chinese Embassy in Washington.

Mr. Chen also asked me to present to you one of his recent photographs which I mailed to you the other day. I enclose a personal letter for you from Mr. Chen.

With kindest regards and sincere greetings,

Yours sincerely,

T. L. Yuan

Director

The list will be included in my personal letter to be mailed by next clipper.

〔平馆(冯平山图书馆转)英文信纸。University of Pittsburgh Library, John Gabbert Bowman, Administrative Files, Box 2 Folder 13, Chinese Material〕

按:陈立夫为匹兹堡大学校友,1925 年获该校矿学硕士学位,其夫人孙禄卿(1898—1992),浙江吴兴人,毕业于上海美术专科学校。此件为打字稿,落款处为先生签名,以航空信方式寄送。

六月四日

先生致信鲍曼,寄上赠送礼物清单,并告自己本年无法赴美访问。

June 4, 1941

Dear Chancellor Bowman:

In addition to the official letter which I wrote to you yesterday, I wish to offer a word of apology for not being able to write to you earlier about my plans. The fact was that I had been obliged to stay in Shanghai for a considerable period of time and I did not want the Japanese there to censor any of my letters.

Although I have been postponing my visit in view of the tense international situation, I did not give up the trip until the other day. It seemed that the more I waited, the worse the situation has become. Since it is now impossible to secure any accommodation, I and my colleagues have to postpone the trip at least for the time being. It is indeed a great disappointment to us not being able to see you and pay our respects.

While in Shanghai, I had a good opportunity of selecting the gift for the China Memorial Room on behalf of our Government. Since the Room is used for seminar classes, it is considered appropriate to send over a humble collection of specimens of articles usually found in a Chinese study. I hope that as soon as they arrive at Pittsburgh, you will secure some Chinese students to help arrange them in the Chinese traditional way.

I enclose herewith a list of the objects in Chinese, as it is rather difficult to translate the names of some of the objects into English. This list may be found useful.

With warmest regards,

Yours sincerely,

T. L. Yuan

〔University of Pittsburgh Library, John Gabbert Bowman, Administrative Files, Box 2 Folder 13, Chinese Material〕

按:该信以航空信方式寄送,此为抄件。

六月十六日

中华图书馆协会撰《为奉令缮送本会民国二十九年度会务报告请鉴核由》,具先生名并钤印。〔台北"国史馆",〈中国图书馆协会请补助(教育部)〉,数位典藏号 019-030508-0015〕

按:该件附中华图书馆协会民国二十九年度会务报告一份,共计4页。

六月二十三日

教育部代电。

国立北平图书馆密

兹支配该馆美金设备费二千元,应即依照规定注意事项,开列请购设备清单四份,于文到两个月内寄部核转。附发国立各学校机关开列三十年度美款购置设备清单应行注意事项一份。

教育部

按:该代电另附吴俊升覆函,内容如下,

守和先生大鉴:

展诵五月廿九日惠书,敬悉一一。贵馆既需添购图书,已转陈核准支配美金二千元,以部电通知。[1] 专此布复,顺颂时祺。

吴〇〇敬复

〔中国第二历史档案馆,教育部档案·全宗号五,国立中央图书馆北平图书馆国立北平研究院等单位动支美借款购运图书仪器的有关文书,案卷号5468〕

六月

《图书季刊》英文本刊登先生所撰编者按(Editorial Comment)。〔*Quarterly Bulletin of Chinese Bibliography* (New Series) Vol. II, Nos. 1-2, pp. 1-3〕

按:该文分两大部分,一为The Vocie of the Press,一为Sino-British Intellectual Cooperation。

七月三日

先生致信王重民,告知平馆本年经费及赴美旅费均有着落,望其早日归国代理馆务,以便自己赴美募集各方资助。

有三吾弟:

兹附上致Smithsonian学院、胡大使及施大使信各一件,请加封寄出。孙君寄上之美金三百元,想已寄到,深盼早日返国代为主持馆务。最近教部补助国币四万元又美金二千元连同运书费共五千元,加以罗氏基金余款美金一千五百元,本年可以勉强渡过,惟明年之经费仍待筹划,故拟候大驾返国后仍来美一行,逗留三月即行返国委员会曾给假三月,尚未开始,可以利用也。晤胡大使时请试探其口气,如不加反对,再在国内进行。本年春假时曾拟在馆中请假一年,曾被孙君阻难,今缩短为三个月,且旅费已有着落(大同书店结束后,赢余有四百美金),可以不动本馆之款,则通过或较容易。惟届时世界大势如何演变,则不可知耳。就大势观察,日本不致与美开仗,故太平洋之交通美国必能维持到底,惟总统船均调至大西洋,今后船支较少,订票更感不易耳。教部之款如不作运书费,拟移作购书费,专购东方学及欧战史料。国会图书馆與图

---

[1] 在此次拨款中,国立中央图书馆为八千美金。

部近购之欧洲地图,并请便中将出版地查出以便采购。每星期六下午及星期日可视察馆中各部之工作概况,俾返国后有所借镜(应先将周年报告读完,再与主任访问)。欧美新出版关于汉学书报,并请刘女士写简单介绍小孩患病想已大愈,以便登《季刊》。馆中迄未添人,辞职者不再补人。钱锺书君已请其就联大教授职矣。兄之失眠症已较前大愈,惟以办事棘手,常常焦灼耳。赴美三月之主要目的在谋罗氏基金补助费之继续美金有八千元即可敷用,并不筹款,以免又生反感也。匆匆,顺颂旅安。

兄同礼顿首

七月三日

子明兄返国拟请其办交换书报事,便中可转达。

〔中国书店·海淀,四册〕

按:钱锺书在平馆上海办事处任职时间约为1941年春夏两季,可对照1941年2月17日李耀南致先生信及《1941年平馆驻外办事处职员表》。①

七月七日

中华图书馆协会撰《为恳请将补助费予以增加以利图书馆事业推进由》,具先生名并钤理事会印。〔台北"国史馆",〈中国图书馆协会请补助(教育部)〉,数位典藏号019-030508-0015〕

按:该文具体内容即请教育部从7月起将协会每月补助增至三百元。

七月十日

教育部部长陈立夫致函先生,就善本运美事方式、途径给予指示。

守和馆长大鉴:

函电均悉,已呈孔副院长,奉复函"为避某方注目,可先分批运港、菲,再行转美,经已急电总税务司仍遵前电饬放"云云,用特函达,即希遵照妥慎办理,是为至要。耑此,并颂公祺。

陈立夫启

七月十日

〔国立北平图书馆用笺。《胡适遗稿及秘藏书信》第31册,页643〕

按:此为抄件。

---

①《中国国家图书馆馆史资料长编》,页340-341。

七月十五日

先生致信王重民，告教育部重启善本运美及馆内困境，并再次表示自己须赴美一行。

有三吾弟：

接上月廿九日来函，详悉种种。致恒君函遵嘱写就，兹随函附上，如能成功，于公私均有利。又致胡大使函，写好后忽接陈部长来信，仍嘱继续进行（此事已逾两月，以为作罢矣。今又旧事重提，可见政府办事之慢）。惟运港与运美在海关出口困难则一，如经菲转运则费用更大，故应请国务院发一切实有力之电报，训令美领按美国财产看待，由其负责启运，再加上总税务司所发之允许证，则不致再有问题矣。现兄在港专候胡大使来电，一俟电到当即赴沪协助一切。至收回租界之说，须看日本态度，而日之态度又须看欧战之如何演变也。陈部长既主张启运，则部中职员拟收回运费之议则可打销。书如能早日运美而美又不参战，则拟乘太平洋无事之时作一短期旅行，至多二三月将存书事作一交代。如胡大使复函对于短期来美表示赞成，则委员会方面决无问题。兄亦愿于明年中基会开年会以前能使罗氏基金补助之款可以继续，届时再到内地进行一切。大驾如不能提前返国，则须请李或曾君先到内地代为主持，因莫太太不善应付，决须派一人前往协助也。孙君所汇之美金叁百元，闻已寄到，甚慰。此款接洽之经过系孙君最初不肯付款，后由兄正式函告罗氏基金，谓出国在即，请执事代理馆长，在离美以前须到美国各地考察，故需此款。该会同意后来电，证明寄洪芬，渠始照付。馆中同人对此颇有烦言（可供昆明同人两个月之薪水），亦是嫉妬之意。故敝意如将来美方能担任一部分旅费，此款似可退还一部分，以免予人以口实，但兄到美后如罗氏基金方面可以延长补助之款，则此区区亦可不必计较，故甚盼个人能早日来美接洽继续之事（该会补助至本年十月截止）也。芝加哥及哈佛聘请燕大之人，其姓名为何，盼查明示复。兄近日失眠之症自服药后业已大愈，惟馆中经费如不设法则难关亦甚多，因之时感忧虑，半夜醒后即不能再眠矣。本馆每年至少须有八千美金，如中基会能拨付此项美金，即不必向外人启齿。晤胡大使时亦盼转告为盼。顺颂旅安。

同礼顿首

七，十五

本馆战前购书费为三万美金，战后一年尚有八千美金。自庚款停付乃改发国币，每年仅有二千美金订购杂志，尚不敷用也。

〔国立北平图书馆用笺。中国书店·海淀，四册〕

按："李或曾君"即李芳馥、曾宪三。

先生致信胡适，谈善本运美、教育部资金分配、《图书季刊》英文稿约稿等事。

适之先生尊鉴：

有三兄返美，想已将沪上一切情形向公详为报告。今后运书事自应改变方式，始能实现。教部前拨付之运费美金叁千元，近忽有部中同人社会教育司主张将款收回，移作他用。而南京伪组织方面自经各轴心国承认后，声势较前浩大友人飞师尔派为德国代办（并非大使），已赴南京，伪欧美司司长为胡道维。报载有收回上海租界之计划见剪报，虽未必即能实现，但将此批书籍寄存沪上，终觉不妥。同礼以责任关系，对此异常焦灼。美方如能商洽，尚希鼎力赞助，继续进行，不胜感祷。教部近以美金八十万元赁款分配国内各大学及各学术机关，多者四万，少者一万，购买大批图书、仪器，既毫无计划，而分配款项又系分赃性质，始终未将平馆列入。经同礼函电申请，始行分配美金壹千七百元。类此之事，足征今日办事之困难。故同礼仍拟明春来美作短期之考察至多三月，并拟搜集欧战史料充实馆藏，最低限度可藉此与美国学术机关保持接触，亦必能得些鼓励，俾能提起精神，再行奋斗。目下经费无着，办事棘手，精神未免颓丧也。近编之《图书季刊》尚为中外人士所欢迎，惟英文稿件稍感缺乏。尊处关于学术方面之讲演稿定必甚多，拟请惠赠一、二篇，以光篇幅。倘承俯允，无任感幸。专此奉恳，顺候道祺。

后学袁同礼敬上

七月十五日

顷奉陈部长来函，录副奉上。由沪运港与运美，在海关方面手续是一样的，如国务院能训令美领代运则较为简捷。届时希赐一电，当即将运费汇沪，并前往协助一切也。

〔国立北平图书馆用笺。台北胡适纪念馆，档案编号 HS-JDSHSC-1636-004〕

按:“部中同人社会教育司”应指刘季洪,1939 年 4 月到部任职。①

七月二十九日

先生致信鲍曼,告知已寄赠送该校的礼物,并谈运费、税费等细节。

July 29, 1941

Dear Dr. Bowman:

Owing to restrictions imposed on foreign travelers to the United States, my friend has been obliged to cancel his trip. I have therefore entrusted the China Travel Service to send you by freight per S. S. "President Madison" one wooden box containing two bronze tripods, one piece of ancient jade and 11 pieces of porcelains. Through freight is paid as far as to Pittsburgh.

I enclose herewith the bill of lading, insurance policy and consular invoice which will enable you to collect the box from the American President Line.

All the articles are over 150 years old, so you need not pay any tax. I do hope that they will reach you in excellent condition as they were packed rather carefully.

Upon the receipt of these gifts, you would perhaps write a letter to Dr. H. H. Kung. I shall be glad to pass it on to him for you.

Trusting you are having a pleasant summer vacation and with kindest regards,

Yours sincerely,

T. L. Yuan

Director

〔平馆(冯平山图书馆)英文信纸。University of Pittsburgh Library, John Gabbert Bowman, Administrative Files, Box 2 Folder 13, Chinese Material〕

按:此件为打字稿,落款处为先生签名,以航空信方式寄送。

七月　香港(般含道旅馆)

先生为《国立北平图书馆藏碑目·墓志类》撰写跋文。〔《国立北平图书馆藏

① 《教育部职员录》,1942 年,叶 15。

碑目·墓志类》,1941年〕

按:此目由范腾端编纂,共收录历朝墓志目37307通,并附佛教塔铭74通,1941年8月由上海开明书店印行,陈垣署耑。

八月七日

先生致信顾毓琇,请其代向陈立夫申请补助,以利在港工作。

一樵次长:

□恳者,弟在港用费,前承地山先生资□□□。半载以来,勉强维持,地山逝世后,景况不佳,昨已函陈。弟所借之款亟须归还,拟请将此中困难情形转陈部长,能否援照。周尚先生前例准予将薪金按照法定汇率由昆汇港。即乞赐以援助,不胜感幸。专此奉恳,敬候道祺。

弟袁同礼顿首

八月七日

〔中国第二历史档案馆,教育部档案·全卷宗5,国立北平图书馆请拨员工学术研究补助费经常费有关文书,案卷号11616(1)〕

按:本月4日,许地山逝世。周尚,字君尚,江苏昆山人,曾长期在侨务委员会任职。9月1日,陈立夫批示"可转财部";9月29日,财政部发函拒绝。此信破损。

八月九日

先生致信王重民,谈其回国主持馆务、善本运美及赴美计划等杂事。

有三吾弟:

接七月二十日函,详悉一一。拟提前返国,尤所企望。由此赴内地之旅费已预为筹划,交孙述万暂为保管矣。前请胡先生继续交涉,不知结果如何。部中原先行运港,拟按私人行李办法分批移运,如万一胡先生交涉成功,则可选运乙库之书也。自美方冻结中国资金后,不识国会圕及私人方面尚能汇款否?馆中出版物已告大同多多寄沪矣。兄赴美护照将于十二月中旬到期,刻下请求延长,中美两方手续繁多,故拟于十二月以前来美。返国护照想大使馆可办春间大驾返国即系大使馆办的护照,下次来函请将此点说明。刻下由美来华之船除Coolidge外均只有头等,故尊处应预定Coolidge三等舱甚好也。余详至胡先生函,不另。顺颂旅安。

兄同礼顿首

八,九

〔国立北平图书馆用笺。中国书店·海淀,四册〕

按:Coolidge 即柯立芝总统号邮轮(S. S. President Coolidge),往返于上海和旧金山之间。

八月十一日

鲍曼致函先生,该校已收到中国政府寄送的礼物,就此表示感谢,并告严文兴在校就读的情况。

August 11, 1941

Dear Dr. Yuan:

By this letter let me acknowledge your letter of June 3, together with the letter from Mr. Chen Li-fu and your letter of June 4. Also let me report that I have just examined a box which has come to the University through your kindness, in which were the following articles:

One square wooden Holder for Stationaries

One red-wood Pen-Holder

One Ink-Stone known as "Tuan Yen"

Four Chinese Ink

Ten Chinese Brushes

Four Paintings by Famous Artists

One Pair of Scrolls with Frame

One Box of Red-Ink for Seals

Complete sets of Reproductions of Chinese Paintings published by Commercial Press, Chung Hua Book Company and Mo Yuan Tang

Samples of Stationery of Classical Style

We understand that some objects in jade, porcelain and bronze are to follow. For the University and for myself, personally, let me thank you for your kindness. For the present we are putting these materials in safe keeping until a more permanent place can be found for them in the autumn in the China Memorial Room.

Time and again I have been sorry that your mission to this country was postponed. Let me assure you again that you would be a most welcome visitor in Pittsburgh.

Mr. Yen Wen-hsing has now completed two years with us in the

Department of Chemistry. A few weeks ago, we arranged to pay his expenses until he completes his work for his doctor's degree, which will probably be about the middle of the year.

Here are all best wishes to you. The good will which has developed between China and the United States since our talk in Hong Kong is to most of us here a great satisfaction.

Faithfully yours,

〔University of Pittsburgh Library, John Gabbert Bowman, Administrative Files, Box 2 Folder 13, Chinese Material〕

按:该函未能及时送到先生处,此件为录副。

八月中上旬

先生由香港赴上海,与海关等方交涉善本运美事宜。〔《王伯祥日记》第 17 册,页 455〕

按:8 月 13 日,赵万里访王伯祥,告知先生已来沪。

八月十六日　上海

先生赴开明书店,与王伯祥晤谈,表示《校辑宋金元佚书》印费两万元后日即可交付,并致谢意。〔《王伯祥日记》第 17 册,页 462 〕

八月二十一日

先生与赵万里赴开明书店,与王伯祥晤谈,商洽董作宾《甲骨丛编》印行,略有眉目。〔《王伯祥日记》第 17 册,页 472〕

按:王伯祥在其日记中将《甲骨丛编》记作《甲骨研究》。

先生发电报给胡适,告知善本书即将运美,请其与美国务院商洽授权并电覆。

AMBASSADOR HU

CHINESE EMBASSY WASHINGTON DC

AMERICAN TRANSPORT COMPANY RECOMMENDS SHIPMENT BOOKS NEXT NAVAL TRANSPORT KINDLY SECURE AUTHORIZATION STATE DEPARTMENT TO CONSUL GENERAL CABLE REPLY YUAN

〔台北胡适纪念馆,档案编号 HS-JDSHSE-0404-082〕

八月二十五日

先生赴开明书店,晤王伯祥,告董作宾所著《甲骨丛编》决定委托该社出

版。〔《王伯祥日记》第 17 册,页 480〕

八月下旬

赵万里将开明书店誊缮之《甲骨丛编》出版合同交来,先生签订。〔《王伯祥日记》第 17 册,页 482〕

八月三十一日

先生访顾廷龙,告知即将返香港。〔《顾廷龙日记》,页 184〕

九月三日

先生离沪赴香港。〔《王伯祥日记》第 17 册,页 496 〕

按:9 月 2 日,王伯祥催开明书店同事赶制《国立北平图书馆馆藏碑目》样书 12 册,并于该日下午送交。

九月十二日　香港

先生致信胡适,告善本运美的两种方法,并略述遇险及沪上生活不易。

适之大使尊鉴:

上月在沪曾与海关当局再度商洽,据云每次如运三、四箱,可保无虞,超过此数则不敢担保。嗣美领介绍,往晤美商转运公司之经理 Gregory 君,渠主张将箱件即日移运美海军仓库,一俟军舰到沪,渠即负责代运,并谓事前无须取得总领事之许可,运到后并不收任何运费云云。同礼当即与洪芬先生商酌,渠颇盼尊处能获得美政府若干之援助,倘国务院能发一电致罗君,则采用此种办法更觉妥当。爰奉上一电,谅荷台察。日前乘荷轮返港,曾携来四箱,途经厦门,检查员开箱检查,幸对于书之内容不甚了然,安然渡过,然已饱受虚惊矣。在沪曾晋谒尊夫人,谓两月以来未接世兄等来信,颇以为念。沪上生活奇昂,然与内地相较,尚远逊之。匆上,顺候道祺。

后学袁同礼顿首

九月十二

〔国立北平图书馆用笺。《胡适遗稿及秘藏书信》第 31 册,页 633-634〕

按:Gregory 应指 F. O. Gregory,时任 Shanghai Stevedoring Co.(上海驳运公司)总经理。[①]

---

① *The North-China Desk Hong List*, 1941, p. 289.

九月十五日

王伯祥致函先生，内附开明书店出版万斯年《唐代文献丛考》契约。〔《王伯祥日记》第17册，页520〕

按：该书出版计划因太平洋战争爆发而中断，1947年7月仍由开明书店印行。

九月十七日

先生致信王重民，告平馆运美书籍已分批运出，并请其在美打探中央图书馆运美书籍拟存何处。

有三吾弟：

上海方面自经再度接洽后，每次可运出四、五箱，已有三十箱安然出口。为节省运费计，拟以五十箱寄存于加利佛尼亚大学，其余者则寄存于国会图书馆。近闻中央图书馆所购之书，约一百三十箱，拟由港运美，深恐国会图书馆感觉麻烦，故拟以一部分存于西美也。中央圕之书是否存于该馆，请询明示复。外四函请分别转寄。专此，顺颂旅安。

同礼顿首

九月十七日

附件：国会圕各人三件，加利佛尼亚大学一件。

〔中国书店·海淀，四册〕

按：中央图书馆拟运美之善本古籍未能及时运出，失陷于香港。

十月八日

先生致信王重民，告知拣选后之善本已全部运出，并谈平馆窘境、亟需其回国代理馆务以便赴美募集美金。

有三吾弟：

九月一号及廿一号两函先后收到。存件于今日完全运完，详致胡先生信中，至所余之箱拟请罗君保护。尊处返国自以乘坐三等舱为宜，犯不上用头等之船费。最好请船公司预为登记，如能于四月间中基会开会时来港最好，否则稍缓亦可。兄必须俟大驾返国后，方能远行，大约要延至六月间也。蒋复聪所购之书已决定经仰光内运矣，善本甚多，已在港看过。近闻又筹到二十万元专购旧籍，本馆则不名一文，故亟愿早日来美。近郭任远在美活动，闻已允为蒋筹募美金，深恐捷足先登,因之愈形焦急。蒋为其季刊致美国征文之函,请觅出录副,寄下一阅为盼。顺颂旅安。

兄同礼顿首

十月八日

余详致吴子明函。

〔中国书店·海淀,四册〕

先生致信加州大学伯克利分校图书馆馆长,告知平馆已寄出七十五箱善本书至该校,如有缩微胶片机可进行拍照,若无空间存储可将其发往国会图书馆。

October 8, 1941

Mr. Harold L. Leupp, Librarian

University of California

Berkeley, Calif.

U. S. A.

Dear Mr. Leupp:

For the past two years, a number of our rare Chinese books and manuscripts have been kept in Shanghai. Owing to the uncertainty of the general situation, we deemed it necessary to release them from Shanghai and send them to the United States for temporary deposit until political situation in the Far East has become more clarified.

In view of the keen interest in oriental studies at the University of California, we are extremely glad to send these books to you on loan in the hope that they will help to facilitate sinological researches carried on in your great institution. If you have microfilm equipment in your library, it would be a good opportunity to make film copies of these books, so that they may be made available to all sinological scholars in the West.

Accordingly, 75 cases have been sent to your Library in several shipments. In order to avoid examination by the Shanghai Customs which, as you know, is now in the hands of the Japanese, the name of this Library as consignor was purposely omitted, but the name of the Chinese Library Service was used instead.

In connection with these shipments, our Shanghai office has not been able to secure consular invoices which, as we understand, will enable you to get the cases through the Customs without any difficulty. But since old books are exempt from duty in the States and since they are not for sale, I hope you will have no difficulty in taking their delivery. But if you have to pay customs duties and other charges in connection with these books, the same will be refunded to you. Freight has been prepaid as far as to San Francisco.

I enclose a check-list showing the number of cases which were shipped to you in five instalments. Kindly have it checked up upon their receipt.

As libraries were usually crowded, we wonder whether you have the necessary space for these books. If it would be possible for you to take custody of them for us, your assistance will be most gratefully appreciated. If you find it inconvenient to comply with our request, you may send it to the Library of Congress in Washington at our expense. I am writing to Prof. Lessing about the details.

Thanking you for your valuable collaboration,

Yours sincerely,
T. L. Yuan
Director

〔National Archives, General Records of the Department of State, Decimal File, 1940–44, Box 5844〕

按:Chinese Library Service 似指中华图书馆服务社,待考。该件为录副。

十月十一日

阿博特致函先生,寄上 Mental Measurements Yearbook 编辑部覆信并告知有关书刊已于九月三十日寄送上海。

October 11, 1941

Dear Sir:

A copy of a letter from the Editor of the *Mental Measurements*

Yearbook dated September 6, 1941, is enclosed herewith, together with the reply made by this Institution thereto.

The publications referred to in the correspondence have been received and have been included in a shipment which left the Institution September 30, 1941, in care of your Shanghai agent, Mr. T. H. Tsien.

Very truly yours,

C. G. Abbot

Secretary.

〔Smithsonian Institution Archives, Records, 1868-1988 (Record Unit 509), Box 1, National Library, Peiping〕

按:该函寄送香港,并抄送给上海办事处钱存训。此为录副。

十月十八日

平馆向教育部呈文一件,题为《为呈覆前奉电令支配职馆美金设备费二千元谨将需要较殷之西文书籍开列清单四份请予鉴核由》,具先生名并钤印。

大部代电内开"密兹支配该馆美金设备费二千元应即依照规定注意事项开列请购设备清单四份于文到两个月内寄部核转"等因附发国立各学校机关开列三十年度美款购置设备清单应行注意事项一份,奉此自当遵办。适职奉令赴沪以致稽延,兹将职馆需要较殷之西文书籍开列清单四份随呈奉上,即乞鉴核准予核转,无任盼祷,谨呈

教育部部长陈

国立北平图书馆代理馆长袁同礼

中华民国三十年十月十八日

〔中国第二历史档案馆,教育部档案·全宗号五,国立中央图书馆北平图书馆国立北平研究院等单位动支美借款购运图书仪器的有关文书,案卷号 5468〕

十月二十九日

先生致信白寿彝,谈合作印书事。

寿彝先生大鉴:

前以未悉尊处最近通讯地址,致稽问候。顷奉手教,敬悉种切。承建议以大著改为敝馆及伊斯兰学会合印之书,印费由双方担任一节,弟极表赞同,兹已函托开明书店先将估价,嘱其先拟一契约草案,

再行奉上，当候尊处与会中商洽也。刻下纸价奇昂，不须先付印费，将纸买下，而昆明之印费如何方能汇沪，亦一问题也。此事迁延已久，深为抱歉，想此中困难当能见谅。匆匆，顺颂大安。

弟同礼顿首

十月廿九日

〔白寿彝《关于袁同礼的两封信》，《文献》，1988 年第 1 期，页 253-254〕

按：白寿彝所撰之书，题名初为《咸同滇变传抄史料（初集）》，由先生选入《西南文献丛编》，本拟在开明书店印行，但因种种原因并未实现。后该书改名《咸同滇变见闻录》，作为《伊斯兰文化丛书》一种，由重庆商务印书馆出版。

十月三十日

先生致信吴光清、王重民，谈平馆善本书七十五箱已运往伯克利大学及平馆经费困难。

子明、有三吾兄大鉴：

接有三十月七日函，详悉一一。寄加省大学之书箱共七十五件，因系抢运，故不能候其覆函寄到再行运寄，但已函告 Lessing 教授如其左右有日本人则 L. C.亦有日人，如该校大学无地可容，尽可函告胡先生设法运至华京。至仍存在上海者，为甲库大部头之书及乙库之书，遇必要时可托罗君帮忙。兹将 Gregory 住址列后，便中可询胡先生之意见也。西谛代中央图书馆所买之书在港装了一百余箱，闻已决定运美，但须先盖上该馆之图章云云。本馆向教部请款，闻又被蒋慰堂破坏，近来对本馆同人，一一代为介绍薪水较高之位置，因之辞职他往者颇不乏人，居心如此，未免太难。今后本馆经费只有在美设法，拟俟明年暑假来美一行，届时两兄必有一人返国可以代劳也。胡先生诚恳态度，至为可感，但内中情节复杂，渠无法知之，亦不便告之（如孙洪芬之无诚意、教部为各司长所把持、蒋慰堂之破坏本馆事业等等），加以地位关系，对于刻苦工作、埋头苦干之人之种种痛苦亦不愿入耳，所谓“富人不知穷人苦”也。郭任远在美活动，胡先生虽不愿意，但似亦无法阻止。渠代中央图书馆征书，并向罗氏基金请款闻请款三万美金，故其组织如能实现，对于本馆恐无任何之好处，此弟亟亟愿早日赴美之一因也。匆匆,顺颂旅安。

同礼顿首

十月三十日

外致胡先生信及英文信两封,请代发。

〔中国书店·海淀,四册〕

按:此信应于11月10日送到,王重民、吴光清二人当即联名致信胡适。①

先生致信胡适,谈善本运美、次女夭折事。

适之大使尊鉴:

平馆善本书籍壹百箱已分数批运美。因海关不肯负责,不得不特别慎重,收件之人必须时常更换,以免引人注意,故内中廿五箱寄国会图书馆,七十五箱寄加省大学。又因抢运性质,故只要能谋到船上舱位若干即寄若干,幸均安然出口,如释重负。今则美轮已停驶沪上,以后再运必更困难矣。箱件到美以后,分存两地或应集中一处,敢请费神代为筹划,一切统希钧裁,径嘱吴、王两君办理可也装箱目录各寄加大及国会图书馆一份。

闻数月以来,贵体与精神俱佳,深慰远怀,惟每晚睡时过晚,未免有损健康,尚冀在可能范围以内多加休息,为国保重,不胜企祷。平馆经费前以中基会无力增加,曾向教育部请求列入国家预算,亦未能办到。近来物价日昂美金一元可换国币三十余元,同人星散,办事尤感棘手,倘不从速设法,则后顾茫茫,真有不堪设想者,未识我公将何以教我。最近舍下长幼三人均患盲肠炎,而次女以割治稍迟,竟因之夭伤。此间医药之费颇属不赀,故私人方面亦告破产,因之心绪恶劣,未能早日握管,想公必能见谅也。近印《石刻题跋索引》,为一有用之工具书,特交邮寄呈壹部,并乞惠存为荷。临颍依依,未尽所怀。专此,顺候道祺。

后学袁同礼顿首

十月卅日

附寄加省大学书籍清单一份。

〔国立北平图书馆用笺。《胡适遗稿及秘藏书信》第31册,页636-638〕

---

①《胡适遗稿及秘藏书信》第24册,页140。

按:“次女”应指袁桂,生卒日期今已无从得知。“临颍”当作“临颖”。

十一月五日

先生致信鲍曼,询问七月十八日寄出的箱件是否收到,如已妥收,请覆函孔祥熙表示感谢。

November 5, 1941

Dear Chancellor:

Sometime ago I was delighted to have your letter of August 11, acknowledging the receipt of a box of material which I sent to you in May.

On July 18 another box was shipped to you on S. S. President Madison. The box contained two bronze tripods, one piece of ancient jade and 11 pieces of porcelains. The Bill of Lading was sent to you by air-mail on July 29. As I have not yet heard from you about its receipt, I feel rather anxious for its safety. As mails are irregular these days, it is possible that your acknowledgment may have been lost during transit. At any rate, I shall look forward to hearing further from you.

If it has been duly received, will you kindly write a letter to Dr. H. H. Kung who was instrumental in sending the two boxes of gifts to the China Memorial Room. The letter may be sent to me for reforwarding.

It is a pleasure to learn that Mr. Yen Wen-Hsing is doing well with his studies at the University. Let me thank you for what you have done for him. I hope he is in every-way worthy of your support.

With the opening of the winter session, I trust you must have been quite busy with the academic work of the University. If you publish your annual report, may I ask you to send me a copy, as I should like to keep in close touch with the work of your great institution.

With cordial regards,

Yours sincerely,

T. L. Yuan

〔平馆(冯平山图书馆转)英文信纸。University of Pittsburgh Library, John Gabbert Bowman, Administrative Files, Box 2 Folder 13, Chinese Material〕

按:此件为打字稿,落款处为先生签名,以航空信方式寄送。

十一月上旬

先生致信王伯祥,寄还签订后的万斯年《唐代文献丛考》契约,并请估算《西南文献丛编》印价。〔《王伯祥日记》第 17 册,页 627〕

按:该信寄送陈贯吾,后者 10 日赴开明书店面交王伯祥。

十一月十日

米来牟致电先生,请简要报告一九三八年以后美国捐赠书刊的分配、利用情况。

November 10, 1941

PLEASE REPORT BRIEFLY BY CABLE AND FULLY BY AIRMAIL DISPOSITION AND USES AMERICAN BOOKS SHIPPED SINCE NINETEEN THIRTY EIGHT. ALSO PRESENT NEEDS.

MILAM AMERICAN LIBRARY ASSOCIATION

〔The American Library Association Archives, China Projects File, Box 2, Books for China 1944-1947〕

按:该电发往香港(冯平山图书馆),此件为录副。

十一月中上旬

先生覆电米来牟,告知书刊分配因运输中断已停止,报告书由航邮寄出。

DISTRIBUTION TEMPORARILY SUSPENDED DUE INTERRUPTION COMMUNICATIONS REPORT SENT AIRMAIL CURRENT PERIODICALS VIA RANGOON NEEDD LETTER FOLLOWS TLYUAN.

〔The American Library Association Archives, China Projects File, Box 2, Books for China 1944-1947〕

按:NEEDD 当作 NEEDED。此电发往芝加哥,收讫时间应为当地 11 月 13 日 18 点 37 分。由该电可知香港寄送西南地区邮件须经仰光转投。

十一月十七日

米来牟覆函先生,告知需中华图书馆协会提供美方捐赠书刊分配报告的缘由并期待收到邮寄的报告。

November 17, 1941

Dear Dr. Yuan:

Thank you for your cable. I shall look forward to receiving a more detailed statement in your promised letter.

You may wonder at the reason for my inquiry at this time. All I can say is that I have become suddenly conscious that the American people appear to be on the verge of putting China in a very prominent place in their thoughts. And if there is to be a revival and extension of interest in cultural relations with China, it is, I suppose, up to you and me and our colleagues to see to it that libraries and librarians do their part.

I need hardly add that when we in America occasionally pause to look in your direction we are filled with admiration, for your country, and for your educational programs.

Very cordially yours.

Carl H. Milam

Executive Secretary

〔The American Library Association Archives, China Projects File, Box 2, Books for China 1944-1947〕

阿博特致函先生，告威廉姆斯学院汤普森物理实验室向中国捐助了大量期刊和课本，史密斯森协会将会寄送上海，并询问钱存训是否有权分发暂存该协会的六百包出版物。

November 17, 1941

Dear Dr. Yuan:

The Thompson Physical Laboratory, Williams College, Williamstown, Massachusetts, recently sent the Smithsonian Institution a large consignment of periodicals and textbooks for transmission to China. The publications will be included in the next consignment to your agent in Shanghai. Correspondence regarding the matter is enclosed herewith for your information.

In this connection I beg to say that there are on hand here about 600 packages of publications for correspondents in Shanghai. Could you authorize Mr. T. H. Tsien, your Shanghai agent, to distribute these packages? If so, they will be included with one of the regular shipments made to his address.

Very truly yours,

C. G. Abbot

Secretary.

〔Smithsonian Institution Archives, Records, 1868-1988 (Record Unit 509), Box 1, National Library, Peiping〕

按:Williams College 通译作威廉姆斯学院,1793 年创办,美国著名的文理学院。该函抄送钱存训。

十一月中下旬

王伯祥覆函先生,告白寿彝《咸同滇变传抄史料(初集)》印行的估价及《滇南碑传集》校对进展。(《王伯祥日记》第 17 册,页 649)

按:此函应写于 19 日之前,附在王伯祥致陈贯吾信中。

十一月二十八日

先生致信白寿彝,告知开明书店略估印书成本,建议早日付印以免纸价再涨。

寿彝先生大鉴:

奉到十一月十一日手教,藉悉种切。顷接开明书店复函,照录如下:"迩来纸价日高,排印装订诸工,时时罢工增值,委实无法悬揣确数。就今日市情略计,此书如印三十二开本五百部,最低成本须二千元。如承委印,须俟出版时照实支成本计数,此时确估则为事实所限,无法接受。"以上所云,谅系实际情形,敝意如能早日付印则成本较轻,已函告敝馆上海办事处,先付开明一千元,并盼学会方面亦能汇寄该书店一千元,以便先将需用之纸予以买下,以免再涨,请通知马子实先生将该款径行送交四马路开明书店王伯祥先生手收。因系委托该书局代印性质,故将来两机关平均分书,并无稿费。二千元不敷时,再由两机关津贴开明,该书店不负赢亏之责任也。如何之处,并盼示复为荷。顺颂道棋。

弟同礼顿首

十一月廿八

香港平山图书馆转

〔白寿彝《关于袁同礼的两封信》,页 253-254〕

按:“马子实”原名马坚,云南人,毕业于伊斯兰师范学校,1931 年由中国回教学会(上海)派往埃及学习,1939 年 10 月离开埃及返国,后由滇赴上海,时应在沪上翻译《古兰经》。[①] “学会”即伊斯兰学会。

十二月二十五日

晚,日军占领香港全境,先生与家人均陷于此地。

① 《月华》第 11 卷第 28-30 期,1939 年 10 月,页 16;《申报》,1940 年 4 月 22 日,第 11 版。

一九四二年　四十八岁

二月十日

先生赴般含道马鉴宅，告知摩罗街书摊状况，后二人同往该处，见各摊陈列之书均系乱时匪徒自官署、学校或私人寓所劫掠者，现普通书以重量贱卖，善本则散见于各摊，极难配全，且索价甚昂。〔香港中文大学马鉴档案〕

先生访陈君葆，与之谈寄存图书事甚久，晚留宿其家。〔《陈君葆日记全集》第2卷，页56〕

二月

先生托陈君葆设法在香港图书馆内为孙述万谋取职位。〔《陈君葆日记全集》第2卷，页61、112〕

> 按：2月28日，陈君葆向日人肥田木中卫呈请加孙述万、尹鸿恩为馆员，照准。

三月四日

下午，先生访冯平山图书馆，与陈君葆晤谈。〔《陈君葆日记全集》第2卷，页63〕

三月三十一日

先生致信陈君葆，请其担任先生和陈寅恪离港返沪申请的保人，并请利用与日军关系加快登记。

> 陈君葆吾兄：
>
> 兹托沈乃正先生面交寅恪兄及弟返沪之申请书，请费神在保证人格内填写大名，并盖章为感。又介绍人方面拟请在友邦军人中代恳绍介，俾能提前登记。无任欣感。屡渎清神，感激不尽。专此，顺颂道安。
>
> 弟袁同礼顿首
>
> 三，三十一

〔谢荣滚主编《陈君葆书信集》，广州：广东人民出版社，2008年，页116〕

按:沈乃正(1899—?),字仲端,浙江嘉兴人,1921 年毕业于清华学校,后赴美留学,获哈佛大学法学博士学位,回国后历任南开大学政治系教授,军官团上校教官,南京国民政府内政部民政司科长,浙江大学政治系主任,清华大学政治学系教授,时与陈寅恪一家合住香港九龙城福佬村道 11 号 3 楼。"友邦军人"应指日军,此种说法实在是不得已而为之。先生确有返沪计划,如王伯祥在 3 月 3 日日记中写道"贯吾来……知孙洪芬已自港来,守和亦将踵至也。"① 5 月 5 日,陈寅恪一家离开香港,途经澳门,后到广州湾,再从广西转入内陆。

是年春

先生陷于香港时,生活颇为困顿,常常向叶恭绰告贷。〔《顾廷龙日记》,页 274〕

按:日伪组织曾邀请陈焕镛、陈寅恪、先生等人赴伪广州大学教书,先生断然拒绝。②

四月二十一日

先生访颜惠庆,告正在撰写一本评曾国藩的著作,并谈某书店正在出售廉价书。〔《颜惠庆日记》第 3 卷,页 425〕

五月中下旬

先生致信钱存训,请代表平馆与王伯祥等人协商解除《甲骨丛编》印行合约,并收回预付印费。〔《王伯祥日记》第 18 册,页 119〕

按:先生欲以此款就平馆沪上办事处急需,5 月 28 日钱存训持此信访王伯祥,后王伯祥与章锡琛磋商,允诺暂缓合同。翌日,预付款八千元退回孙洪芬,稿件则交钱存训代管。

六月上旬

先生偕家人离港,前往内陆。〔台北"国史馆",〈中国图书馆协会请补助(教育部)〉,数位典藏号 019-030508-0015〕

按:今人"香港沦陷后滞留数月得以脱险经上海回昆明"之说③,

---

① 《王伯祥日记》第 18 册,页 25。

② 《竺可桢全集》第 8 卷,页 500。

③ 王成志《袁同礼、费正清与抗战时期中美学术文化交流》,《安徽大学学报》(哲学社会科学版),2019 年,第 43 卷第 2 期,页 80。

是不切实的。

六月二十三日

先生及家人抵达广州湾，致电任鸿隽，告知成功脱险。〔台北"中央研究院"近代史研究所档案馆，〈中华教育文化基金董事会〉，馆藏号 502-01-08-057，页 38〕

按：任鸿隽时任中基会董事、干事长，6 月 25 日，任鸿隽致信顾临，转告这一好消息。

是年夏

先生致信王伯祥，请暂缓执行赵万里校辑《宋元明佚书》印行合约，并请将预付印费两万元退回。〔《王伯祥日记》第 18 册，页 164、76、183〕

按：7 月 9 日，钱存训持此信访王伯祥，与之商洽，翌日王伯祥回覆钱存训，表示开明书店可以接受此请，但须等正式公函后才能照办。此书稿前由郑振铎策动，因牵涉公私藏家太多，王伯祥认为印行恐难实现，而撤销则须先生出面主持。平馆撤销之意，约在本年 4 月时已有所表示。8 月 3 日，钱存训再往相商，王伯祥表示实无经费可退，故暂以开明书店作担保方，由平馆驻沪办事处向新华银行借九千元周济，该约由李芳馥代表平馆订立，11 月 27 日偿还。

七月中下旬

先生抵达桂林。〔沈亚明《千里书来慰眼愁：陈寅恪致沈仲章函》，《上海书评》，2017 年 12 月 30 日〕

八月十一日

先生致信蒋志澄、刘季洪，告知已抵桂林，平馆存沪之善本书籍分存法租界私人住宅，并请二人协助将平馆经费列入教育部正式预算。

养春、季洪司长学兄尊鉴：

敝馆善本图籍前奉部令移运美洲，因沪上海关不肯放行，至十月初旬始行办理完竣。当时曾上部长一函，计达台览。十二月初旬接到美国复函知已全部安全运到，正拟再行呈报，适香港沦陷航邮阻隔，未能早日奉闻。至敝馆存沪之中西文书籍于本年四、五月间亦由英美仓库分批移存至法界私人住宅，仍由驻沪职员分别保管，可告无虞。堪慰廑注。弟将沪港经手事件办理就绪，乃于六月初旬离港，因缺乏交通工具，于日前始抵桂林，一俟获到车位，再行赴筑转渝，届时当再趋谒面陈一切。敝馆经费前承鼎力赞助,本年曾拨四万八千八百元,于馆务发展裨益良多,惟物价狂涨,仍感拮据,近在沪专租私人住宅所费尤属不赀。近与梦麟先生电商,拟请大部在明年预算内特予增加为十万元购书及经常各半。并恳两公在部长、次长前力为关说,俾能列入正式预算,不胜企祷之至。先此申谢,顺候道祺。

弟袁同礼拜启

八月十一日

赐覆请寄昆明敝馆为感。

〔中国第二历史档案馆,教育部档案·全卷宗5,国立北平图书馆请拨员工学术研究补助费经常费有关文书,案卷号11616(1)〕

按:蒋志澄(1897—1949),字养春,浙江诸暨人,时任总务司司长。① 该信首页左侧有批注"先请彭百川先生核示,弟澄,八,十七、十八"。彭百川,江西宁冈人,时任教育部秘书。

八月十二日

先生致信陈立夫,告知已抵桂林,平馆存沪之善本书籍分存法租界私人住宅,并申请将平馆经费列入教育部正式预算。

部长钧鉴:

职馆善本图籍于上年九月分批运美,至十月初旬办理完竣。当时曾上一书,计达钧览。十二月初旬接到美国复函,知已全部安全运到。正拟再行呈报,适值香港沦陷航邮阻隔,曾乘立法委员全增嘏君赴渝之便,托其代为陈述,谅荷鉴察。至职馆存沪之中西文书籍于本年四、五月间亦由英美仓库分批移存法界私人住宅,仍由驻沪职员分别保管,可告无虞,堪慰廑注。职将沪港经手事件办理就绪,乃于六月初旬离港,因沿途缺乏交通工具,于日前始抵桂林,一俟获到卡车车位,当即来渝述职。又职馆经费本年承大部补助四万八千元,于馆务发展裨益良多,惟年来物价狂涨,仍感异常拮据,近与梦麟先生电商,拟请大部在明年预算中特予增加职馆经费为十万元购书及经常费各半,即希赐以鉴核,准予列入正式预算,无任欣感、屏营之至。专此,敬候道祺。

职袁同礼拜上

---

①《教育部职员录》,1942年,叶3。

八月十二日

〔中国第二历史档案馆,教育部档案·全卷宗5,国立北平图书馆请拨员工学术研究补助费经常费有关文书,案卷号11616(1)〕

按:此信于8月19日送达教育部。

八月中下旬

先生及家人由金城江乘资源委员会便车前往贵阳。〔台北"国史馆",〈资源委员会所属各单位搭乘运务处便车等案〉,数字典藏号003-010503-024〕

按:8月14日,资源委员会致金城江运务处,告知先生将前往该处乘车,请预留车位。

九月四日

陈立夫覆函先生,告平馆下年度经费已编列,无法再增补。

守和先生大鉴:

接诵八月十二日大函,敬悉贵馆运美善本图籍及存沪图籍均已安全寄藏。至为欣慰。关于贵馆下年度经费预算,已遵照行政院规定增加三成之原则编呈,无法多列,特此复闻。顺颂时绥!

陈〇〇拜启

〔中国第二历史档案馆,教育部档案·全卷宗5,国立北平图书馆请拨员工学术研究补助费经常费有关文书,案卷号11616(1)〕

按:此件为底稿,拟于8月25日,实际发出为9月4日。

九月二十四日

先生抵达贵阳。〔《贵州日报》,1942年9月26日,第3版〕

九月二十五日

先生向教育部呈文一件,题为《为呈报到馆照常视事请予备案示遵由》。

窃职前奉令移运存沪善本图书至美保存,曾数次到沪,办理其事。业于上年十月全数运毕,于太平洋战事发生之前,即已安抵美京,并由驻美大使馆照数点收,移交美国国会图书馆代为保管在案。嗣以香港沦陷,交通梗阻,在职未返国以前,由中华教育文化基金董事会公举本馆委员会主席蒋梦麟暂行主持馆务,曾于本年三月五日具函陈明,奉四月八日总字第一二九九五号指令,准予备查在案。现职既脱险归国,自应回馆照常视事,理合具文呈报敬祈鉴核,准予备案,指令祗遵,实为德便。谨呈

教育部部长陈

代理国立北平图书馆馆长袁〇〇

〔《北京图书馆馆史资料汇编(1909-1949)》,页752-753〕

按:10月28日,教育部指令第43267号。“令代理国立北平图书馆馆长袁同礼,九月二十五日呈一件——为呈报奉令移运存沪善本图籍至美保存,已公毕回籍照常视事,祈鉴核备案由。呈悉。准予备案。此令。”

十月初

先生抵达重庆。〔John K. Faribank, *Chinabound, a fifty-year memoir*, 1982, p. 209〕

十月七日 重庆

上午,费正清假中基会开会,顾毓琇、杭立武、叶企孙等人出席,先生最后到场。会后,费正清、先生、梁思成一起午餐。〔Harvard University, John K. Fairbank Personal Archive〕

按:费正清认为经历了近一年的疾病折磨和禁闭,先生显然受到明显的影响,但整体而言尚好。

十月八日

先生与李济访翁文灏。〔《翁文灏日记》,页844〕

十月十三日

先生亲自向教育部呈文一件,题为《为呈报本馆职员生活补助费及食米代金请援最近颁布之公务员战时生活补助办法准予自十月份起由国库及粮食部继续核发示遵由》。

窃职馆职员之生活补助及特别生活补助食米代金等均先后经国库署及粮食部核发在案。近政府对于公务员战时生活补助办法业经予以修正,除食米按照年岁长幼核发外,其战时生活补助费在陪都及迁建区者,除以二百元为基本数外,并按其薪俸额加五成发给,凡在各省市之中央机关,其基本数额由行政院按当地物价及其生活情形分别核定等因。查职馆设在昆明其生活指数实较各省市为高,兹附呈职馆职员薪俸表二份,拟恳钧部准予转送行政院鉴核,援照该院新颁布之办法自本年十月份起继续由国库署及粮食部发给战时生活补助(包括基本数及依俸额加增之百分之五十)及食米代金,是否有当,理合具文。呈请鉴核施行指令,示遵,不胜感激,待命之至。谨呈教育部计呈本馆职员薪俸表二份。

代理国立北平图书馆馆长袁同礼

卅一年十月十三日

〔中国第二历史档案馆,教育部档案·全卷宗五,国立北平图书馆员工生活补助费名册及俸薪表,案卷号11614(1)〕

按:此时先生薪俸每月680元(实支640元)并已含特别办公费,故不拟再领依俸额百分之五十之补助。教育部收到呈文后,核准照办。

十月十八日

先生、费正清、蒋梦麟三人访翁文灏。〔《翁文灏日记》,页847〕

十月中下旬

先生致信竺可桢。〔《竺可桢全集》第8卷,2008年,页417〕

按:此信内容极有可能为问询张荫麟病情,于23日送达。

十月二十日

先生亲自向教育部呈文一件,请将平馆经费比照中央图书馆标准列入一九四三年年度教育部正式预算,教育部及中基会分别担任一半。

敬陈者,窃查职馆经费向由中华教育文化基金董事会于美国退还庚子赔款项下按年拨给。当职馆开办伊始,美国庚款用途较少,得以大宗供给职馆应用。其后分润之事业日增,职馆之经费锐减,久有左支右绌之感。自二十九年度起,蒙钧部发给补助费两万元。三十年度加为四万元,三十一年度又加为四万八千八百元,于馆务进行裨益殊多。惟中华教育文化基金董事会所拨常年经费,逐年虽亦稍有增加,然本年度亦仅有十九万五千元。值此物价暴涨之际,指数递高,动辄倍蓰,比诸经费所增指数,恒为什与一之比。目下公务人员最低薪给米贴合计岁需万元,而近年以来书价奇昂,大学用书每册辄需数百元。以此戋戋之十余万元全数充作人员费,只能支配十余人;全数充作事业费,亦仅能购入图书千册而已。顾自抗战以来,职馆人员大减而事务倍增。职馆本为全国学术界服务,目下各方面工作紧张,对于文化食粮需要迫切,范围尤广,一方则固有者多已沦陷,而新刊者供应不及,供不应求,恐慌尤甚。为此,职馆虽于经费支绌之中而采购新书,扩充工作未敢稍有懈怠。连年增购中西文图书以供各大学、各研究所应用者不在少数，尤其关于战后建设问题，更属立法、行政各机关之所特需。此项资料必须与英、美文化机关密切联络，随出随购，多方赶运。否则时机一过，不仅价高倍蓰，而且购寄维艰。一方则沦陷区内散佚之珍本图书，仍须继续密派妥员择尤收购。此外又须征集抗战史料、西南文献、西北文献，近复编辑《西南文献丛刊》、《西北边疆书目》以及《新疆书目解题》等等，工作概属继续前此规定之计划，而又为目前之所必需。所幸上承钧部之补助提倡，下赖各大学、各研究所以及各出版机关顾念文化所关，协力扶助，又得美国罗氏基金董事会补助美金一万八千元，分作三年，以资弥补。比年以来乃获按照预定计划勉为措施。上年罗氏基金补助之款业已用罄，同礼乃有赴美筹款之拟议。旋以馆藏善本书籍运美保存，以海关阻难，滞留沪上将近一载，赴美之举又未获见诸实行，而物价日高不知所届，积年训练有成之优秀员司多已别有高就。以此人少事繁，左支右绌，瞻念前途，实深忧虑。伏念国立图书馆事业乃国家百年大计之所关，职馆经费当年由中华教育文化基金董事会拨给开支，原属一时权宜之计。年来若干私立教育文化机关一经改归国立之后，其经临开支亦即由钧部统核列入国家预算。职馆名称虽属国立，而国库拨给之款为数甚微。且职馆自民国十八年改组以来，职司典藏，为国家搜集重要图籍以及所以供应于国内、国外各学术机关者，其事务之重要似亦不亚于中央图书馆。为此建议钧部恳自三十二年度起，将职馆经费开支列入国家正式预算，其数字并请以国立中央图书馆为准，由钧部及中华教育文化基金董事会双方各任半数。如此一转移间，不仅职馆经费有着，馆务得以继续进行，即顾名思义似亦觉名正言顺。方今多数之教育文化机关先例具在，职馆似亦应与从同也。是否有当，伏候钧部鉴核批示祇遵。如荷愈允，再当敢编概算呈候鉴核。谨呈

部长陈

次长顾、余

代理国立北平图书馆馆长袁同礼

三十一年十月二十日

〔中国第二历史档案馆，教育部档案·全卷宗五，国立北平图书馆请拨员工学术研究补助费经常费有关文书，案卷号 11616(1)〕

按:“次长顾、余”即顾毓琇、余井塘,时分别任政务次长、常务次长。

十月二十三日

竺可桢覆函先生。〔《竺可桢全集》第8卷,页417〕

十月二十七日

先生路遇顾颉刚。〔《顾颉刚日记》卷4,页755〕

先生亲自向教育部秘呈一件,汇报平馆存沪善本书运美经过。

敬密陈者,窃职于上年一月,奉令前往港沪,办理移运馆藏善本书籍,送往美国保存。当时以书存上海法租界震旦博物院,由法租界移运大批箱件,每有被阻之虞;且海关既由敌伪把持,码头左近更多间谍耳目,一经惹起宵小注意,势必发生安全问题,为此频与有关系之方面,密商妥善运法,以策万全。嗣又奉令与美国詹森大使先行接洽,拟将是项书籍,作为中国政府暂行借与美国政府,由美国派人在沪接收,即由该国运输舰自行装运。职当即与詹森大使接洽,由詹大使电商美国国务院,由该院训令上海美总领事负责协助,惟该总领事要求必须先由法租界移至公共租界,又必须江海关发给出口允许证,方肯代运。爰于三月间将上项存书分批秘运,移入公共租界之美籍仓库,同时并向总税务司商洽手续。总税务司于五月间始行奉到财政部训令,饬令发给出口允许证,免验放行,此项允许证书,向由江海关填发,一经总税务司行文转饬,难免泄漏,且码头工人多被敌伪收买,骤见大宗箱件出口,难免检查阻止。总税务司以此为虑,故尔再三劝阻,属为另策万全。此中经过情形,迭经电文承报在案。嗣又奉钧部转下孔副院长手谕,属为分批先运香港,再由马尼剌转运美国,惟由沪运港,仍须向江海关申请出口允许证,方能启运,总税务司既已爱莫能助,职不得已,转与中国旅行社负责人密商,作为职馆在沪新购书籍,赠送美国,委托该社分批代运,冀以掩饰敌伪注意,减少被扣危险。但化整为零,手续较繁,需时较久,直至上年十月初旬,分作十余批之存书,始获全部运毕,共计分装一百零二箱,均由驻美胡大使转交美国国会图书馆代为寄存,并由该馆以小型缩影方式,全部概行摄影,除自留一份外,并允赠职馆一份,一俟邮运恢复,当可寄到。此项运出善本,均以宋元明刊本及名人钞本校本为限,其较次之清刻善本,时间不及装运。本年四月经辗转托人设法,从原寄存之美仓库,分批运至法租界私人住宅,化名寄托,由职馆留沪职员妥为料理处置,均甚秘密,今后谅不至有意外危险。其业经运美之书目,原已编写同样四份,二份随书带美,一份存沪,一份由港转渝,以供呈报钧部,不意原件甫经带至香港,即遭沦陷;拟恳稍假时日,再行设法抄录正本,补呈备案。其运美费用,前蒙钧部拨给美金三千元,当时因承运之轮船公司 American President Lines 未能将抵美后之各项费用预为确定,故将该款全数付交该公司,订明缺则补给,多则缴回。嗣据函报,尚余美金六百〇二元二角五分,由旧金山总公司汇交纽约华美协进社,由该社主任孟治君,代为保管,并已奉钧部令准,留充职馆增购书籍之用。此项运费单据,现存香港金城银行保险库内,只可俟交通恢复再行补报。所有职馆善本藏书运美保管之经过情形,理合先行呈报钧部鉴核备案。谨呈

部长陈

次长顾、余

三十一年十月廿七

〔国家图书馆档案,档案编号 1942-※045-外事 4-001010 至 1942-※045-外事 4-001013〕

按:此件为底稿。11 月 14 日,教育部密令准予备案,并对先生“不畏艰阻”、“多方设法”、“忠勇慎密”予以嘉奖。American President Lines 应指来往于沪(港)美国的邮轮,如 Cleveland、Pierce、Coolidge 等号。《中华民国史档案资料汇编第五辑第二编文化(二)》收录该密呈,但错排较多。

十月二十八日

先生亲自向孔祥熙密呈一件,恳请行政院拨款以支持中美出版品交换事业。

敬密陈者,窃自我国抗战以来,赖我公主持中枢,国际地位日益增高。战后东方世界之政治经济文化,当然仍以中国为中心,届时生产之资金、技术须求助于美国者,不只一端,而美国亦有向东亚发展之必要,不仅有以偿其多年之夙愿,且在政治、经济两方面并须扶助中国,以防日寇之再起复仇。比年以来,美国对于战后之国际组织各项问题,已在详密研究,而中美之如何合作,即为其中大纲要。

美国国务院近派哈佛大学副教授 John K. Fairbank 博士来渝，组织美国学术资料供应处，即属担任此项工作，其第一步则首先将美国最近发表之学术资料以及科学文献由美国国务院文化部根据中国之需要制成小型影片 Microfilm，按期交飞机运华供给于中国学术团体以及行政业务机关，既以救济精神食粮，兼供各方建设参考，该供应处业在渝市求精中学开始工作，预计一阅月以内我国即可利用此项设备，藉以获得最新之资料。其第二步则系统的搜罗战时及战后各项建设之文献，互相交换，俾便双方之公私团体获有研讨之便利途径，此时邮递虽有若干困难，但各项资料若不及时搜罗，日后□至散佚湮没，无从采集，方今美国具有上项研讨之学术机关，除有国会图书馆外，尚有哥仑比亚、哈佛、耶鲁、普仁斯顿（以上东美）、芝加哥（以上中美）、加里佛尼亚、华盛顿（以上西美）大学，每机关均设有中国文化讲座，随时供政府之咨询，实为研究中美文化合作之中心。各该机关对于我国战时及战后关于建设之文献资料需要至为迫切，似应由我国代为择要收集，以供研究，一俟日后通邮即可寄出，作为中国交换之赠品。假定每一机关须费国币叁万元，上列八机关共需国币二十四万元，而易回之资料则以美金计算且必有若干新奇可贵之品，此不仅有以交换文化、沟通思想，且于战后建设之研讨大有裨益。

伏念钧座效忠党国，智烛几先，年来提倡国民之邦交，引导文化之互注，恒先人以图始，收意外之成功。此与中美两国友谊关系至为重大，且美国学术资料供应处既由美国国务院担任经费推动一切，我方似亦宜由行政院提倡以资酬答。

同礼今兹所陈，如蒙采纳，可否即恳钧座属北平图书馆负责筹办，其经费除由该馆担任四万元以及日后由华寄美之运费外，其余之二十万元拟恳钧座惠予筹拨，俾得着手筹备。此项赠品之寄赠可否借重钧座台衔，以示隆重，伏候钧裁，无任屏营，待命之亟。谨呈

行政院副院长孔

三十一年十月廿八日

〔国家图书馆档案，档案编号 1945-※057-综合 5-009002 至 1945-※057-综合 5-009004〕

按：此件为先生所拟之底稿，有大量修改。

是年秋

先生在重庆街头遇张申府，知悉其生活无着，立刻邀请他到平馆重庆办事处工作，负责《图书季刊》中文本的编纂。〔《所忆：张申府忆旧文选》，页115-117〕

按：时，张申府处于无业状态，且被国民政府视为异己人士，生活不易。11月，张申府到馆开始办公，教育部对此项聘用颇为不满，曾责备先生。① 作为《图书季刊》中文本的编纂，张申府勤勉负责②，虽1944年起把精力转到政治生活上，但仍在平馆领薪，至1946年冬被迫脱离平馆。

十一月二日

先生致信赵学海，为《中华图书馆协会会报》联系建国纸厂购纸事宜。

师轼学长大鉴：

奉到一日手教，以患病未能入城走访，此次未克一望颜色，至以为怅。敝处接洽建国纸，远在八九月之间，以尊处无货，嘱于双十节左右携款取纸，故盼尊处对于所需之八令纸特予优待，公私均感。其价若干，请径告李小缘先生金大文化研究所，以便将纸价送上携款至乡间颇觉不妥，能用支票否。琐琐渎神，感谢无已，顺颂大安。

弟袁同礼顿首

十一月二日

〔国立北平图书馆用笺。南京大学图书馆特藏〕

按：赵学海（1898—1943），字师轼，江苏无锡人，清华学校毕业，后赴美留学获威斯康星大学化学学士学位，又赴耶鲁大学等处深造，1924年归国，先后在清华大学、北洋大学、北平师范大学等处任教，1942年起在经济部与中国银行所属的建国纸厂主持工作。

十一月三日

竺可桢致函先生。〔《竺可桢全集》第8卷，页423〕

按：该函可能为一邮包，中含一斤白木耳，由竺可桢家人帮忙购入。

---

①《张申府文集》第3卷，页498。

②《战云纪事——常任侠日记集（1943-1945）》下册，2012年，页376、386。

十一月十一日

先生亲自向教育部呈文一件，题为《为呈请在本年度社会教育经费追加预算图书费项下拨给购书费十万元由》。

窃查抗战建国，各种基本事业莫不需要书籍，而后方之精神食粮，目前尤感缺乏。职馆对于全国教育文化团体以及行政业务机关负有供给图书之义务。历年以还，分途搜集，逐日增加。近一年来物价腾贵、经费支绌，大宗采购未能如愿。虽目前正未易恢复，惟有必不可缓之二项，敢为钧部陈之：一为敌伪出版各项书籍，以及军事、政治、经济、财政、文化种种资料，莫不与抗战情报及现代史料有重大之关系。此类书籍殊鲜再版，定期刊物尤难搜求全份。前此职馆所藏业已略具规模，前年钧座莅滇视察，谬蒙加奖，今后似应继续订购，以免中断。二为沦陷区散佚之各种图书文献，亟有继续搜集之必要，其中善本此时或力有未逮，然间有廉价机会，必需预筹的款以免失之交臂。目前伪币日涨，需款较多。职馆历年委派妥员分赴沦陷区，采访旧籍，对于藏书之家、贩书之肆以及书估经纪较为熟悉。现拟就上列二项范围，向上海、南京、北平、苏州、杭州、广州各处分别采购，所有应用款项拟暂以六十五万元为准。除上月业承钧部分配追加临时费五万元外，拟请在本年度追加经费图书费项下再行拨给十万元。其余之五十万元，并恳准其在三十二年度社会教育经费项下尽先拨给，专供职馆购买上项书籍之用。如发见善本书籍求售者为数较多，款不敷用时，并恳准其再行请款，列入临时费项下开支，匪特充实职馆设备，实与目前抗战建国有极密切之关系。事关国家大计，用敢密陈，谅荷采纳。所有拟请增拨图书费情由是否有当，敬候鉴核批示祇遵。谨呈

部长陈

次长顾、余

代理国立北平图书馆馆长袁同礼

〔中国第二历史档案馆，教育部档案·全卷宗五，国立北平图书馆请拨员工学术研究补助费经常费有关文书，案卷号11616(1)〕

按：12月29日，教育部指令（社字第53059号）准拨平馆经费。“呈悉，准拨给搜购散佚文献及敌伪书刊费叁万元。随令汇发，仰即查收，补具印领呈部。至所请于三十二年度拨给五十万元一

节,应候下年度呈奉行政院核准追加后再行饬知。此令。”

十一月十四日

万斯年致函先生,谈采访西南少数民族语言文献事。

守公先生馆长左右:

十月二十三日曾上一函,并附合作办法,计达钧览。嗣即策动工作,准备离丽,并迁居蒙藏会调查组。二十八日奉到十九日电,当即选书、编目,计先后选书共一百册,带鹤庆四十册。本欲携昆转渝,因不知教部收件日期,恐有所误,昨已交邮快递,包寄情形,另单附上,即请检收。另六十册,周君在整理编目中,昨已函周,嘱其由丽寄渝矣。

据年所知,东巴经典之可以表现于美术者,可分四端:(A)卷端或封面内页有图像者,(B)写法灵活工正者,(C)卷中加有颜色者,至于(D)其封面亦有种种,设计不同,形式亦异,故所寄经典亦分此数类,凡此均与书籍文字美术表现有关,是以寄上,送展与否,敢望卓裁。此外丽江北门坡墓碑之浮雕,亦足为墓碑装饰之美术表现,所拓拓片,亦交周君寄上矣。而鹤庆土司明宣德间墓志碑头之浮雕亦复壮丽伟大,前日手自拓出,昨亦交邮。所有拓片,如欲送展,则请先交托裱,庶可整齐好看也。

十月十九日赐电,因合标准者后文为:“携新幼书盛望速完成,暂缓赴兰”,嗣经交查,乃知为携渝,而下语仍不明,意者或左右催新疆书目之交卷也。倘然,则返昆后,当即杀青,请教,不知可能出版否?

年系于十一月八日离丽,九日抵鹤,因得莫电,有“何日返昆”之语,乃即电渝请示也。

此行系带张文炳君同来,日来忙于踏查工作,高土司之碑头,即在鹤工作成绩之一也。拟略有所得,既往剑川,倘事实许可,沿途略行工作,即当返昆。尊示前请寄喜洲华中大学汪典存先生交年,或已有尊示在喜洲,亦未可知。函件迟慢,交通梗阻,无奈何也。

兰州设馆计划如何?东巴经典现已入藏近四千册,已嘱周君,此后再行努力,期最近能达四千之数,以观厥成,钧意然否?周君于年离丽后,即已迁入丽江师范,依照合同开始工作矣。

道翁想当常见？见请代候，并问汇款已否收到为幸，慧熙先生等是否在筑？便请见示。专上，敬请道安。

万斯年谨上

三十一年十一月十四日在鹤庆

〔国家图书馆档案，档案编号 1943-※036-采藏 8-001019 和 1943-※036-采藏 8-001020〕

按：喜洲位于大理古城以北，白族在此聚居。汪懋祖（1891—1949），字典存，江苏苏州人，教育家，1916 年赴美留学，入哥伦比亚大学并获硕士学位，1920 年回国，历任国立北京师范大学教务长兼代理校长、国立东南大学教育系主任兼教授、江苏省督学等职。

十一月十七日

先生致信蒋志澄，请将教育部补助购书费尽快拨付以便汇往上海应用。

养春司长钧鉴：

最近部中补助敝馆购书费五万元系专购敌伪刊物之用，亟待汇沪应用。前承惠允于一次提前拨付，足征热心赞助，尚希早日交下，不胜感祷。耑此承恳，顺候道祺。

弟袁同礼顿首

十一，十七

〔中国第二历史档案馆，教育部档案 · 全卷宗五，国立北平图书馆请拨员工学术研究补助费经常费有关文书，案卷号 11616(1)〕

十一月十九日

平馆向教育部呈文一件，题为《为呈请拨给职员宿舍建筑费敬祈鉴核示遵由》，具先生名并钤印。

窃查本年公布之战时改善公务员生活办法，内中对于职员公共宿舍，曾经规定由公家供给。查本馆职员向无宿舍，而薪水低微，在外租用民房居住负担过重。爰经再三考虑，拟建筑极简单之临时宿舍六间，最低估价需洋六万元，除拟在本年钧部补助之四万八千八百元内提出三万元作为一部份建筑费外，其余之三万元拟请准予在本年度社会教育追加经费内照数拨给，俾此项临时宿舍得以早日完成。所有拟请赠拨建筑职员宿舍经费三万元缘由是否有当，理合具文呈请鉴核批

示祇遵。谨呈

部长陈

次长顾、余

代理馆长袁同礼

三十一年十一月十九日

〔中国第二历史档案馆,教育部档案·全卷宗五,国立北平图书馆请拨员工学术研究补助费经常费有关文书,案卷号11616(2)〕

十一月二十二日

《大公报》(重庆)刊登先生文章,题为《新中国之建设与中英文化之沟通》。〔《大公报》(重庆),1942年11月22日,第3版〕

按:该篇文章失收于《袁同礼文集》。

十一月二十五日

顾颉刚访先生,不值。〔《顾颉刚日记》卷4,页767〕

十一月二十九日

晚,先生假重庆南开中学(忠恕图书馆)设宴,王世杰、翁文灏、张伯苓、李卓敏等人受邀与席。席间,先生曾向王世杰表示愿意前往印度协助转运图书。此外,翁文灏对时政颇多指责。〔《王世杰日记》,页471;《翁文灏日记》,页862〕

按:王世杰对翁文灏的言辞甚为不满,认为其不分场合任意指述军事机密、妄论十中全会决议,认定其只能为一技术人员,而非政治人物。李卓敏(1912—1991),广州人,金陵大学毕业后赴美留学,获加州大学伯克利分校哲学博士学位,时应在南开大学经济研究所任教。①

十一月三十日

王世杰致函先生,商赴印主持图书转运计划。

守和先生:

昨谈一节,今晨已与陈立夫部长谈过,彼且十分赞成,鄙意将来或可由教育、宣传两部委托足下在印主持办理此事。如得便,足下能将现时运输手续及困难情形查明,杰当再斟酌,提一办法于何

① 《王世杰日记》,页474。

部长(运输局主持者),一面当即与宋部长洽定办法。匆此,即颂日祺。

王世杰敬启

十一月卅日

〔中国第二历史档案馆,教育部档案·全宗号五,教育部关于委派北平图书馆馆长袁同礼办理各院校在美所购图书仪器接收转运事宜的有关文书,案卷号 5465〕

按:“何部长”应指何应钦,“运输局”实指运输统制局,1940 年 4 月 1 日由国民政府军事委员会成立。①

蒋志澄覆函先生,告知教育部拨发购书款项实情。

守和吾兄勋鉴:

十一月十七日惠书敬悉。查该款五万元已经财部拨到半数,即日汇发。其余半数系由财部直拨,到后即转,本部未便垫发,尚希见谅。耑此奉复,顺颂勋祺。

弟蒋〇〇拜启

〇年〇日

〔中国第二历史档案馆,教育部档案·全卷宗五,国立北平图书馆请拨员工学术研究补助费经常费有关文书,案卷号 11616(1)〕

按:此件为底稿,标注 11 月 30 日发,故系于此日。

十二月二日

先生致信陈光甫,约其参观美国提供的缩微胶片机。

光甫先生尊鉴:

抵渝以来,屡欲晋谒,闻公务甚忙,未敢相扰。前在港时,鉴于我国学术界需要新资料之迫切,曾向美订购 Microfilm 设备五套,不意两套运到后,香港即告沦陷。近美国国务院派 Dr. John K. Fairbank 来渝,源源供给此项资料,教育部特组织一委员会,共策进行。该设备业已布置就绪,拟约我公前来指示,本星期五(四日)中午十二时半,如无他约,可否屈驾惠临卡尔登饭店(中四路五九号)便餐,座中多系英美新闻处同人,千祈勿却,餐毕可到金大理学院三楼参观,新到之杂志

① 《建设》旬刊,1940 年 5 月,第 10 期,第 15 版。

已有二百余种矣。专此,敬候道祺。

后学袁同礼顿首

十二,二日

如复初大使仍寓尊处,并乞代约,不胜企盼。

〔国立北平图书馆用笺。《上海市档案馆藏中国近现代名人墨迹》①,页 515-516〕

按:信笺左上角注有"已覆,十二,四,求精中学二楼五号袁守和"似为陈光甫亲笔。陈光甫(1881—1976),原名辉祖,字光甫,江苏丹徒人,银行家,时任中英美平准基金委员会主席。

十二月初②

先生以平馆馆长、国际文化服务社执行秘书(Executive Secretary, International Cultural Service of China)身份与国会图书馆远东代表(Far Eastern Representative, Library of Congress)、外国出版物采购部间委员会中国区主任(China Director, Interdepartmental Committee for the Acquisition of Foreign Publications)费正清共同撰写了一份名为《中美文化关系的备忘录》(Sino-American Intellectual Relations)的文件。

按:该文件共六页,分为两个部分,先概述后枚举具体措施。概述部分首先强调战争期间中美两国必须尽快制订计划、开展文化类相关行动,为重建战后国际关系、区域和平奠定基础;其次,概述了美国对中国援助的现状,指出虽然美国制定了较为详尽的"租借法案"(Lend-Lease Program),但这一援助仅仅只是出于赢得战争的目的,并没有涉及文化领域,而后者则须尽快制订长期计划并着手落实;再次,明确了备忘录的两个基本原则:一是思想与技术并重(ideas are as important as technics),二是两国间文化关系必须是互惠的(reciprocal);最后,备忘录包括两部分内容,分别涉及学术出版物、学者交流和培训。

---

① 该书将此信错系为 1943 年,特此说明。

② 该文件因提交给美国政府、私人基金会、学术团体、高校研究机构,落款时间各不相同,但撰写完成时间应该在 12 月初,参见雷强《袁同礼、费正清联署〈中美文化关系备忘录〉初探》,《国际汉学》,2022 年第 3 期,页 177-185。

十二月四日

中午,先生与费正清前往卡尔登饭店参加便餐,Fisher、Sargent、Frank Price、任鸿隽、魏学仁、曾虚白、温源宁、杭立武等人亦到场。〔Harvard University, John K. Fairbank personal archive〕

按:魏学仁(1899—1987),字乐山,江苏南京人,1922 年毕业于金陵大学,1925 年赴美留学,后获芝加哥大学物理学博士学位,时应任金陵大学理学院院长,费正清记作 Dean Wei;曾虚白(1895—1994),原名曾焘,字煦白,笔名虚白,小说家曾朴长子,毕业于上海圣约翰大学,时任行政院新闻局副局长。

十二月六日

先生访翁文灏。〔《翁文灏日记》,页 865〕

十二月中上旬

先生访运输统制局指挥处,与谭耀宗副处长谈教育部图书转运事。

按:谭耀宗,字子筹,广东台山人,邮传部铁路管理传习所英文高等班毕业,后长期在铁道部任职,曾发明国音电报。①

先生致信竺可桢。〔《竺可桢全集》第 8 卷,页 444〕

按:该信于 12 月 17 日送达。

十二月十四日

先生致信刘节,告知《图书季刊》中文本新书介绍撰写人员及体例,以求统一,并谈联系方式及杂费问题。

子植吾兄:

昨日返沙坪坝,得十日手书,敬悉一一。新书介绍现由张申府前清华大学教授及龚家骅云白,大理民族学院教授与尊处合编,体裁似须一致,拟请一律改为文言。凡尊处不愿介绍之书请交邮寄还寄求精中学二楼五号,以便张、龚两君为之。季刊第一期现定下月二十号付印委托商务办理,时间上尚宽裕也。尊处稿件嗣后请径寄"求精中学二楼五号张申府先生"弟或须赴滇及印度,每月以六千七百字左右为限,再多则不敢奉扰矣。邮费、纸费等等均由本馆担任,径寄张申府或何国贵现由城内办公均可。匆匆,顺颂大安。

① 《北平交大校友录》,1949 年 1 月,页 32;《世界交通月刊》第 1 卷第 1 期,1947 年 7 月,页 46。

弟同礼顿首

十二，十四

〔《瓯越此门两代贤——刘景晨诞辰一百四十周年、刘节诞辰一百二十周年纪念展》，页 195〕

十二月十五日

先生致信傅斯年，告知《图书季刊》将复刊，请寄来史语所近况及研究计划等消息。

孟真先生大鉴：

敝馆近拟恢复《图书季刊》，特侧重于国内及国际学术界之消息。我公主持历史语言研究所，成绩斐然，为海内所景仰，拟请将近年工作概况及进行中之研究计划代写一稿中西文各一，约三百至五百字，如英文不便，仅有中文亦可，于两旬内寄下。如承惠允，钦感莫名。专此奉恳，顺候著祺。

弟同礼顿首

十二，十五

英文本将在美国出版，内中有一栏 Notes on Personal，注重个人之研究工作，贵所人才济济，如承转恳每人各写一短篇之工作计划，尤所感荷。

〔国立北平图书馆驻渝办事处信纸。台北"中央研究院"历史语言研究所傅斯年图书馆，"史语所档案"，李 18-7-6〕

十二月十六日

先生致信史蒂文斯，告知已与费正清开始合作为美国图书馆购买中文出版物，国民政府教育部和中基会正在资助推广缩微胶片阅读器，洛克菲勒基金会可否考虑资助平馆购买纸本外文书刊，并告《图书季刊》英文本即将复刊。

Room No. 5, Second Floor

Chiu Ching Middle School

Chungking, China

December 16, 1942

Dear Dr. Stevens:

Owing to the interruption of mails, I have not been able to write to you as often as I wished. I am asking my cousin to bring this letter to you and as he is going straight through, I hope it will reach you by New Year. May I, therefore, send you and Mrs. Stevens my sincere greetings of the Season?

Since the arrival of Dr. John K. Fairbank, I have been collaborating with him in the selection and buying of Chinese material for American libraries. I have been able to secure Ch $ 100,000 for this purpose. These books and periodicals are now stored in our Chungking office and will be sent to the States as soon as shipping facilities return to normal. I shall appreciate receiving additional information from you and Dr. Graves concerning the needs of American scholars and oriental libraries in the States.

With the regular supply of most important journals on microfilm, Chinese scholars have been able to keep in touch with the intellectual world of the West. With a grant from the Chinese government and the China Foundation, we are now making 100 projectors to be distributed to various scientific centers. Robbed of foreign contact through mail difficulties, the supply of microfilms from the State Department has been gratefully appreciated by Chinese intellectual workers.

For reference books and scholarly publications, we should have original copies instead of microfilms. As it is almost impossible to secure foreign exchange from our Government, I wonder whether the Rockefeller Foundation could find it possible to make a grant for this purpose. If you could arrange to do so, this timely assistance will be greatly appreciated. I enclose herewith a copy of our purchasing program for your information.

The war has disrupted the world-wide exchange of information on progress in all fields of science. Research in China does continue, however, in spite of all kinds of difficulties and to keep American scholars informed of the work being done in China, we shall resume the publication of the *Quarterly Bulletin of Chinese Bibliography*. A microfilm copy will be sent to Dr. Hummel and if we can secure financial assistance, it could be reprinted in Washington for the use of American and European scholars.

Yours sincerely

T. L. Yuan

〔平馆（昆明）英文信纸。Rockefeller Foundation. Series 601: China; Subseries 601.R: China-Humanities and Arts. Vol. Box 47. Folder 390〕

按：my cousin 应指韩权华。此件为打字稿，落款处为先生签名。

十二月十七日

先生致信胡适和顾临，告知平馆已从中基会、教育部两方筹集资金用以购置 100 台显微胶卷阅读机；由于该项设备的局限，平馆计划印行"胶卷文摘"，但尚需资金保障；并告《图书季刊》英文本将复刊以及自己计划赴印度组建购买英美书刊的渠道；希望中基会能够按照战前惯例，将其美元收入的百分之十以上拨付平馆，用以购买美国出版物；另告中华图书馆协会将为美国图书馆购买战时出版的中文书刊等事。

December 17, 1942

Dear Dr. Hu and Greene:

Since arriving at Chungking, I have been busy in organizing the International Cultural Service of China. As you have already been informed by Mr. Zen, the China Foundation has made an appropriation of $ 100,000 towards the microfilm project. Recently I have been able to squeeze out from the Ministry of Education's budget an additional appropriation of $ 300,000. With these funds made available, we are now able to make 100 projectors to be distributed to various scientific centres. I now enclose a statement for your information.

The great drawback in the public use of microfilms is the fact that only a very limited number of machines can be made available. If the reading center possesses only one machine, it means that only one single periodical or book can be read at a time. The public also finds that reading on the films is slower and is a strain on the eyes. In view of these considerations, I have been trying to raise a small publication fund. So that we can carry out our plans in publishing the "Microfilm Digest" and in reprinting a selection of important articles. We are moving very slowly towards these objectives, largely because of the lack of funds. The American "*Readers Digest*" is having a pirated edition, costing $ 30 (US $ 1.50) per copy and is the best seller here. So you will see that the cost of living in Chungking today is much higher than the United States.

The work of the National Library is being carried on very satisfactorily. We have resumed the publication of the *Quarterly Bulletin of Chinese Bibliography*, copies of which will be microfilmed here and sent to the Library of Congress by diplomatic pouch. The Book Committee, both Chinese and Western sections, have been organized and we are going ahead with our purchasing program. I am going to India in order to organize a system whereby we shall have a constant flow of new journals and books from India and soon, it is hoped, from England and the United States. I also enclose herewith our purchasing program for our information and shall be grateful to you if you could circulate this letter and the attached documents to other Trustees of the Foundation as well as to those who are in interested in our projects.

During the pre-war period the China Foundation, in making appropriations to the National Library, usually granted us 10%－15% of its available income. I have urged Dr. Wong and Mr. Zen to stick to this policy if they could possibly arrange it. As we are able to ship the most needed books from the United States to India where our agent will put the packages on U. S. army planes, to Chungking, I hope very much that at least 10% of the Foundations income in U. S. dollars will be granted to the National Library for the purchase of American books. As soon as the request is granted, I hope you will get in touch with Dr. Hummel. Several of my assistants, Wu, Wang and Tseng are doing practice in American libraries and they should be asked to attend to the routine as soon as money is available.

I have been able to secure $ 100,000 to be used for the purchase of

Chinese material for American libraries. The Chinese Library Association has organized a book service similar to Mr. T. K. Koo's Peking Union Bookstore and I hope that through this service foreign libraries will be guided in the selection of material which seems most important in wartime.

I shall write you again after my return from India and I hope to hear from you from time to time. You can always reach me by cable care of the American Embassy. Dr. John K. Fairbank has been collaborating with me since his arrival and since our two offices are in the same compound, we are sharing the services of one typist. You will be surprised to hear that the salary of a typist in Chungking is ＄2,000 a month while in Kunming it is ＄3,000 or more!

With greetings of the Season and with kindest regards,

Yours sincerely,

T. L. Yuan

Director

Encl.

1)International Cultural Service of China, Press Release

2)A statement concerning the "Microfilm Digest."

3)Purchasing Program, National Library.

〔Wesleyan University, Meng Archive〕

按:信中所言 We have resumed the publication of the *Quarterly Bulletin of Chinese Bibliography* 并不准确,《图书季刊》英文本新第 8 卷第 1-2 期(再次复刊)应在 1943 年夏印行。此件为打字稿,落款为其签名,于翌年 1 月 29 日送达。

十二月十八日

谭耀宗覆函先生,告知从印度转运图书适宜办法。

守和吾兄勋鉴:

顷劳枉顾,得接清谈,快慰无似,承告到印图书仪器多校需要正殷,亟宜内运事。关教育前途,倘棉力所及自当设法,惟该项物资重量(大吨)共有若干,每月约需飞机内运若干,卅一次空运优先会议决议应请先行查告,以凭酌办。又各箱重量以(30)至(50)公斤为佳,不宜过重,盖现时机数无多,运量甚弱,必须适合上项重量,始便分月分批设法带运也。专此布意,即颂大安。

弟谭耀宗拜启

三十一年十二月十八日

〔中国第二历史档案馆,教育部档案·全宗号五,教育部关于委派北平图书馆馆长袁同礼办理各院校在美所购图书仪器接收转运事宜的有关文书,案卷号5465〕

十二月中旬

先生致信徐旭生。〔《徐旭生文集》第10册,页1295〕

按:28日,该信由平馆昆明办事处馆员胡英面交。

十二月二十日

中华图书馆协会撰《为恳请增发补助费以利图书馆事业推进由》,具先生名并钤印。〔台北"国史馆",〈中国图书馆协会请补助(教育部)〉,数位典藏号019-030508-0015〕

按:该件内容为恳请教育部自1943年起,每月补助壹千元。

十二月二十一日

竺可桢晤先生,请送一份缩微胶片至浙江大学。〔《竺可桢全集》第8卷,页446〕

按:是日,竺可桢至中英文化协会看缩微胶卷,约一百三十余种,请寄送遵义和贵阳①一份。

十二月二十八日

上午十时许,梅贻琦及西南联合大学两位教授赴求精中学访先生。〔黄延复、王小宁整理《梅贻琦日记(1941-1946)》,北京:清华大学出版社,2001年,页120〕

按:其中一人似为饶毓泰。

十二月三十一日

上午,先生访梅贻琦。〔《梅贻琦日记(1941-1946)》,页121〕

先生撰写 Memo Re the Balance of the Foundation's grant to the National Library of Peiping.

During the academic year 1941-42, two payments of US $ 750 each

① 贵阳者,似指国立湘雅医学院。

were received from the Manila Office of the Rockefeller Foundation. The first payment of US $ 750 was spent by the Library under the supervision of Mr. Clarence L. Senn, the Hon. Treasurer of the Library. All the vouchers are still being kept by him in Shanghai. In view of the censorship at Shanghai by the Japanese, it does not seem possible for him to mail them to Chungking. However, the undersigned has requested him to send a statement whenever he finds it feasible. The same document will be transmitted to Dr. Balfour as soon as received.

The second payment of US $ 750 was received at H. K. from the Foundation in October, 1941. At the outbreak of the Pacific War, only US $ 250 out of this amount was actually spent. The balance of US $ 500 equivalent to HK $ 2, 000 was deposited at the Bank of Canton, Hongkong. Between December 8, 1941 to June, 1942 it was not possible to withdraw any amount of money out of this bank. On June 18, 1942, the Japanese in Hongkong suddenly declared that the said Bank was being liquidated by military authorities and depositors were asked to send their applications before June 30, 1942. Up to the time of writing, no further news has been received concerning the result of liquidation.

Respectfully submitted,

T. L. Yuan

Director

December 31, 1942.

〔Rockefeller Foundation. Series 601: China; Subseries 601.R: China-Humanities and Arts. Vol. Box 47. Folder 390〕

按:该件为打字稿,先生略有修改,落款处为其签名。该备忘录附在翌年 1 月 4 日致 Marshall C. Balfour 信后。

一九四三年　四十九岁

一月二日

翁文灏致函先生，告胡适在美处理平馆运美善本书事宜。

守和吾兄大鉴：

兹接胡适之先生上年十二月七日自美来书，其内有言及书物之保存者。原文如下：

"(1)汉简全部寄存美京国会图书馆(收条及锁钥均存弟处)(适之自称)。

(2)北平图书馆善本书一百零二箱，先由袁守和兄分存国会图书馆廿七箱、喀利福尼亚大学图书馆七十五箱。本年二月，弟去喀利福尼亚交涉，将此七十五箱一并移交国会图书馆保存，故此百零二箱现皆存一处。由弟特许该馆将全部摄影 microfilm 三份，一份赠予该馆，二份将来于全书归还中国时一并归还中国，以便可以分存各地图书馆。

(3)叶玉虎先生本年十二月初拟运美保存之善本书未及运出，故均沦在香港。"

以上事实，知关尊注，专以奉闻。敬希察照，并颂时绥。

弟翁文灏敬启

三十二年一月二日

〔经济部资源委员会用笺。国家图书馆档案，档案编号 1943-&244-027-1-3-001003、1943-&244-027-1-3-001004〕

按："喀利福尼亚大学"即加州大学伯克利分校(University of California, Berkeley)。"本年十二月初"一句抄错，胡适原信实为"去年十二月初"。[1]

---

① 参见 1942 年 12 月 7 日，胡适致翁文灏、王世杰、蒋梦麟、傅斯年等人信，潘光哲主编《胡适中文书信集》第 3 册，台北："中央研究院"近代史研究所，2018 年，页 277。

一月初

教育部筹设国际学术文化资料供应委员会，顾毓琇任主席、任鸿隽为副主席、先生为执行秘书、叶企孙为会计，其他委员有杭立武、陈可忠、吴俊升、刘季洪、魏学仁、蒋复璁，共计十人。[①]〔《大公报》(重庆)，1943 年 1 月 3 日，第 3 版〕

按：美国国务院文化事务委员会鉴于中国学术界近况和空运配额紧张，委托国会图书馆将美国新出版的科学期刊等一律制成缩微胶片运华，赠送教育部。美国大使馆参赞柯乐博、学术资料服务处主任费正清代表美方与国际学术文化资料供应委员会合作。放大阅片机由金陵大学理学院定制，在重庆沙坪坝、成都、昆明、贵阳等处设立阅览室，提供服务。

一月四日

先生致信 Marshall C. Balfour，附上洛克菲勒基金会资助平馆款项余额的备忘录，告知已经与有关部门商妥在加尔各答到重庆的航线上预留一定运力，以便空运书刊，可否由洛克菲勒基金会拨付五百美金用以在印度购书。

January 4, 1943

Dr. Marshall C. Balfour,

c/o Dr. C. C. Chen,

Provincial Health Administration,

Chengtu.

Dear Dr. Balfour:

Enclosed herewith please find a memo re the balance of the Foundation's grant.

As you will note, there is a balance of US $ 500 deposited under the name of the Hongkong Office of the National Library of Peiping in the Bank of Canton, Hongkong. Since this bank is now under liquidation by the Japanese, it does not seem likely that we can expect to be able to withdraw our deposits as long as the present war lasts.

---

① 《大公报》原文还记有委员蒋廷黻，但其似并未参与该会，见本年 1 月 8 日之记录。

In your travels throughout Free China, you will no doubt realize that the most pressing intellectual need at this moment is for western publications. Practically all of our intellectual workers have not been able to see new books published since 1940.

Recently I have been able to arrange with the Priority Board of the Military Affairs Commission to give us a certain quota for new books on the CWAC planes from Calcutta to Chungking. We expect to ship by air two tons of new books every month.

Since it is not easy for us to secure foreign exchange from the Government at this time, I wonder whether the Foundation could find it possible to render some timely assistance. Dr. J. K. Fairbank and I have prepared a joint memorandum which we shall present to you upon your return to Chungking.

Personally, I hope you will find it feasible to arrange to send us $ 500 US currency in exchange for the amount now under liquidation by the Japanese in Hongkong, so that the whole amount may be used for book purchases in India. I expect to spend three weeks in February in India in connection with a book buying trip.

With Season's greetings,

Yours sincerely,
T. L. Yuan
Director

〔平馆重庆办事处（Chungking Office, c/o Nankai Institute of Economics, Shapingpa, Chungking）英文信纸。Rockefeller Foundation. Series 601: China; Subseries 601.R: China-Humanities and Arts. Vol. Box 47. Folder 390〕

按：Dr. C. C. Chen 应指陈志潜（1903—2000），祖籍江苏武进，生于四川华阳，北平协和医学院医学博士，哈佛大学公共卫生学硕士，时任四川省卫生处处长。2 月 5 日，Marshall C. Balfour 致信史蒂文斯，转交了先生信及备忘录，但他表示不相信先生可以谋得每月两吨的空运配额。

一月五日

中午,澳大利亚使馆 Sir Frederick W. Eggleston 设宴,先生与梅贻琦受邀与席。饭后围炉闲谈,颇为惬意。〔《梅贻琦日记(1941-1946)》,页 123〕

按:Frederick W. Eggleston(1875-1954),澳大利亚律师、政治家,1941 年授予爵士,时担任驻重庆外交官。

一月七日

先生访顾颉刚。〔《顾颉刚日记》卷 5,页 8〕

一月八日

教育部发聘书,任命先生为国际学术文化资料供应委员会委员兼秘书。〔国家图书馆档案,档案编号 1949-※055-综合 3-002001、1949-※055-综合 3-002002〕

按:随后,该委员会在重庆沙坪坝中央大学、成都金陵大学及华西大学、昆明西南联大①、桂林广西大学设立图书影片阅览室,提供缩微胶片阅览,并自 2 月份起印行《图书影片指南》。②

先生致信中国国防物资供应公司(China Defense Supplies Inc.)驻印度新德里代办处,初步洽商在印购买书刊运输问题。

按:该公司由中国银行行长宋子文筹建,约在 1941 年 4 月成立,其初衷是为中美两国政府签署的租借项目服务。③

徐旭生致函先生。〔《徐旭生文集》第 10 册,页 1299〕

谭耀宗致函先生,谈航运图书事。

守和先生史席:

展诵瑶章,敬聆一是。西书内运事关充实文化食粮,已与优先会诸君一再恳商,容当促其实现……

弟谭耀宗拜启

元月八日

〔中国第二历史档案馆,教育部档案·全宗号五,教育部关于委派北平图书馆馆长袁同礼办理各院校在美所购图书仪器接收转运事宜的有关文书,案卷号 5465〕

---

① 西南联合大学收到胶片及阅览机约在 1943 年 3 月中旬,参见《国立西南联合大学史料》第 2 卷,页 276。

②《中华图书馆协会会报》第 17 卷第 3-4 期合刊,页 5。

③ *The China Press*, Apr. 30, 1941, p. 1.

按;此为抄件,原就不全,特此说明。

一月九日

谭耀宗致函先生,请教育部就航运图书一事致公函与军委会运输会议商洽。

守和先生大鉴:

昨复寸笺,度达清览。关于航运书籍,本可即提出空运优先管制委员会讨论,惟运输统制局已自本年起奉令撤销,本处并入交通部空运统制,改由军委会运输会议决定,由钱次长慕尹召集。请速以教育部致该会公函寄下。弟当尽力设法并转交该会,提出讨论。专此奉复,顺颂时祺。

弟谭耀宗拜启

元月九日

〔中国第二历史档案馆,教育部档案·全宗号五,教育部关于委派北平图书馆馆长袁同礼办理各院校在美所购图书仪器接收转运事宜的有关文书,案卷号5465〕

按:钱次长即钱大钧(1893—1982),字慕尹,江苏吴县人,国民党政要。先生在收到谭耀宗两函后,抄呈教育部,并在其后注明"教部公函如尚未发出,应要求每月二吨,同礼"。

一月十一日

刘景山覆函先生,收悉来信并附上介绍函两份,会将图书转运一事转告宋子文。

1943, January 11

Dear Mr. Yuan,

I have received your letter dated January 8, in regard to the shipment of books. Enclosed, please find letter of introduction to Mr. Tweedy and Mr. Shen Shih hua, our General Representative in India. I trust that they will make some arrangement to help you bring in small quantity of books for the Library on a semi-official basis. Many thanks for the publication you have enclosed. I shall bring it to the attention of Dr. Soong, who, I know, has taken a good deal of interest in such matters of cultural relations in Washington.

Sincerely yours,

C. S. Liu

P. S. Mr. Shen is still here. I have talked to him about your worthy object. He has promised full help, and noted down your name. So, I am omitting Mr. Shen's letter.

按:刘景山(1882—?),字竹君,生于天津,时在中国国防物资供应公司负责交通器材[①],抗战胜利后曾任交通部次长;Shen Shih hua 即沈士华(1900—?),浙江吴兴人,中华民国外交官,时任国民政府驻印度专员;Dr. Soong 即宋子文。11 日,刘景山致信 Mr. Gordon G. Tweedy(Representative, China Defense Supplies, New Delhi),希望协助先生处理运输事宜。

1943, January 11

Dear Mr. Tweedy,

I have the pleasure of introducing you to Mr. T. L. Yuan, Director of National Library of Peiping, who is trying to bring in a small quantity of current books for universities and colleges in China. He has approached General Stilwell on the matter, who expressed small parcels of books may be brought in by the planes from time to time, if it is handled privately with the understanding of the Air Transport Command of the U. S. Army Forces in India. I shall feel greatly obliged if you would be kind enough to help Mr. Yuan to make the necessary arrangement.

Very sincerely yours,

C. S. Liu

〔中国第二历史档案馆,教育部档案·全宗号五,教育部关于委派北平图书馆馆长袁同礼办理各院校在美所购图书仪器接收转运事宜的有关文书,案卷号 5465〕

一月十七日

《大公报·星期论文》刊发先生文章,题为《南美各国最近动态及其与中国之关系》。〔《大公报》(桂林),1943 年 1 月 17 日,第 2 版〕

按:该文分四部分,依次为引论、南美洲地理概要、南美各国政情之最近动态、结论,后又被《今日文选》第 1 号、《新新新闻旬刊》

① 胡光麃《忆刘瑞恒同学》,《刘瑞恒博士与中国医药及卫生事业》,台北:台湾商务印书馆,1989 年,页 2。

第 5 卷第 13、14 期转载，但各处排印均有出入。

一月十八日

先生访顾毓琇，谈赴印转运教育部图书，并希望加入赴印文化访问团，以利工作。

一月十九日

先生致信陈立夫，商谈教育部在印图书转运计划并请部中拨给旅费。

部长钧鉴：

上月奉雪艇先生来书嘱将部中在印度所存之西文书设法运渝，藉以解决目前之饥荒。当即与美国史迪威将军及运输统制局进行接洽，尚称圆满。兹将两方复函录副奉上，即希钧阅。惟印度方面尚须前往接洽，俾每月均能有若干之新书及杂志可以按期运至内地，拟于下月中旬前往印度约四星期，即可返渝，惟刻下雪艇先生既不在中宣部，赴印旅费似须由部中担任。昨与一樵次长面商未识能否加入赴印文化访问团，尚希尊裁为荷。

钧座何日得暇，拟请约定时间以便前来晋谒，面陈一切。专此，敬请崇安。

职袁同礼谨上（印）

一月十九日

〔中国第二历史档案馆，教育部档案·全宗号五，教育部关于委派北平图书馆馆长袁同礼办理各院校在美所购图书仪器接收转运事宜的有关文书，案卷号 5465〕

一月二十一日

顾颉刚访先生，不值。〔《顾颉刚日记》卷 5，页 14〕

一月二十二日

中午，先生、蒋梦麟、费正清等人赴卡尔登饭店午餐，保君建等人亦在场，席间曾讨论美国援华联合会（United China Relief）对西南联合大学援助办法。〔Harvard University, John K. Fairbank Personal Archive〕

按：保君建时任驻印度加尔各答领事。

顾颉刚访先生，不值。〔《顾颉刚日记》卷 5，页 15〕

一月二十七日

先生致信 Marshall C. Balfour，可否由洛克菲勒基金会给予临时贷款用以在印度购买书籍并将通过恒慕义归还300美金,另告自己抵达加尔各答后将会联系兰安生。

January 27, 1943

Dr. Marshall C. Balfour,

Regional Director for the Far East,

Hotel Cecil,

Delhi, India.

Dear Dr. Balfour:

I was sorry not being able to see you before you leave for India. I am, however, looking forward to seeing you in your headquarters in Delhi.

With reference to the US $500 under liquidation by the Japanese in Hongkong as noted in my letter of January 4th, I trust you have already passed on the information to your New York Office. As I would like to have some foreign exchange with which to buy current books in India, I wonder any arrangement can be made to obtain this objective. Perhaps a temporary loan from the Foundation would seem to be a way out of the present difficulties.

As it is easier to secure foreign exchange to be remitted to the United States, I shall arrange to have US $300 refunded to your New York Office through Dr. Hummel, if it is agreeable to you.

I expect to leave here around February 10 and as soon as I arrive at Calcutta, I shall get in touch with Dr. J. B. Grant.

With kindest regards,

Yours sincerely,

T. L. Yuan

Director

City address:

Room No. 5, second floor, Chiu Ching Middle School.

〔平馆重庆办事处英文信纸。Rockefeller Foundation. Series 601: China; Subseries 601.R: China-Humanities and Arts. Vol. Box 47. Folder 390〕

按:此件为打字稿,落款处为先生签名,于2月4日送达。

一月

先生致信向达(敦煌),为《图书季刊》组稿。〔《向达先生敦煌遗墨》,页 397〕

按:是年春,向达拟将《蛮书校注》寄先生,但查《图书季刊》各期,并未刊登此文。

先生将王重民一九四二年十二月十四日致向达信转发后者。〔《向达先生敦煌遗墨》,页 433〕

按:此信谈王重民在美情形,并告海外诸君近况,向达于 3 月 9 日覆函王重民。

二月四日

Marshall C. Balfour(印度德里)覆函先生,就前信所提临时贷款方案表示怀疑,但其将会等待纽约总部的决定。

Hotel Cecil,
Delhi, India
February 4, 1943.

Dear Dr. Yuan:

I have forwarded your letter of Jan. 4th and memo which you gave me in Chungking to Mr. Stevens in New York. Regarding the balance of US $ 500 which remained in the Bank of Canton, Hongkong, I am doubtful that this can be replaced as you suggest; at least not unless an additional grant is made since the money was paid and already appears on our books as a disbursement. However, we will await news from Mr. Stevens.

In the meantime, I have received your letter of Jan. 27th in which you mention a temporary loan for the purchase of books in India. I will, of course, be quite ready to act if cabled instructions are received from New York.

It was a pleasure to see you again in Chungking and I enjoyed the luncheon with you, Mr. Fairbank and the other guests. I will write you again shortly about the joint memorandum which you have sent.

Looking forward to see you soon in India, I am

Very truly yours,

M. C. Balfour

〔Rockefeller Foundation. Series 601: China; Subseries 601.R: China-Humanities and Arts. Vol. Box 47. Folder 390〕

按:该函以航空信方式寄送昆明,此件为录副。

二月十日

先生路遇顾颉刚。〔《顾颉刚日记》卷5,页24〕

二月十一日

先生访顾颉刚。〔《顾颉刚日记》卷5,页25〕

二月十六日

顾颉刚致函先生。〔《顾颉刚日记》卷5,页28〕

匹兹堡大学校长秘书致函先生,再次告知所有礼物均已妥收。

February 16, 1943

Dear Dr. Yuan:

We have just learned through Dr. Chih Meng that you have never received from Dr. Bowman his acknowledgment and thanks for the gifts of Dr. Kung to the China Memorial Room. Two sets of these letters were sent at different times, and it is a matter of regret to us that you received neither.

I am sending copies to you at the address given to me by Dr. Chih Meng of the China Institute in America, and I am sending copies to Dr. Meng with the suggestion that they might be put in the diplomatic pouch.

The gifts have been exhibited here since their arrival and they have been much admired.

Very sincerely yours,

Secretary to the Chancellor

〔University of Pittsburgh Library, John Gabbert Bowman, Administrative Files, Box 2 Folder 13, Chinese Material〕

按:该函寄送重庆美国大使馆转交,此为录副。

二月十八日

徐旭生和韩儒林访先生。〔《徐旭生文集》第10册,页1308〕

二月二十日

教育部函聘刘季洪、先生、陈东原、刘国钧、岳良木、郑通和、陈训慈、蒋复璁、蔡孟坚九人为国立西北图书馆筹备委员会委员，并指任刘国钧为筹备主任。〔《中华图书馆协会会报》第17卷第3-4合期，1943年2月，页4〕

按：郑通和（1899—1985），字西谷，安徽舒城人，早年赴美留学，获哥伦比亚大学教育学硕士，时应任甘肃省教育厅厅长。蔡孟坚（？—2001），字侔天，江西萍乡人，青岛大学毕业，后赴日留学，时任兰州市长。

二月二十五日

竺可桢（遵义）致函先生。〔《竺可桢全集》第8卷，页514〕

二三月间

先生致信王重民，嘱其联络在美人士为平馆募捐。〔《胡适论学往来书信选》，页46〕

三月三日

先生和费正清联名撰写备忘录，题为 Preservation of Chinese Scholarly Personnel。〔Library of Congress Archives Box 674 Asia-3〕

按：该备忘录指出自抗日战争爆发以来，中国学者不得不与疾病、通货膨胀斗争，有些人被迫放弃学术研究，而一些优秀的年轻学人如张荫麟则由于无法得到恰当的医治不幸去世，这对中国学术研究乃至世界范围而言都是极大的损失。因此，在抗战进行的紧要关头，美国有必要对中国学者伸出援手，如同洛克菲勒基金会援助从德国流亡的犹太学者一样。本计划拟由傅斯年、陈寅恪、袁同礼三人成立资助管理委员会，并请费正清担任顾问，覆盖范围则以汉学研究为主要对象，包括历史、语文学、考古、科学史、社会学和哲学，时间计划以两年为期，每年资助额为20,000美金，每人1,000美金，用以确保受资助者的研究能够继续并出版相关成果。该份备忘录附上了八位候选人的介绍和他们各自研究计划的概述，分别是董作宾、郭宝钧、丁山、陈梦家、贺昌群、陈述、陈寅恪、张申府。

三月六日

先生致信叶理绥，寄送与费正清联署的补充备忘录，并告《图书季刊》中英文本均将出版新期,将尽可能向哈佛燕京学社寄送一套胶卷版本,另表自己将赴印度负责转运书籍、仪器。

March 6, 1943

Dear Prof. Elisséeff:

I hope you have duly received my letter of December 16, 1942 and the joint memorandum prepared by Dr. Fairbank and myself.

Here is a further proposal from Dr. Fairbank and myself and we hope it will receive your attention.

Both the Chinese edition and the English edition of our *Quarterly Bulletin* will be issued next month and I shall try to send microfilm copies to your Institute in order to keep you informed about our work.

The Ministry of Education has asked me to take a short trip to India and to arrange the transportation and research institutions. I am leaving within a few days and I shall write you more fully after my return.

Will you kindly convey my greetings to your colleagues in Cambridge and inform them of the close collaboration which I am having with Dr. Fairbank in the promotion of closer Sino-American cultural relations.

With kindest regards,

Yours sincerely,

T. L. Yuan

Director

〔平馆(昆明)英文信纸。Harvard-Yenching Institute Archives〕

按:该信应于4月12日前送达叶理绥手中,信中所附备忘录也寄送美国图书馆协会东方和西南太平洋委员会。

三月十二日

史蒂文斯覆函先生,表示洛克菲勒基金会不会考虑资助平馆购买美国出版的书刊,但将会与恒慕义讨论《图书季刊》英文本缩微胶片寄美后可能采取的进一步措施。

March 12, 1943

Dear Mr. Yuan:

On December 16 your letter raised a question on reference books and scholarly publications. I have taken some time since the letter reached New York on January 29 to get data on all that this implies. I regret that it is not now possible to encourage a request for a grant for this purpose. Your purchasing program shown in the attached statement is most informing. I have loaned it in quarters where it will be effective, and I have circulated it within our own office. This is the kind of information to be used when we are able to take up further work in library development in the Far East. You and your colleagues will be glad to hear that the publishers of our country are becoming more interested daily in the possible ways of collaboration. Naturally they are much aroused by such reports as we have had this week. A start on producing the Encyclopedia Britannica in Chinese and the publication of your President's new book in such enormous editions imply great things for the future of general culture in your country.

I note particularly your intent to send a microfilm copy of your *Bulletin of Chinese Bibliography*. I shall talk with Dr. Hummel to see what steps he intends to take promptly to get it into circulation in some form for American scholars.

Yours very sincerely,

David H. Stevens

〔Rockefeller Foundation. Series 601: China; Subseries 601.R: China-Humanities and Arts. Vol. Box 47. Folder 390〕

按:此件为录副。

三月十三日

先生抵达印度,并致信 Marshall C. Balfour。〔Rockefeller Foundation. Series 601: China; Subseries 601.R: China-Humanities and Arts. Vol. Box 47. Folder 390〕

按:此次,先生赴印为奉教育部令赴印度为各国立院校购置西文图书、仪器。先生留印一月有余,代订急用图书、仪器甚多。七月起,此批书籍、仪器开始运抵昆,教育部训令由平馆派人前往接收并转寄西康技专、西北医学院、西南联合大学、交通大学、浙江大学、云南大学等十四校。[①]

三月十六日

Marshall C. Balfour 覆函先生，希望先生提前告知何时前往德里，并就此前中基会向洛克菲勒基金会暂贷一千美金购书费的请求致电纽约总部，现正在等待史蒂文斯的回覆，但表示这一申请似乎并不符合常理，至于沈祖荣的请求，已给予两百美金的支票，并询问汇款方式。

March 16, 1943

Dear Dr. Yuan:

I was glad to learn from yours of March 13th that you had arrived in India. I had several meetings with the Chinese Educational Mission while they are in Delhi. I trust you would give advance notice of your visit to Delhi as I expect to be travelling during the next month or two.

Referring to my letter of Feb. 4th I have not yet had any reply from Mr. Stevens. Unfortunately, mail both to China and the U. S. has been somewhat delayed and uncertain. A fellow-up copy to Mr. Stevens was also subsequently sent by air-mail. In reference to Dr. H. C. Zen's request, I cabled Mr. Stevens yesterday as follows: Reference my letter February Four H. C. Zen Director China Foundation requests loan US one thousand dollars to T. L. Yuan National Library Peiping in India for book purchases subject reimbursement by Roger Greene. Greene can remit Yuan my care stop advise. I believe the immediate question that will arise in the mind of our New York office is that if Roger Greene will make the proposed reimbursement, why could not he remit directly by T. T. to you in India and if desired in my care? The effect will be the same and in fact that remittance will be exchanged at 329 1/2 as against the customary 326 1/2 from my New York check, if I am authorized to make the payment here. I know it is difficult for our New York office to make any payments or advances unless they are supported by an existing appropriation. I will act

① 徐家璧《袁同礼先生在抗战期间之贡献》,《传记文学》第 8 卷第 2 期，页 42。

promptly on such instructions as I receive.

With reference to Dr. Seng's request, I will issue you a check for US $200 against the Boone Library School account. Do you wish this sent to Calcutta now or will you prefer its being paid when you are in Delhi? Further payment will await information which has been requested from Dr. Seng.

Very truly yours,

M. C. Balfour

Dr. T. L. Yuan

c/o Chinese Consulate General,

Calcutta.

〔Rockefeller Foundation. Series 601: China; Subseries 601.R: China-Humanities and Arts. Vol. Box 47. Folder 390〕

按：T. T. 所指，待考。此件为录副。

三月十七日

教育部代电，电发赴印旅费及购汇通知。

国立北平图书馆袁馆长同礼：

兹拨发该馆长赴印旅费国币一万五千元，及外汇管委会准购外汇通知书渝管一字第一九二四号一件，应即持据赴渝部取款并径往洽购。附发通知一件。

教育部

〔中国第二历史档案馆，教育部档案·全宗号五，教育部关于委派北平图书馆馆长袁同礼办理各院校在美所购图书仪器接收转运事宜的有关文书，案卷号5465〕

按：该件左侧标注"此款系在去年度国际与文化宣传费项下开支"。

三月三十日　拉哈尔

先生与 Marshall C. Balfour 聚餐，先生再次确认转运书刊任务获批每月两吨的运输配额，后者仍对此深表怀疑。〔Marshall C. Balfour's Diaries, Rockefeller Archive Center, Rockefeller Foundation records, Officers' Diaries, RG 12〕

四月十二日

哈佛燕京学社董事会举行会议，经社长叶理绥提议并获得批准，学社拨款

1500 美金委托先生为哈佛燕京图书馆购买新出版的中文书刊,并将其暂时保存在中国。〔《裘开明年谱》,页 286〕

按:该处记录与 8 月 25 日先生覆信之表述有相当差异,后者表示此笔购书款用途为 US $ 1,500 in connection with the purchase of the writing of Ming Dynasty Royalists,待考。

四月二十二日

教育部代电,准予拨款与平馆搜集西南民语文献。

国立北平图书馆袁馆长:

本年三月十日函暨马学良君原函均悉。该凤土司署内所藏凤氏自宋迄今家谱既为研究民族学及考古之重要资料,所请拨收购费十万元,准予随令汇发,仰即查收,补具印领呈部,并将收购情形报核教育部。

〔国家图书馆档案,档采藏 8〕

按:马学良(1912—?),字蜀原,山东荣成人,1938 年 7 月获得北京大学文学士,1941 年 9 月获文学硕士,同年 11 月赴中央研究院历史语言研究所任助理研究员。①

四月二十四日

先生收到赴印旅费,开具收据。

兹收到中央信托局印度办事处拨付本人赴印办理国立各校院美购图书仪器内运事宜所需旅费,印币二千四百九十三盾十二安正,此据(渝管一字第 1924 号通知书核准)。

国立北平图书馆馆长袁同礼

卅二,四,廿四

〔中国第二历史档案馆,教育部档案·全宗号五,教育部关于委派北平图书馆馆长袁同礼办理各院校在美所购图书仪器接收转运事宜的有关文书,案卷号 5465〕

五月十七日　重庆

晚,先生与傅斯年、金岳霖、竺可桢谈至十二点。〔《竺可桢全集》第 8 卷,页 565〕

---

①《国立中央研究院人员录》,1948 年,页 32;《国立中央研究院概况》,1948 年,页 255。

五月二十七日

先生致信董作宾，告为其谋取美方学术界捐助进展，并谈《甲骨丛编》送美石印之议。

彦堂吾兄：

本日交邮汇上五月份研究费五百元，请连同四月份收据一并寄下为荷。又，二月间曾向美方接洽为吾兄谋一研究费，在该研究费未寄到之前，暂由敝馆每月垫付五百元。近接美方复函，拟赠研究费美金壹千元（约二万元），俾《甲骨丛编》早日完成，惟该款须七、八月间方能拨付，故六、七月份之研究费仍由敝馆暂垫。又，政府对于美国捐款用于教育文化方面者，闻每元可换国币叁拾元，但申请手续较繁，一俟该款汇到当为进行。此事尚未到发表时期，请暂秘是荷。又，郭宝钧君研究费事，曾为进行，未能如愿，深为歉然。弟在印逗留两月，见彼方学术研究空气远胜于吾人，而物价稳定，学者生活不似吾人之贫困也。专此，顺颂著祺。

弟袁同礼顿首

五月廿七

《甲骨丛编》完成后在美石印似无问题，惟运费甚钜且不易运出也。

〔中华图书馆协会用笺。清风似友·台北古书拍卖会(2024)〕

六月一日

蒋廷黻在其家召开会议，先生、叶企孙、费正清等到场，讨论傅斯年就哈佛燕京学社批准援助中国学者所撰写实施草案。会议商定，(1)将资助范围限定在中国学领域，包括经济史、考古、文献学，即哈佛燕京学社所关注的学术范围；(2)考虑地域（机构）的分布，譬如中央研究院、清华、北京大学和其他高校；(3)拟授予一千美金的学者为陈寅恪、董作宾、汤用彤、梁思成、潘光旦、萧公权，拟授予五百美金的学者为李方桂、罗常培、梁方仲、陈梦家、郑德坤、王崇武、邵循正、李剑农。〔Harvard University, John K. Fairbank personal archive〕

按：5月3日，哈佛燕京学社通过美国国务院致电重庆驻华大使馆，就3月3日费正清、先生联署的Preservation of Chinese Scholarly Personnel备忘录给予积极回应，但因费正清前往昆明考察，并未在立刻筹划落实,先生曾将此计划告知傅斯年,后者在返回李庄前撰写了救助草案。该项资助后应由美国驻华大使馆将美元以一比三十的汇率换成法币发放。

六月二日

下午四时,平馆委员会假资源委员会会议室召开会议,蒋梦麟、任鸿隽、叶企孙、先生出席,蒋梦麟为主席,先生记录。首先报告本年度馆务、沪平藏书保管近况,后讨论以下事项:

一、组织购书委员会。本年度西文购书费美金三千元,除去一千五百元外,拟将所余之款及下年度拨付之购书费委托胡适在美组织购书委员会,暂以数学、物理、化学、生物、工程、东方学、政治、经济为限,建议胡适商请陈省身、赵元任、王守竞、周鲠生等人为委员。采购手续和寄存地点由平馆与胡适商洽后报会备案。

二、平馆提议以上年度中文购书费国币两万五千元,本年春始行领到,预计勉强够今年购中文书,本年度中文购书费三万元尚未使用,拟改为本年度追加之经常费。照案通过。

三、下年度经费。决议:中文购书费国币三万元,西文购书费美金一万元,经常费国币二十八万元。

五时散会。〔《北京图书馆馆史资料汇编(1909-1949)》,页762-763〕

按:翁文灏本拟出席,但因临时有事未能到场。

六月十四日

竺可桢致函先生。〔《竺可桢全集》第8卷,页584〕

六月二十二日

万斯年致函先生,略述其赴云南武定旅途经过,并告联系方式。

守公馆长左右:

在富民曾上一函(十八日写,十九日发,航平),当已寄达钧览?十九日发富民,住冷村。村南三十里有鸡街坡者,向称险塞,地属富民、武定交界,爬将及顶,竟闻山头枪声二响,幸有富民派队保护,乃得安然度过,然已一场虚惊矣。

二十日冒雨来武定,道途在山坡上,泥滑路泞,三时方始抵武,衣被均湿。回忆鸡坡之惊,盖能安然抵达,亦云幸矣。

连日遍访县政当局及地方绅士,情形颇好,现在准备一切,拟于日内,即向茂连进发,此行亦为三站,据闻山之险遥,正不下于昆武间者。意者当较迤西山势为小,武定县长力许妥为保护,并已通令茂连乡乡长协助矣。年拟抵达后即与马君会商一切,迅即决定,总期妥善以达目的,请释廑念。惟茂连不通邮,带信须有便人,否则须专人饬送,通信恐须稽迟。倘有钧示,请寄"武定县城内邮局留交"即可。最好能用航空挂号,以免万一遗失也。此行吴佩南不来,欲带一随行,而无妥人,馆中无一工友可带者,而工作不便久候,是以支身出发,虽多不便,无如何也。

钧示嘉靖石刻,据闻字迹尚不止此,容当至禄访拓,年抵茂连,自当将一切情形,详为报告也。专上,敬请教安。

斯年谨上

三十二年六月二十二日

原来搰干,不肯深入山地,索价甚昂,交通工具现成问题,盖须此一问题解决,不能动身也。此外,年有友人葛君秉曙国文系毕业,为人勤慎,暑假联大毕业,可以翻译俄文,彼意拟愿参加史料会工作,不知史料会现可增用人员否?敬候钧示是祷。

斯年再上

三十二年六月二十二日

雇马则须候街子天,大后日始为街子也。

〔国家图书馆档案,档案编号 1943-※036-采藏 8-001016 至 1943-※036-采藏 8-001018〕

按:"马君"应指马学良,以下皆同。

六月二十八、三十日

万斯年致函先生,告其已抵达万德并与马学良商妥协力购买彝文经典,并略谈该地所藏民语及中文文献概况。

守公馆长左右:

在富民、武定各上一函,计达钧览。现年已于二十三日发武定,沿途宿插甸、永兴、多只立等村舍,于二十六日安抵万德,万德即土署所在也。沿途崇山峻岭,第一日尚多平路,此后则几全行山岭间,山势极大,且连互盘结,行旅艰苦,幸行次仅遇雨一阵,余皆晴明,武定县政府并派干警保护,故能平安抵达也。

抵达后即晤马君学良，商谈一切，惟该土司无售意，且即售亦恐过昂，故恐须徐为设法办理。年已将钧意此等书册将托史语所整理意告马君，马君方治此事，自无不协同尽力也。

其夷文经册，已见数册，写法整齐，实较丁文江氏《爨文从刻》所印者以及一般夷文经册为优，大抵为明代写本，据马君云不及千册，但夷文经典大都厚册，其每册中则又包括数种经文，初不若麽些文经之薄，而大抵仅一种经订为一册也故数百册可及千余种。

此外，中文方面，土署尚藏有档册若干，大抵清代之物，如土司出征记录、诉讼记录及田册等，年意亦当为馆入藏。至于古物方面，马君无鉴定能力，初无若何价值也。次则经版，当亦在蒐购之列。总之，年意当以夷文中文经档为主，与之商购，务期一网打尽，庶不负此行也。

此间气候恶劣，早晚颇寒，午中颇热，加以饮食不便（几无青菜可吃），年今日起竟患腹疾，意乃不欲在此多留，期以十天左右之力，进行商洽，无论成否，年当先行返回武定，报告一切也。且此间不通邮政，必须托人至城取信，往返须七八日，亦无如何也。年初以为此间距昆为近，当较迤西方便，不意重山互阻竟乃如此。要之年虽力期工作成功，以报钧命，使不能成，自问此行辛苦，已足无负馆命矣。诸容再上，敬请教安。

斯年上

三十二年六月二十八日

再者，此间虽为滇康之交，地极荒僻，无医无药，幸年于出发之前略购药品，此次腹疾，可请释念。又连日阴雨，极为烦人，昨幸晚晴，今又复阴，此信写就即拟交人带至武定投邮，行者阻雨，故乃候至今日也。日来，购书事仍在进行，尚无眉目也。

斯年谨再上

三十日晨

武定慕连土署

〔国家图书馆档案，档案编号 1943-※036-采藏 8-001011 至 1943-※036-采藏 8-001015〕

按：《爨文从刻》即《爨文丛刻》（甲编），丁文江编纂，1936 年商务印书馆初版。

六月三十日

《社会教育季刊》(三届全国美展专号)刊登先生文章,题为《如何发扬我国之艺术》。〔《社会教育季刊》第1卷第2期,1943年6月30日,页44-47〕

按:该文共分三部分,依次为“艺术乃民族性之特殊表现”、“我国艺术之特点”、“今后改进之道”。该刊由社会教育季刊社(重庆青木关)编辑,独立出版社(重庆江北香国寺上首)印刷发行。

六月

《图书季刊》英文本刊登先生所撰编者按(Editorial Comment)。〔*Quarterly Bulletin of Chinese Bibliography* (New Series) Vol. III, Nos. 1-2, pp. 1-6〕

按:该文分五部分,依次为 To our Readers、Microfilms for Chinese Libraries、Visit of Professor Dodds and Dr. Needham、Scientific Research and National Defense、Preservation of Chinese Scholarly Personnel、Sino-British and Sino-American Treaties.

七月八日

万斯年致函先生,详述那氏家藏彝文经典文献、雕版数量,并与马学良初步商妥购买办法,另告此中种种困难。

守公先生馆长左右:

在慕连托人交邮一函,当已寄达钧览?计年在慕连八日,始与马君晤面时,马君即先问吾馆愿出价若干,年以未经观书,不便多给,乃告以袁先生欲将该土司所存经典古物等事,一网打尽,馆中拟出三四万元,意者当可先行观其所藏,再定价格也。年抵达之日,即在马君架上,见有夷文经典多束,马君谓年其中即有那氏藏书也。马君且谓彼在土署借读经典如何困难,费二月之力,始能读到,且每次借读至多不过十数册,且语年见那安氏时不必提到伊有经典古物之事,即提及亦勿告以由马君知之,以那氏秘密其事也。及年语及家谱、中文档册及古物,马君则谓恐须俟一年始能睹及。方年之至也,马君似意谓年专为购置整理而去,故若是刁难,年告以钧意购入经典仍将交由语所交彼整理,彼乃允为帮忙设法进行也。故年抵达之日,虽晤那氏,未谈书事,于次日谈及藏书,那氏力加否认,此后诸日乃均由马君间接接洽,至年离开之日为止,未尝直接一谈也。初马君尚谓那氏无售意,此则六月二十六日至三十日年在慕连上函时接洽之大致情形也。

方年抵达之际，那氏之内侄（系该乡乡长之子）为匪刀伤极重，卧床二十余日，命在旦夕，故那氏时往看视，马君不便催问。嗣经年以不能在彼因循语马，七月一日马君谓六月二十九日已托那氏之姐为一进言，那氏已有售意。初年到达之日，马君语云，清华研究所已筹万元，亦购那氏藏书，至此时，马君仍谓恐书款不够，年乃告以可向钧座力恳，或可连同中文档册，书价再加万元，至多至五万元也（按此时马君已告年，那氏宗谱极为简单，而中文档册中有田租册子）。

次日（七月二日）马君语年，那氏以内侄死丧需款，确有售意，但那安氏意，谓基本书每册千元始可（普通书每册可在千元以下）。于是乃与马君估计其藏书册数，及其基本书与非基本书问题。马君所谓基本书，据云以内容言，为外间所稀见者，其书如次：

一、汉夷四十九人合集	二册
二、列国	五册？
三、三国	五册？
四、女圣普确荷葛传	六至七册
五、沙苴内维传	四册
六、夷族古代史	十册
七、古诗歌集	十册
八、七十贤人集	五册
九、神话集	三册
十、穆古芮那	五册

以上总计夷文书五十五册，而其中二、三、四三种，马君对其册数，亦未能确定，仅暂以六十册估计，倘以那氏索价论，则已需六万元左右矣。

此外那氏尚藏有刻本罗罗文经十一册（中有复本），书板十余块，且其他道场用经，因那氏无全部出售意，马君谓连同基本书，需购四百册左右，始足略称够用也。按那氏虽谓普通书每册可在千元以下，如以每册五百计，则所需之款，已超过专款之数矣，况中文档册，尚不在内乎？

年□□此事，自始即抱下列原则：

一、视书之所值，给以书价，不能一视□□之意而付款也。

二、总算一笔书价，不以册论，亦不分夷文中文。

三、必要时，嘱那安氏作半售半送。

如此，则可量物入藏，庶几可省公帑于浪费矣。

既略有进步，当日（二日）年即就马君手边及架上所用那氏之书，加以检阅，见其册之大小、厚薄，出入甚钜，以年所见者论，十之八九，尽皆残缺（如夷文三国，完整而薄，可以勿论，夷汉四十九人合集及普确荷葛传，则多已残缺破损）。且那氏之书，比较观察，其粗布及皮皮之大本，大抵较旧于他书，但即此等书之是否明代写本，马君前上傅公函中，虽有明代写经之语，至此亦不能断言其事，要之，有无明写本未可知。年观其纸张、写法，以所见者论，清代中叶及其以后写本，当占百分之九十以上，使有明写本，亦极少也。

斯年本欲审定全部经典档册，再与初步议价，专函请示，然后决定。今乃所见经典，情形如此，自觉不敢负此全责，益恐将来必有非议也。于是向马君表示，非观全部藏书，不能议价，因以年观察，使其他藏书完整者不占大多数，即四五万元，亦未必值也。至此马君乃谓那氏藏书，虽颇有缺帙，但尚有复本可以校补，彼自愿负选订经典之责，而以价格问题，交由斯年负之。年不敏，选书之事，出之马君，安敢以议价之事，自任也耶！？因见马君与那氏过从密切，关系颇深，出言多据那氏立场，且此事既非能由斯年，亦不愿由斯年商决，而全部观览，尚须待马君整理选订，要在一二月之后。在彼消费时日，殊无意义，乃于四日离开慕连，于昨日（七七）返回武定矣。

临行与马君商定，

一、选订经典，仍由马君负全责。

二、仍由马君进行购书事。

三、由年请钧示最高价格，转告马君。

四、购书原则，以总值论，不以册数论。

五、书价应包括中文档册、木板、刻本、夷经在内，不仅夷文写经也。

六、夷文经典，非那氏藏书全部，乃应选入研究夷文够用之书，约四百册左右，中文档册则应尽量全部购藏。

以年观察，

一、马君知年为购藏而去，一旦成功，其功在年，故有妒意，多方阻难，离开最好。

二、马君似将年为购书而去，告之那氏，年倘不离开，那氏更将视为奇货，索值过苛，议价较难，故年于离开之际，曾声言我馆并不是非购不可。

三、年既离开，马君与那氏更好商量。

四、据马君口吻观察，五六万元，可以办到。

五、如上所述，夷文经中即有明写本，亦为数极少（其刻本夷经，年已见一册，马君谓为明代刻本，以年观察，要为清初所刻，盖其板式作中国形式，可由而见也。此事尚待考订，但其刻本整齐完全，足备文献之一格，亦可贵也）。且大抵残破不全，而中文档册，年所见者二册，皆清代物，如亦无明本，则五万之数，未始不超书之所值也。

至于此后之事，依年意，

一、似须请马君，将全部拟购经册，作一详细纪录，以为议价根据，且免我馆将来无从典收，及掉换之事。

二、马君现虽须问我馆出价之最高数字，但似仍须马君将清单开出，然后决定也。

三、购妥后，书之运送，应请马君负责，其运费等，当由我馆负之（此事已语马君）。

四、购妥后，款项当可在昆支付。

现在重要情形，已如上述，归纳起来，应请钧裁者如左：

一、是否待马君将全部经典档册木板作一记录，再定价格，抑一面选订，一面议价？

二、□购□全值，请钧座决定，抑四万元，抑五万元，抑五六万元，请示最大数字（但此系马君要问之事，年意不问书，先问价，似不□理也）。

三、交涉此事，此后仍由年转函马君，抑由馆中直接？

此则目前即须决定之问题也。

此外尚有一事，拟请斟酌办理：按马君整理夷经需靠"毕摩"（即罗罗巫师)，现有二人在慕连为之工作，故马君倘为我馆选订编目，亦须就地办理，盖彼不能离开毕摩也。但现史语所催彼返川甚急，彼之工作，尚未竟事，倘加上我馆工作，势须延长，故马君意，拟请左右于晤傅公时或函傅公时一为道及，请略宽其时日。好在书如入藏，几为该所而购，傅公当无不帮忙也。

要之，年慕连之行，既得实况如此，马君前致傅公函，未免过甚其辞，而年之所以如此办理者，盖为节省公帑及合理计，不然，专款之数，为年所知，充量付价，落得人情，则不必费此周折矣。

按由武定至慕连，山岭极多，曲折连亘，各岭脊要口，每有匪患，慕连界滇康之交，地荒民陋，时生匪情，且有川蛮之扰。返来之际，二营卫保护，幸告平安，行程略如去时，但途中多冒雨耳。□□□途所住，蚊蚤蝇虱，终夜烦扰，未尝安眠。抵武后，所住旅店亦复如之，其苦可知。疲劳已甚，拟日内即往禄劝访查凤氏石刻，束装返昆，当在旬日之内。赐示请寄昆明，年当可在昆聆得训示也。

所陈已多，诸容再上，敬请教安。

斯年恭上

三十二年七月八日

〔国家图书馆档案，档案编号 1943-※036-采藏 8-001021 至 1943-※036-采藏 8-001027〕

按：该函有些许破损。

七月中上旬

先生致信竺可桢。〔《竺可桢全集》第 8 卷，页 601〕

按：此信可能是接到竺可桢 10 日致国际文化资料供应委员会函之后的覆信，7 月 16 日，竺可桢(湄潭)收悉。

教育部代电，题为《电饬督导国立北平图书馆昆明办事处人员办理由印内运图书仪器转运事宜》。

国立北平图书馆袁馆长(同礼)览：

本部代各校院在美所购图书仪器，现由印度内运。该项物品运抵昆明者，共有四十三箱计重二三〇九公斤，迭准交通部滇缅路运输总局电请派员接收。兹派该馆长督导该馆昆明办事处人员办理各院校图书仪器接收转运事宜，凡滇黔桂粤赣各省校院之物品，即在昆分别交运，川康甘陕各省校院之物品应汇运重庆本部。该馆长及该馆昆明办事处人员均可由部酌予津贴办公费用，关于运输费，应即据实拟定预算呈报核夺，除电复滇缅路运输总局外，令亟检发运昆物资表一纸，电仰遵照。仍应将经办情形，随时具报察核。

教育部

〔中国第二历史档案馆，教育部档案·全宗号五，教育部关于委派北平图书馆馆长袁同礼办理各院校在美所购图书仪器接收转运事宜的有关文书，案卷号5465〕

按：该代电约在7月14日（后）发出。

七月

《中美文化协会丛书》第四种《战后中美文化关系论丛》出版，内载先生撰写的文章，题为《战后中美文化之关系》。〔《战后中美文化关系论丛》，页51-79〕

按：该书实为"中美文化协会"悬奖征文的结果，其所登各文，除序言、引言外，均以《战后中美文化之关系》为题名（Chinese-American Cultural Relations After the War），第一奖为李絜非、第二奖为陈锡康①、第三奖为乐森璧，先生所获为"名誉奖"，因事先声明不受奖金。该篇文章失收于《袁同礼文集》。

八月二日

平馆向教育部呈文一件，题为《呈为关于办理代各校院在美所购图书仪器接收转运之两项运费及查点分配清单请提前拨发由》，具先生名并钤印。

窃职前奉钧部七月十五日高字第三四三六一号代电，饬职督导职馆昆明办事处人员办理钧部代各校院在美所购图书仪器接收转运事宜。遵经电饬该处人员妥慎办理去后，兹接函电，内称此项图书仪器之箱支运到昆明存栈者，共四十四箱；由印运昆之运费，据滇缅路运输局人员核算，约一万七千元左右，须于接收箱件以前支付，请即向部速领汇下，俾便接收；其由昆转运各地之运费，亦请向部先行预支若干，以备接收后分别转运等语前来。查以上两宗款项，拟请钧部提前发

① 此人文章为英文，其他诸位皆用中文所写。

下,以利进行。又各箱查点清单及分配各校院图书仪器清单,拟请一并寄下,以凭清点而便分配。谨呈

教育部部长陈

国立北平图书馆代理馆长袁同礼

三十二年八月二日

〔中国第二历史档案馆,教育部档案·全宗号五,教育部关于委派北平图书馆馆长袁同礼办理各院校在美所购图书仪器接收转运事宜的有关文书,案卷号5465〕

八月三日

先生致信教育部高等教育司司长吴俊升,谈办理各校院在美所购图书仪器接收转运费用事。

士选司长大鉴:

关于奉令办理各校院在美所购图书仪器接收转运一案,昨日曾呈部一文,想邀洞鉴。兹又接敝馆昆明办事处来函,略谓此项箱件由印度运到者共四十九件,其运费分为两项,(一)由昆明巫家坝空运站运至黑林铺仓库之运费装卸接转及保管(自四月卅日至七月卅一日)等费一万七千四百四十六元零二分,(二)由黑林铺仓库(黑林铺在市区西北部,距城约十七八公里,除用汽车提取外无其他工具,此次运输亦托滇缅路运输局代办)运至敝馆之运费计五千八百三十八元九角六分,以上两项合计二万三千二百八十四元九角八分(附该局原函抄件一纸)。查昆明汽油昂贵,自属实情,但上述费用未免过钜,除由敝馆向其索取详细清单外,拟请用大部名义根据教育用品之运输,请其核减。又各箱查点清单想已由美寄到,至分配各校院图书仪器清单,均请从速掷下,以便转寄昆明查点分配。其上述两项运费共合国币二万三千二百八十四元九角八分,及转运各院校之运费(因各地运率多寡不同而分配数量之多寡,以缺乏详单无从估计,拟请预支三万元)。务希从速径汇昆明(拓东路迤西会馆)敝馆办事处,俾利进行,不胜感盼望。专此,敬颂大绥。

弟袁同礼谨启

八月三日

附抄件一纸。

按:所附抄件亦为先生亲笔,内容如下,

接准贵处七月廿九日大函,敬悉。查本馆自四月卅日至七月廿一日止,计代接转教育材料四十九箱,业经全数送交滇缅公路运输局第一运输段仓库接收清楚,计应收运杂费国币二三,二八四.九八元。相应开具运费清单二份,随函送请查照如数惠付,以便函知第一运输段仓库交货为荷。此致

国立北平图书馆昆明办事处

滇缅公路运输总局

附运费清单二份

〔中国第二历史档案馆,教育部档案·全宗号五,教育部关于委派北平图书馆馆长袁同礼办理各院校在美所购图书仪器接收转运事宜的有关文书,案卷号5465〕

八月十一日

先生致信顾临,寄上前在印度购书发票并解释因为需要申请出口故无法提前寄送,略述在印购书经过及协助教育部转运此前滞留在印的书籍、仪器,另告中基会董事会会议决定向平馆拨款五千美金请胡适在美主持购书事宜。

August 11, 1943

Dear Mr. Greene:

Your letters dated April 14 and 28 have recently been forwarded to me here from the Chinese Consulate-General, Calcutta. I hasten to write to thank you for the information which you so kindly furnished me.

With regard to the appropriation of US $ 3,000 for western books granted by the Emergency Committee in January, both Mr. Zen and I thought that the communication from the Foundation had duly reached your hands in March, hence Dr. Balfour was requested by Mr. Zen to make a temporary loan of US $ 1,000.

The amount of the US $ 1,000 which you remitted through the Rockefeller Foundation was duly received and a copy of my report was sent to you through Mr. Zen in May. I am enclosing herewith a duplicate copy of this report together with all the invoices in connection with the purchase of these books. These invoices were needed in India in order to secure the export license from the Government of India, hence I was not able to send them to you earlier.

The securing of export license in India has taken a much longer time than we expected. These books packed in one large wooden box and seven packages were dispatched by air from Calcutta to Kunming. They are now kept in our Kunming office. I hope you will kindly inform other Trustees of the Foundation who may be interested in knowing their safe arrival in China.

In addition to our own books, I also helped in the transport by air of 66 cases of books, scientific instruments and medical supplies bought by the Ministry of Education through the Universal Trading Corporation in New York and held up in India for over a year. Our Kunming office has taken delivery of these 66 cases and is now engaged in their distribution. Considering the demands on the limited transportation by air from India, it seems gratifying that it has been possible for me to make these arrangements in spite of all sorts of difficulties.

A part of our book fund can be transferred to India with which we can buy more books to be sent to China by air. But all these arrangements mean so much work for me personally. We are having a very small staff and I feel that I deserve a temporary rest at least.

You will have received communication from Mr. Zen that at its June meeting of the Trustees, it was decided to appropriate an additional amount of US $ 5,000 for book purchases in America for this Library. The Library Board passed a resolution requesting Dr. Hu Shih to organize a small working committee for the purchase of books and a letter was sent to Dr. Hu sometime ago to this effect.

The Ministry of Education has recently decided to subscribe 20 sets of 200 American journals for universities and libraries in China. I now enclose a list of these journals for your information. As one of these sets will be given to this Library, it necessitated a change in our purchasing program for periodical subscriptions. I shall, however, write you more fully at a later date.

Thanking you again for your interest and with kindest regards,

Yours sincerely,

T. L. Yuan

Director

P. S. I am asking the American Embassy to send this letter to you together with the invoices for books bought from India. These invoices are being sent to you at the suggestion of Mr. Zen for your auditing purposes.

Mr. Roger S. Greene,

The China Foundation,

119 west 57th Street,

New York, N. Y.

U. S. A.

〔平馆(昆明)英文信纸。台北"中央研究院"近代史研究所档案馆,〈中华教育文化基金董事会〉,馆藏号 502-01-08-058,页110-111〕

按:信中提及 20 sets of 200 American journals 至 1947 年初,仍未得实际分配完毕。

教育部代电《电知抵昆图书仪器可由西南运输局运滇应速洽办》。

国立北平图书馆袁馆长览:

关于由印内运之各校院图书仪器,业经电派该馆长督同昆明办事处人员负责接收在案。兹准交通部公路总局公运字第四二四三二号代电内诵"转原文"等由,应即迅速派员前往滇缅西南两运输局洽商进行,并将已到物品,依照附发箱号校名对照表详细检查,倘系滇省校院之物品应在当地转发,至粤桂湘赣闽黔等省院校之物品应商请西南运输局分别转运,其余各校院物品,应全数运至重庆本部,所有运费及办公费用暨员工津贴,可编拟概算呈部核夺。附发对照表一纸,仰即遵照办理,仍将办理情形随时报部备核。

教育部

按:该代电另附公函,内容如下:

径启者,关于由印内运之各校院图书仪器接收运输事宜,现

又由部加派王树基君协助办理，除函知该员前往贵馆昆明办事处秉承台端意见办理外，相应函请查照。此致

袁馆长同礼

教育部高等教育司启

〔中国第二历史档案馆，教育部档案·全宗号五，教育部关于委派北平图书馆馆长袁同礼办理各院校在美所购图书仪器接收转运事宜的有关文书，案卷号5465〕

八月十二日

马学良致函先生，谈采访西南文献进展。

守和馆长先生赐鉴：

手谕拜悉。所示各项自应仰承尊意尽心办理，况此系先生奖掖后进，便利学良研究之事，文化界固所颂戴，而私衷尤为铭感，异日稍有成就，皆先生之所赐也。此间购书困难情形，万先生必已详述，惟以此种经籍关系一个民族之文化，故万先生曾尽最大之努力，方得物主允售之结果。其后学良仅以万先生所示各点与其交涉价值，并希获得全数，经月余之周旋，方允全数出让，惟最低价值必需八万五千元，且物主要求将来如翻印，必须每种赠彼一份，因此为其祖上根本，不能由彼手中断绝。关于后一条件，似无何重要，已允其请。惟价值问题虽较原定之数字减低十分之九（初时索价每本一千元，今不以册数论，而以总值与其交涉，则就其存书册数与价值之比例，每本仅百余元），且最近物主以地方匪炽，将其营盘山所藏一部分最珍贵之夷经运回，约百余册，较原见者尤为整齐，内容价值较大。据云此为明代老祖避乱时所藏之遗物，曾遭回禄，此为焚余之一部分，查其版本及内容当为明本（因有些年代在文中可考出，如称其当时皇帝之年号，亦有注写书之年代，又依万先生在此所见之册形断定，则多近似）。学良来此数月，今始得见，固为幸事，惟彼坚不允售，几经交涉，则此百余本必须每本千元，学良以为此种价值太苛，曾与其交涉，统属于八万五千元价值之内，彼仍不肯。嗣经种种开导，截至昨日止，其姊谓土司虚荣心大，意欲由购书机关出一奖状，并允将来印此书时，于册中附土署名义以扬其名，则此百余本作为捐赠。学良以为此种条件本无所谓，为急于得书故亦允其请，惟其妹（物主）尚未吐口。窃以为先生若以无何妨碍，

可否以贵馆名义出一奖状,则此百余本作为彼之捐赠(其名为那安和卿)方易收效,如此则较原册数又增加三分之一的善本,而每本百余元之价值似亦差强人意。如何之处,伏乞裁示为祷。肃此,敬叩道安。

晚马学良敬上

八月十二日

〔国家图书馆档案,档案编号 1943-※036-采藏 8-001028 至 1943-※036-采藏 8-001030〕

八月十九日

平馆撰《为由印内运之各院校图书仪器案兹送呈滇缅公路运输局运费清单及通知书请将上项运费径汇该局由》,具先生名并钤印。〔中国第二历史档案馆,教育部档案·全宗号五,教育部关于委派北平图书馆馆长袁同礼办理各院校在美所购图书仪器接收转运事宜的有关文书,案卷号 5465〕

八月二十一日

竺可桢致函先生。〔《竺可桢全集》第 8 卷,页 620 〕

八月二十四日

竺可桢致函先生。〔《竺可桢全集》第 8 卷,页 621〕

八月二十五日

先生致信叶理绥,收到书款并已兑换且设立单独账户,出于经济考虑卷数较多者建议由费正清在桂林一带寻找抄写人员,并告知将会编写文章补充《晚明史籍考》,另再次感谢哈佛燕京学社给予中国十四位学者资助。

August 25, 1943

Dear Prof. Elisséeff:

I beg to acknowledge the receipt of your cable remittance of US $ 1,500 in connection with the purchase of the writings of Ming Dynasty Royalists. The above remittance was converted into local currency at the rate of 51/2 equivalent to Chinese national dollars 19,268.29. A separate account has been opened in a local bank for this special fund.

While waiting for your further instructions, I wish to state that the writings of the Ming Dynasty Royalists have now become rather rare. For the thinner volumes I am asking several libraries to make duplicate copies by hand at cost, but for bulky volumes it is cheaper with Dr. Fairbank who is now on a short visit to Kweilin.

You are no doubt familiar with the bibliography of the writings of Ming Dynasty Royalists (in 10 volumes) which this Library published ten years ago. I am compiling a supplementary list including periodical articles recently published in "Free China". These articles, after being cut down, could be sent by air to your Institute from time to time through the courtesy of Dr. Fairbank.

In a previous communication I reported that we are very much gratified that the Trustees of your Institute appropriated US $ 10,000 as a grant-in-aid of research for 14 Chinese scholars. May I repeat that this action on the part of your Institute will have a great effect on the lives of these scholars and your courtesy in making the necessary arrangements has been very much appreciated.

With kindest regards,

Yours sincerely
T. L. Yuan
Director

〔Harvard University, John K. Fairbank personal archive〕

按:bibliography of the writings of Ming Dynasty Royalists 应指《晚明史籍考》,谢国桢撰,著录明代万历年间至清朝康熙年间文献一千一百四十余种,未见书目六百二十余种,1932 年 8 月平馆印,确为 10 册。a supplementary list,似并未发表。此件为录副。

九月八日

先生致信米来牟,告知中华图书馆协会愿意为美国图书馆购买战时中文出版物,并将成立由先生、沈祖荣、李小缘、严文郁、蒋复璁组成的委员会,提供意见并负责挑选出版品,并就出版品的内容范围、存放问题、期限等细节给予意见。

Sept. 8, 1943

Dear Dr. Milam:

We learn with pleasure that the American Library Association is interested in the organization of co-operative purchase of Chinese materials for certain American libraries. In view of the valuable assistance which the A. L. A. has extended to Chinese libraries in the past, the Library Association of China is glad to assist in this undertaking.

In order to carry out the project, it is proposed to set up a sub-committee to advise and to collect a selected number of current publications for American libraries. The personnel of the sub-committee are to be made up as follows: T. L. Yuan, Director, National Library of Peiping, Chairman; Samuel T. Y. Seng, Director, Boone Library School; S. Y. Li, Research Fellow, Institute of Chinese Cultural Studies, University of Nanking; Wen-yu Yen, Chief, Division of Acquisitions, National Library of Peiping; and F. T. Chiang, Director, National Central Library.

In view of various handicaps in wartime, such as poor printing and paper, lack of adequate accommodation, danger of bombings, etc., a rigid selection should be made of the publications issued currently. For periodicals only journals of value and permanence should be bought, such as in serial publications of research institutes and learned societies, and of certain agencies of the Government. As for books, works on (1) sinology, (2) economic and statistical materials on wartime China, (3) source materials on China and things Chinese, and (4) scientific and technical publications, are to be preferred.

The members of the above committee will be glad to assist in this work as a lobar of love. But the amount of work involved requires the services of a full-time trained assistant, whose salary may be shared by the A. L. A. and the Library Association of China.

Arrangement for storage in China for the duration of the war is to be made by the American Publications Service, American Embassy. As none of the Chinese libraries has facilities for film reproduction, this work will have to be done by the American Publications Service. The Director, J. K. Fairbank, will be glad to cooperate but cannot guarantee the extensive use of his office's facilities because of the scarcity of film and supplies.

Quarterly statements of the purchases will be submitted to the A. L.

A. through the American Embassy. In view of the uncertainties in wartime, we propose to limit this program to a small scale, utilizing the first year as an experiment, to be renewed next July if agreed upon by both parties.

Assuring you once more our hearty co-operation in this enterprise.

Yours faithfully,

T. L. Yuan

〔平馆（昆明）英文信纸。The American Library Association Archives, China Projects File, Box 2, Yuan T L 1943-1945〕

按:American Publications Service 即美国学术资料服务处,隶属于美国驻华大使馆。此件为打字稿,落款处为先生签名, 9 月 11 日该信由费正清寄出。

九月二十日

先生具文密呈教育部报告战时损失情况。

职馆系由钧部所属之京师图书馆及中华教育文化基金董事会所办之北海图书馆合组而成。国立之初,计京师图书馆藏书二十万册,北海图书馆藏书十万册,自民国十六年至二十六年六月底,历年增益中外文图书十五万册,共四十五万册。此“七・七”事变以前之大概情形也。职馆所藏图书,如善本部甲库之宋元明旧椠,乙库之清代精刻批校以及罕见之本,文津阁本《四库全书》,敦煌唐人写经,以及内阁大库明清舆图,皆为国家瑰宝,非仅能以货币价格估计。除宋元旧刊一部分于二十四年冬间运往上海妥慎保管,并于三十年十月奉令运往美国,商妥该国国会图书馆代为保管,订有契约外,其余北平全部馆舍建筑及设备,以及留在北平未及运出之藏书,于二十六年七月底北平失守后,悉数沦陷。职馆在南京分设之工程参考图书馆,于二十六年十二月亦随首都之沦陷而全部损失。二十六年冬间,职馆在长沙设立办事处,积极进行复兴工作。后派员在香港设通讯处,征集图书,因运输困难,大部分暂存该埠。三十年十二月,太平洋战事爆发,此项图书亦沦敌手。先后沦陷损失,估计约值国币壹千万圆,依照战前汇率,折合美金约叁佰叁拾万圆。至北平馆舍建筑及现存该处图书,将来敌军撤退时,是否遭遇毁坏,未能预卜。是以战后复原之计划,一时无从详拟。其现存昆明、重庆两地图书,将来运回北平,所需运输费用,以及工作人员回平旅费,约需国币一百万圆,依现时汇率,折合美金五万圆。上开数目,系照最低价格估计。另开职馆战时损失项目估价表及战后复原需用费用表各二份,一并附呈,即希鉴核汇转,实为德便。谨呈

教育部部长陈

国立北平图书馆代理馆长袁〇〇

三二,九,二十日

〔《北京图书馆馆史资料汇编(1909-1949)》,页 765-769〕

按:此件为先生所拟之底稿,后附"国立北平图书馆战时损失估价表"(共计战前国币捌佰贰拾万元,折合战前汇率美金贰佰伍拾万元)。8 月 6 日,教育部密电第 39495 号,令平馆速报战时财产损失情况。

九月二十二日

竺可桢致函先生。〔《竺可桢全集》第 8 卷,页 640〕

九月二十七日

竺可桢致函先生。〔《竺可桢全集》第 8 卷,页 645〕

十月一日

王重民致函先生,就馆务发展提出意见并告知美图书馆界拟帮助中国图书馆计划情形。

守和吾师道鉴:

上周在纽约见王信忠先生,伊称行前见吾师,身体甚好,闻之颇慰!尚望格外保重,为祷!又闻昆明分馆已取消,一部分书借与外部应用。吾师除赴印度一行,未离重庆,而将馆务集中陪都,俾政府中人见到馆务发展之速,渐渐发生密切关系,则目前补助,不致被人歧视,而将来经费,冀得一较高数目,必不难达到。外间舆论,虽尚不无嫉妒之言,事业发达,自所难免。更望吾师遇到于馆有利机会,能胜则争之,不信必胜则撒手,以免多树敌人。吾师竭尽心力,完全为图书事业,今后自当有人知之。韩愈所谓:"懦者不能修,而忌者畏人修。"盖人之常情,顺此常情以应付之,亦可免时人之讥。作战胜利之后,图书与金钱,尤须赖外人帮助。欧洲各国,亦必均乞助于美,故欧人不能助

我。而美国朝野人士，莫不信仰吾师，那时发为言论，必得大效果。在美能帮助吾师作此运动者，国人则胡适之先生，美人则顾临先生，在平时无妨稍作预备。国会马馆长上周请胡先生吃饭，胡先生提出美国一图书馆帮助一中国图书馆，如国会图书馆便应专帮北平图书馆是。马氏很赞成，惟不知能帮到何种地步耳。（大约仅能给复本书，绝对不能帮钱。柯德思亦在坐，他必要谈到。）柯先生到后，一切无问题，自能完全合作，慰堂方面，不必顾也。生等情况颇佳，柯君自要详告。子明兄行后，国会一缺，虽尚未正式说明，自然要属之刘女士，则子明兄未回以前，均可代理，而生活不成问题。带上之文稿，想图书季刊均可继续发表。胡先生积稿很多，再要可再寄也。买一皮钟，略表微意，美国亦已不易得。闻傅维本兄已寄瑞禾五百元，除前后寄上之三千元外，又托柯君带上美金五十，托维本到黑市兑换，所得必多也。闻教育费得多换三分之一，然否？专此，即请钧安！

受业王重民敬上。

十月一日

有机会请介绍维本兄与柯君相识，如能来美，柯君或可办免费航票也。

〔国家图书馆档案，档案编号 1945-※057-综合 5-016007〕

按："懦者不能修，而忌者畏人修"与《原毁》原文略有出入，应为"怠者不能修，而忌者畏人修"。"马氏"即 Archibald MacLeish（1892-1982），美国诗人、作家，1939 年 7 月至 1944 年 12 月担任国会图书馆第 9 任馆长。"柯德思""柯君"即 George N. Kates（1895-1990），中国文化、家具爱好者，著有 *The Years that Were Fat: Peking 1933-1940*；*Chinese Household Furniture*，时在美国国务院服务，1943 年底前往重庆接替费正清，负责在华收集出版物及其他文献资料。

十月初

先生致信竺可桢。〔《竺可桢全集》第 8 卷，页 649〕

按：竺可桢（湄潭）10 月 5 日收悉该信。

十月上旬

先生致信竺可桢。〔《竺可桢全集》第 8 卷，页 654〕

按:竺可桢(湄潭)10月13日收悉该信。

十月十一日

先生具文呈报教育部,恳请自一九四四年起平馆经费全部由教育部拨给。

窃查职馆经常费向由中华教育文化基金董事会于美国退还庚子赔款项下按年拨给。自二十九年度起,蒙钧部发给补助费二万元,三十年度加为四万元,三十一年度加为四万八千八百元,三十二年度又加为十六万三千四百四十元,最近又蒙追加五成计八万一千七百二十元。以上各款虽属补助费性质,而于馆务进行裨益匪浅。惟中华教育文化基金董事会所拨经费本年度仅有三十一万二千元,值此物价暴涨之际,维持馆务已属支绌万分。自中美新约成立以后,庚款停付,该会收入来源已穷,所拨职馆经费今后能否继续维持尚难预卜,更难期其随物价之高涨而量力增给。伏念国立图书馆事业之发展,乃国家百年大计之所关,职馆经费当年由中华教育文化基金董事会拨付,原属一时权宜之计。近年以来,钧部对于全国教育文化事业正在统筹扩充,通盘计划,此后职馆经临开支,似应与其他国立各馆各校,一律由钧部统筹列入国家预算。如此一转移间,不仅职馆经费来源巩固,即顾名思义亦觉名正言顺。倘承俯允,拟请自明年度起,于本年度拨给之补助费十六万三千四百四十元及最近追加之八万一千七百二十元以外,另增加三十一万二千元,计全年经费预算共为五十五万七千一百六十元,与国立中央图书馆及国立民众教育馆明年度之预算相较,尚远逊之。至中华教育文化基金董事会所拨经费,下年度如其仍能继续,拟请改充事业费之用,俾留伸缩余地。是否有当,伏候钧部鉴核。

〔《北京图书馆馆史资料汇编(1909-1949)》,页771-773〕

按:此件为先生所拟之底稿。

十月十四日

先生致信王云五,商洽与商务印书馆合作出版《图书季刊专刊》第二种。

云五先生惠鉴:

久未晤教,唯兴居安善为颂。敝馆续刊《图书季刊》已出一、二两期,谅业邀览。兹拟应读者需要,于季刊之外另编专刊丛书一种,不定期出版,每册字数由三万至五万之谱,内容与季刊大同,以国学考订为主。已编定之第二种为冯沅君女士之《孤本元明杂剧题记》

第一种在沪出版，亦为元明杂剧，字数适为三万，所述甚为新颖充实，乃根据菊生先生借敝馆原稿排印之本而成。此项专刊颇愿与贵馆合作出版，稿件由敝馆编辑，至印刷发行则由贵馆担任，并照惯例略抽版税。素仰先生热心文化事业，想必乐观其成。如何之处，尚请拨冗见示，俾取进止，至为感盼。专此，顺颂著祺。

袁同礼拜启

十月十四日

附原稿七十四页，请予审查，如不合用并希掷还。

〔瀚義堂拍卖(http://www.kongfz.cn/56558969)〕

按：冯沅君(1900—1974)，原名恭兰，笔名沅君，河北唐河人，作家、古典文学研究者，1919 年入北京女子高等师范学校，1922 年考入北京大学国学门，1932 年赴法入巴黎大学留学，1935 年归国，先后在河北女子师范学院、中山大学、武汉大学等校任教。《孤本元明杂剧题记》最终定名为《孤本元明杂剧钞本题记》，1944 年 6 月商务印书馆初版。

十月十九日

先生亲撰公函致外交部亚洲司，请惠赠《日本当代人物志》。

谨启者，贵司曾于民国廿六年出板《日本当代人物志》一书，内容丰富，极便参考，因属密件，坊间不易蒐购。如贵司存有复本，拟请赐赠一部，以光典藏。如已无存书，拟请将第一、第二两辑暂借一用，以利研究，无任感荷。此致

外交部亚洲司

国立北平图书馆驻渝办事处启

十月十九日

〔国立北平图书馆用笺。台北"国史馆"，〈参考资料及敌伪纪要等刊物(二)〉，数位典藏号 020-010199-0167，页 141〕

按：国民政府外交部亚洲司收到此信后，10 月 28 日回覆平馆驻渝办事处，表示没有复本，请自行购买商务印书馆所印新版(上下两辑)。

十月二十六日

竺可桢(遵义)致函先生。〔《竺可桢全集》第 8 卷，页 662〕

十月二十八日

先生致信吴宓。〔《吴宓日记》第9册，北京：生活·读书·新知三联书店，1998年，页153〕

十月三十一日

王重民致函先生，谈柯德思之为人及资历，并希望其能协助傅振伦来美留学。

守和吾师道鉴：

想柯君刻已抵渝，而范君行将回美矣。范氏夫妇，与Graves关系颇深，亦有相当学识与干材，将来很有成为Graves之继承人的趋势，将来和范家的关系正多，以后友谊，仍当永久继续。柯君新出马，其态度与敢作敢为方面，恐不及范君，然为人颇聪明，正给他一练习机会。所可虞者，在美国资望太浅，又无十分相知之后台，一时力量尚不够，不敢放胆去做，固其宜也。Cultural Relations派来之王教授，一年期满，大约尚能继续一年。生曾与柯君谈过，以后再有派人机会，可提议增加博物馆一人，冀能使傅维本兄来美。否则(一)我国家如能给生活费，(二)或由吾师向美方博物馆函荐，荐妥以后，柯君可照王信忠等之例，向(美)外部办免费航票，如此来美亦可。近美国各机关，需要中国人甚多，只要能来，自有工可做也。维本兄为人太好，只因十余年来，虽忠于人，而不为人所忠视，未免郁郁。敬希吾师相机，多予提掖，为祷！美国情形，无大变化，惟那一些青年汉学家，因受战争关系，刻几乎均在华府，为政府服务如此可免兵役。于学术暂不能深造，如Graves所计划者，不过制造中、日语留声片，读本，与开各种补习班而已。我文化界中人来此者，于捐教育费，捐图书等等，亦稍有活动，然无多大成绩自我大学教授不接受外国帮助，成大批的钱，一时不至再有，零星募捐，为数总不至太大。国会图书馆到拿出了一点重本书，让来的教授们，为联大及其他大学选了一些，预备停战后，方运中国。石曾先生近在L.C.要了一间房子，叫生看管，有想零星捐助吾馆书，而暂不需要者，可交生存此处。善本film已照四百五十余卷(一千零八十种书)，国内如需要，只请吾师来信，现可送重庆一份也。专此，即请道安！

生重民敬上。

十月卅一日

〔国家图书馆档案，档案编号1945-※057-综合5-016008〕

按:"范君"即费正清,1943 年 12 月 8 日,费正清离开重庆,后途经印度等地回到华盛顿。"王教授",应指王信忠。"自我大学教授不接受外国帮助",此事可参见费正清回忆录。①

十一月三日

先生亲撰公函致粮食部民食司,询问国立机关重庆、昆明两地每石食米的代金数。

径启者:敝馆职员分在重庆及昆明两地办公,关于本年七月以后之食米或食米代金,迄今尚未领到,除已呈请教育部准予提前办理外,兹亟须询明本年七月以后重庆及昆明两地每石食米之代金数,以资参考,即希惠予查明,早日赐覆,不胜感祷。此致

粮食部民食司

国立北平图书馆谨启

十一月三日

赐覆请寄沙坪坝敝馆。

〔台北"国史馆",〈北平图书馆及故宫博物院〉,档案编号119000005853A〕

按:本月 19 日,该司函覆平馆。1944 年 7 月,平馆重庆部分公粮改照国立学校教职员战时生活补助办法办理。

十一月四日

先生亲撰公函致教育部会计处,催问十月两件呈文批复结果。

敬启者,敝馆于十月二日寄部呈文二件。(一)请示关于三十一年七月至十二月,敝馆主管人员之特别办公费国币一万零二百元,能否在三十二年经常费或最近追加经费内予以支付(二)尊令缴还二十九年度一月至十二月米贴结余款五三八.六五元,开具中国银行支票一纸,请核收赐据。迄今月余尚未奉到指令,拟请贵处一查,早日批示,俾有遵循,不胜感盼。此致

教育部会计处

国立北平图书馆谨启

十一月四日

① John K. Fairbank, *Chinabound: a fifty-year memoir*, 1982, p. 252.

赐覆请寄重庆沙坪坝敝馆。

〔中国第二历史档案馆,教育部档案·全卷宗五,国立北平图书馆请拨员工学术研究补助费经常费有关文书,案卷号11616(2)〕

十一月五日

陈立夫致函先生,请密荐馆员担任平馆人事管理员。

守和馆长大鉴:

本部筹设附属各机关人事管理机构案,经咨商铨叙部,顷准贾部长函复决定贵馆设置人事管理员。在此初次设置之时,并请遴选具有委任资格及有人事行政学识与经验人员,开具履历送铨叙部审查任用,即希就贵馆现有工作人员密荐一人或二人函复,以便核转为盼。此颂公绥。

陈立夫启

卅二年十一月五日

〔教育部部长室用笺。国家图书馆档案,档案编号1945-※057-综合5-003003〕

按:铨叙部为中华民国考试院的两个附属部门之一,负责对政府公务人员的资历、功绩等进行评估,"贾部长"即贾景德(1880—1960),字煜加,号韬园,山西泽州人,时任铨叙部部长。此件应为油印,上款处手书、落款处钤印。

十一月十六日

先生致信吴宓。〔《吴宓日记》第9册,页153〕

按:此信与十月二十八日函似都与英文稿件有关,吴宓本月二十三日校阅完毕,送莫余敏卿转交先生。

十一月十七日

中华图书馆协会撰《呈请领本年一至十二月补助费请准予照发》,具先生名并钤理事会、协会两印。〔台北"国史馆",〈中国图书馆协会请补助(教育部)〉,数位典藏号019-030508-0015〕

按:内文称明年初计划举办图书馆年会,需款颇急,拟请将整年度补助费两千四百元核发。

十一月十八日

先生路遇顾颉刚。〔《顾颉刚日记》卷5,页190〕

十一月二十二日

万斯年致函先生，谈西南访书事。

守公馆长钧鉴：

九日谕，敬悉一一。

（一）马君日前抵昆，莫君来函通知，年当于昨日（廿一日）入市，至靛花巷同运经典至迤西会馆，典收文献并办手续，当日算是了去武定夷经问题，书款亦当面算清矣。想莫君当亦函陈？兹以有关诸端条陈于后：

a. 马君此次携昆之书，其精品与普通书相混杂，精品较年在慕连所见者并未增加多少。

b. 夷文经板，亦非全部，该土司处尚有所存，本馆共十五块，且有两面刻刊者，堪称难得，其刻本经典亦已入藏。

c. 款系面交马君，收据仅有土司私章。

d. 残本很多，如年所见，薄册亦颇多残本，马君并未订补。

e. 马君意此批夷经将来由史语所正式函借，马君或返李庄或留昆，现未定。

f. 目录之中文部份，马君谓返李庄后再写，则须延迟，可否先以夷文目录报部，以清专款公案。专款已超过，可否请追加？

g. 马君夷文目录，全为一巫师所写，拟请我馆付以报酬，马君已将钧处地址要去，当亦有信致左右也。

h. 马君意将来借去夷经，拟由史所择要录副。

i. 经典现存迤西会馆，由莫君函范君押运至桃园存放。

j. 土司仍请馆中转请教部发给奖状。

关于本馆整理此批经典问题，年意：

a.此间既无巫师，年亦无暇，故所谓整理，仅为版本方面之注意事项，年意须以专册登记，所登记事项，一如年在丽所订者。

b.丽江所用图章，拟请速制，便中带昆，好在范君处有印泥，章到，即可请其先在此批经典上加盖图章，有馆章有详细登记，自可免人偷或换也。

c.年拟最近至桃园，告范君登记事项，请其作初步登记。钧意何若？

（二）新疆书目，已在犁订，钧意分为二辑，甚善甚善，自当遵办。惟年之撰写，现止于廿五年年底，故拟即以二十五年以后者为第二辑，但如此分期，则二辑著录论著，当远不若一辑之多也。

（三）丽江年虽欲再去，但以此间责任颇重，事实或不许可，容许图之。周汝诚君，是否可请函告，俟经典整理完竣，调其来昆？彼倘来昆，则昆明可多一人工作，一方面且可运书来昆，一举两得。钧意如何？（但此事不妨略缓发表，倘蒙钧允，当由年先函询彼意见，以免函调而彼不来也。）

（四）张君待遇情形，已转告，现在工作中，俟三个月后一月底止再定继续与否，亦已转告。届时当函请定夺。诸容再上，敬请教安。

万斯年谨上

三二，十一，廿二

育伊兄是否在南开中学办公，请便中见示是幸。

〔国家图书馆档案，档案编号 1943－※036－采藏 8－001031 至 1943－※036－采藏 8－001034〕

按：1944 年 4 月 18 日，平馆向教育部呈文，请给予那安和卿褒奖证书，6 月 8 日教育部指令，认为符合捐资兴学褒奖条例，颁发一等奖状一张。

米来牟致先生两函，其一，告知 Charles H. Brown 将负责制订中美图书馆合作采购计划、在华筹设美国图书馆等提案。

November 22, 1943

Dear Dr. Yuan:

Your letter of September 8 in answer to our cable was received by Mrs. Fairbank and by her and us made available to the several people particularly concerned. You gave us the information we needed and we are making progress.

The key man in this situation is Charles H. Brown of Ames, Iowa, Chairman of the Committee on Library Cooperation with the Orient of the A. L. A. International Relations Board. He has been hard at work. Within a few days letters will go from him to research libraries proposing a cooperative purchasing scheme. It would involve contributions of $ 1,000 each, including full salary for an assistant to you, and incidental administrative expenses both here and in China. It is hoped that about 15 libraries will participate.

Mr. Brown has been working also on a general plan for library cooperation between the United States and China. This has been somewhat delayed because Mr. Brown can give only limited time to such matters, but is nearing completion.

Nearing completion also is a proposal for an American Library in China. It will be sent to the Department of State.

Mr. Brown is coming in to talk about all of these matters on Wednesday. We may be able to reach conclusions also on another question-how to round up a few Chinese students now in this country for a year's library school instruction.

We appreciate your interest in our problems and your always prompt response to our inquiries. It will be highly gratifying if we can get into actual operation some of the plans which you and we have put down on paper.

I suppose my secretary usually addresses you as Director of the National Library of Peiping. We do not forget that you are also the ranking man in the Library Association of China. That is an added reason for carrying through our plans of international cooperation.

And aren't we lucky, you and I, to have Mr. and Mrs. Fairbank as our collaborators?

Cordially yours

Carl H. Milam

Executive Secretary

其二,代表美国图书馆协会国际关系委员向先生致力于中美图书馆合作表示由衷的感谢。

November 22, 1943

Dear Dr. Yuan

It is my pleasant duty to transmit the following resolution of thanks, which was adopted on October 28, 1943, by the International Relations Board of the American Library Association:

RESOLVED, that this Board express on behalf of the American Library Association sincere and emphatic appreciation of the interest shown and the help given by Dr. Tung-Li Yuan, in connection with the efforts of librarians of the United States to obtain closer connection with the librarians of China, and more particularly to secure books and other publications now available in China.

Cordially yours,
Carl H. Milam
Executive Secretary

〔The American Library Association Archives, China Projects File, Box 2, Yuan T L 1943-1945〕

按:Charles H. Brown(1875-1960),美国图书馆学家,本谱中译作"布朗",早年获卫斯理大学(Wesleyan University)学士、硕士学位,1901年获纽约州立图书馆学校学位,随后在卫斯理大学图书馆、国会图书馆、布鲁克林公共图书馆服务,1922年至1946年担任爱荷华州立大学图书馆馆长,1941至1942年兼任美国图书馆协会主席。此两件皆为录副。

十一月二十三日

吴宓致函先生。〔《吴宓日记》第9册,页153〕

十一月二十八日

费正清致函先生,恳请协助哈佛大学购买中文现代出版物。

November 28, 1943

Dear Dr. Yuan:

I wish by this letter to request you to act on my behalf and make a collection of Chinese publications for the Library of Harvard University. I understand that you are already acting for the Harvard-Yenching Institute, using funds sent to you by it for certain purposes. My object in the present request is to ensure that a buying program in contemporary publications in social sciences will continue, even if the Harvard-Yenching funds now available are all used for other purposes or become exhausted. It is most important for the Harvard Library, of which the Harvard-Yenching Chinese Library is a part, to maintain its files of leading Chinese publications and government documents, and I wish to guarantee that a sum of US $ 500 can be made available for that purpose, if you will proceed with a program and find it necessary to spend such an amount over and above what is now available from Harvard-Yenching. Please communicate with me on this subject through this office, as need arises.

Sincerely yours

J. K. Fairbank

〔美国学术资料服务处(American Publications Service)信笺。Harvard University, John K. Fairbank personal archive〕

十一月

先生致信向达(重庆附近),告知或可向美国方面筹款,为其子女支付上学费用。〔《向达先生敦煌遗墨》,页425〕

十二月二日

先生致信米来牟,寄上抗日战争爆发后中国图书馆状况报告,希望战后美国图书馆学家可以来华考察帮助恢复,愿意为美国图书馆获取并存储战时中文出版物,并告将会寄上一九三九年至一九四零年间美国援助中国图书的分配情况说明。

December 2, 1943

Dear Dr. Milam:

Sometime ago you were kind enough to suggest that this Association should send you a statement about library situation in China since the outbreak of the Sino-Japanese War. Owing to shortage of staff and the pressure of my other duties, I have not been able to send it to you earlier.

Our Association has suffered a great deal owing to the departure of a trained staff. As all of our members are so anxious to keep in touch with American librarians, I would like to issue a circular letter provided we can secure some financial support. It is proposed to include in this circular all the facts about Chinese libraries and their problems.

We hope very much that after the War is over, we may be privileged to have American librarians visit China and help us in our work of rehabilitation. Meanwhile it would be most helpful to us if a number of duplicates in American libraries can be reserved for China and put the names of our libraries on the mailing lists of your libraries and research institutions.

On our side, we shall be extremely glad to help American libraries in securing Chinese current material which is so easily out of print. A communication regarding these arrangements was sent to you through the Department of State and we are waiting for your reply.

Most of the donors to Books-for-China will be interested to know the fate of the books they sent to us in 1939 and 1940. The Japanese have looted a number of them, but a great portion is still kept in Hong Kong. The custodian is now on his way to Chungking and we shall send you a statement later on.

With kindest regards,

Yours sincerely,

T. L. Yuan

Chairman, Executive Board

〔中华图书馆协会(重庆沙坪坝)英文信纸。The American Library Association Archives, China Projects File, Box 2, Yuan T. L. 1943-1945〕

按:此件为打字稿,落款处为先生签名,于 1944 年 1 月 12 日送达。

十二月上旬

先生寄洋一千元与竺可桢。〔《竺可桢全集》第 8 卷,页 684〕

按:此款似为美元,应为先生所争取之美方学术界的援助。

十二月十一日

先生具文呈教育部,汇报采购云南武定县那土司家藏经典经过并呈缴用费单据。

窃职馆前在昆明,即留意于西南各省文献之蒐集,历年以来入藏各省方志及其他文献，蔚为大观。此项目录，前曾呈缴钧部，谅邀洞鉴。本年三月间，访闻云南武定县那土司家藏有明清两代写本及刻本罗罗文经典，并存有木版及汉文档册，数量虽不甚多，但均为世所罕觏，对于西南民族之语言文化历史制度之研究，有绝大之参考价值。旋蒙钧部拨发国币十万元进行收购，随于本年五月间具领在案。职馆当于本年六月间，派编纂万斯年前往武定调查访购。该员冒涉暑雨匪警，几经艰险，抵达那土司家，当即会同正在该处作调查研究工作之国立中央研究院历史语言研究所助理研究员马学良，研究审订，断定确有特殊价值。该土司那维新外出，其职务例由其母那安氏即那安和卿代行。万、马两员当向那安氏进行磋商，那安氏初谓家藏经典文献，为其祖宗数百年传家宝物，未便割让，嗣则要求按册给价国币一千元，始肯出售。经万、马二员再三与其商洽，一面喻以国家文化机关保存文献之盛意，一面央请该土司亲友多方从中劝导，历时数月，该土司之母附带要求职馆代为呈请钧部颁给奖状或匾额，并要求职馆将来如刊印该项经典文献时，于册中附书该土司姓名，并检赠印本一部，以资显扬而存手泽，始允将其家藏经典文献之一部分廉价出让，一部分作为捐赠归诸国有。经职考虑该土司之母所有附带要求，于情理尚无不合，其所要求价让之部分，代价已低至无可再低，职当命万斯年会同马学良迅即付款收购。所有该土司出让附捐赠之件，计夷文即罗罗文写经五百零七册、夷文写经卷子一轴、夷文刻经十五册、夷文刻版十五块、汉文档册十二册，共用代价国币九万元。上述各件，现已运抵昆明，其目录容由夷文译成汉文后再行呈报。兹请将此次收购、寄运等费用共国币拾万叁千叁百柒拾肆元正单据一宗，随呈附缴，恳予核销。其超出之款三千三百七十四元，暂由职馆挪垫，是否由钧部拨还抑由职馆在事业费下报销，谨候鉴核批示。其那安和卿收据一纸，以该土司地在僻乡，于法令亦稍有隔阂，无从购贴印花，合并陈明。至该土司那维新或其母那安和卿，拟恳钧部颁给奖状或匾额以示褒奖而资观感，是否可行，理合呈请鉴核批示祗遵。谨呈

教育部部长陈

国立北平图书馆代理馆长袁〇〇

中华民国三十二年十二月十一日

附单据一宗,计八件,共十二纸,又三纸。

〔国家图书馆档案,档案编号 1943-※036-采藏 8-001035、1943-※036-采藏 8-001036〕

按:该件应属底稿性质。

十二月十六日

国立西北图书馆筹备委员会假中央图书馆召开第二次筹备会议,刘国钧、先生等人出席。刘国钧为会议主席,报告数月来的筹备工作,并讨论通过暂时馆址、组织条例等案,拟于明年 4 月 1 日或 6 月 1 日开馆。〔《大公报》(桂林),1943 年 12 月 18 日,第 2 版〕

平馆文书撰《呈为办理接收转运钧部代各院校在美所购图书仪器箱支缮具报告请予鉴核并请示转运所余箱支办法由》,具先生名并钤印。〔中国第二历史档案馆,教育部档案·全宗号五,教育部关于委派北平图书馆馆长袁同礼办理各院校在美所购图书仪器接收转运事宜的有关文书,案卷号 5465〕

按:7 月 28 日,教部高字第 34361 号代电命平馆负责此事。具体经办人为莫余敏卿、胡英两位馆员,涉及箱件原为 57 箱,后因分发之便析成 61 箱,云南大学、西南联合大学及西康技艺专科学校提取 29 箱,余下者则须转运黔、湘、粤、赣、渝等地。但转运工作并未就此持续开展,原因有二,一是在印度并无书可运,二是运费无着,导致虽有空运吨位配额,但该项工作暂时中断。①

十二月十七日

上午十时,竺可桢与汪懋祖赴求精中学国际文化资料供应处访先生,不值。〔《竺可桢全集》第 8 卷,页 690〕

十二月二十日

上午十时许,竺可桢至求精中学访先生,晤谈。〔《竺可桢全集》第 8 卷,页 692〕

十二月二十四日

顾颉刚赴求精中学访先生,晤谈。〔《顾颉刚日记》卷 5,页 207〕

按:此时,王育伊已回平馆工作。

十二月下旬

平馆撰《为呈覆收到本部物资一箱系缩绘器及量表情形请予鉴核由》,具

① 台北"中央研究院"近代史研究所档案馆,"中华教育文化基金董事会",馆藏号 502-01-08-061,页 9。

先生名并钤印。〔中国第二历史档案馆,教育部档案·全宗号五,教育部关于委派北平图书馆馆长袁同礼办理各院校在美所购图书仪器接收转运事宜的有关文书,案卷号5465〕

按:该件似于25日撰写,28日送达教育部高等教育司。

十二月三十一日

《社会教育季刊》刊登先生的文章,题为《国立北平图书馆工作概况》。〔《社会教育季刊》第1卷第4期,1943年12月,页10-12〕

按:该文共三部分,依次为采购、编辑、出版。本期刊有国立各社会教育机关概况,如国立北平故宫博物院、国立中央博物院筹备处等。另,该刊目录页标题遗漏"工作"二字。

先生撰写平馆年度英文报告 National Library of Peiping, Report for 1943。〔Rockefeller Foundation. Series 601: China; Subseries 601.R: China-Humanities and Arts. Vol. Box 47. Folder 390〕

按:该报告分为五页,主要涉及 Acquisition of source materials、Editorial work、Republication of the *Quarterly Bulletin*、Reference work and other services、Staff changes 五个方面。该件抄送至洛克菲勒基金会,后者对平馆在此艰难时局下的表现十分赞赏。

十二月

《图书季刊》英文本刊登先生所撰编者按(Editorial Comment)。〔*Quarterly Bulletin of Chinese Bibliography* (New Series) Vol. III, Nos. 3-4, pp. 1-8〕

按:该文分五部分,依次为 To our Readers、British Scientific and Cultural Mission to China、Visit of Professor Cressey、Scientific Liaison Between China and the West、The Need for Humanistic Sciences、Sino-Indian Cultural Cooperation.

是年

先生通过王重民请朱士嘉兼任平馆采购外文图书的工作。〔朱士嘉《我所了解的袁同礼先生》,页90〕

按:时朱士嘉在哥伦比亚大学研究生院深造,感经济拮据,得此职务后,他颇为积极,前后三年间为平馆募集相当数量的西文书刊。

一九四四年　五十岁

一月一日

范腾端致函先生，谈武定那土司家藏倮倮文经典及其他汉文谱系案卷清点事。

守和先生馆长座右：

去岁十二月廿五日航遽上书，计已彻尘钧鉴。端昨将本馆购入武定那土司家藏倮倮文经典及其他汉文谱系案卷等件，按照马学良君新写番字标检及洋文编号一一清点钤印已毕。惟无汉字经名，留待他日译定之后再行登记簿籍而已，兹另具清单一纸寄呈察览。查此类经典大半为明清两朝钞本，所惜那氏似不珍重宝爱此物，料想庋置不得其处，甚或积年未尝为之一顾，是以历岁未久，其中篇幅不尠朽败累累，且多残阙不全之本，几难有一完帙。若或信手拈取，略不措意即可立见破绽之点，端因之特为小心倍慎，幸无此虞，堪慰廑系。又其写经纸质类用劣楮应事，复经日染薰烟，其色益增黝暗，故虽以极佳印泥而钤识之，然其赤耀之光亦终为彼所掩，而难独放异采者矣。专肃，敬请崇安，伏乞垂鉴。

职范腾端谨上

三十三年元旦

附呈清单一纸。

武定那土司家藏倮倮文经典及汉文谱系案卷等件清单：

倮倮文经典　五百二十三册内十四册刊本，余均为写本

倮倮文经典刊版　十五面

汉文传家谱系　一册

汉文词禀呈稿　一册

汉文嘉庆十七年立嗣案卷　一册

汉文那沙氏呈控那振兴状藁　一册

汉文祖父故后案稿卷一　一册

回覆禀贴卷一　一册汉文

回覆禀贴卷五　一册汉文

回覆承袭禀卷二　一册汉文

禀报乌蒙、普耳、东川军务案稿雍正五年、八年、十年　一册汉文

那振兴在万德衙内日行号簿　一册汉文

回覆州内禀贴簿道光十一年　一册汉文

劝君修行歌唱本　一册汉文

共计一十四种

〔国家图书馆档案，档案编号 1943-※036-采藏 8-001047 至 1943-※036-采藏 8-001050〕

一月八日

上午，竺可桢至国际文化资料供应处访先生，不值。〔《竺可桢全集》第 9 卷，2006 年，页 8〕

按：竺可桢似欲谈浙大所需幻灯机、胶片事，先生助手告已由胡刚复带走。

一月二十一日

先生路遇顾颉刚。〔《顾颉刚日记》卷 5，页 227〕

一月二十七日

陈立夫致函先生，仍请按照要求密荐平馆人事管理员一人。

守和馆长大鉴：

十一月十一日函悉。本部附属各机关设置人事管理机构一案，系遵人事管理条例之规定，办理、管理对象并非限于应铨叙人员，各机关自宜一律设置。前以贵馆职员不多，经咨准铨叙部核定，仅设人事管理员一人，事关通案，仍希就现有馆员中密荐一人（将来仍可兼任馆内其他职务）函复，以便核转为盼。此颂公绥。

陈立夫启

三十三年一月廿七日

〔教育部部长室用笺。国家图书馆档案，档案编号 1945-※057-综合 5-003004〕

按：此件为文书代笔，落款处钤印。左下角标注有“三三，一月廿九日到”。

二月十一日

米来牟覆函先生，告知收到客岁十二月二日寄来的中国图书馆界报告，其中所附未来计划尤其受人瞩目，该文将刊印在*Library Journal*，对美国图书馆协会收到先生与费正清联署中美文化备忘录后行动迟缓表示歉意，并对中美图书馆合作的方式和细节谈已有的进展和设想。

February 11, 1944

Dear Dr. Yuan:

Your good letter of December 2 arrived late in January. Both the letter and the report which you enclosed are of great interest to us. We had asked, if I remember correctly, primarily for a report on damage to libraries. We are much pleased that you added a section on plans for the future.

Copies of the report and letter were sent promptly to all the members of our International Relations Board, its Committee on the Orient, the President of the ALA, Mrs. Fairbank of the Department of State and various others. We have suggested publication of the report in whole or in part in *Library Journal*.

Mr. Charles H. Brown of Ames, as Chairman of the Committee on the Orient, was of course particularly interested. I quote a few sentences from his remarks:

"This report made me thoroughly ashamed. We have proposed a number of projects but have made little progress since November. Many of the projects are mentioned in A PROPOSED CULTURAL PROGRAM FOR SINO-AMERICAN RELATIONS INVOLVING LIBRARIES. Dr. Yuan mentions the same projects which we discussed last October at the meeting of the Board on International Relations.

We were early in outlining what ought to be done for China. We have been slow in really putting any our plans into operation.

We have avoided some duplications in the book purchases for the University of Peiping. We have helped out the Universal Trading Corporation, but we have really not done very much for China during the last three or four months."

I share Mr. Brown's regret that we have not done more. Several of us would like to say, however, that Mr. Brown himself has done a lot. He is mainly responsible for the existence of the first three items mentioned in the next paragraph.

I enclose A PROPOSED CULTURAL PROGRAM FOR SINO-AMERICAN RELATIONS INVOLVING LIBRARIES, A PROPOSAL FOR AN AMERICAN LIBRARY IN CHINA, OUR STAKE IN CHINA BY Charles H. Brown, and LIBRARY WAR GUIDE, February 1944.

As indicated above, we are very much interested in our plans for the future. Mr. Brown is informed about the orders which are being placed by the Chinese Ministry of Education through the Universal Trading Corporation, about the purchases which are being made by the Associated Boards of Christian Colleges for Non-Governmental Institutions, and about purchases being made by the China Foundation. Some effort has been made to bring about a coordination of these activities. You know, I think, that the ALA with Rockefeller Foundation funds is spending approximately $70,000 a year in the purchase of current scholarly American journals for distribution to libraries in war areas after the war. We have made a recommendation that funds be provided for the purchase of important current reference books for similar use but have not yet obtained the money. The possibility of making a national campaign for books for foreign libraries is now being explored.

Mr. Brown hopes our Committee on the Orient can help arrange for an extension of the pair off of Chinese and American college libraries.

We are much interested in your proposal to issue a circular letter about Chinese libraries and their problems. If you find it possible to carry this plan to conclusion, we shall want to distribute a good many copies in this country for there are many librarians among us who are eager for more information about Chinese libraries.

We all hope that there will be many students from China in our library schools as soon as transportation is available. We shall be glad to have your comments on this aspect of our possible relations.

I was delighted to learn from Mr. Fairbank a few days ago that the Boone Library School is still in operation. Will you please accept and extend my congratulations? Is there anything we can do to assist that school or the Library Association of China in making full use of its facilities? What plan have you, if any, for the development of other library schools in the future?

Recently I suggested to Dr. Steven A. Duggan, Director of the International Institute of Education, that one or more of the Chinese students stranded in this country might be interested in attending a library school. He thought well enough of the suggestion to offer to explore the possibilities.

The American Library Association is also interested in having American librarians visit China to become better acquainted with your library and other educational developments and to learn more of the character of the Chinese people. If they can assist in some small way in the rehabilitation of your libraries, that will give us added pleasure.

Ten large libraries have indicated to Mr. Brown their desire to participate in the plan for cooperative purchase of current Chinese material. I believe that Mr. Brown is delaying final action on the scheme until he can talk with Mr. Fairbank, and others in the East later this month.

I am glad to have the report on the fate of the books which were sent in 1939 and 1940 and hopefully look forward to the time when we can start much larger shipments in your direction.

This letter is already too long. I must add, however, a good word for Mr. and Mrs. John Fairbank. You have in them two of the best friends you could ever hope to have. They are constantly providing us in friendly helpful ways to give you every possible assistance. We need and welcome their knowledge and assistance. We earnestly hope soon to find ways of increasing our activities. Please therefore continue to keep us informed.

Cordially yours,

With all good wishes, I am

Carl H. Milam

Executive Secretary

〔The American Library Association Archives, China Projects File, Box 2, Yuan, T. L., 1943-1945〕

按:Steven A. Duggan 当作 Stephen P. Duggan。此函应请费慰梅代为转寄。

二月二十一日

先生致信胡适,感谢赐稿,谈拍摄美国藏中国古籍善本计划及平馆财务困难。

February 21, 1944

My dear Dr. Hu:

We are much thrilled by the two scholarly articles which you so kindly sent to us through Mr. Wang. As the academic world has missed so much your articles for such a long time, we immediately sent your manuscripts to the printer. As soon as they are published, we shall forward copies to you care of the Library of Congress. Nothing would give us greater pleasure than receiving your further articles from time to time.

The project of filming Chinese rare books in American libraries has been in mind for sometime. I am enclosing a letter addressed to Dr. Mortimer Graves which is self-explanatory. If you approve it, will you mail the enclosed letter with your recommendations if necessary.

Enclosed herewith please find a copy of our report for 1943. To carry on the work of an institution these days is by no means an easy task. The China Foundation has not been able to get the cash from the Government, although the loan was promised last winter. Up to the time of writing we have neither received our allowance for January from the Foundation nor the rice allowance for December from the Government. Meanwhile the cost of rice per 石 has jumped to $5,400 in Kunming and $3,300 in

Chungking.

It has occurred to me that some friends of the Library in the States might be willing to make a gesture at this time. As you probably know, it is not advisable to remit money through the bank from which we get only the official rate of 1∶20 plus 100% government subsidy if it is intended as contribution to cultural or missionary institution. The best way would be to transmit the amount through the Department of State which would authorize the Embassy here to pay in bank-notes, the black market rate of which has jumped to 1∶200 in the course of last three weeks! If the Department is not willing to do so, the other alternative would be to send the contribution to Rockefeller Foundation in India where books can be purchased and transported by air to China. Both Mr. Hsing Ta and Mr. L. K. Tao are here and we discussed the advisability of informing you these facts if there should be any possibilities of sending remittances in the immediate future.

Thanking you again for the two articles and wishing you good health.

Sincerely yours,

T. L. Yuan

〔平馆(昆明)英文信纸。台北胡适纪念馆,HS-JDSHSE-0393-013〕

按:“two scholarly articles”应指《两汉人临文不讳考》《读陈垣史讳举例论汉讳诸条》,均刊于《图书季刊》新第5卷第1期(1944年3月),该两文的手稿似由柯德思携带至重庆。[①] L. K. Tao应指陶孟和(履恭)。落款处为先生签名。

先生致信格雷夫斯,感谢美国学术团体理事会推动《图书季刊》英文本在美复刻出版,并询问有无可能进一步扩大拍摄善本古籍的范围。

February 21, 1944

My dear Dr. Graves:

Since receiving your cable last November, I should have written to you long ago to express to you our sincere appreciation for your interest

① 台北胡适纪念馆,档案编号HS-JDSHSE-0250-018。

in the reprinting of our *Quarterly Bulletin*, having had no secretary for so long, I must apologize for my inability in keeping up my correspondence.

You are no doubt familiar with the project of microfilming our rare books now stored at the Library of Congress. As this work will be nearing completion very soon, it is time to consider the possibility of enlarging the program by filming Chinese rare books in the collection of the Library of Congress and in other American libraries.

A list of the desired items to be filmed could easily be compiled by Mr. Wang Chung-min, an old student of mine now with the Asiatic Division of the Library of Congress. It is necessary for Mr. Wang to visit the leading sinological centers such as New York, Princeton, Cambridge, Chicago, etc. before providing the list. But with his expert knowledge of Chinese books the whole job could be completed in a few weeks' time. Owing to the war many public and private collections in China have been dispersed. The items considered rare by Mr. Wang may not be easily procurable in China now.

The amount of money needed for this program depends upon the number of items to be filmed. In view of the immense value to scholarship, I don't think it difficult to raise the necessary funds. If desired, a part of our book fund granted by the China Foundation can be used for this purpose subject to approvals by the Trustees in America.

I am seeking Dr. Hu Shih's advice in regard to this program and I shall be grateful to you if you would consult Dr. Hu and Dr. Hummel before asking Mr. Wang to make the survey. In view of your great interest in the promotion of sinological studies, I hope the project will receive your favorable consideration.

With kindest regards,

Yours sincerely,

T. L. Yuan

〔平馆（昆明）英文信纸。台北胡适纪念馆，档案编号 HS-JDSHSE-0393-014〕

按：就拍摄美国各大图书馆所藏中文善本书计划，先生除致信格雷夫斯外，如本信提及"I am seeking Dr. Hu Shih's advice in regard to this program"，曾致信胡适(由王重民转寄)。[①] 此件为打字稿，落款处为先生签名。

二月二十二日

平馆撰《为呈请拨发五万元以便由印空运之图书仪器早日运至各地请察核示遵由》，具先生名并钤印。〔中国第二历史档案馆，教育部档案·全宗号五，教育部关于委派北平图书馆馆长袁同礼办理各院校在美所购图书仪器接收转运事宜的有关文书，案卷号5465〕

二月二十三日

先生致信史蒂文斯，已将洛克菲勒基金会赞助过的几位中国图书馆员近况告知访华的美方人员，其中李芳馥应在上海，并附上1943年平馆报告。

Chungking, February 23, 1944

Dear Dr. Stevens:

When Mr. Sloane was here, he told me that you inquired about several former fellows of the Foundation. I gave him all the information which I hope will reach you in due course.

Mr. F. F. Li is still in Shanghai and we have entrusted him with the collecting and storing of Japanese material. I enclose herewith a copy of our report for 1943 from which you will have some idea about the work we are doing. I hope you have met Dr. Fairbank by this time and he will tell you about my work here.

I shall write again before very long. With kindest regards,

Yours sincerely,

T. L. Yuan

〔国立北平图书馆(重庆求精中学二楼)用笺。Rockefeller Foundation. Series 601: China; Subseries 601.R: China-Humanities and Arts. Vol. Box 47. Folder 390〕

按：Sloane应指William Sloane，纽约Henry Holt and Company出

① 台北胡适纪念馆，档案编号HS-JDSHSC-0808-003，该信于3月7日送达。

版社的贸易部主任。[1] 该信为打字稿,落款处为先生签名。

二月二十五日

哥伦比亚大学图书馆馆长 Carl M. White 致函先生,请为该校图书馆“购置、接收、存放和发送美国出版物服务中心(American Publications Service)或美国大使馆安排的图书资料”。〔王成志《袁同礼先生和哥伦比亚大学》,页 247〕

按:Carl M. White(1903-1983),美国图书馆学家,本谱中译作“怀特”[2],1943 年至 1953 年担任哥伦比亚大学图书馆馆长,同时兼任图书馆学院(School of Library Service)主任。

二月二十八日

先生致信吴俊升,请高教司再拨五万元以支付转运各院校图书仪器费用。

士选司长尊鉴:

前于廿二日寄奉一函,计邀察阅。敝馆近接西南公路运输局通知,该局业已允予提前将各院校之图书仪器赶速运渝。兹将该局其曲靖办事处、曲靖调配所电文一通录副附上,即希台察。查该次箱件须由昆明运到曲靖后,再交西南公路运输局,方能转运各地,所有由昆明运曲靖火车费约二万余元,及西南公路运输局预缴运费约三万元。本月廿二日曾呈请大部准予再拨五万元,以资应用。此事务乞鼎力从旁催促,提前将该款交下(请送求精中学),俾该件早日付运。无任感荷。耑此,敬请公绥,并候赐覆。

弟袁同礼顿首

二,廿八

〔中国第二历史档案馆,教育部档案·全宗号五,教育部关于委派北平图书馆馆长袁同礼办理各院校在美所购图书仪器接收转运事宜的有关文书,案卷号 5465〕

按:落款处为先生亲笔。

三月三日

中华图书馆协会撰《为恳请自三十三年一月份起按月赐补助费壹仟元以利

① Zhou, Yuan, and Calvin Elliker. “From the People of the United States of America: The Books for China Programs during World War II.” *Libraries & Culture*, vol. 32, no. 2, 1997, p. 205.

② 该人译名参照严文郁著《中国图书馆发展史:自清末至抗战胜利》,页 235。

全国图书馆事业之推进由》,具先生名并钤印。〔台北"国史馆",〈中国图书馆协会请补助(教育部)〉,数位典藏号 019-030508-0015〕

按:该件提及拟于 4 月 1 日召开协会年会,教育部接到此件后实发每月四百元。

三月八日

先生致信米来牟,表示中华图书馆协会愿意与美国图书馆协会开展一系列合作,但因为财政问题部分项目只得暂缓,并对布朗提出的合作办法给予客观的、可操作性评价。

Chungking Office
c/o Nankai Institute of Economics
Shapingpa, Chungking
March 8, 1944

Dear Dr. Milam:

I am extremely glad to receive your letters of November 22nd and February 11 together with the documents enclosed therein. It gives us great pleasure to learn your plans for closer collaboration between Chinese and American libraries. Some of the projects mentioned in Mr. Brown's proposed program have already been started by the Chinese Library Association, but its financial difficulties have delayed their completion.

Since January a Chinese Book Service has been organized under the auspices of our Association, the object of which is to assist foreign libraries in the acquisition of Chinese material to store them at safe places in China for the duration of the war. A new building cost Ch $ 200,000 is being constructed at the campus of the Nankai Institute of Economics situated at the university center at Shapingpa, Chungking. The building is being constructed with funds from the National Library of Peiping, but when completed it will be loaned to the Association for this purpose.

The Association has already collected much material in connection with a survey of the present status of our libraries and their immediate and post-war needs. This compilation (in English) will be extremely useful to Mr. Brown and other members of your Committee on the Orient.

I have loaned your proposed program to Mr. Hall Paxton of the American Embassy who is in charge of cultural matters and I shall make some comments later on. Meanwhile, I may say that your plans for the training of librarians would meet a very timely need. Mr. Mark Tseng who was a member of our staff has been working in the Claremont College Library and if his chief feels that he needs further training in library work, I shall greatly appreciate your and Dr. Duggan's assistance if he can be given a fellowship to pursue advanced studies at the University of Chicago.

We shall most heartily welcome American librarians if they can arrange a visit to this country. But I am afraid that they will be greatly disappointed with the physical difficulties which we are facing in war-time. But the moral support which an American librarian can give us will be very great. Among other things, you will be able to give us hope that we can count on your assistance in our work of rehabilitation after the war.

Mr. Brown's suggestion that American and Chinese libraries be paired off is not very practical, because most of our librarians do not read English and it would be difficult for them to conduct correspondence, not to say that in war-time we have no typewriters, ribbons and even carbon paper. I am typing this letter myself as I have no secretary nor typist, not to say stenographers and dictaphones.

Your suggestion of asking some of the Foundations to support your program for the purchase of reference books is indeed an excellent idea. If it could be carried out, many foreign libraries will be benefited.

You will be interested to know that the Chinese Library Association is planning to present 25 sets of 25 Chinese books on America to 25 Chinese libraries with a view of obtaining a wider knowledge of culture of the United States. This program could be enlarged if finances permit.

It has occurred to me that if your Association could make a small grant to the Chinese Library Association to enable it to enlarge its program along such lines, a great deal can be done and our Association could be put on a more permanent footing, instead of depending on the National Library of Peiping for its support as it has been doing all these years.

In my last letter to Dr. Fairbank, I urged that all the ALA funds should be transmitted here through the Department of State, so that we can secure the American notes which have a higher value four times than the official rate.

I am trying to catch the pouch to-morrow, so I shall leave other matters in my next letter.

With sincere appreciation for your assistance,

Yours sincerely,

T. L. Yuan

〔The American Library Association Archives, China Projects File, Box 2, Yuan T L 1943-1945〕

按:Hall Paxton 即 J. Hall Paxton(1899-1952),美国外交官,中文名包懋勋,字有功,曾任美国驻南京副领事,时应在美驻华大使馆中负责文化事务,后转任他务,并由费慰梅继任。曾宪三本拟于1939 年 5 月归国,但因为时局问题,先生建议其继续在美,他先在哈佛燕京图书馆服务,约于 1941 年 8 月入克莱蒙特学院(Claremont Colleges),负责该校图书馆中文馆藏,似并未赴芝加哥大学学习。此件为打字稿,落款处为先生签名。

三月九日

先生撰写 Memorandum Re Chinese Tanslations of Outstanding Books on America。〔Rockefeller Foundation. Series 601: China; Subseries 601.R: China-Humanities and Arts. Vol. Box 47. Folder 390〕

三月十一日

米来牟覆函先生,其已与布朗达成一致,希望尽快派一位美国图书馆学家赴华考察,一是藉此了解中国各类型图书馆、图书馆学校的信息和困难,二是培养未来十年美国图书馆界的领军人物,如果同意该计划请中华图书馆协会正式函请美国图书馆协会,并将此议报备中华民国教育部。

March 11, 1944

Dear Dr. Yuan:

Charles H. Brown and I are becoming more and more convinced that if we are to do our part in preparing for and participating in library relations with China, we should send to China soon one of our American librarians.

The purpose of the visit would be twofold: 1, to gather specific information about the needs of various types of libraries, library schools and other agencies, and to learn, as one can learn only from personal conversation, some of the problems and difficulties; and 2, to have someone who is likely to be prominent in the counsels of the A. L. A. for the next decade or two who has at least some direct acquaintance with some Chinese librarians and some knowledge of Chinese libraries.

We have in mind two or three persons, all relatively young. One is the head of a large public library who will soon be an officer of the A. L. A.; the other two are connected with university libraries and are very active in A. L. A. affairs. Because of the uncertainties we have not discussed the matter with them.

We have not as yet attempted to explore the possibility of finding the rather sizable sum of money which would be necessary for such a visit under present circumstances. We have been, however, assured of the active and sympathetic interest of persons of influence in our government and others connected with American foundations.

The purpose of this letter therefore is to ask whether you agree that such a visit would be desirable. If you do, we suggest a letter from the Library Association of China to the American Library Association with the endorsement, if you think wise, of the Chinese Minister of Education.

Unfortunately, I cannot say with certainty that we will be able to respond promptly and favorably to such an invitation because the funds and priorities may be difficult to obtain; but we shall do our best. A letter from you as mentioned above will be of assistance to us.

Cordially yours,

Carl H. Milam

Executive Secretary

〔The American Library Association Archives, China Projects File, Box 2, Yuan T L 1943-1945〕

按:One is the head of a large public library 应指怀特。该函抄送给费慰梅、Miss Ludington、布朗、Mr. Ulveling、莱登伯格。

三月十三日

教育部高教司吴俊升致函先生,告知已拨接运图书仪器经费三万元,将由中国农业银行汇发。〔中国第二历史档案馆,教育部档案·全宗号五,教育部关于委派北平图书馆馆长袁同礼办理各院校在美所购图书仪器接收转运事宜的有关文书,案卷号5465〕

三月十五日

平馆向教育部呈文一件,题为《为呈送职馆卅三年一月份请领生活补助费名册及编制员额俸给预算表又卅三年度一月份本馆员工请领食米代金名册昆明重庆两部分各二份恳祈鉴核示遵由》,具先生名并钤印。

案奉钧部本年三月八日会字第一一七三九号训令内开:(略)"查关于卅三年一月份请领食米代金名册等业经本部转饬编造分别送核在案复奉前因合亟令仰遵照限文到日覆实编造卅三年一月份请领生活补助费名册四份填明职别姓名年龄月支薪俸数额并附具编制员额俸给预算表于二月十五日以前并同前案所编米代金名册以二份径行汇送国防最高委员会秘书厅核办以二份呈部备核为要此令"等因。奉此,查职馆前奉令编造卅三年度一月份请领员工食米及代金名册及一月份请领生活补助费清单俸给费说明表各一份,曾于二月十四日径送国防最高委员会秘书厅并赍呈钧部备核各在案。兹再遵令编造卅三年一月份请领生活补助费名册并附具编制员额俸给预算表及一月份请领食米代金名册各四份,除以二份径送国防最高委员会秘书厅外,并以二份随文赍送,理合具文呈请鉴核批示祇遵。

谨呈

教育部部长陈

国立北平图书馆馆长袁同礼(印)

三十三年三月十五日

〔中国第二历史档案馆,教育部档案·全卷宗五,国立北平图书馆员工生活补助费名册及俸薪表,案卷号11614(1)〕

先生致信史蒂文斯,附上翻译中文书籍备忘录并告知已经开始为美国图书馆购买中文书报杂志,建议往来信件借用美国国务院的外交渠道以保证稳定。

March 15, 1944

Dear Dr. Stevens:

I hope you have received a copy of our report for 1943.

Knowing that you are interested in cultural interchange, I am enclosing herewith a memo re the translation of books on America. The object of this program is to promote understanding by Chinese scholars of the cultural values of the United States. Our main difficulty lies in the choice of books because we have not got many books to choose. In this connection we hope your office in Delhi might render some assistance, as books intended for the Library can now be transported here by air from India. I hope you will discuss these matters with Dr. Balfour if he is still in New York.

You will be interested to know that our Library and the Library Association of China have been assisting American libraries in securing Chinese material. Books and journals for the Library of Congress are being transported by air to Washington through the Embassy Channels. Material for other institutions is being stored in this Library. A temporary building costing Ch $ 200,000 is now under construction. It will be used mainly for this purpose.

A survey of Chinese libraries is being conducted and when completed copies will be sent to the American Library Association with a request that some priority be given to China in the national book campaign as planned by the ALA.

It is gratifying to report that though harassed by exigencies of war, our cultural program is continuing.

Ordinary air mail between China and the United States is slow and uncertain. May I suggest that any communication relating to cultural program from your Foundation be transmitted here through the Department of State?

With kindest regards,

Yours sincerely,

T. L. Yuan

〔平馆（昆明）英文信纸。Rockefeller Foundation. Series 601: China; Subseries 601.R: China-Humanities and Arts. Vol. Box 47. Folder 390〕

按:此件为打字稿,落款处为先生签名。

Library Jouranl 刊登先生文章,题为 Library Situation in China。〔T. L., Yuan. "Library Situation in China." *Library Jouranl*, vol. 69, no. 6, 1944, pp. 235-238〕

按:此篇文章最初是因先生受美国图书馆协会要求,对中国图书馆所遭受的损毁作一份正式报告,本附在先生写给米来牟的信中,后者认为极为重要,遂请该协会东方及西南太平洋分委会主任布朗凝练、加注,最终在*Library Jouranl* 正式发表。本文分为信件节录、Destruction of Chinese Libraries、Library Situation in Free China 1937-43、Plans for the Future 四部分。此文后附布朗的文章 Implementation of China Program,以示美国图书馆协会支持中国图书馆重建事业的态度和方针。该篇文章失收于《袁同礼文集》。

三月十六日

先生致信秘鲁国立图书馆馆长 Jorge Basadre,代表中华图书馆协会表示慰问。〔《中华图书馆协会会报》第 18 卷第 5-6 期,1944 年 12 月 15 日,页 10〕

按:Jorge Basadre(1903-1980),秘鲁历史学家,曾任秘鲁教育部长及秘鲁国家图书馆馆长。1943 年 5 月,秘鲁国立图书馆不幸被焚毁。该信由中华民国驻秘鲁领事馆李骏转交。7 月 6 日,Jorge Basadre 覆信表示感谢。

三月二十九日

史蒂文斯致函先生,告知 William Sloane 已回到美国,并收到先生发来的 1943 年度报告。

March 29, 1944

Dear Dr. Yuan:

I am happy to report in replying to your letter of February twenty-third that Mr. Sloane is back in New York City, bringing excellent reports of his months in China. Yesterday, I heard him speak to the publishers whom he represented in China. They were most appreciative and very much interested in all that he had to report. My thanks to you and all your colleagues who have contributed to the success of his mission.

Your own report for 1943 is very informing. I have shown it to Mr. Winter, who still is in New York. He is very sorry to see what prices you have been compelled to pay for even Chinese books and says your record is extraordinarily fine in view of all the difficulties you encounter.

I hope that the plan of re-issuance of the Bulletin of bibliography can be maintained. During the week, I shall see the chairman of the International Board of the American Library Association. I will show your report to Miss Flora B. Ludington and have no doubt that she will wish to report on it to her colleagues.

Sincerely yours,

David H. Stevens

〔Rockefeller Foundation. Series 601: China; Subseries 601.R: China-Humanities and Arts. Vol. Box 47. Folder 390〕

按:此件为录副。

三月三十日

中华图书馆协会撰《奉令填具工作报告表呈请鉴核并恳发给补助费由》,具先生名并钤印。〔台北"国史馆",〈中国图书馆协会请补助(教育部)〉,数位典藏号 019-030508-0015〕

四月二日

竺可桢(重庆)致函先生。〔《竺可桢全集》第 9 卷,页 69〕

四月七日

先生致信 Harry M. Lydenberg,呼吁美国图书馆协会(国际关系委员会)在美国国务院文化关系项目下派遣专家来华考察中国图书馆蒙受的损失和战后复兴的需求，并告知为美国图书馆购买战时中文出版物，存放空间问题将在本月末得到解决。

April 7, 1944

Dear Dr. Lydenberg:

It was only recently that I learned that you had been serving as Chairman of the Board on International Relations of the A. L. A. Knowing your past achievements at the New York Public Library, I am confident that under your inspiring guidance the Board will accomplish a great deal in promoting closer international cultural relations.

Since the outbreak of the Sino-Japanese War, we have been fully blockaded and isolated from the rest of the world. It is easy, therefore, to visualize our need for closer contact with our colleagues in the West. It is on this account I proposed that an American library expert be sent to China by the A. L. A. In order to secure for him an official status in war-time, it is suggested that he be designated as one of the experts to be sent under the Cultural Relation Program of the Department of State.

A survey of Chinese libraries is being conducted which, we hope, will facilitate the work of such an expect if and when he comes, I am only afraid, however, that our poor means of transportation in war-time will be a source of disappointment to such a new comer.

Through the Chinese Book Service of this Association, we have purchased and stored a number of Chinese materials for American libraries. Those items purchased for the Library of Congress are being transported to Washington by air through the courtesy of the American Embassy. Those intended for other American institutions are stored here for the duration of the war. Storage space is a most serious problem here, but a temporary building is in the course of the construction and will be completed at the end of this month. We are waiting for the book funds as well as other specific information from the A. L. A. Headquarters.

Both your work and ours may be described as intellectual Lend-Lease in both directions; so, it is a source for gratification that we are able to contribute our share toward the war effort.

With best wishes and kindest regards,

Yours faithfully,

T. L. Yuan

P. S. Will you kindly forward the enclosed letter to Dr. Bishop?

〔中华图书馆协会(平馆沙坪坝办事处转)英文信纸。The American Library Association Archives, China Projects File, Box 1, Correspondence about China, National Library at Peiping, 1943－1944〕

按:Harry M. Lydenberg(1874－1960),美国图书馆学家,本谱中译作“莱登伯格”,1931 年至 1932 年担任美国图书馆协会主席,1934 年至 1941 年担任纽约公共图书馆馆长,1946 年出任美国图书馆协会国际关系委员会主席。Lend-Lease 即租借法案,1941 年 3 月 11 日生效,其目的是在美国不卷入战争的同时为盟国提供战争物资。此件为打字稿,落款处为先生签名,于 5 月 5 日送达。

四月十一日

先生致信米来牟,商洽美国图书馆协会专家来华访问事宜。

April 11, 1944

Dear Dr. Milam:

I am most happy to receive your letter of March 11 and to learn that a visit from an American library expert to China could possibly be arranged. That is a most welcome news. On behalf of the Library Association of China, I hasten to write to extend to you a most cordial invitation. I can assure you that in doing so I am voicing the sentiment of all of my colleague in China in welcoming such a delegate from the A. L. A.

You may probably recall that in the spring of 1937, Dr. W. W. Bishop, then Librarian of the University of Michigan, was invited by our Association to visit China and to make a survey of Chinese libraries with a view to promoting closer cooperation between Chinese and American Libraries. The sudden outbreak of the Sino-Japanese War in July 1937 prevented Dr. Bishop from coming to the Orient-a matter which all of us have deeply regret.

Since China and the United States have been united in war, there has been an earnest desire for closer cultural cooperation between the two countries. We are confident that such a visit from the A. L. A. delegate will greatly promote that closer cooperation desired by both countries.

I shall secure the endorsement from the Chinese Minister of Education and I shall not fail to communicate with you in the immediate future.

In order to secure an official status for such a delegate, may I suggest that he be designated as one of the experts to be sent to China under the Cultural Relation Program of the Department of State. Such an official status, as you will no doubt realize, is most desirable in war-time.

With kindest regards,

Yours sincerely,

T. L. Yuan

Chairman, Executive Board

〔The American Library Association Archives, China Projects File, Box 2, Yuan T L 1943-1945〕

按:此信先发送至华盛顿费慰梅处,后由她转与米来牟。此件为打字稿,落款处为先生签名,于 5 月 10 日送达。

四月十二日

先生呈教育部部长陈立夫,商洽美图书馆协会派遣专家访华事宜,并请教育部批注该请。

……溯自倭寇内犯以来,我国图书损失不可胜计。刻下胜利在望,复员计划亟待拟订,西文图书仪器之供给前已由钧部先后拨付美金壹佰万元,以之分配各院校,尚虞不敷,似更无余力顾及省立市立各图书馆,故今后我国图书馆之复兴颇赖国际间之援助。近月以来,美国图书馆界方面屡次表示愿加赞助。爰定于本年内发起全国捐书运动,以为之倡,并拟派一专家来华视察。近接美国图书馆协会总干事 Milam 博士来函,嘱先得钧座之同意,再行派遣。爰将该总干事来函录副奉上,即祈钧阅。至该专家来华一切费用,拟提议由美国国务院担任,列为派遣来华服务专家之一,并援 Eaton 教授前例,指定在钧部服务,为时约八个月,是否有当。敬候尊裁,并恳赐覆为感。

(袁同礼)

〔国家图书馆档案,档案编号 1943-※052-协会 6-002001 和 1943-※052-协会 6-002002〕

按:Eaton 即 Paul B. Eaton,美国机械工程学家,曾任拉法耶特学院(Lafayette College)机械工程系主任,1943 年由美国国务院派华访问。此为抄件,前文空缺。

四月十三日

先生撰写 Comment on Mr. William W. Schwartzmann's Project,该份英文报告包括该计划概述、相关制约因素、结语三部分,先生认为运输极为不易、分类索引卡片绝无可能在短期内实现、经费支绌不宜新设专门机构。〔台北"国家发展委员会档案管理局",〈国际文化合作——美国〉,档号 A309000000E/0030/640.66/0001〕

按:William W. Schwartzmann,相关档案中译作奚华滋曼,曾在国会图书馆任职,时在昆明担任红十字会工作,其计划为在华盛顿设立一小规模办事处,与国会图书馆等联络,为中国搜集有关科学文化资料。

四月十四日

先生覆信哥伦比亚大学图书馆馆长怀特,表示愿为该校购买、收集、存放、运送中文出版物。〔王成志《袁同礼先生和哥伦比亚大学》,页 247〕

四月二十七日

先生致信米来牟,感谢美国图书馆协会通过美国国务院寄来两份缩微胶卷正片,涉及编目规则、分类和院校图书馆建筑。

April 27,1944

Dear Dr. Milam:

We beg to acknowledge with many thanks the receipt of two positive rolls of microfilms which the American Library Association has so kindly transmitted to us through the Department of State. The two rolls consist of the following films:

A. L. A. Rules for Filing Catalog Cards, 1942. pp. 1-109.

Introduction to Cataloging and the Classification of Books, by Margaret Mann, 1943. pp. 1-277.

College and University Library Buildings, by Edna Ruth Hanley, 1939. pp. 1-152.

We appreciate very much your thoughtfulness in sending us these films which will not only be useful to our libraries, but also to our library schools. We shall see to it that they are circulated among interested agencies, in order to make the best use of the material you so kindly put at our disposal.

Very sincerely yours,

T. L. Yuan

〔中华图书馆协会(平馆沙坪坝办事处转)英文信纸。The American Library Association Archives, China Projects File, Box 2, Yuan T L 1943-1945〕

按:此件为打字稿,落款处为先生签名,于5月31日送达。

四月二十九日

先生致信李济,请其更正购书发票抬头信息并将书款降至八折。

济之吾兄赐鉴:

四月廿二日惠书及内附发票一纸,拜悉一一。《苍洱考古报告》系中华图书馆协会所购,兹将该发票奉还,还请将原写之"国立北平图书馆"抬头字样改写为"中华图书馆协会"抬头,以便报销。又该书书价并盼赐予八折,如荷同意,当将书款汇上。专此敬复,并颂著安。

弟袁同礼谨启

四月廿九日

〔台北"国家发展委员会档案管理局",档号A335000000E/0033/400/001/001/007〕

按:《苍洱考古报告》即《国立中央博物院专刊乙种之一:云南苍洱境考古报告》,吴金鼎、曾昭燏、王介忱合著,1942年出版。该件全文皆为文书代笔,落款处钤先生名章。

布朗覆函先生,谈图书运输问题、邹秉文在美收集农业相关书刊和政府出版物,并就中美高校图书馆合作、选派图书馆员赴美留学等事发表意见。

April 29, 1944

Dear Dr. Yuan:

I have been wanting to write you for some time, but I have delayed my letter until I could hear reports of the interest aroused by your excellent article in the *Library Journal* on the library situation in China.

I have had a very considerable correspondence from librarians in this country who have been deeply stirred by your account of the destruction of Chinese libraries and by your proposals for the future. I regretted deeply that it was necessary to abridge your report somewhat. The editor of the *Library Journal* was unable to allow more space to the two articles, and he was unwilling that I give to you some of the pages assigned to me.

I understand that twelve copies of the reprint of your article have been sent to you through the Department of State. If you want more copies, please let me know. I thought you might like to distribute them to members of your government and to your colleagues.

Librarians in the United States are greatly interested in the library development in China, possibly more so than in the proposed development in any other country. Many of them have written me asking what they can do to assist in the rehabilitation of your libraries. You can count on the support of all of us. It would be a help if from time to time you can send me information that would be of interest to my colleagues here. Such notes can be published in the *Library Journal* and ALA *Bulletin*, and if they are too extensive for such publication, I can mimeograph a more complete statement as I did with your report, a digest of which appeared in the *Library Journal*.

I have talked with most of the Chinese professors now visiting in this country. They have been of great assistance in giving us information on the methods which will be of most help to China.

The great difficulty is in the shipment of books, but we hope to be able to get at least a few books through each week, and possibly the difficulty of transportation will be eased considerably in the not too distant future.

You are probably aware that the Universal Trading Corporation has many orders from your Ministry of Agriculture. I understand these orders of books were compiled originally about 1939 and do not include books for the last four years. The Universal Trading Corporation has not been able to arrange for the purchase of many of these books as yet, but we hope that they will be able to proceed with the buying. The space allotted to the Universal Trading Corporation for transportation to China is extremely limited and does not make possible the inclusion of books.

Dr. P. W. Tsou, who represents your Ministry of Agriculture in this country, has been very energetic in collecting government publications in the field of agriculture and also bulletins of state experiment stations. These are being stored for shipment to China when opportunity offers.

I am afraid my proposal for the pairing off of Chinese and American libraries was not clearly stated. The proposal is only considered in connection with postwar planning; not for immediate operation. There is considerable pairing off now between the mission colleges and universities in this country. Unfortunately, this pairing off is very uneven. Yenching University is paired off with six different American universities; Ginling has affiliations with a number. Yale University is now collecting many books for its sister institution, Yale in China.

I have had several discussions with Dr. Hu Shih who first proposed this pairing off arrangement between Chinese and American universities and would like to see it developed after the war. The pairing off proposed was only for university libraries, not public libraries.

A similar pairing off is being arranged between British and American universities and has been proposed as possibility for American and continental European universities. There is not much that can be done about it now except to give the matter thought. If there are to be close relationships between individual institutions of this country and other countries, I would not want to see China left out of the arrangements. The universities in this country will be much more international after the war than now.

We understand from your scholars, and we agree, that it would be desirable to bring as many Chinese and American librarians as possible into close understanding with each other and into correspondence if this pairing off can be extended. If, for instance, one of your large scientific and technical colleges were paired with Iowa State College, exchanging books and students, it would bring the librarians and educators of these two institutions into close and mutually helpful relationships.

Your friends Mr. and Mrs. Fairbank and I have been appointed a committee of three to try to expedite shipments to China and to arrange for coordination. I have a note that books on postwar planning are especially needed. I have sent two or three to Mr. Fairbank to see if they could be forwarded through State Department channels. If you will be good enough to inform me of any special needs at any time, we shall be glad to see what we can do to meet them.

I have been astonished to find how much all these Chinese students appreciate what you have done under difficult circumstances. Several professors are deeply interested in their own libraries and have asked about the distribution in China of the books and periodicals collected in this country. I have talked with these scholars and a representative of your government on this subject. Their advice was to continue our close relationships with you as an official of the Chinese Library Association. Some of them expressed their own convictions that eventually it might be necessary for you to appoint a committee of three to avoid too much criticism. One of them suggested that a committee composed possibly of you, Chiang Fu-tsung of the National Central Library, and a certain university president who was a liberal and sympathetic with American thought and who was a close friend of yours would form an excellent group. However, I was informed by one of your scholars in whom I have great confidence that it probably would be better to delay such an appointment for the time being and continue our very close relationships with you as the head of the Chinese Library Association.

We are very much pleased to learn that the Boone Library School has received a grant from the Rockefeller Foundation of US $ 5,000 a year for the next three years. This is, indeed, welcome information.

There is another matter on which I should like your help. I am proposing to issue an inexpensive mimeographed news letter to American librarians who are interested in China and naturally would like to make sure that their interest continues. If you can send me notes to include in this publication, I shall appreciate it. Dr. T. F. Tsiang gave us a very interesting account of the destruction of his very valuable personal library.

We should like also your ideas of what should be done to assist in the development of library schools in China after the war. Can the Boone Library School take care of all your needs? Would it need any instructors from this country or do you have instructors in China who can assist in the teaching? Is there any possibility you could send some librarians to this country to prepare themselves for teaching in China after the war?

For your information, I have written a letter to Dr. P. W. Tsou saying that this library would be glad to grant a fellowship to some Chinese Student who wishes to become a librarian. The salary would provide employment in the Library on a half-time basis, the balance of the time being given over to studies in the college. The compensation would be US $ 75 a month, which is sufficient to live on in this rural section. The University of Minnesota is proposing to make a similar arrangement.

This letter is extremely long, but the librarians of this country are very eager to get all the information they can about China. I wish I could send to you the very many expressions of sympathy at the great destruction of your irreplaceable collections. Every day I receive letters from librarians not personally known to me asking what they can do to help China.

Yours very truly,

Charles H. Brown, Chairman

Committee on the Orient and Southwest Pacific

〔The American Library Association Archives, China Projects File, Box 2, Yuan T L 1943-1945〕

按:P. W. Tsou 即邹秉文(1893—1985),江苏苏州人,植物病理学家,1915 年获康乃尔大学农学士,归国后历任金陵大学教授、东南大学农科主任、上海商品检验局局长,时任国民党政府驻美农业代表。此件为录副。

四月

先生致信王重民,谈国内物价高涨,《四部丛刊》已售至三十万元,请其代为向胡适索求稿件,并附《图书季刊》目录。〔台北胡适纪念馆,档案编号 HS-JDSHSC-0797-004〕

按:该信于 5 月 10 日送达。索稿之请,胡适似并未积极回覆,因直至《图书季刊》新第 8 卷第 1-2 期(1947 年 6 月),才再次登载其文章。

五月一日

米来牟致函先生,告知美国图书馆协会正在物色美国图书馆学家赴华考察、洛克菲勒基金会拨款为战区图书馆购买书刊的进展。

May 1, 1944

Dear Dr. Yuan:

Mr. Brown and I have delayed our reply to your good letter of March 8 until we could both write. Following his recent extended trip to New York and Washington, Mr. Brown has now written and is eager to get his letter off. I am therefore writing briefly.

I have written to Mr. Willis Kerr, Librarian of Claremont Colleges, asking for his advice concerning Mr. Mark Tseng but have not yet had a reply.

We shall investigate further the possibility of arranging for a librarian from this country to visit China. For reasons previously explained we are exceedingly eager to give one of our leading librarians an opportunity to get acquainted with you and your colleagues.

The Rockefeller Foundation has appropriated $100,000 for the purchase of reference and research materials for libraries in war areas. This is a comparatively small sum and will not go very far but it will do something. As a part of this general program of assisting foreign libraries we are now having lists prepared-lists of books which librarians and scholars think the foreign librarians will want. These should be helpful to men like yourself who are concerned with problems of selection and purchase.

You are certainly most enterprising in planning to purchase 25 sets of 25 Chinese books on America to be presented to 25 Chinese libraries. I wish we had some funds which could be allocated to your organization to enable it to expand this program. Unfortunately, we do not have.

We have telegraphed a message to Mr. John Fairbank who will undertake to get it to you in time for your meeting on May 5 and 6. Again my congratulations. We are not having a conference this year.

I believe Mr. Brown has answered your other questions.

With most cordial greetings and full appreciation of the importance of the opportunity we have to work together, I am

Very sincerely yours,

Carl H. Milam

Executive Secretary

〔The American Library Association Archives, China Projects File, Box 2, Yuan T L 1943-1945〕

按:Willis Kerr 即 Willis H. Kerr(1885-1953),美国图书馆学家,1927 年至 1948 年担任克莱蒙特学院图书馆馆长。20 世纪 40 年,曾宪三的确作为研究生在克莱蒙特学院学习,根据洛克菲勒基金会档案,Porter Fund 为其提供了奖学金,但时间似在 1944 年之前,待考。① 此件为录副。

五月四日

教育部部长陈立夫覆函先生,同意邀请美国图书馆协会派员来华考察。

---

① Rockefeller Foundation, Rockefeller Foundation records, Fellowships, RG 10, New China Program-Humanities-Social Sciences (H-SS), Series 18.

守和馆长大鉴：

四月十二日大函敬悉。关于美国图书馆协会拟派专家来华考察一节，可予同意。专复，并颂公祺。

陈立夫顿首

三十三年五月四日

〔教育部部长室用笺。国家图书馆档案，档案编号 1943-※052-协会 6-002003〕

按：该函非陈立夫亲笔，落款处钤印。

五月五日

下午一时，中华图书馆协会第六次年会假国立中央图书馆杂志阅览室召开，先生、蒋复璁、沈祖荣、洪有丰、陈训慈、岳良木、陆华深、严文郁、徐家麟、汪长炳、皮高品、傅振伦、张申府、王育伊、何国贵、爨汝僖、徐家璧、贾芳、罗香林、李之璋、童世纲、孙述万、颜泽霪、蓝乾章等六十五人出席，另有文华图书专科学校学生二十三人列席。先生以理事长身份作为会议主席，李之璋记录。先生致开会辞，首对中央图书馆筹备招待表示感谢；次对第五次年会以后本会工作略作总结，希望会员能够团结配合、克尽文化工作者职责；表示本次年会之旨趣，一为集思广益，二为联络感情，克服当下之困难；最后谈及到场人员仅为协会会员十二分之一，希望本次年会成果不辜负未能出席会员的希望。继由蒋复璁、邓光禄（华西协和大学图书馆主任）相继发言，随后讨论提案七件。

以上事务结束后，首由先生报告会务，除会报、本日《中央日报》报道者外，涉及会员、经费、调查工作、美国图书馆协会派专家来华考察诸方面。此后，讨论二十四位会员在 5 月 4 日提交的修改本会组织大纲临时提案，涉及第四章组织、第六章选举、第八章事务所三部分，就此与会人员态度不一，但表决为赞成由出席会员修改组织大纲者占多数。此时已六时半，先生建议请于便餐后再行讨论，但留下人数过少，未能继续。〔《中华图书馆协会会报》第 18 卷第 4 期，1944 年 6 月 15 日，页 6-9〕

按：本日，中国教育学术团体第三届联合年会亦在中央图书馆举行，中华图书馆协会第六次年会将首要提案三件送交联合年会审查。

《中央日报》刊登先生文章，题为《中华图书馆协会之过去现在与将来》。

〔《中央日报》1944年5月5日，第6版（中华图书馆协会年会特刊[①]）〕

按：该文共三部分，依次为过去会务之简溯、现在会务之概况、将来事业之展望，后又刊登于《中华图书馆协会会报》第18卷第4期（6月15日）。

五月六日

上午十时，中华图书馆协会第六次年会假国立中央图书馆继续召开。先生、蒋复璁、陈训慈、岳良木、陆华深、严文郁、徐家麟、汪长炳、皮高品、童世纲、孙述万、颜泽霮、蓝乾章、罗香林等四十七人出席。先生为主席，李之璋记录。继续讨论修改协会组织大纲案，诸人意见并不统一，有人表示理应修改，但须慎重。结果如下：第六条以汪应文修正提议（本会设理事十五人，由出席年会会员照定额二倍票选候选人，再由会员通讯公选之，但于候选人意外选举者，听之）获得二十二票通过；第八条以二十四人修正提议（理事会设常设理事五人，由理事票选之，常务理事中推出理事长，书记、会计各一人）多数通过；第七条以二十四人修正提议多数通过。此时已过十二点，本应赴中央党部午餐，但严文郁等建议立刻选举理事、监事，结果当选理事候选人共三十人，先生仅得14票，远远落后沈祖荣、蒋复璁、汪长炳、洪有丰、陈训慈、徐家麟、严文郁等人；当选监事候选人十八人，先生则以21票名列第一。〔《中华图书馆协会会报》第18卷第4期，页9-11〕

按：此时，中华图书馆协会已有明显裂痕，二十四人在5月4日的临时修改案即征兆，而因出席人数较协会注册会员甚少，且第二日又少十八人，所谓“修正提议”被众人裹挟，先生作为会议主席亦无办法。此次会议有“严重分裂倾向”，先生十分不悦，“面有怒色”。[②]

五月八日

先生以中华图书馆协会执行部主席身份致信米来牟，感谢发来年会贺信并祝愿两国图书馆协会能够在未来紧密合作。

May 8, 1944

The officers and members of the Library Association of China wish

---

① 该版另有蒋复璁《战后我国图书馆事业之瞻望》、沈祖荣《战后图书馆发展之途径》、陈训慈《闲话省立图书馆》三篇文章。

② 严文郁著《中国图书馆发展史：自清末至抗战胜利》，沈宝环序（17）。

to express our profound appreciation for the friendly message and cordial greetings which you and President Warren sent to us on the occasion of our conference on May 5 and 6. For many years Chinese librarians have watched with constantly increasing admiration your magnificent contribution to library service and to international library cooperation. The achievements of the A. L. A. under your inspiring leadership have been a constant source of inspiration to our work in China. Today we are proud to stand united with your country not only in winning the war, but also in winning the peace. This identity of aims coupled with the friendship born of mutual interest and understanding has now developed into a spirit of firm solidarity which will furnish a basis for still closer cooperation in the years ahead. We share with your determination to build a world in which vandalism cannot flourish and we firmly believe that our united effort will not only contribute materially toward hastening the restoration and rehabilitation of cultural and educational institutions in war areas but will also assure to humanity a happier world based on foundations of liberty, democracy and cooperation.

Library Association of China,
T. L. Yuan, Chairman,
Executive Board

〔The American Library Association Archives, China Projects File, Box 2, Yuan T L 1943-1945〕

按：President Warren 即 Althea H. Warren（1886-1958），时任洛杉矶公共图书馆馆长并担任美国图书馆协会主席。此件为打字稿，落款处为先生签名，于6月29日送达。

五月九日

李济覆函先生，所嘱各节均已照办并寄上购书发票。

守和吾兄赐鉴：

奉四月廿九日惠书，属将苍洱境考古报告发票抬头改为"中华图书馆协会"并将书价以八折计算，自当遵命。兹另开发票一纸寄呈。敬悉收转为感。专此，敬颂著安。

弟〇〇谨覆

卅三年五月九日

〔台北"国家发展委员会档案管理局",档案编号 A335000000E/0033/400/001/001/007〕

按:此件为底稿。

莱登伯格致先生两函。其一,告知美方寄送武昌文华图书专科学校的书刊将由国务院发送,并随信附上清单,另预祝中华图书馆协会年会顺利召开。

May 9, 1944

Dear Dr. Yuan:

Through the kindness of the Department of State, the American Library Association is able to send to the Boone Library School the publications on the attached list. They go with the compliments of the American Library Association in general and the International Relations Board in particular. We hope that they may be of interest to the staff and students of the school and in addition that they may give a light indication of some of the things American librarians are doing and thinking.

The conference of the Chinese Library Association, according to the information received here, was to have taken place on the fifth of this month. All of us here were wishing a fruitful and worthwhile gathering of minds for that occasion. So too we shall be awaiting news of what was said and done then.

I know Mr. Carl Milam, Mr. Charles Brown and your countless other friends here want me to extend their greetings with mine.

Truly yours,

H. M. Lydenberg

〔The American Library Association Archives, China Projects File, Box 2, Yuan T L 1943-1945〕

按:该函寄送重庆,此件为副本。

第二,告知毕寿普近况,并表示有幸出任国际关系委员会主席职务,对先生和中国图书馆界在战时不利局面下的坚持表示钦佩。

May 9, 1944

Dear Dr. Yuan:

It is a real pleasure to report arrival of your letter of 7 April and to say the enclosure to Dr. Bishop is now on its way to him in Ann Arbor.

You will be glad to hear that he stopped in to see us in Washington on his way to Florida early in the winter and also on his return to Michigan, looking much better and feeling much fitter on the return trip than on the outbound.

It is sad, however, to have to say he lost his wife last summer, and then this last month lost his mother. Both women had lived fruitful and useful lives, his mother adding the distinction of attaining an age well over ninety.

Yes, thank you, I left Mexico last July to take this post in Washington which gives me a fine chance to keep in touch with the marvelous work you are doing in China. The ‘you’ there is both individual and collective as to Yuan and to China, for I get extensive reports from Charles Brown as to what you are accomplishing as well as what the other Chinese librarians are setting to their credit against such distressing odds.

I'm glad of this chance to extend not only my congratulations on past achievements but my assured conviction of even greater things to be done by you in future. For the part we are fortunate enough to play in help, you may be sure of the happiness felt by us, all and sundry.

Truly yours,

H. M. Lydenberg

〔The American Library Association Archives, China Projects File, Box 1, National Library at Peiping 1943-1944〕

五月十日

先生致信费正清，告知中华图书馆协会年会修改组织大纲及改选的经过，重提在华设立美方图书馆的重要性，此外为美国十三家图书馆购买书刊存放问题已与何廉商妥解决。

May 10, 1944

My dear Dr. Fairbank:

We are greatly touched by the message from the A. L. A. which conveys direct expression of solidarity. On behalf of our Association, I sent a reply to Dr. Milam, thanking the A. L. A. for this friendly message.

At our recent Conference I made a full report about our plans in connection with the proposed visit of an American library expert to China in the immediate future. I also read the letter from the Minister of Education giving his approval to such a visit. The news was received with great enthusiasm.

Due to difficulties of travel in war-time, only 60 out of 700 members were able to attend the Conference and half of this number were either students in the library schools or newly admitted members. This situation gave the radicals an opportunity for manoeuvring. The methods they used were: (1) revision of the constitution of our Association at the Conference and (2) election of officers by those attending the Conference.

The constitution in force provides that 15 members of the Executive Board are to be elected by correspondence by members at large throughout the country from among 30 candidates nominated by the Executive Board. The amendment now proposed by the radicals reads: "15 members of the Board are to be elected by those attending the Conference".

After much discussion another amendment was introduced whereby 15 members of the Board are to be elected by members at large from among thirty candidates nominated at the Conference. This resolution was finally adopted. Since the new officers are to be elected by correspondence throughout the country and since mails in war-time China are very slow, they will not be able to assume office until August or September. It appears, therefore, that in the interim no one is likely to be fully responsible for the affairs of the Association.

Although liberal elements of our Association tried to remedy the situation to the best of our abilities, yet in these times libraries in China are always in minority and are not able to match the growing number of radicals. With radicals in majority, it is difficult to foresee the repercussions from the new situation.

In view of these and other considerations, it is advisable to reconsider our previous proposal of asking the Association to supervise the joint purchasing program of Chinese publications for American libraries. In the interest of this program, I have consulted several members of our Board of Management. They feel that since of the functions of the proposed American Library in China is to facilitate the acquisition of Chinese materials by American libraries, this purchasing program should very adequately be supervised by that Library as soon as established. But pending its establishment in the immediate future, this Library, in recognition of the assistance which it had received from American libraries in the past, should give our support to the A. L. A. in carrying out this project. In rendering assistance to this program at this time, we shall make tangible our very real interest in the development of Chinese collections in American libraries.

While the program should be conducted with the minimum of publicity, they feel that an agreement should be drawn up and approved by authorities on both sides. A draft agreement is herewith enclosed and we would welcome suggestions and comments from A. L. A.

Storage is a tough problem in war-time. With the cooperation of Dr. Franklin L. Ho, there is no question about storage space in the Nankai Middle School as you will see from the enclosed letter from Dr. Ho.

It seems rather awkward for me to write officially to the A. L. A. in regard to these details, but after consulting Mr. J. Hall Paxton of the Embassy, he suggested that I should send you a full report in order to serve as a basis for background understanding. As this project was proposed in our joint memorandum dated December 31, 1942, both you and I are morally bound for the success of the undertaking. Whatever advice you may be able to offer will be gratefully appreciated.

Sincerely yours,

T. L. Yuan

Director

Dr. John K. Fairbank

c/o Mr. Lauchlin Currie

The White House

Washington, D. C.

〔The American Library Association Archives, China Projects File, Box1, Correspondence about China 1944〕

按:此为抄件,附录各件未存。

五月十六日

竺可桢(遵义)致函先生。〔《竺可桢全集》第9卷,页103〕

五月十七日

先生致信外交部亚洲司杨云竹,请补赠该处发行刊物。

云竹司长台鉴:

顷承惠赠《敌伪集要》第六十一一号、《参考资料》第六十六-九号各一册,高谊隆情,至深感荷。除妥慎保存外,用特具函申谢。又查以前各期已承邮寄昆明,但近一年以来,尚未收到,拟恳贵司将现存各期检赠一份,俾成完帙,藉供参考,有渎清神,统俟面谢。又敝馆所编之参考资料已陆续寄赠贵部矣。耑此,即颂公祺。

弟袁同礼顿首

五,十七

附敝馆英文本参考资料目录乙纸。

〔国立北平图书馆(重庆沙坪坝)用笺。台北"国史馆",〈参考资料及敌伪纪要等刊物(二)〉,数位典藏号020-010199-0167〕

按:杨云竹(1901—1967),河北蠡县人,北平师范学校毕业,中华民国外交官。此信为文书代笔,落款和日期则为先生亲笔,附平馆英文本考藏资料目录1页。

五月二十四日

先生致信布朗,感谢其寄赠*Library Journal* 抽印本,并对中美两国图书馆结伴互助、组建分发美国图书期刊委员会的建议提出实操层面的问题和解决途径。

May 24, 1944

Dear Mr. Brown:

I am greatly indebted to you for your letter of April 29 and for your courtesy in arranging to have my article printed in the *Library Journal*, 5 copies of the reprints of which have just been transmitted here through the courtesy of the Department of State. I am particularly grateful to you for the great interest you take in library development in China. All of us here are confident that under your inspiring leadership much will be accomplished in the near future.

The magnificent achievement of American librarianship has been a constant source of inspiration to our work in China. Although we have lost contact with each other especially since Pearl Harbor, it is most gratifying to learn that librarians in the United States are keenly interested in the library situation in this country. I shall be glad to send you from time to time the information you require and I hope our efforts here will deserve your support.

Your proposal for the pairing off of Chinese and American libraries is most excellent and I endorse it heartily. On our side, however, there are many practical difficulties because a great number of our librarians find it difficult to conduct correspondence in English. But such difficulties can be overcome by soliciting the assistance of the faculty of each educational institution. I feel that the proposed arrangement could be made much simpler if it is limited at the start to colleges and university libraries, as you suggested.

One of my proposals to Chinese college and university presidents is to have a library committee set up in each institution whose duty is to advise the librarian not only in the selection and acquisition of material, but also in maintaining closer contacts with foreign libraries and scientific institutions. The lack of trained librarians in China today is one of our major difficulties-a fact of which you are already aware.

I am much obliged to you for your thoughtful suggestion re the appointment of a committee of three charged with the duty of the distribution in China of the books and periodicals to be collected in the United States. The formation of such a committee is most desirable, and I feel that it should include not only librarians, but also representatives of National Government and the universities. Fifteen members at least would be required.

From our past experience in China, we are fully aware of the delicate situation which will be faced by such a committee. It is by no means an easy task to have the books and periodicals distributed in such a manner as to satisfy the needs of all parties concerned. But the work of this Committee can be greatly reduced and made much simpler if the pairing off arrangement between Chinese and American libraries can be carried into effect. While it may be too early to think about these matters, it is worthwhile to consider the whole question from all angles. At any rate I would suggest that we keep up our correspondence in order to keep each other informed about the developments in each country.

Chinese librarians are extremely grateful to you and to all members of your Committee for the pioneering work you are doing. I appreciate especially the opportunity to work together with you in this great task. I am confident that our continued and fruitful collaboration will bring our two countries together in thought and in feeling and will pave the way for larger plans for the promotion of closer Chinese-American cultural relations.

With most cordial greetings,

Yours sincerely,

T. L. Yuan

Director

〔The American Library Association Archives, China Projects File, Box1, Correspondence about China 1944〕

按:此为抄件。

五月二十九日

先生致信费正清,告知已与柯德思、包懋勋等人谈过合作计划,倘若美国图书馆协会(十三家图书馆)汇来启动资金,购买中文出版物工作即可展开。

May 29, 1944

Dr. John K. Fairbank,

Office of War Information

Washington, D. C.

Dear Dr. Fairbank:

With further reference to my letter of May 10, I wish to report that after Mr. G. N. Kates returned from his northwestern trip, we discussed the A. L. A. purchasing program in China at considerable length. Mr. Kates consented to serve as a member of the Advisory Committee, but prefers to do so in the capacity of the Far Eastern Representative of the Library of Congress.

Both Mr. Kates and I feel that Mr. J. Hall Paxton of the Embassy should also serve as a member of the Advisory Committee. After consulting Mr. Paxton, he assured me that he would be glad to serve with the approval of the Ambassador.

Mr. Liang Sze-Cheng has been added as a member of the Committee of Selection to look after materials on art and archaeology.

In a cable to the A. L. A. I advised to hold the fund temporarily, but if some means can be found to transmit the money to Mr. Kates, say $ 1,000 or $ 1,500, the program can be started right away.

I shall be glad if you will kindly transmit this message to the A. L. A.

Yours sincerely,

T. L. Yuan

Director

〔The American Library Association Archives, China Projects File, Box 1, China Publications for American Libraries 1945〕

按:此为抄件。

五月三十一日

布朗覆函先生,就曾宪三在美学习、工作给予意见,并告知正在联系十三家参与馆获得相应的授权,另告副总统华莱士来华班机上有相当数量待分配给中国大学的书刊,希望先生能够与之晤谈。

May 31, 1944

Dear Dr. Yuan:

Mr. Milam has written asking me to see what arrangements can be made for Mr. Mark Tseng to enter an American library school. I find, at the present time, that he is employed at Stanford University Library and is doing an outstanding piece of work. It is my opinion that he will gain more at present by his employment at Stanford University in the temporary position he is holding than he would by leaving his position and attending a library school. On the other hand, if he is about to return to China, I should hope that he could spend one semester or one quarter either at Chicago or Columbia.

I am enclosing, for your information, a letter from Mr. Kerr to Mr. Milam and my letter to Mr. Tseng. I shall be happy to have your advice on this matter.

Mr. Milam is spending the next two or three months in South America; therefore, I shall have to handle the matters relating to China without his assistance. I shall write you within a few days on the cooperative purchasing plan, I have asked authorization from the cooperating libraries to send a token payment of U. S. Dollars 1,000 to you for this purchase program. Mrs. Fairbank has suggested that Mr. Wallace might bring back on his plane some Chinese publications for these thirteen cooperating libraries. I talked with Vice-President Wallace before he left Washington. He knows of you and your work. I hope you will have an opportunity to meet him. You can refer to my conversation with him about Chinese Libraries. Mr. Fairbank has probably informed you that he is taking with him on his plane 600 pounds of books for distribution to Chinese Universities. I am sincerely hoping you will have an opportunity to talk with him personally. He is a graduate of Iowa State College and is an outstanding liberal. He also has a great interest in the development of libraries and knows something of the work we are attempting to do. I have known him personally for some time.

Your article in the *Library Journal* is meeting with warm approval. There is so great an interest in this country in China that many librarians hope to visit your country after the war. There is a great increase in the study of your language. The proposal to send an American librarian to China is progressing favorably. I feel confident that we shall be able to send to China by next fall at the latest, one of the outstanding members of the American Library Association who can represent both Universities and Libraries.

Yours very truly,

Charles H. Brown, Chairman

Committee on the Orient and Southwest Pacific

〔The American Library Association Archives, China Projects File, Box 1, Correspondence about China 1944〕

按:Vice-President Wallace 即 Henry A. Wallace(1888-1965),美国政治家,1941 年任副总统,1944 年访问重庆。此件为录副。

六月二日

杨云竹覆函先生,告知其将尽可能补寄刊物并抄录《日苏渔约(协定)》。

同礼馆长吾兄勋鉴:

接奉五月十七日大函,敬悉一一。查本司所编刊物曾逐期寄至昆明棉花街二二号贵馆办事处,从未间断,至于本司现存者大都已残缺不全,兹谨就所有之《参考资料》十四册、《敌伪纪要》十二册随函附奉,即希密存参考!又□贵馆五月廿一日函开:嘱抄一九三六年日苏渔约草案及一九三九日苏渔业协定一节,自当遂办,兹特将各该约及协定要点各摘录乙份,一并附上,即祈查收,并祈赐复!顺颂公绥。

弟杨〇〇顿首

〔台北"国史馆",〈参考资料及敌伪纪要等刊物(二)〉,数位典藏号 020-010199-0167〕

按:此件为底稿。

六月三日

先生致信布朗,告知已与柯德思、包懋勋等人谈过购买中文出版物计划,并将来函转给沈祖荣;至于赴美学习图书馆学人员虽有合适者但因为战时交通不便难以成行。

June 3, 1944

Dear Mr. Brown:

I trust that Dr. Fairbank has informed you as to the desirability of reorganizing the committee in China to supervise the ALA project for cooperative purchasing of Chinese publications.

I am writing to say that both Mr. George N. Kates, Far Eastern Representative of the Library of Congress, and Mr. J. Hall Paxton, Second Secretary of the American Embassy in Chungking, expressed great interest in the success of this project and are willing to serve on the Advisory Committee. As soon as a part of your funds is received here, we shall start immediately and a monthly report will be sent to you for circulation to the participating libraries. This program, already much delayed, should be started on July 1st, if possible.

I have sent a copy of your letter to Mr. Samuel T. Y. Seng, Director of the Boone Library School. He will answer you soon about the various points mentioned in your letter concerning the needs of his School.

In view of the need for trained personnel in China, it is a pleasure to learn that the Iowa State College has made arrangements to grant a fellowship to some Chinese student who wishes to become a librarian. No doubt this fine example will be followed by other institutions. We do have a good number of trained assistants who can be recommended for such fellowships, but the present difficulty lies in obtaining priority for their travel in wartime.

We are extremely glad to learn that you hope to be able to get a few books through each week. It will be a blessing indeed if the plan can be carried into effect. Books on postwar planning, international relations and social sciences are urgently needed.

I enclosed a table of contents for Reference Series which we publish monthly. We have tried to supply a need for official documents concluded by foreign governments, and with limited source materials at our disposal, we have carried on this work to the best of our abilities.

With cordial regards, yours sincerely,

T. L. Yuan

Director

〔The American Library Association Archives, China Projects File, Box 1, Correspondence about China, 1944〕

按：此件为录副，附一页 Reference Series, National Library of Peiping，自 1943 年 1 月至 1944 年 7 月，以月度为单位汇总平馆就国际关系方面所作的参考服务工作。

六月八日

郑天挺致函先生，请代为寻找《满洲字典》。〔《郑天挺西南联大日记》，页 844 〕

六月十三日

先生致信傅斯年，询问《图书季刊》英文本发表冯汉骥论文的可能性。

孟真先生大鉴：

敝馆编印英文本《图书季刊》，刻由美国翻印，在华京重版。关于学术方面之论文亟愿多所介绍。上年成都发掘王建墓，于我国历史颇多考证，前请冯汉骥先生为敝刊撰一论文，业已脱稿，如荷赞同准予在敝馆发表，无任感幸。即希见复为荷。专此，敬候著祺。

弟袁同礼顿首

六，十三

〔台北"中央研究院"历史语言研究所傅斯年图书馆，"史语所档案"，李 22-37〕

按：此信为文书代笔，落款处为先生签名，似乎并未送到傅斯年手中。

六月十四日

先生致信布朗，寄上书单一份并附马廷英论文，希望为美国十三家图书馆购买中文出版物的计划可以自七月一日实施，建议每家参与馆每月出资五十美金。

June 14, 1944

Dear Mr. Brown:

I enclose herewith a list of Chinese publications which are sent to your Library with our best compliments. We hope they will be transmitted to you through the courtesy of the Department of State, as they will probably be placed on Vice-President Wallace's plane on his return trip.

Thirteen sets of Dr. Ting-Ying Ma's recent treatise entitled: Research on the Past Climate and Continental Drift for thirteen American libraries are also included in the shipment. As no funds from the A. L. A. have been received as yet, we are sending these publications in advance. They are addressed to the Division of Science, Education and Art, Department of State, with a request that they be redistributed according to the enclosed list.

In spite of printing difficulties and high cost of paper, a good number of useful books have appeared as you will see from the *Quarterly Bulletin of Chinese Bibliography*, copies of which are also being sent to you.

In view of the difficulty of obtaining the back issues of scientific publications in China which are now printed in limited editions, we hope that the cooperative purchasing program could be started here on July 1st, already a year and half late since Dr. Fairbank and I submitted our joint memorandum.

In view of the unrealistic rate of exchange, it is difficult to advise about remitting money to China. But if you could arrange to remit $ 50 per participating library at the beginning of each month, it would enable our Committee here to go ahead with this project. If you could arrange to remit through the official channels, it would simplify matters a great deal.

With best wishes,

Yours sincerely,

T. L. Yuan

Director

〔The American Library Association Archives, China Projects File, Box1, Correspondence about China 1944〕

按:Ting-Ying Ma 即马廷英(1899—1979),字雪峰,辽宁金州人,

地质学家、古生物学家,早年赴日本东京高等师范学校理科学习,后入仙台东北帝国大学地质古生物学教室,1929 年获得地质古生物学教室理学士。毕业后继续攻读博士,1934 年获得日本东北帝国大学、德国柏林大学博士学位,1940 年任中国地理研究所研究员兼海洋组主任,1942 年率领中国地理学会海洋组专家考察福建省沿海地区,Research on the Past Climate and Continental Drift 一般译作《古气候与大陆漂移之研究》。此为抄件。附一页书单,包括三部分,分别为 Publications sent to the Iowa State College Library, Research on the Past Climate and Continental Drift 和 Sent by the Naitonal Library of Peiping to the thirteen American libraries。

六月二十日

中华图书馆协会撰《为赉呈工作报告表检附收据请核发四五六三月补助费由》,具先生名并钤印。〔台北"国史馆",〈中国图书馆协会请补助(教育部)〉,数位典藏号 019-030508-0015〕

六月二十七日

先生覆信莱登伯格,告知已收到来华副总统华莱士携带的赠给武昌文华图书馆学专科学校的书刊,并寄赠《图书季刊》英文本。

June 27, 1944.

Dr. H. M. Lydenberg

International Relations Office

American Library Association

Library of Congress Annex, Study 251

Washington (25), D. C., U. S. A.

Dear Dr. Lydenberg:

I beg to acknowledge the receipt of your two letters dated May 9. The publications which the ALA sent to the Boone Library School were brought over here by Vice-President Wallace last Wednesday. They were immediately sent to the Boone Library School for the use of the faculty and students. Your courtesy and assistance in transmitting them to China is very much appreciated.

Through the courtesy of the Vice-President, we have sent to you and the ALA headquarters copies of our *Quarterly Bulletin of Chinese Bibliography* which, we hope, will give you the information about books and libraries in China. Future issues will be sent to you as issued.

With kindest regards,

Yours truly,

T. L. Yuan

Director

〔平馆(重庆办事处)英文信纸。The American Library Association Archives, China Projects File, Box 1, Boone Library School 1944-1948〕

按:此件为打字稿,落款处为先生签名,于7月12日送达。

六月底

先生致信傅斯年,告知哈佛燕京学社继续补助史语所、营造学社,询问汇款方式及补贴人员等事。

孟真吾兄:

前上一书,询问冯汉骥君所写关于王建墓论文一篇能否在英文本《图书季刊》发表,务希早日见覆,以便决定办法是荷。顷接哈佛燕京社来电,对于吾请求继续补助研究费一案,已获通过,并补助贵所美金五千元,营造学社美金五千元。兹奉上来电□请告思成,弟即不另□□□,即希台阅。至该款应汇何机关,并盼见示。如径汇中央研究院,恐每元仅能得四十元。弟仍拟设法使其径汇大使馆或可能得钞票也。如何之处,希尊酌示复或电复寄沙坪坝为荷。本届人选,弟拟加向觉明、贺昌群、姚从吾、唐兰、徐中舒、王崇武、张正烺诸人,未□尊意以为如何?并盼示复,以便电告前途,该款方能汇来也。匆匆,顺颂□□。

又Parlism来谈,谓美国方面托人携来美金钞票五百元每元行市为160元左右,两月以来大跌也,系赠尊处及李庄诸友,此款应交何人,或换成国币径汇李庄,亦盼示知,以便转达。

同礼

关键在美国国务院,因该院不肯代罗氏基金及UCR汇款也。

〔台北"中央研究院"历史语言研究所傅斯年图书馆,"史语所档案",李69-3-2〕

按:华盛顿时间 6 月 27 日下午 3 点 44 分,哈佛燕京学社给重庆美国大使馆发电报,告知给予资助史语所、营造学社各五千美金。UCR 即美国援华联合会(United China Relief)。“张正烺”即张政烺。该信各页左侧部分均有少许未能扫描,且无落款时间,“中央研究院”历史语言研究所将该件标注为是年 6 月。

六月三十日

美国大使馆向先生转交美国图书馆协会汇款一千美金。〔The American Library Association Archives, China Projects File, Box 1, Correspondence about China 1944 07-08〕

先生致信布朗,告知马廷英论文的印刷、运输成本,询问十三家参与购买中文出版物的图书馆是否愿意购入。

June 30, 1944

Dear Mr. Brown:

Vice-President Wallace was kind enough to bring back 13 sets of Dr. Ting-Ying H. Ma's Research on the Past Climate and Continental Drift, vols. 1-3. The parcels were addressed to the Science, Education and Art Division, Department of State, to be redistributed to the 13 libraries which participate in the cooperative purchasing program.

The book was printed at Yungan, Fukien. The cost of transportation from Yungan to Chungking is quite high. The total cost including transportation charges is US $36.00.

As it is rather costly, we would like to refer the decision of its purchase to the 13 libraries concerned. If they agree to buy it, I should like to hear from you, so that I can pay Mr. Ma here. Otherwise, will you be good enough to inform them that the book be turned over to Messrs. G. E. Stechert & Co., New York City.

I shall be much obliged to you if you will circulate this note to the libraries concerned.

Yours sincerely,

T. L. Yuan

Director

〔The American Library Association Archives, China Projects File, Box 1, China Publications for American Libraries 1945〕

按:Yungan 即永安,抗战时期为福建省会所在。由 7 月 27 日布朗致美国图书馆协会执行秘书 Julia Wright Merrill 信可知,13 家图书馆接受该份论文,并愿意承担相应的费用。该件为副本。

七月一日

怀特覆函先生,对本年 2 月 25 日函件中的建议略作修改,并愿意向先生预付酬劳。〔王成志《袁同礼先生和哥伦比亚大学》,页 247〕

按:此函具体内容似为,哥伦比亚大学图书馆在华美协进社预存 200 美金,用以支付平馆(先生)为该校购买中文书刊。此外,预支 500 美金,作为先生担任此项任务的酬劳。

七月三日

先生致信布朗,告知华莱士所乘专机返回美国时只能搭载少量书籍,其他代购者则只能经加尔各答并由海运送抵美国。摘件如下:

We prepared about 500 pounds of Chinese publications to be put on Mr. Wallace's plane, but only 100 pounds were brought back, while the rest will be sent to Calcutta and shipped by sea. I am keeping Mrs. Fairbank informed about the details.

〔The American Library Association Archives, China Projects File, Box 1, China Publications for American Libraries 1945〕

七月六日

傅斯年致先生两函,谈美款补助如何分配事。其一:

守和吾兄左右:

惠书敬悉,一切极感。所询冯汉骥文能否在英文本《图书季刊》发表一事,弟并未接此信,故未及先复也。兹承询及,自然可以,若能先寄下此文交济之兄一看,俾文字上有所增进,更是佳事,因冯君作此等文,恐亦是初出茅庐,而大刊在美翻印,亦此时之重要事也。此为《图书季刊》着想耳。

哈佛电敬悉。此皆吾兄努力之效也。敝所何缘得分此惠,亦可感矣。此项五千元之补助费,自本为工作之补助,然如分人补助之,亦即变之为生活补助,乃为今日最切要之事,盖各人不能维持,工作更不能维持也。此法未知有困难否?或者他们也要报账,如一切政府之不通。然弟固可名之为每人之 Research grant,仍给穷极病极者也。此当无碍,详细办法开会后写呈就商。兄去电时,先代思成及弟一致谢意也。

继续补助研究费,诚大佳事,兄之努力至可佩也。名单中兄所拟加入"向觉明、贺昌群、姚从吾、唐兰、徐中舒、王崇武、张政烺"末二位在敝所者,皆堪此任,弟均同意。皆妙选也。其中有若干人,去年即当有之矣。李方桂兄,去年之一事,弄得不上不下,弟意可改为全份,其学力足以当之(亦寅恪之次也)。未知吾兄以为如何?联大各人,似乎除锡予应给全份外,(年老、资深、病多、累重。)其余似均可给半份,以免纠纷。萧公权、潘光旦二位,似皆不是汉学 Sinology,此亦兄去年未同意者,萧闻亦尚不太窘,此点乞兄斟酌。已赴美或即赴美者,似不当更给。因报告中甚难提及,奉派赴美,而又领此,美国人或不解耳。兄名单之外,弟意可加闻一多,彼专心治学者也。总之,一切乞兄斟酌,弟无不同意。兄定即定矣,不必再找大人物去商量,如去年之生枝节也。敝所兄拟加之人外,尚有可考虑者,有凌纯声、芮逸夫二兄,二人皆极困难,又有陈槃兄,更有梁思永,只惜在病中。然既分配不下,弟可在敝所之 grant 中,给予等于二万元(前二人)之数,不敢请再加入,弟只顺便附陈此一节,以此事与 Fairbank 之计画有关,故及之也。

汇来之法,弟觉我们总不便请求他带票子来,除非美大使馆自想此法。然则只有复电请其速汇贵馆或中研院,事前并与张厉生(或俞鸿钧)接洽,汇到后照捐款算,如必要,乞示知,弟当函之。

五百元票子,弟尚不知来源,或是元任兄之惠,然彼一时亦或分不出如许钱,故猜不到也。此款须料理得当,乞暂存兄处,待下回分解。大约其中与我无涉,即有涉,而是送多人者,弟亦不取也。一切费神,感何有极。专颂道安。

弟斯年

三十三年七月六日

再启者:王献唐先生著作甚多,其最近大著《中国古代钱币史》,尤为考古界第一流钜著,盖近年在本所,材料多,工力更勤矣在本所住,非本所职员，甚窘，近又丧子，负债累累。五百元之一份，未知可以有法列入否？（假如潘、萧除去，赴美者不给，因有余额时。）然此须在兄拟新加"向、贺、姚、唐、徐中舒、王崇武、张政烺"之外，不便以其更易兄所拟诸人，弟觉兄所拟诸人皆甚当，弟极其同意。

弟斯年又白。

〔《傅斯年遗札》，页 1500-1502〕

按：张厉生（1900—1971），字少武，河北乐亭人，时任行政院秘书长兼国家总动员会议秘书长。俞鸿钧（1898—1960），广东新会人，上海圣约翰大学毕业，时应任外汇管理委员会委员及中央信托局局长。1943 年 2 月底，王献唐赴李庄史语所。[1]《中国古代钱币史》实指《中国古代货币通考》，王献唐生前并未正式出版，是书于 1979 年由齐鲁书社初版。

其二：

守和兄：

顷上一信，计达。末节所言票子 $ 500 事，弟又思之，以为是费正清送梁思成兄者。盖弟处既无关于此事之来信，弟之中国友人在美者皆穷极，其外国友人可以有此事者至多只有一人，亦欠他信债四年矣，故以为应是梁家事也。兄原信及此意已送山下给思成兄看矣。专颂道安。

弟斯年

三十三年七月六日

此票子在未查明来源前，乞存兄处。

〔《傅斯年遗札》，页 1502〕

Jorge Basadre 覆函先生，表示秘鲁国家图书馆愿与中国图书馆（平馆）开展交流合作。

Lima

July 6, 1944

My dear Mr. Yuan:

Due to the kindness of the Minister of China in Peru, his excellency Senor Li Tchuin who forwarded your kind letter of March 16 of the

---

① 《王献唐年谱长编》，页 836。

present year, I have the pleasure of expressing my lively desire to initiate a Section China in the new Bibliotheca Nacional of Peru.

In the enclosed memorandum summarizing the state of the work of reorganization and in nos. 2 and 3 of the *Boletin* which I sent you (I was not able to send no. 1, as it is out of print) you can obtain a general view regarding this project. In a word, what we desire is that our library be able to give the best in the way of services and technique among modern librarians, which is precisely what you incarnate and symbolize before the China of today.

There are several reasons why we have a special interest in initiating for the first time in our history a China section. In the first place, China and Peru, as they have interests in the Pacific Ocean, possess a common interest, in spite of the distance, as the present war demonstrates. For China, Japan has been a rapacious aggressor; for Peru, where he has come, favored by the collective negligence, as a suspicious alien, the gracious Japanese in the last 20 years has been a potential threat, which only by the change of events in the Pacific theater of war has not turned into a tremendous reality.

On the other hand, Peru has had for almost a century a numerous and industrious Chinese colony which has contributed, in my estimation, to the development of the country. I will never forget that my first lessons that the librarian of an institution should be of service to the community were given to me in the library of the Universidad de San Marcos in Lima, from 1923 until his death in 1925, by a man exceptionally wise and good, Pedro Zulen, whose father was Chinese. In Lima there now appear two Chinese dailies, "Man Shin Po" founded in 1911, and "Vos de la Colonia China". "Last but not least," we hold in highest esteem the embellishment, the quality, and the antiquity of the culture of this great country, not well known in South America, by whose ancestral virtues the Chinese today unite a martyrdom and heroism which bring forth the admiration and renewed respect of the entire world.

That which we desire is your assistance and that of Chinese librarians for counsel and initial orientation, and for such practical assistance as circumstances permit, so that we might receive regularly the periodicals, journals, pamphlets and books of your country. We are intending to place in our future budgets a sufficient sum to care for these needs.

Recently my old friend Carl H. Milam, Secretary of the American Library Association, passed through Lima, and he was greatly interested in these ideas, promising me that the North American librarian who left for China on the mission of interlibrary solidarity would take with him a copy of my letter.

I send my kindest regards, offering my services to all who would cement and increase the relations between China and Peru.

Jorge Basadre

Director

〔The American Library Association Archives, China Projects File, Box 1, Correspondence about China, 1943-1944〕

按:Senor Li Tchuin 即李骏(1892—1948),字显章,广东梅县人,外交官,1934 年至 1944 年担任中华民国驻秘鲁全权公使。*Boletin* 西班牙语,意为《通报》。此件为副本。

七月七日

周达夫覆函先生,告知中印学会无款购书,并简述印度购书情形。

守和先生:

五月卅日示,近日始奉到。季刊英文本已得读,印友另函道谢。炅于四月间即须回国,延至现在。先生八月来印,是否赴美,抑仍回国,在印至新德里否?兹附上朱骝先先生一笺,如中印学会无款再购书,尊处可购否?炅经手已购之书,有属于中研院历史语言研究所者,傅孟真先生之意拟交涉教育部吨位,不知结果如何。炅知教部有运输吨位,每月空余,如可拨给,则尊处如购书,亦可运矣。应购之书尚甚多,Lahore 梵文书店有书尤亟需购,炅希望先生来印时能在新德里晤面详商,□□专员及印政府教育、考古、Archives 各部门友人均可相助。先生来印后如仍返渝,炅甚愿同行。匆请道安！

周炅（达夫）敬上

卅三，七，七

按：周达夫（1914—1989），中国大辞典编纂处派其赴印度留学，先在国际大学（Visva-Bharati）中国学院学习梵文，1945 年获得孟买大学博士学位①，归国后曾任中山大学文学院教授。Lahore 为拉合尔，今属巴基斯坦；Fergusson College 为印度弗格森学院。原信第二页附与傅斯年信一封，并请先生转达，内容如下，

Chou Tafu, Fergusson College, Poona, India

孟真先生：

近得袁守和先生信，云于八月间来印。前方桂先生曾云：先生拟向教育部交涉吨位，不知结果如何？炅知教部有运输吨位，每月空余。Lahore 有一梵文大书店，颇有书亟需购。鄙意①欧洲（大陆）出版者，②印度坊本，二者最需购，印学术机关、团体及政府出版者，当可赠若干。敬乞于守和先生来前函商，炅自当尽力遵办。敬请道安！

周炅（达夫）谨上

卅三，七，七

〔台北“中央研究院”历史语言研究所傅斯年图书馆，“史语所档案”，杂 36-59-4、杂 36-59-5〕

七月十二日

先生致信傅斯年，谈补助款申请细节及注意事项。所存者如下：

……考虑一折衷办法。

（二）除李庄外，其他中心点之汉学家似应顾到，但值得考虑者似亦不多耳。

（三）得到补助费之人，原可得美金一千元者，如付其四万元 official rate，难免有怨言（如寅恪）。

（四）在渝昆兑换美钞乃一极困难之事，因国人购买力太差。如市上有一万美钞，则行市必又大跌（见附件）。如每人均付美钞，则邮

① 高山杉《辨析〈金克木编年录〉中的几个片段》，《上海书评》，2022 年 12 月 9 日。

寄又多困难。

（五）名单应从速决定，仍希按寄上之名单加以改正及补充，暂按四十额或三十额分配何如？宁缺勿滥。

（六）中美汇率近月将在华盛顿商妥大约为1:100，亦谣言也，如此则以上之计划恐又须完全推翻，故弟如此希望能在新汇率未决定之前将美钞寄到也。

吾兄为文史界之泰斗，例应得到补助，故决定将兄加入。另约孟麟、叔永及弟三人成立一分配委员会，完全为对外之性质。在今日状况之下，只可任劳任怨，费力而又不讨好也。

至贵所及营造社之款，如得美钞，每机关可约八九十万元，亦一笔意外之财，务希将用途计划先为拟定，以便寄哈佛也。

又此事务须严密，万勿声张，深恐政府当局从中作梗，因之尽弃全功。此中困难想能洞鉴（兑换美钞为不合法之举），故张厉生、俞鸿钧处决不能预先告之也。匆复，顺颂大安。

弟同礼顿首

七，十二

〔台北"中央研究院"历史语言研究所傅斯年图书馆，"史语所档案"，李69-3-5〕

按：该信落款页左侧有批注"此信原不全"，似只缺少首页。

先生致电叶理绥，感谢再次赠予研究费用，史语所和营造学社也一并表示感谢。

GRATEFULLY APPRECIATE ACTION TRUSTEES RENEWAL RESEARCH GRANT. MESSRS FU SZE NIEN AND LIANG SZE CHENG NOW IN LICHUANG CONVEY TRUSTEES EXPRESSION SINCERE THANKS FOR GRANTS TO THEIR RESPECTIVE INSTITUTIONS. SUGGEST FUNDS BE TRANSMITTED TO NATIONAL LIBRARY. SHALL SUBMIT FULL REPORT AFTER FUNDS RECEIVED.

〔Harvard-Yenching Institute Archives〕

按：此次赞助费共计两万美元，其中平馆一万，史语所和营造学社均为五千，于8月21日先统一汇付平馆，再分发。该电应由美驻重庆大使馆发送予费慰梅，由后者在7月17日转寄。

七月十六日

中国教育学术团体联合会在教育部(川东师范学院)举行集会,先生出席。黄炎培被推选为主席,张伯苓、常道直、杨卫玉、艾伟、郝更生担任常务理事,黄炎培、彭百川、沈祖荣为常务监事。〔《黄炎培日记》第8卷,页290〕

按:原文集会有“第一次”加以限定,但据1942年2月8日黄炎培日记可知,该会时正举办“第二届开会”,其中“开会”应为年会之笔误,故笔者认为“第一次”极有可能是本年度者。另,先生似久未出席如此类型的会议,故黄炎培有“平时不常见者”之语。

七月十八日

平馆向教育部呈文一件,题为《呈为呈送补具部发职馆三十三年度购书费十二万元印领一份请予鉴核备案由》,具先生名并钤印。

案奉钧部本年六月二十七日社字三〇九六四号指令内开:“呈悉准拨给该馆给关本年度购书费拾贰万元随令汇发仰即查收补具印领呈部备查并专案报销此令”等因,计发国币拾贰万元。奉此,职馆采购工作今后自可顺利进行,除后方各省市出售之国学书籍及各地新出版之新书及各种期刊续予订购,一俟年度终了,另案报销外,兹补具印领一份,理合具文呈请鉴核备案。谨呈

教育部部长陈

国立北平图书馆馆长袁同礼(印)

三十三年七月十八日

〔中国第二历史档案馆,教育部档案·全卷宗五,国立北平图书馆请拨员工学术研究补助费经常费有关文书,案卷号11616(2)〕

七月十九日

刘节覆函先生,请代为婉拒顾立雅所赠美金,并告其可能赴中山大学历史系执教。

守和先生惠鉴:

□书藉悉,顾立雅先生从前在北平,弟并没有什么帮助他,况且也是替馆中应尽的义务。在此时得伊馈赠,尤为不安,因为立雅先生已入军队服役,我们在后方很相安。美金百元敬恳先生婉言退还,弟已另函谢。弟承中大邀约,或许暑后要到历史系教书,届时所处相近,可

以时常晤教也。耑复，即颂撰祺。

弟刘节顿首

七月十九日

按：“□书藉悉”，洪光华识别为“损书藉悉”，笔者存疑，故用□标识。先生收到后即覆，表示除刘节外，顾立雅还赠款与梁思成、梁思永、董作宾等四位学者，倘若不收，恐与他人不便。另，本日刘节写给顾立雅函件也应由先生转交。函件内容如下，

立雅先生惠鉴：

别来已十年，全世界都遭战祸。正如贵国威尔基先生之书所说，将要造成四海一家的局面。先生为国服役，已入军队，至为欣幸。弟自从战争起始，曾沦陷杭州，于匆遽中逃出，一切无恙，可以告慰。一九三八年冬末到云南，曾在各大学中教书。自从一九四〇年以后，即专任中英庚款会研究工作，住重庆已经四年了。今年五月间曾有一作品《中国古代宗族移殖史论》，得教育部学术奖励金。承赠 Academia Sinica 百元，当此时期，更是不能收受的。因为我们中国正在捐款给前方军人。我如果收受前方军人的钱，要给人大笑话的。□□我如先生，必定能相信我的话，把这一百元收回去。况且弟帮助先生者很有限，而屡承先生在大作中提及，已经很感谢了。此前弟在北平图书馆任事，本有帮助同好研究的义务，这样一点事不算什么。

拙作《中国古代宗族移殖史论》[①]行将出版，届时当设法寄赠。还有一件很重要的事，就是 Your Student □□□定要奉还，以后惠书，仍旧称朋友。很希望战争早日胜利，我们重聚于北平，那是最快乐的事。

敬祝康健。

弟刘节顿首

七月十九日

以后惠书，请由北平图书馆袁守和先生转。

〔洪光华《刘节退还顾立雅赠款的三通书信》，《文史荟萃》，2018年3月〕

① 《中国古代宗族移殖史论》，1948年5月正中书局初版。

七月二十四日

刘节覆函先生,再次婉拒顾立雅通过中央研究院转赠美金百元。

守和先生惠鉴:

手书奉悉。美钞百元还是请为退回,其余四公如何办法,弟不能代为设想。惟弟之情形与四公不同,前函已详细说明,我公实有为弟解释之义务也,否者于馆誉有关也。顾君函已照原样寄去。耑复,即颂公绥。

弟刘节顿首

七月二十四日

〔洪光华《刘节退还顾立雅赠款的三通书信》〕

按:该件左上部标有⑧字样,似为刘节所注二人通信编号。

七月二十九日

先生致信傅斯年,谈费正清筹集哈佛大学捐助款项事。

孟真吾兄:

两次手教均拜悉。哈佛之款正由费正清设法,因数目较大已告分两次来电,或须因之延搁,并非携现钞而来。只由该院来一受权 authorization 之电报,则此间即可付款。如果能如弟所期,则亦不必退还一笑。吾人仅不声张而已,此点已与思成谈过,渠亦谅解也。顷又致费正清一函,告其弟九月中旬必须赴印,务在九月初旬以前办妥,想届时大驾来渝,一切分配之事可面商也。Creel 赠思永及彦堂之款,已交思成。匆复,顺颂大安。

弟同礼顿首

七,廿九

……是否已受贵所之聘?

〔国立北平图书馆用笺。台北"中央研究院"历史语言研究所傅斯年图书馆,"史语所档案",李 69-3-10〕

按:该件应已装订成册,扫描后缺少左侧边沿,故补语处当有某人姓名未能扫入。

布朗覆函先生,此前因病未能及时付款,告知可以按月汇上一千美金但汇率则须听取先生意见,十三家图书馆愿意购买马廷英的论文,并谈中美图书馆互助合作、怀特访华计划等事。

July 29, 1944

Dear Dr. Yuan:

I owe you a most sincere apology and an explanation.

When you were writing me on June 14, I was undergoing a minor surgical operation on my right eye. My recovery has been greatly delayed and, therefore, I have not been able to give my attention to your many interesting and illuminating letters. Although I am not yet released from the attention of my doctor, I am nevertheless returning to work. I expect to be in Chicago, Washington, New York, and Boston for two weeks commencing August 7.

We expect to be able to make arrangements to send you US $ 1,000 each month through the State Department. Our chief worry is the question of exchange. We note that certain relief organizations have obtained an exchange rate of 100-1. We do not know whether this rate would apply to the money sent to you by the American Library Association or not. In any case, we must leave the matter to your judgment.

Your organization of an advisory committee and a committee on selection for the handling of Chinese publications to be bought for the thirteen cooperating libraries seems to us most excellent. I have sent the information to the thirteen cooperating libraries.

In your letter of June 30, you raised the question of the cost of Dr. Ma's "Research on the Past Climate and Continental Drift" and suggested that we refer the question to the cooperating libraries. I am positive the cooperating libraries will agree to accept the volumes at the price mentioned. I am sure they will be delighted to have volumes brought back from China on the plane of the Vice President. You may, therefore, proceed to make payments on this shipment. I shall notify the cooperating libraries at once that the shipment has been made. I have not heard from Mrs. Fairbank yet as to whether or not the Department of State has shipped the books to the thirteen libraries. Our new fiscal year in this country starts on July 1, and governmental departments are extremely busy during July with budgetary questions.

We are planning over here an extensive book campaign for devastated libraries in war areas. Your proposal to set up a committee on your side, to include university presidents, librarians and some representatives of your government, seems most excellent. Scholars from your country have expressed their eagerness to have their own university libraries included in any distribution. Obviously, we in this country do not know the needs of their libraries; neither do we have exact information as to the damage caused by the war.

In this country the associations and agencies, such as the American Library Association, work closely with government agencies and departments, especially the Department of State, but the committees and boards of the American Library Association conduct correspondence as we have done. With such persons as Mr. and Mrs. Fairbank we have maintained cordial relations. Our Department of State is eager to continue our present arrangements. In order to be of mutual help to each other, there is need both of governmental and personal relationships. We are very happy that you and your government are pursuing this policy.

We cannot do much on pairing off of university and college libraries in our two countries until after the war. The plan applies only to college and university libraries. I understand that there may be some reorganization in the field of higher education in your country after the war, and such a reorganization would naturally affect the pairing off of university libraries. One object in the eventual pairing off is to bring more Chinese and American librarians into personal correspondence and relationships.

You will be glad to know that conversations in this country in regard to sending an American librarian to China are progressing. We hope we can make arrangements to send the Director of Libraries of Columbia University, Dr. Carl White. I am to meet him in Washington on August 9 and 10 to have consultations with officials of the Department of State and the Office of War Information.

I am sending an appeal to the *Library Journal* for copies of the latest reports of university and college libraries to be sent to me at Ames to be transmitted to you. I think I shall ask for the reports for the last four years. I do not know whether you desire that a few of these be sent through the Department of State or whether you wish us to hold them until shipment by ordinary channels is possible. You may be assured, however, that we shall attempt to collect reports of at least the larger university and public libraries. If you desire also the reports of the smaller public libraries, please let me know. Many of them in this country do not print reports, however.

A student at Harvard, Mr. Zunvair Yue, is working in the library of the Harvard Divinity School. He has written me about possible fellowships for librarians. I hope to meet him when I am in Boston on August 14.

I hope that in the future my answer to your letters will not be so greatly delayed. The work you are doing is greatly appreciated in this country. The American librarians all hope for an opportunity to express their appreciation in more tangible forms after the ending of the war. If the arrangements to send Dr. White to China are consummated, you will find that he will be of very great assistance in perfecting and extending the unusually cordial relations which have been maintained for some time between Chinese and American librarians.

Yours very truly,

Charles H. Brown,

Chairman Committee on the Orient and Southwest Pacific

〔The American Library Association Archives, China Projects File, Box 1, Correspondence about China, 1944 07-08〕

按:Zunvair Yue 即于震寰(1907—1999),字镜宇,山东蓬莱人,1933 年毕业于私立武昌文华图书馆学专科学校,1927 至 1935 年在北京图书馆、平馆工作。此件为副本。

七月

先生覆信柯育甫,商李女士来馆工作事宜。

育甫先生尊鉴：

昨由□□□□大札，承介□□□□□□□□□厚意。敝馆在南开借地办公，甚为狭小，且无女职员宿舍，故无法增聘新职员。如李女士宿处已承尊处设法，而又不嫌简陋者，则来馆工作甚表欢迎。其待遇每月二百四十元，生活补助米贴等均照政府规定办理，此外另行津贴菜钱六百元，其工作则注重采购新书兼管购书账目及编目，每日工作七小时，须有恒心，方易见成绩也。如愿一试，请于八月一号或九月一号到馆办事，即希费神转达，见复是感。此上，顺候道祺。

弟袁同礼顿首

七，□

〔https://www.ruten.com.tw/item/show? 21908910748065〕

按：柯育甫（1904—1961），原名德发，安徽庐江人，1928 年东南大学外文系毕业，1936 年赴欧美考察教育，时应任教于四川大学，并担任该校训导主任。“李女士”似指李宛文，1944 年 8 月入馆。①

八月四日

顾颉刚致函先生。〔《顾颉刚日记》卷 5，页 321〕

八月五日

先生致信董作宾，谈哈佛燕京学社补助款及印书事。

彦堂吾兄左右：

奉到廿五日手教，深慰远怀。美钞百元已面交思成，至哈佛补助费尚未汇到，届时当托贵院转奉也。《殷历谱》一书明春可以写成，允称不朽之作。春间大驾来渝，得亲教益，至为欣幸。惟如与甲骨分属两地，则材料不在手下，编辑甲骨丛编必感困难，此亦值得考虑者也。哈佛津贴明年六月期满，弟当设法继续，极盼能在抗战结束以前将丛编予以完成，至印刷方面可送美石印仿英文本图书季刊前例，毫无困难也。中文本季刊目前需稿颇亟，贵所同人如有关于目录版本或题跋考证之文字，盼费神代为接洽每千字赠稿费二百元。无任感荷，匆复，顺颂大安。

弟袁同礼顿首

八月五日

---

①《北京图书馆馆史资料汇编》，页 1370。

哈佛津助事，孟真自应列入，并闻。

〔国立北平图书馆用笺。2016 年上海泓盛拍卖有限公司春季艺术品拍卖会〕

八月七日

先生致信史密斯森协会，询问有无可能暂存 Woodrow Wilson Memorial Library 为平馆挑选的复本图书。

August 7, 1944.

Dear Sir:

Before the outbreak of the Pacific war, your Institution rendered invaluable assistance in the shipment of American books and journals to this Library. Your scholarly collaboration has been sincerely appreciated.

We have recently learnt from Woodrow Wilson Memorial Library that they will reserve a part of their duplicates for this Library. But since they have not much storage space for these duplicates, we wonder if your Institution would be willing to store them for this Library for the duration of the war. If you are willing to do so, please write direct to Miss Harriet Van Wyck, Librarian, Woodrow Wilson Memorial Library, 8 West 40th Street, New York City, so that their duplicate material intended for this Library can be sent to you at our expense.

This letter is being mailed to you by the Woodrow Wilson Memorial Library. Fully confident of your desire to assist foreign libraries, we wish to express to you our sincere appreciation for your assistance.

Sincerely yours,

T. L. Yuan

Director

〔平馆（重庆沙坪坝）英文信纸。Smithsonian Institution Archives, Records, 1868－1988 (Record Unit 509), Box 1, National Library, Peiping〕

按：该信应寄送史密斯森协会，并由该会直接联系 Woodrow Wilson Memorial Library。此件为打字稿，落款处为先生签名，于 9 月 18 日送达。

八月九日

布朗致函先生，就于震寰、曾宪三在美学习图书馆学询问先生意见，并告知其已向各图书馆征求一九四〇年以后报告，另谈怀特访华计划。

August 9, 1944

Dear Dr. Yuan:

I have had some correspondence with Mr. Zunvair Yue, now at Harvard. Since the end of the war is approaching, it might be desirable for him and Mr. Mark Tseng to spend a few months at one of our library schools, more to study the curricula and methods used than to profit directly by the instruction. Such an experience might be valuable to them in the organization of education for librarianship in your country. You might advise us on this point.

When the Pacific war looked as though it might continue for two or three years, I was perfectly willing to let these gentlemen wait until they obtained more experience in American libraries. Now that the end of the war is approaching, it might be desirable to make sure that they do spend a few months at a library school before they return to China. I expect to see Mr. Yue at Harvard on August 14.

I have asked university and research libraries to send me, for transmission to you, copies of their reports since 1940. I shall hold their reports here until I hear from you. Possibly Mrs. Fairbank might send a few of the latest reports in shipments from the Department of State.

I expect to spend the next two weeks in Washington, New York, and Boston in conferences. We are hoping to make final arrangements for an American librarian to go to China. Dr. Carl White, Director of Libraries at Columbia University, has the assignment under consideration. I shall report more on this point later.

Thanks to some help from you, I hope to rewrite "A Proposed Cultural Program for Sino-American Relations Involving Libraries". I hope also to make arrangements for forwarding of US $ 1,000 each month for the purchase of publications for the thirteen cooperating libraries.

I shall also attempt to collect material on training programs on library science and museum work and shall send you the reports and curricula of our library schools. There has been very little work done as yet in this country in training for museum work, but I shall see what material is available. The most extensive program with which I am acquainted is one proposed by the librarian of Harvard University, but I doubt if he has any of it ready for publication yet.

Yours very truly,

Charles H. Brown,

Chairman Committee on the Orient and Southwest Pacific

〔The American Library Association Archives, China Projects File, Box 1, Correspondence about China, 07-08〕

按:该件为录副。

八月十日

先生致信布朗,告知为美国十三家图书馆购买中文出版物近况,请其联系国务院相关机构以便转寄分发。

August 10, 1944

Dear Mr. Brown:

Enclosed herewith please find a list of 22 publications which we purchased in July for 13 American libraries under the ALA Cooperative Purchasing Program and a financial statement ending July 31, 1944.

The American Embassy in Chungking has been most helpful in arranging to have these books (wrapped in 4 parcels for each library) sent by air to India and from there by sea pouch to Washington. Presumably the Science, Education and Art Division of the Department of State will assist in their distribution and I would like to suggest that you get in touch with the Division before the arrival of these books.

I hope it would be possible for you to make copies of the enclosed documents for distribution to various libraries concerned.

We shall be glad to take care of special material for special libraries, although I must say that the amount of material produced in war-time is limited owing largely to the shortage of paper and the high cost of printing.

Yours sincerely,

T. L. Yuan

〔The American Library Association Archives, China Projects File, Box 1, Correspondence about China, 1944 09-10〕

按:该信应于9月16日前送达。此为抄件,另附书单及收支各一页。

八月十六日

平馆撰《呈为职馆办理各校院图书仪器箱支到昆接配转运谨将卅三年一月至八月办理经过报告及卅二年四月至卅三年八月所有开支编造会计报告呈请鉴核指令祇遵由》,具先生名并钤印。〔中国第二历史档案馆,教育部档案·全宗号五,教育部关于委派北平图书馆馆长袁同礼办理各院校在美所购图书仪器接收转运事宜的有关文书,案卷号5465〕

按:1944年1月至8月,各校院图书仪器箱转运的具体经办人为莫余敏卿、孙平两位馆员,涉及箱件总计119箱。

八月二十一日

平馆撰《呈为现存昆明各校院图书仪器六十三箱拟恳钧部派车转运或函国际救济委员会转嘱公谊救护队代运来渝请示遵行由》,具先生名并钤印。〔中国第二历史档案馆,教育部档案·全宗号五,教育部关于委派北平图书馆馆长袁同礼办理各院校在美所购图书仪器接收转运事宜的有关文书,案卷号5465〕

九月五日

先生致信吴俊升,告知平馆为空运吨位配给事呈文一件,并请从旁协助。

士选司长尊鉴:

前承枉顾,得聆教言为快。敝馆申请空运吨位事荷承赞助,至为感幸。兹备具呈文一通,即希提前批准,无任感荷。专此,敬候道祺。

弟袁同礼拜上

九月五日

〔中国第二历史档案馆,教育部档案·全宗号五,教育部关于委派北平图书馆馆长袁同礼办理各院校在美所购图书仪器接收转运事宜的有关文书,案卷号5465〕

按:该信为文书代笔,落款处为先生签名。

平馆撰《呈为职馆在美在印购西文书五箱拟恳拨给空运吨位半吨运滇请鉴核示遵行由》,具先生名并钤印。〔中国第二历史档案馆,教育部档案·全宗号

五,教育部关于委派北平图书馆馆长袁同礼办理各院校在美所购图书仪器接收转运事宜的有关文书,案卷号5465〕

先生致信布朗,欣悉其右眼恢复健康,建议怀特在明年春季以后访华,并对曾宪三、于震寰、王恩保等人在美学习、实习等给予意见。

September 5, 1944

Dear Mr. Brown:

I beg to acknowledge the receipt of your letters of July 29 and August 9. I am glad to learn that you have fully recovered from the operation of your right eye and have returned to work.

We are happy to learn that Dr. Carl White of Columbia will be asked to visit China in the immediate future. I can assure you that a hearty welcome will be given him during his stay in China.

Owing to the war operations in Hunan Province, communications between S. E. China and S. W. China have been cut off. If Dr. White could find it possible to come out next spring, the war situation in interior China would no doubt be different, as we hope that by that time internal communications will return to normal and Dr. White would be able to travel that part of the country.

I must thank you once more for the attention you gave to Chinese students now specializing in the library science in America. Mr. Mark Tseng, although not in good health, is a careful worker and upon his return to China would be a good cataloguer for our library where he had spent a number of years in the Cataloging Department. I concur with you that a few months' experience at one of your library schools would be more valuable to him. To spend even a few weeks in a summer library school would help him a lot.

Mr. Zunvair Yue, handicapped by his English and academic training, is not so much an asset to us as we would like to him to be. However, I learn that Mr. Joseph En-Pao Wang (B. L. S., Syracuse, 1943) is serving as Assistant Cataloguer at Syracuse University. If his work proves good, I hope you will extend to him some help if he needs it.

We should like so much to see the reports of university and research libraries, and if you can ask Mrs. Fairbank to send them by sea pouch to India, we shall receive them within two months' time. Your assistance in collecting these reports and training programs for us is very much appreciated.

I hope you have received our report for book purchases for July. As soon as your second remittance is received, we shall submit the report for August-September, 1944. No doubt you have learned from the American Embassy about the exchange rate which is very much better than July.

Yours sincerely,

T. L. Yuan

Director

〔平馆(重庆沙坪坝)英文信纸。The American Library Association Archives, China Projects File, Box 1, Correspondence about China, 1944, 09-10〕

按:Joseph En-Pao Wang 即王恩保(承栋),后赴宾夕法尼亚大学图书馆工作,1947 年离职转往国会图书馆任职。

布朗致函先生,就在华负责为美国十三家图书馆购买中文出版物的联席委员会人员、主席人选给予建议,并告怀特访华尚未最终确定而温德教授也因船位问题无法立刻回到西南联合大学。

September 5, 1944

Dear Dr. Yuan:

I have sent a letter to all the thirteen cooperating libraries asking them to approve a change in the original contract to provide that the cooperative purchase of Chinese publications will be administered by a committee to be appointed by you, with the approval of the Joint Committee of the ALA and ARL in this country. As you know we propose that the committee should consist of Mr. J. Hall Paxton, Mr. Hung-chun Zen, and you. It seems desirable that you act either as Chairman or Executive Secretary of this Committee. Dr. Roger Greene would prefer that Paxton act as Chairman, but it is possible that the American Embassy would prefer that Zen act as Chairman. Whether you should take the Chairmanship of the Committee or ask Mr. Paxton or Mr. Zen can be left to you. In any case, we shall recognize this permanent committee as a committee to administer the funds in regard to the cooperating libraries. We will, of course, be glad to know the results of the reorganization of the Library Association of China, in case there is a reorganization.

There are one or two matters to be cleared up on this side before we can announce that Dr. White can and will go to China this fall. As soon as definite arrangements are made, I shall cable or write you. In the meantime, no public announcement should be made.

Dr. White and I had a profitable and enjoyable talk with a group of Chinese professors, most of whom have recently arrived in this country. All of them apparently knew you. Apparently, Chinese universities are suffering greatly from the inability to obtain recently published books and journals and laboratory supplies. Dr. Winter, who expects to return to Southwestern University in the near future, could take a considerable quantity of books with him, but up to the present time has not been able to obtain shipping space. If arrangements are made for Dr. White's visit, we shall hope to send a collection of the latest books with him. American technicians returning from China also report that these is a great lack of books published in this country during the last few years. The difficulty on this side is not alone concerned with the transmission of books from India to China, it has to do with shipping space which seems to be taken up chiefly by the requirements of the military forces. I certainly hope this condition can be remedied. As soon as the lines of communication are open, I hope we can clear the books and periodicals available at ALA offices as well as the periodicals being held by the Universal Trading Corporation upon requisition from your Minister of Education.

Any notes from you which can be published in our library periodicals will be most welcome in this country. Librarians are greatly interested in the development of schools and libraries in your country. The concern of the State Department is shown by its proposal to send a university librarian to China to give you whatever help you may desire and to keep us informed in this country of what aid we can best render. It is fortunate that the American Library Association has the advice of the persons like Mr. and Mrs. Fairbank and Roger Greene as well as the counsel of eminent Chinese scholars now in this country.

I have quite recovered my health, and hope that I can accomplish more in the next few months than I have in the last two.

Yours very truly,

Charles H. Brown, Chairman

Committee on the Orient and Southwest Pacific

〔The American Library Association Archives, China Projects File, Box 1, Correspondence about China, 1944, 09-10〕

按:ARL 应指美国研究图书馆协会(Association of Research Libraries)。Universal Trading Corporation 一般译作"美国世界贸易公司",该机构与中华民国教育部应有较为密切的合作,负责在美代购图书、仪器。①

九月十一日

董显光致函先生,请约定时间面洽拜谒蒋介石事宜。

同礼先生大鉴:

前奉委座谕,召见台端。曾请雪艇先生转奉,想达左右。亟盼于趋谒之前得与先生一谈,祈接函后即赐电话(电话号码二九七三号)约定时间为荷。此颂台祺。

弟董显光谨启

九月十一日

〔《北京图书馆馆史资料汇编(1909-1949)》,页 778〕

按:此信为文书代笔,落款处似为董显光签名,并钤印。

先生致信竺可桢。〔《竺可桢全集》第 9 卷,页 185〕

按:此信于 9 月 18 日送达。

① 《国立西南联合大学史料》第 2 卷,页 196。

九月十三日

向达覆函先生，寄上文章两篇或可登载于《图书季刊》，哈佛燕京学生补助款可转赠夏鼐用以提携后辈，并谈归期及现下敦煌一地搜集写本的困难。

守和先生侍右：

奉七月廿七日手教，敬悉一一。今寄上《记敦煌石室出晋天福十年写本寿昌县地境》及《评张大千近著》二种，凡两篇，又关于《敦煌艺术研究所发见北魏写本残经消息及目录》，敬求指正。两文如可用，即付《季刊》，消息则请斟酌为之。《评张大千近著》一文，曾写一份付敦煌艺术研究所常君书鸿。常君为人多顾虑，不一定能登，今寄之本，又加修定，不妨两存。唯此与《记寿昌县地境》一文俱不必赐稿费，能各予抽印本二三十份即为惠多矣。《季刊》两册亦已先后收到矣，并此谢谢。哈佛燕京社方面承为推毂，铭感无既。达意此款如可成，还不如补助夏鼐先生作考古工作，夏先生在今日考古学界中最年青，而学识修养又极丰富，学术界先进俱应予以扶持爱惜也。至于达则恃联大薪给，勉强可以敷用，区区之意，惟先生有以察之。承询达等在敦煌工作需款情形，极感垂注之殷。达等今日在此，一方面固感款项不足，以致只能为小规模之发掘，费时既多而程工无几，时间精力，两不经济。一方面则孟真先生屡次声明研究院自身亦极为困难，彼所能为力者，即止于此，此外更不能增益一文。达等自五月中抵敦工作，三月至今，所余款项约二十万，如全以之为工作费用，大约尚可维持四五个月，如达等归来之旅费亦须在二十万内开支，则只有立即停工，束装东归之一法。自七月以后，西北公路亦复涨价，自敦煌至兰州汽车票价为四千余，自兰州至渝为八千余飞机亦八千余。合计约一万三千，行李运费、沿途食宿不与焉。故一人自敦反渝，最少亦须三万，以三人计，即为十万。发掘所得物品，虽不甚多，今只以十箱计，十万元能运至渝即是大幸。然跋涉数千里至此，不为发掘工作未窥百一，即敦煌以北汉代长城废塞、玉门遗址，尚不可以工作之处，亦未能一事凭吊，岂不有虚此行？早知如此，则不如不来之为愈矣。上月函孟真先生，曾为略陈此种情形，并请其函西北公路局何竞武先生，洽商达等归来免费办法，万一公路局免费不能办到，则先生为史语所代筹之五千美金，盼能抽出若干，作为达等东归旅费。此事是否可行，敬恳与孟真先生一商，即为电告,幸甚盼甚电报寄敦煌向达或夏鼐即可收到,最多加县政府转四个字。达个人则以离校过久,益以舍下在川,渐复多事,是以意兴阑珊,久思返川。未来以前,屡向孟真、济之两先生声明此行不过引路性质,余不过问。五月抵敦,复亦曾告孟真先生,工作站既已成立,三个月后达即准备东归。上月函孟真先生,重申此请,现拟于十月中旬离敦,归途并欲至天水一访麦积之胜,抵渝或须在岁暮矣。夏鼐先生及北大派来之阎文儒先生如经费稍有办法,当可留至明春,然后返川也。石室写经残留敦煌,本尚不少,民初张广建督,以此为买官之券,大事搜罗,是为一劫。民廿七湖北郭曙南(此君现在国家总动员会)长敦煌县事,于石室写本有特嗜,因此迭兴大狱,锁郎当者不绝于途,一时动色相告,视为祸水。有石室写本者,俱不敢视人,是为再劫。去岁敦煌艺术研究所至后,所中诸公于石室写本既一无所视,为古董横肆搜求,甚且威胁利诱,以致对簿公庭,成为笑柄,结果所至,石室写本大都割裂求售,长或一尺,短至数寸,索价可至数千,且多恶扎,求如去岁达所获之《稻芊随听手镜记》及《羯磨戒本》,已不可得矣,是为三劫。经此三劫,其情可知。先生命为搜求古文献,只有随缘,任不敢必也。率复,不尽覼缕。即叩道安。

后学向达载拜上自敦煌鸣沙山下

九月十三日

《记寿昌县地境》一文随函附呈,余一文及目录另寄。

〔台北“中央研究院”历史语言研究所傅斯年图书馆,“史语所档案”,李 38-4-15〕

按:《记敦煌石室出晋天福十年写本寿昌县地境》《敦煌艺术研究所发见北魏写本残经消息及目录》刊《图书季刊》第 5 卷第 4 期,前者为该期首篇“论著”,后者改题为《国立敦煌艺术研究所发见六朝残经》,列为“学术界消息”首则;《评张大千近著》,似未刊登。郭曙南(1900—1964),湖北京山人。此为抄件,“民初张广建督”后有校补之“甘”字。10 月 5 日,先生曾将此函示于傅斯年,后者当日致信夏鼐。

九月十五日

先生致信傅斯年,谈哈佛燕京学社补助款分配事。

孟真吾兄：

梦麟先生复函已到，一切均表同意。兹拟一分配清单，请赐考虑，于星期二以前寄下，即可汇款。弟须星期二十九日方能入城另有油印通知已印好矣。

不幸被遗漏下的有下列诸人，李剑农战区左近无法汇款、石璋如据兄言未从事研究工作、顾颉刚、徐旭生均参政员，如何之处，仍候尊裁。顺颂大安。

弟同礼顿首

十五日

〔国立北平图书馆用笺。台北"中央研究院"历史语言研究所傅斯年图书馆，"史语所档案"，李 69-3-7〕

按：傅斯年在此信上眉批"我院吴禹铭今年未从事研究工作（在一单上）特别提出，兄□列入，乃反有张冠李戴之误也"。另，原信徐旭生处亦有批示"后来又□□□□"。吴金鼎（1901—1948），字禹铭，山东安丘人，考古学家，早年毕业于齐鲁大学，后入清华大学国学研究院，从李济学习人类学，城子崖遗址的发现者，时投笔从戎，任四川新津美国空军第二招待所主任。

中华图书馆协会撰《呈送七八九月份工作报告及同月份补助费收据请鉴核赐发》，具先生名并钤印。〔台北"国史馆"，〈中国图书馆协会请补助（教育部）〉，数位典藏号 019-030508-0015〕

九月十六日

布朗覆函先生，收悉八月十日来信及沈祖荣的信件，怀特预计于十月十五日乘军机赴华，但仍须等待国务院的官方消息，并告其已寄出十三家图书馆就委托购买中文出版物的合同修订版，询问中华图书馆协会改选结果并表示不必太过在意，希望先生能够选派一些在图书馆学专业上并无太多学习履历的人来美深造。

September 16, 1944

Dear Dr. Yuan:

I acknowledge receipt of your letter of August 10. I have had it mimeographed and sent to all the cooperating libraries. I think you should be congratulated for your accomplishments. You have done much better that I had thought possible. I assure you that your colleagues in this country appreciate your efforts.

I am also indebted to you for an extremely interesting letter from Mr. Samuel T. Y. Seng of the Boone Library School. Through the acquaintance of many of our librarians and Mary Wood, there is a great interest in this Boone Library School.

I think you will be glad to know that the arrangements now seem to be completed for Dr. White to visit your country for a number of months. I have had several conversations with him in regard to this trip, and he and I met with a group of some of your eminent scholars visiting in this country. Dr. White expects to leave here about October 15, by Army plane, but, of course, he may be very greatly delayed. I do not think any public announcement should be made until I can obtain an official release from the State Department.

There will be some difficulty in the distribution in China of the books and periodicals collected in this country by gift or by purchase from Rockefeller funds. The group of scholars I met in Cambridge proposed that a committee be set up. I have asked Dr. White to discuss this matter with you and with others. The group at Cambridge proposed that some of the scholars associated with the Academia Sinica, together with two or three librarians, possibly a representative of the Minister of Education, probably Mr. Paxton of the American Embassy, and some others, be organized into a committee to cooperate with our committee on this side and to advise as to the distribution of cultural material collected in this country. There is always a possibility that the war may be over earlier than we think.

You will be happy to know that we have sent out to the librarians of the thirteen cooperating libraries a request for an amendment to the contract for the purchase of Chinese material. I enclose a copy of the amendment to which the cooperating libraries have agreed. You will note that the contract now is made with a permanent committee to be appointed by "by Dr. T. L. Yuan, Director of the National Library of Peiping, with the approval of the Joint committee of the ALA and ARL, with the understanding that the permanent committee shall include Dr. T. T. Yuan." We understand the permanent committee at present consists of you, Mr. Paxton, and Mr. Zen. There is a little disagreement on this side as to who should be chairman, but I think probably you can arrange that as you see fit. Certainly, you should be either chairman or executive secretary of the committee.

I shall be interested in knowing how the mail ballot for the reorganization of the Chinese Library Association turns out. Occasionally we have had similar occurrences in this country, but you knew enough about our country to realize that we do not take these matters too seriously.

We are hoping to arrange for an increase in the shipment of books to your country and, more especially, for the sending within a short time the books available to the American Library Association. As I wrote you, I shall attempt to collect library reports. When I get my letter out, I think I shall ask for two copies-one for the National Library of Peiping, and one for the Boone Library School. Please let me know in case you wish priority for any of this material. In any case, we shall hold the reports at this library.

I noted your suggestions made some time ago that it might be well for Mark Tseng and Zunvair Yue to take further courses of instruction at some library school. I find that both of them are rendering valuable services-Tseng in the Stanford University Library and Yue in the Library of the Yenching Institute at Cambridge. It seems to be the general opinion over here that both gentlemen would profit more by employment in American Libraries than they would by further attendance at library school. I hope that eventually you can arrange for some persons with possibly less experience in education to come to this country for professional education.

The opinion seems to be quite general over here that both Tseng and Yue have made such a good start under your direction that further professional education would not be of great help to them. This is another matter you might discuss with Dr. White when he reaches Chungking.

With cordial regards, I am,

Yours very truly,

Charles H. Brown, Chairman

Committee on the Orient and Southwest Pacific

〔The American Library Association Archives, China Projects File, Box 1, Correspondence about China, 1944, 09-10〕

按:此为录副。

九月中下旬

先生拜谒蒋介石。〔University of Pittsburgh Library, John Gabbert Bowman, Administrative Files, Box 2 Folder 13, Chinese Material〕

按:其间,先生请蒋介石为匹兹堡大学题词,后者为之撰"菁莪乐育"。

先生将蒋梦麟、翁文灏、任鸿隽三人具名致郑天挺函转交予其本人。〔《郑天挺西南联大日记》,页932〕

按:此函于9月23日送达,内容为哈佛燕京学社拨专款支持中国文史研究界学者,蒋梦麟、翁文灏、任鸿隽三人共同商定,给予郑天挺四万元。

先生应罗香林之约,撰写纪念朱希祖的文章——《朱逷先先生与目录学》。〔马楚坚主编《罗香林论学书札》,广州:广东人民出版社,2009年,页365〕

按:1944年7月,朱希祖在重庆因病去世,翌年《文史杂志》(朱逷先先生纪念专号)[1]刊登此文,该篇失收于《袁同礼文集》。

九月二十日

国民政府军事委员会代电,照准先生赴美。

国际宣传处董副部长九月三日国渝字7478号报告所请先派袁同礼出国一节,可予照准,名义可照给。除知照行政院外,其川旅费美金

---

① 《文史杂志》第5卷第11-12期,1945年12月,页44-45。

六千元并已饬财政部照发。希即洽领可也。

中正申养侍秘

〔《北京图书馆馆史资料汇编(1909-1949)》,页777〕

先生与傅斯年商谈分配哈佛燕京学社补助事。〔《傅斯年遗札》,页1532〕

多尔西覆函先生,表示史密斯森协会因空间局促,无法暂存 Woodrow Wilson Memorial Library 赠送给平馆的复本。

September 20, 1944

Dear Sir:

I have your letter of August 7th and in reply would say that the Institution regrets that it is unable, on account of lack of space, to store here the duplicates which the Woodrow Wilson Memorial Library is reserving for the National Library of Peiping. The Institution has stored here many tons of publications for shipment abroad when the war is ended, and the space available for storage is now overcrowded.

A copy of this letter is being sent to the Woodrow Wilson Memorial Library.

Very truly yours,

H. W. Dorsey

Acting Chief

International Exchanges

〔Smithsonian Institution Archives, Records, 1868-1988 (Record Unit 509), Box 1, National Library, Peiping〕

按:该信寄送重庆。此件为录副。

先生致信布朗,收到第二笔购书汇款并已结汇,并告知自己可能赴美进行短期访问。

Chungking, September 20, 1944

Dear Mr. Brown:

Your second remittance of $ 1,000 was duly received and exchanged by the American Embassy at 210:1. A statement will be sent to you at the end of this month.

It is indeed a pleasure to learn that Dr. White has been asked to come out to China and I can assure you of our most hearty welcome to his forthcoming visit.

There is a possibility of my taking a short trip to the States in October and I shall know definitely sometime next week. My stay in America would be very brief, so it would be very nice if I could accompany Dr. White to China. We certainly should not miss seeing each other. I shall therefore keep you informed about my movements.

With kindest regards,

Yours sincerely,

T. L. Yuan

Director

〔The American Library Association Archives, China Projects File, Box 1, Correspondence about China, 1944, 09-10〕

按:此件为打字稿,落款处为先生签名。

九月二十二日

先生致信叶理绥,告知收到哈佛燕京学社赠予的研究经费并附上分配方案,感谢其支持中方学者的举措。

September 22, 1944

Dear Prof. Elisséeff:

On September 6, I requested the Embassy to transmit you a telegram informing you that the research grant of US $ 10,000 from your Institute was exchanged at 206:1.

Since then, the Committee had two meetings to consider how the fund was to be used to the best advantage. A report is herewith enclosed which is the result of our deliberations.

I need hardly say that the action of the Trustees of the Institute is very much appreciated in China. To you personally we wish to express our sincere appreciation for your assistance which enables the recipients to maintain the tradition of free inquiry in the midst of all handicaps.

With kindest regards,

Yours sincerely,

T. L. Yuan

Director

P. S. The grant of $5,000 each for the two institutes will be received from the Embassy early in October and will be acknowledged by Messrs. Fu and Liang respectively.

〔平馆(重庆办事处)英文信纸。Harvard-Yenching Institute Archives〕

按:收到此项捐助后,蒋梦麟、翁文灏、任鸿隽、傅斯年、先生五人组成资助款分配委员会,入选者均为哈佛燕京学社所关注的传统汉学领域的学者,分为三档,金额依次为六万、四万、三万法币,陈寅恪、李方桂、董作宾、梁思永、梁思成、向达、凌纯声、姚从吾、韩儒林、汤用彤、徐森玉、朱自清、贺昌群,以上十三人为第一等,李济、芮逸夫、陈槃、傅乐焕、张政烺、劳榦、雷海宗、闻一多、潘光旦、郑天挺、王献唐、徐中舒、陈乐素、刘敦桢,以上十四人二等;高去寻、马学良、王崇武、岑仲勉、丁山、陆侃如、陈述、罗庸、毛准、浦江清、刘节、罗根泽、郑德坤、傅振伦、曾昭燏、徐旭生、魏建功、方壮猷、王育伊、王庸、谭其骧、邓广铭,以上二十二人为第三等。此件为打字稿,落款处为先生签名。

九月二十三日

先生致信罗香林,感谢赠书,其所邀稿件随信寄上。

香林先生著席:

前奉手教,并承惠寄大著数种,至为感谢。嘱件仓卒草成,尚希教正,恐不能用也。尊处近著之书均拟撰一英文提要,在敝馆英文季刊予以发表,知注并闻。专此申谢,顺颂大安。

弟袁同礼顿首

九,廿三

〔国立北平图书馆用笺。《罗香林论学书札》①,页 365〕

按:"尊处近著之书"似指罗香林《中夏系统中之百越》,1943 年独立出版社初版,其英文提要刊《图书季刊》英文本新 4 卷 1-4 期(页 75-76)。

① 《罗香林论学书札》将此信系于 1942 年,实无可能。

董显光致函先生，告知蒋介石已经核准先生赴美宣传之请。

守和我兄大鉴：

关于台端赴美作演讲宣传一事，已奉委座核准。即祈惠临敝处，面洽为荷。顺颂台安。

弟董显光谨启

九月廿三日

〔《北京图书馆馆史资料汇编(1909-1949)》，页779〕

按：此函为文书代笔，落款处为董显光签名，并钤印。

九月二十九日

竺可桢致函先生。〔《竺可桢全集》第9卷，页192〕

按：该函内容似为推荐涂长望《中国夏季风之进退》，极可能附此篇论文。

九月下旬

吴俊升覆函先生，告知所需空运吨位已与交通部沟通。

守和吾兄大鉴：

九月五日手书敬悉。贵馆在美在印购置西文书五箱，已由部电知交通部驻加尔各答代表王慎名先生，准在本部核定空运吨位内，分批运滇，即希吾兄径行洽办。专此复闻，顺颂勋绥。

弟吴○○敬复

九月□日

〔中国第二历史档案馆，教育部档案·全宗号五，教育部关于委派北平图书馆馆长袁同礼办理各院校在美所购图书仪器接收转运事宜的有关文书，案卷号5465〕

按：王慎名，湖北恩施人，清华大学毕业，时任交通部专门委员之一。该件落款时间付诸阙如。

十月二日

先生致信布朗，寄上截至九月三十日的购书单及费用支出情况，并告八、九两月所购书刊已由美国大使馆寄出。

October 2, 1944

Dear Mr. Brown:

Your second remittance of US $ 1,000 was exchanged by the American

Embassy at the rate of 210:1 which was much higher than July.

13 items of Chinese publications were purchased in August (Nos. 23-35) and 29 items were purchased in September (Nos. 36-64). The lists of these books and the financial statement ending September 30, 1944 are herewith enclosed for your information.

In order to enable the 13 libraries to identify the books, the cover of each volume is marked by a serial number which corresponds with the number on the bill, copies of which, we hope, will be distributed by you to the libraries concerned.

As usual, the books bought in August and September have been sent to the American Embassy which will arrange their shipment by air to India and by sea to Washington. It is hoped that the Department of State will assist in their redistribution in America,

Your sincerely,

T. L. Yuan

Director

〔The American Library Association Archives, China Projects File, Box 1, China Publications for American Libraries 1945〕

按:此件为打字稿,落款处为先生签名,附有三页清单,于 11 月 3 日送达。

十月三日

午间,金毓黻至国际文化资料供应处访先生,不值。〔《静晤室日记》第 7 册,页 5687〕

十月五日

先生致信李济。〔刘以焕《从袁守和遗存在大陆的一件墨迹说起》,《新亚论丛》第 5 期,2003 年〕

十月二十一日

先生致信徐旭生。〔《徐旭生文集》第 10 册,页 1385〕

按:该信于 27 日送达。

王献唐致函先生。〔《王献唐年谱长编》,页 886〕

按:其中附"研究计划"一份,为向哈佛燕京学社申请资助所需材料。

十月二十五日

平馆撰《呈为呈覆职馆先后收到图书仪器箱支情形再为声复请鉴核备案由》,具先生名并钤印。〔中国第二历史档案馆,教育部档案·全宗号五,教育部关于委派北平图书馆馆长袁同礼办理各院校在美所购图书仪器接收转运事宜的有关文书,案卷号5465〕

先生致信布朗,告知已对怀特访华略作安排,并告为美国图书馆购买中文出版物委员会成员。

October 25, 1944

Dear Mr. Brown:

I have pleasure in acknowledging the receipt of your letters dated September 5 and 16th.

Since receiving a telegram from the Department of State informing us the probable date of Dr. Carl M. White's arrival in China, we have made a tentative itinerary for him, a copy of which is enclosed herewith for your information. A small reception committee has been organized to look after Dr. White and to assist him in his investigation.

Concerning the permanent committee to administer the funds for ALA cooperative purchasing pool, I may inform you that it now consists of Mr. H. Ze. Zen, Chairman; Mr. J. Hall Paxton, and myself, as you proposed. I shall serve as Executive Secretary to keep up our correspondence with you, copies of which are sent to Messrs. Zen and Paxton for their information and files. I trust their arrangements will be acceptable to your Joint Committee.

Yours sincerely

T. L. Yuan

Director

〔The American Library Association Archives, China Projects File, Box 2, Carl White Trip 1944-1945〕

按:该信于12月7日送达。

十月二十九日

徐旭生覆函先生。〔《徐旭生文集》第10册,页1386〕

十月三十日

先生致信 H. L. Milbourne(重庆),旋即得其覆函,告知今后美方汇款只得以官方汇率支付。

October 30, 1944

Dear Dr. Yuan:

The cable remittance mentioned in your letter of today has not been received.

In this connection it may be stated that the Embassy has been instructed by the Department of State that hereafter when paying special deposits of unofficial funds only those for officers and employees of the United States should be paid in United States currency and that others should be paid at the official rate.

Sincerely yours

H. L. Milbourne

〔The American Library Association Archives, China Projects File, Box 1, Purchasing Pool 1943-1945〕

按:H. L. Milbourne 时任美国驻华大使馆二等参赞。

十月三十一日

先生致布朗两信,其一,告知中美汇率最新定价并表示平馆可以垫付购买出版品费用,以便等待更合适汇率时再行汇寄美金,另外先生愿意推迟访美计划以便迎接怀特。

October 31, 1944

Dear Mr. Brown:

I enclose herewith copy of a letter from Mr. Milbourne of the American Embassy, Chungking, which is self-explanatory.

Under the new arrangement the monthly remittance of US $ 1,000 will be exchanged at 40:1 which will, no doubt, reduce the purchasing program considerably.

In regard to future remittance facilities, I hope you will explore the possibilities at your end with a view to obtaining better exchange rate before sending us the third remittance of US $ 1,000. Meanwhile, this

Library will be glad to advance necessary funds, so that the program will be continued without serious interruptions.

I have delayed my trip to America in the hope of meeting Dr. White in China. Since he is coming out by sea, I hope to meet him at Bombay if satisfactory arrangements can be made.

Yours Sincerely

T. L. Yuan

Director

〔The American Library Association Archives, China Projects File, Box 1, Correspondence about China, 1944 11-12〕

按:Bombay 即孟买。此为抄件。

其二,寄上十月购买中文出版物清单和财务报表,并告购买经费将用尽。

October 31, 1944

Dear Mr. Brown:

With reference to my letter of October 2, I am enclosing herewith a list of 24 Chinese publications purchased for 13 American libraries in October. The financial statement ending October 31, 1944 is also enclosed for your information.

In order to enable the 13 libraries to identify the books, the cover of each volume is marked by a serial number which corresponds with the number on the bill, copies of which, we hope, will be distributed by you to the libraries concerned.

As usual, these books have been sent to the American Embassy in Chungking which will arrange their shipment by sea pouch to Washington for redistribution to various libraries.

As the purchasing fund is nearly exhausted, we trust that your further remittance is on its way to China.

Yours sincerely,

T. L. Yuan

Director

〔The American Library Association Archives, China Projects File, Box 1, China Publications for American Libraries 1945〕

按:此为抄件。

十一月二日

平馆撰《呈为各校院图书仪器五十六箱恳祈径电交通部转饬昆明川滇铁路公司特拨车皮并按照国内教育用品核减运费呈请鉴核示遵由》,具先生名并钤印。

> 窃职馆前以各校院图书仪器由昆运渝一案,曾遵部令派员前往川滇东路运输局苏局长处接洽,据称该局在昆无车启运,须将箱支由昆明运至曲靖,方能装车运至泸县,再行转渝。所有由昆明至曲靖之火车须向川滇铁路公司接洽特拨车皮,该公司并索取运费约三四万元之多,拟恳钧部径电交通部转饬该公司请其按照国内教育用品,准予将该箱支五十六件核减运费,俾便进行。又钧部前拨之运输费,职馆所存无几,并祈再拨国币陆万元,以资应用,理合具文呈请鉴核指令示遵。谨呈
>
> 教育部部长陈
>
> 国立北平图书馆馆长袁同礼
>
> 民三十三年十一月二日
>
> 〔中国第二历史档案馆,教育部档案·全宗号五,教育部关于委派北平图书馆馆长袁同礼办理各院校在美所购图书仪器接收转运事宜的有关文书,案卷号5465〕

十一月五日

竺可桢致函先生,附卢守耕论文。〔《竺可桢全集》第9卷,页216〕

按:卢守耕(1896—1989),字亦秋,浙江慈溪人,作物育种学家、农业教育家,曾赴康乃尔大学学习,时任浙江大学农学院教授。

十一月中上旬

先生致信竺可桢。〔《竺可桢全集》第9卷,页224〕

按:此信于16日送达。

十一月二十一日

平馆撰《呈为呈复职馆昆明办事处接收各院校图书仪器箱支前与钧部商定概不开箱因为内容不详无法办理报关手续请鉴核示遵由》,具先生名并钤印。〔中国第二历史档案馆,教育部档案·全宗号五,教育部关于委派北平图书馆馆长袁同礼办理各院校在美所购图书仪器接收转运事宜的有关文书,案卷号

5465〕

按：平馆收到的箱件，既无国外提单也无物资详细清单，无法办理报关手续。

十一月二十三日

平馆撰《呈为各院校图书仪器箱支由昆运渝须派员押运恳祈从速拨款并乞鉴核示遵由》，具先生名并钤印。

窃职馆昆明办事处寄存各院校图书仪器箱支待运来渝一案，顷据昆明职馆来函称十一月十八日接奉川滇东路运输局电话告知，该局可将图书仪器箱支五十六件由曲靖运至泸县，但不能再由泸县运至重庆，同时该局并云不负任何保管之责，尚须由馆派员沿途押运，至由昆明至曲靖之火车运输须由职馆自行接洽等语。查由昆明至曲靖之火车须与川滇铁路公司接洽，特拨车皮，前于十一月二日呈请钧部迅电交通部转饬该公司，请其按照国内教育用品准予将该箱支核减运费，想钧部已在办理之中。该箱支既须派人沿途照料而火车运费及由泸县至渝之运费需款甚亟，前请拨下陆万元，恐不敷用，拟请一次拨付十万元以资便利，除候覆电到馆，再与该局接洽外，是否有当，理合具文呈请鉴核迅予示祗遵。谨呈

教育部部长陈

国立北平图书馆袁同礼

中华民国三十三年十一月廿三日

〔中国第二历史档案馆，教育部档案·全宗号五，教育部关于委派北平图书馆馆长袁同礼办理各院校在美所购图书仪器接收转运事宜的有关文书，案卷号5465〕

十一月二十四日

先生致信布朗，建议美国十三家图书馆将购买中文书刊、出版品的款项由国会图书馆馆长转汇时在重庆的该馆舆图部馆员。

November 24, 1944

Dear Mr. Brown:

With further reference to my letter of October 31 re the transmission of the ALA purchasing funds to China, I beg to inform you that our Committee here has been co-operating with Mr. Floyd E. Masten, Map

Bibliographer of the Library of Congress, who is now in Chungking in connection with some mutual overlapping library interests. If your Committee has not been able to ascertain the best means of transmitting funds to China, may I suggest that your monthly remittances be sent to Mr. Masten in U. S. Post Office money orders. He will administer the deliverance of these funds to Mr. K. K. Ho, Treasurer of this Library, who is to carry on your purchasing program in China during my temporary absence. Mr. Masten's address is as follows: Headquarters, U. S. A. F., China Theatre, APO 879, c/o P. M., New York, N. Y.

I suggest that your Committee deliver these money orders to Dr. Luther H. Evans of the Library of Congress who will handle the forwarding of the money orders to Mr. Masten in the usual way.

I expect to meet Dr. Carl M. White at Calcutta and shall probably come to the States by boat. I am looking forward to the pleasure of meeting you at Ames.

Yours sincerely,

T. L. Yuan

Director

〔The American Library Association Archives, China Projects File, Box 2, Carl White Trip 1945〕

按:Mr. K. K. Ho 应指何国贵,下同。Luther H. Evans(1902－1981),美国政治学家,1945 年至 1953 年担任国会图书馆第十任馆长,本谱中译作"埃文斯"。此为抄件。

Melin A. Bishop 覆函先生,就美方图书馆汇款途径和汇率问题给予建议。

24 November, 1944

Dear Dr. Yuan:

Thank you for your letter of November 16th in regard to bringing US dollars from the American Library Association to China. If this remittance comes in regularly, it would be possible to open an account for you so that it would come through without any difficulty.

I think it would probably be better if you would have the

American Library Association contact Mr. Carl Evans of the Associated Board for Christian Colleges in China, 150 Fifth Avenue, New York City, and ask Mr. Evans to include this in his remittances to the China Educational Institutions. Then when this comes through designated for your work, I shall be glad to take it out and pay it over to your institution.

It is hard for me to give you the rate of exchange that you would realize on this money as our rate changes from time to time and I do not know when it would be deposited. Our rate for money bought in this month will probably average around 133 Chinese dollars for December, but I cannot give you that figure until late next month.

I hope that this gives you the information that you desire and hope that we will be able to serve you in the future.

Yours very sincerely,
Merlin A. Bishop
Treasurer

〔The American Library Association Archives, China Projects File, Box 1, China Publications for American Libraries 1945〕

按：Melin A. Bishop 是 United Clearing Board of Mission, Educational and Relief Agencies 的司库，其办事处位于重庆金正银行（Kincheng Bank Building）内。此件为附录。

十一月下旬

先生致信李书华、徐旭生。〔《徐旭生文集》第 10 册，页 1390〕

按：该信于 28 日送达。

十一月二十九日

下午五时，中华图书馆协会假中美文化协会举行理事、监事联席会议，沈祖荣、陈训慈、蒋复璁、戴志骞、先生、岳良木、毛坤、严文郁、徐家麟、王文山、陆华深出席，先生为会议主席，李之璋记录。首由蒋复璁报告募集捐款经过和结果，继决议五项议案，分别为招待美国图书馆专家怀特、向怀特建议事项、先生赴美期间代本会向美国图书馆协会致意、组织本会基金保管委员会、本会改选唱票。其中票选结果为，沈祖荣、蒋复璁、刘国钧、先生、毛坤、杜定友、洪有丰、汪长炳、王云五、严文郁、王文山、陈训慈、徐家麟、桂质柏、李小缘十五人担任理事,监事为柳诒徵、何日章、沈学植、徐家璧、陈东原、裘开明、汪应文、戴志骞、姜文锦九人。

晚七时,沈祖荣、蒋复璁、先生、毛坤、严文郁、王文山、陈训慈、徐家麟作为当选理事继续理事会议,决议推选先生为协会理事长,在先生出国期间,会务由蒋复璁代理。〔《中华图书馆协会会报》第18卷第5-6合刊,页11-12〕

按:此时,中华图书馆协会设在平馆驻渝办事处内。

先生致信布朗,寄上十一月购买中文出版物清单和财务报表,虽然汇款有困难但平馆已经垫付费用以免项目中断。

November 29, 1944

Dear Mr. Brown:

Enclosed herewith please find a list of 39 titles of Chinese publications purchased for 13 American libraries in November, 1944. The financial statement ending November 30, 1944 is also enclosed for your information.

As usual, the cover of each volume is marked by a serial number which corresponds with the number on the bill. All of these books have been sent to the American Embassy which will arrange their shipment by sea to Washington.

Pending the arrival of your funds, this Library has advanced the necessary money in connection with the purchase of these books, so that the program is continued without interruption. Owing to a limited supply of paper and high cost of printing only 1,000 copies each of these books are printed. It is practically impossible to obtain them after the supply is exhausted.

I trust that my letter to you dated November 24th and transmitted through Mr. Luther H. Evans of the Library of Congress will reach you safely.

The rate of exchange quoted by the United Clearing Board is by no means satisfactory, because the open market rate of US bank-notes at present has jumped to 600:1. Copy of a letter from that Board is enclosed herewith for your reference.

During my absence from China, Mr. K. K. Ho, Treasurer of this Library, will carry on your purchasing program in China. Communications should be addressed to Mr. Ho who will maintain close contact with Mr. Paxton, Mr. Zen and Mr. Masten here.

Yours sincerely,

T. L. Yuan

Director

〔The American Library Association Archives, China Projects File, Box 1, China Publications for American Libraries 1945〕

按:此为抄件。

十一月三十日

先生乘飞机离渝赴印度。〔《中央日报》,1944 年 11 月 30 日,第 2 版〕

按:先生拟由印度经转非洲飞赴美国,此次访美不仅考察美国图书馆事业、高校和研究机构、争取各方援助,似还受行政院委托考察战后农业恢复事业。

十二月下旬

先生抵达美国。〔《中华图书馆协会会报》第 19 卷 1-3 期合刊,1945 年 6 月,页 13〕

十二月二十八日　迈阿密

先生致信陈梦家,告知已到美国,预计明年春至芝加哥。

梦家吾兄:

到美以后,贤伉俪工作如何,颇以为念,想一切安适,较国内便利多多矣。弟于日前飞此,在美约有四个月之逗留,约明年三四月间方能来芝城一聚。芝城中国学生名单及所习科目请便中代觅一份是荷。匆匆,顺颂教祺。

弟同礼顿首

十二,二十八自 Miami 寄

美国通讯处

To Mr. C.M. Wang 王重民转

Division of Orientalia

Library of Congress

Washington, D. C.

罗莘田君已到否?

〔方继孝藏札〕

按:1944 年,罗常培受美国波莫纳学院(Pomona College)邀请,前往该校讲学,后又赴耶鲁大学等校访问。

先生致信福开森,告知已抵美并寄上马衡信一件。

En road to Washington

Dec. 28, 1944

Dear Dr. Ferguson:

All of your Chinese friends have been greatly concerned about your welfare since Pearl Harbour. It is a pleasure to hear that you and Miss Ferguson have settled down in New York.

I have just arrived from China and I am looking forward to have the pleasure of seeing you soon. I enclose a letter from Mr. Ma Heng who wish to be remembered to you.

With kindest regards and season's greetings.

Yours sincerely,

T. L. Yuan

按:该信为先生亲笔,翌日于亚特兰大寄出。马衡信如下,

茂生先生赐鉴:

七年违教,时企清辉。王世襄君去岁南来,备述先生经历艰险之状及挈同世妹安抵珂乡经过,差为欣慰。衡典守文物、迁徙流离,除少数未及迁出外,余均安顿后方,幸无重大损失,堪慰垂注。此间各关系方面颇有意将一部分艺术品选运贵国展览,所虑者空运、海运皆欠安全,须俟胜利后方可议及耳。唐立庵君南来时赍来历代著录吉金目一册,在书荒之际获读大著受益良多,深愧年来见闻寡陋、学殖荒芜,实为个人莫大之损失也。舍弟季明鉴自香港沦陷后展转内移,今在成都燕京大学任教,与贵记室张君同事,内子则于四年前在上海逝世矣。如有赐示,请寄重庆海棠溪故宫博物院为感。专肃,敬颂颐安。

受业马衡上言

卅三年十一月廿五日

〔Freer Gallery of Art and Arthur M. Sackler Gallery Archives, Box 3 folder 67 of the John Calvin Ferguson Family Papers〕

一九四五年　五十一岁

一月三日　华盛顿

先生至费慰梅办公室访问，并一起午餐。〔The American Library Association Archives, China Projects File, Box 1, Correspondence about China, 1945 01-03〕

按：先生寓 Bellevue Hotel, 15 E Street, N. W. (Telephone Metropolitan 0900)，此时预计在华盛顿盘桓一月。

一月六日　弗吉尼亚州温泉城

先生致信顾临，告知已至温泉城（Hot Springs），将参加太平洋国际学会第九次年会，预计二月中旬回到纽约。〔The American Library Association Archives, China Projects File, Box 2, Books for China Correspondence 1945-1946〕

按：本次会议的会期为1945年1月6日至1月17日，蒋梦麟率中国代表团出席会议，会议的主题是——战后太平洋地区的安全和发展。

莱登伯格致函先生，得知先生赴美考察，代表美国图书馆协会同仁表示欢迎，并期待见面。

January 6, 1945

Dear Dr. Yuan:

We have just learned from Dr. Carl White of your arrival. May we on behalf of your friends of the American Library Association extend to you our cordial greetings and express our great pleasure at having you with us in the United States?

Mr. Carl Milam, Executive Secretary of the Association, Mr. Keyes D. Metcalf, Chairman of the International Relations Board, and Mr. Charles Brown, Chairman of the Committee on the Orient and Southwest Pacific, I know, would want me to send you a special word of greeting did they know you are here.

This office is at your service, and I hope soon to have the privilege and pleasure of greeting you in person.

Truly yours,

H. M. Lydenberg

Director

〔The American Library Association Archives, China Projects File, Box 1, Correspondence about China, 1945 01-03〕

按:Keyes D. Matcalf(1889-1983),美国图书馆学家,历任纽约公共图书馆、哈佛大学图书馆馆长,时应任伊利诺伊州大学图书馆系主任。此件为录副。

一月八日

米来牟致函先生,得知先生赴美考察,代表美国图书馆协会表示欢迎,期待面谈,尤其企盼可以赴芝加哥、艾姆斯商洽合作事宜。

January 8, 1945

Dear Dr. Yuan:

I was very happy to learn some weeks ago that you were actually coming to the United States again without waiting for the war to end. Now I am delighted to know that you have arrived.

I extend my cordial welcome, as I am sure many others have already done, on behalf of the American Library Association and on my own account.

You will have learned from White and Lydenberg and Brown and from Mrs. Fairbank what we are thinking about, trying to do, and, in some small measure, doing. It will be of great advantage to all of us to have an opportunity to talk with you personally and to get your advice.

Mrs. Fairbank says that you are to be in Washington for three or four weeks and that you hope to get to Chicago and Ames. By all means come out this way if you can! If you cannot, then let me know and I will make certain to meet you somewhere else.

Cordially yours,

Carl H. Milam

Executive Secretary

〔The American Library Association Archives, China Projects File, Box 2, Yuan T L 1943-1945〕

按:希望与先生面谈的诸事中涉及美国务院向美国图书馆协会拨款五万美金,用以购买新书捐赠中国。①

孙念礼致函先生,表示葛思德东方藏书库馆藏中文书籍已超过十万卷,希望先生能够在二月份来普林斯顿大学作短暂停留,该校高等研究院主任 Frank Aydelotte 等人皆希望面谈,商讨葛思德东方藏书库与平馆间的合作。

Jan. 8, 1945

Dr. T. L. Yuan
c/o Orientalia
Library of Congress
Washington, D. C.

Dear Dr. Yuan:

When in Washington in November last Dr. Hummel told me that you were expected to pay a visit to the States; and through the courtesy of Mr. Wang I have just heard of your arrival in Washington. If you can spare the time, we would very much like to have you come for a visit to the Gest Library.

You have had some exchange of courtesies through Mr. Lawrence Heyl, Associate Librarian, with Princeton University Library, and very likely you would like a conference with Mr. Heyl, and perhaps would like to meet the University Librarian, Dr. Julian Boyd. You have seen part of the Gest Collection when it was deposited at McGill University, although at the time I was away on vacation. Since our removal to Princeton the remainder of the collection came over from Peking, and the present holdings of something over 100,000 Chinese stitched volumes are on the shelves. As yet we are not in permanent quarters, nor have we undertaken even the ordinary routine activities of library since we have not yet been

① Rockefeller Foundation, RG: 1.1 Series, 200R Box 203, Folder 2426.

able to have a staff required to make the necessary preparations for such activities.

We would like to have you talk with Dr. Aydelotte, the Director of the Institute for Advanced Study, and I would like to plan with you any suggestions which we may be able to work out for the cooperation of the Gest Oriental Library with the National Library of which you are Director in so far as can be done for the mutual advantage of the two institutions.

If you can arrange it when you are in New York City, or en route to or from that city, some time in February, or later, if necessary, would you pay a visit to The Gest Library to be the guest of The Institute for Advanced Study? I would appreciate the help such a visit would be to us all.

Very sincerely,

(Dr.) Nancy Lee Swann, Curator

〔Princeton University, Mudd Manuscript Library, AC123, Box 415, Folder Peiping, National Library of, 1937-1944〕

按:Lawrence Heyl(1893-?),长期担任普林斯顿大学图书馆总馆副馆长,1962 年 7 月退休;Julian Boyd(1903-1980),美国历史学家,1964 年任美国历史学会主席;Frank Aydelotte(1880-1956),美国教育家,1939 年至 1947 年担任普林斯顿高等研究院第二任院长。此件为录副,打字稿上有修改,特别是将右上角正确的年份错改为 1944。

一月上旬

裘开明致函先生。〔《裘开明年谱》,页 307〕

按:该函附在 1 月 8 日裘开明致吴光清函中。

一月九日

米来牟致函先生,转达美国图书馆协会国际关系委员会在去年十月会议上就先生(平馆)为美国十三家图书馆采购中文出版物致以的谢忱。

January 9, 1945

Dear Dr. Yuan

I have pleasure in transmitting to you the following brief expression of thanks voted by the International Relations Board of the American Library Association at its meeting on October 7-8, 1944:

> On behalf of the thirteen libraries cooperating in Chinese purchase, the American Library Association expresses its great appreciation of the energy and wisdom shown by Dr. T. L. Yuan in the execution of this project.

American libraries and the American Library Association are under obligation to you for many favors. This particular item was singled out for a formal action because we believe that it is putting an unusually heavy burden on you.

Cordially yours,
Carl H. Milam
Executive Secretary

〔The American Library Association Archives, China Projects File, Box 2, Yuan T L 1943-1945〕

按：该函寄送 Bellevue Hotel, Room 420，此为录副。

一月十日

莱登伯格致函先生，希望尽快与先生开始讨论为中国购买书刊的项目计划，并希望了解先生行期以便安排晤谈和聚会。

January 10, 1945

Dear Dr. Yuan:

Are your plans beginning to take definite shape enough to let us have some suggestions as to how we can best help you put your time to good use when you get back to Washington? Are there any things in particular you wish to see-any people? If so, we shall be glad to try to make appointments for you, though in that case it will be more fruitful if we know of any engagements you have made or any you would like to have made.

One thing certain is that it would be well for you to get together with the State Department force and with Messrs. Milam and Brown as well as our office to tell us just what kind of books you feel will be most appreciated by and most useful for China. We want to begin buying as soon as possible. We want likewise to avoid as many mistakes as possible. We feel your advice and counsel on this point will be of first importance.

Some of your friends, many indeed, would like to get together with you informally around the dinner table. We feel this is so important as to make us want now to know whether you have any particular dates you would favor or any to avoid.

With kindest greetings to all your friends.

Truly yours,
H. M. Lydenberg
Director

〔The American Library Association Archives, China Projects File, Box 2, Books for China Correspondence, 1945-1946〕

按:该函由费慰梅转交,此为录副。

一月十二日

先生覆信孙念礼,八日来函收悉,告知或将在二月中旬抵达纽约,届时再联系。

January 12, 1944

Dear Dr. Swann

I am much obliged to you for your kind of letter of January 8th which has been forwarded to me here.

The Gest Oriental Library which has been developed under your able direction is one of the institutions which I am looking forward to visit. I should like very much to call on Dr. Aydelotte, Dr. Boyd and Mr. Heyl and discuss with them measures of cooperation.

I shall probably be in New York City in the middle of February and I shall write you again before my arrival.

With kindest regards,

Yours Sincerely,
T. L. Yuan

〔Princeton University, Mudd Manuscript Library, AC123, Box 415, Folder Peiping, National Library of, 1937-1944〕

按:此信为先生亲笔,左上1944应作1945。

一月十三日

先生致信布朗,告知抵达华盛顿的时间并期待面谈,寄上去年十一月二十四日有关美国图书馆协会汇款信函的副本。

January 13, 1945

Dear Dr. Brown:

Many thanks for your good letter of January 6th. I am particularly happy to learn that you expect to be in Washington for a few days beginning January 24 and I am looking forward with keen pleasure to meeting you.

Before leaving Chungking, I wrote you on November 24 with regard to the remitting of ALA funds to China. For fear that you may not have received it, I am enclosing copy of that letter for your reference.

It is possible that I could arrange to be in New York City when you are there, so that we can talk over matters of mutual interest. I am also anxious to visit Chicago and Ames during this trip.

With renewed thanks for your interest and cooperation.

Sincerely,

T. L. Yuan

〔The American Library Association Archives, China Projects File, Box 2, Carl White Trip 1945〕

按:此为抄件。

加斯基尔致函先生,邀请先生前往康乃尔大学做客。

January 13, 1945

Mr. T. L. Yuan

Division of Cultural Cooperation

Department of State

Washington, D. C.

Dear Mr. Yuan:

I was delighted to learn from Knight Biggerstaff that you are in this country, and I hope that you will have time to come to Ithaca before long. Dr. Kinkeldey joins me in extending to you a cordial invitation to visit Cornell as the guest of the University. We are forever grateful to you for all you have done to help us build up our library of Chinese books, and we should be so glad of an opportunity to have a visit with you. A considerable interest in Chinese studies have developed here, not yet all one could hope for, but a beginning, and it would be helpful to have several of those concerned with it meet you, too. To me it seems much too long since the many pleasant occasions on which I enjoyed your hospitality during the year I spent in Peiping.

Sincerely yours,

〔Cornell University Library, Wason Collection Records, 1918-1988, Box 1, Folder Koo, T. K. Letters〕

按:Knight Biggerstaff(1906-2001),美国汉学家,中文名毕乃德,毕业于加州大学伯克利分校,1934 年获得哈佛大学博士学位,后在燕京大学学习,1946 年后长期在康乃尔大学执教。

一月十五日

先生回到华盛顿。〔方继孝藏札〕

一月十六日

先生致信陈梦家,告知行程并表示愿意赞助其出版铜器目录专著事。

梦家吾兄:

上星期曾到太平洋学会会议旁听,昨日始返,奉到四日手教,欣悉种切。承示各节,尤以为感。美国各杂志颇欢迎我国学者投稿,大著原为序文体裁,似可改为论文,登入艺术杂志较印单行本效力更大,不识有暇为之否?关于重编海外铜器之事,弟拟愿赞助,惟此时美国纸张缺乏,无法付印,似不如利用此时机会搜集资料,但此项工作亦非得有确定之款项不易进行。未识尊处能代拟一计划否?俟弟三月间到芝后,面谈何如?弟拟下月初到纽约转波士顿,约三月中旬可到芝加哥,此行见其进步之速,深资借镜,惟限于时间,未能多留,颇以为憾耳。贤伉俪任课余暇尚能从事研究,健羡何似,望能作一久留之计划,俟战事结束再行返国。匆匆,顺颂旅安。

同礼顿首

十六

弟之住址为 Bellevue Hotel, 15 E Street, N. W, Washington,离华京

后为 c/o China Insititue, 125 East 65th. St. N. Y. City

〔方继孝藏札〕

按："大著"似指 Style of Chinese Bronzes，是年 11 月 30 日，陈梦家以此为题在大都会艺术博物馆学术会议上发表演讲，后又刊登于*Archives of the Chinese Art Society of America*。① 时，赵萝蕤应在芝加哥大学攻读英语文学博士学位，并翻译艾略特《荒原》，1948 年获博士学位，后归国。

布朗致函先生，告知其将于二十四日上午前往先生所在酒店，期待与先生一起访问国会图书馆与相关人士面商一切，并代米来牟无法前往华盛顿表示歉意，最后对先生仍任中华图书馆协会执行部主席表示祝贺。

January 16, 1945

Dear Dr. Yuan:

Your telegram was received with much pleasure. I am planning to arrive in Washington Wednesday morning, January 24, probably about 9 o'clock. I am staying at the Hotel Washington, but it is very probable that no room will be available for me until late in the day. I shall, therefore, check my suitcase and proceed over to your hotel, which I should reach before 10 o'clock.

I thought you might like to go with me to the Library of Congress to confer with Mr. Lydenberg and Mr. Milczewski, and then we would go over to see the Acting Librarian of Congress, Dr. Luther Evans. I am writing both Milczewski and Evans today. Later on in the day we might check over some future appointments with Mrs. Fairbank, and then we can commence on various conversations which will probably take some time. We shall want to spend some time with Dr. Carl White also, if he is still in Washington.

I am leaving for New York late Thursday evening, January 25, but shall return to Washington on the evening of January 29 and shall be

① Meng-chia, Ch'en. "Style of Chinese Bronzes." Archives of the Chinese Art Society of America, Vol. 1, 1945, pp. 26-52.

available January 30–31, and February 1. I have many matters which we should discuss frankly without the difficulties imposed by the restrictions in correspondence.

I have talked with so many Chinese scholars who are warm friends of yours and have been so interested by your approach to library problems that I am looking forward with the greatest pleasure to talking with you personally. I feel that we have been friends for many years.

I talked with Mr. Milam over the phone yesterday. He would have liked to have gone to Washington to greet you personally, but he thought that in view of the difficulties in travel and the pressure upon his time you would make allowances for his delay. Both of us are expecting to see you in Chicago and at Ames later in the year. In the meantime, I trust you will accept me as a representative of our Executive Secretary. I know he shares with me my warm respect for you personally and, officially, for the librarian of the National Library of Peiping and the Chairman of the Executive Board of the Library Association of China.

May I add also that some anxiety on this side has been much relieved by your signature in your letter of November 20. We were very glad to know that you are still the Chairman of the Executive Board of the Library Association of China.

Yours very truly,

Charles H. Brown, Chairman

Committee on the Orient and Southwest Pacific

〔The American Library Association Archives, China Projects File, Box 1, Correspondence about China, 1945 01–03〕

按:Mr. Milczewski 即 Marion A. Milczewski(1912–1981),美国图书馆学家,本谱中译作"米尔泽夫斯基",后曾担任华盛顿大学图书馆馆长。此件为副本。

一月二十日

先生致信加斯基尔,收悉一月十三日函,并告有可能赴康乃尔大学访问。

Jan. 20, 1944

Dear Miss Gaskill:

I was so glad to have your letter of January 13.

It is a pleasure to learn that there is a considerable interest in Chinese studies developed at Cornell, and I learn also that you have made great progress in Slavonic studies. I shall certainly look forward to seeing you and meeting Dr. Kinkeldey. Before coming to Ithaca, I shall write to you a week ahead. It will probably be in March at the earliest.

Thank you again for your letter which I highly appreciate.

Yours sincerely,

T. L. Yuan

N. Y. address: c/o China Institute

125 East 65th St.

New York City

〔The Homestead (Hot Springs, Virgina) 信纸。Cornell University Library, Wason Collection Records, 1918-1988, Box 1, Folder Koo, T. K. Letters〕

按:该信为先生亲笔,左上 1944 应作 1945。加斯基尔收到此信后,应在 2 月 16 日再次致函先生。

一月下旬

先生因腿部发炎,入院治疗。〔方继孝藏札〕

一月三十一日

晚七点,美国图书馆协会国际关系委员会假 Hotel Willard Cabinet Room 宴请先生,出席者有该会东方委员会主席布朗,国务院代表费慰梅、Harry Warfel,战时情报局代表费正清,国会图书馆执行馆长埃文斯和东方部主任恒慕义,农业部图书馆执行馆长 Mildred Senton,以及美国图书馆协会国际关系委员会委员等数十位。〔"A. L. A. News." *Bulletin of the American Library Association*, Vol. 39, no. 3, 1945, p. 118; The American Library Association Archives, China Projects File, Box 1, Correspondence about China, 1945 01-03〕

一月

叶理绥致函先生,请在华盛顿时协助鉴定王文山所售古籍。〔《裘开明年谱》,页 308〕

按：后先生与王重民都看过此批图书，做出了大致判断，认为价值一般，售价太高，虽然建议哈佛购入，但请其与中间代理人刘驭万协商。2月23日，裘开明致信刘驭万，表示愿以1500美元购入王文山藏书。

二月二日

下午三时[①]，先生在国会图书馆 Whittall Pavilion 发表演讲，讲述日本侵华的种种暴行、中国图书馆界的现状和战后复兴计划，呼吁美国各界积极援助中国，尤其是捐赠西文出版物。〔美国国会图书馆网页 https://lccn.loc.gov/2001660343〕

按：本次演讲由埃文斯和恒慕义做开场介绍，并由国会图书馆录音并永久保存。

二月三日

先生覆信陈梦家，就其研究计划书提出意见并告知行程。

梦家吾兄：

奉到廿四日及三十一日手教，适以腿部发炎，曾在医院小住数日，以致未能早覆为歉。承寄下英文计划，至为感谢，内中尚有待奉商者数点列后：(一)第一集，商务曾制版，序文亦排好，此时或已出版。第二集之资料已运沪，大致亦未被毁，内中美国、欧洲各半(尊处想有详细目录)。今日之计划拟专限美国较易办理，未识尊意以为如何；(二)如能先将美国部分出版则筹款较易，惟商务以版权关系难免不抗议，因商务原拟在国外多销数百部方肯承印，其经过想尚记忆；(三)照片费用、参考用书等可由北平馆担任不必列入预算，此外旅费及其他费用，可在美设法，惟数目敝意二千左右，如何？以愈少愈妙，不识应规定若干，请赐考虑，示知至感。第三月间在波士顿一带，须三月底来芝或四月初，请告邓君仅□□，不敢作讲演(因无资料)也。嘱索各方□□铜器照片，当另为设法随时寄上以供参考。公超想已赴英，端升在纽约通讯处：孟治君收转。怀主教处当先去信接洽，卢君处弟到纽后即奉访。现定十五日至三十一日在纽，通讯处亦由孟君平收转，不误。匆匆，顺颂大安。

① Library of Congress Archives Box 673 Asia-3.

弟同礼顿首

二，三

日前，丁声树、全汉昇经此赴波士顿，谓罗莘田或尚未到。尊夫人同此致意，弟到芝后须让弟参加洗碗方来叨扰。

〔方继孝藏札〕

按："邓君"应指邓嗣禹。陈梦家在此信上标注"着重三事：(1)铜器以美国为主、(2)目录为主、(3)美国其它古物"。

米来牟致函先生，告知其计划前往华盛顿、纽约的日期。

February 3, 1945

Dear Dr. Yuan:

I am expecting to be in Washington at the Hotel Washington on February 15 and 16. I hope you will be in the city at that time and that we can have an hour or two of conversation on the state of the world.

Incidentally, I shall be in New York at the Algonquin Hotel on February 13 and 14.

Cordially yours

Carl H. Milam

Executive Secretary.

〔The American Library Association Archives, China Projects File, Box 2, Yuan T L 1943-1945〕

按：此件为录副。

二月五日　纽约

先生覆信米来牟，二月中旬前往费城无法在华盛顿相见，但三月或许有机会碰面。

Feb. 5, 1945

Dear Dr. Milam:

I thank you for your note of February 3. I am extremely sorry that my engagement at Philadelphia on February 15 and 16 will prevent me from meeting you here or Washington.

I am looking forward to our meeting at Chicago sometime next month. Perhaps I may be able to see you at the President Butler dinner, if you could arrange to come on the 17th.

With Kindest regards,

Yours sincerely,

T. L. Yuan

〔The Bellevue Hotel 信纸。The American Library Association Archives, China Projects File, Box 2, Yuan T L 1943-1945〕

按:该信为先生亲笔。

二月七日

哥伦比亚大学校长巴特勒致函先生,拟于十七日晚设宴款待。函文摘抄如下:

I wish to express my satisfaction that we are to have the pleasure of entertaining you at the University at dinner on Saturday, February 17. We have issued invitations to a group that will be interested in greeting you. Dr. White has or will give you the details of the arrangements, but I will set down here the basic fact that dinner is at seven o' clock at the Men's Faculty Club, 400 West 117 Street.

〔王成志《袁同礼先生和哥伦比亚大学》,页 245〕

Ernest J. Reece 致函先生,邀请先生于本月二十一日赴哥伦比亚大学图书馆学院茶会。

February 7, 1945

Dear Mr. Yuan:

I have been hearing for some time about your plans for being in this country and about your arrival, and the moment seems to have come for me to get in touch with you.

Dr. White writes that you would consider coming to the School of Library Service some afternoon while you are in New York and giving some of us here a chance to meet you. This would be a pleasure to our group, especially in view of your connection with the New York State Library School, which contributed to the founding of the present School of Library Service.

Could you, accordingly, give us some time on the afternoon of

Wednesday, February 21? We should plan to arrange an hour for tea, probably 4:00 to 5:00, in the social room, 523 South Hall, at which there would be opportunity to grasp your hand and perhaps to hear a word about what you have been doing all these years.

We shall be happy in case you can come, and if you can send us an answer soon this will help us in making our plans.

With best wishes,

Sincerely,

Ernest J. Reece

Associate Dean

〔Columbia University Library, New York State Library School Collection, Series 2 Student Records, Box 65, Folder Yuan, T. L.〕

按：Ernest J. Reece（1881－1976），美国图书馆学家，1926 年至 1948 年在哥伦比亚大学图书馆学院执教，时任院长助理。该件为录副。

米来牟致函先生，表示无法参加巴特勒二月十七日的宴席，但其在本月底、三月中旬均将前往华盛顿，或者可在芝加哥碰面。

February 7, 1945

Dear Dr. Yuan:

Unfortunately, I am unable to attend the Nicholas Murray Butler dinner in New York on the 17th. But I shall be back in Washington again at the end of February and near the middle of March.

As soon as you can make up your schedule, I hope you will let me know when you expect to be in Chicago so that I can be certain to be here. Difficulties of transportation make it necessary for us these days to plan several weeks ahead for any trip we intend to take.

Cordially yours,

Carl H. Milam

Executive Secretary

〔The American Library Association Archives, China Projects File, Box 2, Yuan T L 1943-1945〕

按:该件为录副。

二月八日

先生覆信 Ernest J. Reece,接受返校邀请,表示谢意。

February 8, 1945

Dear Prof. Reece:

Thank you so much for your letter of February 7th.

It is most kind of you to arrange a tea for me on Wednesday, February 21. It is a great honor to me and I shall be glad to come.

I am looking forward with keen pleasure to meeting you and other members of the faculty of my alma mater.

Yours sincerely.

T. L. Yuan

〔The Bellevue Hotel 信纸。Columbia University Library, New York State Library School Collection, Series 2 Student Records, Box 65, Folder Yuan, T. L.〕

按:该信为先生亲笔。

二月十日

先生覆信哥伦比亚大学校长巴特勒,感谢设宴并表示将如约前往。信文摘抄如下:

I appreciate very much your kind letter of February 7th. I wish to thank you very heartily for the great honor you give me in arranging the dinner on Saturday evening which I accept with much pleasure.

Your achievement has been the source of inspiration to my work in China and I am looking forward with keen pleasure to my visit to my Alma Mater after an absence of ten years.

I should like to call on you and pay my respects on Saturday morning and shall get in touch with your Secretary after my arrival.

〔王成志《袁同礼先生和哥伦比亚大学》,页 245〕

Ernest J. Reece 覆函先生,很高兴先生将于二十一日访问哥伦比亚大学图书馆学院,并将茶会时间略作调整。

February 10, 1945

Dear Mr. Yuan:

We are much pleased that you can be with us on February 21st. There will be present members of the School of Library Service faculty and a few from the staff of the libraries, including those having to do with the Chinese collection. We think it will be pleasant.

The chairman of our social committee desires to make a slight change in the hour I mentioned to you. Subject to your convenience the tea will be scheduled from four to five-thirty.

Sincerely,

Ernest J. Reece

Associate Dean

〔Columbia University Library, New York State Library School Collection, Series 2 Student Records, Box 65, Folder Yuan, T. L.〕

按:该件为录副。

二月十七日

晚七时,哥伦比亚大学校方设宴款待先生,洛克菲勒基金会、大都会博物馆、美国图书馆协会、纽约公共图书馆、华美协进社、美国政府馆员等受邀前往作陪。〔王成志《袁同礼先生和哥伦比亚大学》,页 245-246〕

按:本次宴会嘉宾名单本有 58 人之多,但最终应邀出席者约为 35 人,中方人员有赵元任、张彭春、刘廷芳、孟治、王际真。胡适本受邀参加,但因邀函送达太迟且身在哈佛大学,最终未能出席。[1]

二月中下旬

中美文化协会改选职员,先生被推举为研究委员会主任委员。〔《大公报》(重庆),1945 年 2 月 23 日,第 3 版〕

按:本年 2 月 22 日是中美文化协会成立六周年纪念日,新一届职员名单即在此日公布。

二月二十一日

下午四时,先生赴哥伦比亚大学,与图书馆学院教师、校图书馆馆员等茶叙。〔Columbia University Library, New York State Library School Collection, Series 2

① 台北胡适纪念馆,档案编号 HS-JDSHSE-0102-011。

Student Records, Box 65, Folder Yuan, T. L.〕

二月二十三日

米尔泽夫斯基致函先生,感谢先生寄赠《图书季刊》英文本。

February 23, 1945

Dear Dr. Yuan:

Please accept our thanks for the *Quarterly Bulletin of Chinese Bibliography*, New Series, Volumes 1-2, 3-4, which have just arrived. They are indeed interesting publications, true evidence of the indomitable spirit of your people.

Sincerely yours,

Marion A. Milczewski

Assistant to the Director

〔The American Library Association Archives, China Projects File, Box 1, Correspondence about China, 1945 01-03〕

按:此件为录副。

二月二十五日

中午,国会图书馆执行馆长埃文斯等人在 Cosmos Club 设宴款待先生,米来牟等人作陪。先生表示四月初会前往芝加哥,米来牟则表示计划邀请先生在芝加哥大学、Cliff Dwellers Club 各做一次发言。〔The American Library Association Archives, China Projects File, Box 1, Correspondence about China, 1945 01-03〕

按:米来牟感慨战争带给人的冲击,觉得先生已经不再精力充沛、活力四射,与十年前刚认识时已截然不同。

先生致信陈梦家,谈编印铜器目录计划。

梦家吾兄:

到纽约后接到十日及廿一日手教,敬悉一一。关于编印铜器目录之事,曾与张彭春及孟君平商议,渠等虽热诚赞助,但对筹款一事,仍感棘手。敝意只有二处可以设法:(一)哈佛燕京社、(二)罗氏基金会。哈佛方面或愿自行出版,故另须将敝馆 sponsor 的话予以删去;罗氏基金方面似须由 Graves 从旁进行,但渠有一友 Davides 君亦愿作此项工作,且不愿中国学者完成此事,故敝意仍向哈佛进行。兹将大稿改正，请签署后再寄 Elisséeff 一函，说明系 Revised Copy 可也。弟不日再致函 Elisséeff 说明一切。大约三月底方能到剑桥，所需 Freer 照片□□□私人藏器照片当分别进行。到芝日期仍难预定，余容再函。顺颂大安。

弟同礼顿首

二，廿五

〔方继孝藏札〕

三月二日

先生致信鲍曼，告知因故无法如约前往匹兹堡大学，但已请刘师舜大使携带蒋介石所题匾额和沈尹默、沈兼士所撰书法作品前往该校。

March 2, 1945

Dear Chancellor Bowman:

Before leaving for America, I told President Chiang Kai-shek about the China Memorial Room in the Cathedral of Learning. I requested him to send you a tablet in the form of four characters, which he did with pleasure.

I have been hoping to bring it to you personally, but owing to a previous engagement at Washington, I shall not be able to come to Pittsburgh with Ambassador Liu. I am, therefore, asking him to present it to the University on my behalf.

I am also asking Ambassador Liu to bring two scrolls for the China Memorial Room. They were written by Shen Yin-mo and Shen Chien-shih, two of our noted contemporary calligraphers. Please accept them with my best compliments.

With cordial regards,

Yours a sincerely,

T. L. Yuan

c/o Chinese Embassy

Washington, D. C.

〔University of Pittsburgh Library, John Gabbert Bowman, Administrative Files, Box 2 Folder 13, Chinese Material〕

按:Ambassador Liu 即刘师舜(1900—1996),字琴五,江西宜丰人,清华学校毕业后赴美留学,1925 年获哥伦比亚大学博士学位,时任中华民国驻加拿大大使。此信为先生亲笔。

三月初

先生赴波士顿。〔《裘开明年谱》,页 310〕

按:裘开明似与先生晤面。

三月八日

鲍曼覆函先生,收到沈尹默、沈兼士书法卷轴及蒋介石所题匾额,表示感谢。

March 8, 1945

Dear Dr. Yuan:

It is good this morning to have your letter of March 2. It has come with the two scrolls of calligraphy that take my breath. These scrolls are indeed beautiful, and we plan promptly to see how they may best be put on exhibition in the China Memorial Room. Further, the tablet in the form of four characters done by President Chiang Kai-shek is also here. We shall try to work out a plan by which faculty and students may see this tablet. For these courtesies let me now, on behalf of the University, most heartily thank you.

Personally, I should be delighted to see you, and I hope that you will have some time to spend in Pittsburgh before you return to China. In the meantime, let me express again our gratitude to you and our deep appreciation for the two scrolls and the tablet.

With kind personal wishes, I am

Faithfully yours,

〔University of Pittsburgh Library, John Gabbert Bowman, Administrative Files, Box 2 Folder 13, Chinese Material〕

按:该件无落款,应为录副。

三月十日　华盛顿

先生致信陈梦家,告知叶理绥来函之消息。

梦家吾兄:

在纽约奉到手书,曾覆一函内附计划书二份,谅已收到。日前返华京，接到 Elisséeff 来信此旅馆未曾转寄，询及一切，当即作复。内称此项工作自以中国人为之较易见效。本月廿二日至廿八日在康桥，当再面托，促其成功。因四月初或中旬哈佛燕京社即开董事会也。弟原定四月一日来芝加哥，兹又因事改四月十二日前来，请届时预定旅馆不愿住□□□□为感(住一星期)。兹致邓君一函，请转交是荷。顺颂大安。

弟同礼顿首

三月十日，华京

通讯处 China Insit.转。

〔方继孝藏札〕

三月十七日

布朗致函先生，随信寄上其发给十三家图书馆的通知，期待与先生在芝加哥、艾姆斯面谈，因收到许多来自中国的购买、合作信函，期望与先生讨论后再作出对中国各机构的答复，此外蒋复璁、岳良木都曾写大量信件请求美方将捐赠书籍通过包裹方式寄送中国，但其就这些捐赠的复本书刊是否应该集中于重庆表示质疑。

March 17, 1945

c/o China Institute in America

125 East 65th Street

New York

Dear Dr. Yuan:

I am enclosing a notice just sent out to the thirteen cooperating libraries. I shall also insert a note in the *Library Journal*. You have made an excellent record with the money available for you to spend. I am hoping that the exchange rates will stay down so that we can resume shipment of books.

As soon as you can arrange your schedules, I would like some idea when you will be in Chicago and in Ames. I find I will have to go East sometime within the next month or two and I do not want to miss our proposed extensive conversations.

I have been receiving many letters in regard to the purchase of individual books in China and the future of our cooperative buying program. These matters I shall want to discuss with you. In the meantime, I hope you will not make any definite commitments until we can discuss the future of this program.

Chiang Fu-tsung has flooded American libraries with the request that publications be sent by parcel post. As you know, these parcels, up to the present time, are forwarded at the risk of the sender. Now I am receiving similar request from Peter L. Yoh, who signs himself Associate Director of the Library of the Central Planning Board. I am wondering what relation the Library of the Central Planning Board has to the National Central Library. Furthermore, I wonder how far we should go in duplicating books in the field of librarianship. We have sent many of these publications to the Boone Library School and to the National Library of Peiping in Chungking. Shall we also send the same books to the Library of the Central Planning Board, or shall we attempt to use the available copies we have for libraries in cities other than Chungking?

Yours very truly,

Charles H. Brown, Chairman

Committee on the Orient and Southwest Pacific

〔The American Library Association Archives, China Projects File, Box 1, Purchasing Pool, 1943-1945〕

按:a notice 应为运送美国的中文出版物收到,正待分发的通知。Library of the Central Planning Board 应指国民政府中央设计局设计委员会图书馆,岳良木的确曾兼任该馆副馆长。

三月十八、十九日 纽约

先生与史蒂文斯、John Marshall 晤谈,就重建平馆缩微胶片实验室和在美购买中国缺藏的文献胶片等议题交换意见。〔Rockefeller Foundation. Series 601: China; Subseries 601.R: China-Humanities and Arts. Vol. Box 47. Folder 391〕

三月二十日

先生致信史蒂文斯,提交备忘录希望洛克菲勒基金会给予考虑。

c/o China Institute

125 East 65th Street

New York 21, N. Y.

March 20, 1945

Dear Dr. Stevens:

With reference to my conversation with you and Mr. John Marshall, I enclose herewith a memorandum and I hope it will receive due consideration from officers of the Foundation.

With kind regards,

Yours sincerely,

T. L. Yuan

Director

〔平馆（重庆沙坪坝）英文信纸。Rockefeller Foundation. Series 601: China; Subseries 601.R: China-Humanities and Arts. Vol. Box 47. Folder 391〕

按：此件为打字稿，落款处为先生签名，附本日撰写的 Memorandum Re The Establishment of a Central Repository of Western Books and a Photoduplication Laboratory in China，共计 4 页。

先生致信布朗，欣悉此前代购中文出版物运抵美国，并告赴芝加哥、艾姆斯的行期。

c/o Chinese-Japanese Library

Cambridge, Mass.

March 20, 1945

Dear Mr. Brown:

Thank you so much for your letter of March 17. I am glad to know that the books we bought for the thirteen libraries have been received.

I expect to be at Chicago April 12–18. From Chicago I should like to visit the University of Minnesota and come to Ames about April 23–24 if that would suit your schedule.

I am on my way to Boston. You can reach me through Mr. Chiu. I shall urge Mr. Chiu to have printed cards made for the Chinese books which will save the labour of the libraries considerably.

The library of the Cultural Planning Board is a very insignificant institution. I hate to see Mr. Yoh bother you with such unreasonable requests. I shall look forward to meeting you in Ames if not at Chicago.

Yours sincerely,

T. L. Yuan

〔The American Library Association Archives, China Projects File, Box 1, Correspondence about China, 1945 01-03〕

按:The library of the Cultural Planning Board 应指中央设计局设计委员会图书馆,此处拼写似有问题,应为 Central 而非 Cultural。该信于 3 月 26 日送达,此为抄件。

三月二十三日

布朗致函先生,期待在芝加哥面洽联合购买中文出版物计划,请代向裘开明转达对哈佛燕京图书馆排印卡片计划的称赞,并对沈祖荣、文华图书馆学专科学校表示极大的关注,对邹秉文拟将所有存于此地的图书复本运往华盛顿并最终运送到中国农业部的计划表示质疑,另告一月份的购书款项已汇出。

March 23, 1945

Dear Dr. Yuan:

I was very glad to hear from you. I am asking Carl Milam to see what day you will be free in Chicago, and then I shall arrange to come in to take up some matters on the cooperative buying program with you, Mr. Beals, and Mr. Milam.

I hope you will assure Mr. Chiu that we appreciate greatly his offer to furnish printed cards. I hope you will also give him my warm personal regards.

Yoh's various communications do not trouble me especially. I am afraid Harry Lydenberg fussed over them more than I did. I have quite a collection now. He has sent form letters all over the United States.

On the other hand, I am beginning to have a considerable esteem for Dr. Seng. I want to talk with you in regard to professional education at the Boone Library School when you are here. Dr. Tsou will be here April 8 and 9, and our Chinese students are making quite a fuss over it. He would like to take all of our duplicates and have them shipped to Washington to be sent to the Minister of Agriculture and the Agricultural Society of China. We have sorted out certain books, but there are some matters connected with schools of agriculture which I think should receive consideration and which might be ignored in the distribution at Chungking. I also want to take up with you some matters relating to Mrs. Fairbank's visit to China.

I do not know whether you have written to Chungking in the hope of obtaining a list of scientific periodicals published during the war or not. If not, possibly you might do so and get someone started on it.

We sent \$1,000 to Chungking in January for the cooperative purchase program, making \$3,000 we have sent altogether. You have done wonders with this money. I do not know yet what exchange rate we got for the \$1,000 sent in January. The exchange rates have gone up to \$600 to \$1 at least, so I am informed. You and I must decide what we are going to do in regard to additional funds.

I cannot tell you adequately the pleasure with which I am looking forward to our future conversations.

Yours very truly,

Charles H. Brown, Chairman

Committee on the Orient and Southwest Pacific

〔The American Library Association Archives, China Projects File, Box 1, Purchasing Pool, 1943-1945〕

按:Ralph A. Beals(1899-1954),美国图书馆学家,时任芝加哥大学图书馆馆长、图书馆学系主任。该函由裘开明转给先生,并抄送给莱登伯格、Metcalf和米来牟。此为抄件。

三月二十四日　波士顿

中午,在哈佛大学的中国学者梁方仲、全汉昇、丁某、桑恒康设宴招待先生,杨联陞作陪。晚,先生在该校学生会做演讲。〔《杨联陞日记》(稿本)〕

按:梁方仲(1908—1970),生于北京,经济史学家,时受邀在哈佛大学研究。桑恒康(1915—1997),河北故城人,经济学家。

三月二十六日

Margaret Boothman 致函先生,告知已收到此前寄送洛克菲勒基金会的申请备忘录。

March 26, 1945

Dear Dr. Yuan:

Mr. Stevens has asked me to acknowledge and thank you for your letter and memorandum of March 20.

The proposals in behalf of the National Library of Peiping will have careful consideration.

Sincerely yours,

Margaret Boothman

Secretary to Mr. Stevens.

〔Rockefeller Foundation. Series 601: China; Subseries 601.R: China-Humanities and Arts. Vol. Box 47. Folder 391〕

按:此函由华美协进社收转。

三月二十七日

中午,先生出席美国援华联合会(United China Relief)午宴,Mrs. Arthur Hartt、G. Nye Steiger、Mrs. William Tudor Gardiner、Mrs. William P. Wharton 等人出席。〔*The Boston Daily Globe*, 27 Mar., 1945, p. 11〕

按:午宴地址为 367 Boylston Street Boston,G. Nye Steiger 为美国西蒙斯学院(Simmons College)历史学教授,曾任上海圣约翰大学教授。

三月二十九日

上午八时,先生致电米来牟,接受四月十三日之邀请。

THANKS TELEGRAM, LUNCH AND CONVERSATION APRIL 13TH SUIT ME ADMIRABLY.

TUNGLI YUAN.

〔The American Library Association Archives, China Projects File, Box 2, Yuan T L 1943-1945〕

波士顿大学(Boston University)主席 Daniel L. Marsh 在 Algonquin Club 设宴款待先生。席后,先生在该校文学院大厅发表了题为 Friends of the Library 的演讲。〔*The Boston Daily Globe*, 29 Mar. , 1945, p. 6〕

四月一日

先生致信傅振伦、齐念衡二人,谈帮助其来美学习博物馆专业事。

维本、树平仁兄大鉴:

关于两兄来美研究博物馆学,弟到美后即为进行。正日昨大致决定,此中办法系由哈佛大学之 Fogg Museum 聘维本兄为研究员,费尔特费城本雪文尼大学 University of Pennsylvania 之 University Museum 聘树平兄为研究员,其在美经费每月一百五十元左右及往来川资则由罗氏基金会担任言明返国后必须发展中国博物馆事业,为期一年。想不日,罗氏基金会 Far Eastern Office,Rockefeller Foundation 驻印度代表 M. C. Balfour 先生必有公函通知。尊处所需之经费须到印度之新德里领取,此外两大学必有聘函寄到,俟寄到后请即办理护照七月动身为宜,并可申请少许外汇,以备第二年之用(如成绩良好,则第二年在博物院中实习,可由院中设法津贴)。此外,在重庆除到美英领事馆签字外,并应到加拿大使馆签字,因 Toronto 有一博物馆 Royal Ontario Museum 值得参观也。如乘船到美多半由孟买乘船,在洛仙机 Los Angels 上岸,东来时务到 Kansas City 之 Nelson Gallery of Art 参观一次芝加哥及旧金山博物馆均可参观,以免将来再往西方徒耗旅费也。到华京后可到王重民处得些消息,弟六七月间离此,恐不能在此晤面,所以应接洽之事当留交王君转交。匆匆,顺颂大安。

弟同礼顿首

四月一日

〔平馆(昆明)英文信纸。国家图书馆善本组手稿特藏〕

按:傅振伦将此封信错记于 1944 年。①

四月二日

先生致信鲍曼,告知预计四月八日前往匹兹堡大学。

c/o China Institute

125 East 65th St. N. Y. C.

April 2, 1945

Dear Chancellor Bowman:

Thank you so much for your letter of March 8.

① 《蒲梢沧桑·九十忆往》,页 24。

It will be such a treat to see you and your great university. I expect to arrive Sunday afternoon April 8th and shall spend next day at Pittsburgh. I have to leave for Chicago Tuesday morning.

Looking forward with keen pleasure to seeing you.

Yours sincerely

T. L. Yuan

〔University of Pittsburgh Library, John Gabbert Bowman, Administrative Files, Box 2 Folder 13, Chinese Material〕

按:此信为先生亲笔。

先生致信孙念礼,预计四月五日前往普林斯顿大学(高等研究院)。

April 2, 1945

Dear Dr. Swann:

Since meeting you in New York, I have been hoping to have the pleasure of visiting the Institute of Advanced Study.

Now I have returned from a trip to New England, I expect to come to Princeton Thursday morning, April 5, from Philadelphia, and return to New York in the afternoon.

After arrival I shall take a taxi to the Institute and perhaps visit the University in the afternoon.

Looking forward to seeing you,

Sincerely,

T. L. Yuan

〔Hotel Commodore(Washington, D. C.)信纸。Princeton University, Mudd Manuscript Library, AC123, Box 415, Folder Peiping, National Library of, 1937-1944〕

按:此信为先生亲笔所书。

米来牟致函先生,美国图书馆协会交际委员会于四月十七日在芝加哥 Cliff Dwellers Club 设宴款待先生,请尽快回覆是否出席。

April 2, 1945

Dear Dr. Yuan:

On behalf of the Entertainment Committee and the President of the

Cliff Dwellers Club, I invite you to be the guest of the Club at luncheon on Tuesday, April 17. You will be expected to make some remarks after lunch and they may be as informal as you wish. You will know by now in what subjects Americans are likely to be interested.

The Cliff Dwellers Club, as you may remember, is a club of painters, architects, sculptors, musicians, writers, and laymen interested in those subjects.

Please let me know as soon as you can whether you will be able to accept this engagement so that announcement can be made to the members in plenty of time.

This is not to be confused with the luncheon conversation which is already scheduled for April 13 at the same place.

Cordially yours,

Carl H. Milam

Executive Secretary

〔The American Library Association Archives, China Projects File, Box 2, Yuan T. L. Chicago Visit, 1945〕

按:该函寄送了三份,分别是纽约华美协进社、哈佛燕京汉和图书馆、Hotel Commodore(华盛顿)。此件为录副。

四月五日

先生前往普林斯顿大学。〔Princeton University, Mudd Manuscript Library, AC123, Box 415, Folder Peiping, National Library of, 1937-1944〕

按:先生此次访问目的是考察葛斯德东方图书馆馆藏古籍情况,讨论该校(高等研究院)与平馆开展合作的具体措施,尤其是商讨请王重民前往葛斯德图书馆编目的可能性。

匹兹堡大学校长秘书 Mildred E. Stegeman 致电先生,告知校长因事外出,询问是否按计划来校访问。

April 5, 1945

MUCH REGRET DR. BOWMAN OUT OF CITY NOT TO RETURN FOR TWO OR THREE WEEKS. HE WILL BE SORRY TO MISS YOUR VISIT. OTHERS HERE WILL BE DELIGHTED TO WELCOME

YOU. HAVE RESERVED ROOM FOR YOU AT HOTEL SCHENLEY. PLEASE LET ME KNOW SHOULD YOU DECIDE TO POSTPONE YOUR VISIT.

Mildred E. Stegeman

〔University of Pittsburgh Library, John Gabbert Bowman, Administrative Files, Box 2 Folder 13, Chinese Material〕

四月六日　纽约

先生覆信米来牟,接受邀请并将演讲。

New York City

April 6, 1945

Dear Dr. Milam:

I have just received your letter of April 2. I shall be glad to accept your invitation to luncheon on Tuesday, April 17, and speak informally afterward.

Looking forward to seeing you,

Yours sincerely,

T. L. Yuan

〔平馆(重庆沙坪坝)英文信纸。The American Library Association Archives, China Projects File, Box 2, Yuan T L 1943-1945〕

按:该信为先生亲笔,4 月 13 日送达。

四月上旬

先生覆电匹兹堡大学,告知将推迟访问。

JUST RECEIVED YOUR TELEGRAM SINCE CHANCELLOR BOWMAN IS OUT OF TOWN SHALL POSTPONE TRIP UNTIL JUNE. INFORM DR CHIU AND CANCEL HOTEL ACCOMMODATION MUCH OBLIGED

TUNGLI YUAN

〔University of Pittsburgh Library, John Gabbert Bowman, Administrative Files, Box 2 Folder 13, Chinese Material〕

四月十日

米来牟致电先生,是否参加十七日的宴会请先生电覆。

PLEASE WIRE REPLY APRIL 2 INVITATION TO CLIFF DWELLERS LUNCHEON, APRIL 17.

〔The American Library Association Archives, China Projects File, Box 2, Yuan T L 1943-1945〕

按:该电发往纽约华美协进社。

四月中上旬

先生拜访美国学术团体理事会中国学研究委员会秘书格雷夫斯,恳请其协助获得两本哈佛大学燕京学社《汉和图书馆分类法》。〔《裘开明年谱》,页315〕

按:5 月,先生收到了《汉和图书馆分类法》。

四月十七日

中午十二时许,美方图书馆界、学术界人士在 Cliff Dwellers Club 设宴款待先生。〔*Chicago Tribune*, Chicago,17 Apr. , 1945, pp. 13-14〕

布朗覆函先生,再次表示美国图书馆协会、图书馆收到了大量来自中国各机构求助的信函,而收件方没有能力辨析各求助方的实际情况,建议先生撰写一条国立北平图书馆为何优先需要各类书籍的说明文字。

April 17, 1945

Dr. T. L. Yuan
c/o Chinese Consulate General
551 Montgomery
San Francisco, California

Dear Dr. Yuan:

I have your letter written from the International House in Chicago. The difficulty in the sending out of a letter of this sort is that librarians have received a host of letters from Chinese institutions, societies and organizations. I enclose a copy of one that came this morning. It is almost impossible for librarians to know the merits of the various institutions requesting books. Furthermore, we are receiving many requests from such libraries and organizations as the National Central Library, Central Planning Board and Ming Sung Industrial Company, Ltd.

If the proposed letter is sent out to institutions, there should be some explanation why the National Library of Peiping should have priority in the requests being received. I am enclosing a short note which you may wish to send out with your letter. Of course, you are at perfect liberty to send out the letter you propose without any reference to the ALA, to the Committee on the Orient or to me. If you wish, however, to enclose the attached statement, I would have no objection and, of course, you are under no obligation to consult me on this matter. Certainly, other librarians in China have not been so meticulous.

The three possibilities are (1) send out the letter as you have written it, or (2) send out the letter with the attached statement from me, or (3) let the matter drop for the time being. You will have to decide what step to take.

Yours very truly,

Charles H. Brown, Chairman

Committee on the Orient and Southwest Pacific

〔The American Library Association Archives, China Projects File, Box 1, China Publications for American Libraries 1945〕

按：Ming Sung Industrial Company, Ltd.即民生公司。此件为副本。

四月中旬

先生与美国图书馆协会东方和西南太平洋委员会主席布朗、芝加哥大学图书馆馆长 Ralph A. Beals 等人数度会面。布朗就很多事项向先生征求意见，尤其是中英文双语图书目录的问题。〔《袁开明年谱》，页 311、314〕

按：此次会面可能极为成功，一方面美国图书馆协会东方和西南太平洋委员会对中国采购计划的进展做出了评估，虽然有些书刊因为运输问题遗漏或者延后，但就投入产出比而言，该会认为先生以相当优惠的价格购买了出版物，尤其是在中国国内通货膨胀严重的局面下，难能可贵。此外，先生向布朗提交了一份中国科学期刊目录。

四月二十四日　旧金山

先生致信陈梦家，谈募集资助事。

梦家吾兄：

哈佛燕京社想尚无信寄到，只好听之，以后小规模蒐集可也。

Bishop White 处尚未写信，拟六月初往彼一游，藉可面谈，较为便利。弟在此又移一旅馆，较以前者清静许多。匆匆，顺颂教祺。

弟同礼顿首

四，廿四晚

承转下三信已收到，代洗之小褂可寄此处。新住址 Hotel Stewart, Geary Street, San Francisco, Calif.

〔方继孝藏札〕

按：Bishop White 即怀履光。此信翌日寄出。

四月二十五日

联合国国际组织会议在旧金山举行，先生被聘为中国代表团咨议并列席。〔《中华图书馆协会会报》第19卷1-3期合刊，页13〕

按：本次会议会期为4月25日至6月20日，中国代表团共一百余人，其他咨议有司徒美堂、邝炳舜、施思明、刘选萃、翁秀民。①

四月二十六日

先生致信陈梦家，告知哈佛燕京学社愿意资助其研究计划，并请其代购图书。

梦家吾兄：

昨日甫发一信，即接到 Elisséeff 来函，谓对于编印目录事已允补助叁千元，并将致尊处之函十九日录副寄下，欣悉种种，敝意可先写一信致谢，以后再拟详细计划。七月一号以后始能发款也。兹需用下列各书，请到大学出版部代购一部，告其径寄是感。款请代垫约二三十元，发票写北平图书馆。匆匆，顺颂大安。

弟同礼顿首

四，廿六

Room 630, Hotel Stewart, 353 Geary Street, San Francisco, Calif.

F. A. Hermans: *Tyrants War and Peoples Peace,* 1944

凡关于国际组织、国际法庭，Trusteeship System, peaceful settlement of international dispute, international organization, international court of justice, and all legal institute of judicial organization 均可购。

〔方继孝藏札〕

---

①《传记文学》第22卷第2期，页11。

按：*Tyrants War and Peoples Peace* 准确题名为 *The Tyrants' War and the Peoples' Peace*，芝加哥大学出版社初版。

五月一日

鲍曼致函先生，告知匹兹堡大学将授予先生名誉法学博士学位。

May 1, 1945

Dear Dr. Yuan:

It gives me pleasure to tell you that the Honorary Degrees Committee, at a meeting held yesterday afternoon, voted to invite you to receive at Commencement of Monday morning, May 28, the honorary degree of Doctor of Laws. This action was taken because of the distinguished service which you have given to your country. The Committee was also pleased to take action as an expression of our good will toward China and of our hope that such relationship may long continue. Personally, it gives me great pleasure to send you this note.

If it is possible for you to be here on May 28, we shall be glad to send you details of the occasion later.

With kind personal wishes, I am,

Faithfully yours,

〔University of Pittsburgh Library, John Gabbert Bowman, Administrative Files, Box 4 Folder 23, Commencement, 1944-1945〕

按：此件为录副。

五月十日

先生致信陈梦家，告知行程，并请其代收信件。

梦家吾兄：

前奉廿七日手教，并寄下小褂二件，均拜收。今日又收到书 *Tyrants War and Peoples Peace* 一本。刻下邮件甚慢，请勿再寄任何刊物。弟定廿二晚离此径赴 Pittsburgh，接受名誉博士学位，如火车不迟到则可在芝城停留二小时，俟到站后再行电告；如迟到则不及一晤矣（廿五日八时三十分至九时三十分之间，当有电话）。由 Pittsburgh 径至加拿大怀主教处已函托寄照片，再由彼返芝城，故各地信件均告由尊处收转，请代为收留是荷。由芝再到 Minneapolis 时间不能预定，余面谈。顺颂大安。

弟同礼顿首

五，十

邓先生同此不另。

〔方继孝藏札〕

五月十二日　伯克利

先生列席美国加州图书馆协会的地区性会议，并作为嘉宾发言。〔*The Petaluma Argus-Courier*, 16 May, 1945〕

五月十四日

赛珍珠致函先生，对中国作家在美出版其文学作品给予意见和忠告。

May 14, 1945

My dear Dr. Yuan:

I have been thinking a good deal about our conversation on the morning you so kindly came to call on me, and about your suggestion that I should write out some of the ideas which might be useful to Chinese writers trying to find American readers.

Of course, I feel embarrassment in doing this, since Chinese writers are so successful in their own country, and it seems very presumptuous of me. I can only proceed on two grounds first that there may be some young writers who might be helped by knowing something of my own experience, and second, that I am so anxious that the work of Chinese writers should become known, here in my own country, in order to further the understanding between our two peoples.

For the first, I may say that I, myself, began to write for Americans very much as a young and inexperienced Chinese might begin. I had lived so long in China that I had no knowledge of any other people, even my own, except by hearsay and the acquaintance of a few individuals. It was impossible for me to write about American life. I remember at first, I had many rejections from American editors and I got quite in despair. Only a lifelong determination to write kept me trying again. The usual reply from these editors was that Chinese subjects would not interest their readers. I succeeded at last only by making the characters in my books primarily human beings and secondarily Chinese. I must confess that then I fell under the criticism of some Chinese, who did not like the human beings!

But all that is past. Even the times have changed. There is a real eagerness now among the people of America to know more about China, and the market is open for Chinese writers, even in translation.

I know that this statement will bewilder some Chinese writers who have tried in vain to get their work published in this country, but I think it is true, nevertheless. The market is here and it is ready, but that is not to say that anything a Chinese writes will find publication. We all know that in order to sell anything, one must consider to some extent the demands of those who want to buy. I don't want to put literature on a commercial basis, by any means, but unfortunately what editors and publishers put into their magazines and books has to seem to them, at least, what their readers will want and enjoy. For this reason, I will put down what I think is essential for Chinese writers to know, who want American readers.

1. The casual, subjective, informal essay type of writing, which delights Chinese intellectuals, find little interest here. I do not know why this is so. But it is true that the informal essay is almost non-existent in this country. Americans are not much interested in the internal workings of the writer's mind, nor in his opinions and vague thoughts, especially if these are tinged with a sort of pretentious melancholy. Americans are an extremely realistic people. They like their literature realistic and human. They are non-intellectual, and much of the material sent here by Chinese intellectuals does not interest them American intellectual writing, too, finds little publication.
2. A good deal of the modern Chinese writing is derivative. Modern plays which may seem original to a Chinese audience

unversed in Western Literature do not seem so to an American audience who recognize the source of the inspiration. I have in mind a Chinese play I have recently read, which achieved great fame in China. I hear, but which would be impossible to present on the American stage, because obviously it is modeled after the plays of our own Eugene O'Neill.

This brings me to another point, which is that the whole attitude toward literary influence is different in China and America. In China it is quite permissible, through long tradition, to write "after the manner" of some great master but here it is simply called plagiarism or imitation and is rejected. Originality is our most highly prized quality in writing.

If a young writer is called imitative, it is the most damning thing that can be said about him. It means his own creative genius is weak. It is extremely important, therefore, that Chinese writers create out of their own material and in Chinese ways, not in the least reminiscent of western literature. The western flavor at once makes the American reader feel that the writing is not fresh and good.

3. Another difference between us is that Chinese quite willingly tolerate stories and novels which have no plot, but just begin and go on and then stop. Not so in this country. Americans like their stories with some complication and with some clear conclusion. They like their characters clearly defined, not vague and romantically cloudy, not sighing and weeping and over-intellectualized. If a man weeps, as often happens in a Chinese story, Americans are shocked at the weakness. Men do weep, I suppose, in America, but if they do, it is behind a closed door, and nobody wants to hear about it! Let us say that strong men, such as are heroes in stories, ought not to weep! Clearness in story structure, clearness in character development, are essential

to American enjoyment.

4.Americans enjoy humor very much. Even in very tragic works they enjoy a touch of humor in some character put in for contrast. Tragedy unrelieved is not much read. Least liked of all is the sentimental *Sorrows of Werther* type of □□□.

5.The form which writing can take, except for the informal essay, can be almost anything. There is a wide market for short stories, and if these are accepted by popular magazines, they bring good prices. Articles have also a good market, and many publishers would like to have novels, especially if they deal with the modern scene. Good translations are also welcomed. The market for poetry exists but is small. Short stories are usually about forty-five hundred words in length, but may be as little as one thousand. Two and three part stories may also be acceptable, if material and technique are good. By *good*, I mean human and living and naturalistic in mood.

I do think that American writers work harder than the Chinese writers do at a given piece of writing. Chinese writers "dash" something off-so I am told. But an American will write and re-write, endeavoring to have his work the best of which he is capable. Writing is a serious and difficult job-not at all an easy or casual one. Only the writer long accustomed to his work can, like a painter, knows just where his strokes should lie in order to make the coordinated whole. A good deal of the writing now sent to us from China seems to us, if I may venture to say so, done too quickly and casually.

To sum up, I should say that Americans enjoy realistic clear writing. They like good character delineation, they dislike sentimentality and most of all they dislike intellectualization, especially the sort which seems to be an intellectual pose. Affectation of any kind the American despises.

One thing which Chinese writers might wish to know in dealing with western editors and publishers is not to be personally offended if their work is rejected or if it is severely cut or criticized, and changes suggested. American editors are accustomed to this, without any personal feelings of loss of face, etc. One reason for Lin Yutang's great success in this country is his utter disregard of his own "face". He accepts criticism and suggestion with good humor and a genuine desire to do a job the best he can, without hurt feelings.

I may say that there is no writer in the United States who can expect always to have his material accepted as he writes it, unless actually it does fit the editorial demands of the magazine to which he submits it. At the same time, of course, no true writer will consent to write at the dictation of anyone else. The final judge is the writer, but the real writer wants to know how his work can be improved.

In closing this overlong letter, I might say on the constructive side that any one writing about China in a true, human way will find an audience today in America. Americans are much interested in how the real Chinese think and feel and live. They are not interested in intellectual gymnastics, in false pretentious writing, in imitative writing, nor in writing obviously for sale. But the writer who can dig deep into the real Chinese mind and heart and reveal its essential humanity, without propaganda and without pose, can succeed with American readers.

One more word; the propaganda plays and stories and poems which have performed a real service in China during the war will not be read here. Such writing has also been done on a large scale in Russia, and is really unpopular in this country. Americans feel they do not have the need for such propaganda and have no interest in it.

I feel that there is a great opportunity for Chinese writers to make their people known now to our people. In honesty and simplicity this should be done, without false shame. The Chinese people are so great. After ten years in my own country, I still feel that the Chinese people are perhaps the greatest on earth-I mean, the Chinese common man and woman, the ninety-eight percent of any nation. Their strength, their humor, their goodness, their reality, will win Americans to China, if they can only be made plain to us. And no one can do this as Chinese writers can. I send them all my good wishes, and would like to say that if, in my humble way I can do anything to be of service in getting their works published here, I shall do it gladly.

Yours cordially,
Pearl S. Buck

Dr. T. L. Yuan
Kings Crown Hotel,
420 West 116th Street,
New York City, N. Y.

〔Wilma C. Fairbank, *America's Cultural Experiment in China, 1942-1949*. pp. 210-213〕

按:该函后被译成中文,刊于《周报》(上海)第36期,题为《中国作家与美国读者》。[1]

五月十五日

先生致信陈梦家,告知行程安排。

梦家吾兄大鉴:

奉到十三日手教,拜悉一一。哈佛工作完成以后到加拿大继续研究,弟极愿力促其成。俟到芝面商后,再与怀主教进言。弟定廿五号(星期五)上午八时三十分乘 Chicago and North-Western 之第二十八号车由 Omaha 开来时到芝,因时间太早不敢惊动,且恐尊处有课也。车站为何,弟尚未打听明白,大约 Chicago & Northwestern 必有一站也。明日赴南加往访罗莘田、陈受颐、莫泮芹诸君。本星期日仍返金山。匆匆,顺颂俪安。

弟袁同礼顿首
五,十五

〔方继孝藏札〕

① 《周报》(上海),第36期,1946年5月,页10-13。

按：Chicago and North-Western 即 Chicago and North Western Railway，通译作“芝加哥和西北铁路”。

五月十六日

布朗致函先生，希望先生可以提供一份战时期刊、社团出版物清单，并愿意就联邦能源署计划发展工业图书馆听取先生和吴光清的意见，蒋梦麟表示愿意成立相关委员会用以分配美国各机构为中国图书馆复兴事业收集的书刊，此外，告知先生被推举为美国图书馆协会国际关系委员会顾问。

May 16, 1945

Dr. T. L. Yuan

Room 630, Hotel Stewart

353 Geary Street

San Francisco 2

California

Dear Dr. Yuan:

I have asked Mr. Beals and Mr. Dooley to arrange for a shipment once a month of ＄1,000 for China. The latest report we have is that the exchange was consummated at over 300:1, which is not too bad. I hope you can obtain at list of periodicals and society publications issued in China during the war. We should have at least one copy of such publications in this country. This is one matter we must talk over when you are here.

I believe you know something about the report of the FEA in regard to the development of industrial libraries and the training of engineers and agricultural specialists. I offered to the FEA to compile some notes on the training of Chinese students who have a background in science and engineering for filling the positions of librarians in these industrial libraries. This would have to be done in consultation with you, and possibly later with Dr. Wu, now of the Library of Congress. I also talked with Dr. Wu in connection with the possibility of working out some guide to the reorganization of libraries in China. Should, for example, the scientific and industrial libraries proposed by the FEA be organized as separate libraries or as sections of existing libraries? Anything we do would necessarily be only suggestive and would have to be done by some Chinese scholars and librarians in consultation with some of us who know the background in this country and possibly can advise you how to profit by our experiences. We are following the example of FEA, the report of which was worked out by authorities in your country with the assistance of authorities over here. The matter would have to be handled tactfully.

Dr. Chiang Mon-lin told me last week that when he returns to China in the fall, he hopes to set up a committee representing Chinese colleges and universities which could study the organization, curricula, and location of Chinese universities in the postwar period. He proposed that his committee might also serve as a committee on the distribution of books and publications collected in this country. He proposed that we ask the Academia Sinica or, preferably, the Chinese National Research Council to organize a committee on book distribution at once and then let this committee serve as a subcommittee of his larger committee when and if it is organized. I have acquainted Mrs. Fairbank with this proposal.

There are a number of principles on the distribution of books in China which we can lay down for the benefit of your committee, in regard to the destruction of Chinese libraries, certainly, a library which was completely destroyed would need more assistance in the way of books published before 1939 than a library which has been able to preserve its collection.

There subjects are some of those which we must talk over when you are here, Mr. P. W. Tsou's proposal for a system of agricultural libraries in China will also require some consideration.

I am happy to inform you that the ALA Board on International Relations voted to elect you as consultant to the ALA Committee on the

Orient and Southwest Pacific. This will, in a way, give you recognition in China no matter what happens to the Library Association of China, and will make possible our continued relationships.

When you have your schedules for your travels east made out, please let me have it. There is always a possibility that something may come up which will require immediate action.

Yours very truly,

Charles H. Brown, Chairman

Committee on the Orient and Southwest Pacific

P. S. I have copies of the FEA reports on industrial libraries in China, training of engineers, and training of agriculturists. I shall have to return these reports before you reach here, but I will make extracts of important features.

〔Rockefeller Foundation, RG: 1.1 Series, 200R Box 203, Folder 2426〕

按:FEA 似指联邦能源署(Federal Energy Administration)。此件为录副。

五月二十日　旧金山

下午二时三十分,加州图书馆协会在 Commerce High School 礼堂举办圆桌讨论会,主题为“图书馆在联合国中的角色”(Role of the Libraries in United Nations)。加州大学图书馆系主任 Sydney B. Mitchell 作为主持人,先生、Elena Braceras 女士(乌拉圭国家图书馆)、Octavio Mendez Pereira(巴拿马大学)、Mohamed Awad(埃及代表)、Solomon V. Arnaldo(菲律宾大学)、Antonin Obrdlik(捷克斯洛伐克驻美大使)等人受邀与会。其中,先生作为三位演讲人之一发表主旨演讲。〔*The San Francisco Examiner*, 20 May, 1945, p. 18; *The Petaluma Argus-Courier*, 23 May, 1945, p. 4〕

五月二十八日

匹兹堡大学举行毕业典礼,其间授予先生名誉法学博士、Igor Sikorsky(航空发动机工程师)名誉科学博士学位、Henry Lee Mason Jr.名誉法学博士、Louis M. Hirshson 名誉神学博士。该校学术委员会对先生的评价如下:

Tung-li Yuan, man of highest wisdom, at home in the East or the West, ambassador of good will to this country, the wide world needs you at this hour in its seeking for lasting peace. We confer upon you the honorary degree of Doctor of Laws, with all of the rights and privileges pertaining thereto. ①

典礼结束后，鲍曼校长、普林斯顿大学哲学系教授 Theodore M. Greene 与各位名誉博士合影留念。

按：Theodore M. Greene 发表学位典礼演讲，主题为战后世界的教育（Education in the Post War World）。〔*The Pittsburgh Press*, May 28, 1945, p. 2〕

五月底

先生赴加拿大，参观各大学及文化机构，并与国立博物馆议定合作办法，介绍陈梦家前往该馆，协助整理馆藏中国古铜器及甲骨文字。

六月初

先生访问布朗。〔Rockefeller Foundation. Series 601: China; Subseries 601.R: China-Humanities and Arts. Vol. Box 47. Folder 391〕

按：布朗对先生印象颇佳。另就先生向多家基金会申请资助的这一行为，他在6月22日致信史蒂文斯，认为不应该苛责，而是应该理解，并告先生应该获得了哈佛燕京学社的一笔数额不大的资助。

六月五日

史蒂文斯致函先生，告知美国图书馆协会有可能扩大购买书刊规模，特别是用于协助中国图书馆复兴，但洛克菲勒基金会暂时不能给予特别资助，须等待战局结束后考虑。

June 5, 1945

Dear Dr. Yuan:

May I answer for Mr. Marshall two questions that have added answers since he wrote you on May 7.

Larger funds are being made available through the American Library Association for book purchase, specifically for use in China. I wish very much that you would discuss your chances of special attention by seeing someone in the Chicago office. This money from the government is quite apart from money of the Association used by Dr. Lydenberg for all

① University of Pittsburgh Library, John Gabbert Bowman, Administrative Files, Box 4 Folder 23, Commencement, 1944-1945.

countries in need of special help. The condition of the market and of transportation suggest that you should rely on such sources as the Association both for purchase and for storage, but you will need to give the lists that you wish considered into their hands.

Under all the circumstances I am not able to recommend to our trustees the desired special fund of \$18,000 for book purchase. This means that I am certain this is not a favorable time, but I am interested as ever in your future plans in a permanent location.

We still are waiting to get word from the men who are to write us to support requests for fellowships for your friends from China. I understand that it is to be more difficult for the time just ahead to get releases or to offer invitations to fellows from the Far East. Perhaps this will take a turn for the better before you are back in the east. I hope so.

Sincerely yours,
David Stevens

Dr. T. L. Yuan
c/o Mr. Chen Meng-chia
226 Oriental Institute
University of Chicago
Chicago, Illinois

〔The American Library Association Archives, China Projects File, Box 1, Requests, 1945 – 1948; Rockefeller Foundation. Series 601: China; Subseries 601.R: China-Humanities and Arts. Vol. Box 47. Folder 391〕

按:该函抄送给米来牟、莱登伯格等人。

六月十一日

加斯基尔致函先生,寄送康乃尔大学文学院开设的有关中国、俄国的课程表,给予先生五百美金购书款并委托购买战时中文出版物,并告其赴华盛顿的日期。

June 11, 1945

Mr. T. L. Yuan
c/o China Institute

125 East 65th Street

New York 21, N. Y.

Dear Mr. Yuan:

I have sent you under separate cover Arts College announcements which list courses in Russian and Chinese. Because of present unsettled conditions, the announcements are not so nearly complete and up-to-date as one might wish, but they give some information which may be of interest to you.

Enclosed is a check for $ 500 as a deposit to cover the cost of books and periodicals published in China recently which you so kindly agreed to have sent to us. You know better than I, I am sure, what we should have, but we do need sinological publications and source materials on wartime China, including widely read literary works.

I expect to go to Washington Wednesday and hope to see you there before you go back to China. It was a privilege and pleasure to have you here, and we appreciate very much your interest in Chinese studies here and in the Wason Collection.

Sincerely yours,

Gussie E. Gaskill

Curator, White Library and Wason Collection

〔Cornell University Library, Wason Collection Records, 1918-1988, Box 1, Folder Koo, T. K. Letters〕

按:此件为录副。

六月十三日

先生与布朗制订 Suggestions for the distribution in China of books and periodicals purchased by the ALA, collected by gift by the NLA council or individual libraires.〔The American Library Association Archives, China Projects File, Box 1, General 1941, 1945-1947〕

按:该分发意见仅为初稿。

先生覆信史蒂文斯,此前布朗告知只有在美国出版的书籍才能在国务院的资助下购买,且不能包含有关苏俄以及批评国民政府的书刊,这让先生非常遗憾,希望洛克菲勒基金会能够在平馆有限外汇外提供更多的资助,用以购买欧洲出版的书刊尤其是有关斯拉夫语研究的文献。

My address after June 17: care of Hotel Bellevue, Washington, D. C.

c/o International House
University of Chicago
Chicago, Ill.
June 13, 1945

Dear Dr. Stevens:

Upon my return from Minneapolis, I was glad to have your letter of June 5. I am much obliged to you for the information you gave me.

When I was at Ames, I discussed with Mr. Charles H. Brown about the lists of books which he has compiled for the A. L. A. for use in China. I was given to understand that only books published in this country are to be bought under the grant of the Department of State. The Department, however, insists that books on Russia and materials criticizing the Chinese Government should be eliminated. As they are just the sort of material that I should like to have for China, I cannot very well submit my lists of desiderata.

As I explained to you in our last conversation, I am very much interested in the promotion of Slavic studies in China. Aside from the question of personnel, we need urgently basic materials. I feel strongly that the availability of basic materials in our Library will help promote such studies at postgraduate level.

I have obtained a small grant of $ 3,000 from the China Foundation for books and journals published in Europe since 1937. This amount is, of course, not sufficient to meet our needs, especially in view of the fact that the cost of books has gone up tremendously in Europe.

The memorandum which I submitted to you in March was meant for a long-term project. Whenever you find it possible to recommend a grant, it will be used to supplement our existing sources of support and will meet our special needs not covered by government appropriations. Above all, a gesture from your Foundation will induce the Chinese Government to make larger grants to us in the future.

I shall be in New York after the 25th and shall sail for Europe in July. I hope to be able to see you and Mr. Marshall before my departure.

Yours sincerely,

T. L. Yuan

P. S. I trust you have heard from Pennsylvania and Harvard about the two men I recommended for training in museum work.

〔Rockefeller Foundation. Series 601: China; Subseries 601.R: China-Humanities and Arts. Vol. Box 47. Folder 391〕

按:此件为打字稿,落款处为先生签名,于6月19日送达。

六月十五日

中央研究院院长朱家骅、评议会秘书翁文灏召集有关人士,商组英美捐赠图书期刊分配委员会,设委员十一人,推选翁文灏为主席,先生为秘书,吴有训、周鲠生、陈裕光、杭立武、傅斯年、楼光来、李四光、任鸿隽、蒋复璁为委员,在先生回国之前,秘书之职由傅斯年代理。〔《中华图书馆协会会报》第19卷1-3期合刊,页5〕

六月十七日

先生致信陈梦家,告知行程及通讯地址。

梦家吾兄:

芝城小留又扰□府,感谢无似。临别匆促,竟将旅馆地址写错,请再告校中转信之人,是15 E Street, N. W.为荷。弟定廿四日离此赴纽约,希望在彼可一晤教。匆匆,顺颂大安。

弟同礼顿首

六,十七

嫂夫人同此致谢。

〔方继孝藏札〕

六月十九日

先生致信加斯基尔,附上购书款收据,并邀请其赴国会图书馆看中文馆藏。

June 19, 1945.

Dear Miss Gaskill:

On my return to Washington, I am glad to have your letter of June 11 enclosing a check for $500 as a deposit to cover the cost of books and periodicals being published in China. I enclose herewith a receipt which you may need for your Treasurer's files.

I am writing to our Library to secure for you a representative set of scholarly publications especially those which may not be reprinted after the war.

I am usually at the Library of Congress in the afternoons and I shall be here until Saturday. I hope you will find it possible to come to the Library of Congress and see the Chinese collection here.

I hope you have found a suitable apartment in Washington which is not easy these days. It was a pleasure to see you at Ithaca and I do want to thank you once more for all the courtesies which you so kindly extended to me.

Yours sincerely,

T. L. Yuan

〔Cornell University Library, Wason Collection Records, 1918-1988, Box 1, Folder Koo, T. K. Letters〕

按：此件为打字稿，先生略加修改，落款处为其签名。

六月二十一日

先生致信陈梦家，告知行程及通讯地址。

梦家吾兄：

承转下□君电报，谢谢。顷又接十八日手教，拜悉一切。弟定明日赴纽约，所有尊处代存之刊物，均请改寄下列地址，

T. L. yuan

c/o China Institute

125 East 65th Street

New York 21, N. Y.

并请转告贵校转信之人是荷。弟在纽约至少有两星期，当在该处候

驾,电话为 Rhinelander 4-8181,余俟面谈。顺颂大安。

弟同礼顿首

六,二十一

〔方继孝藏札〕

六月二十二日

先生致电杭立武。

重庆外交部请译转教育部杭次长钧鉴:

承部拨三十万元购置图书,曾请允准代购外汇除孔院长已电中央银行提前办理外,请部文早日送中央银行是盼,下月中旬赴英。

袁同礼

〔中国第二历史档案馆,教育部档案·全卷宗 5,国立北平图书馆经常费预概算书及有关文书,案卷号 11617〕

按:重庆收到此电的时间为 23 日,但应为时差之故。

六月下旬

先生给布朗发电报,希望美国图书馆协会东方和西南太平洋委员会在美国世界贸易公司为中国各大学、机构代购书籍前审查书目清单,国民政府将为此支付两千美金的费用。

WITH VIEW TO COORDINATING EFFORTS SHALL RECOMMEND CHINESE GOVERNMENT REQUEST YOUR COMMITTEE LOOK OVER ALL BOOK-LISTS BEFORE ORDERING BY UNIVERSAL TRADING CORPORATION. SHALL RECOMMEND MAKE GRANT TWO THOUSAND DOLLARS TO YOUR COMMITTEE MEET NECESSARY EXPRENSES, KINDLY ADVISE WHETHER YOUR COMMITTEE COULD ASSIST IN THIS PROGRAM.

布朗收到该份电报后即覆电,表示同意并告知随后将发送正式文件。

AM RECOMMENDING TO EXECUTIVE BOARD AMERICAN LIBRARY ASSOCIATION ACCEPTANCE YOUR PROPOSAL WITH APPRECIATION. PERSONALLY AM HIGHLY GRATIFIED AND HAVE NO DOUBT FORMAL ACCEPTANCE WILL FOLLOW. GRANT IF ALLOWED SHOULD BE MADE TO AMERICAN LIBRARY ASSOCIATION FOR USE OF A. L. A. COMMITTEE ON

ORIENT. LETTER FOLLOWS.

〔The American Library Association Archives, China Projects File, Box 1, Requests, 1945-1948〕

按:6月27日布朗致信米来牟,将两份电报内容寄上,翌日米来牟函复,表示十分赞成。

六月三十日

先生致信 Ernest J. Reece,请其赠予哥伦比亚大学图书馆学院的课程大纲和明年的公告。

June 30, 1945

Dear Mr. Reece:

I have just returned to New York and I hope to call on you soon to thank you for all the courtesies which you so kindly extended to me.

I shall greatly appreciate your assistance if you could send me any outline of courses that are offered at the School of Library Service. I need also two copies of your announcement for the next year, and I shall hope to receive them from you.

Yours truly,

T. L. Yuan

〔平馆(重庆沙坪坝)英文信纸。Columbia University Library, New York State Library School Collection, Series 2 Student Records, Box 65, Folder Yuan, T. L.〕

按:此件为打字稿,落款处为先生签名,于7月2日送达。

是年夏

朱士嘉陪同先生访问美国国家档案馆(National Archives of the United States),会见 Oliver Wendell Holmes 和 Hammer,商洽复制中美外交档案胶卷。〔朱士嘉《我所了解的袁同礼先生》,页90〕①

按:Oliver Wendell Holmes (1902-1981),美国档案学家,1935年美国国家档案馆成立即在此服务,时应任研究部主任。Hammer,待考。后先生募集1200美金从该馆复制中美外交关系档案324卷

① 该文错将此次拜访回忆为1942年,实无可能,特此说明。

缩微胶片，主要涉及19世纪美国在华各使领馆的报告。

先生在国会图书馆遇李璜，本拟吃中餐，但因后者匆忙，只得在馆内咖啡室内简餐。〔《传记文学》，第10卷第5期，页25〕

按：时李璜陪同张君劢访美，拜访国会议员。

中基会在美董事给予先生临时拨款7440美金，其中3000美金用于在欧洲购买图书，3000美金用于购买期刊及运费，另外1440美金则用于平馆在纽约代表的薪水。〔台北"中央研究院"近代史所档案馆，〈中华教育文化基金董事会〉，馆藏号502-01-08-060，页70〕

按：平馆在纽约代表即朱士嘉。[①]

七月四日　纽约

先生致信朱家骅，请在教育部所获中美借款余额下增拨平馆购书费，以便在美就近选购。

骝先部长钧鉴：

此次到美为全国文化机关征募图书，颇著成效，并由美政府专拨美金十万元选购图书分赠各大学，故未便为职馆单独进行。查中美借款二十万元项下尚有未购余款一万五千余元，而八十万元项下亦有余款至少一万余元。除上海商学院三四四五.一七元已承令取销外，尚有重庆商船专科学校（前承令停办）八一三七.二三元，福建研究院三〇〇〇元，闻在停顿中等等。此外，各院校所开书单所列绝版之书为数甚多，坊间既无法购到，故预料将来尚有大批余款。截至目前为止，尚有三十余院校之书单未曾配购。窃念两次中美借款共计美金一百万元，职馆仅蒙大部支配美金二千元，当此书价高涨之际，选购实感困难，且北平收复在即。职馆藏书极待补充，用特再申前请，恳乞大部在该借款余额项下增拨北平图书馆美金一万五千元俾便就近选购，以实国藏，除专电请求外，尚希俯允径电财政部转电纽约世界贸易公司，查照办理，无任感荷。专此奉恳，敬候道祺。

职袁同礼拜上

七月四日，纽约

〔中国第二历史档案馆，教育部档案·全卷宗5，国立北平图书馆经常费预概算书及有关文书，案卷号11617〕

---

① 台北"中央研究院"近代史所档案馆，〈中华教育文化基金董事会〉，馆藏号502-01-02-003，页226。

Ernest J. Reece 覆函先生,附上图书馆学院教学大纲的简述并愿意廉价出售全本。

July 4, 1945

Dear Mr. Yuan:

It will be good to see you when you are able to get in. Kindly let me know when you are likely to be coming.

We shall send you the two copies you request of the current School of Library Service Announcement. As for outlines, the most useful and significant thing would be a set of the syllabi, which are described on the sheet I am enclosing. The prices specified are those for students, but we can give you the advantage of them if you care to buy the syllabi at the office of the School of Library Services.

Sincerely,

Ernest J. Reece

Associate Dean

〔Columbia University Library, New York State Library School Collection, Series 2 Student Records, Box 65, Folder Yuan, T. L.〕

杭立武覆电先生。

美国华盛顿中国驻美大使馆译转袁馆长同礼兄鉴:

已养电悉贵馆购外汇三十万元,部文支已发出,特复。

杭立武

〔中国第二历史档案馆,教育部档案·全卷宗 5,国立北平图书馆经常费预概算书及有关文书,案卷号 11617〕

七月五日　艾姆斯

先生访问爱荷华州立大学(Iowa State College),拜会布朗,商讨战后中国图书馆重建、美国援助图书、中国出版期刊运美等事。〔*Ames Daily Tribune*, Ames, Iowa, Sat Jun 9, 1945, p. 1; *Manson City Globe-Gazette*, Jun. 8, 1945, p. 4〕

七月八日　纽约

王重民夫妇、陈梦家、尤桐、陈鸿舜、朱士嘉、冯家昇、王毓铨、胡先晋、杨联陞在羊城(Yank Sing)酒家设宴款待先生,胡适作陪,并饮葡萄酒。〔胡颂平编著《胡适之先生年谱长编初稿》第 5 册,台北:联经出版事业公司,1984 年,页

1888〕

按:王重民和刘修业来自华盛顿,陈梦家自芝加哥,尤桐来自普林斯顿。王毓铨(1910—2002),山东莱芜人,历史学家;胡先晋(1910—1984),王毓铨的夫人,湖北沔阳人,古物学家。

先生致片孙念礼,谢谢寄赠书刊并预祝王重民协助葛斯德图书馆编写中文善本书目顺利。

July 8

Thanks for the books and periodicals which you so kindly sent to me in New York. They are useful to our work in China. Glad to know that you are asking Mr. C. M. Wang to look over your collection and I hope he can spend longer time with you.

Best wishes.

T. L. Yuan

〔Princeton University, Mudd Manuscript Library, AC123, Box 415, Folder Peiping, National Library of, 1937-1944〕

七月十日

先生乘船离开美国。〔The American Library Association Archives, China Projects File, Box 1, Requests, 1945-1948〕

七月中旬

先生致信 John Marshall,商讨资助中国学者前往美国学习博物馆事业的方式。

c/o China Institute
125 East 65th Street
New York, N. Y.
July 1□, 1945

Dear Mr. Marshall:

With reference to our conversation regarding the possibility of giving assistance to two Chinese scholars to study museum work in the United States, I quite readily appreciate the general policy of the Foundation vis-a-vis getting men out of China at this time.

In view of these considerations, may I venture to suggest another possibility? This would mean that the Chinese Government would arrange their transportation and pay their travel expenses to this country. Upon their arrival here, would the Foundation be prepared to give fellowships to them for one year and pay their passage back to China?

I shall be glad to hear your views in regard to this possibility.

Your sincerely,

T. L. Yuan

Director

〔国家图书馆善本组手稿特藏〕

按:two Chinese scholars 应指傅振伦、齐念衡。该件为副本,右上日期处有修改,或为 11 日或为 14 日,无法确认,特此说明。

七月二十三日　爱丁堡

先生致电陈源,告明日到伦敦。〔陈源著、傅光明编注《陈西滢日记书信选集》(下),上海:东方出版中心,2022 年,页 639〕

按:本日,British Council(英国文化协会)有人前往火车站迎接。另,先生并未如期抵达伦敦。

七月下旬

先生途经苏格兰爱丁堡、格拉斯哥、阿伯丁、圣安德鲁等市。〔《陈西滢日记书信选集》(下),页 643-644〕

七月二十五日

先生致电陈源,告知今晚抵达伦敦,请代联系各方人士、机构。晚九时半,陈源赴先生预订住所,先生仍未到。〔《陈西滢日记书信选集》(下),页 642-643〕

七月二十六日

晨七时许,先生抵达伦敦借宿寓所,后赴中英文化协会(Sino-British Cultural Association)办事处,遇陈源,告此前行程,预计在英盘桓一年,并将赴法。十时半,钱存典[①]来,先生、陈源与之同赴英国文化协会下属图书和期刊委员会,Sir Ernest Barker 为该会主席,与会人员有 Alfred Zimmern[②]、

① 《陈西滢日记书信选集》记作“钱树尧”,或为陈源错写钱存典(字述尧)之字,该书以下有关“钱树尧”者,笔者均自行转写为钱存典。

② 《陈西滢日记书信选集》记作 Alfred Zimmerman,应为编注者误识陈源的英文字迹所致。

Sommerfeld、White、Photiades 等人，请先生作报告，先生略述中国图书馆近况，陈源又稍作补充。十二时半，先生与陈源赴中国驻英使馆，晤傅冠雄、陈尧圣、梁鉴立、翟瑞南、吴权等人。下午一时，陈源在 Cafe Royal 请客，Waley、杨振声、萧乾、先生、钱存典与席，席间 Waley 与杨振声讨论《离骚》的真伪问题。〔《陈西滢日记书信选集》（下），页 643-644〕

按：Sir Ernest Barker（1874-1960），英国政治学家，1920 年至 1927 年任伦敦国王学院（King's College London）校长，1944 年被封为爵士。Sir Alfred E. Zimmern（1879-1957），英国古典学者、历史学家、国际关系学家，对联合国教科文组织的筹建贡献颇多。傅冠雄（Fu Kuan-hsiung，？—1962），字筱峰，河北永清人，1921 年北京大学毕业，入外交部学习，1923 年夏派往驻英国使馆服务，后长期担任顾维钧的中文秘书。Waley 应指 Arthur Waley（1889-1966），通译作亚瑟·伟利，英国汉学家。

七月二十七日　伦敦

晚七时，施肇夔在新探花楼招宴，金问泗夫妇、董霖夫妇、杨振声、汪敬熙、萨本栋、先生、陈源、傅冠雄、郭泽钦等人受邀与席。〔《陈西滢日记书信选集》（下），页 646〕

按：施肇夔（1891—1957），字德潜，浙江绍兴人，清末赴美留学，获硕士学位，归国后供职于北洋政府外交部，并追随顾维钧，时应代理驻英大使职务。董霖，时任驻荷兰大使。

先生致信爨汝僖、何国贵（重庆），谈在渝为哥伦比亚大学购书及在欧行程计划。原信如下：

颂声、驭权吾兄大鉴：

离美以前曾寄一函，想已收到申请由印至昆空运吨位事想已呈部。莫太太应得之薪水米贴等，曾请汇联大陈福田教授，想已照办。又，哥伦比亚大学购书费共国币叁万肆千元，想已用毕。如尚未用完，请速购其他书籍，以便早日报账是盼。弟于日前来英，住一个月即赴巴黎，大约九月中旬可由英启程返国，到印度时大约在九月底，如有要件请随时电告是盼。顺颂大安。

同礼顿首

七，廿七，伦敦

九月十五日以前通信处均寄伦敦大使馆收转，九月十五日以后寄加尔加答总领事馆留交。

〔国家图书馆档案，档案编号 1945-※057-综合 5-025001〕

按：爨汝僖，字颂声，曾任编纂、总务主任等职；何国贵，字驭权，抗战前任平馆西文编目组组长，1940 年 12 月起任平馆驻渝办事处主任。[①]“莫太太”即莫余敏卿，时可能已前往美国。

七月二十八日

中午，先生路遇陈源，遂一同吃饭，谈国际教育文化机构事，先生告于斌在美声誉不佳，因其下属潘朝英私德不济，并告于斌在华盛顿购房产，设立 Chinese Culture Society，并在旧金山、纽约、波士顿等处设立分会。此外，先生对顾维钧的下属颇有微词。〔《陈西滢日记书信选集》（下），页 647〕

按：潘朝英（1905—1987），广东顺德人，北平辅仁大学毕业，后赴美留学。

七月二十九日

晚七时半，傅冠雄在上海楼招宴，陈源、先生、郭秉文等人受邀与席。〔《陈西滢日记书信选集》（下），页 648〕

七月三十日

晚七时许，顾维钧在中华民国驻英大使馆为于斌饯行，潘朝英、先生、陈源、国民党加拿大党部代表三人受邀与席，叶公超、钱存典作陪。十时许，散席。顾维钧、叶公超、先生、陈源等人又谈至十二时，先生对清末以来历任驻英大使之姓名均非常熟悉，并言使馆馆舍为曾纪泽时所买，顾维钧表示该所历史颇为久远。〔《陈西滢日记书信选集》（下），页 650-651〕

按：国民党加拿大党部代表前赴重庆参加国民党大会，归途中路过伦敦。

七月三十一日

晚七时半，郭秉文在上海楼招宴，蒋廷黻、杨振声、汪敬熙、陈源、先生、傅冠雄、谭葆慎、蒋彝等人受邀与席，九时许散。〔《陈西滢日记书信选集》（下），页 652-653〕

按：谭葆慎（1896—?），字敬甫，广东新会人，早年赴美留学获加

① 台北“国史馆”，〈北平图书馆经费〉，典藏号 018000026234A。

州大学政治学硕士学位，归国后曾任武汉大学教授，后入外交部服务，1928年任外交部秘书。

八月二日

上午，先生访陈源，后者约午饭于上海楼，但先生迟到，而另一客 Sir John Pratt 有事，二时即离去。先生与陈源又谈半小时，先生有意撰写曾纪泽传记，对外国史料颇留心搜集。此外，先生告朱家骅有意来英参加教育文化会议，此前报端发表的人员名单并不可信，另谈到吴俊升、蒋志澄在美互相攻讦。〔《陈西滢日记书信选集》(下)，页653-654〕

按：Sir John Pratt(1876-1970)，曾任英国驻天津、南京、上海等使领馆领事。

八月三日

晨，先生给陈源打电话，告在报纸上看到五国外交部长会议报道，王世杰必将出席，建议准备剪报资料以供届时参考。〔《陈西滢日记书信选集》(下)，页654〕

按：《波茨坦协定》中约定由美、苏、英、法、中五国外交部长开会，处理二战遗留问题，第一次会议在伦敦举行，中国代表团由王世杰、顾维钧、胡世泽、董显光等人组成。

八月六日

晚，叶公超约先生一同吃饭并晤谈。〔《陈西滢日记书信选集》(下)，页659〕

八月七日

下午，先生赴中英文化协会办事处与陈源晤谈，告叶公超、熊式一互相攻讦，互相指责宣传不力并有夸大之嫌。此外，先生从使馆处得到消息，王世杰、傅秉常将同来伦敦。〔《陈西滢日记书信选集》(下)，页661〕

八月十三日

中午十二时半，先生赴陈源处，二人同至 China Institute，先生即兴演讲，从战争谈到文化合作，并言英美的东方学研究，特别是英国汉学后继乏人，希望造就很多年轻学者。听者极多，翟林奈亦出席。晚七时，赵志廉在上海楼招宴，先生、王云槐、朱抚松受邀与席，席间谈国内局势，均表忧虑，待日本战事结束，中国前途问题愈多，叶公超未到。〔《陈西滢日记书信选集》(下)，页668〕

按：赵志廉，时应在国民党中央宣传部驻英办事处任职。王云

> 槐,江苏江阴人,武汉大学英文系教授,后在英国驻重庆使馆工作。朱抚松(1915—2008),湖北襄阳人,外交官,沪江大学毕业,后赴英国伦敦大学留学,时为国民党中央宣传部驻英办事处处长。

八月十四日

下午一时,陈源在 Cafe Royal 招宴,Alfred Zimmern、Grayson N. Kefauver、先生受邀与席,忽有传闻日本接受投降条件。席间,先生谈旧金山会议时,美国代表不赞成联合国教科文组织使用"教育"一字,只用"文化"一词,经中国代表特别提出才获保留。此外,先生对国联时期此类文化机构组织秘书处皆是法国人,表示无奈。〔《陈西滢日记书信选集》(下),页 669-670〕

> 按:Grayson N. Kefauver(1900-1946),时为盟国教育部长会议美方联络人、联合国教科文组织成立会议美国代表团成员。

八月十五日

上午九时许,英国文化协会邀请外国嘉宾赴议会开幕大典(State Opening of Parliament)观礼,陈源、先生、陈占祥、陈纪彝、黄翠峰、商素英、周美玉、伊朗外交部长等人乘车前往,十一时,英皇乔治六世亲临。结束后,英国文化协会在 Brown's Hotel 宴请各国嘉宾,后陈源和先生走回中英文化协会办事处。晚六时,先生赴陈源处,同去 Claridges Hotel,蒋廷黻在此举行招待会,客人以联合国善后救济总署各国代表团成员为主,中方人士有李卓敏、刘瑞恒、熊式一、陆晶清、陈甲孙、杨志信,顾维钧因故晚到。会后,陈源、王云槐、先生等人步行离开,但各处庆祝胜利、人群聚集,几无法坐车。〔《陈西滢日记书信选集》(下),页 671-673〕

> 按:陈占祥(1916—2001),城市规划专家、工程师,生于上海,1938年赴英留学,在利物浦大学、伦敦大学学习。陈纪彝、黄翠峰、商素英、周美玉四位女士,依次为妇女指导会副总干事、妇女慰劳会总干事、女青年会代理总干事、军医看护队上校。[1] 刘瑞恒(1890—1961),字月如,河北南宫人,早年赴哈佛大学留学,获医学博士,归国后曾任卫生部次长、部长等职务。陆晶清(1907—1993),女,云南昆明人,王礼锡夫人,1944 年以特派记者身份赴

---

① 《陈西滢日记书信选集》(下),页 831。

欧洲采访。杨志信,辽宁辑安人,燕京大学法律系毕业,曾在四行联合总处服务。“陈甲孙”待考。

八月十七日

下午,先生访陈源。晚八时许,Sir John Pratt 在其寓所招待,先生和王景春受邀前往,陈源因故晚到。九时,三人告辞,乘王景春车同赴驻英大使馆,百余人在此举行庆祝胜利大会,顾维钧、蒋廷黻、桂永清、恽震、连瀛洲等人演说。〔《陈西滢日记书信选集》(下),页 675-676〕

按:桂永清(1900—1954),字率真,国民党将领。恽震(1901—1994),字荫棠,江苏常州人,电气工业专家,1921 年上海交通大学毕业,后赴美留学、工作,归国后任国民政府建设委员会技正,并兼全国电气事业指导委员会主任委员、中央电工器材厂总经理。连瀛洲(1906—2004),广东潮汕人,南洋华商领袖。

八月二十一日

先生致信伯希和,告知自己已在伦敦盘桓许久,并谈预计前往巴黎的时间,期待见面。

20 F New Cavendish Street
London, W.1.
Aug. 21, 1945

Dear Prof. Pelliot:

I have been in England for a few weeks already, and I have been hoping to have pleasure of seeing you in Paris.

The sudden conclusion of the war made it necessary that I should return to China at the earliest moment. So I could not stay longer in Paris as I had planned.

I expect to be in Paris August 29-Sept. 2. I look forward with much pleasure to seeing you and the friends.

Your sincerely
T. L. Yuan

〔韩琦《袁同礼致伯希和书信》,页 131〕

八月二十三日

朱家骅覆函先生,婉拒平馆增拨购书款之请。

守和吾兄惠鉴：

七月四日发自纽约大札敬悉。查第一二两次中美借款均经支配无余，关于贵馆拟再予增拨美金订购图书一节，歉难照办。尚希鉴原为荷！专复，顺颂旅绥。

弟朱〇〇顿首

〔中国第二历史档案馆，教育部档案・全卷宗5，国立北平图书馆经常费预概算书及有关文书，案卷号11617〕

按：此件为底稿，标注"卅四年八月廿三日发"。

八月二十四日

先生致信爨汝僖、何国贵，谈平馆复员事宜并告返国计划。

颂声、驭权吾兄大鉴：

北平收复后所有同人薪津应由中央担任，应请声明原委，将名单呈报教部，以便与其他中央在平机关一并办理。一俟渝方与平沪通电报后，请告顾子刚及钱存训设法接收日人印刷机厂或机器，以便本馆自办一印刷所。此外，并函询顾子刚本馆旧存之照书机Photostat需用何种材料，请开一单寄渝以便在美购置。又，广州何多源、香港陈君葆冯平山图书馆转处均请各寄一函，托其搜集日伪刊物，恐以后即不易得，沪平亦然。此外，应办之事另纸写出。弟大约九月十号左右乘美军用机返渝，过印度不停留，请告舍下。匆匆，顺颂大安。

弟同礼顿首

八，廿四日，伦敦

外汇迄未收到，至念。

〔国家图书馆档案，档案编号1945-※057-综合5-025002〕

按：该信右侧下方标注"三四，九月十三日由城内转到"，应为送达后的记录。

八九月间

先生赴法国，在巴黎盘桓一周，购旧书甚多。〔《陈西滢日记书信选集》（下），页700〕

九月六日　伦敦

晨，先生给陈源打电话，告知已回伦敦。陈源赴先生住处，堆满旧书，先生表示伦敦的旧书物美价廉。后，二人同赴中英文化协会办事处，先生表示已花七八百镑购书，前向教育部申请汇款三千镑，如不汇来，则无法离英，原本计划十日出发，现只能延期，并请陈源与其一同致电杭立武催款。晚，陈源约饭，先生告法国物价昂贵，旅馆每日二、三镑，每餐也需二镑，但中国学生大都过得很好，其中很多人做黑市生意，使馆人员也参与其间，只有钱泰奉公守法。〔《陈西滢日记书信选集》（下），页700-701〕

九月八日

十二时半，陈源在 Cafe Royal 招宴，吴秀峰、杨永清、先生受邀。〔《陈西滢日记书信选集》（下），页703〕

按：吴秀峰（1898—1993），广东人，早年赴法留学，就读于巴黎大学和巴黎外交学院，获法科硕士及政治经济学博士学位，1939年担任国际反法西斯同盟代理秘书长。杨永清（1891—1956），字惠庆，浙江镇海人，早年赴美国留学获华盛顿大学硕士学位，后历任驻英使署随员、国际联合会代表办事处及华盛顿会议中国代表团秘书、东吴大学校长等职。

九月十日

先生赴中华民国驻英大使馆，收讫教育部拨付给平馆的购书款支票，金额为3750英镑。〔中国第二历史档案馆，教育部档案·全卷宗5，国立北平图书馆经常费预概算书及有关文书，案卷号11617〕

晚，蒋彝在上海楼招宴，周宪章、先生、刘圣斌、陈源等人受邀与席。〔《陈西滢日记书信选集》（下），页706〕

按：周宪章（1897—?），字显承，安徽当涂人，海军将领，曾派至英国格斯威治海军学校、朴茨茅斯海军学校留学，时应任军政部副处长。刘圣斌（1910—1956），辽宁绥中人，东北大学预科、清华大学外文系毕业，后赴英留学，时任《时与潮》特派员。

九月十一日

上午十时半，先生访陈源，出示一份有关中国图书馆损失情况的报告，陈源交办事员 Mrs. King 打印，三时方打好。下午四时许，先生又访陈源。〔《陈西滢日记书信选集》（下），页707〕

九月十三日

上午十一时，陈源、先生参加图书和期刊委员会会议。本次会议主要讨论翻译问题，由 Publishers Association 主席及英国文化协会医药部 Howard

Jones 报告。陈源代钱存典提出有关国立编译馆的备忘录，先生则提交中国图书馆战时损失的备忘录。下午一时，杨振声、汪敬熙、先生在 Brown's Hotel 宴请英国文化协会人士，White、Parkinson、Salisbury、Mrs. More、Mrs. Day、Bryans。饭后，英人想听中国话，杨振声朗诵诗歌，陈源请先生用中文演说。〔《陈西滢日记书信选集》（下），页 710〕

按：此后，先生当选盟国书籍中心分配委员会委员，该组织将向各国分配图书，共计约一百万册。

九月二十三日

先生离开巴黎，行前曾致信王重民。〔袁同礼家人提供〕

按：此信应由朱士嘉转交王重民。

九月二十七日

先生抵达昆明。〔袁同礼家人提供〕

十月三日　重庆

下午，先生赴中央研究院，遇梅贻琦，稍谈。〔《梅贻琦日记（1941－1946）》，页177〕

十月六日

先生向国民政府（蒋介石）呈欧美访查报告一份。

窃同礼去冬奉派赴美，于十二月间行抵美国，历赴华府等各大城市，访问教育文化以及政治舆论各界之名流，或个别谈话或公开演讲，就双方所提出之时事问题互相研讨。同时，又于联合国国际组织会议开会之际，奉派参加。本年七月，承顾大使之嘱托，由美转英参加伦敦联合国教长会议图书委员会内之各项工作。又于中途就便赴巴黎、罗马等处参观，至本年九月下旬始得结束归国，所有工作情形，除历次呈送报告外，合再综合始末扼要缕述如下：

(一)对美学术界之访问。单独访问者有大学校长四十人，大学教授七十七人，著作家三十二人，舆论界三十四人，政界五十九人，其谈话大都从教育文化问题入手，比及发生兴趣之后，乃引至政治问题，尤以目前时事为主，关于我国政府当局之处境、困难颇能谅解，虽有若干不感兴趣或情形隔阂者，究属少数。

(二)对美公私团体之演讲。承美国公私团体之邀，公开演讲或于宴会后即席讲演先后二十余次，其尤重要者如在美国国务院文化部、美国学术团体联合会、美国图书馆协会、国会图书馆、哥伦比亚大学、波士顿大学、必珠卜大学、本雪文尼亚大学、芝加哥大学、加利福尼亚大学、加省图书馆协会、司丹佛大学等处之演讲。又于联合国国际组织会议时,在旧金山美国新闻处广播二次,所讲问题以中国之民主政治及中美文化合作等项为主。

(三)太平洋学会会议之参加。本年一月间,该会举行第九届年会时,我国代表团胡适之先生中途缺席,公推同礼代表继续参加,并曾即席演讲太平洋各国文化合作问题,提供材料、发表意见。

(四)中美文化协定之私人商榷。美国人士对于中国问题之研讨兴趣日浓,但亦时有误解,双方知识分子均感文化沟通之重要、迫切,拟议仿照泛美各国间之文化协定以建立沟通文化之初基,交游往还屡曾讨论及此,并承挪威国前外交部长 Koht 氏于赴美商讨美挪文化协定之际,示以美挪、英挪两项文化协定之原案以供我国参考。我国如有此意,似可相机向美政府正式协商。同礼尚采集有其他资料可供参考。

(五)联合国国际组织会议之参加。本年四月,承宋院长之命,聘为中国代表团咨议,协助代表团搜集专门资料,共采得一千余种,并在会外访问各国代表团之学术界人士,取得密切联络,我国建议案内第三款曾列国际教育文化合作一条,即公同商讨之结果也。

(六)美国情报处之访问。此行原以沟通文化为主,故参观接洽亦多属于此方面,但文化所涉及之范围颇为广泛,凡机构虽不属于文化范围而由文化人主持其事者,亦在调查之列,如美国情报处系由哈佛大学 Langer 教授主持,向来谢绝参观。同礼因与该教授私交关系获予特允,观其组织工作之宏伟、研究分析之细密,实属出人意表,其主要之二部分:1.为研究与分析,2.为地图之绘制与复印。世界各大都会都有其情报之采集,所得材料概集中于此,由学者专家按其区域作分部之研究,所得结果则径行送存于白宫所贮。地图尤为应有尽有,比各国自身之所绘制或且更为精确。对于中国与苏联尤为注重,关于中国部分特聘各大学教授分端研究,至为详密,搜集中国日报及新书以及政府负责人之生平事迹及过去历史至为详尽,对于苏联研究则侧重于学术性的纯用科学方法以分析,而研究之所存关于苏联之资料尤为丰富。

(七)美国之捐书运动。英法各国先后派国立图书馆长等赴美接洽征书办法,同礼因亦代表我国相与呼应,美国爰于本年五月间发起全国捐书运动,由学术机构合组联合办事处将所捐图书集中分配,预计可得一百万册,一俟交通恢复,分别运送我国及欧洲诸国。

(八)美国图书事业之联系。国民外交应以沟通文化为基础,美国颇知注重此点,历年对于我国文化事业多所尽力,亦尝属托我国人士宣扬我国文化,以资互换而交益。此次同礼就便接洽并承美国图书馆协会聘同礼为顾问,俾两国图书事业密切联系而中美文化日渐趋沟通。

(九)必珠卜大学之赠予学位。美国必珠卜大学创立于一八七八年,乃美国历史较古之大学,设有中国文化讲座,提倡中国文化颇见成效,于本年五月举行毕业典礼时特赠同礼名誉法学博士学位,因得前往参观并作学术讲演。

(十)加拿大之访问。五月杪由必珠卜便道访问加拿大参观各大学及各文化机构,并与国立博物馆议定合作办法,介绍我国古物学者陈梦家君应该馆之聘,助其整理所藏之中国古铜器及甲骨文字。

(十一)伦敦教长会议之参加。本年七月间在伦敦召集联合国之教育部长会议,事前承顾大使属托同礼前往参加。前此,因我国并未正式参与其事,而分配捐赠之书籍初议以欧洲各国为限,嗣经同礼出席说明中国在抗战期中图书损失之重大,并将备忘录分送各国代表,我国乃获同等分享此项捐书,亦仿美国办法集中分配,同礼并被选为分配委员会委员。

(十二)影摄有关史料。英美法各国所藏外交档案,关于我国外交史者为数甚多,而英法所储敦煌旧藏、西藏文写本尤关重要。同礼业向各该主管机关分别接洽,将各项有关文件分别摄影以供我国政学各界之参考。

以上为十阅月来之工作概略,至于耳目所及,头绪颇繁,其尤堪注意者二点,缕陈如下:

(一)美人对于我国之观察。(1)美国若干年来政府当局对于中国问题虽亦时切注意,但仍不免于隔阂,国民方面更欠普遍,自九一八事变以后,愈感中美之关系重要,而且国人对于中国之认识研究兴趣日浓。(2)美国之关心中国不仅为经济贸易之发展,而且认为政治上有安危与共之关系,工商企业多侧重于前者,而政治学术人士则侧重于后者。(3)美国人士之研讨中国事项甚至比我国人士更为热心,此固由于教育普及、识见深远,亦由于机构完善、资料丰富,人人具有研讨之便利而易引起其兴趣。(4)美人对于我国前途至为关心,例如本年元旦,主席发表之新年告国民书及国防最高委员会通过之第一期经济建设原则,各报纷纷登载,发生极良好之影响。(5)共产党在美宣传不外二种方式(甲)延安英语广播(乙)利用左倾之美籍记者助为宣传,其宣传之资料则除夸张其游击战略、民主政治之外,尤以分田减租、优待佃农一事为最有力量,但有识之士观察较为深刻,窥见其隐,则不以为然。(6)美国人之厌恶战争较任何国人为甚,但有识之士对于未来之世界颇不乐观,故其倚重中国以谋安定东亚之念,实属出于爱国以爱世界之诚意。(7)美人建国最晚,其国民又为集合多数民族而成,故其世界观念至为浓厚,而且今后趋重于此,此与狭隘之国家观念趋向迥异。

(二)我国应如何使美国人了解我国。(1)美人重事实不尚哲理,遇有问题,辄以统计数字为询,而统计数字又为我国之所缺乏,故我国必须注重此点,无论政治经济文化,各种设施总以实践为第一要义,但既已见诸实行之成绩则宣传之技巧亦不可少。(2)美国民主政治之主旨要在民治、民有、民享,实与我国之三民主义暗合,虽其政权久为资本家暗中操纵,以致民主政治之本旨不获澈底实现,但近年已大见改善,社会政策之实施日有进步,劳工、劳农之实力日见增强,我国但能依照三民主义之政策切实推行,必受美人欢迎,尤为两国合作之本。(3)延安方面之擅自增兵,欲假武力以窃取政权,美国人士多不谓然,但亦有若干浅见者流睹其刻苦劳作以及解放佃农等事,辄为赞扬鼓吹,彼固见其表而未睹其里,知其一而未知其余也,今后中央似须加强地方政治之努力,消灭贪污、盗贼、豪滑一切蠹国殃民之障碍,以及烟赌迷信各种不良之嗜好,而整饬交通、生产、教育、卫生、治安,以及城乡之公用设备,使觇国之外人一入其境而即感觉有太平兴国之气象,庶几使抗战八年赢得之国际地位愈得坚凝而长久矣。

以上谨就管见所及略述梗概，所有此次采辑资料因其数量较多，须待交通恢复始克寄回，日后再当译纂整理，择要进呈，是否有当，理合先行报告鉴核。谨呈

主席蒋

国立北平图书馆馆长袁同礼谨呈

三十四年十月六日

〔台北"国史馆"，〈出国留学暨回国服务申请案〉，数字典藏号 001-098325-00001-024〕

按："必珠卜大学"即匹兹堡大学，"本雪文尼亚大学"应为宾夕法尼亚大学(University of Pennsylvania)，"Langer 教授"即 William L. Langer(1896-1977)，哈佛大学历史系主任，二战期间执掌战略情报局研究与分析处(Research and Analysis Branch of the Office of Strategic Services)，对东亚、南亚、中东、非洲、拉丁美洲以及欧洲区域广泛进行政治、文化、社会状况的分析。该件应为誊抄件，钤"国立北平图书馆关防"印。

先生致信布朗，告知邓衍林、岳良木二人赴美进修计划暂时无法落实。

October 6, 1945

Dear Mr. Brown:

Mrs. Fairbank was good enough to consult me with regard to Mr. Den and Mr. Peter Yoh, both of whom have expressed desire to study in American Library Schools.

I am writing to Mr. Den today and have suggested to him that he might as well postpone his trip to the States until transportation facilities between Shanghai and San Francisco return to normal. At present it is impossible for him to go to Shanghai from the interior. Even he gets there, he will not be able to board on an American steamer. He will also have difficulties in getting accommodation at Bombay, as all American steamers are loaded with troops returning home.

Mr. Yoh is now working in the Ministry of Education. If the Chinese Government feels the need of sending him to the United States for further study, he will be sent at the Government's expense.

As a matter of principle, in arranging for fellowships for Chinese students studying library science, preference should be given to those who have never been in the United States before, and those who have made a good record in China. At present, practically every librarian is anxious to return to his home, but due to the lack of transportation facilities, none of them can leave until next summer.

I shall keep you informed about developments here from time to time.

Yours sincerely

T. L. Yuan

Director

〔Rockefeller Foundation, RG: 1.1 Series, 200R Box 203, Folder 2426〕

按:该信于12月13日送达,此为抄件。

十月十一日

王重民覆函先生,谈到平接收馆务、复员的建议及其在美杂事。

守和吾师道鉴:

前天士嘉兄转来九月二十三日吾师从开罗发来手谕,捧读至慰!窃自计算,到今天吾师当已平安抵渝近两周矣。在最近两月内,因不知吾师行迹所至,除寄英伦一信外,又捎渝一短信,但均不长。吾师此次抵渝,想更要十二分忙,盖即准备到平接收,并安插港、沪分馆事务。而最困难者,则为经费。接收要钱,安插与保管亦要钱,不知我政府及基金会,肯十分帮忙否?更念目前旧馆员分散各地,眼前未免缺少得力帮手,生远在海外,每念及心甚不安。此中最要者,似以平馆稍觉辣手,因其中冗员不少,但若说他们在陷落期中,维持保管有功,则不易裁,——裁了亦一时没有人。所以这一个大好"分别"时期,很难为将来大计打基础,总望吾师拿定主意,能作多少算多少。港、沪两方,留人愈少愈好,只求维持,不要再发展。

目前另一大问题,当为接收日本文物与我如何分配问题。不知教部或其他政府机关,有通盘计划否?恐此中最容易引起争端。其在沪、宁各处日本旧有文化机关所遗下之书籍,我们缄口不言,最好。至于北平方面,不论如何,我们应分一些。若是我们不干预沪、宁,最好慰堂等也不要干预平、津。生前信所论联合朋友机关者,即文物不要离开本地,以止外来之争,而朋友机关,则看性质与须要,可商议如何分配也。此事吾师当亦有成竹矣。

国外所闻,我国都似有迁回北平之趋势,则吾馆又有占据重要地位之希望矣。不知慰堂随迁北平,抑仍留南京?如伊亦要迁平,则以后纠纷仍未已。又此次统一之后,实行宪政,则"国会"不久要成立,而且此次成立以后,不论党政如何变化,希望那个国会要与民国同存。因此生想到:慰堂既以"中央"名馆,隶属教育部,我们盍不将来照着美国国会图书馆及英国大英博物院之趋势,隶属我"国会"之下,岂不既免纷争,而我们更直接有所属乎。这是生一时梦想。此事颇长,颇不易,请作为一个参考看,准备我们将来应走的道路。

以下分禀琐事:(1)韩寿萱兄处,已允卜给三百元,但恐尚缺二百元上下,伊别有信,请酌。(2)哥大明春方开班,故陈鸿舜学费暂不用。(3)朱士嘉兄每月廿元,遵命扣下。(自九月份起)(4)寿萱、士嘉、子明诸兄,想回国后开一书铺,大约如大同书店性质,如顾子刚先生决定不办,将来可否由我们大家来继办?(6)查镇湖(字阜西)君交来五卷琴书 film,寄存吾馆,生暂代收,想吾师能同意,或由馆方备一公函,承认接受,更好。(谨将原信附上。)(7)李石曾先生回来,拟商议迁平编辑计划。Davidson 不能合作,愧未听吾师忠告。(8)前有五十美金寄王世圻,转瑞禾;兹闻世圻兄赴沪,该款又转陕西,如再递不到,请吾师代收。瑞禾又要一笔实习路费约三万元,寄至重庆或北平均可,有款时,请汇去一些,生再从此奉还。(9)美档案馆档案,关于中国者,使馆有 130 册,外部训令 13 册,各领馆 155 册,全照 film 约须 3000 美金。陶孟和拟向王雪艇写信,请外部照,而社会所加洗。加洗约五六百元,我们亦可洗一份否?(10)打字机收条下次寄上。新的稍后有了即买。(11)善本书已照一千余卷,下月内定可完。尚未见 Graves,但不久先去 Princeton 编目。(12)胡、赵廿三日赴英,教育会毕会后仍回来。生若不编辞典,则明春或明夏可回国矣。(13)film 机存协和者丢了没有,得信后请示知。将来如何买法,或请外汇,或由罗氏会买,得消息后请示知。(14)生寄存香港之三箱书,(是不是五箱)既与中央书同丢,请列入赔偿单内。(15)子明兄日内可将离婚手续办清,因慧如甚坚,不能挽回也。(16)前寄石曾先生重庆一信,请他把傅维本兄带出,恐他不办。但颇望他能出来,则生回国后,此间一切事情,可托他办也。

受业重民敬上。

十月十一日

〔国家图书馆档案,档案编号 1945-※057-综合 5-016005 和 1945-※057-综合 5-016006〕

按:10 月 27 日,胡适与赵元任从纽约乘飞机前往伦敦,参加联合国教科文组织筹备会。① 王世圻(1901—1980),字可孙,福建闽侯人,王世襄堂弟,1920 年清华学校毕业,赴美留学,1926 年归国任职福建省建设厅,抗战时任西南运管局长,抗战胜利后任上海接收特派员,1949 年去台,先后任台船公司、机械公司董事长。

十月十五日

平馆向教育部呈文一件,题为《呈为拟送职馆组织条例并具说明呈请鉴核示遵由》,具先生名并钤印。

窃查职馆于民国十八年六月由钧部与中华教育文化基金董事会协议合组并订合组办法九条,及国立北平图书馆委员会组织大纲呈请行政院鉴核备案。其馆内组织原分八部十六组,设置员额一百三十余人,历年以来仍依旧贯相沿未改,比及抗战军兴,馆基随平市以俱陷,仅有局部馆员暂移渝昆两地工作。鉴于抗战时期财政困难,竭力缩小范围,今平市既已收复,全部馆务亟须复员,整理所有业务,分配员额,设置自应斟酌。现实恢复旧观,兹经职馆委员会本照钧部最近所订国立北平图书馆组织条例,参酌既往历史现在事实,拟议条例草案十一条,其中纲领悉依钧部规定,惟分组及员额二项,则就战前组织加以修改。查职馆战前组织,原分总务、采访、编目、阅览、期刊、善本、金石、舆图八部,八部之下又分十六组。今拟依照现章改部为组,并将原有期刊部职掌并入采访组,而保留原有之参考组,改名为研究组,取消原有之金石部,改名为特藏组,合诸原有之总务、采访、编目、阅览、善本、舆图六部分,共为八组。研究、特藏、舆图所以特设三组者,研究事项,

① 赵新那、黄培云编《赵元任年谱》,北京:商务印书馆,1998 年,页 281 页。

原于阅览部内附设一组，其后因编纂出版研究参考以及行政机关文化机关咨询事项日增，代为采辑资料或编辑书目逐年有加，关系重要，今后并须继续扩充，故仍留置一组；特藏事项，专收满蒙藏回以及东方语文各项典册，数量繁多，性质亦与善本有殊，须为分别庋藏保管，故于善本之外另设一组；舆图事项，亦因所收中西舆图，为数甚多且有不少珍品，其编目保藏及阅览之方式亦与普通书籍不同，故向来独设一组。以上三组之设置，实因事实使然，此应声明者一也。至于馆员员额分配，战前原有一百三十余人，抗战期间于渝昆两地分设办事处，仅留三十余人，司临时之采访、编纂、阅览各项工作，其留平事务亦已大减，因阅览室较多，仍有职员六十余人。战后馆务视战前已大增恢复，战前百三十人之原额实属事实上不得已，此项数字虽比他馆为高，但念官为事设，员额多少自应以事务繁简为衡。职馆藏书已达一百万册以上，数量为全国之冠，北平向称文化中心，阅览频繁亦非其他都市所可比拟，而且职馆成立较早，国内外文化机关之联系向趋重。于职馆历年编印各项书目、各项索引、各项辞典字典、各项中英文刊物，以供各界需求，兼受公私机关委托代为搜采资料编纂文件，逐年有增。主司人员几于日不暇给，战后万事维新，注重学术，此项联系益形繁重，故恢复战前员额实乃万不得已之举，此应声明者二也。所有拟议职馆组织条例原由，理合连同条例草案及说明具文呈请鉴核指令祇遵，实沾德便。谨呈

教育部部长朱

国立北平图书馆馆长袁同礼

后附组织条例草案十一条。

〔中国第二历史档案馆，教育部档案·全卷宗五，中央宣传部组织法草案、国立北平图书馆组织条例草案及有关文书，案卷号235〕

按：10月4日上午9时，立法院法制委员会召开审查国立北平图书馆组织条例草案，意欲消减人员编制，教育部派参事王伯琦[①]列席。此后，王伯琦分别于10月9日、16日撰写报告，认为平馆作为重要学术机构，不应缩减人员，且现有馆员尚不及国立中央图书馆

① 王伯琦（1909—1961），江苏宜兴人，1931年毕业于东吴大学法学院，旋即赴法留学，归国后历任云南大学教授等职位，时应朱家骅之邀任教育部参事。

法定名额。本呈文极有可能是应教育部（王伯琦）要求而呈。

十月十六日

先生与 C. G. Copley 晤谈，告知平馆此前的缩微胶片设备被日军劫掠，但已设法委托各方开始追索，如果无法找到，史蒂文斯曾承诺将资助购买新机器一台。〔Rockefeller Foundation. Series 601: China; Subseries 601. R: China-Humanities and Arts. Vol. Box 47. Folder 393〕

先生致信史蒂文斯，告知已由巴黎返回中国，伦敦和巴黎的敦煌经卷中藏文文献已被两地的保存机构拍摄为缩微胶片，此前洛克菲勒基金会赞助的缩微拍摄机被日军从协和医学院掠走，平馆将展开追索，平馆馆藏善本书籍完好无损。

October 16, 1945

Dear Dr. Stevens:

I left Paris on September 23 and arrived Kunming on September 27. While in Paris, I was very much impressed by the amount of scholarly work carried on by French scholars during German occupation, and I could not help comparing with what Chinese scholars suffered under Japanese occupation.

The French scholars suffered because of shortage of food and fuel, but scientific work was not interrupted. On this account the Chinese Government recently made a grant of US $10,000 to support Prof. Pelliot's Institute.

The Tibetan MSS formerly preserved at Tun Huang are scattered in London and Paris. In London, they are kept at the India Office Library and arrangements have been completed to have them reproduced by microfilm. Similar arrangements are being made with the Bibliothèque Nationale for reproduction of these manuscripts kept there. After these films are made, we shall be glad to reproduce them for the use of American libraries.

The Draeger Machine was taken away by the Japanese from the Peking Union Medical College, as you may recall. We are taking immediate steps to trace it and I hope to send you a report after my return from Peiping.

You will be glad to learn that our rare books kept in Shanghai and other cities are intact. As they are extremely rare, we shall have to do a great deal of reproduction work for both Chinese and American libraries. So, the need of a photo-duplication laboratory is most urgent. I hope that my application dated March 20, 1945, may be considered by your Trustees at their meeting next year.

Our collection of books on Soviet Russia in the Russian language have been taken away by the Japanese. We are making plans for the restitution of these books.

I shall leave for Peiping early next month, but shall return to Chungking in December.

Yours sincerely

T. L. Yuan

Director

〔平馆（重庆沙坪坝）英文信纸。Rockefeller Foundation. Series 601: China; Subseries 601.R: China-Humanities and Arts. Vol. Box 47. Folder 391〕

按：India Office Library 应指英国印度事务部所辖图书馆，该部门于 1858 年设立，是英国与殖民地印度之间重要的政治、商业纽带。此件为打字稿，落款处为先生签名。应于 12 月送达。

十月十七日

先生致信吴光清、王重民，邀二人回国任事。

子明、有三吾兄大鉴：

弟于上月廿三日离巴黎，廿七日抵昆明。关于本馆组织大纲，正在立法院审议中，内分八部总务、采访、编目、阅览、善本、特藏、舆图、研究，极盼台端能于明夏返国，俾能共策进行。静生生物调查所所址或可由本馆接收，因该所或须与科学社之生物调查所合并为一也。又本馆将与北大合作，在北平办一训练机构，凡目录、版本之课程由北大担任，凡分类、编目及技术课程由本馆担任，亦盼台端返国协助训练高级人才。弟定月杪赴北平，住一月再返重庆，大约须与政府同时迁移，或须在明年四月间也。钱存训君已请罗氏基金会资助，于明秋赴美研究。兹致 Graves 一函，又致舆图部一函，请分别加封寄出。影照美国所藏罕见本事，并希从旁催促是荷。匆匆，顺颂大安。

弟同礼顿首

〔国立北平图书馆用笺。中国书店·海淀四册〕

按：该信落款处残缺，但由王重民抄呈胡适[1]可知写于10月17日。先生致信史蒂文斯，告知傅振伦、齐念衡因公务无法如期赴美学习，但请资助谭卓垣在美参观、钱存训赴芝加哥大学学习。

October 17, 1945

Dear Dr. Stevens:

The two museum curators, whom I recommended last March for fellowships, are unable to leave for the United States, as their services are now needed in China for taking over cultural institutions in Japanese occupied areas. I shall seek the assistance of the Foundation on their behalf as soon as they are released.

I am writing on behalf of Dr. C. W. Taam and Mr. T. H. Tsien.

Dr. Taam got his Ph. D. degree in library science at the University of Chicago. Since 1937 he has been developing the Chinese collection at the University of Hawaii. In view of his excellent training, I am asking him to join our scientific staff as Chief of the Division of Research. He will have charge of our training centre for librarianship at Peiping. Since he has not visited the mainland at least for 15 years, it is desirable that he should be given an opportunity to visit American libraries and the leading American Library schools. On account of his important work in China, I would like to solicit the assistance of the Foundation in giving him a grant-in-aid to enable him to visit the United States before returning to China. The grant-in-aid will cover his travel expenses from Hawaii to New York and return as well as his living expenses for a three-months period. I estimate that $ 900 would be sufficient. If it would be possible for you to grant him a

---

① 《胡适王重民先生往来书信集》，北京：国家图书馆出版社，2009年，页438。

grant-in-aid, may I suggest that you communicate with him at the following address: c/o University of Hawaii Library, Honolulu, T. H.

Mr. T. H. Tsien has charge of our Shanghai Office since 1935, and has been largely responsible for removing our rare books from Japanese occupied areas to Washington. He is a graduate of the University of Nanking and has had more than 15 years practical experience. I should like to see that he be given the first priority to come to study at the University of Chicago and I wish therefore to request the Foundation to consider the possibility of giving him a fellowship beginning from September, 1946.

The proposed training centre will be organized on a graduate level. All general courses of bibliography and librarianship will be offered at the National University of Peiping, while technical courses will be offered by the staff of the National Library. There will be close collaboration between the two institutions.

Both Dr. Taam and Mr. Tsien will be asked to give courses at the training centre upon their return. I shall therefore greatly appreciate whatever assistance you and Mr. Marshall may extend to us in furthering professional training for librarianship in China.

Yours sincerely,

T. L. Yuan

〔平馆(重庆沙坪坝)英文信纸。Rockefeller Foundation. Series 601: China; Subseries 601.R: China-Humanities and Arts. Vol. Box 47. Folder 391〕

按:Dr. Taam 即谭卓垣(1900—1956),广东新会人,图书馆学家,长期担任夏威夷大学东方图书馆馆长。此件为打字稿,落款处为先生签名,应于 12 月送达。

十月十九日

王访渔、顾子刚致函先生,报告沦陷时期北平馆务情况。

守和先生赐鉴:

违教八载,顷获光复旧物,我公不日回平,得以继续供其奔走,快慰无极。九月八日曾电周季梅先生,转请大驾回平,谅蒙入察。本馆兹于十月十七日经教育部特派员沈兼士先生接收复员。凡属三十年十二月八日以前到馆、现仍供职之职工,准予一律留馆;三十年十二月八日以后到馆者,均行即日离馆。接收现款,计伪联银券二十三万九千七百五十六元五角九分(包括罗氏基金及借书保证金等,一切帐目暂时封存,容后详报)。所有事务仍交访渔、子刚暂时保管。访渔等遵即照办,督率同人共维现状,并照常公开阅览,敬候钧座回馆主持。惟此数年中,本馆沦陷于敌伪之手,同人等为恪遵我公临行手示,仍以馆产为重,未敢擅离职守,隐忍于伪组织管理之下,与之相周旋数载,于兹终获重睹天日。现除调赴内地及自行离馆者外,此次留馆职员四十九人,另附名单,伏冀察览。

数年中,本馆图书大体损失甚小。《四库》及留馆之善本书籍毫无损失,由沪运回之中西文书亦均完整无缺;普通书库内关于党义及国家法令以及俄文书籍,伪新民总会均认为违禁之书,于二十七年五月三十一日强行提去三十箱。又静生生物调查所借用之生物书四百六十余种亦未及归还。该所即被敌军盘踞,此项书籍,闻一部份已移存伪理学院。此外,除敌伪强行借阅之书籍、报纸、杂志未能尽数归还者,均不过六七十种。顷已陈请沈兼士先生,将上开各项书籍代予设法索还。此藏书之大略情形也。

馆舍亦大体仍旧,惟大楼书库内暖汽管于三十三年冬季因敌方管制用煤,严冬尚未生火,以致冻裂,一部分尚未修复。西偏发电厂因敌军盘踞生物调查所,遂亦连带被其占据。顷生物调查所与本馆同日接收,该发电厂日内即可收回。派工检查、修理其所有机件,大体亦尚完整。至中海本馆馆舍,于三十二年经伪教育总署强令将增福堂借给伪华北电业公司使用;三十四年春季,伪华北政务委员会迁移居仁堂,又强将来福堂及西跨院迫令迁让,因是此项馆舍已全部损失无存。现亦并请沈先生代向此间当局索还。

至于阅览事务,历年尚无停顿,仅阅览时间因治安关系,只限于昼间而已。全部文卷及原奉部发铜质关防、馆长小印各一颗,经文书组设法保管,完全无缺。北平沦陷八年有余,只有本馆损失比较轻微,斯固文化界之大幸。已略奉闻,伏希垂察。

又沈先生携带爨颂声、王育伊两先生函，已敬悉所言。航寄数函均未收到，未识何故。乞予转达渝、滇同人，并祈代为致意为幸。晤教匪遥，诸容面罄。专此，敬候台祺。

附名单、预算各一份。

弟王访渔、顾子刚仝启

十月十九日

〔《北京图书馆馆史资料汇编(1909-1949)》，页802-805〕

十月二十二日

先生致信吴鼎昌，请协助暂缓立法院公示平馆组织条例。

达诠前辈尊鉴：

日前趋谒，适值公出，未得一瞻颜色为怅。兹有恳者，敝馆组织条例本年夏间由教育部拟订十一条，呈由行政院转送立法院，予以审查，闻已于本月十六日照案通过。谨查教育部原拟之条例第二条及第三条关于分组及员额，仅包括后方昆明、重庆两办事处现有职员人数。今北平既已收复，似应参照战前组织加以调整，而业务增加，所有职员亦须维持战前之数目。业经呈明教育部转呈行政院，将以上两条予以修正，再由该院咨送立法院，予以审查。如万一立法院将本月十六日通过之组织条例呈送国府，拟请暂予保留，一俟该院修正后，再为公布，以免周折。敝馆事业素蒙赞助，用特专函奉恳。敬祈俯允，无任感祷。专肃，敬请勋安。

后学袁同礼敬启

十月廿二日

〔国立北平图书馆用笺。台北"国史馆"，〈教育部所属机构组织法令案〉，数字典藏号001-012071-00243-017〕

按：吴鼎昌时任国民政府文官长兼中国国民党中央设计局秘书长。此信为文书代笔，落款处为先生签名。

十月二十三日

中华图书馆协会举行理事会，沈祖荣、蒋复璁(缪镇藩代)、徐家麟、陈训慈等十一人出席，先生报告以下事项，一为美国图书馆专家怀特未能访华的原因，二为美国对欧亚各国图书馆的援助，三为英国对于欧亚各国图书馆的援助，四为十年来美国图书馆的进步。此后，理事会议决五个议案，一由本会函请教育部特派员对收复区图书损失予以调查并委托收复区会员供给资料;二提升会费标准;三本会经常费自明年起除向教部申请增加补助费外,并请社会部与宣传部予以补助;四呈请教部恢复国立西北图书馆,并请分区增加国立图书馆;五呈请教部拨发磐溪国立造纸学校所产纸张,供会报印制使用。〔《中华图书馆协会会报》第19卷第4-6期合刊,1945年12月,页12-13;《中央日报》,1945年10月23日,第3版〕

按:先生在会上分发英伦教育会议所拟向德、意索取赔偿文物损失办法。

先生致信费慰梅,询问可否将暂存平馆重庆办事处的数箱书籍送往美国驻华大使馆,并由后者安排运往哈佛燕京学社、芝加哥大学等处。

October 23, 1945

Mrs. Wilma Fairbank

Cultural Relations Officer

American Embassy

Chungking

Dear Mrs. Fairbank:

We have stored in this Library cases of books for the following institutions:

Harvard-Yenching Institute 5 cases

University of Chicago 1 case

University of California 1 case

The books contained in these cases were purchased by Dr. Fairbank in 1943 and were stored in this Library soon after he left for the United States.

We shall be obliged to you if you would inform us whether the Embassy would be in a position to arrange their transportation to the United States in the future, so that we can send these cases to the Embassy.

Yours sincerely

T. L. Yuan

Director

〔Harvard University, John K. Fairbank personal archive〕

十月二十四日

上午九时,清理战时文物损失委员会假教育部召开第六次会议,顾树森、先生、鲍扬廷、刘真、张道藩、马衡、闻钧天、金毓黻、杭立武出席，其中杭立武为主席，郭志嵩为记录。〔台北"国史馆"，〈战区文物保存委员会〉，数位典藏号020-050207-0050〕

先生致信史密斯森协会，请其将寄送平馆的出版品以特殊木箱标识，以便中国有关部门分拣。

October 24, 1945

Dear Sirs:

With the gradual improvement of transportation facilities between United States and China, we trust that you are now making plans to forward to China the consignments of U. S. documents and other scientific publications held up by the interruption of communications as a result of the Japanese war.

As you may recall, this Library is the leading research library in China; and before the war we received from your Service monthly shipments of books and documents. On account of the large number of packages addressed to us, we requested you to put all packages for this Library in special boxes, so as to save the Chinese Exchange Service from sorting them out. This arrangement, which worked out very satisfactorily before the war, should be continued.

As soon as we are able to set up a sub-office in Shanghai, we shall notify you immediately, so that regular shipments can be arranged.

Assuring you once more our sincere appreciation of your valuable assistance,

Yours sincerely

T. L. Yuan

Director

〔平馆（重庆沙坪坝）英文信纸。Smithsonian Institution Archives, Records, 1868-1988 (Record Unit 509), Box 1, National Library, Peiping〕

按：此件为打字稿，落款处为先生签名，于 12 月 10 日送达。

十月二十五日

先生致信董作宾，告为其联系赴北美地区从事研究之事的进展，并告即将前往上海,便中将会与开明书店商讨刊印《甲骨丛编》事务。

彦堂吾兄惠鉴:

奉到十月十五日手教,欣悉种切。致顾立雅先生函已代转寄。关于吾兄在美研究工作,弟曾推荐吾兄于加拿大之皇家博物院,该院主持东方部之人为怀履光主教(Bishop White),渠亦久慕盛名,极愿罗致,且年老本应退休,因工作未完迟延至今。该院因经费困难,未能延聘,必须向他处另谋援助,方有具体答覆。俟弟与彼通讯时,当再一托。弟甚盼吾兄将《甲骨丛编》早日完成,如研究所不□□联,则请□□到敝馆□□纂,大约□□明秋方能□□。现因组织□有更改,正在□之中也。匆匆,□颂□□。

弟同礼顿首

十,廿五

弟不久到沪,当将尊稿觅出,恐开明一时亦不能印。

〔中华图书馆协会用笺。清风似友·台北古书拍卖会(2024)〕

按:该信上沿因折叠关系未能拍摄全幅。

十月二十七日

中华图书馆协会撰《呈请拨发盘溪造纸学校所产纸张十令以供职会印刷会报之用仰祈核示》,具先生名并钤印。〔台北"国史馆",〈中国图书馆协会请补助(教育部)〉,数位典藏号 019-030508-0015〕

按:11 月 13 日,教育部批示请协会与该校洽办。

十月二十八日

朱家骅覆函先生,收到参加旧金山联合国会议记录文稿。

守和先生大鉴:

□□□十四日惠书,早经奉悉。承示参加旧金山联合国会议情形,具见辛劳,感佩无似,其时国内正在筹备出席英伦教育会议事宜,因将尊函交由主管同志研究,致稽裁复,尤为歉悚,特复布臆,并希亮察是幸。顺颂台祺。

弟朱家〇顿首

〔台北"中央研究院"近代史研究所档案馆,〈朱家骅〉,馆藏号 301-01-23-770〕

按:此件残破,首有“卅四,十,廿八,航”字样,尾有“亲签”字样,文稿应为他人代拟或誊抄。

十月三十日

十一时半,中美文化资料供应委员会(Sino-American Cultural Service)假中央研究院(国府路)会议室召开第二次会议,杭立武、魏学仁、林伯遵、周鸿经、先生、费慰梅、E. H. Cressy 出席,费正清、陈□庭、萨本栋、岳良木受邀列席。杭立武为会议主席,徐家璧为记录。议决事项如下:

(一)中美文化资料供应委员会之显微影片分配,至本年十二月底结束。

(二)中国科学报道继续编印与显微影片分配工作同时结束。

(三)现代西文杂志论文选继续编印。

(四)请美国国务院继续赠送美国出版杂志,至一九四六年六月止。

(五)协助大学及学术机构订购美国出版杂志并设法代请外汇。

(六)中央研究院设置图书分配委员会于中美文化资料供应委员会之关系,前者为顾问性质,后者为执行机构。

(七)除在美原设之中国文化奖学金三十五名外,另设中国战区美国服务人员奖学金十名。

(八)派遣中国著名学者教授赴美国大学讲授中国文化或文学,并邀请美国著名学者二人来华讲授艺术与科学。

(九)拟于一九四六年或一九四七年在美国举行中国美术展览会,由中国运物品前往展览。〔台北“国家发展委员会档案管理局”,〈国际文化合作——美国〉,档号 A309000000E/0030/640.66/0001〕

按:周鸿经(1902—1957),字纶阁,江苏徐州人,数学家,1922 年入国立东南大学算学系,毕业后任教于厦门大学、清华大学,后赴英留学,1937 年归国,任中央大学数学系教授、系主任、训导长,时似已升任高等教育司司长。

十、十一月间

任鸿隽委托先生携三十万元作为静生生物研究所复员经费,其中二十万用于房屋家具修理添置。〔胡宗刚撰《胡先骕年谱》,南昌:江西教育出版社,2008 年,页 381、386〕

按:后,先生向任鸿隽表示款项颇不够用,因静生损失甚大。对比,胡先骕并不以为然,参见 12 月 26 日胡先骕致任鸿隽信。[1]

十一月五日

先生致信顾子刚,请核对平馆前馆员孙述万所说书款之归属。

November 5, 1945

Dear Mr. Koo:

Mr. Sun Shu-wan resigned from our Library over a year ago. He has joined a coal mining company and will leave for Manchuria soon.

When he was in Hongkong, I asked him to sell some of my books entitled "*Japan's Aggression and Public Opinion*", using the name of the Hongkong Branch, Peking Union Book Store. The profit from the sale of this book and other publications amounts to US $ 60.00. But according to his own story, part of the money belongs to his relative. Please look up your file and let me know the exact amount deposited at Stechert under the name of the P. U. B. S.

Your sincerely

T. L. Yuan

Director

〔国家图书馆档案,档案编号 1945-※057-综合 5-023056〕

十一月七日

吴鼎昌覆函先生,告知平馆组织条例已暂缓公布。

守和先生大鉴:

接奉手书,嘱将贵馆组织条例暂予保留,一俟立法院修正后再为公布。正饬局注意间,适准立法院函请转陈将贵馆组织条例予以保留,暂不公布。经即转陈,奉批准予暂缓公布。除函复立法院外,特此奉复。顺颂文祺。

弟吴〇〇拜启

〔台北"国史馆",〈教育部所属机构组织法令案〉,数字典藏号 001-012071-00243-018〕

按:此件为底稿,标注 11 月 7 日发出。

---

① 胡宗刚撰《胡先骕先生年谱长编》,页 384。

十一月十二日

下午，先生由上海搭乘飞机，返抵北平。〔《光华日报》（北平），1945 年 11 月 14 日，第 2 版〕

十一月十三日

上午十时，先生抵平馆，召集全体馆员训话，并处理接收事宜。〔《光华日报》（北平），1945 年 11 月 14 日，第 2 版；《大公报》（上海），1945 年 11 月 16 日，第 2 版〕

按：此次，先生携来维持费五百万元。

中华图书馆协会撰《呈请恢复国立西北图书馆及分区增设国立图书馆并充实已有之国立图书馆仰祈鉴核采纳施行》，具先生名并钤印。〔台北"国史馆"，〈中国图书馆协会请补助（教育部）〉，数位典藏号 019-030508-0015〕

博文致函先生，告知此前设在协和医学院的缩微设备被日方劫掠而去。

Peiping Union Medical College
Peiping, China
November 13, 1945

Dear Mr. Yuan:

This will certify that to my own knowledge the Draeger semi-automatic microphotographic camera for the filming of books and other printed matter on standard movie film, complete with lighting equipment, and dark room equipment consisting of tanks for developing 200-ft films and automatic water circulator and heater and two reading machines, of the National Library of Peiping was housed in the premises of this College on December 8, 1941 at the time the Japanese declared war on America, and that it was no longer in our premises when immediately after the peace was declared in August 1945 I again inspected the premises. Therefore, the complete apparatus had been taken from here during the occupation of this College by the Japanese armed forces.

Sincerely yours,
Trevor Bowen
Controller

〔Rockefeller Foundation. Series 601: China; Subseries 601.R: China-Humanities and Arts. Vol. Box 47. Folder 391；台北"国史馆"，〈要求日本归还科学仪器及标本〉，数字典藏号 020-010119-0019〕

按：该函（抄件）附在本月 15 日致史蒂文斯、费慰梅的信中，及翌年 1 年 15 日先生给朱世明、杨云竹的信中。

十一月十五日

先生致信史蒂文斯，告知平馆正在多方寻找被日军劫掠的缩微设备。

November 15, 1945

Dear Dr. Stevens:

Upon my return to Peiping, I immediately proceeded to ascertain the losses sustained by the Library during the period of Japanese occupation. An important object which the Library lost is the Draeger semi-automatic microphotographic camera for the filming of books, donated by the Foundation and installed in the premises of the Peiping Union Medical College. According to a letter from Mr. Bowen, copy of which is herewith enclosed, the aforesaid camera is still missing. Most probably it has been removed to Japan.

I am referring this matter to Mrs. Wilma Fairbank, Cultural Relations Officer of the American Embassy in China, in the hope that she would be able to trace the whereabouts of the camera in Japan through General MacArthur's Headquarters in Tokyo.

I shall write more fully by next mail.

Yours sincerely,

T. L. Yuan

Director

〔平馆（北平）英文信纸。Rockefeller Foundation. Series 601: China; Subseries 601.R: China-Humanities and Arts. Vol. Box 47. Folder 393〕

按：此件为打字稿，落款处为先生签名，于 1946 年 1 月 10 送达。

先生致信费慰梅，恳请其协助向日本追讨缩微设备。

November 15, 1945

Dear Mrs. Fairbank:

Upon my return to Peiping, I immediately proceed to ascertain the losses sustained by the Library during the period of Japanese occupation. An important object which the Library lost is the Draeger semi-automatic microphotographic camera for the filming of books, donated by the Foundation and installed in the premises of the Peiping Union Medical College. According to a letter from Mr. Bowen, copy of which is herewith enclosed, the aforesaid camera is still missing. It is learned that it had already been removed to Japan for military use.

We would be very grateful to you if you could take the matter up with General MacArthur's Headquarters in Tokyo in an effort to trace the whereabouts of the aforesaid camera in Japan.

As we are to film books and newspapers for American Libraries, we are in urgent need of the camera. It would be gratefully appreciated if the American authorities could assist us in its return to the rightful owner.

For identification purposes, we are also enclosing a reprint describing the camera in question.

Yours sincerely,

Director

〔平馆(北平)英文信纸。Rockefeller Foundation. Series 601: China; Subseries 601.R: China-Humanities and Arts. Vol. Box 47. Folder 391〕

按:此为抄件。

十一月中旬

教育部长朱家骅赴北平视察,为接收平伪组织设立的各专科及大学,决定设立学生补习班,并设置顾问委员会负责规划,函聘陈垣、陆志韦、李麟玉、沈兼士、何基鸿、张伯谨、萧一山、陈福田、先生为委员。〔《大公报》(重庆),1945 年 11 月 17 日,第 3 版〕

按:此外,还聘请邓以蛰、张准、郑天挺、张佛泉等人任各分班主任。

十一月十六日

先生与平馆留守且仍在在职同仁摄一合影。〔"欢迎袁馆长回馆摄影"相片〕

十一月十九日

先生呈文教育部,报告接收平馆大致情况。

同礼前奉部令接收国立北平图书馆,遵即来平,于本月十三日上午十时到馆办理接收事宜。经视察所及得悉,本馆藏书仅有二十七年五月三十一日经伪新民会强行提去政府出版品及俄文书籍一部份,除已函达北平市市党部请予清理归还外,其他留平之善本图籍、《四库全书》及普通中西文图书均幸无残佚毁损,房舍器物亦尚完好。一面督饬留平员司力加整理,俾能早复旧观,再图积极发展,用以上副钧长推行教育文化事业之盛意。所有接收本馆大概情形理合具文呈复,伏乞鉴核备案,实为公便。再,本馆前于二十年四月奉发国字三一三八号铜质关防及馆长小印各一方,沦陷期内经主管员司慎密保管,未被敌伪毁损。本文系在平馆缮呈,故仍盖用旧关防,合并呈明。谨呈教育部。

〔《北京图书馆馆史资料汇编(1909-1949)》,页806-809〕

按:"新民会强行提去政府出版品及俄文书籍",应在1938年5月23日,数量为30箱。① 收到此呈文后,翌年1月12日,教育部令该件准予备案。

十一月二十日

中美文化资料供应委员会致函先生,请出席该委员会第三次会议。

敬启者,本委员会第三次会议订于本月二十七日(星期二)上午十一时假国府路中央研究院举行,继续商讨中美文化合作事宜,特缄奉达,至祈届时拨冗出席,是所企盼。此致

袁委员守和

中美文化资料供应委员会启

十一月廿日

〔中美文化资料供应委员会用笺。国家图书馆档案,档案编号1945-※045-外事4-001006〕

按:该件右下方有批注"三四,十二月十日由城内交到",应为先生笔迹,其"城内"应指北平,特此说明。

十一月二十一日②

先生致信钱存训,请其转告徐森玉在南京时访查平馆被日寇掠走的藏书、舆图,并设法收回。

---

① 台北"中央研究院"近代史研究所档案馆,〈中华教育文化基金董事会〉,馆藏号502-01-08-068,页117-118。

② 此信被《北京图书馆馆史资料汇编(1909-1949)》错系为1942年,实无可能。

存训先生大鉴：

兹阅南京伪行政院文物保管委员会三十年《年刊》第一五页，载故宫博物院南京保存库移管之文物，有旧工程参考图书馆藏书十四箱（一二箱开箱排架），旧工程参考图书馆地图类十五箱（全部开箱排架），又一四页载旧工程参考图书馆藏地测图约四千种（假目录系作三千九百种），旧工程参考图书馆挂绘图约一千九百种（此两项系与第一五页所载之地图原注参见）。此当系本馆之物，未识徐森玉先生在京时曾见及否？遇机会时请转告，设法收回为要。另有致周连宽先生函一件，请代寄。专此，顺候台祺。

袁同礼顿首

十一，廿一

〔国立北平图书馆用笺。国家图书馆档案，档案编号 1947-※010-年录 6-006001 和 1947-※010-年录 6-006002〕

按："南京伪行政院文物保管委员会三十年《年刊》"即《行政院文物保管委员会年刊（民国三十年）》，其中"第一章本会之成立"下"三、移交接收情形"第 14、15 页有先生在信中所说之记录。周连宽（1905—1998），广东潮州人，图书馆学家，时应任上海市立图书馆馆长。此信为文书代笔，落款处为先生签名。

十一月三十日

中午，韩振华在泰丰楼设宴，先生、王昭贤、张伯驹、梅贻琦等人与席。〔《梅贻琦日记（1941-1946）》，页 186〕

按：韩振华时任北平盐业银行行长。

十一月

先生作为政府代表接收北京大学图书馆，并暂代馆长之职。〔栾伟平《木犀轩藏书的整理、编目与书目出版》〕

按：不久，先生即聘请余光宗担任秘书主任，12 月底后者到校任职。翌年 8 月毛准就任该校图书馆馆长前，馆务均由先生代理。

十二月一日

先生致信爨汝僖，告知复员费用及请来平人员酌情携带后方出版物。

颂声先生大鉴：

兹寄上陈福田、李济之中央研究院转、尹石公中央圕等人收据，请归账或转寄。部款二千万元,领到后以五百万元暂留本馆,其余一千五百元设法交中央银行汇平,如汇兑仍不通即请令王育伊君携带来平。如王君因事不能即来,可令张全新来平,其机位请教部总务司第二科函行政院核准。俟部函发出后,再函陈克文君参事予一优先机位,并将后方出版之刊物选其重量较轻者,按公物航运办法交其携平。公物航运可十公斤至十五公斤(由沪航空运平每公斤法币二千七百元)。又王念伦君亟盼有中央各机关名称及关于公文程式之书及会计章则,俾能便利办公,并希检寄为盼。专此,顺候台祺。

弟袁〇〇

附收据三纸。

温源宁函一件、王育伊函二件,分别转交

lettres, sciences et arts, supplément hebdomadaire

(此为法国大使馆出版之期刊,馆中如尚未备,请即函索。)

〔国家图书馆档案,档案编号 1945-※057-综合 5-024006 和 1945-※057-综合 5-024007〕

按:"一千五百元"应为"一千五百万元"。张全新(1913—1984),生于吉林市,后入哈尔滨工业大学读书,精通俄文,笔名"铁弦",1944 年入平馆工作。① 此件为文书誊缮稿,但补语"lettres, sciences et arts, supplément hebdomadaire(此为法国大使馆出版之期刊,馆中如尚未备,请即函索)"为先生亲笔。

十二月二日

下午二时半,北平图书馆协会假平馆召开光复后第一次会员大会,百余人到场。松坡图书馆馆长叶景华为会议主席,平馆西文编目组组长李锺履任司仪和记录。首由主席致辞,次由先生报告后方及欧美图书馆事业情况,继由李锺履报告本会目前应办事宜,一为会员登记,二为会所借用南池子政治学会,三位调查各馆损失,四为恢复馆际互借办法,五为通告书业公会转告书商请其拒绝收买公共图书馆旧藏书籍并随时报告本会会员,六为函请北平市政府扩充市立图书馆并多设分馆,七为函请教育局嘱本市中小学增设图书馆。讨论结束后推举本会临时负责人,由各图书馆派一人。〔《中

① 戈宝权《老友铁弦》,《人民日报》,1985 年 1 月 22 日,第 8 版。

华图书馆协会会报》第19卷第4-6期合刊,1945年12月,页9;《光华日报》(北平),1945年12月1日,第2版〕

十二月六日

下午,梅贻琦来访,与先生晤谈。〔《梅贻琦日记(1941-1946)》,页188〕

某记者来访,请先生谈平馆文献损失概况及欧美考察印象。〔《世界日报》,1945年12月7日,第2版〕

按:先生表示除被新民会运走书籍三十余箱外,平馆所幸并无大的遗失;图书馆事业发展今后要以引导大量读者来馆阅读为最重要的职责,美国图书馆事业值得中国学习。

先生致信爨汝僖,复员费用及在美购书费用可用电汇不必由来平馆员携带。

颂声先生大鉴:

前寄两函想均寄到,现在渝平汇兑已通,教育部发下之款,请不必派人送来,可先拨壹千伍百万元交由中央银行电汇,既省时间又较派人所用旅费为廉。美国购书费前拟请傅孟真先生便中带来,兹以汇兑既通,亦无须托带,请由中央银行汇平贰百万元为要。闻故宫博物院追加预算书年内可以成立,本馆预算亦应呈请追加,可先向徐科长一询为盼。专此,顺候台祺。

弟袁〇〇

十二月六日

〔国家图书馆档案,档案编号1945-※057-综合5-024004和1945-※057-综合5-024005〕

按:此件为文书誊写稿,后附先生铅笔草拟之要点,因内容一致,不再赘述。

十二月七日

晚,韩振华设家宴,李莲普、傅铜、邝寿堃为主,先生、梅贻琦为客,饭后谈甚久始散。〔《梅贻琦日记(1941-1946)》,页188〕

按:李莲普、傅铜、邝寿堃、梅贻琦皆为韩耀曾女婿。

十二月八日

中午,先生、张庭济在故宫博物院招宴,梅贻琦、吕文贞①、张伯谨、Meslin少

---

①《梅贻琦日记(1941-1946)》此处只记"吕",未注全名,另根据《梅贻琦传稿》(页74)得悉此人姓名,但该书将此日之事记作12月7日,笔者根据《梅贻琦日记(1941-1946)》归于8日,特此说明。

校、何基鸿受邀与席,谈故宫博物院接收问题。〔《梅贻琦日记(1941-1946)》,页188〕

按:吕文贞(1909—1995),字石如,河北人,将领,时应任华北受降区北平前进指挥所主任。其中,梅贻琦因应李宗仁之公宴而晚来。

十二月十二日

上午十一时许,先生搭乘英国首相私人代表魏亚特(Adrian Carton de Wiart)及驻华英大使薛穆夫人飞机南下上海。〔《世界日报》,1945年12月13日,第1版〕

按:魏亚特(1880-1963),英国陆军中将,曾随丘吉尔出席开罗会议。

十二月十六日

先生抵达南京。〔孔夫子旧书网(https://book.kongfz.com/0/83197669/)〕

十二月十七日

先生赴上海。

先生致信柳诒徵,请其在南京代为留意工程参考图书馆藏书、内阁大库舆图去向。

翼谋先生尊鉴:

日昨来京,本拟前来拜访,适接沪电嘱即返申,匆匆离京,未及一望颜色,至以为怅。兹附上敝馆公函一件,如荷于清点藏书时特予注意,至为感荷。专此,敬候道祺。

弟袁同礼顿首

十二,十七

上海宝庆路十七号。

〔孔夫子旧书网(https://book.kongfz.com/0/83197669/)〕

十二月十九日

史蒂文斯覆函先生,请先生继续寄来相关数据信息以便考虑照相复制(缩微)实验室的申请,随函附留学申请表两份,请候选人填好尽快寄来,但须等到1946年秋才有可能实现。

December 19, 1945

Dear Dr. Yuan:

Your two letters dated October 16 and 17 present useful information. When data are at hand regarding the operative basis for a photographic laboratory, please send them to us.

We now are taking measures to secure the essential fact on the two men proposed for fellowships in the field of library science, presumably to begin work in the autumn of 1946. The appropriate blanks are enclosed for dispatch to us as soon as convenient, but any action will be impossible until after a visit to the field by an officer. This may not occur until the autumn of 1946.

Sincerely yours,
David H. Stevens
Director for the Humanities

〔Rockefeller Foundation. Series 601: China; Subseries 601.R: China-Humanities and Arts. Vol. Box 47. Folder 391〕

按:该函以航空信方式寄送重庆沙坪坝,并抄送 Balfour。随函附有空白的申请表。

十二月二十日

杭立武致函先生,询问美国教育总署是否曾函聘各国专家从事远东各国国情研究和编译。

守和吾兄惠鉴:

七月廿二日令弟志仁兄由美来缄,谓美国政府自一九四二年在其教育总署内聘有远东教育专家从事远东各国国情及状况之总和研究及编译,并建议由本部遴派专家参加,惟经美国大使馆文化专员费正清夫人(Mrs. Fairbank)函询美国教育总署,据复并无是项设置。吾兄返国未久,在美想或有所闻,即祈函示为感。耑此,顺颂时绥。

弟杭立〇

〔台北"国家发展委员会档案管理局",〈国际文化合作——美国〉,档号 A309000000E/0030/640.66/0001〕

按:10 月 12 日,岳良木奉教育部指令联系费慰梅询问该事原委,

16 日后者致信美国国务院，11 月 28 日收到 11 月 8 日覆函告知并无此说。岳良木得悉后即向教育部签呈报告，12 月 1 日杭立武批示"函询袁守和馆长"。此件为底稿，标记 20 日发出。

十二月二十七日

先生由上海出发乘飞机前往重庆。〔《光华日报》(北平)，1946 年 1 月 6 日，第 4 版〕

十二月二十八日　重庆

先生致信胡适，谈收购善本古籍事，希望可以获得美方支援。

适之先生著席：

战事结束以来，故家文物纷纷散出，除海源阁已收归国有外，正在接洽中者尚有傅沅叔、伦哲如在平，潘明训、刘晦之、刘翰怡及潘氏滂喜斋均在沪。目前沪上之房租地产均按美金或金条计算，潘明训名宗周去世后屡闹家务，各支主张分书析产，尤有提前收购之必要。渠家索价美金五六万元，虽力请政府设法，但宋院长对于文化事业之赞助似尚不如庸之先生。故甚盼美方可以给予少许至少三万美金之援助，则在国内进行较易办理。除在沪时曾奉上一电外，兹又奉上致 Stevens 先生电稿副本及说明一纸，仍希相机进行，不胜感盼。专此，敬候道祺。

同礼叩上

十二，廿八，重庆

〔中美文化资料供应委员会(重庆曹家岩求精中学内)用笺。〕

按：刘体智(1879—1963)，字晦之，安徽庐江人，清淮军将领、四川总督刘秉璋第四子，曾任中国实业银行董事、上海分行总经理，著名藏书家。信中附致史蒂文斯电文及说明，内容如下，

Dr. David H. Stevens:

Postwar China witnessing dispersal of valuable private libraries. For the sake of scholarship immediate steps should be taken to acquire these library treasures valuing at one hundred thousand US dollars. Chinese Government already pledged half and has purchased the famous Yang Family Library for the National Library. The Pan and Liu Family Libraries in Shanghai are now in the process of dispersing. Would the Foundation be able to assist in this cause by contributing fifty thousand US dollars? Please consult Mr. Jayne of Metropolitan Museum who knows the situation here. Suggest photoduplication laboratory set up in Shanghai to film Pan and Liu collections for American libraries if the Foundation could finance it. Appreciate cable reply 17 Route Pottier Shanghai.

Tungli Yuan

Chinese Incunabula in the Pan Family Library

Chinese incunabula, or books printed in the Sung Dynasty, included books published before 1280 A. D. They form the pride of any Chinese bibliophile not only because they are the earliest specimens indispensable for textual criticism, but also for the fact that the art of printing reached its climax during this period-the penmanship, carving work and the quality of paper and ink far surpass those of later periods. Even single leaves of Sung editions are highly treasured by book lovers.

Among the modern book collectors one of the most noted is Mr. Pan Tsung-chou of Nan-hai, Kwangtung, who worked in the Shanghai Municipal Council for many years. During thirty years of active collecting, he concentrated his efforts to the acquisition of Sung editions. His private library was known as Pao Li Tang named after the Sung edition of Li-Chi Cheng-I published by Huang Tang of the Southern Sung Dynasty. The library rivals that of Huang Pei-lieh, the most famous collector of Chinese incunabula in modern history. As a matter of fact, many of the books in the Pan family collection can be traced to Huang Pei-lieh's Pei Sung I Ch'an, "a market-place of hundred Sung editions", which has long been considered as a unique landmark in the history of Chinese book-collecting.

According to the Annotated Catalogue of the Sung Editions of Pao Li Tang, the library consists of 107 Sung editions besides six

Yuan editions. All of them are first editions and beautifully printed.

〔《胡适遗稿及秘藏书信》第 31 册，页 640－641；台北胡适纪念馆，档案编号 HS-JDSHSC-1636-009、HS-JDSHSE-0393-015〕

先生致信朱家骅，告平馆收购海源阁残存旧藏书价仍未商妥，请教育部电“存海学社”有关股东，并申请外汇以便赴美时为平馆采购书刊。

骝先部长钧鉴：

海源阁藏书收归国有，股东方面希望甚奢，故截至目前止，书价尚有问题，兹代拟电稿致股东代表，表示书价不能再增，倘荷同意，即希拍发，不胜感盼。又同礼拟乘赴美之便，为北平图书馆采购图书，拟购外汇美金二万元，奉上呈文。即希迅予批准，以便价购，无任盼祷。专此，敬候道祺。

职袁同礼拜启

十二，廿八

附电告及呈文各一件。

〔中国第二历史档案馆，教育部档案·全卷宗 5，国立北平图书馆经常费预概算书及有关文书，案卷号 11617(2)〕

按：此前，行政院院长宋子文视察平津，曾与时任天津市长的张廷谔商议，并商请“存海学社”股东同意，将海源阁残存旧藏 92 种 1207 册作价 1500 万元收归国有，交平馆收藏，并在馆内辟专室纪念。

十二月二十九日

先生向教育部呈文一件，请迅速陈请行政院拨付北平馆务经常费、临时费，以解燃眉之急。

查本馆北平部份经、临各费自太平洋战事发生后即奉令停拨，旋由伪华北政务委员会派周作人主持馆务，留平保管人则处境艰危，仅能在可能范围内尽力维持。曾密饬总务部主任王访渔及编纂顾子刚率同保管人员留守监护、相机应付。数载以来，该留守人员虽经敌伪再三压迫，仍忍辱负重、艰苦支持，存平图籍赖以无恙。现北平馆务已于本年十月十七日由钧部特派员沈兼士予以接收，并将伪组织时代所用职员一律解聘，事变前任用之职员六十三人则仍继续供职。职于十一月十二日返平，当即到馆接收，视察所及，见馆藏书及舍均无任何损失。惟复员伊始经费无着，员工生活急待救济，所需经、临各费实难再缓。爰将北平部份本年九月至十二月份之全部馆经、临各费核实、编制追加概算书，拟请俯念事关战时紧急措施，可否转陈行政院，特准以紧急命令拨付，俾便转汇北平，以应急需。是否有当，理合检同概算二份，具文呈请鉴核。伏乞迅赐核转批示遵行，实为德便。谨呈

教育部部长朱

国立北平图书馆馆长袁同礼

三十四年十二月廿九日

〔《北京图书馆馆史资料汇编(1909-1949)》，页 812-813〕

按：此件为文书所拟之底稿，先生删改甚多。

十二月三十一日

中午，顾颉刚来访，先生告知其留存北平书物现状。〔《顾颉刚日记》卷 5，页 578〕

十二月

平馆复员后，因馆中书库不敷用，欲借静生研究所房屋。先生致信任鸿隽、中基会，请代为从中说项。〔《胡先骕先生年谱长编》，页 386〕

是年冬

艾克借阅平馆馆藏《国华》，后放置于德国使馆内，被封查。经先生证明，方得归还。〔台北"国史馆"，〈德国杂卷(五)〉，数位典藏号 020-042399-0008〕

北京大学图书馆设立编目委员会，由先生、余光宗、赵万里、周祖谟、孙楷第组成，并由赵万里、周祖谟具体指导李盛铎藏书的整理与编目。〔栾伟平《木犀轩藏书的整理、编目与书目出版》〕

一九四六年　五十二岁

一月二日　重庆

清理战时文物损失委员会假教育部召开第八次会议，张道藩、梁思成、先生、张政烺、傅斯年、陈训慈、朱家骅、顾树森出席，杭立武为会议主席，郭志嵩为记录。〔台北"国史馆"，〈战区文物保存委员会〉，数位典藏号 020-050207-0050〕

先生致信史密斯森协会，就太平洋战争前遗失的六箱书籍，请该会考虑重新寄送平馆。

January 2, 1946

Dear Sirs:

On October 8, 1941, the U. S. Government Despatch Agency at 45 Broadway, New York City, informed us that 6 cases of books weighing 1, 093 lbs. were sent to Shanghai from New York per M/S "Sea Witch". It was consigned to Mr. T. H. Tsien of our Shanghai Office at Room 404 National City Bank Building, 45 Kinkiang Road, Shanghai.

On December 5, 1941 we were informed by the American President Lines to the effect that owing to existing conditions in Pacific, M/S "Sea Witch" was not able to proceed to Shanghai and all cargo to Shanghai will be discharged at Manila. Copy of its letter is herewith enclosed for your information.

We are writing to the American President Lines at Shanghai about the fate of the 6 cases of books in question. But in view of the terrible destruction at Manila, we seriously question the possibility of being able to locate the cargo.

In view of these considerations, we wonder whether it would be possible for you to arrange to supply the books contained in these 6 cases. As you keep a record of every case sent out from Washington, we trust you will be able to find out the titles of books and documents contained therein. While you may not be able to supply all of them, we hope you will be able to acquire a number of them for us.

With renewed thanks,

Yours truly

T. L. Yuan

Director

〔平馆(重庆沙坪坝)英文信纸。Smithsonian Institution Archives, Records, 1868-1988 (Record Unit 509), Box 1, National Library, Peiping〕

按:此件为打字稿,先生对信文有略微改动,落款处为先生签名,附证明、John Carey 致钱存训信两页,于1月25日送达。

一月三日

先生致信史密斯森协会,告知平馆上海办事处地址,请将美国政府出版物及其他寄送平馆的书籍优先发送。

January 3, 1946

Dear Sirs:

Under the date of October 24, 1945, we advised that you put all packages of books intended for this Library in special boxes, so as to facilitate their delivery in China.

We have established a sub-office at Shanghai to which all cases of books and documents should hereafter be sent. The full address is as follows:

Shanghai Office
National Library of Peiping
17 Route Pottier
Shanghai, China.

We have received notification from the Librarian of Congress stating that this Library has been added as a depository for a full set of U. S. Government documents beginning from January 1945. We trust you have been duly informed regarding this matter.

As soon as you are able to arrange priority for the shipment of books and documents to China, we hope that those intended for our Library could be included in the shipment, so that Chinese and western scholars in Peiping would be able to consult them after eight years of Japanese occupation and blockade.

Thanking you once more for your valuable assistance,

Yours truly

T. L. Yuan

Director

〔平馆(重庆沙坪坝)英文信纸。Smithsonian Institution Archives, Records, 1868－1988 (Record Unit 509), Box 1, National Library, Peiping〕

按:此件为打字稿,落款处为先生签名。

一月六日

下午,金毓黻至南友村访先生,先生告其抗战前在南京存书或有可能在今日中央图书馆接收京内外书籍之中,似可致信一问。〔《静晤室日记》第 8 册,页 5992-5993〕

按:金毓黻听从先生建议,于本月 13 日致信柳诒徵、缪凤林、蒋复璁,询问藏书下落。

一月七日

先生致信史蒂文斯,请洛克菲勒基金会考虑资助平馆购买潘氏宝礼堂藏书。

January 7, 1946

Dear Dr. Stevens:

When I was in Shanghai, I sent you a cable copy of which is herewith enclosed.

In view of the importance of the Pan family collection to sinological research, I sincerely hope that funds will be available to purchase it en bloc. Out of Chinese Government appropriation we have just set aside a sum equivalent to US $ 10,000 which will serve as a deposit if and when it is required.

We have asked the Pan family to preserve the collection intact and have promised them to raise money within a reasonable period. If we are unable to raise the necessary amount of money (about US $ 50,000), I am afraid that the collection will be sold at a public auction, which would, of course, yield a large amount of money to the Pan family.

Mr. F. F. Li is in charge of our Shanghai Office at 17 Route Pottier, Shanghai, and is in touch with the Pan family. During my temporary absence from China, Mr. Li will keep you informed about future development.

Yours sincerely

T. L. Yuan

Director

〔平馆(重庆沙坪坝)英文信纸。Rockefeller Foundation. Series 601: China; Subseries 601.R: China-Humanities and Arts. Vol. Box 47. Folder 391〕

按:此件为打字稿,落款处为先生签名,似由美国大使馆负责转寄。

一月八日

先生致信史蒂文斯,告知就日军掠去的缩微胶片机所做追讨尝试,并表示平馆馆藏文献除俄文略有损失外均保存完好,北平仍将是汉学研究的中心,希望洛克菲勒基金会考虑客岁三月二十日提交的备忘录,资助筹建照相复制实验室。

January 8, 1946

Dear Dr. Stevens:

Upon my return from Peiping, I was glad to have your letter dated December 19, 1945 for which I wish to express to you my hearty thanks.

While in Peiping I wrote to you in regard to our failure of tracing the Draeger Machine formerly kept at P. U. M. C. Both P. U. M. C. officials and the OSS staff were unable to locate it at Japanese headquarters in Peiping. Everyone concerned seems to think that the machine must have been taken away to Japan.

I wrote to the American Embassy in regard to this matter (copy of my letter was enclosed in my previous correspondence), but I was informed the other day that since the machine legally belonged to a Chinese institution, it is up to the Chinese Government to trace its whereabouts in Japan. Accordingly, I shall solicitate the assistance of

General Chu Shi-ming of the Chinese Military Mission in Japan in regard to this matter.

I am glad to inform you that our library building and our collections at Peiping are both intact. All of our Russian material, however, have been taken away by the Japanese. The Russian collections in other libraries, such as the Tsing Hua University and the National University of Peking, were also removed to Japan.

After my survey of the resources of Peiping libraries, it is safe to say that no Russian books and journals are to be found in Peiping.

However, all collections of Chinese documents (entirely in manuscript form) in the Palace Museum, the National University of Peiping, and the Historical Museum are intact. This fact alone will make Peiping the leading centre of sinological research in China.

As the need of reproducing this unique archive material is more than apparent, I hope that my memorandum dated March 20, 1945 may be given due consideration. In this connection, I beg to enclose a letter from Mr. Eugene B. Power of the University Microfilms which is self-explanatory. I shall solicit the assistance of Mr. Power when the funds for a photo-duplication laboratory are available.

While in Peiping, I secured a historical temple near our library which, after some alterations, can be used most advantageously as a training centre for librarians and museum curators. I expect to visit some training centres in the United States this spring and I shall look forward to seeing you and Mr. Marshall before very long.

With kindest regards,

Yours sincerely

T. L. Yuan

Director

〔平馆（重庆沙坪坝）英文信纸。Rockefeller Foundation. Series 601: China; Subseries 601.R: China-Humanities and Arts. Vol. Box 47. Folder 391〕

按:Eugene B. Power(1905-1993),美国使用缩微胶卷复制学术文献的开拓者,1938 年在安娜堡(Ann Arbor)成立 University Microfilms,即今日 ProQuest 有限责任公司的源头;二次大战期间,他曾指导英国各图书馆拍摄善本古籍,并将其带至美国。此件为打字稿,落款处为先生签名。

一月上旬

朱家骅覆函先生,谈收购海源阁遗存及购汇等事。

守和先生大鉴:

十二月廿八日大札展悉。关于收购海源阁藏书事,已照电张市长呈请向各有关股东妥为解释矣。至采购图书,拟购外汇美金两万元一节,经于十二月二十七日以总字六五七一五号令指复。专复,顺颂文祺。

弟朱〇〇

卅五年一月

〔中国第二历史档案馆,教育部档案·全卷宗 5,国立北平图书馆经常费预概算书及有关文书,案卷号 11617(2)〕

按:此件底稿,实发时间待考。客岁 12 月 29 日,朱家骅急电北平盐业银行王昭贤并转天津市长张廷谔,告知书款一千一百五十万元已汇平,并嘱古籍运平时应派军护送。就申请外汇事,"总字六五七一五号令"之内容,待考,似未如数批准。

一月十一日

Eugene B. Power 覆函先生,就平馆搭建缩微实验室所需设备、耗材等给予意见。

January 11, 1946

Dear Mr. Yuan:

Your letter of October 31 is received, and I am hastening to answer. Naturally, I am delighted to know that you are planning to go ahead with your laboratory and want to assure you at the beginning that if we can be of any assistance, either in the purchasing of equipment, recommending what equipment should be obtained, or in its installation and initial operation, I trust you will feel free to call upon us.

In considering the list of equipment which you enclosed, one must know what type of work you are going to do, and how much of it. Not having too much information on this point, I can only guess, and give you an opinion based on that estimate.

I. CAMERA. I do not believe that you require a Microfile Model C-2 unless you are planning to copy engineering drawings exclusively. The model C-1, with the oscillating cradle, is particularly useful for large volumes such as bound newspapers, and by clamping a top on the cradle it can be used for large drawings. The Microfile Model D is a very useful camera for the photographing of books and periodicals, particularly if used in combination with a book-holder.

The cost of the C-1 is $ 3600.00, and of the D about $ 1300.00.

II. PROCESSING. You have made no provision in your list for suitable processing equipment. There are two types which would probably be satisfactory for you; either Stineman reels or rack and tank built on the spot. In the hands of skilled operators Stineman functions satisfactorily. We used them for some years. A 200-foot reel costs $ 60.00, and you would probably need at least two such reels. In addition, you will need stainless steel trays and washer, and a squirrel cage dryer.

The reels can be purchased in this country, and I would recommend the purchase of the stainless-steel trays and the washer made after a design described on page 213 of Volume V. No. 4 of the *Journal of Documentary Reproduction*. With two such Stineman reels as mentioned above, you should have a capacity of around 1200 feet per day, which should be all that you would need, I believe. Rack and tank can be used, but I am not so familiar with this method. More chemical is required, and more space, although it is a dependable method as well.

The Stineman reels are manufactured by:

III. PRINTERS. The Depue microfilm printer is without a doubt the most satisfactory piece of equipment for that use made at present. We have used one for a number of years with complete satisfaction, and I would certainly recommend it.

IV. ENLARGER EQUIPMENT. The Recordak Model. An enlarger is an excellent piece of equipment, and is thoroughly satisfactory for microfilm work, I am not intimately familiar with the Omega D－11 enlarger, inasmuch as we have not used them here. I know that it is good equipment, however, but I wonder if you have reason to duplicate, whether the Recordak enlarger might not serve all your needs adequately.

V. PAPER DRYER. The Pako Dryer is a good one, and should do the work satisfactorily. The size you will need will depend somewhat upon the size of enlargements you anticipate making. Ordinarily a 30” belt is sufficient.

VI. PRINT WASHING EQUIPMENT. If you are making enlargements, it will be necessary to have a suitable washer for your points. We have experimented with a considerable number of these, and have concluded that the Pako Rotary Washer is by far the most satisfactory. This sells for $ 125.00

VII. MISCELLANEOUS EQUIPMENT. In addition to what we have listed above, you will need a rather considerable amount of miscellaneous equipment. This involves such things as tin reels, inspection lenses, light boxes for inspection of film, splicing equipment, cartons for the storage of film, etc. In other words, the amount of miscellaneous equipment which one accumulates and requires in the operation of a laboratory is surprising.

VII. MICROFILM READER. The Recordak library film reader Model C is the most satisfactory one on the market at present, and you should have one in your laboratory.

I am attaching to this letter a list of equipment which you will need and the probable cost, as well as the addresses of the manufacturers. I trust that what I have written will be of assistance to you, and want to repeat what was said at the beginning of this letter. We will be very glad to assist you in any way possible.

When you were here you suggested that we might help you get your laboratory started. I hope that you will feel free to make that request when the time comes. My sincere regards.

Sincerely yours,

University Microfilms

Eugene B. Power

〔Rockefeller Foundation. Series 601: China; Subseries 601.R: China-Humanities and Arts. Vol. Box 47. Folder 393〕

按:附各种设备价目表,共计美金一万五千元。该函抄件附于5月11日致史蒂文斯信中。

一月十四日

先生致信布朗,就教育部尚未支付美国图书馆协会协助审读、完善购书清单所需经费表示歉意,并告已催请拨付。

January 14, 1946

Dear Mr. Brown:

Upon my return from Peiping, I was surprised to find that the $2,000 which I recommended as a grant to the A. L. A. has not been paid by the Ministry of Education. I have already requested the Ministry to send you the above amount through the Universal Trading Corporation.

Neither you nor Mr. T. Y. Fan of U. T. C. have informed me of the non-receipt of the grant and I have taken it for granted that this amount has long been received. It was only yesterday when the Ministry asked me to proceed to the United States to expedite the purchases made by U. T. C. that I discovered this error.

I expect to be in the United States in March and April and I should like to seek you and your Committee's advice regarding closer cooperation between Chinese and American Libraries.

Yours sincerely,

T. L. Yuan

Director

〔平馆(重庆沙坪坝)英文信纸。Rockefeller Foundation. Series 601: China; Subseries 601.R: China-Humanities and Arts. Vol. Box 47. Folder 391〕

按:T. Y. Fan 即范祖淹,江苏昆山人,毕业于中央大学,后赴美留学,获哥伦比亚大学硕士,时应任世界贸易公司(Universal Trading Corporation)代办[①],二十世纪六十年代曾任教于新亚书院。落款处为先生签名。

一月十五日

先生致信朱世明、杨云竹,请协助在日调查平馆复制影片摄影机下落。

世明、云竹先生大鉴:

前闻大驾因公赴日,未及走送,至以为歉,近维为国宣勤,无任钦仰。兹有恳者,敝馆前有复制影片摄影机 Draeger Camera 一架,前曾寄存北平协和医院。太平洋事变发生后,由日本军部接收该院,并将该项复制影片摄影机移至日本。据各方报告,大约存于东京参谋本部。现敝馆需用至为迫切,拟恳惠予协助,代为访查其下落,遇必要时可请美军军部派员协同追查,随函附上说明一份及协和医院证明书一件,即希查照,并祈赐覆为荷。专此奉托,敬候勋祺。

弟袁同礼顿首

一月十五日

按:朱世明(1898—1965),字公亮,湖南湘乡人,清华大学毕业,曾任国民政府驻苏联大使馆武官,时任国民政府驻日本军事代表团中将团长。该信由文书代笔,落款及日期为先生亲笔,另附英文信一页,内容如下,

Draeger microphotographic camera

Among the important objects which the National Library of Peiping lost during Japan's occupation of Peiping is the Draeger semi-automatic microphotographic camera for the filming of books and documents, donated to the National Library by the Rockefeller Foundation and installed in the premises of the Peiping Union Medical College. From the information supplied by many quarters in Peiping, the camera had been removed to Japan for military use.

For identification purposes, a reprint describing the camera in

---

① 《竺可桢全集》第 8 卷,页 652。

question is herewith attached, it is hoped that the OSS attached to General MacArthur's Headquarters in Tokyo may be able to assist in the tracing of the whereabouts of the said camera. A letter from Mr. Bowen, controller of the Peiping Union Medical College, is also attached.

T. L. Yuan

Director

National Library of Peiping

January 15, 1946

〔国立北平图书馆用笺。台北"国史馆",〈要求日本归还科学仪器及标本〉,数字典藏号 020-010119-0019〕

一月十八日

先生致信布朗,告知已请国民政府教育部催促财政部支付美国图书馆协会款项。

January 18, 1946

Dear Mr. Brown:

With further reference to my letter of January14, I beg to state that the Ministry of Education has asked the Ministry of Finance to send to the A. L. A. the sum of US $2, 000 through the Universal Trading Corporation. I hope very much that it will be received in due course.

Since Mr. T. Y. Fan is returning to China very soon, I am asking the Managing Director of U. T. C. to send you the above remittance as soon as it receives the official notification from the Ministry of Finance.

I enclose a letter to Mr. Eugene Power and I shall be grateful to you if you could forward it for me. I shall be glad to attend the meeting of the International Federation of Documentation if it is held at Ann Arbor in March or April when I expect to be in the United States for a brief visit.

With kindest regards,

Yours sincerely

T. L. Yuan

Director

P. S. Please inform Mr. Roger S. Greene that the Ministry of Education has accepted my recommendation of making a special grant of US $ 18,750.00 to the American Book Centre, Inc.

〔平馆(重庆沙坪坝)英文信纸。Rockefeller Foundation. Series 601: China; Subseries 601.R: China-Humanities and Arts. Vol. Box 47. Folder 391〕

按:此件为打字稿,落款处为先生签名。

一月二十五日

先生致信朱家骅,接钱泰大使来函,称伯希和夫人已允将伯希和之中文藏书售与中国,请教育部在寄存驻英使馆外汇中暂拨经费用以支付书款。

骝先部长钧鉴:

法国汉学家伯希和教授于上年十月逝世,身后萧条,其藏书势将出让。前曾函请驻法钱大使加以注意,随时函告。顷接复函,内称伯氏去世后比国鲁文大学及英法各学术机关纷纷争购,其夫人正待价而沽,内中大批西文善本书,法国政府将禁止出境且索价甚昂,商洽不易就绪,惟中文图书占全部藏书三分之一,其夫人已允秘密售于我国,索价三四百万法郎(约一万余美金),事不宜迟,应从速决定等语。窃查伯希和氏于四十五年前来华搜集燉煌写本及古刻本以及我国学者之稿本为数甚多。曾见有燉煌出土五彩印刷之佛像,为人间之孤本,允宜收归国有,以免散佚。此事既应从速进行,拟下月先到巴黎从事选购,未识能否在钧部寄存英大使馆之外汇准予暂借一千五百磅(美金六千元)以资采购,一俟取得伯夫人之收据及发单再行根据申请外汇归还上项垫款。是否有当。敬祈尊酌示复为感,祇请道安。

职袁同礼敬上

一月廿五日

〔中国第二历史档案馆,教育部档案·全卷宗5,国立北平图书馆经常费预概算书及有关文书,案卷号11617(1)〕

按:最终,平馆并未购入伯希和旧藏敦煌写本或其他善本古籍。

多尔西覆函先生,告知史密斯森协会无法补寄书籍。

January 25, 1946

Dear Sir:

The Institution regrets that it is not possible to comply with the request contained in your letter of January 2, concerning the contents of the six boxes sent you in October 1941, which were discharged at Manila. No record is made here of the titles of publications contained in packages passing through the Service.

Very truly yours,
H. W. Dorsey
Acting Chief
International Exchanges

Dr. T. L. Yuan

〔Smithsonian Institution Archives, Records, 1868 - 1988 (Record Unit 509), Box 1, National Library, Peiping〕

按:该函寄送重庆,此为录副。

一月二十六日

先生致信王重民,谈在美购买资料、仪器及将赴欧商洽购买伯希和旧藏善本。

有三吾弟:

接一月六日来书,详悉一一。普仁斯敦所有之书为本馆所无者,均应影制复本。原因(一)国内古书日少,想今后能购到之可能并不甚多;(二)照相需时,势非用中国人帮忙不可,如此则吾馆可源源派人到美实习;(三)本馆所得之一份如能受赐最好,否则根据此理由申请外汇亦可。

傅维本亟愿返平,已为之设法由教部派其到平协助调查文物在团城办公损毁事。至罗氏基金方面,前曾作函推荐,尚无覆音,大约须今年秋间方能决定。朱士嘉申请国务院奖学金事,已作函推荐,大致无问题,惟渠拟接家眷去美,实不容易。刻下由沪开行之船位极少,而护照亦不易也。

图书博物专科事曾与孟真谈过,渠谓北大方面不赞成太职业化,故目前计划拟由北大、故宫及本馆合组一研究部,趋重自由讲学,为高级班。至于初级班则为三机关在职人员之进修而设。日前师资颇成问题，俟到美后，当约美籍教授数人来华参加工作。此次赴美系教部派侧重搜集大量之仪器及各大学所需之设备，例如美国战时机构，今已裁撤，而所存之科学设备能否售与我国，亟待调查。此事应如何进行请先赐考虑是盼。下月九号到港飞欧，拟买伯希和所藏之燉煌写本及名人稿本，伯夫人千嘱西文书不卖须绝对秘密，故不必向外人言，能否成功亦无把握。在法在英均无多大停留，即行来美，如确知伯希和有中文古籍值得吾人购买，请速函告，径寄巴黎汪德昭先生留交是荷，Ouang Te-Tchao, 24 bis rue Tournefort, Paris 5e。

估价单及鱼肝油丸均存尊处可也。

同礼

一月廿六日

海源阁书已购妥，共一千五百万元，四经四史皆在内。

〔中国书店2017年秋季书刊资料文物拍卖会〕

按："普仁斯敦所有之书"应指时隶属于普林斯顿高等研究院的葛斯德东方图书馆馆藏文献，1945年夏，先生返美期间曾前往该所商讨合作事宜，后王重民分五次前往该图书馆协助编纂善本书目。①

一月二十七日②

先生致信钱存训，谈本馆所藏内阁大库之舆图装裱细节及寻找本馆特藏英国印刷珍本图书事。

存训吾兄：

廿五日自京来函已悉。本馆内阁大库旧藏地图均系黄绫装裱并未盖馆章但海内并无第二份，原存故宫保存库朝天宫。依据伪组织之文物保存会报告，应在鸡鸣寺中央研究院。此事将来仍须请森玉先生代为调查，或请王以中庸赴京之便代为查询，请分别接洽。至于印刷样本，原存中英文化协会，亦未盖章，但本馆之英国印刷展览目录均详载无遗，国内亦无第二份也目录已寄上海。此间拟派来京工作之杨君一时不易启程，将来需人时由顾斗南君介绍一助手可也自备宿处。匆

---

① 雷强《普林斯顿大学图书馆藏王重民孙念礼往来书札》，《精一文献》，2020年10月27日。

② 此信被《北京图书馆馆史资料汇编(1909-1949)》错系为1943年，实无可能。

复，顺颂大安。

弟同礼顿首

一月廿七日

工程图书馆现既无人办公，征求工作暂用上海办事处名义可也。

国外寄工程馆之图书□□尊处函□□□邮局□改寄金大圕转交为□，再函托金大同人。

〔国立北平图书馆用笺。国家图书馆档案，档案编号 1947-※010-年录 6-006003〕

按：本年 10 月左右，工程参考图书馆（平馆驻京办事处）恢复办公。原信左侧边缘破损，无法识别。

先生致信顾子刚，有意安排钱存训负责罗斯福纪念图书馆（上海），并请物色主持中文编目人员。

January 27, 1946

Dear Mr. Koo:

I have your letters of January 21 & 25.

Regarding Mr. Tsien, I am hoping to have him run the Roosevelt Memorial Library to be set up in Shanghai. I have a voice in the administration of that Library when organized.

Please suggest someone to take charge of the Chinese Cataloguing Section. We can assign Mr. Y. C. Yuan in charge of the printing of catalogue cards.

Yours sincerely

T. L. Yuan

Director

〔国家图书馆档案，档案编号 1945-※057-综合 5-023059〕

按：1945 年 4 月 12 日，美国总统罗斯福突然去世。罗斯福纪念图书馆（Roosevelt Memorial Library）本拟在上海设立，翌年秋由蒋介石决定改为重庆，定名为国立罗斯福图书馆，严文郁担任筹备委员会秘书并最终出任馆长。[①] Y. C. Yuan 应为袁涌进。

---

①《传记文学》第 16 卷第 4 期，页 47-52。

一月二十八日

先生致信布朗，告知即将访问欧美，并请就中国各院校提交的购书单予以订正。

January 28, 1946

Dear Mr. Brown:

I hope you have received my letters dated January 14th and 18th stating that the Universal Trading Corporation had been asked to remit to your Committee the sum of US $ 2,000 as a grant to the A. L. A. As I wrote to you on January 14th, I took it for granted that this amount had long been paid, so I did not inquire about it before I left for Peiping.

On my return from Peiping, the Ministry of Education asked me to take a short trip to America to expedite the purchases made by UTC and it was on this occasion that I inquired about it. When I learned that this amount was not sent, I immediately asked Minister Chu Chia-hua to make a prompt payment. I also wrote to the Managing Director of UTC to send you this remittance without waiting for my arrival.

I have much pleasure in acknowledging the receipt of your letter of December 24th informing me about the allocation to China of the periodicals subscribed by the A. L. A. I am sure all of my colleagues in China appreciate very much the assistance given by the A. L. A. in granting China the highest priority.

As I expect to leave for Europe very soon, I am not sure whether I could receive Mr. Lydenberg's letter before my departure. I have, however, told my secretary to send me copies of correspondence from you and other officials from the A. L. A.

As to the revision of the book lists submitted by various institutions, you are requested to exercise authority to make changes as you see fit. You will no doubt include the latest books and latest editions, using these lists only as a basis. I am afraid that very extensive revisions have to be made in view of the fact that these lists were compiled in 1939-40 when China already had several years of blockade.

I think I had written to you informing you that a grant of US $ 18,750 was made by the Chinese Government to the American Book Centre, Inc. to meet its administrative expenses. I hope to call on the Centre immediately after my arrival in March.

With sincere thanks for your valuable assistance.

Yours sincerely,

T. L. Yuan

Will you forward the letter to Mr. Greene?

〔平馆(重庆沙坪坝)英文信纸。Rockefeller Foundation. Series 601: China; Subseries 601.R: China-Humanities and Arts. Vol. Box 47. Folder 391〕

按:1月上旬,教育部曾发布训令,请各校将拟添图书及有关研究必备之基本参考书籍开列书目并呈核。[①] 由该信可知,先生此时已知各校提交购书单的问题,即编制于1939年至1940年间,严重滞后于美国教育界、出版界的现实情况。此件为打字稿,落款处为先生签名。

一月二十九日

先生致信洛克菲勒基金会人文部副主任 Marshall,告知前函已录副转发给在日工作的傅振伦,此前申请给予旅费资助的谭卓垣因病无法赴平馆任职,并告国民政府已经出资收购郭葆昌旧藏瓷器、杨氏海源阁遗书并将其分别存于故宫博物院与平馆,教育部在美设立奖学金等事。

January 29, 1946

Dear Mr. Marshall:

I have pleasure in acknowledging the receipt of your letter of January 7, copy of which has been sent to Mr. Fu Chen-lun who is now busily engaged in conducting a survey of Chinese cultural materials now stored in Japan.

In my letter to Dr. Stevens dated October 17, 1945, I mentioned Dr. C. W. Taam of Honolulu as deserving some support from the Foundation

① 《国立西南联合大学史料》第2卷,页410。

in regard to his trip to the United States. I have recently heard from Dr. Taam stating that owing to ill-health he has to remain at Honolulu, and he regrets that for the time being he will not be able to join our staff at Peiping.

In my letter to Dr. Stevens dated January 17, I mentioned the dispersal of private collections in China, particularly the Pan family library. As it is not easy to raise the necessary amount of money before my departure, we have urged the owner to keep the collection intact until funds are available.

You may be interested to know that the Government has purchased the late Mr. Kuo Shi-wu's famous collection of Chinese porcelains and the Yang family library of Chinese incunabula and has deposited them in the Palace Museum and the National Library of Peiping respectively.

The Government has increased the total number of fellowships offered for Chinese studies at American universities to 45. With these fellowships they can spend their second or third year in Peiping. Unfortunately, the choice of universities has not been a happy one. For instance, the University of Southern California has been provided with five fellowships, while Cornell, Pennsylvania and Pomona have all been left out.

The Ministry of Education has made a grant of US $ 18,750 to the American Book Center and US $ 2,000 each to the A. L. A. and the Inter-Allied Book Center in London.

I am leaving for Paris next week and I hope to have the pleasure of seeing you and Dr. Stevens in March or early in April.

With kindest regards,

Yours sincerely,

T. L. Yuan

Director

〔平馆（重庆沙坪坝）英文信纸。Rockefeller Foundation. Series 601: China; Subseries 601.R: China-Humanities and Arts. Vol. Box 47. Folder 391〕

按:“Dr. Stevens dated January 17”似有误,应指1月7日信。此件为打字稿,落款处为先生签名。

一月三十一日

先生致信史密斯森协会,再次询问可否补寄六箱被日本劫去的美国交换品,并告知今后寄送平馆的书刊均应将地址改为驻沪办事处。

January 31, 1946.

Dear Sirs:

With further reference to our letter of January 2, 1946, regarding the six cases of books sent to this Library per M/S “Sea Witch” on October 8, 1941, we beg to enclose herewith copy of a letter from the American President Lines, Shanghai, dated January 26, 1946 stating that the Manila Office of the American President Lines has informed it that the above cargo was either looted or taken by the Japanese at the time of their occupation.

From your record you would no doubt, ascertain whether these six cases of books contained U. S. government documents, or scientific publications sent to us by various correspondents in the United States. We shall be exceedingly grateful to you if you could take steps to supply us with the missing publications if any of them is still available.

As stated in our letter dated January 3, our Shanghai office is now situated at 17 Route Pottier, Shanghai, to which all of the publications addressed to this Library should be sent. We hope that it will not be very long before you could obtain priority in your shipment of book cases to China.

Yours faithfully,

T. L. Yuan

Director

〔平馆(重庆沙坪坝)英文信纸。Smithsonian Institution Archives, Records, 1868-1988 (Record Unit 509), Box 1, National Library, Peiping〕

按:此件为打字稿,落款处为先生签名,于2月14日送达。

二月九日

先生抵达香港。〔《胡适遗稿及秘藏书信》第24册,页56-58〕

按:先生原计划先赴欧洲,然后转往美国,但并未成行。

朱家骅覆函先生,告知教育部已遵前请致电驻英大使馆垫拨购书款。

守和先生大鉴:

本月廿五日惠示敬悉。关于收购法国汉学家伯希和教授中文藏书事,已遵嘱电驻英大使馆暂垫拨美金六千元。希抵英后径往洽取。耑此布复,并颂公绥。

朱家〇

〔中国第二历史档案馆,教育部档案·全卷宗5,国立北平图书馆经常费预概算书及有关文书,案卷号11617(2)〕

按:该信实发为2月9日,故虽拟于1月,与"本月廿五日"之说并不矛盾。2月9日,教育部电驻英大使馆,请准备垫拨美金六千元。

二月十八日

平馆向教育部呈文一件,题为《呈为呈复职馆收购海源阁藏书及点运各情形钞同书目呈请鉴核备案示遵由》,具先生名并钤印。

案奉钧部三十五年元月廿四日渝社字第〇四九八四号代电内开"海源阁藏书收归国有,已由宋院长批定为一千五百万元合亟电仰转饬就近拨付并派负责人员协携同沈特派员与张市长洽商运书事宜,仍将洽办经过报部"等因。奉此,查聊城杨氏海源阁藏书九十二种,前经平津士绅潘复、常朗斋、王绍贤及现任天津市市长张廷谔等组织存海学社,购存于天津盐业银行,已历有年,所上年十一月中,职馆以平津故家文物散佚堪虞亟应收归国有以资保存,曾呈请钧部拨给专款。旋奉指令照准,并拨发专款备用,各在案。窃以海源阁藏书首在拟购之中,即与该学社各股东商谈办理,适宋院长视察平津经与张市长面洽,将原书作价一千五百万元收归国有交由职馆购藏并在馆特辟存海学社专室,以资纪念。职馆当于一月廿二日派员赴津洽办,将价款一千五百万元交由张市长派李秘书家镆代表到场监视,比经一一点交清楚,计原书九十二种,一千二百零七册,分装七大箱,于二月一日起运来馆并经张市长委托杜副市长建时亲自率队督运，书既到馆连同原箱保藏于善本书库内。二月五日，由行政院驻平办事处特派员张冠儒先生暨钧部平津区特派员办公处特派葛信益先生会同莅馆开箱查验无误。除俟将该项书籍登记编目，遵照宋院长指示成立存海学社专室用资纪念外，理合将本馆收购海源阁藏书及点运各情形并钞同点收书目二册具文呈请鉴核备案示遵。谨呈

教育部部长朱

国立北平图书馆馆长袁同礼（印）

中华民国三十五年二月十八日

〔中国第二历史档案馆，教育部档案·全卷宗5，国立北平图书馆收购杨氏海源阁藏书及要求归还日本劫掠我国图书的电文，案卷号11610〕

二月中下旬

先生致电法国友人，称将于二十八日抵达巴黎。〔《胡适遗稿及秘藏书信》第24册，页61〕

按：友人可能是戴密微、杜乃扬等人，收悉电报时间为22日。事实上，先生并未如期赴欧。

三月二日

胡先骕致函先生，告知静生生物调查所房屋不能借与平馆，并谈复员经费交割事宜。

守和先生惠鉴：

不通音信又隔多日，敬以兴居为念。骕已于日前来沪，一俟与中基会任叔永先生接洽后，即将飞平，布置静生所复员工作。顷得敝所庶务主任夏纬琨报告，云贵所欲借用敝所房屋成立西文部，并已将书架百个运至敝所，将植物标本室占满。闻之至为诧异，此等事何以事先不同骕商洽取得同意，竟自由行动！且敝所复员在即，图书、标本均将运回陈列应用，原有房屋不能让借，且贵馆房屋极多，似无更借用敝所房屋之需要，应请将书架运回为要。再闻中基会曾拨与敝所复员经费三十万元，交与台从手收，请将此款交与夏纬琨先生收用。又骕曾电任叔永先生，电汇十万元与夏先生收用，此款汇出已久，而夏先生来信云尚未收到，若此款系由台从转交，亦乞即日交与夏先生为感。专

此，敬颂台绥。

弟胡先骕拜启

三月二日

〔中国第二历史档案馆，全宗号409，案卷号41〕①

按：夏纬琨，生平待考，时负责静生生物调查所在平复员、接收事务。②

三月七日

杨云竹覆函先生，告知已收到协助访查复制影片摄影机下落的请求。

守和馆长吾兄大鉴：

大示敬悉。嘱协助访查被敌掠去之贵馆复制影片摄影机下落一节。因盟国对日委员会即将成立，我国参加该会代表团即将赴日，拟交我代表团设法调查，俟有结果后，再行奉闻。耑此，并候勋祺。

弟杨云〇启

〔台北"国史馆"，〈要求日本归还科学仪器及标本〉，数字典藏号020-010119-0019，48页〕

按：此件为底稿，标注3月6日拟，3月7日发出。

三月二十一日　上海

先生与岳父袁道冲访徐森玉，后顾廷龙至，遂同赴合众图书馆参观。〔《顾廷龙日记》，页449〕

按：袁道冲在合众图书馆阅览其父袁昶的稿本。

四月一日

先生覆信范腾端，嘱托其离昆北返前注意事项。

九峰仁兄大鉴：

接奉三月二十五日大函，备悉种切。留昆书箱既承蔡、俞二君允代照料，甚善甚善。兹再函二君恳托并致谢忱，即希转交是荷。台端将此项书籍运存完毕即可赴沪，至由沪至津一段可乘轮船，已托夔君代为预定舱位。东巴经典一包既经周君寄昆，如包件到时台端业已离去，务请先期通知当地邮局转寄北平本馆。又嗣后凡有寄昆明本馆信

① 转引自《胡先骕先生年谱长编》，页388-389。

② 胡宗刚《北平静生生物调查所的复员》，《中国科技史料》，2000年第1期，页52-60。

件，均请函告龙头村邮局转寄北平为要。专复，即候时祉。

弟袁同礼顿首

四月一日

〔国家图书馆档案，档案编号 1946-※039-采藏 11-005020 和 1946-※039-采藏 11-005021〕

按：蔡、俞、周三人，待考。此件为文书代笔，落款处为先生签名，所附致他人信件皆不存。

四月十日　旧金山

先生致信邓嗣禹、陈梦家，告知最近行踪并请代收信札。

嗣禹、梦家吾兄大鉴：

别来忽将一载，想著作日宏为慰。弟于昨日来美，日内即东行，大约本月廿一或廿二日可到芝城（廿二及廿三在芝城），逗留二日即赴纽约。已函告朱士嘉兄，将弟之信件寄至尊处转交，并祈转告收发处暂代收存是荷，余容面陈。匆匆，顺颂教祺。

弟袁同礼顿首

四，十，旧金山

旅馆无须代订。

〔方继孝藏札〕

先生致信王重民，告知已抵旧金山。〔《胡适遗稿及秘藏书信》第 24 册，页 70〕

按：暂将此信系于此日，另该信于 12 日送达。

四月二十日　纽约

先生访问洛克菲勒基金会总部，与史蒂文斯晤谈。〔Rockefeller Foundation. Series 601: China; Subseries 601.R: China-Humanities and Arts. Vol. Box 47. Folder 393〕

四月二十六日　华盛顿

先生致电朱家骅，告知美国捐赠书刊已开始起运，请在上海预备暂存场地。

南京外交部请转教育部朱部长钧鉴：

美国捐赠图书，首批三百余箱，已托联总运沪，径送沪中央研究院暂存，请转告该院准备存书房屋。

袁同礼

〔台北"中央研究院"近代史研究所档案馆，〈朱家骅〉，馆藏号 301-01-09-054〕

按:该电于4月30日译出。

先生致信英国图书馆协会,祝贺其即将召开的年会并希望加强两国图书馆协会间的合作。大意如下:

兹当贵会在黑池举行年会之际,中国圕界同人谨掬亲热之忱,以申贺意。当此和平复员之初,吾人即欣闻贵会计划贵国圕之善后与复兴工作,以贵国人士对于学术爱好之传统精神,组织能力之优长与经济援助之适当,深信贵会在最短期内定可完成巨大之收获。当前工作至为艰巨,吾人谨祝贵会圆满成功。

回顾过去可怖之岁月中,我中英两国圕与文化机关同受暴力之摧残,吾人不得不信现代战争对于文明与人类进步之威胁。现代战争之本格即属毁灭,积数世纪始获艰难缔造之成绩,在极短之时间内,即可毁灭无遗。

在八年长期抗战中,中国牺牲极巨,圕与文化机关遭受严重与无可补偿之损失,中国学者缺少适当之资料与设备,以致研究工作,无从进行,文化发展因此阻滞不前。惟在此重重困难之中,吾人犹挣扎于保持此学术火炬之光明,不计其成就之微细,此则差足引以为慰者也。

我国当前复兴工作之中,急需代表英国学术研究之各种出版物。吾人希望联合国圕中心征集之图书及刊物于分配遭受战祸各国家时,中国能居于优先之地位,中国业已组织一图书分配委员会,以备接收此项来自图书中心及各方捐赠之书籍。吾人并当筹划将此项图书及杂志得以平均分置于各处冲要地点,以供研究。

倘若战争所赐者,仅为破坏,则其至少可以惊醒吾人,使知文化上之孤立,实应自吾人之思想及行动中永予驱除。我国图书馆界同人当可努力于此,以求其实现。过去中英两国在文化事业上之关系素甚密切,此项联系将来当可更见增强,而贵我两会之合作,将来当更增其紧密。深信此次年会在贵会辉煌之事业中,将为一重要之指标焉。

〔《中华图书馆协会会报》第20卷第1-3期合刊,1946年6月,页14〕

按:英国国会馆协会定于5月6日在Blackpool举行战后首次年会,商讨善后与复兴事宜。中华图书馆协会派徐家璧代表出席。原信应为英文,此处为其译本。

四月三十日

先生赴国会图书馆,与馆长埃文斯、副馆长 Verner W. Clapp 晤谈,感谢该馆向平馆捐赠并交换图书。〔The Library of Congress ed.,*Information Bulletin* (May 6–12, 1946, P. 4)〕

按:此时,国会图书馆交换部准备了 675 箱书刊,待运往中国分发给各图书馆、机构。Verner W. Clapp(1901–1972),美国作家、博学家,本谱中译作"克莱普",1922 年毕业于三一学院(Trinity College),1931 年担任国会图书馆阅览室特别助理,自此在该馆服务,时任副馆长。

先生交给吴光清美金五百元,作为将来归国旅费。〔University of Chicago Library, Yuan T'ung-li Papers, Box 3〕

四月

国民政府教育部获得联合国善后救济总署四百万美金资助,由部聘萨本栋、汪敬熙、先生、蒋复璁、贝时璋、吴有训、杜殿英、施嘉炀、谢家声、周鸿经等人负责组织分配。〔《竺可桢全集》第 10 卷,2006 年,页 93 〕

按:联合国善后救济总署(United Nations Relief and Rehabilitation Administration,简称 UNRRA),创立于 1943 年,发起人为美国总统罗斯福,其名称内之"联合国"并非指后来于旧金山组成的联合国组织,而是指第二次世界大战期间的同盟国参战国家。贝时璋(1903—2009),生于浙江镇海,生物学家,1921 年毕业于上海同济医工专门学校医预科,后赴德留学,1928 年获图宾根大学(Eberhard Karls Universität in Tübingen)博士学位,1948 年当选中央研究院院士。杜殿英(1893—1978),字再山,山东潍县人,同济大学机械系毕业,后赴德留学,时应任资源委员会工业处处长。谢家声,江西九江人,早年赴美留学,获康乃尔大学农学硕士学位,后任中央农业实验所所长。《竺可桢日记》(排印本)此处将汪敬熙记作"汪戢哉"。

四五月间

先生嘱王重民在方便时归国,并许诺资助旅费。〔《胡适遗稿及秘藏书信》第 24 册,页 78–81〕

按:此后,平馆资助王重民回国旅费美金贰百元、刘修业返国旅费美金伍百元，二人撰写收据的时间均为本年8月1日。[①]

五月二日

加斯基尔致函先生，询问中国政府对美国学生设立汉学研究奖学金计划的进展，并询问可向中国何所图书馆捐赠地理学出版物。

May 2, 1946

Dr. T. L. Yuan

c/o Division of Orientalia

Library of Congress

Washington, D. C.

Dear Mr. Yuan:

It is good to know that you are in this country again. Is there any chance of your coming to Ithaca?

I received two lists of books you had for us in Chungking and I sent word to Mr. Biggerstaff asking him to try to arrange to have the books sent on to us. I hope they will arrive before long and that others from Shanghai and Peiping will follow.

Last winter, at the suggestion of Mortimer Graves, and remembering that you said we ought to have some of the Chinese government fellowships for American students in Chinese studies here, I suggested to the Vice-President, Mr. Sabine, that he write to Mr. Chen Chi-mai about the matter. In December Mr. Chen wrote that he was recommending that the fellowships be established at Cornell. Since then, we have heard nothing more about them. I wonder if you have any suggestions as to anything we might do in order, if possible, to make them available for students here for next year. Mr. Kok is going back to Yale but the language work is to be carried on as before, Mr. Biggerstaff will be back to give courses in Chinese history, and Mr. Shadick, formerly at Yenching, is to come to teach courses in Chinese literature, so that with all these courses and the Wason Collection, we feel that facilities for work in

① University of Chicago Library, Yuan T'ung-li Papers, Box 3.

Chinese studies here will be as good or better than in most other universities in this country. We shall appreciate very much any help you can give us in this connection.

A day or two ago this list of geological publications was given to me with the suggestion that the Paleontological Research Institute would be glad to give them to any Chinese library which would like to have them. If you know of such a library and will tell me where the books should be sent to be forwarded to it, I shall be glad to pass the information along to the Institute.

With all good wishes,

Sincerely yours,

〔Cornell University Library, Wason Collection Records, 1918-1988, Box 1, Folder Koo, T. K. Letters〕

按:Mr. Sabine 即 George H. Sabine,美国哲学家,1943 年至 1946 年担任康乃尔大学副校长。Mr. Shadick 即 Harold E. Shadick,中文通译作"谢迪克",曾任燕京大学外国文学系主任。Mr. Chen Chi-mai 应指陈之迈(1908—1978),祖籍广东番禺,生于天津,1928 年清华大学毕业,旋即赴美留学,获哥伦比亚大学哲学博士,时应任驻美大使馆参事。Mr. Kok 待考。Paleontological Research Institute 即古生物学研究所,隶属于康乃尔大学,是北美最大的化石收藏馆之一,出版历史悠久的学术期刊《美国古生物学通报》(*Bulletins of American Paleontology*)等。此件为录副,其中提及欲赠予出版物的清单未存。

五月四日　哈佛

中午十一时,先生至赵元任家,路遇杨联陞。下午,先生前往 Charles S. Gardner 家饮茶。〔《杨联陞日记》(稿本)〕

按:Charles S. Gardner(1900-1966),美国汉学家,中文名贾德纳,曾以哈佛大学远东语言系助教身份来华,1939 年回国,翌年邀请杨联陞赴美留学。①

① 杨联陞著《哈佛遗墨》(修订本),北京:商务印书馆,2013 年,页 52-53。

五月七日 纽约

先生致信教育部(朱家骅),告诸事。大意如下:

……协会同人对于我国图书馆之复兴热诚赞助,至可感佩。如彼等对于国内需要更加了解,则援助之程度当更扩大。敝意似可由大部延请美国专家一人于明春来华视察,并由部中资助美金三千元。如荷同意,请即电告(寄伦敦)是感。(七)联合国教育科学文化会筹委会之参加,前承尊电,嘱参加此会,已与该会接洽,准备届时参加,现定五月二十日赴英,当出席六月六、七日之会议,届时当再函述。专此,敬候道祺。

职袁同礼顿首

五月七日,自纽约发

伦敦通讯处,大使馆收转。

〔中国第二历史档案馆,教育部档案·全卷宗5,国立北平图书馆请拨员工学术研究补助费经常费有关文书,案卷号11616(4)〕

按:该信残,根据内容似应为致朱家骅。

五月十一日

先生致信史蒂文斯,继续就申请洛克菲勒基金会资助平馆筹建缩微实验室与其沟通,并请考虑资助钱存训前往美国接受技术培训。

May 11, 1946

Dear Dr. Stevens:

With reference to my memorandum of March 20, 1945 and our subsequent conversation regarding the need of a photoduplication laboratory in China, I beg to enclose herewith copy of a letter from Mr. Eugene Power of the University Microfilms, Ann Arbor, Michigan.

Attached to his letter you will find a list of equipment with their present prices. It does not, however, include chemicals nor the dark room set up. I have also consulted Mr. Tate of the National Archives who has gone over this list very carefully and found it in order.

In order to have a trained man in charge of this laboratory, it is desirable that one of my assistants in China be given an opportunity to come to the United States for further technical training. I therefore propose that Mr. T. H. Tsien of our Shanghai office be sent over for a period of one year under a Rockefeller Foundation fellowship. He will take courses at the School of Library Service, Columbia University, and at the same time get practical training and experience at the laboratory of the New York Public Library and Columbia University Libraries. Since I have not received the blank forms which you sent me in January, I would appreciate very much if you will kindly send me another set so that I can forward them to Mr. Tsien. Should an interview with Mr. Tsien by your field representative in Shanghai be necessary, Mr. Tsien can be reached at our Shanghai Office, 17 Route Pottier, Shanghai.

I would like to add that the above plan, as well as the plan of sending over Mr. Tsien for further training in this country, have been endorsed by the Board of International Relations of the American Library Association at its meeting held in Washington on April 26, 1946.

If a decision is made after my departure and if you desire additional information regarding our plans, I would suggest you communicate with Dr. K. T. Wu, Library of Congress, Washington, D. C. Dr. Wu has been a member of the National Library of Peiping, now on leave to serve in the library of Congress.

I presume your purchasing department may be able to assist us in ordering and shipping the equipment to China, if the above request receives favorable consideration of your trustees.

I hope to call on you and Mr. Marshall again sometime next week before I sail for Europe.

Yours very sincerely,

T. L. Yuan

〔平馆(重庆沙坪坝)英文信纸。Rockefeller Foundation. Series 601: China; Subseries 601.R: China-Humanities and Arts. Vol. Box 47. Folder 393〕

按:Mr. Tate 应指 Vernon D. Tate(1909−1989),美国图书馆学家、档案学家,时应兼任美国缩微胶片协会(National Microflim

Association)秘书。此件为打字稿,落款处为先生签名,于5月23日送达。

五月十三日

先生覆信加斯基尔,告知将会设立奖学金管理委员会,再次推荐梁思庄女士前往康乃尔大学协助编写中文藏书目录,并推荐清华大学接受古生物学研究所出版物。

May 13, 1946

Dear Miss Gaskill:

On my return to New York, I am delighted to have your letter of May 2nd.

With regard to the books which we have bought for you, I have just had word from Chungking, stating that they had been sent to the American Embassy for transmission to you. I hope you will receive them before very long.

Concerning the fellowships for American students in Chinese studies, I strongly recommended that this fellowship be established at Cornell, but things are moving very slowly in China. I understand that a small committee will be organized to consider the whole question of Chinese Government Fellowships for American students, which totals forty-six. You will no doubt hear officially our plans for next year.

You may recall that last year I recommended Miss Liang Sze-Chuang, a graduate from Columbia School of Library Service and now librarian of Yenching University, to assist you in cataloging the Chinese collection. I trust that as soon as her services are needed at Cornell, you will write to her direct. Her address is "care of Yenching University Library, Peiping, China."

Thanking you also for a list of geological publications. As Tsing Hua University suffered much in her scientific literature, may I suggest that you ask the Paleontological Research Institution, at Ithaca, to send these publications to that University. They should be sent to the American Book Center, Inc., Deck A. Library of Congress, Washington, D. C., for transmission to Tsing Hua University, Peiping, China. As I am leaving for Europe on May 20th, I regret that I shall not be able to pay you a visit, but I hope to see you in China before very long.

Yours truly,

T. L. Yuan

〔国立北平图书馆英文信纸。Cornell University Library, Wason Collection Records, 1918–1988, Box 1, Folder Koo, T. K. Letters〕

按：此件为打字稿，有轻微修改，落款处为先生签名。加斯基尔收到此信后于 17 日覆函先生。

五月十五日　新泽西

先生赴普林斯顿大学拜访 George Rowley，并前往葛斯德图书馆与孙念礼晤谈。〔Princeton University, Mudd Manuscript Library, AC123, Box 415, Folder Peiping, National Library of, 1937–1944〕

按：George Rowley（1892–1962），美国艺术史学者，长期执教于普林斯顿大学，著有 *Principles of Chinese Painting*。所谈议题中，应涉及拣选平馆在国会图书馆暂存的善本书赴该校参加二百周年校庆活动的可能性。

五月十七日　纽约

先生赴洛克菲勒基金会，与史蒂文斯晤谈，内容涉及筹建缩微胶卷实验室和资助钱存训留美学习图书馆学等。〔Rockefeller Foundation. Series 601: China; Subseries 601.R: China-Humanities and Arts. Vol. Box 47. Folder 393〕

Dorothy J. Comins 致函先生，寄上运往上海中央研究院期刊的各类型目录，并告知此前要求编制的三份专业目录尚未完成。

May 17, 1946

Dear Dr. Yuan:

I am enclosing several lists that have to do with the sets of periodicals that are now being sent to the Academia Sinica in Shanghai for distribution to Chinese libraries. The enclosures include the following:

1. An alphabetical list of the titles being sent showing the number of sets and the dates or volumes covered by each set.

2.A list of publishers who are making shipments. As is indicated by the symbols, some of these shipments are going by direct mail, others we hope to send through some special facilities since the shipments will be very large. At present it looks as though the American Book Center would take care of these shipments. We have also indicated on this list all the shipments which have been reported shipped up to the time the list was prepared.

3.A single page list showing the expiration dates of all subscriptions that do not expire in December 1946. All those that are renewable through June have already been ordered but we will assume that the later subscriptions will be taken care of by the libraries receiving the sets.

4.A form letter addressed to you which describes the sets of sample copies of periodicals which I believe I mentioned to you in one of your visits here.

I am sorry that it has not been possible to complete the three periodical lists which you requested last week. The Army Medical Library did prepare a medical list which is ready except for the addition of a few prices. We asked the Department of Agriculture for an agriculture list but what they have given us is not satisfactory and I am working on the revision which should be ready sometime next week. We asked Mr. Brown to prepare the engineering list and have not yet heard anything from him. It is possible that it will reach us tomorrow or that he has sent it directly to you in New York. We hope to be able to get all the lists off to you in London sometime next week.

I hope that the enclosed lists are reasonably accurate. Some of the work has been done in a great hurry and it is very likely that some errors have crept in. Please let us know if you do have discrepancies that cannot be explained. Since we do not see the journals before they are shipped, we shall have to rely on you for reports on any errors in packing that are made by the publishers.

Sincerely yours,

Dorothy J. Comins

Executive Assistant

P. S. Mr. Brown has sent us, in connection with your request for a list of medical journals, the enclosed list of those ordered from the State Department grant. Most of these journals are also on the list prepared by the Army Medical Library.

〔The American Library Association Archives, China Projects File, Box 2, Periodicals for Chinese Universities, Correspondence and Lists, 1944-1947〕

按:three periodical lists 应分指医学、工程、农业三类专业期刊目录。该函寄送纽约华美协进社转交,此件为录副。

五月二十日

上午,先生前往世界贸易公司(Universal Trading Corporation)。

先生致信世界贸易公司,坦言此前提交的订单与现实情况不符,中华民国教育部已委托美国图书馆协会国际关系委员会(华盛顿办公室)制订参考书清单,提交一份中国大学、学院名单,前者需要综合性参考书而后者只需要专业性书刊,并告知国际关系委员会联系方式。

May 20, 1946

Universal Trading Corporation

630 Fifth Avenue

New York City

Dear Sirs:

With reference to our conversation this morning, I wish to confirm the arrangements which we agreed to follow in connection with the placing of the book orders for Chinese universities.

It is realized that one of the main difficulties which you encountered in the past in placing the order was due to the fact that the book lists were compiled in China during 1939-40 and many titles contained in these lists either lacked bibliographical data or were already out of print. In many cases a number of titles were not even published in this country. For this reason, your agents were reluctant to executive the orders which you placed.

In order to overcome this difficulty, the Ministry of Education has requested the American Library Association to draw up lists of basic reference books published in the United States during the last ten years which are especially needed by Chinese universities. Accordingly lists of such books for Colleges of Arts, Sciences, Law, Commerce, Agriculture, Engineering, Medicine and Education are being compiled by the Washington Office of the ALA. If a university consists of these faculties, the books listed in all of these lists will be ordered for that University. On the other hand, if a certain university is made up of only two or three faculties, only the books listed for those faculties will be purchased. Under this arrangement books are supplied according to the number of faculties and departments of instruction which each institution maintains. Each institution is thus enabled to obtain the basic reference books concerning the special field of concentration in which it is particularly interested. For your convenience, I am enclosing a list of Chinese universities and colleges indicating the departments of instruction in each institution. It is suggested that you consult this list before placing the order.

After you have purchased these books as well as scientific apparatus, you will be in a better position to know how much is left in the appropriations for each institution. The Ministry will appreciate such information as early as possible so that the order for additional books and apparatus can be placed. In this connection the Ministry will appreciate your assistance if you would ask American publishers to send their book-lists and recent catalogue to various institutions in China as noted in the attached list. With the help of these lists and catalogues, Chinese universities will be able to select additional titles necessary for teaching and research.

As to the book lists now being compiled by the Washington Office of the American Library Association, I have requested that Office to have them mimeographed at Washington and to send as many copies as you wish to have. Please contact that office at the following address: International Relations Office, American Library Association, Library of Congress Annex, Study 251, Washington, D. C.

Yours faithfully,

T. L. Yuan

Director

〔The American Library Association Archives, China Projects File, Box 2, Yuan T L, 1946-1947〕

按:事实上,国内各院对久未收到订购书刊多表不满,譬如竺可桢在其 1947 年日记中曾 4 次①提及此事,认为先生在美时将各校提交的订单遗失,导致迟迟未订一本。笔者认为这应是某些人有意造谣中伤,首先各院校提交订单肯定会有副本,其次美国与中国邮件通讯更未断绝,以"大衣丢失"解释无法订购,显然与实际情况不符。由该信即可知实际困难之一为 the book lists were compiled in China during 1939－40 and many titles contained in these lists either lacked bibliographical data or were already out of print。此外,竺可桢认为"要 American Library Association 美国图书馆协会开单为各校购书,此亦可笑之至"。此件为副本。

先生致信 Dorothy J. Comins,附上致世界贸易公司信的副本及中国各大学、院校清单,十分赞同油印书目由美国图书馆协会国际关系委员会负责印制,并告知离美时间。

China Institute in America

125 East 65th Street

New York 21, New York

May 20, 1946

Miss Dorothy J. Comins

American Library Association

① 《竺可桢全集》第 10 卷,页 366、369、373、548。

International Relations Office

Library of Congress Annex

Washington, D. C.

Dear Miss Comins:

I appreciate very much your good letter of May 17 enclosing several lists that have to do with the sets of periodicals that are being sent to China by the ALA. The lists will be transmitted to China for immediate attention and I shall have occasion to write to you from time to time.

I now enclose a copy of my letter to the Universal Trading Corporation together with a list of Chinese colleges and universities. From this list you will readily see how Chinese universities are made up. I hope it might be of some assistance to you in drawing up the book lists.

With regard to the mimeographing of the booklists, I would urge your Office to do it in Washington, because there is no trained librarian in the UTC and I am afraid that they might get things mixed up. I really feel that the matter is placed in safe hands if the A. L. A. Washington Office would undertake the job.

Thanks for sending me the list of medical journals which is extremely useful to us. As to the lists of engineering and agricultural journals, you can send to me at my London address: care Chinese Embassy, London. My steamer S. S. Washington has postponed its sailing until Wednesday, so it has given me two extra days here.

Please convey my hearty thanks to Mr. Milczewski and Miss Kelly for their assistance which means a great deal to us.

Sincerely yours,

T. L. Yuan

〔The American Library Association Archives, China Projects File, Box 2, Yuan T L, 1946-1947〕

按:先生离美时间应为 5 月 23 日。此为抄件。

五月二十一日

先生致信 Marshall C. Balfour,介绍钱存训并希望洛克菲勒基金会考虑给予其奖学金资助。

May 21, 1946

Dear Dr. Balfour:

Dr. Stevens told me that you will soon establish an office in Shanghai. I trust that you and Mrs. Balfour will soon return to Shanghai from New Delhi.

Dr. Stevens further informed me that the Humanities will soon send a representative to China to make preliminary surveys and to interview applicants for fellowships.

In connection with our request for a photo-duplication laboratory at Peiping, I have recommended Mr. T. H. Tsien for a fellowship.

If it is granted, he will make special studies in microphotography in American libraries.

I am asking Mr. Tsien to call on you and I hope you will introduce him to the Foundation's representative as soon as he arrives. I hope you will also give Mr. Tsien a blank form in connection with his application for a fellowship.

Thanking you once more for your interest in our work.

Yours sincerely,

T. L. Yuan

〔Rockefeller Foundation. Series 601: China; Subseries 601.R: China-Humanities and Arts. Vol. Box 47. Folder 393〕

按:此为抄件,标注8月21日打电话(76275)联系,并简述钱存训的履历,金陵大学毕业、交通大学图书馆任职。

先生致信米尔泽夫斯基,寄上中国学术、文化机构名单及分配给各所的大致购书金额,以便美方工作人员据此编制购书清单。

125 East 65th Street

New York 21, N. Y.

May 21, 1946

Dear Mr. Milczewski:

With reference to my letter of May 20 to Miss Comins, I now

enclose a list of Chinese institutions for whom the basic reference book-lists should be compiled. In this list I indicated the approximate amount allotted to each institution which, I trust, will help Miss Kelly and Miss Comins in compiling these lists.

If there are points that you are not clear, will you write to me at the following address: care the Chinese Embassy, London, until July 20 when I expect to fly back to China.

Thanking you again for your assistance,

Yours sincerely

T. L. Yuan

〔The American Library Association Archives, China Projects File, Box 2, Chinese Universities, Correspondence, 1946-1947〕

按:此件为打字稿,落款处为先生签名,于5月27日送达。

五月二十二日

先生致信陈梦家,告知赴英行程。

梦家吾兄:

奉到手教,欣悉大驾将于下月来纽,工作进行至为顺利,健羡何似。弟定明日赴英再转大陆,闻入德困难万分,恐不能如愿矣。在英出席联合国教育科学文化组织之筹委会后,拟七月杪即行返国。目前国内战云密布,焦灼万分,真不知能□善其后也。顺颂俪安。

弟同礼顿首

五,廿二

〔方继孝藏札〕

是年夏

先生介绍朱士嘉前往美国国家档案局学习档案管理方法,并从美国图书馆协会申请奖学金1200美金,支付其生活、学习费用。〔朱士嘉《我所了解的袁同礼先生》,页90-91〕

按:该项学习持续半年,在此期间朱士嘉不仅深入了解美国机构设置、人员配备、档案整理和利用的办法,还继续搜集中美外交关系档案。

先生撰写公告,表示平馆希望与欧美学术机构恢复出版物交换。

The Director of the National Library of Peiping takes pleasure to inform you that the Library has returned to its permanent headquarters at Peiping, China. It is now ready to receive current publications from foreign institutions and to send its own publications in exchange.

Before the war the National Library received regularly your publications. It is hoped that you will continue to place it on your mailing list to receive your publications which may be sent by mail direct, or through the International Exchange Service, Smithsonian Institution, Washington, D. C.

T. L. Yuan, Director

〔Cornell University Library, Wason Collection Records, 1918-1988, Box 1, Folder Koo, T. K. Letters〕

按:此件于6月4日送达康乃尔大学图书馆。

五月二十三日

先生离开美国,乘坐华盛顿号邮轮(S. S. Washington)前往英国。〔方继孝藏札〕

五月二十八日

米尔泽夫斯基覆函先生,询问代拟购书清单所涉及的中国学术机构数量、科目、购买金额等细节,并预估工作量及项目费用。

May 28, 1946

Dear Dr. Yuan:

Thank you for your letter of May 21 and for the enclosed list of institutions for whom the lists of basic reference books are to be compiled. In the initial steps preparatory to the compilation of the bibliographies, several questions have arisen. May we please ask you to assist us in clarifying the following points:

①On the list of institutions you enclose with your letter (List A), there are some nine universities and twenty colleges or institutions. However, on the previous list you sent to Miss Comins (List B) there are forty-one universities, national and private, and thirty-five colleges.

Are we to understand that the book lists are to be compiled taking into consideration only the nine universities and twenty colleges, or do you plan eventually to purchase books for all those institutions mentioned in the longer list?

②Is the National Academy of Peiping divided into separate faculties, and if so, what are they? There is no institution of that name listed in List B.

③Enclosed you will please find a chart breaking down the separate faculties into departments of instruction, primarily to show the wide divergence in subjects taught at the various institutions. This chart would tend to indicate that the lists should be prepared not merely by faculties, such as Arts, but also by departments of instruction, such as Chemistry or Biology. For instance, these two universities vary in the number of departments in the college of Science:

Tung Chi University	Chekiang University
Mathematics	Mathematics
Chemistry	Chemistry
Biology	Biology
	Physics
	Pharmacy

Then, too, in some universities there is a combination of faculties, such as in the National University of Yunnan's College of Arts and Public Affairs which has the following departments of instruction, some of which would not be included normally in an Arts list:

Chinese literature and history
Western languages
Law
Political Science
Economics
Sociology

In your letter to the Universal Trading Corporation, you imply the possibility of making up the list by departments of instruction in these sentences:

"……Under this arrangement books are supplied according to the number of faculties and departments of instruction which each institution maintains. Each institution is thus enabled to obtain the basic reference books concerning the special field of concentration in which it is particularly interested. For your convenience, I am enclosing a list of Chinese universities and colleges indicating the departments of instruction in each institution. It is suggested that you consult this list before placing the order."

If the bibliographies are compiled by department, the mimeographed lists can be assembled in this office and so marked that the Universal Trading Corporation can ship the desired sets to the proper institution, thereby relieving them of the difficulty of sorting. This would in effect be equivalent to preparing a special list for each university.

④In regard to the total amount to be spent, it was our understanding that each subject list such as Science, was to total approximately ＄2,000. However, on your List A you indicate ＄3,000 as the amount to be spent on each of the nine universities. There are three faculties in the Tung Chi University, and five faculties in the University of Yunnan. Do you intend that ＄3,000 be spent of each university regardless of the number of faculties, or departments of instruction, or that ＄3,000 are to be spent on each of the faculties within the university? In the latter case Tung Chi would receive ＄9,000 and Yunnan ＄15,000.

In the desire to compile the best type of lists to meet the individual needs and interests of each institution and at the same time to facilitate the distribution of the books by the Universal Trading Corporation, American Library Association recommends the following procedure:

1) Compiling lists by subject, such as Arts or Commerce, and subdividing each list by department such as Philosophy or Economics.

2)Marking the mimeographed lists for U. T. C. so as to indicate which subdivision (or departments) should be sent to any one university.

Our estimate of the cost of this selection job still comes within the $ 2,000 allocated to the A. L. A. There are a number of unknowns, particularly the amount of time, which is involved which may raise the cost. May we feel free, if that should prove necessary, to raise with you later the question of additional funds to complete the work?

Awaiting your further instructions, I am

Very truly yours,

Marion A. Milczewski

Acting Director

〔The American Library Association Archives, China Projects File, Box 2, Yuan T L, 1946-1947〕

按:此件为录副。

六月初　伦敦

先生参加联合国教育文化科学机构下属的图书馆及博物馆特别委员会,并被推举为该会副主席。〔《中央日报》,1946 年 6 月 19 日,第 3 版〕

六月四日

先生致信顾临,附上联合国教科文组织筹备委员会下属的图书馆、博物馆、出版品及特别项目委员会文件。摘件如下:

I enclose documents issued by the Committee on Libraries, Museums, Publications and Special Projects of the Preparatory Commission, UNESCO. I have been asked to serve as Vice-Chairman of the meeting and shall preside over the conference on International Museum Services. After you have read them, will you send them to Mr. Brown and suggest to him to have them mimeographed for wider circulation. I am surprised that the United States will not send any delegates to our Conference.

〔The American Library Association Archives, China Projects File, Box 1, Correspondence about China, Requests, 1945-1948〕

按:6 月 18 日,顾临致函布朗并将此信附上。

先生致信米尔泽夫斯基,就代拟购书清单所询问各节给予答复。

c/o Chinese Embassy

London

June 4, 1946

Dear Mr. Milczewski:

Thank you for your letter of May 28 with the enclosed chart which you were so good to have drawn up. In answer to your inquiry, I beg to offer the following information:

1)Lists of basic reference books should be prepared for each of the 29 institutions, the list of which was enclosed in my letter of May 21. Consult the "longer list" only when you wish to know the location and organization of a particular institution.

2)The National Academy of Peiping is a research institution and is made up of institutes of physics, chemistry, radium, botany, zoology, etc. Booklists should emphasize the natural sciences.

3)Your list should be prepared for each institution under departments of instruction. The titles should be assembled at your office, so that the UTC's business will be to place the orders only.

4)The amount specified for each institution is only approximate. It is allotted to each institution regardless of the number of faculties and departments of instruction. For instance, Yunnan and Tung Chi each get $3,000, not $9,000 or $15,000.

5) I am in entire agreement with your proposed procedure as indicated in your letter. Please be sure to have a special list for each institution, so that the UTC can place the order immediately without any further sorting. In fact, the same list can be used for all engineering colleges. There will be economy of time and labor.

6)Further requests from China will be forthcoming and I hope you will let me know whenever additional funds are needed. If there are points which are not clear to you, you may consult Mr. K. T. Wu of the Library of Congress.

7)I think it would be of great help to China if the ALA would send out a circular to all publishers asking them to mail their catalogues and booklists to Chinese institutions in strategic centers, so that they will be regularly informed about American current publications. In my letter to UTC, I suggested that they attend to this matter, but I find they are incompetent even to do this. Please consult Mr. Wu as to the institutions in China interested in receiving such catalogues and book-lists from American publishers.

I expect to visit Germany after June 25. The Chinese Embassy at Pairs will forward my mails.

With renewed thanks,

Yours sincerely,

T. L. Yuan

〔The American Library Association Archives, China Projects File, Box 2, Chinese Universities, Correspondence, 1946-1947〕

按:UTC 即 Universal Trading Corporation。此件为打字稿,落款处为先生签名,于 6 月 10 日送达。

六月十一日

米尔泽夫斯基覆函先生,收到答复细节,已经初步选择列入清单的书目,并将向顾问及吴光清寻求建议。

June 11, 1946

Dear Dr. Yuan:

Thank you so much for your prompt and enlightening reply to our letter regarding the many questions that had arisen in preparing the lists of purchases for Chinese universities.

We are happy to learn that you agree with our proposed procedure inasmuch as we feel that by following it the individual needs of each institution can best be met.

The comparison of available bibliographies has already begun in our office for the initial selection of titles to be placed on the lists. Letters will be sent to a select number of Consultants this week so that we may have the benefit of their authoritative advice.

We shall contact Mr. Wu in the near future to ask about the

institutions in China interested in receiving book catalogues, and shall request the most important American publishers to send them as soon as possible.

Sincerely yours,

Marion A. Milczewski

Acting Director

〔The American Library Association Archives, China Projects File, Box 2, Chinese Universities, Correspondence, 1946-1947〕

按:该函寄送中华民国驻英大使馆,此件为录副。

六月十六日

九时五十分,先生至伦敦维多利亚车站,陈源等人送行。〔《陈西滢日记书信选集》(下),页771〕

按:同行人或有王承绪夫妇,待考。先生拟先赴巴黎然后转往瑞士、德国。

七月七日

教育部举行罗斯福图书馆筹备委员会首次会议,朱家骅任主任委员,翁文灏、陈立夫、王世杰、蒋梦麟、蒋廷黻、胡适、傅斯年、吴有训、先生等被推为委员。〔《申报》,1946年7月8日,第6版〕

按:该筹备委员会后又陆续增聘委员,如蒋复璁、张群、张笃伦、张洪沅、卢作孚、晏阳初、龙文治、向传义、胡子昂、沈祖荣、严文郁等。[①]该馆本拟在南京或上海设立,沪市尤其欢迎,但政府考虑再三,决定将其设于陪都重庆,以原中央图书馆为馆舍。

七月十四日

先生从法国福尔巴赫出发前往柏林。〔袁同礼家人提供〕

按:同行者应有李景枞,前欧亚航空公司经理。[②]

七月中下旬　柏林

Wolf Haenisch 在其位于西柏林的寓所设宴款待先生,Wolfgang Seuberlich 应邀作陪。〔《思忆录》,英文部分 p. 39〕

按:Wolf Haenisch(1908-1978),德国汉学家海尼士之子,生于牯

① 《国立中央图书馆馆刊》复刊第1号,1947年,页58。

② 《世界日报》,1946年7月18日,第1版。

岭，时任 Deutsche Staatsbibliothek（东柏林）副馆长。Wolfgang Seuberlich（1906－1985），德国汉学家，后曾撰写文章追忆与先生的交往。

七月二十六日

莱登伯格致函先生，告知由于洛克菲勒基金会的资助，美国图书馆协会购买了数套一九三九年至一九四四年间在美国出版的参考、研究书籍，其中四套已通过联合国善后救济总署发往中国，一九四四年出版者将由出版社直接寄送，并告知这些书籍的拣选依据。

July 26, 1946

Dear Dr. Yuan:

The American Library Association is privileged through the generosity of the Rockefeller Foundation to distribute sets of outstanding publications of a reference and research value published during the years 1939－1944 in this country. We know that those publications would not have found their way during the war to the countries in the war areas, and there was a great likelihood of their not being available later because of paper and other factors limiting production.

It is our pleasure to be able to tell you that four sets of these books, one set of approximately 747 titles (853 volumes) and three sets of approximately 544 titles (593 volumes) published during 1939－1943 were dispatched to you from our office July 12th, through the shipping facilities of the United Nations Relief and Rehabilitation Administration, for distribution to the libraries of China.

The titles for the year 1944 are being sent directly to you from the publishers. A number of these may already have reached you. We shall be most deeply grateful if we can leave to your Committee the distribution of these volumes to the libraries in China which need them most.

The books themselves were selected on the basis of two lists prepared for the Committee on Aid to Libraries in War Areas of the International Relations Board: "Books published in the United States, 1939－43; a selection for Reference Libraries", and "Books published in the United States, 1944; a selection for Reference Libraries". The lists were prepared with two purposes in mind (1) to inform reference libraries, governmental agencies, and individual scholars in war areas of important American books published since the beginning of the war, and (2) to serve as buying lists for the sets of books mentioned above which were purchased for libraries in war areas with funds provided by the Rockefeller Foundation. Three hundred copies of the first list mentioned above have been included with the shipment.

Enclosed are the check lists of the titles selected in both shipments. The numbers refer to the titles as numbered in the first list noted above.

Our Board and the Rockefeller Foundation hope that the books sent will be made available to the students and scholars of China and that they will find them useful.

With expressions of high esteem, believe me to be,

Sincerely yours,
H. M. Lydenberg
Director

〔The American Library Association Archives, China Projects File, Box 2, Books for China, 1944－1947〕

按:该函寄送中央研究院(上海白利南路37b),由此转交分发中央研究院英美赠书分配委员会(Chinese Committee on the Distribution of Books)。此件为录副,附件未存。

七月

先生查明德国收藏中国古代珍贵铜器颇多,其主要公藏机构有慕尼黑国立民族学博物馆(Museum Fünf Kontinente)、科隆东亚艺术博物馆(Museum für Ostasiatische Kunst Köln)、弗莱堡,拟以外交途径索回。〔《东南日报》(上海),1947年1月16日,第10版〕

先生托留学生闵乃大在德购买图书、仪器设备。

按:闵乃大(Ming Nai-ta,1911—2002),江苏如皋人,中国计算机科学先驱。1936年清华大学电机工程专业毕业,后赴德国柏林夏洛滕堡工学院(Berlin-Charlottenburg, Technische Hochschule

Charlottenburg)留学,1948年[1]获博士学位,1949年归国,旋即任教于清华大学电机系,1958年中国科学院吴有训副院长批准闵乃大全家返回东德,在东柏林的洪堡大学工作,后迁入联邦德国。

七月二十七日

先生由德国返回法国。〔袁同礼家人提供〕

七月下旬

中国政府参加巴黎和会代表团人员组织公布,代表为王世杰、郭泰祺、傅秉常、钱泰,副代表金问泗、于焌吉、张谦、梁龙、谢寿康,外交部欧洲司长吴南如、驻意大利使馆参事薛光前、外交部专员黄正铭、先生等担任顾问。〔《申报》,1946年7月30日,第3版;台北:"国史馆",〈法占南海九小岛(三)〉,数位典藏号:020-049904-0016〕

按:7月29日巴黎和会召开。于焌吉(1900—1968),字谦六,天津人,南开大学毕业,后赴美留学,获哥伦比亚大学博士学位,时应任国民政府驻意大利大使。张谦(1888—?),字公捴,广东新会人,早年赴美留学,获宾夕法尼亚大学法学学士学位,时应任国民政府驻葡萄牙公使。黄正铭(1903—1973),字君白,浙江海宁人,1928年毕业于东南大学,1933年赴英留学,后曾任国民政府外交部东亚司司长。

八月九日　巴黎—布鲁塞尔

金问泗、金咸霖与先生一同乘汽车至布鲁塞尔,并在使馆吃晚饭。〔《金问泗日记》下册,2017年,页788〕

按:金咸霖为金问泗长子。

八月十日　根特

圣伯铎禄修道院(Saint Peter's Abbey, Ghent)举办陆征祥领受名誉院长祝圣典礼,金问泗、谢寿康、先生等人出席。晚,金问泗设宴款待谢寿康、尹国祥、先生等人。〔罗光著《陆征祥传》,香港真理学会,1949年,页236;《金问泗日记》下册,页788〕

按:谢寿康时任外交部驻教廷公使,后又升任大使;尹国祥(1910—?),河北唐县人,陆军将领,1945年底赴法,时在法国陆

① 一说为1944年,此处暂依《中国留欧大陆各国博士论文目录》中的记录。

军参谋大学深造，1947 年秋返国。①

八月十一日

金问泗与先生访当地的中国图书馆，遇见 M. Spruyt 及 Mlle. Blomberg。〔《金问泗日记》下册，页 788、866〕

按：M. Spruyt 为比利时首都布鲁塞尔中国图书馆主任，另一人待考。

八月下旬

教育部指派沈兼士、胡适、傅斯年、梅贻琦、袁敦礼、先生等人在平组织图书处理委员会。〔《民国日报》，1946 年 8 月 25 日，第 6 版〕

按：该会主要工作是寻找、发还被日伪掠走的各公藏机构及私人图书，没收日伪各机构、人物、汉奸的藏书并分配。

是年夏

先生将"我国在德文物清单"两页寄呈教育部清理战时文物损失委员会。〔台北"国史馆"，〈清理战时文物损失委员会及交涉文物归还〉，数字典藏号 020-010119-0031〕

按：1946 年 11 月 4 日，清理战时文物损失委员会②举行第 12 次会议，会间曾讨论该项，并决定由教育部转外交部办理。此次在德国调查，尤其涉及平馆回纥文写本，内载玄奘法师列传，1936 年由德国普鲁士学院商借，运抵柏林后由该院 Annemarie von Gabain 女士研究，完成著述两种。该件写本后由普鲁士学院委托英国军用飞机空运至伦敦，再由英国皇家学院航运寄华，约在 1947 年 1 月交还平馆。③

九月四日　巴黎

先生致信陈梦家，谈《海外铜器图录》编录进展及德国古物情况。

梦家吾兄惠鉴：

奉到十九日手书，欣悉铜器总目约明年春夏之交可以完成，至为欣慰。哈佛燕京社既肯资助完成，美国所藏者自应先将已有成绩陆续呈送，如能在美先刊印一部分，尤所企盼，一俟工作完成再请该社资助

---

① 《尹国祥先生访问记录》，台北："中央研究院"近代史研究所，1993 年，页 1-3。

② 该会于 1945 年 4 月 1 日成立，原名为"战区文物保存委员会"。

③ 《大公报》(上海)，1947 年 1 月 14 日，第 11 版。

调查欧洲各国所藏者，至少在欧应留一年，方能完成也。弟此次赴德调查德国所藏铜器及其他文物，内中大部分仍在装箱，且疏散在乡，不易提取。此批中国文物，我国拟要求退还明年和会中当提出，将来拟请吾兄来德协助，此时拟请先将德国各机关所藏之铜器先编一简目（根据德国各博物院之目录及日本著作又 Toledo 博物院集女士编一简目，前请其寄上亦可参考），以便按图索骥。此项工作或较在国内编制为易也，兹将教部所编之目录随函奉上，可供参考（恐系张政烺所编），亦请予以补充。可惜馆藏德国铜器照片仍存在商务，一时不易提取也。弟日内赴瑞士再转意大利，由意飞沪，大约十月初旬可以抵平。匆匆，顺颂俪安。

弟袁同礼顿首

九月四日，巴黎

兹致邓嗣禹一函，并请转交，如已返国，即商诸 Creel。如何之处，并盼示复（寄北平）。

〔方继孝藏札〕

按："Toledo 博物院"即托莱多艺术博物馆（Toledo Museum of Art）。集女士，待考。

九月十一日　瑞士因特拉肯

先生与顾毓琇游览圣女峰。〔《顾毓琇自述（三）》，《传记文学》第 68 卷第 4 期，页 98〕

是年秋

先生致信相关机构（人员），证明周作人担任伪北京图书馆馆长期间，图书毫无散失。〔《申报》，1946 年 9 月 20 日，第 2 版〕

按：9 月 19 日，南京最高法院开始公审周作人，该日主要审查各方提供证据，其中胡适、先生等人的证言、函件多对其有利。

九月下旬

先生由开罗出发，抵达香港。〔《经世日报》，1946 年 10 月 13 日，第 4 版；《益世报》（北平），1946 年 10 月 7 日，第 4 版〕

按：先生抵港日期有两种说法，一为 26 日，一为 29 日。

十月四日

先生返国路过昆明。〔《申报》，1946 年 10 月 7 日，第 8 版〕

十月五日

先生由昆明搭乘飞机抵达上海。〔《华北日报》,1946年10月21日,第3版〕

十月八日　上海—南京

先生由沪转往南京,向教育部接洽平馆经费、组织事宜。〔《北京图书馆馆史资料汇编(1909-1949)》,页837;《华北日报》,1946年10月21日,第3版〕

十月九日

先生赴教育部报告国际图书购买及赠与事宜,表示美国已有一千箱图书运至上海,英国则有七万册书籍尚在途中。另,先生赴平馆驻京办事处,处理馆务。〔《申报》,1946年10月12日,第8版;《北京图书馆馆史资料汇编(1909-1949)》,页837〕

按:自9日至21日,先生每日均赴平馆驻京办事处,此时该处设在金陵大学图书馆内。①

十月中旬

先生与地质调查所洽商,得该所赠送平馆驻京办事处(原工程参考图书馆)大号书架十余件。此外,先生主持购置办公桌椅、书橱、图箱等必要用品,又函上海办事处交来手提英文打字机一架。〔《北京图书馆馆史资料汇编(1909-1949)》,页838〕

十月十六日

平馆向教育部呈文一件,题为《为加拿大教士明义士旧藏甲骨文字散佚堪虞拟请钧部派胡厚宣前往济南调查保存情形并设法收归国有由》,具先生名并钤印。

窃查加拿大传教士明义士 Rev. Menzies 于二十年前在河南安阳小屯一带从事发掘,共得甲骨文字三万余片,关系我国文化至为重要。民国二十五年明氏返国,除携回之一部分现存加拿大博物馆外,余件均存于济南齐鲁大学文学院内。抗战军兴,该大学不悉甲骨文字之重要,并未移存安全地点,日人投降后,职曾托友人前往视察,据报该甲骨文字现尚无恙,惟该大学对此不加重视,散佚堪虞,亟应移交国立图书馆妥为保管云云。窃查该教士明义士在内地擅自发掘,已违中央颁布之古物保存法令,且二十余年以来对此批贵重史料未加研究,今则

① 《北京图书馆馆史资料汇编(1909-1949)》,页862。

散佚堪虞，不得不亟谋安全办法。兹由职馆派甲骨文字专家胡厚宣君前往济南调查该批甲骨文字保存情形，拟请钧部再加委任并致函齐鲁大学，由部委托胡君商洽收归国有办法，俾能永久保藏而免散佚。是否有当，敬候批示遵行，不胜待命之至。谨呈

教育部长朱

国立北平图书馆馆长袁同礼（印）

〔中国第二历史档案馆，教育部档案·全卷宗5，国立北平图书馆请拨员工学术研究补助费经常费有关文书，案卷号11616(4)〕

按：Rev. Menzise即James Mellon Menzies（1885-1957），中文名明义士，加拿大长老会传教士，考古学家，1910年赴河南北部传教，1914年春开始收集、整理、研究商代甲骨。朱家骅批复"可先询问傅斯年。但似由中研院接收，非属意平馆"。

十月十七日

英美赠书分配委员会致信各委员，召集第一次会议。

径启者，英美捐赠书籍将陆续运沪，亟待将分配办法予以决定。兹定于本月十八日（星期五）下午三时在鸡鸣寺中央研究院举行本会第一次会议，即希惠临参加为荷。此致

〇〇〇先生

英美赠书分配委员会谨启

十，十七

〔国家图书馆档案，档案编号1946-※046-外事5-006004〕

按：此件为先生所拟之底稿，该信应分致杭立武、蒋复璁、严文郁等人。

十月十八日

下午三时，英美赠书分配委员会假中央研究院举行第一次会议，翁文灏主席、杭立武、傅斯年、吴有训、蒋复璁、陈裕光（李小缘代）、先生、严文郁出席，顾斗南纪录。先生作为该会秘书报告事项如下：

（一）去岁奉派赴美与彼邦朝野人士接洽发起捐书运动，当时因战事尚未结束、运输困难，仅能作筹备工作，遂决定先由美国图书馆协会联合全国学术团体及出版机关共同组织成立"美国图书中心"。去冬开始进行募集，现仍在继续，预计将募到书刊约二百万册至三百万册，现

向美方申请捐赠者共三十六国。今春赴美后,本人再与接洽,表示中国战事历经数年,需书尤殷,终被列为第一位,约得全部赠书总数十分之一,并能予以分配全套之丛书及期刊,现运到上海者仅一小部分。又美国图书馆协会得洛克菲勒基金会之补助,订购一百四十余种学术期刊二至五份不等,又赠战时出版书籍四套,每套约六百册,此四套该会愿分配于学术中心区域,请分配委员会特予注意。以上两批书刊均委托联总由美运沪,此外尚有教育部订购之学术期刊二十份(自一九四〇年至一九四七年),共装七百余箱,业已运沪,并将传单传阅。

(二)英国方面成立之联合国图书中心原为教长会议下属事业,两年以来共捐书七十万册,性质大都偏重专门学术,经本人接洽,中国可得十分之一,惟装运时均须自购木箱并交联总由英运华,具体事宜正在接洽中。

严文郁报告事项如下:点收美方赠书第一批二百〇五箱、第二批二百五十七箱,均标注受赠机关,另有三十六箱业已到沪,正在申请提领。余下各箱以联总除粮食外暂时停运其他物资,故尚未运到。

随后,讨论事项如下:

(一)拟定分配原则及办法请公决案。决议,本日先行通过下列二原则,俟大批书籍到沪较多再行计议。1. 捐募之书可分研究资料、普通书报两大类,前者应分配与研究性质之图书馆,促成专门化或使之成为有系统之书藏;后者应分配于普通性质之图书馆,但均应顾及区域之分配。2. 受赠之图书馆应尽量公开阅览,凡受赠之书如与该馆已有之书相重复时,应尽量与其他图书馆复本交换,本会发通知时应对此予以特别说明。

(二)分配教育部订购学术期刊二十种由本会建议案。决议,建议教育部尽量先分配与国立大学并授权先生、蒋复璁、严文郁三委员根据各大学现有院系拟订分配办法。

(三)各机关申请分配图书如何办理案。决议,先予存记容再统筹办理。

〔国家图书馆档案,档案编号 1946-※046-外事 5-006045 和 1946-※046-外事 5-006046〕

按:“联总”即联合国善后救济总署,以下各处皆同;“美国图书中心"即 American Book Centre。该会记录存有毛笔、油印件数份,并附"分配原则草案"两页,共计七条。

十月二十一日

先生致信朱家骅,请教育部通知国库紧急支付平馆复员费用以收购傅增湘、伦明、邢端等人藏书。

骝先部长尊鉴:

顷陈援庵先生面告近月以来平津物价奇昂,故家藏书不可自保,江安傅氏、东莞伦氏、南宫邢氏之藏均将散佚,亟应收归国有,以资典藏。前曾呈请钧部在追加复员费项下拨发两亿元,谅荷惠允,拟请通知国库以紧急命令支付,俾能及时收购而免散佚,事关保存文献,至恳提前批准,无任感祷之至。专此,敬候道祺。

职袁同礼谨启

十月廿一日

〔中国第二历史档案馆,教育部档案·全卷宗5,国立北平图书馆经常费预概算书及有关文书,案卷号11617(2)〕

按:朱家骅收到此信后,于24日批复"追加复员费内照拨两亿元"。

先生致信王重民,请其于一九四七年初归国并谈北平馆务、北京大学设立图书专科等事。

有三吾弟:

北平自张家口攻下后,已毫无危险,故吾人计划之事业均可逐步推行。北大校务积极进行,且此次接收之房屋甚多,大可发展。本日适之先生来京,嘱转告务于明年二月以前返国,韩君亦然。北大并与历史博物馆合作(现属中央博物院)作为实习机关,而故宫又将接收古物陈列所合并为一,故图书及博物人材均更感需要也。本馆经费亦大增,近又购入好书不少,足供研究之用。尊处在美各项工作务请予以结束,何时定妥轮船并望先期示知,以便接洽海关免验事。关于L.C.继任人选拟荐钱存训君 Tsun Hsun Tsien 金大毕业,交大圕及本馆服务共十五年,渠中文亦甚佳,且应付外国人较万君为优也。如 Hummel 同意,请寄来一聘书以便办理护照,并盼能于大驾离美以前渠可赶到华京渠稍缓再去似亦无妨,似亦是一好办法。至前往日本照古书一节,因目前日美汇率未定，而美方又不能用黑市相差甚大，故用美金行使极不合算，只好稍缓再为进行矣。北平研究院已聘冯家昇为研究员，如冯君已赴欧即希转告是荷。今晚赴沪，住十日即返平，来函均寄“北平金鱼胡同一号”。又刻拟恢复《大公报·图书副刊》，尊处如有短篇之稿，盼即寄下。蒋慰堂之英文寄刊已寄美，想已看见。近蒋又聘郑振铎及王庸编辑中文季刊，接收陈群之书亦有三十余万册，故藏书亦甚可观也。顺颂大安。

同礼顿首

十月二十一日，南京

关于善本书装箱事，想已筹划，不识应新购之箱已定做否？将来除送 Princeton 展览之百种外，余箱均请于大驾离美前办妥。夏间如交通恢复，再托子明兄运回，以觅直航天津之船为佳，因目前 Handling Express 在国内甚大也。

友人由美返国遗失箱件者甚多，志仁遗失大铁箱一个，均因送入行李房内发生毛病，或未送入行李房被人窃去。大驾返国时应将各箱均编成号数，并须到行李房内 check 一下。敝处所购之皮大衣存于 storage 之件及箱件二件，均请费神携回，重要之件可置于 cabin 内较为安全。

〔中国书店·海淀，四册〕

按：“韩君”应指韩寿萱，“万君”应指万斯年。“蒋慰堂之英文寄刊”当作“蒋慰堂之英文季刊”，即 *Philobiblon: a quarterly review of Chinese publications*（《书林季刊》），钱锺书（C. S. Ch’ien）任编辑，1946 年 6 月创刊，共发行两卷。“往日本照古书”，该事似本拟与美方于 1947 年开展合作，但因困难重重未能成行。[①] 陈群（1890—1945），字人鹤，号中之，福建长汀人，国民党政要，1932 年曾出任内政部政务次长，抗战爆发后，历任维新政府内政部长、汪伪政权内政部长，1942 年在南京颐和路 2 号建泽存书库，1945 年 8 月 17 日服毒自杀。“Princeton 展览”即普林斯顿大学二百周年时举办的中文善本书展览，其展品部分为借自平馆运美之古籍，由吴光清、王际真等具体操办。

① 《经世日报》，1947 年 9 月 10 日，第 4 版。

先生离开南京前往上海，携馆中旧藏德文植物年鉴第四十九卷一册。〔《北京图书馆馆史资料汇编(1909-1949)》，页839〕

按：此册在抗战前应为某机关或个人向平馆借出者。

十月二十三日 上海

先生致信 Dorothy J. Comins，此前两函皆已收到，但寄赠的样刊仍未送达，另告知已成立书籍分配委员会制订援华书刊分配原则。

October 23, 1946

Dear Miss Comins:

Upon my return from Europe, I find your letters of May 16 and July 31 awaiting me here. The three cases of sample copies of periodicals have not yet been received. They will firstly be used for exhibits, and as you kindly suggested, sample copies will be circulated to various cities together with information as to where the sets for the war years are located.

We have had a meeting of the Committee on the Distribution of Books to decide on the principles to be followed in the distribution of materials received from the American Library Association and the American Book Centre. I have taken note that the American Academy of Political and Social Science has been sending complimentary copies of their ANNALS to the National Central Library, and shall see to it that no duplication will be made in this case. As to the disposition of the four sets of the ANNALS, I shall let you know by next mail.

Sincerely yours,

T. L. Yuan

Executive Secretary

Chinese Committee on Distribution of Books

〔国立北平图书馆英文信纸。The American Library Association Archives, China Projects File, Box 2, Yuan T L, 1946-1947〕

按：Committee on the Distribution of Books 应指(中央研究院)英美赠书分配委员会。此件为打字稿，落款处为先生签名，于11月26日送达。

十月三十一日

布朗致函先生,希望中国政府给予额外三千美金用以支付为中国各高校编辑采购书目的相关费用。

October 31, 1946

Dear Dr. Yuan:

We have compiled a report on the present status of our selection of comprehensive purchase bibliographies for the Universities of China for your information. Actually, a great deal has been accomplished, probably far more than the report reveals. The groundwork is well-laid, but our conception of the scope of this project has greatly changed.

We had so little time for practical conversation with you that it has taken us some time to realize all the needs which these purchase bibliographies must meet. Therefore, we now feel that an increased budget at this point will make possible far more valuable bibliographies and will, in the end, be a truer economy. It is our hope that the American Library Association bibliographies will cover, not only your present needs, but also your possible and future needs.

Before arriving at this decision, we have discussed the problem with some of our distinguished consultants. Such discussion has confirmed our impression that additional care and time will be more than compensated for by the greater usefulness of the bibliographies.

You will note that the Medical Bibliography is ready for mimeographing and will be forwarded to Universal Trading Corporation within a very few days. We will continue to forward each bibliography as it is completed with the names of the universities to whom allocations have been made and explicit instructions for purchase. The major bibliographies should move forward fairly rapidly now; that is, the Science, Technology, Agriculture, and Education lists.

Our request for an additional $ 3,000.00 which we wish to present at this time, is designed; (1) to cover the expansion of the remaining bibliographies; (2) to cover the mimeographing cost; (3) and to cover any incidental expense which may arise, not only in the first few months of 1947, but in the completion of the orders for the remaining universities later in the year.

We leave the matter in your hands, Dr. Yuan, with the simple assurance that we consider this additional amount necessary in order to meet the objectives which you so carefully stated when you were in Washington.

Very sincerely yours,

Charles H. Brown

Chairman Committee on the Orient and Southwest Pacific

〔The American Library Association Archives, China Projects File, Box 2, Yuan T L, 1946-1947〕

按:此函寄送重庆,该件为录副。由下文可知,先生并未及时收到原件,但由于 Rae Cecilia Kelly 在 12 月 10 日函中附录了此件,先生得以知悉美方的具体要求。

十月

国民政府行政院令设立北平文物整理委员会,主管北平文物整理事宜,奉派马衡、熊斌、谭炳训、朱启钤、胡适、先生、谷钟秀、梁思成、关颂声等为委员,马衡任主任委员。〔《行政院北平文物整理委员会三十六年度工作概要》,1948年5月,页1〕

按:该会于 1947 年 1 月 1 日正式成立,在北海团城办公,设工务、总务两科。行政院本以朱启钤为主任委员,但其以病请辞,故改派马衡主持。[1] 熊斌(1894—1964),字哲明,湖北礼山人,国民革命军高级将领,时任北平市市长。谭炳训(1907—1959),山东济南人,1931 年毕业于北洋大学土木工程科,时任北平工务局局长。谷钟秀(1874—1949),字九峰,河北定县人,时应任北平市参议会议长;关颂声(1892—1960),广东番禺人,建筑工程师、企业家,营造学社社员,1949 年后赴台。

---

① 《行政院北平文物整理委员会三十五年度工作概要》,1947 年 5 月,页 1。

十一月四日

先生致信吴宓，谈《图书副刊》集稿事。〔《吴宓日记》第10册，北京：生活·读书·新知三联书店，1998年，页171〕

按：本月23日，吴宓覆信推荐程会昌（即程千帆）代自己为该刊集稿，并撰《近十年来中国之文学研究》一文，又代先生致信笪远纶①，催促曾宪三速就平馆职务。

先生致信王重民，谈归国前所需注意事项。

有三吾弟：

近寄一函，内附500元支票一纸前函附200元支票。当时忘言携带现钞，务须选最新者，否则贬值也。教部之九千余元，曾与适之先生联名又致朱部长一函，催其再电使馆，请便中再询陈参事。如仍无电来，请即来一函说明原委，当将原函转呈教部，再催一次。此次到部观察，内中杂乱不堪设想，办公事向不调卷，故往往不接头也。接北平转来上月十一日来函，所述各节与敝见完全相同。前函请担任研究组主任，该组之下即设有目录股，专编专题目录亦在进行之中。近又恢复《图书副刊》，需要短篇文字，有现成者可径寄北平。查台端即将返国，善本书木箱请速做成以便装箱，所需之款如存款不敷用，可在子明兄保管款内支取，至Princeton展览之百种均交子明保管，届时由渠送往陈列可也。《季刊》仍在申印刷，由李芳馥及王育伊分任英文及中文本编辑事项，每年印行二次，尚不难也。关于返国遗失行李者，据云其毛病往往出于转运公司未曾送到船上，故台端返国须于开船前三日赶到金山，将行李由车站取出后，自雇大货车送到船上较为稳妥，凡返国者均望以此告之。后日返平前日由港返申，正接洽购伦氏藏书。匆匆，顺颂

大安。

同礼顿首

十一，四，上海

适之先生编《文史周刊》，在《大公报》发表，想已见过。

钱存训来美继任，如无问题，请Hummel来一电报或聘函，方能申

---

① 笪远纶（1900—1976），字经甫，江苏镇江人，清华学校毕业后赴美留学，获麻省理工学院工程学学士学位，归国后历任清华大学、沪江大学、武汉大学工程院教授，时任教于重庆大学。《吴宓日记》将其错排为"竺远纶"，特此说明。

请护照。

北平研究院已聘冯君,请转告速归。

〔中国书店·海淀,四册〕

按:1946 年 10 月 16 日,《文史周刊》作为《大公报》(上海)副刊之一创办,实际应由毛准负责主持。“冯君”即冯家昇。

十一月五日

先生致信莱登伯格,告知已回到中国,此前美国洛克菲勒基金会和图书馆协会购买、捐助的科学期刊均按期运抵中国并将分配给各参考图书馆,四套美国参考出版物刚刚收到并将分发各馆,表示再次感谢。

November 5, 1946

Dear Dr. Lydenberg:

I have recently returned to China after having spent four months in Europe. Your good letter of July 26 has been awaiting me here, and I am taking the first opportunity to acknowledge its receipt with grateful thanks.

The various issues of American scientific and learned journals have arrived regularly, and are being distributed to those reference libraries which can make the best use of them. The four sets of American publications of reference value have just been received, and we are now checking over them before distributing them to various libraries.

We are very much indebted to the American Library Association for the splendid effort in supplying us with the much-needed American publications in connection with the replenishment of Chinese libraries. We also appreciate highly the foresight and generosity of the Rockefeller Foundation in making the gift to China possible. The presence of these publications in this country will form an everlasting token of American friendship toward Chinese scholars.

With kindest regards, I remain,

Sincerely yours

T. L. Yuan

Director

P. S. When you write me, please use the above address.

〔国立北平图书馆英文信纸。The American Library Association Archives, China Projects File, Box 1, National Library at Peiping, 1946-1947〕

按:此时莱登伯格已退休,由米尔泽夫斯基接替出任美国图书馆协会国际关系委员会主席。此件为打字稿,落款处为先生签名,于12月30日送达。

十一月六日

先生由上海搭乘飞机返回北平,下午三时,抵达西郊机场。某记者来访,先生略谈此次出国任务:(一)奉政府令,赴欧美募集图书,以供国内各大学研究机关之用,此次募集三十万册,美国即占二十万册,多系参考资料,即可由各国运回,分配应用。(二)赴德国调查我国文物,前据德人云,我在德文物,已悉遭炸毁,但经调查证明系德人之妄言,其中重要者,有一九〇四年在新疆吐鲁番抢去之壁画多幅,即可用外交方式索回。(三)参加巴黎和会,担任我国顾问,专事搜集各国资料共两箱,外交部与平馆各有一份完全者,实为二次大战中之珍贵材料,足供研究。① 〔《经世日报》(北平),1946年11月7日,第4版〕

十一月七日

某记者来访,先生略谈平馆复员情况、欧美各国图书馆复兴近况,并谓平馆将以高深研究为将来之前途,协助市立图书馆为一般民众服务,拟设立苏联、日本两个专门研究室,并继续开展抗战史料的征辑和整理工作。〔《大公报》(天津),1946年11月8日,第3版〕

十一月八日

下午四时,中国政治学会在南池子会所召开光复后首次理事会,到者数十人。胡适为会议主席,讨论会务事宜并选举正副会长,先生、陈岱孙分任之,此外通过增选王季高等二十余人入会。六时许,事毕始散。〔《华北日报》,1946年11月9日,第3版〕

按:王季高(1905—?),湖南常德人,清华大学毕业,后赴美留学,获哥伦比亚大学博士学位,归国后在中央大学政治系执教,后任北平特别市教育局局长等职。

---

①《申报》,1946年11月9日,第8版。

张伯苓致函先生，请将教育部平津特派员公署接收日本各华北机构旧藏及在欧美募集书刊酌情分配南开大学，以充实馆藏。

守和先生座右：

敬恳者，查本校复校伊始，原有图书早已荡然无存，刻正各方搜集，以备充实。兹闻教育部平津特派员公署接收日本图书保存会存储图书四十二万册，已交贵馆保存。该项图书想已整理就绪，其中或不乏复本，拟请惠赐本校，以供浏览。

再，先生再次赴美各方奔走，获得图书珍品颇多，可否酌予分赠。倘承协助，实拜嘉惠无涯矣。特函奉恳，诸希鉴察是幸。敬颂公绥。

张伯苓拜启

十一，八

〔《张伯苓私档全宗》，页1157、1377〕

按：1948年2月，教育部平津区图书处理委员会拨交近六百余种日文书籍与南开大学。

十一月十八日

上午十时，先生赴北洋大学北平分部，应邀于国父纪念周上演讲。〔《经世日报》(北平)，1946年11月15日，第4版〕

十一月二十日

下午，先生访徐旭生，晤谈。〔《徐旭生文集》第10册，页1485〕

十一月二十一日

下午，平馆馆员丁濬引季羡林来见，先生与之晤谈，谈借书事。〔《此心安处是吾乡：季羡林归国日记(1946-1947)》，重庆：重庆出版社，2015年，页118〕

按：季羡林时为北京大学东语系主任，商借平馆所藏梵文和巴利文文献。

先生致信顾斗南，谈平馆西南馆员来平事宜。

斗南先生大鉴：

兹有重庆同事贾芳、卢延甲二君，不日由川取道飞京返平。请在京先予代备住处，附证明书一件，并请转交为荷。专此，顺候台祺。

弟袁〇〇

卅五，十一，廿一

附证明书一纸。

〔国家图书馆档案，档案编号 1945-※057-综合 5-023061〕

按：此件为底稿。

十一月二十二日

Marshall C. Balfour 至平馆，与先生晤谈。〔Marshall C. Balfour's Diaries, Rockefeller Archive Center, Rockefeller Foundation records, Officers' Diaries, RG 12〕

按：此次来访，应受先生电话邀请。Balfour 认为先生积极、乐观如恒。

十一月二十三日

下午四时半，先生在家召集冯至、毛准、郑昕、郑华炽、季羡林等人，讨论中德学会留存问题，约六时散。〔《此心安处是吾乡：季羡林归国日记（1946－1947）》，页 119〕

按：郑华炽（1903—1990），广东中山人，物理学家，1928 年南开大学毕业，后赴德留学，后转奥地利继续深造，1934 年获得博士学位，时执教于北京大学。中德学会失去德国政府的资金支持，但却拥有大批珍贵书籍、刊物，亟待接管。8 月 13 日中德学会中方会员蒋复璁、冯至、毛准、姚从吾与傅吾康商谈，决定将学会图书和设施并入平馆，续聘曾在学会学习德语的刘东元管理学会图书。此外，先生还曾介绍傅吾康结识朱家骅。①

十一月二十四日

先生致信徐旭生，告陈寅恪拟售其所藏《百衲本二十四史》，询国立北平研究院史学研究所是否有意购买。〔《徐旭生文集》第 10 册，页 1485〕

十一月二十五日

下午，先生访徐旭生。〔《徐旭生文集》第 10 册，页 1485〕

十一月下旬

某记者来访，先生告知平馆决定增设国际问题研究室、舆图研究室，预计十二月一日开放。此外，先生告知聘任情况，吴光清回国后将任秘书主任兼总务主任，顾子刚任西文秘书，曾宪三任采访主任，赵万里任善本主任，于道泉任特藏主任，王访渔任舆图主任，王重民任研究主任，莫余敏卿任阅览

① 《为中国着迷：一位汉学家的自传》，页 154。

主任,张凤举任日本研究室顾问,John J. Gapanovich 任苏联研究室顾问,陈寅恪、周一良、陈梦家等出任编纂委员会委员。〔《时事新报》(上海),1946 年 11 月 27 日,第 2 版〕

按:John J. Gapanovich(1891-1983),俄国历史学家,中文名噶邦福,圣彼得堡大学毕业,1931 年 8 月到清华大学任教,1953 年离开中国前往澳大利亚,何兆武在《上学记》中对其有相当记述。

十一月二十六日

平馆同人联名呈请先生彻查沦陷时期王访渔附逆之罪行。〔《东南日报》(上海),1946 年 11 月 28 日,第 8 版〕

十一月二十七日

先生代表平馆致信欧美各高校、图书馆、研究机构,告知平馆已经关闭重庆、昆明办事处,馆务迁回北平原址。

November 27, 1946

Dear Sirs:

We wish to inform you that we have closed down our offices at Chungking and Kunming and are now concentrating our work at Peiping, where our address is as follows:

National Library of Peiping,
1, Wen Ching Chieh,
Peiping, China.

We should be much obliged to you if you would kindly make the necessary change in your mailing list, so that we may receive your publications regularly in the future.

Thanking you for your continued cooperation.

Yours very truly,
T. L. Yuan
Director

〔国立北平图书馆英文信纸。Columbia University Library, New York State Library School Collection, Series 2 Student Records, Box 65, Folder Yuan, T. L〕

按:此件为打字稿,落款处为先生签名,寄送哥伦比亚大学图书馆。

十一月底

某记者来访，先生略谈三事，一为王访渔媚敌传闻辩白；二教育部拟在西北增设图书馆，先生建议广州、武昌、上海也应有所考虑；三北平接收日文图书四十余万册，现置于太庙编目整理，等待分配。〔《经世日报》(北平)，1946年12月1日，第2版〕

十一、十二月间

朱家骅致函胡适、沈兼士、梅贻琦、傅斯年、袁敦礼、先生，告教育部对分配兴亚院、东方文化协议会等五单位旧藏书籍的意见，尤其考虑将其分润东北各省院校及山东大学。

适之、兼士、月涵、孟真、志仁、守和诸兄大鉴：

奉诵惠札，忻聆种切。关于兴亚院、东方文化协议会等五单位书籍分配问题，诸兄拟以《清实录》、《明实录》两书分拨北平图书馆与历史语言研究所一节，自应照拨。至余书处理办法原当同意，惟念北平一地如北平图书馆与北大图书馆等藏书颇多，而东北各省与山东等地极为缺乏，今东北大学、长春大学、长白师院既已恢复，图书设备一无所有，一时未能购置，但不能比伪满时代为差。弟意此项书籍以百分之二十拨交清华大学外，似均应统筹分配于上列各校院及山东大学较为合理，且甚望北平各图书馆之复本图书肯能分赠以上各校院也。各书如何分配，并请处理会先将目录送部。至关于日本图书保存会之正本书籍移交北平图书馆整理后，成立日本研究室及日文书库一节，亦应照办，惟其中所有复本亦应分配东北、长春、长白三校院为妥。至所需迁移费壹千万元、整理费伍千万元，均可照拨。耑此奉复，顺颂公祺。

弟朱家骅拜启

〔《北京图书馆馆史资料汇编(1909-1949)》，页849-850〕

按：此件为打字稿，落款处为朱家骅签名。左侧有胡适亲笔标注"胡适看过。卅五，十二，五夜"。

十二月九日

费慰梅覆函先生，告知由美国国务院拨款购买的书籍只有一小批抵达中国，并已分发给西部各高校图书馆，上海收到箱件不多且并未开箱，此外该类书籍的分发与美国图书馆协会毫无关系，不受其监督。

American Embassy

Nanking, December 9, 1946

Dear Dr. Yuan:

In reply to your letter of December 2nd, of the books purchased by the American Library Association under a grant from the Department of State, only a very small shipment has arrived in China and that one came last year to West China and was distributed to university libraries in that area. No books have yet been unpacked in Shanghai and, in fact, none of these books have been received for nearly a year.

We are at the present time doing our best to trace these shipments, and arrangements for their distribution will be made as soon as they are received. The distribution will be made by the United States Information Service under the supervision of the Embassy, and the American Library Association will have no voice in the distribution of the books.

Yours sincerely,

Wilma Fairbank

Cultural Relations Officer

〔The American Library Association Archives, China Projects File, Box 2, Books for China Correspondence, 1947〕

按:United States Information Service,一般译为美国新闻处。此件为抄件。

十二月十日

先生致信史蒂文斯,告知平馆接收了大量的日文文献因此正筹备日本研究中心,此外还筹设苏俄研究中心。

December 10, 1946

Dear Dr. Stevens:

Since I had the pleasure of meeting you in New York, I have spent four months in Europe. While there I bought a great number of books which have already been shipped to Peiping. I returned to Peiping four weeks ago and found them already on our shelves.

You will be interested to know that in spite of inflation and political instability, our work at the National Library goes forward. In addition to the main library which has been kept intact, we have just established a branch library containing about 300,000 volumes of Japanese books which were left over by the Japanese in Peiping and are now turned over to the National Library by the Government. Several experts are studying the collection and we are trying to bring it up-to date by securing material issued since Japanese surrender. It will serve as a centre for Japanese studies in China.

We are also engaged in collecting Russian material; and I am glad to inform you that we have been successful in obtaining extremely rare items from private collections in Peiping. I am confident that if further financial support is coming, we shall be able to maintain a centre for Russian Studies having close liaison with the work of Russian studies in Europe and the United States. As you may recall, this is a matter which has been in my mind during the last few years.

I understand that both you and Mr. Marshall were in Europe recently, but I regret that I did not have the opportunity of meeting you there. I sincerely hope that you will soon arrange to pay us a visit as you promised me. It would give us great pleasure to see you and Mr. Marshall here and to show you how we could do things much cheaper than Americans can do either in China or in the States.

With best wishes for a Merry Christmas and Happy New Year,

Yours sincerely,

T. L. Yuan

Director

〔平馆（重庆沙坪坝）英文信纸。Rockefeller Foundation. Series 601: China; Subseries 601.R: China-Humanities and Arts. Vol. Box 47. Folder 391〕

按：此件为打字稿，先生略加修改，落款处为其签名。

Rae Cecilia Kelly 覆函先生，询问中国专业院校和研究所所需购买书籍是以专业知识为界限还是也需要一般通识类书籍，并告知医药、农学、艺术和一般参考书的书目即将发给美国世界贸易公司。

December 10, 1946

Dear Dr. Yuan:

We were pleased to learn from your letter of October 23rd to Miss Comins of your safe arrival in China and hope that your work is going forward.

You should have received in early November our progress report on the bibliographies for Chinese universities, together with our request for additional funds. However, as the mails are not yet completely regular, we are enclosing copies of the report and of Mr. Brown's letter.

The information which we requested will be required soon for compilation of the bibliographies for the special institutions, i. e., curricula outline for N. Mercantile Marine College, N. Kweiyang Teachers College, N. College of Social Education, Fukien Research Academy and N. Institute of Compilation and Translations; also, the statement of needs of the N. Central Library will be necessary.

Since writing the letter referred to, we have needed to know whether certain special institutions will require books other than in their subjects and general reference. To be exact, will N. Mercantile Marine College and N. Institute of Pharmacy require the books in general arts, philosophy, Western language and literature, Chinese history, Western history and geography?

It is a pleasure to report that the lists in medicine, agriculture, the arts and general reference will probably be in the hands of Universal Trading Corporation when you receive this letter. Copies will be forwarded to you as each subject list is mimeographed.

Please be assured of the desire of all of us concerned with this work to see it move forward rapidly to its culmination in the shape of books on Chinese library shelves.

Hoping to hear from you soon, I am

Very sincerely yours,

Rae Cecilia Kelly

Assistant

〔The American Library Association Archives, China Projects File, Box 2, Yuan T L, 1946-1947〕

按:Rae Cecilia Kelly 时任美国图书馆协会国际关系委员会助理,其办公场所位于华盛顿。N. Mercantile Marine College, N. Kweiyang Teachers College, N. College of Social Education, Fukien Research Academy and N. Institute of Compilation and Translations 依次为国立吴淞商船专科学校、国立贵阳师范学院、国立社会教育学院(时应在南京和苏州)、福建省研究院和国立编译馆,N. Institute of Pharmacy 似指国立中国医药研究所。该函寄送重庆办事处,翌年 1 月 21 日送达先生处。此件为录副。

十二月十一日

中午十二时,平津国立院校长谈话会假清华园举行,梅贻琦、陈荩民(北洋)、袁敦礼、郑天挺、徐佩琨(铁院)、徐悲鸿(艺专)、先生、李麟玉、杨光弼、牛文清(大辞典编纂处)等十余人出席。讨论议案四项,依次为学生公费米价,继续补助公教人员医药、生育、子女教育费用,冬季购煤方式,兼任教员待遇。〔《新中国报》(北平),1946 年 12 月 12 日,第 2 版〕

按:陈荩民(1895—1981),原名陈宏勋,浙江天台人,早年赴法入里昂中法大学,获理学硕士学位,时任北洋工学院院长。徐佩琨(1892—1980),字叔刘,江苏吴江人,南洋公学毕业,后赴美留学,获俄亥俄大学经济学硕士学位,时应任国立北平铁道管理学院院长。

十二月十四日

中华图书馆协会撰《为呈送职会本年秋冬二季工作报告表检附收据祈核发七至十二月补助费并呈报职会通讯处等由》,具先生名并钤印。〔台北"国史馆",〈中国图书馆协会请补助(教育部)〉,数位典藏号 019-030508-0015〕

十二月二十六日

中午,先生与马衡假太庙事务所设宴款待司徒雷登,梅贻琦、郑天挺、毕正宣、沈兼士等人作陪。〔《申报》,1946 年 12 月 27 日,第 1 版;《大公报》(香港),1946 年 12 月 27 日,第 2 版〕

按:上午,叶剑英赴燕京大学访问司徒雷登。中午,宴毕,司徒雷登又至军调部。

十二月二十七日

先生致信蒋梦麟,请其从旁催促教部有关机构从速拨付平馆存美善本书籍运费,以利钱存训启程协助。

梦麟先生尊鉴:

敝馆存美善本书籍,近经部中决定运回并发下美金叁仟陆百元在案。兹因该项书籍亟待装箱,拟派敝馆编纂钱存训君前往协助,其所需旅费即在部款拨付,拟请通知主管部分,对于此案加以注意,不胜感祷。专此,敬候道祺。

后学袁同礼拜

十二,廿七

〔《北京图书馆馆史资料汇编(1909-1949)》,页818〕

按:此为抄件。

是年冬

刘树楷商借款项为王重民父亲及族人购买衣被,先生慨然借予百万元。〔台北胡适纪念馆,档案编号HS-JDSHSC-0939-009〕

按:本年10月,王步霄携其孙辈赴北平避乱,因姻亲关系投奔刘树楷。

一九四七年　五十三岁

一月三日

米尔泽夫斯基致函先生，告其已经接替莱登伯格担任美国图书馆协会国际关系委员会主席，表示乐于继续承担为中国高校挑选图书的重任。

January 3, 1947

17 Pao-King Road,

Shanghai, China.

Dear Mr. Yuan:

Please accept our thanks for your letter of November 5 in which you note that you had returned to China after having spent four months in Europe. I know that you must be glad to be home even though your absence has meant that a great deal of work has piled up for you. We are looking forward to renewing our most pleasant relationship with you in the months to come.

Since Mr. Lydenberg has retired from the Directorship of this office, I have been privileged to be named as successor. It will give me a great deal of personal pleasure, as well as professional, to work with you.

We are especially glad to have your word that the periodicals and the books have now been received. We were worried about them since we were afraid that something might have happened to them. In your hands, we know that they will receive the kind of distribution which needs to take into account all of the library needs of China, both governmental and non-governmental.

Because I know that other members of our Board will be pleased to have word of your return to China and to know that the distribution of books and periodicals is taking place, I am having a copy of your letter sent to each member of the Board.

We trust that by this time you will have received the communication about the selection of books for Chinese universities. This is one of the most interesting jobs it has been our privilege to be able to carry out and we hope that we may be able to continue it.

Sincerely yours,

Marion A. Milczewski,

Director

〔The American Library Association Archives, China Projects File, Box 1, Correspondence about China, National Library at Peiping, 1946-1947〕

按:此件为录副。

一月四日

《大公报》(天津)刊登先生撰写的《图书周刊》复刊词。

二十二年九月,我和几位对于中外图书目录学有兴趣的朋友,在天津《大公报》创刊了一个《图书副刊》。每周一期。直到二十六年七月二十二日,出至第一百九十一期。因卢沟桥事变突起,炮声震撼平市,本刊编辑人仓皇离平而停刊,到如今整整十年了。我们这次又应《大公报》之约,自今年一月起,在津沪两地同时复刊。这是非常值得庆幸的事。缅怀过去,瞻望未来,有不能已于言者。

在那年九月二十二日创刊号"卷头语"里,我曾说过下边这几句话:中国是印刷术最先发明的国家,西元后第二世纪便已知道造纸,第八世纪左右便已发明雕版印刷,第十一世纪左右便已知道利用活字。到了十七世纪左右,又已有了世界上最古而又最精美的五彩套印书籍。然而近二十几年书籍出版的数字非常低落,据统计不过二四八〇〇种,这真是一个可怜的数目。到今日印刷术最先发明的民族,反成了出版业最低落的国家。

我又说:一国图书出版的盛衰,就是一个民族生活力强弱的表现。我们打算从这方面去找出我们这民族再生的源泉和优良的品种,培植起来,积垒起来,以求达到理想的境界。

因此,我们想用一部分的力量,来作中外新旧图书的介绍和批评,给予一般人以书籍选择的尺度，并着重于有系统的评介，以便读者能够“触类旁通”。此外又拟尽力来传达学术界的消息，使一般人士也能知道中国和外国学术界进展的轮廓。为了实现此种理想起见，除常常刊登“学术消息”外，又拟仿照外国学术年报办法，每年作一次概括的总账，综合论述这一年内学术界出版界进展的实况。

这些老生常谈，在抗战胜利周年后的今日，依然是针对现实的说法，依然是我们所怀抱惟一的愿望。

回想这八年来，敌寇肆虐，空袭频繁，以及其他种种天灾人祸，无论前方后方，被敌寇间接的或直接的摧毁和掠夺的图书，真难以数计。同时相反地，转移到后方的出版界，因为原料缺乏，工价高翔，运输困难，种种客观条件的束缚，生产量也萎缩到了极点。影响所及，精神食粮的供应，顿时失去平衡，学生说书贵，教授闹书荒，都是常见的事。这不仅中国如此，除美国外，英国及其他欧洲各国也遭逢到同样的厄运。

现在大战已成过去，出版界亟应急起直追，加紧复员，至少限度须立刻恢复到战前的生产量，以适应当前需要。而全国各处以“精神食粮仓库”自命的公私立图书馆，尤应早日得到政府和社会的协力，设法充实起来，健全起来，而善尽其职责。

我们这个《周刊》，不前不后，恰于此时复刊，所负时代的艰巨使命，自非往日可比。一方面要评介战后八年来，尤其近二三年来中外新版图书，作为《周刊》的主要任务，同时我们也要尽力报道学术界和出版界的消息，以供读者观摩和参考。此外目录、版本、校勘之学，本是历史方法亦即科学方法的一部分，我们也将以新姿态、新资料与读者相见，并请求专家批评，以期有所改进。

以上这一点点的愿望，我们也不敢自信是否能够顺利做到。我们惟有恳切地盼望国内外朋友们和读者们，给予我们伟大的同情和协助，以加强我们的信心与努力。

〔《大公报·图书周刊》第1期，1947年1月4日，第7版〕

按：该文失收于《袁同礼文集》。

一月六日

顾斗南致函先生，请代询相关人士汪精卫赠日本皇室屏风是否为故宫博物院旧藏。

守和先生赐鉴：

敬启者，汪逆于三十年六月访问敌国日本时，赠送其皇室翡翠屏风四扇，是否故宫旧物，莫得而知，然国宝不宜流传于外，可否由我诸公建议教部追还之处，自钧裁。专此，敬请道安。

顾斗南谨启

一月六日

〔《马衡年谱长编》，页 937〕

按：先生收到后将该函转与马衡，后者批复“非故宫物。衡”。

一月八日

中午十二时，平津地区国立院校长第五次谈话会在北平艺专举行，先生应参加。〔《民国日报》（天津），1947 年 1 月 5 日，第 4 版〕

一月上旬

外交部部长王世杰致电先生，邀请提前赴京，并担任中国对日要偿代表团外交部代表赴日工作。〔《华北日报》，1947 年 1 月 13 日，第 2 版〕

一月十一日

中午，先生在馆中设宴，胡适、陈垣、向达、周一良、赵万里、邵循正、容肇祖、季羡林等人与席。饭后，先生引导诸位参观最近购入之宋版书，胡适谈《水经注》版本问题。〔《此心安处是吾乡：季羡林归国日记（1946－1947）》，页 144；《华北日报》，1947 年 1 月 12 日，第 3 版〕

先生致信 Laurence J. Kipp，澄清英美赠书分配委员会与经济部毫无关系，前者隶属于教育部，并由中央研究院负责接收英美捐赠图书期刊，另向其询问美国图书中心此前发送给中国各基督教大学六百箱书籍的航运等信息。

January 11, 1947

Mr. Laurence J. Kipp

Acting Executive Director

American Book Center

Study S 46, Deck A

Library of Congress

Washington 25, D. C., U. S. A.

Dear Mr. Kipp:

A copy of your letter of November 4, 1946, addressed to H. E. Y. W. Wong, Minister of Economic Affairs, has been forwarded to me for reference.

I am afraid the Chinese Embassy in Washington has misunderstood the relation between the Ministry of Economic Affairs and the Committee on Distribution of Books because of our Chairman, Dr. Wong Wen-hao, who was once Minister of Economic Affairs. Our Committee was appointed by the Academia Sinica, but the Ministry of Education is paying our expenses, though it does not interfere with our work. Our Committee so far has had no relations with the Ministry of Economics.

The Academia Sinica in Shanghai has furnished work space to our Committee. Hereafter, please send shipments by UNRRA-CNRRA to Chinese Committee on Distribution of Books, c/o Academia Sinica, 37-B Brenan Road, Shanghai. Correspondence may be addressed there too. In case there are matters requiring my personal attention, please send a copy to me here in Peiping.

Please look up your files whether you have ever sent 600 cases of books addressed to Christian Universities, and give me all information you have regarding their shipment. These cases, according to Dr. Y. W. Wong, were addressed to the Ministry of Economic Affairs, but the Ministry has not received them. Our Committee is now locating the whereabouts of these cases.

I hope this matter will receive your attention.

Yours sincerely,

T. L. Yuan

〔The American Library Association Archives, China Projects File, Box 2, Books for China Correspondence, 1947〕

按：Laurence J. Kipp，美国图书馆专家，北达科他州河谷市州立师范学院（Valley City State Teachers College）毕业，后获得伊利诺伊大学图书馆学硕士学位，曾任尤里卡学院 (Eureka College) 图书馆馆长。“H. E. Y. W. Wong”应指翁文灏（Wong Wen-hao），时任经济部长；CNRRA 即 China National Relief and Rehabilitation Administration（中国善后救济总署）。该件为副本。

先生致电布朗，告捐赠图书尚未分发，随后寄上相关报告。

DONATED BOOKS NOT YET DISTRIBUTED. CHRISTIAN UNIVERSITIES RECEIVE EQUAL ATTENTION FROM COMMITTEE. REPORT FOLLOWS.

〔The American Library Association Archives, China Projects File, Box 2, Books for China Correspondence, 1947〕

一月十三日

先生致信布朗，告知曾发电报，虽然已收到四类书刊，但因教育部一直没有公布一九四零以来订购的二十套美国期刊的分配方案，只得暂缓书刊发放工作，并告中央研究院英美赠书分配委员会对教育部订购期刊没有分发权，但对美国图书馆协会、美国图书中心捐赠的书刊会严格遵守国际关系委员会制订的“书刊在中国分发原则”，坦言这一工作的艰巨性，极难让所有接受机构满意。

January 13, 1947

Dear Dr. Brown:

On receiving your letter of December 24, I sent you the following radiogram:

DONATED BOOKS NOT YET DISTRIBUTED. CHRISTIAN UNIVERSITIES RECEIVE EQUAL ATTENTION FROM COMMITTEE. REPORT FOLLOWS.

Pending a fuller report to be submitted later, I wish to advise that the following four categories of books have been received by our Committee. (a) American publications issued during war years allocated to China by the ALA. They have not been distributed because our Committee has been waiting to know just what would be done with the $100,000 worth of books donated to Chinese libraries by the Department of State. I contacted Mrs. Fairbank, but as you can see from the enclosed copy of her reply, we did not get anywhere. Our Committee feels that the distribution of books should be coordinated, even if handled by two separate organizations. Though the Committee is at present unable to effect the desired coordination, I hope this objective may ultimately be achieved. Any assistance your Committee may be able to lend us in this matter will be appreciated.

(b) American journals allocated to China by the ALA. They have not been distributed because our Committee has been waiting for the decision of the Ministry of Education regarding the distribution of the 20 sets of American journals which the Ministry subscribed since 1940. If the Ministry decides to allocate these journals to national institutions, a large part of the journals donated by the ALA will go to private colleges, taking into account the subscriptions already placed on their behalf by the Associated Boards of Christian Colleges in New York, and also taking into account the courses of study offered in each of these private colleges.

(c) Books shipped by the American Book Center but consigned to various institutions. They represent the duplicates selected from the Library of Congress, books collected by the Associated Boards of Christian colleges, cases and packages sent via the Smithsonian Institution, etc. In each case the name of the address was marked on the book case and our Committee has distributed them according to instructions received from the American Book Center. Among them, 257 cases of books were designated to private colleges by the American Book Center and all of them have been sent to the National Christian Council at 163 Yuan Ming Yuan Road, Shanghai, as instructed.

(d) Books shipped to China by other agencies than the American Book Center and the ALA. Cards are being made for these books and they will be distributed equally between National and Christian universities.

The special representative in China referred to in your letter must evidently have mixed up the distribution of the 20 sets of American journals subscribed by the Ministry of Education with the journals and books donated by the ALA and the American Book Center. He might wish to exaggerate his statements with a view to securing larger financial support from the Associated Boards of Christian Colleges!

As I explained to you previously, our Committee has no control over the distribution of the journals subscribed by the Ministry of Education. As to the distribution of the books and periodicals donated by the ALA and the American Book Center, our Committee shall observe strictly the "Principles in Regard to the Distribution of Books in China" as approved by the ALA Board on International Relations. At the same time, we shall see to it that at each institution there shall be no duplication of donated books and periodicals received from various sources.

I assure you that this is not an easy task. So many requests have been received that we feel overwhelmed, and there are practical difficulties that make it difficult for us to make decisions. Different libraries have suffered damages to different extent, but are equally clamorous for donated books. For us to satisfy everyone is hardly to be hoped for, but it will help the Committee greatly if libraries, desiring to share in the distribution, would communicate with us directly and not send exaggerated statements to New York as the special representative has done.

In sending the cases to China, the American Book Center has not used the correct address. I enclose herewith copies of correspondence for your information.

Yours sincerely,

T. L. Yuan

〔The American Library Association Archives, China Projects File, Box 2, Books for China Correspondence〕

按:此为抄件。

潘光旦致函先生,商谈日伪图书分配事。〔《潘光旦文集》第 11 卷,北京:北京大学出版社,2000 年,页 230〕

按:敌伪图书由五部分组成,分别为兴亚院华北联络部调查所、东亚文化协议会、桥川时雄、久下司、小谷晴亮。

一月十四日

朱家骅覆函先生,告知教育部已拨专款负责美英运来图书、仪器运费,并设立专职机构负责在上海办理该项事务。

守和吾兄大鉴：

客岁十二月十六日惠书拜悉。关于上海提领国外捐购图书运费事，近已由部拨汇一千万元交李芳馥君，谅可敷用。兹以该项图书源源入口，提领清理工作至为繁重，已在沪设立国外捐购图书仪器提运清理办事处，专办此事，今后入口箱件当可迅捷处理矣。专复，即颂时祺。

弟朱家骅顿首

元月十四日

〔教育部部长室用笺。国家图书馆档案，档案编号1945-※057-综合5-005003〕

按：1945、1946年先生在欧美订购的图书、仪器确须由国民政府教育部支付运费，因此有专款拨付的必然需求，但先生募捐的图书则多不在此列。此件为打字稿，落款处钤朱家骅印。

一月十五日

某记者来访，先生告以下诸事：一、坚辞外交部对外要偿代表团代表一职；二、收缴约四十一万册日文书籍，现已移至太庙，正派员整理并待分配，平馆在此基础上将成立日本研究室；三、平馆已收到美方（杜威博士）捐赠西文图书一百三十余箱，日内将编辑整理；四、夜间阅览室待煤炭供应恢复后继续承办；五、奉教育部令代为接收伪教育总署档案；六、教育部拨款委托平馆上海办事处提运、整理国外捐赠的图书。〔《世界日报》，1947年1月16日，第3版〕

下午，潘光旦、张准至金鱼胡同宅访先生，谈日伪图书分配事。先生告知待分配的图书均已自东厂胡同运至太庙，仍分别堆放，近日正准备添置木架用以插放，如何整理分配、复本如何处置、教育部处理意见如何答复，均需与平馆协商后解决。〔《潘光旦文集》第11卷，页231〕

按：是日，潘、张二人先拜访了敌伪产业处理局孙越崎，询问五单位图书有无清单，但未得结果。与先生谈后，又至东厂胡同见分配委员会委员沈兼士、胡适，希望他们帮助清华大学获得该批图书的八成。

一月十六日

上午十一时，教育部视察平津地区高等教育专员吴正华、刘求南前往平馆，

先生负责接待并报告馆务，二人对平馆馆藏和业务情况极为称许。〔《民国日报》(天津)，1947年1月17日，第4版〕

按：吴正华，字西屏，安徽庐江人，曾任北京大学历史系讲师，1940年6月入教育部，时应任学术审议委员会委员。刘求南，安徽南陵人，1946年9月入教育部训委会工作。

一月十九日

李芳馥致函先生，告接收整理美国赠书上海临时办事处前后收到寄到书刊批次情况，指出问题关键在于联总运输困难，另将飞回武汉脱离该项事务。

守和先生赐鉴：

关于分配处前后收到及待提书箱，谨报告如下：

(一)第一批收到205箱，系美图书中心寄来，其中只有七箱寄交图书分配委员会分配，书单另邮寄上。

(二)第二批收到257箱，箱面概注明受赠机关，分配处只分别通知而已。

(三)第三批收到72箱，系赵主任夫人筹用United China Relief名义所捐得，现在整理中。

第四批收到壹箱，系教部在英国所购书，箱面写明寄中央信托局。

第五批70箱，系教部托British Council在瑞典所购英文书，尚未提到分配处。

第六批18箱，由联总运来，只收到提单并未注明来源，大约系美中心书。

第七批74箱，情形同上

第八批101箱，系教部在英所购书，在待提中。

此外分配处收到ALA所赠之Outstanding publications of a reference and research value published in 1944 and sent directly from the publishers 178种(书单另邮寄上)，每种四部，及1946出版之美国杂志而已(亦系由出版公司直接由邮寄来)。至于ALA所赠由联总运来之1939至1943年出版之书籍又3 cases of sample copies of periodicals。又所赠1946年以前出版之期刊全未收到(教部所订购之期刊清单、ALA所赠期刊清单、又本馆所编清单皆已另邮挂号寄上)。美中心将书籍交联总，但联总迟迟不运来，国内各学校因未配得书向教部及美方发怨言，美方亦以为何至今未收到分配报告为言，其实此间收到美心中书籍待分配者只有书七箱、1944出版之书籍及1946出版之期刊而已。书籍未运到，教吾人如何分配。此层似应通知美心中及ALA，前美中心通知于七月二日运来书籍36箱，至今未收到，联总运书之慢如此（此层或者应由行总负大部分责任）。分配处改组，事前吾人不得而知，教部做事每每如此。杨维庆见此情形决定仍回中基会，林先生处一月份亦不支薪，此后分配处事暂由王醒吾负责（蒋慰堂已定渠为事务组主任），以待正式接收。回汉飞机票已购得，明日（星期一）上午七时起飞，抵汉后当航函报告。匆此，敬请道安。

后学李馨吾上

卅六年一月十九日晚

又美图书中心通知于十一月四日由联总运来160箱（我馆38箱在内），十一月廿七日运来78箱，则不知何时可到。

馨吾又及

〔教育部接收整理美国赠书上海临时办事处①信纸。国家图书馆档案，档案编号1946-※046-外事5-006037至1946-※046-外事5-006042〕

按：两处"美心中"似当作"美中心"。"赵主任夫人"或指杨步伟，待考。"行总"应指联合国善后救济总署（"联总"）。王醒吾，浙江平阳人，早年赴日留学，时应任教育部专员，后竞选国民大会代表。杨维庆，生平待考。该信附一页清单，题为Books received from American Book Center，分前后两批，各为205、257箱。

一月二十日

Rae Cecilia Kelly致函先生，此前递交的各院校计划购买书目大都过时，相应书籍早已绝版，建议经过各学科顾问的审查后购买现下美国最好的书刊。

January 20, 1947

Dear Dr. Yuan:

On August 13, 1946, you sent us an appropriation for the following Chinese universities:

---

① 该处似位于中央研究院上海理工实验馆内，待考。

	Total Appropriation	Book Appropriation
National Sunyatsen University	$ 21,256.00	$ 12,000.00
National Teachers College for Women	12,750.00	6,000.00
National School of Commerce	1,700.00	800.00

Dr. Wei of the Universal Trading Corporation provided the definite figures for book purchases. The matter has rested here, up until this time, due to the fact that we wish to complete our bibliographies before handling these specific requests.

In comparing the request lists from these universities with the completed bibliographies, we find that the bibliographies supplied by these schools pertain to many titles which are now out of print. Therefore, it is our considered opinion that a much more useful collection could be purchased for the schools or universities, if the selection were made from the bibliographies compiled. In order to carry out such a suggestion, we should need a clarification of the faculties and subject departments of the schools, with the exception of the National Sunyatsen University which is included on your original list.

It is not only a question, Dr. Yuan, of the endless task of checking the bibliographies in question, but rather the waste effort involved in such a procedure. The material is hopelessly out-dated, and out-of-print market today is almost non-existent. We sincerely feel that the purchase of the best available material in America today, as approved by consultants in each subject field, would be a far more intelligent procedure for the universities of China. Will you please let us know how you feel about this particular point as we are most anxious to send off some orders for these schools? If you will give your approval to the aforementioned plan, we should be very happy to proceed.

Very sincerely yours,

Rae Cecilia Kelly

Executive Assistant

〔The American Library Association Archives, China Projects File, Box 2, Yuan T. L., 1946-1947〕

按:Dr. Wei,待考。该函寄送上海宝庆路办事处,此件为录副。

一月二十一日

先生致信 Rae Cecilia Kelly,对刚收到去年来函表示歉意,并对编纂书目工作表示感谢,另告其中国专业院校只需要专业领域的书籍。

January 21, 1947

Dear Miss Kelly:

Your letters of December 20 and December 28 were received this morning. As both of them were addressed to our office at Shapingpa, Chungking, it was with considerable delay that they were reforwarded here. As we have returned to our headquarters at Peiping, will you kindly note that all communications should henceforth be sent to our Peiping office.

We are profoundly grateful to you and your colleagues for the great assistance you have rendered to China in compiling the bibliographies for Chinese universities! In looking over the medicine bibliography, I fully realize the vast amount of labor involved. You can rest assured that these lists will not only meet our present, but also our future needs.

I enclose my letter to Mr. Charles H. Brown, which gives additional information you requested. May I ask you to forward it to Mr. Brown after you have read it?

Specialized institutions require only books in specialized fields. For instance, N. Mercantile Marine College (which now forms a part of the National University of Communications, Shanghai) requires books only in the field of marine engineering, and the Institute of Pharmacy requires books only in the field of pharmacology and medicine. I hope it will not take up too much of your time to compile these lists of specialized subjects.

The copies of your letter and memoranda, dated December 27, to the Universal Trading Corporation meeting with our hearty approval, and I would advise you to continue in that way. We shall greatly appreciate your assistance if copies of your future lists and correspondence could be sent to us at the same time as to Mr. Boggs.

Thanking you and your colleagues once more for your valuable assistance,

Yours very sincerely,

T. L. Yuan

Director

〔国立北平图书馆英文信纸。The American Library Association Archives, China Projects File, Box 2, Chinese Universities Correspondence, 1946-1947〕

按:此件为打字稿,落款处为先生签名,于2月4日送达。

先生致信布朗,感谢国际关系委员会为中国各院校编制采购书籍清单所付出的努力,并已按照要求联系各家机构,此外就国立编译馆、国立中央图书馆所需书目给予意见,澄清需要编制书目院校的数量,并希望能够在三月底前完成此项工作。

January 21, 1947

Dear Dr. Brown:

I have just received Miss Kelly's letter dated December 10, enclosing copies of your letter dated October 31 and a report on the selection of purchase bibliographies for Chinese universities. Miss Kelly's letter was addressed to our office at Shapingpa, Chungking, and it took considerable time to have it forwarded to Peiping.

On behalf of Chinese librarians, I want to express our sincere appreciation of your painstaking work in compiling these bibliographies. It is really too much a demand made upon the resources of the International Relations Office of your Association.

Concerning the information you requested, I am communicating with the different institutions and I shall write you again before very long. Meanwhile I can report that the Preparatory School for College Students was abolished last year, so lists of books for that school are no longer necessary.

Regarding the requirements of the National Institute of Compilation and Translation and the National Central Library, I would suggest that only lists of reference books such as dictionaries, encyclopedias, biographical dictionaries, who's who, geographical gazetteers, social science encyclopedias, handbooks and dictionaries in the field of natural and applied sciences, art encyclopedias and dictionaries, periodical indexes and bibliographies, should be compiled with Miss Mudge's Guide to Reference Books and the supplements as a basis of selection.

Lists for only twenty-eight institutions will be required. Regarding the remaining thirty institutions, either they have already received grants from the government or they will not receive anything. So, under these circumstances, they need not solicit any assistance from the International Relations Office of your Association.

It is our hope that the work of compiling these bibliographies will be completed by the middle of March 1947. Will you let me know how much additional funds will be required if you do not go much further than the present program. Upon hearing from you I shall take up the matter with the Chinese Government. Owing to the strict control of foreign exchange, I am afraid that the government may not be willing to spend additional funds on the program, though it is most desirable in every way.

I have just received Miss Kelly's letter dated December 29, enclosing the medicine bibliography, which, I think, is a very fine piece of work and which, I am sure will be extremely useful to our medical colleges in China.

With renewed thanks for your assistance,

T. L. Yuan

Director

P. S. Your letter of January 2 just received. Mr. Greene's supposition was correct, as I explained to you in my letter of January 13, 1947. Please inform Dr. and Mrs. Lydenberg that a hearty reception will be accorded them when they are able to arrange the proposed trip to China.

Your original letter of October 31, with the enclosed report, has not been received. Your secretary may have sent it by ordinary mail.

〔The American Library Association Archives, China Projects File, Box 2, Yuan T. L., 1946-1947〕

按:此件为录副。

一月二十五日

先生致信朱家骅,告知英美捐赠图书运华进展和运费问题。

骝先部长钧鉴:

奉到十四日赐书,藉稔钧部在沪设立国外捐购图书仪器提运清理办事处,今后入口箱件自可迅速整理。惟国外捐赠之书以运输关系,大部分仍未运寄,故沪上提运工作在本年四月以前无法结束。又同礼上年在英国捐募之书已装就二百九十八箱,由联总伦敦办事处运往上海中央研究院收转分配委员会,装箱费由图书中心担任,运费由联总担任,我方无须付款也。又整理及分配工作至关重要,李芳馥君近因母病暂行请假,近又加派职馆编目组主任曾宪三君前往上海协助一切,并希鉴核备案是幸。肃此,恭候勋祺。

〔国家图书馆档案,档案编号 1945-※057-综合 5-005002〕

按:此件为先生所拟之底稿,并注有“一月廿五日发”字样。

一月三十一日

先生致信 Laurence J. Kipp,汇报已在上海收到的六批书刊箱数,其中前两批已经分发给不同学术机构,而教科书只有七箱且大部分于一九三零年前出版,无法分发给相关院校。

January 31, 1947

Dear Mr. Kipp:

In view of the wrong address which the American Book Center has used, I am now giving you a brief report as to the actual number of cases which we received from you at Shanghai.

1st instalment-205 cases

2nd instalment-257 cases

3rd instalment-18 cases

4th instalment-74 cases

5th instalment－160 cases

6th instalment－78 cases

Among the cases in the first instalment only 7 cases of books were received, which consisted largely of text-books published before 1930, while the rest were consigned to different institutions. All the 257 cases in the second instalment were also consigned to different institutions, and our Committee has distributed them immediately after their receipt.

So far, we have only received the bill of lading for the third instalment of 18 cases, but they have not yet arrived. This applies also to the 74 cases of the fourth instalment.

Recently we have received your notification dated Nov. 4 of the shipment of 160 cases and also your notification dated November 27 re the shipment of 78 cases, but how soon we shall be able to receive them we do not know.

It seems that everything is very slow with regard to the shipment through UNRRA. I shall be grateful to you if you would check up from your end the cause of the delay. We have received complaints about the slowness of distributing work, but, as you will note, we have so far received only 7 cases of textbooks, which were out of date and which we find it difficult to place in the hands of our colleges.

〔The American Library Association Archives, China Projects File, Box 2, Periodicals for Chinese Universities, Correspondence and Lists, 1944－1947〕

按:此件为录副,无落款。

一二月间

先生致信王重民,告知平馆宿舍能有三间房子供其及家人使用。〔《胡适遗稿及秘藏书信》第 24 册,页 84－85〕

按:该信应于 2 月 7 日前送达,王重民认为并不敷用,因上有父母下有小孩,刘修业也有寡母需要照顾。

二月一日

先生致信布朗,告知已将李芳馥和曾宪三留在上海协助分发援助书刊,并将工作进展告知金陵大学 Fenn 教授，避免误会。

February 1, 1947

Dear Dr. Brown:

For your information I enclose herewith a copy of my letter addressed to Mr. L. J. Kipp of the American Book Center. As you will note, only 7 cases of books will be distributed by our Committee, while the rest were consigned to different institutions. These have been distributed according to the wishes of their donors.

Although I could not remain in Shanghai too long, I have sent two of our staff to assist in the distribution of books-Mr. F. F. Li, who studied in the Graduate Library School of the University of Chicago and also the Columbia University, and Mr. Mark Tseng of the Columbia University, who worked at Stanford University Library for the last seven or eight years. Both are men of experience and know thoroughly American publications. From time-to-time directives are sent from Peiping, and I enclose herewith a memo on the Allocation of American Periodicals.

I suppose Professor Fenn of the University of Nanking serves as special representative of the Associated Boards of Christian Colleges, and I am keeping him informed about our distribution work, so there will be no more complaints in the future.

With kindest regards,

Sincerely yours,

T. L. Yuan

Director

〔The American Library Association Archives, China Projects File, Box 2, Periodicals for Chinese Universities, Correspondence and Lists, 1944-1947〕

按：Professor Fenn 即 William P. Fenn（1903－1993），中文名方恩[①]，生于美国长于中国，1932 年担任私立金陵大学外文系主任，

① 《私立金陵大学一览》，1933 年，页 385。

1942年担任亚洲基督教高等教育联合董事会(United Board for Christian Higher Education in Asia)主任,时为该会执行秘书;其父为Courtenay H. Fenn(1866－1953),美国长老会(American Presbyterian missionary)来华传教士,中文名芳泰瑞,曾编著*The Five Thousand Dictionary*等。此为抄件,另附1月31日致Laurence J. Kipp信及备忘录各1页。

朱家骅覆函先生,感谢先生为国节省开支、增派曾宪三前往上海协助提运、整理美英捐购图书仪器。

守和先生大鉴:

顷获本月廿五日手书,得审台候胜常,忭慰何量。吾兄前在英国捐募之书将由联总装运来沪,我方无须付款可省国币开支,具仗贤劳,尤用忻感。承示已派曾宪三君前往上海协助工作,甚善。耑此奉复,顺颂时祺。

弟朱家骅顿首

二月一日

〔教育部部长室用笺。国家图书馆档案,档案编号1945-※057-综合5-005004〕

按:此函底稿撰写时间应在一月底,故有“顷获本月廿五日手书”之语,但实际发出则在2月1日。此件为打字稿,落款处为其签名。

二月三日

先生致信陈梦家,告知收悉赠书及所托查找目录进展。

梦家先生:

奉到一月四日手教,欣悉种种。近月以来北平及上海所出铜器甚多,惜无款未能由公家购买,大约均为美人购去定价按美金计算,故无人敢问津。《芝加哥铜器目录》业已拜收,至谢至谢,当在《大公报·图书周刊》写一介绍。《陶德曼铜器集》不易觅得,兹由艾克送上一部作为交换,至《Lochow目录》更不易办,现秘藏某处,恐藏器被没收也。弟今年无法赴欧,将来接收德国铜器,当推荐吾兄前往,惟须俟对德和约何日生效,方能派人前往接收也。匆匆,顺颂大安。

弟袁同礼顿首

二月三日

外二信请分别转交。

〔方继孝藏札〕

按:《芝加哥铜器目录》即*Chinese Bronzes from the Buckingham Collection*,1946年芝加哥艺术博物馆初版,后由张全新撰写书评,刊于《大公报·图书周刊》第13期。① Lochow应指Hans-Jürgen von Lochow(1902–1989),德国收藏家,1934年来华参与策划铁道建设规划,1940至1950年间留居北平,对中国文物兴趣极浓,以青铜器为主,兼收陶瓷、家具、书画等,1950年获得中国政府发给签证离境,并特准携带收藏离开,他的珍藏以青铜器最为著名,后捐赠科隆市的东亚美术馆。信中所提目录应指*Sammlung Lochow: Chinesische Bronzen*,中文题名为《冯洛侯饶斋吉金录》(两卷本),1943年、1944年由辅仁大学印字馆、彩华印书局合作刊印②,艾克则作为该书的发行人(Herausgegeben)。

二月五日

先生致信Rae Cecilia Kelly,此前其寄送重庆的书目尚未转到,请将历史、中国历史、地理、哲学、西方语言和文学的书目及其他油印书目送往北平,再次重申中央图书馆、国立编译馆、社会教育学院、贵阳师范学院所需参考书类型。

February 5, 1947

Dear Miss Kelly:

I have just received your letter of January 15 which you addressed to me at Shanghai. Of the bibliographies which you sent, only the bibliographies for medicine and agriculture have been received. These, as you will note, were enclosed in your previous correspondence. The bibliographies you sent to Chungking have not been forwarded. May I ask you to send me extra copies of the bibliographies in History, Chinese History, Geography, Philosophy, Western languages and Literature, as well as all the other bibliographies that you have mimeographed.

I have already informed you about the needs of the National Central

---

① 《大公报》,1947年3月29日,第6版。

② 辅仁大学印字馆负责文字部分,彩华印刷局负责珂罗版印制铜器图片。

Library. The Institute of Compilation & Translations has been engaged in the standardization of technical terms, in the translations of Western standard works on history and literature, and in the compilation of text books for university students. So, they need reference books such as dictionaries, encyclopaedias, both general and special, indexes, historical atlases, collected biographies, geographical gazetteers, etc. They need particularly dictionaries of scientific terms, and if you could include these in your bibliographies, it would help the work tremendously.

The requirements for College of Social Education and Kweiyang Teachers College are about the same. Both are colleges of education and are in need of books on various aspects of education, including reference books in the field of education and social sciences.

I shall write you later on about the requirements of the Fukien Research Academy.

Thanking you again for your valuable assistance,

Yours very sincerely,

T. L. Yuan

Director

P. S. Will you kindly ask the publisher to send us 2 copies of the latest edition of Dewey's "*Decimal Classification*"? If the Memorial Edition of 1932 is still available, will you ask the publisher to include that also. Please ask him to send us these two volumes by registered book-post with his bill in duplicate. Thank you.

T. L. Yuan

〔国立北平图书馆英文信纸。The American Library Association Archives, China Projects File, Box 2, Chinese Universities, Correspondence, 1946-1947〕

按:此件为打字稿,落款和补语皆为先生亲笔,其中补语在背面书写,于2月24日送达。

二月七日

张伯苓致函先生等人,告平津国立各院校长谈话会第六次例会举办时间、地点。

敬启者:

兹订于二月十二日(星期三)正午十二时假北京大学总办事处(松公府夹道)举行平津国立各院校长谈话会第六次例会,届时务请台端拨冗出席为荷。此致

袁馆长守和 国立北平图书馆

黎锦熙 北平中国大辞典编纂处

徐院长 北平铁道管理学院

徐院长悲鸿 北平艺术学院

袁院长 北平国立师范学院

李校长圣章 北平国立中法大学

梅校长月涵 国立清华大学

金校长通尹 天津西沽北洋大学

胡校长适之 北平松公府夹道北京大学

陈院长荩民 北平端王府夹道北洋大学工学院

李院长 北平国立研究院

张伯苓拜订

三十六年二月七日

〔《张伯苓私档全宗》,页 1192-1193〕

按:"金校长通尹"即金问洙(1891—1964),字通尹,浙江嘉兴人,天津北洋大学毕业,本年 8 月辞去该校校长职务。

加斯基尔致函先生,询问此前委托平馆购买中文出版物运美情况,并希望平馆能够继续刊印书目卡片。

February 7, 1947

Dear Mr. Yuan:

The books you bought for us in Chungking and turned over to the American Embassy to be forwarded to us have never come. Do you know anything about them, or is there anything you can do about it? We are wondering, too, if any other books have been sent from Peiping or Shanghai, where the balance of our deposit was sent when your Chungking office was closed. So far, we've received nothing at all.

I trust you are pretty well re-established in the library in Peiping now.

It must be a constant joy to be back. Have you been able to resume printing catalogue cards and what condition is your stock of printed cards in? We find them exceedingly useful, and should be glad to get more of them.

We shall appreciate very much any information or help you can give us about the books.

With best wishes, as ever,

Curator of the Wason Collection on China and the Chinese

〔Cornell University Library, Wason Collection Records, 1918-1988, Box 1, Folder Koo, T. K. Letters〕

按:此件为录副,无落款签名。

二月九日

下午四时,欧美同学会举行抗战后的复员成立大会,胡适、周炳琳、张伯谨、萧一山、陈福田、袁敦礼、先生、陈莀民、郭麟阁、王霭芬等七十余人到场。张伯谨任会议主席,报告会务及财务状况,并修订会章,最后选举理、监事,因时间关系,改为通信方式投票。〔《民国日报》(天津),1947 年 2 月 10 日,第 4 版〕

按:郭麟阁(1904—1984),字炳汉,河南西平人,1928 年中法大学服尔德学院毕业,后赴法留学获里昂大学文学博士,归国后长期执教于辅仁大学。王霭芬(1911—?),女,字瀛生,祖籍浙江萧山,生于江苏崇明岛,北京大学毕业,后赴法留学获巴黎大学文科硕士学位,1949 年去台。

二月十三日

先生致信米尔泽夫斯基,询问一九三九年至一九四三年间出版物是否委托给美国图书中心,而后者是否通过联合国善后救济总署将书刊发送到中国,以便查找运输状态。

February 13, 1947

Mr. Marion A. Milczewski, Director

International Relations office

American Library Association

Library of Congress Annex, Study 251

Washington 25, D. C.

U. S. A.

Dear Mr. Milczewski:

I am much obliged to you for your letter of January 3, and I want to send you my congratulations for your appointment as Director of the International Relations Office. I am looking forward to our most pleasant relationships with your office in the near future.

As I wrote to Mr. Lydenberg last November, the outstanding publications issued in 1944 donated by the A. L. A. were received direct from the publishers. They are being distributed in accordance with the memo attached to my letter to Mr. Charles H. Brown. As to the publications issued in 1939–1943, we have not had any news about them. May I ask you to be good enough to find out whether you have entrusted them to the American Book Center and, if so, whether the American Book Center has sent them to China through UNRRA. Could you give me the exact date of their shipment so that we can trace them at this end?

I have had a good deal of correspondence with Miss Kelly regarding the selection of books for Chinese universities. I wish to assure you once more of our heartfelt thanks for the painstaking work which you have done in making these lists available to Chinese scholars and institutions.

Sincerely yours,

T. L. Yuan

Director

P. S. Please forward the enclosed letters to Miss Kelly and Mr. Brown.

〔国立北平图书馆英文信纸。The American Library Association Archives, China Projects File, Box 2, Books for China, 1944–47, Folder1〕

按:此件为打字稿,先生对信稿有改动,落款处为其签名,于3月3日送达。

先生致信布朗,寄上美国图书馆协会捐赠书刊的分配情况备忘录,但只限于1944年出版者,向其询问1939年至1943年出版物现在何处,并将寄赠静生生物调查所出版品。

February 13, 1947

Dear Dr. Brown:

With further reference to my letter of February 1, I now enclose a memo regarding the distribution of outstanding publications donated by the ALA. If you have any comments to make, will you let me know?

So far, we have received only 178 titles in 168 volumes, representing the books issued in 1944. Since we have not received those issued in 1939–1943, we are quite anxious to trace their whereabouts. I am writing to Mr. Milczewski in regard to this matter, and I hope to hear from him before very long.

I am writing to you separately regarding the publications of the Fan Memorial Institute. These are being sent to you by registered book-post.

T. L. Yuan

Director

〔The American Library Association Archives, China Projects File, Box 2, Books for China, Correspondence, 1947〕

按：信中的168似乎应为186。[①] 该信附有一页备忘录（Memorandum on the Distribution of Outstanding Publications donated by the American Library Association）。

先生致信 Rae Cecilia Kelly，同意前函建议，请其按专家意见购买现在可购买到的书刊，并告国立商学院院系情况。

February 13, 1947

Dear Miss Kelly:

Thank you for your letter of January 20. I now attach further information regarding the different institutions for whom lists of books should be compiled.

I quite agree that the purchase of best available material in America today would be a far more intelligent procedure for Chinese universities than to follow their outdated and out-of-print lists. I approve of your suggestions and plans, so please proceed placing orders in accordance

① The American Library Association Archives, China Projects File, Box 2, Books for China, 1944–47, Folder 1.

with various bibliographies you have compiled.

Sincerely yours,

T. L. Yuan

Director

P. S. National School of Commerce: The School is made up of seven departments, Banking, Accounting, Industrial Management, Foreign Trade, Statistics, Insurance and Cooperation.

〔国立北平图书馆英文信纸。The American Library Association Archives, China Projects File, Box 2, Yuan T L, 1946-1947〕

按:此件为打字稿,先生对信稿有改动,落款处为其签名,于3月3日送达。

布朗致函先生,就寄送中国的美国书刊、出版物分配方案无法保证私立基督教院校的利益表示深深的不安和疑问。

February 13, 1947

My dear Dr. Yuan:

I have spent the last three weeks in the East due to an accident, as the result of which I was confined to New York hospitals on account of a slight fracture. I shall, however, be in shape by March 1.

The report in regard to the distribution of books in China came not so much from a representative of Associated Boards as from a Chinese authority who has no connection with the Associated Boards. Apparently, however, he had some familiarity with the discussions of your Committee.

There are some matters mentioned in your letter of January 13 which need correction. The lists compiled by the Associated Boards were not lists on which any extensive purchases have as yet been made. The lists were prepared for the Christian colleges in China, from which they could check the books and periodicals they desired, if and when funds become available.

The books and periodicals sent over from appropriations of the State Department for distribution by the American Embassy were not intended so much as publications for permanent rehabilitation as they were intended for immediate use by scholars. The American Library Association has nothing to do with the distribution of these books by American Embassy. It was left entirely to the American Embassy, and I am very happy that such was the decision. Mrs. Fairbank is quite correct in stating that most of these books had been temporarily lost in shipment. I understand, however, that many of the boxes have now been located and are on their way, unless by chance they become lost again. I want to emphasize that the American Library Association has nothing to do with the distribution of these books. The only connection ALA had with it was to aid in the selection and binding.

I was quite aware that our Committee has no authority over the distribution ordered by the Chinese Ministry of Education. On the other hand, the distribution of the twenty copies of 199 periodicals made by the Minister of Education would affect the distributions of the periodicals purchased from Rockefeller funds, as many periodicals are on both lists. If, for example, the *Journal of Biological Chemistry* purchased by the Ministry of Education went to twenty national universities or national libraries, then at least some of the copies shipped to your Committee by ALA might well go to some of the Christian colleges which did not benefit by the twenty copies ordered by the Ministry of Education.

Incidentally, I was informed last November by Mr. Lochhead that these periodicals have not been shipped as of November, 1946, and that the Universal Trading Corporation had not received any priority from your government for the shipment of these accumulated volumes.

I have received directly from the Chinese authority mentioned above information in regard to the distribution of the periodicals and books sent over by the American Library Association and American Book Center which has been confirmed by a letter I have received personally from the library of a Christian college in China; I am quoting from this letter:

“I have made contacts with Dr. T. L. Yuan’s Committee on Distribution of Books in China and also Mr. Wen-Yu Yan, the

Executive Secretary, who has recently gone to Chungking to be the Director of the newly proposed Roosevelt Library, but I was disappointed to find that expected shipments of books from the American Library Association and the American Book Center are intended for the national libraries……, being a private institution, may not be entitled to the donations from abroad. However, we are trying to make some plea for filling up the gaps in our periodical files."

Letters such as these certainly indicate some misunderstanding. It was never the intention of the ALA, as you know by the Tentative Suggestions we sent you, that the distribution of books and periodicals sent over by the ALA and American Book Center should be limited to national libraries. Yet apparently this impression has gone out, and we have had confirmation of this same impression from different independent sources. Possibly your Committee can correct this unfortunate impression.

It might be of assistance to us if we could have a copy of the Minutes of the meeting of your Committee held in November, 1946. As far as I know, neither the American Book Center nor the ALA has received a copy of the action taken by your committee in regard to the distribution of books. Possibly I have been misinformed as to the date of the meeting of this Committee, but I understood it was held in November. If we can obtain full information, it may help us in removing what apparently were mistaken impressions of the policy of your Committee……

I may have written some time ago of the possibility that Harry Lydenberg would go to China to aid the Associated Boards in the reorganization of the libraries of Christian colleges. He has now found it impossible to go, but the Associated Boards is planning to send over a librarian just as soon as feasible. I shall keep you informed as soon as there is any definite decision.

If you can do anything in China to dispel the feeling expressed by my correspondent noted above in regard to distribution of books, it will be greatly appreciated. I understand the difficult position the Committee is in and it has my sympathy. When there is such a great need for publications, there is sure to be some criticism. All we can do is to remove any legitimate cause for criticism, and I am sure your Committee will do so.

Yours very truly,

Charles H. Brown, Chairman

Committee on the Orient and Southwest Pacific

〔The American Library Association Archives, China Projects File, Box 2, Books for China Correspondence, 1947〕

按:此为抄件。

二月

普林斯顿大学邀请中国学者参与建校二百周年纪念活动,陶孟和、陈达、吴景超、吴文藻、吴国桢、费孝通、冯友兰、先生、李济、梁思成、梁思永、邓以蛰、陈梦家等人受邀。〔《申报》,1947 年 2 月 26 日,第 5 版〕

按:该校预计在 4 月初举办演讲会,拟于 3 月 20 日派军舰来华接送中方学者,先生并未前往,但允诺普林斯顿大学借平馆在美暂存的古籍善本,并由吴光清、王际真等人协助举办专门展览。①

二三月间

先生致信王重民,告知须在平馆兼事四小时。〔《胡适王重民先生往来书信集》,页 475〕

按:3 月 6 日,王重民偕刘修业、王黎敦抵达上海,寓安亭路 80 弄 33 号。

三月二日

先生奉教育部令赴津视察省立、市立两图书馆及市立美术馆。〔《大公报》(天津),1947 年 3 月 5 日,第 5 版〕

按:抗战胜利后,天津各界人士筹建一座规模宏大的图书馆,1947 年 5 月组成筹备委员会,先生此次前往天津视察,似与此事相关。省立图书馆即 1908 年开馆的直隶图书馆,后更名为河北省立第一图书馆;市立图书馆应指 1931 年开馆的天津市立图书馆;天津市立美术馆 1930 年设立,其馆址最初在河北公园内。

① *Far Eastern Culture and Society, Princeton University Bicentennial Conferences*, Series 2 Conference 7, 1946, pp. 3, 35.

三月三日　天津

先生会同天津市教育局秘书李天贵及第三科科长曾葆清前往天津日本图书馆视察。〔中国第二历史档案馆,教育部档案·全卷宗5,国立北平图书馆请拨员工学术研究补助费经常费有关文书,案卷号11616(4)〕

按:该馆应位于天津原日租界大和公园内,先生认为该馆"旧藏中西日文图书甚富,现该处为警备司令部借用,图书则归市府教育局保管。惟以缺乏专款,无人驻馆,图书常被窃失。拟请将该馆收归国有,拨款派员保管"。

先生赴生活、远东等书店,购买大批关于苏联的图书。另外,先生与天津某收藏家商谈购买其所藏清末外交家洪钧所绘中俄交界详图。晚七时,先生拜谒杜建时市长,建议增加图书馆之经费、馆员人数,并谈美术馆馆址迁移等事。〔《大公报》(天津),1947年3月5日,第5版〕

按:洪钧(1839—1893),字陶士,江苏苏州人,清末外交家,1889年至1892年清廷驻俄、德、奥、荷四国大臣。杜建时(1906—1989),字际平,河北武清人,民国军政人士,曾赴美国雷文沃兹军事学院攻读炮兵军事学科,归国后曾任第九战区高级参谋,时为天津市市长。

先生致信胡适,请其在中基会年会中为平馆批准中西文购书经费。

适之先生道席:

阅报悉台旌指日赴京,弟顷奉令去津查视日本图书馆事,不及走谭,歉甚怅甚。兹恳者,上年十一月间,敝馆函请中基会于三十六年度补助购书费事(中文书费法币壹仟万元,西文书费美金壹万元)。此次大驾出席中基会年会,附钞原函呈阅,拟恳对于此件赐予赞助。仰荷仁言,玉成斯举,幸甚幸甚。又前在抗战期内,中基会曾代敝馆购置西文书籍多种,兹制成报告,一并送请台察。费神,容再面谢。专此,敬候道祺。

弟袁〇〇

卅六年三月三日

附抄中西文件三件。

〔国家图书馆档案,档案编号1945-※057-综合5-002004和1945-※057-综合5-002005〕

按:此件为先生所拟之底稿,其中有大幅修改,首页标注"民国三十六年叁月叁日发"。

常道直致函先生,请将美国全国教育协会捐赠中国教育学会之书刊收转并送后者在南京办事处。

同礼馆长尊兄道鉴:

久未聆教为念。弟于去年夏赴美出席世教会议,会后赴华府与美国 N. E. A.负责人 W. E. Givens 先生接洽,请其将该会最近约十年来出版之刊物捐赠中国教育学会,每种各一册(书目单交该会)。兹接 American Book Center 副干事 A. D. Ball 女士来函,谓此项书籍即可运到,并告以应与尊处接洽,特此函达,敬希转知前途,即将该类刊物径寄"南京太平路,红花地廿二号"本会办事处为荷。耑颂教安。

弟常道直上

三月三日

Pottier 路是否浦石路,敬祈便中示知。

〔World Conference of the Teaching Profession 英文信纸。南京大学图书馆特藏部〕

按:N. E. A. 即 The National Education Association,一般译作"全国教育协会",W. E. Givens 即 Willard E. Givens(1886-1971),美国教育学家,1935 年至 1952 年担任该协会执行秘书。Pottier 应指 Rue Pottier,上海宝健路,非蒲石路(Rue Bourgeat)。

三月四日

中午十二时许,先生乘车返平。〔《大公报》(天津),1947 年 3 月 5 日,第 5 版〕

季羡林致函先生。〔《此心安处是吾乡:季羡林归国日记(1946-1947)》,页 171〕

Maybelle Bouchard(南京)致函先生,告知费慰梅将回国,另美国国务院和中美文化资料供应委员会均无法资助平馆出版《图书季刊》英文本。

American Embassy

Nanking

March 4, 1947

Dear Dr. Yuan:

Mrs. Fairbank is sailing for the United States tomorrow, to return to "civilian" life at Cambridge. As you probably know, Dr. Fairbank resigned last summer to resume his teaching career at Harvard, and Mrs. Fairbank has been waiting until the appointment of her successor to follow him. You will no doubt be as pleased as I am to know that our old friend Mortimer Graves is evidently to be the Embassy's new Cultural Relations Officer. We have not yet been notified when he will arrive in Nanking. In the meantime, I am carrying on the work in this office.

Before she left Nanking, Mrs. Fairbank referred to me your letter of February 26, inquiring about the possibility of a grant to the National Library of Peiping to subsidize the publication of the *Quarterly Bulletin of Chinese Bibliography*. She asked me to inform you that unfortunately the Department of State has no funds for grants at this time, and has not been notified of any that may be available in the future. Furthermore, she was also told that the Sino-American Cultural Service has no funds from which a grant of this kind might be made.

I am very sorry that we are not able to be of assistance to you, for I am well aware, from my years at the Library of Congress, of the fine reputation the *Quarterly Bulletin* has made for itself. You may be sure that I shall keep this matter in mind.

So far, it has been impossible for me to visit Peiping. I am still hoping to go before too many more months have passed, and I intend to come and see you then. Do Wang Chung-min and Wu Kwang-tsing expect to return to the National Library soon?

With all good wishes, I remain,

Sincerely yours,

Maybelle Bouchard

Assistant Cultural Relation Officer

〔Rockefeller Foundation. Series 601: China; Subseries 601.R: China-Humanities and Arts. Vol. Box 47. Folder 391〕

按:此为抄件,附于 11 日致史蒂文斯信中。

三月五日

先生致信布朗，明确表示美国图书馆协会、美国图书中心发来的书刊尚未分配，并保证只要自己还在分配委员会中就会尽可能保证私立大学、在华基督教院校的利益。

March 5, 1947

Dear Dr. Brown:

I have your letter of February 13. I trust you have received mine dated February 1 and February 13.

As I wrote you before, no books and periodicals from the ALA and the American Book Center have been distributed. So, I hope everybody will not criticize the committee until the books and periodicals are distributed.

With regard to the distribution of' the American periodicals donated by the ALA, it is my opinion that most of them will go to the Christian colleges as well as to national universities which have not been allocated the 20 copies of American periodicals subscribed by the Ministry of Education. I shall make strong recommendations to our Committee regarding this point.

So far, the Ministry of Education has not made any decision regarding the distribution of these periodicals in spite of our repeated requests. As soon as a decision is made, our Committee will immediately distribute the ALA periodicals to Christian colleges. I can assure you that the books and periodicals we received from the American Book Center and the ALA will be distributed both to Christian colleges and national universities. They will receive equal attention from our Committee.

Owing to my various duties in Peiping, I am thinking of resigning as Executive Secretary of the Committee on the Distribution of Books. However, it is difficult to find a man who could succeed me as Executive Secretary and who would like to serve as a target for criticisms from all sides.

As long as I am on the Committee, the interests of Christian colleges will be protected. I am having copies of your letter made and distributed to other members of the Committee. If you could keep me informed about the names of libraries desiring material from the donated books and periodicals, they would receive attention from our Committee.

With kindest regards,

T. L. Yuan

〔The American Library Association Archives, China Projects File, Box 2, Books for China, Correspondence, 1947〕

按:该信应于 3 月 19 日前送达,此为抄件。

三月七日

先生致信史蒂文斯,向其介绍平馆日本研究中心、苏俄研究中心的近况。

March 7, 1947

Dear Dr. Stevens:

Knowing that you are interested in the activities of the National Library, I am afraid that you may be inclined to think that we cannot accomplish anything in view of the inflation and the unsettled political situation in China. However, I am glad to inform you that in spite of our unfavorable situation we have been able to initiate new developments of our work.

As mentioned in my letter to you dated December 10, 1946, we have taken over a huge collection of Japanese literature, numbering over 400, 000 volumes. After spending considerable time in rough sorting, the cataloguing work is proceeding rapidly under the direction of several returned students from Japan. As soon as the collection is organized, we hope that an Institute for Japanese Studies will be set up with the cooperation of local universities.

The Japanese collection is now housed in a beautiful temple-the former Ancestral Hall of the Ming and Ching dynasties-loaned to us by the National Palace Museum. During his recent visit to Peiping, the American Ambassador was very much pleased with our work and he assured us that the Japanese center we have set up would be an important agency for the scientific study of Japan.

The National Library is now organizing a Russian Research Center. Emphasis is laid on history and Sino-Russian relations. Besides buying

Russian literature at Peiping and elsewhere, we have been promised assistance by Russian institutions, though on account of transportation difficulties, only a small portion of publications from the Soviet Academy of Sciences has been received.

According to Prof. J. J. Gapanovich of Tsing Hua University, who serves as Consultant to our Russian Research Center, a great number of the Russian books we purchased at Peiping are no longer available elsewhere. He suggests that we exchange microfilm copies with other Russian collections in the U. S. A. as soon as our photo-duplication laboratory is set up.

Meanwhile we have translated a number of documents relating to Sino-Russian relations. Since the printing cost in China is very high, I shall seek the assistance of Dr. Graves to see if they could be published in the U. S. A.

……

About the photo-duplication laboratory, you will recall the memorandum which I submitted to you on March 20, 1945. Since no action has been taken by the Foundation, we have purchased out of our own funds the following which have been received in Peiping:

1. Depue Microfilm Printer	$ 1,978.00
2. Omega Enlarger	147.50
3. Dryer	381.00
4. Spencer Microfilm Reader	119.70

When the Foundation decides to make us a grant in the future in connection with the photoduplication laboratory, the above items might be omitted from the list of the necessary equipment.

I hope before very long Dr. Fahs will be able to pay us a visit so that he can see our work at first hand.

……

〔Rockefeller Foundation. Series 601: China; Subseries 601.R: China-Humanities and Arts. Vol. Box 47. Folder 391, Folder 393〕

按:Dr. Fahs 即 Charles B. Fahs(1908-1980),本谱中译作“法斯”,美国西北大学博士毕业,曾赴京都、东京两所大学留学,二战期间在战略情报局远东部(Far Eastern Division of the Office of Military Strategic Services)服务,1946 年起出任洛克菲勒基金会人文部副主管,1950 年升任主管。该信残,应于 3 月 17 日送达。

三月十一日

先生致信史蒂文斯,告知《图书季刊》英文本的出版困境,另请其考虑资助美国图书馆编目专家来华指导工作。

March 11, 1947

Dear Dr. Stevens:

Referring to the Russian Research Center which we are setting up here, I am glad to inform you that we have acquired the premises of the famous Rocky Garden in the Winter Palace of Peiping. It is the historical garden built by Emperor Chien Lung and the buildings therein will meet our need for additional space for housing our Russian collection for the next few years.

We are still having difficulties in obtaining foreign exchange from the Chinese Government. So, we cannot undertake extensive acquisition of source materials until we can buy freely foreign exchange in the open market. I have been asked to visit the Soviet Union in the future, and I hope to buy extensively when our financial situation will have improved.

You have taken interest in the publication of *Quarterly Bulletin of Chinese Bibliography* and I wish to take this opportunity to report our present difficulties. When I returned from Europe last October, I had some assurance from the American Embassy that the Embassy would recommend a grant towards its publication from the Department of State under its cultural relations program. After four months' waiting, I received the enclosed letter which is self-explanatory. The *Quarterly Bulletin* has always been printed with subsidies from other sources, as our own budget has no provision for it. The cost of printing the *Bulletin* is higher in China than in the United States (about $890 each issue), so unless financial support is forthcoming, we shall be obliged to discontinue its publication. The table of contents for the issue now in press is enclosed herewith for your information.

The critical shortage of cataloguers of western books forms a serious problem in China today. Chinese college and university libraries are struggling along without any qualified cataloguers of western books. The Boone Library School has lowered the standard of its curriculum to that of a training school, so we cannot expect anything from it. I have been in correspondence with Dr. Milam of the ALA, suggesting that we should explore the possibility of sending out two experienced cataloguers to Peiping to conduct a seminar here for the purpose of training catalogers for Chinese libraries. If Dr. Milam brings up the matter with the Foundation, I hope you will give it your support. This Library will pay their expenses for food and lodging, but we cannot afford to pay their travel expense. Since the Foundation has given similar assistance to Latin America, I trust you would give due consideration to our request. If you would find it possible to make a grant for general operations for $30,000 for the years 1947－1950, we shall be able to render greater service to Chinese and American scholarly world.

By ordinary mail, I am sending a map of the Winter Palace which is the most picturesque spot in Peiping, and I do want to have the pleasure of showing you around when you and Mrs. Stevens come to Peiping.

With cordial regards to you and Mr. Marshall,

Yours sincerely,

T. L. Yuan

Director

〔Rockefeller Foundation. Series 601: China; Subseries 601.R: China-Humanities and Arts. Vol. Box 47. Folder 391〕

按：Rocky Garden 即静清斋，为北海北岸一处独立的院落，今改称"静心斋"。此件为打字稿，落款处为先生签名，于 3 月 20 日送到。

三月十三日

先生致信于震寰,告知在美复制中美外交档案细节,并谈图书馆协会会报及会费。

镜宇仁兄大鉴:

接奉三月四日大函,备悉一切。贵馆拟加照中美等外交史料一节,自当赞助。中美者,约美金壹千元,南京已有二份(一存外交部,一存中央研究院)。贵馆似可以该款另购他书较为经济,但如仍愿影印,请径向美方函洽(地址列后)。中英者系用 Photostat 所照,仅能照一份,且照料之人即将返国,容俟另觅继任人选,再当奉闻。兹因无法取到外汇,此项工作势将停止,颇觉可惜。又美国印制本馆善本影片,因经手人王重民君尚未返平,详情未悉,应候询明再行函告。至抗战期间出版之会报,大部份仍存渝,已告本馆上海办事处在可能之内寄一全份,但不识仍能凑一全份否?关于协会之事,另纸详述,即希分别办理是荷。顺颂时祉。

袁同礼顿首

三月十三日

协会之款经王文山先生保管者,共四一六,六七七.七五元。兹将王先生二月十四来函奉上备查。需用时可径向王君提取。

〔台北"中央图书馆"档案,档案编号 129-0001 和 129-0002〕

按:该信为文书代笔,落款、补语则为先生亲笔,3 月 17 日送达中央图书馆。

中华图书馆协会撰《呈报中华图书馆协会会址及新聘常务干事请予备案由》,具先生名并钤印。〔台北"国史馆",〈中国图书馆协会请补助(教育部)〉,数位典藏号 019-030508-0015〕

按:协会会址为国立中央图书馆内,新聘常务干事即于震寰。

三月十四日

米尔泽夫斯基覆函先生,告知已经转交二月十三日的信件和备忘录与布朗,提供该信中询问的寄出时间并表示愿意协助调查运送记录。

March 14, 1947

Dear Dr. Yuan:

We are appreciative of your congratulations and sincerely hope that our pleasant relationship will continue.

Mr. Brown will be delighted to receive your memorandum and your personal letter which I am forwarding to him today. It is very difficult to trace the shipment, which you inquired about in your letter of February 13, 1947, at this time. Therefore, we are giving you the exact date, July 12, 1946, of their departure from the International Relations Office. We are enclosing, for your information, Dr. Lydenberg's letter to you dated July 26, 1946. Further, we intend to check with the shipping agent; but, since UNRRA operations are closing, we are not too hopeful about the results.

We deeply appreciate your comment on the bibliographies and selection of books,

Sincerely yours,
Marion A. Milczewski
Director

〔The American Library Association Archives, China Projects File, Box 2, Books for China, 1944-47, Folder 1〕

按:该函寄送北平,此为抄件。

Dorothy J. Comins 覆函先生,告知美国图书馆协会战区图书馆援助委员会将所余书刊全部分发,其中相当一部分将分配给中国,附上第一个补充清单,并请将最终分发报告寄送给国际关系委员会。

March 14, 1947

Dear Dr. Yuan:

The Committee on Aid to Libraries in War Areas is now working on final distribution of sets of journals remaining from the stock it has purchased. Now that all countries have had an opportunity to express their need, some additional sets are being assigned to the libraries of China.

The enclosed list is the first of two supplementary lists you will receive. Most of the titles here included were purchased in small quantities. The second list now being compiled, which will probably be sent to you in about a month, will consist of extra sets of journals you have already received.

We realize that some of the sets sent you are incomplete because certain issues are out of print. The Committee is now working on plans to reproduce such issues and these will be sent to you within the next few months, either as original copies obtained from various sources, lithoprint reproductions in reduced size, or as a last resort microfilm copies.

We hope these additional sets of wartime issues of American journals will prove useful. May we once more emphasize that the Committee's subscriptions to these journals, with a few exceptions already reported to you, expired at the end of 1946. The Committee has no funds for continuing these subscriptions, and publishers have been asked to send renewal notices to you. We are also anxious to have a complete report from you showing the exact allocation of all journals sent to you for distribution.

Sincerely yours,
Dorothy J. Comins
Executive Assistant

〔The American Library Association Archives, China Projects File, Box 2, Periodicals for Chinese Universities, Correspondence and Lists, 1944-1947〕

按:该函寄送上海由中央研究院代转,此为抄件,另附1页期刊名单,共计19种。

三月十七日

史蒂文斯覆函先生,告知法斯预计五月份前往北平,建议届时先生与之面对面讨论。

March 17, 1947

Dear Dr. Yuan:

This past week I have seen Dr. Goodrich, and with Mr. Fahs of our office I have gathered many useful reports on circumstances of work in Peiping today. Now I have your own letter of March 7 on the morning when I intended to write to you. Many thanks for all the news in it.

The points that you list in reference to studies in Japanese, Russian, and Chinese will all be studied carefully by us. Also, tomorrow in Washington I will tell Mr. Graves of the news in the matter of translation. He has been working on plans to publish translations from Russian. He also will be much interested in the news you give of the large number of unusual Russian titles available in your Library for exchange in microfilm.

The most helpful way to get on with discussion of such general matters is by direct discussion, and I am glad that seems probable during the spring. Mr. Evans of the Social Sciences Division and Mr. Fahs expect to be in Peiping for some time, probably during May. Since the plans are not finally formed, exact word will not be possible to send very much in advance of their expected arrival. For that reason, the possibility of visit during May should not be taken literally for the time being. I wish that I were to be with them at the time of this visit.

My kindest regards to you.

Sincerely yours,

David H. Stevens

〔Rockefeller Foundation. Series 601: China; Subseries 601.R: China-Humanities and Arts. Vol. Box 47. Folder 391〕

按：Mr. Evans 即 Roger F. Evans，时任洛克菲勒基金会社科部副主任。

三月十九日

布朗覆函先生，已经寄出浙江大学所需农业出版品、实验室记录等，如果北京大学需要某些老旧期刊，他将努力协助补配，对先生辞去英美捐赠图书期刊分配委员会秘书职务表示遗憾。

March 19, 1947

My dear Dr. Yuan:

I have received your letter of March 5. I have received so many requests from Chinese colleges and universities that it will be impossible for them all to be satisfied. We have packed one box of books, agricultural publications, Experiment Station Records, etc., which was sent to your

Committee for trans-shipment to National Chekiang University, Hangchow. The President of the university is now in this country and promised to get out the volumes of the Experiment Station Record to him, together with some bound copies of the Bulletins of State Experiment Stations.

I have been told that the National University of Peking has had difficulty in building up its agricultural library. If they desire some older agricultural publications, files of Experiment Station Record, etc., will you please let me know and I shall earmark some boxes direct from this library to National University of Peking, by way of your Committee.

I had a bad accident which sent me to the hospital for a few weeks, but I am now recovering and expect to spend the next two or three weeks in the East.

We have just received a long list of missing volumes of periodicals from the University of Shanghai. We may try to fill in some of these missing volumes.

It would be very unfortunate if you resigned as Secretary of the Committee. In another six months, the bulk of shipments will be over, and probably by next Fall we can start our exchange shipments through the Smithsonian. The work of allotting books is sure to be filled with difficulty, and all that you can do is to make as fair a distribution as possible.

Yours very truly,

Charles H. Brown, Chairman

Committee on the Orient and Southwest Pacific

〔The American Library Association Archives, China Projects File, Box 2, Books for China, Correspondence, 1947〕

按:此为抄件。

三月二十日

平馆向教育部发代电一件,题为《建议天津日本花园图书馆拟由国立南开大学接收整理》,具先生名并钤印。

教育部钧鉴：

案奉社字第一〇二二二三号代电略开：以据视察员报告天津日本花园图书馆旧藏中西日文图书甚富，现该处为警备司令部借用，图书则归市府教育局保管，惟以缺乏专款，无人驻馆，图书常被窃失。拟请将该馆收归国有，拨款派员保管等情，合亟电仰该馆速派专家，会同天津市教育局点验整理具报，其经费准予报部核发等因。奉此，当由职于三月三日赴津，会同天津市教育局李秘书天贵及第三科曾科长葆清前往视察，经查该馆藏书遗失甚夥，馆舍复为津沧绥靖区党政军联席会报秘书处所借用。既属军事区域，教育局方面实无法派人前往查验整理，因即面晤杜市长建时、林警备司令伟涛，请将该秘书处即日迁让。一方面并请当局制止再有盗窃情事发生，同时与教育局洽议，期谋一永久办法。据教育局表示，该局直辖之天津市立图书馆，其经常费每月仅拨三万元，实无余力再接收其他图书馆，所言当系实情。经职慎重考虑，拟向钧部建议：

（一）由钧部委托国立南开大学接收整理，即在日本公园原址公开阅览，以免迁移。

（二）由该大学成立图书委员会，聘天津市长及教育局长暨地方人士为委员，主持进行事宜。

（三）由钧部电天津市政府及警备司令部，请将津沧绥靖区党政军联席会报秘书处另行迁移，以便南开大学接收房屋（另由后门出入，与警备司令部之间可筑一墙隔离之），一俟该大学接收完毕，职馆可派专家一二人赴津协助整理。奉电前因，理合将视察情形及建议各节特电呈复，伏乞鉴核施行，实为公便。

国立北平图书馆馆长袁同礼寅号叩（馆印）

〔中国第二历史档案馆，教育部档案·全卷宗5，国立北平图书馆请拨员工学术研究补助费经常费有关文书，案卷号11616(4)〕

按：4月9日，朱家骅批复“拟如此办理”。

三月二十一日

中华图书馆协会撰《呈请增加补助费以维持出版刊物由》，具先生名并钤印。〔台北“国史馆”，〈中国图书馆协会请补助（教育部）〉，数位典藏号019-030508-0015〕

按:3 月底,教育部批准此请,在本年度社教事业费内一次性拨给补助费壹百万元。

三月二十二日

上午十一时,故宫博物院理事会在平理事第三次谈话会在该院绛雪轩召开,陈垣、胡适出席,马衡、沈兼士、先生、张庭济、徐悲鸿、邓以蛰、启功列席。会议报告徐森玉在沪觅得宋版《四明志》一册,正在议价收购;讨论米芾尺牍等书画是否收购。〔《马衡年谱长编》,页 943-944〕

按:徐悲鸿、邓以蛰、启功三人为专门委员。

三月二十九日

下午四时,中法汉学研究所举行茶话会,招待 Prabodh Chandra Bagchi 教授,邀请向达、邵循正、Rudolf Löewenthal、陈垣、王静如、先生作陪。该所理事长杜伯秋负责招待一切。〔《民国日报》(天津),1947 年 3 月 29 日,第 4 版〕

按:Prabodh Chandra Bagchi(1898-1956),印度汉学家,佛教研究专家,中文名师觉月,1920 年获得加尔各答大学硕士学位,后赴法国,跟随伯希和、马伯乐、布洛克(Jules Bloch,1880-1953)等人学习,1944 年出版其重要著作 *India and China: a thousand years of cultural relations* (《印度与中国》)。Rudolf Löewenthal (1904-1996),中文名罗文达,生于德国什未林(Schwerin),1933 年获柏林大学经济学博士学位,1934 年来华在燕京大学任教, 曾著有 *The Religious Periodical Press in China* ,时在康乃尔大学任教。

四月一日

先生致信朱家骅,请教育部为汪德昭开具推荐信。

骝先部长尊鉴:

敬陈者,联合国教育科学文化组织之科学部,现由英人尼德汉博士主持,渠近约留法研究生汪德昭君前往该部工作,惟按前例须由我方教育当局推荐方合手续。兹将汪君来电录副奉上,即希钧阅。汪君留法十五载,专研物理学,为郎之万教授之高足,著作甚多,以足充任斯职,定能胜任。又该组织设在巴黎,往返接洽多用法文,汪君精于法语,亦可协助钧部作联络工作。倘荷惠允,拟请钧座电嘱陈通伯先生正式提出。闻四月十号即将开会决定也。专此奉恳,敬候道祺。

〔国家图书馆档案,档案编号 1945-※057-综合 5-005005〕

按:“尼德汉”即李约瑟(Joseph Needham,1900-1995)。“陈通伯”即陈源,时任国民政府驻联合国教科文组织首任代表,常驻巴黎。此件为先生亲笔,无落款,旁注有“寄顾斗南”字样,4月1日发,应由平馆驻京办事处主任顾斗南转呈朱家骅。

先生致信胡适,告知前为北京大学垫付博物馆学应用器械款项、韩寿萱垫付运费,请赐还美金。

适之先生尊鉴:

奉到两示,感谢不尽。博物馆学应用器械各件,敝处曾垫付美金捌佰肆拾元壹角叁分,又韩寿萱君垫付运费美金贰拾捌元,拟请分别写纽约支票,便中赐下至感。至由沪运平之运费已请中国旅行社开列清单,容再奉寄。先此,敬颂道祺。

同礼顿首

四月一日

敝馆之款请写 National Library of Peiping,抬头 $ 840.13。

〔国立北平图书馆用笺。《胡适遗稿及秘藏书信》第31册,页639〕

按:此信暂系于此。

四月三日

平馆向教育部呈文一件,题为《呈报尊令向国立沈阳博物院洽领清实录全书经过情形请鉴核备案》,具先生名并钤平馆印。

案奉社字第九二二四号代电略开:本部接收之《清实录》决定分配于各重要教育文化机关,兹分配该馆一部,仰径向国立沈阳博物院筹备委员会洽领具报为要等因。奉此,当即遵令函达该会,查照邮寄去后,旋准函复,先汇邮递包扎等费,即行寄书等语。复经本馆照汇邮递等费。兹由该会将《清实录》全书一百二十二函如数寄到。经查无误,除函复该会外,理合具文呈报,伏乞鉴核备案,实为公便。谨呈

教育部

国立北平图书馆馆长袁同礼(馆印)

中国第二历史档案馆,教育部档案·全卷宗5,国立北平图书馆请拨员工学术研究补助费经常费有关文书,案卷号11616(4)

按:该呈文应于4月3日发出。

四月四日

下午二时,故宫博物院在会议室举行复员后第二次会议,马衡、沈兼士、先生、张庭济、张德泽、章乃炜、何澄一、黄鹏霄、王世襄、吴荣华(许协澄代)、刘鸿逵、王孝缙、常惠出席。报告第六(七)届理事会第二次会议记录等八项事宜,此外讨论九项议案。先生在临时动议环节,提出本院应聘请法律顾问,议决通过。〔《马衡年谱长编》,页947-949〕

任鸿隽覆函先生,告知中基会本年补助平馆购书费用不便挪用,并谈顾临去世。

守和吾兄大鉴:

顷奉三月卅一日手示,敬悉种切。本会补助贵馆之美金,原系两项:一为购书费,当由本会拨付;一为影印专门论文费,由本会前补助东方图书馆余款项下拨付,此款现存顾临先生处。顾临先生逝世,须待清理后始得知此款下落。至购书费三千元,当即缄在美会计先拨半数(一千五百元),交 Chase Bank 存贵馆帐中备用。唯因敝会会计现在交替中,何时可以签发此款,颇难预料。最好请兄暂勿支用,俟敝处得到美方通知时再行动用可也。

关于运回存美之期刊事,敝意以为最好在他处筹措运费。本会本年补助贵馆之三千美金,指定为购书之用,若用作运费,查帐时恐将发生问题,尊意想以为然。分配美赠书籍,原极烦难。闻教部近组织接收整理委员会,由蒋慰堂、朱国璋两君主持,专办接收及整理事宜。将来分配时,是否由原分配委员会主持,此时尚不明了。中基金对于此事素未参与,此时自不便强为出头。弟此次返国后,偶与教部及适之先生谈及此事,盖因在美时曾得 Dr. Brown 专诚拜托,代为传达,希望公平分配于公私各学术机关(尤注意教会学校)之意。至何人主持此事,弟拟不过问。如兄仍任分配委员会事,则拟请兄早为催促进行,以免夜长梦多,使捐书者更为失望也。

顾临先生忽尔溘逝,实公私各方不可弥补之大损失,此后欲再觅一美国友人如渠之竭忠尽虑以为我国,何可得耶?关于渠所经手之各事件,弟本请兄另行觅人代管,俾免损彼健康。兹则此层已不成问题,未了各事非由尊处直接处理不可矣。余不备悉。此颂春祺。

弟任鸿隽顿首

卅六年四月四日

〔《北京图书馆馆史资料汇编(1909-1949)》,页875-877〕

按:1947年3月27日,顾临在佛罗里达西棕榈滩(West Palm Beach)病逝。[1] 朱国璋(1913—1981),字仲谋,浙江吴兴人,上海商学院毕业,赴英留学,获伯明翰大学商学士学位,归国后曾在中央大学任教,时任上海商学院院长。

四月九日

朱家骅覆函先生,已遵嘱托推荐汪德昭出任联合国教育科学文化组织科学部工作。

守和吾兄大鉴:

顷获本月一日手书,忻聆种切。尼德汉博士近约汪德昭均前往联合国教育科学文化组织科学部工作一节,重以台嘱。经电请陈通伯兄,即为正式提出并为促成矣。知注特复,顺颂时祺。

弟朱家骅顿首

四月九日

〔国家图书馆档案,档案编号1945-※057-综合5-005006〕

按:此件为打字稿,落款处为朱家骅签名。

Jessie Lou Tyler 覆函先生,告知法斯已前往远东地区。

April 9, 1947

Dear Mr. Yuan:

Mr. Stevens has asked me to acknowledge and thank you for your letter of March 11 concerning the *Quarterly Bulletin of Chinese Bibliography*. Mr. Charles B. Fahs, Assistant Director for the Humanities, is now on his way to the Far East and plans to be in Peiping sometime around the latter part of April and first part of May. He now plans to visit the National Library of Peiping and will call on you sometime during his stay there.

---

① David Shavit, *The United States in Asia: a historical dictionary*, Greenwood Publishing Group, 1990, pp. 200-201.

Sincerely yours,

Jessie Lou Tyler

Secretary to Mr. Fahs

〔Rockefeller Foundation. Series 601: China; Subseries 601.R: China-Humanities and Arts. Vol. Box 47. Folder 391〕

按:此件为录副。

布朗覆函先生,因美国图书馆协会为中国各大学、院校编制采购书刊目录费用超出预算,请求中国政府额外支付一千美金。

April 9, 1947

Dear Dr. Yuan:

It has been a great satisfaction to the International Relations Board of the American Library Association to know that the selection of purchase bibliographies for Chinese universities has proceeded so well. In fact, we are informed the other day that the Ministry of Education had recommended that these bibliographies be used for the universities of China in place of incomplete and outdated bibliographies supplied without proper bibliographic checking. We are sincerely pleased to know that we have contributed in some sense to the rehabilitation of educational life in the universities and are most anxious to complete this bibliographic task for you.

We have completed twenty-one bibliographies which we have listed on the attached sheet. At the present time, we have eight bibliographies to complete, namely, Drama, Political Science, Law, Music, Fine Arts, Pharmacy, Natural Science, and Merchant Marine. In some instances, the consultants are still working on the lists, for example, the Merchant Marine and Natural Science lists.

It is quite true that the work of compiling these bibliographies would have been completed by at least the end of March if additional funds had been available; however, the cost of preparing these bibliographies has already exceeded to original \$2,000.00 budget by \$500.00. Therefore, it will require \$1,000.00 to cover the \$500.00 deficit incurred and the \$500.00 for the cost of final operation. The International Relations Office of the American Library Association regrets that it has been forced to stop the project until additional funds are received, as the general office budget is simply not able to absorb these expenses.

It is not our intention to place an additional strain upon you or your committee; but we are sure you will realize that this request for additional funds will barely cover the cost of preparation of lists, mimeographing, clerical assistance, and postage, and does not include the professional direction of the office which the International Relations Board is only too happy to contribute.

The American Library Association believes that these bibliographies are of far more lasting value because of careful consideration and preparation and would like to resume work as promptly as possible in order that your work with the Chinese universities may move forward.

Hoping to hear from you very soon, I remain,

Yours very sincerely,
Charles H. Brown
Chairman
Committee on the Orient and Southwest Pacific

〔The American Library Association Archives, China Projects File, Box 2, Chinese Universities, Correspondence, 1946-1947〕

按:该函寄送北平,此为抄件。

四月十日

先生致信史蒂文斯,提交有关苏俄研究中心的翻译计划并期待与法斯会晤。

April 10, 1947

Dear Dr. Stevens:

I am much obliged to you for your letter of March 17 and for the information you gave me.

Concerning our work in translating Russian documents relating to Sino-Russian relations, I enclose herewith a tentative plan. I have sent a copy to Professor Robinson at Columbia and I have shown it to Dr.

Michael of the University of Washington, who is now visiting Peiping and who is very much interested in our work. Prof. Robert A. Jelliffe of Oberlin College is lecturing at the National University. He says he will write to inform you how little of our academic life is affected by the political situation-a matter which is not much understood by most Americans.

We have moved our Russian Research Center to the Rocky Garden in the Winter Palace, and I now enclose a snapshot of this garden. It is a most picturesque spot in Peiping, and I am sure you would enjoy it when you come to this city.

I am leaving for Nanking next week and I expect to meet Mr. Evans and Dr. Fahs in Shanghai if they will come in May.

With cordial regards,

Sincerely yours,

T. L. Yuan

Director

〔国立北平图书馆英文信纸。Rockefeller Foundation. Series 601: China; Subseries 601.R: China-Humanities and Arts. Vol. Box 47. Folder 391〕

按:Professor Robinson 待考;Dr. Michael 应指 Franz H. Michael (1907-1992),德裔美籍中国学家,时在华盛顿大学(西雅图)任教;Robert A. Jelliffe(1883-1970),中文名为真立夫,时在北京大学任客座教授,后曾协助夏志清留美。① 此件为打字稿,落款处为先生签名,另附有 1 页计划书,于 5 月 6 日送达。

四月十一日

米来牟覆函先生,告知美国图书馆协会国际关系委员会对先生建议美国图书馆编目专家来华考察并指导工作的计划持积极态度。

April 11, 1947

Dear Dr. Yuan:

Your renewal of the suggestion that a cataloger be sent to China-your

① 王洞主编《夏志清夏济安书信集》卷 1,台北:联经出版事业公司,2016 年,页 30。

letter of February 13-has been brought to the attention of the International Relations Board and the International Relations Office. It was also specifically mentioned in a letter to the Rockefeller Foundation asking for another grant for the interchange of persons. We have not yet had a report of notion by the R. F.

We all hope that we may find it possible to cooperate with you in the way suggested. Maybe we can take advantage of the Fulbright Act for this if we don't get private funds.

Cordially yours
Carl H. Milam
Executive Secretary

〔The American Library Association Archives, China Projects File, Box 2, Books for China, 1944-47, Folder 1〕

按:该函寄送北平,此件为录副。

四月十六日

先生致信纳尔逊·洛克菲勒,请其考虑资助北平市政府修复历史古迹。

April 16, 1947

Dear Mr. Rockefeller:

In spite of my long silence, I have often been thinking of you. I trust that Mrs. Rockefeller and your children are all doing well. When you have occasion to write, will you kindly send me a snapshot of your family?

Since I had the pleasure of seeing you at the San Francisco Conference, I have been travelling in Europe, collecting scientific literature for this Library. Upon my return to Peiping last December, I found that our Library was intact and the Japanese did not do much damage.

With the rapid flow of books and periodicals from Europe and the United States, our stack room is now filled up. In order to relieve the congestion, we have bought the premises of the famous Rocky Garden and its attached buildings. Unfortunately, these buildings were badly damaged by the war and it now costs a great deal to have them restored to their original splendor.

In view of your father's interest in the restoration of Williamsburg, VA., I wonder whether he would be similarly interested in assisting us to restore some of the historical buildings in Peiping. I now enclose three photographs of the damaged buildings, including the Buddhist Temple, known as Tien Wang Dian, the restoration of which would cost US $ 100, 000.

It is gratifying to report that the Chinese government has already spent about US $ 150, 000 for the restoration of historical buildings in Peiping, including the Temple of Heaven, the Confucius Temple, the Lama Temple, etc. but in view of the vastness of our need, we have to depend upon private donations.

A special committee for the Restoration of Historical Buildings was set up last year, and I am serving as a member of the Executive Committee. The other members are the Mayor of Peiping, Dr. Hu Shih, Prof. Ma Heng and Mr. Chu Chi-chien, ex-Minister of the Interior.

I shall be most grateful to you if you could find out from your father whether the above project would be of any possible interest to him. If he would give half of the estimated cost of $ 100,000, our Committee will raise the other half in China.

In the interest of preserving the cultural heritage of the Orient, I am taking the liberty of writing to you, and I hope that we may count upon you for your interest and assistance.

In spite of political instability, scientific and cultural work in China goes forward. I hope you and Mrs. Rockefeller will find it possible to pay us a visit before very long.

With kindest regards,

Sincerely yours,

T. L. Yuan

Director

〔国立北平图书馆英文信纸。Rockefeller Foundation, Nelson A. Rockefeller Personal Papers. Box 22 Folder 173〕

按：Williamsburg 即威廉斯堡市，是美国历史最悠久的城市之一，1926 年约翰・洛克菲勒（John Davison Rockefeller, Jr., 1874－1960）斥巨资恢复该市 18 世纪的风貌，持续数十年才得以完工；Tien Wang Dian 应指北海公园西天梵境中的天王殿，始建于明朝。Mr. Chu Chi-chien 即朱启钤。此件为打字稿，落款处为先生签名，于 5 月初送达。

四月十九日

下午三时，故宫博物院第六（七）届理事会在平理事在绛雪轩召开第四次谈话会议，陈垣、李书华出席，马衡、先生、张庭济、张伯驹、徐悲鸿、邓以哲、启功、张允亮、赵万里、王重民列席。〔《马衡年谱长编》，页 950〕

四月二十四日

Marshall C. Balfour 覆函先生，告知法斯的行程，自己因回国无法陪同其前往北平。

April 24, 1947

Dear Dr. Yuan:

Yours of April 12, in reference to Mr. Fahs's visit, was appreciated and has been called to his attention. I have asked Miss Ferguson to keep you informed of his plans, which are now to arrive by CNAC May 2nd, at least temporarily putting up at the Wagons-Lits Hotel. He looks forward to his Peking visit with great enthusiasm.

Unfortunately, I can not join him and Mr. Evans on this visit, since I am leaving with Mrs. Balfour on May 8 for the United States. During my year's absence, Dr. Robert Briggs Watson will assume responsibility of this office, and I trust you will become acquainted in due course.

With cordial regards,

Very truly yours,

M. C. Balfour

〔Rockefeller Foundation. Series 601: China; Subseries 601.R: China-Humanities and Arts. Vol. Box 47. Folder 391〕

按：CNAC 即中国航空公司（China National Aviation Corporation）。

四月二十五日

晚,中国政治学会举行理事会,先生为会议主席,陈岱孙、张德熙、鲍文、Heinrich Kroes、范因博士、钱端升等理事出席,胡适、洪业、吴文藻等因事未到。讨论事项有,鲍文因在抗战期间囚于潍县集中营,后又筹备协和医学院恢复,身体不堪重负,请辞补选他人;本会自五月起恢复定期学术演讲,其范围集中于法政、经济。〔《华北日报》,1947 年 4 月 27 日,第 5 版〕

按:1915 年 12 月 5 日,该会由陆征祥倡导成立,会员多为各大学教授,后有会员二百余人。抗战中,损失藏书甚多,1945 年 12 月 18 日收回一万六千余册。张德熙,字柳池,广东香山人,清末赴美留学,入威斯康星大学,归国后曾任财政部秘书。Heinrich Kroes(1903-1989),生于荷兰,中文名胡鲁士,1934 年起在北平辅仁大学执教,授历史学课程,时任该校教务长。“范因博士”应为西人,待考。

四月二十七日

清华大学校庆,各地校友纷纷赶来参加,胡适、查良钊、先生等六百余人到场。〔《大公报》(上海),1947 年 4 月 28 日,第 4 版〕

按:梅贻琦、胡适在纪念会上呼吁校友踊跃捐款,以解经费不足。

四月三十日

中午,胡适在松公府蔡先生纪念堂设宴,真立夫[①]、师觉月、Bura、先生、梅贻宝、朱光潜、汤用彤、季羡林、王岷源等受邀出席。〔《此心安处是吾乡:季羡林归国日记(1946-1947)》,页 200〕

按:王岷源(1912—2000),四川巴县人,1934 年毕业于清华大学外文系,旋赴美入耶鲁大学英文系学习,时应在北京大学任教。Bura,待考。

五月一日

某记者来访,先生谈国际图书馆协会第十三届年会,如经费无着,拟请国民政府驻挪威使馆代办雷孝敏出席。此外,先生还介绍了平馆苏俄研究室筹备情况。〔《世界日报》,1947 年 5 月 2 日,第 3 版;《经世日报》,1947 年 5 月 2 日,第 4 版〕

按:本届年会在挪威首都举办,会期定于 5 月 20 日至 22 日。雷

---

① 《此心安处是吾乡:季羡林归国日记(1946-1947)》(排印本)记作 Jellife,实应为 Jelliffe。

孝敏,字叔礼,广东台山人,1910 年官费留美。

五月二日

先生赴机场迎接美国洛克菲勒基金会人文部副主任法斯、社会科学部副主任 Roger F. Evans。〔Charles B. Fahs' Diary, Rockefeller Archive Center, Rockefeller Foundation records, Officers' Diaries, RG 12〕

先生致信陈梦家,建议短期访英,并告陈源联系方式。

梦家吾兄:

奉到四月十八日手教,欣悉种切。中德外交关系一时不易恢复,前曾建议由政府派台端赴德接收铜器,此时尚嫌过早。敝意不如先行返国,俟将来有机会时再行赴欧。如此时愿由美短期赴英一行,往返川资约四百元及在英两月住宿旅行约四百元,可托人向 British Council 设法补助,似可由尊处函附介绍函陈通伯源先生。以前杨金甫、汪敬熙赴英均 British Council 招待,惟目前由美赴英及由英返美,订购船票均属不易,似宜早办是荷。敝馆经费困难,已向北大借款,勉维现状,更不易购到外汇也。余容再陈,顺颂旅安。

弟同礼顿首

五月二日

陈通伯通讯处

Dr. Chen Yuan

Sino-British Cultural Association

62 New Cavendish Street, London, W. 1.

〔方继孝藏札〕

五月四日

中午,先生在北海北门等候法斯、Roger F. Evans,陪同其参观平馆新获的俄语文献、日伪史料,后在仿膳用餐,饭后又至静心斋看该批文献,后北京大学真立夫和邓嗣禹来此一同拣阅。〔Charles B. Fahs' Diary, Rockefeller Archive Center, Rockefeller Foundation records, Officers' Diaries, RG 12〕

按:法斯认为这些史料文献作为初具规模的专藏已属不易,且有相当价值。

五月五日

于震寰致函先生,代教育部索取此前商洽美国图书馆专家赴华考察费用公函。

守和先生馆长钧鉴：

六月十三日我公在美所收朱部长同意美国图书馆专家来华考察，并允资助美金三千元函稿，部中百觅不得，祈将原函寄下，俾便持示主管拟办，用毕仍以奉还也。专陈，顺颂道绥。

于震寰谨上

卅六年五月五日

〔国家图书馆档案，档案编号 1947-※046-外事 5-001002〕

五月六日

下午，季羡林来平馆借书，并拜访先生。〔《此心安处是吾乡：季羡林归国日记(1946-1947)》，页 204〕

按：本年 3 月 4 日，季羡林、王森二人在平馆找到了藏文《甘殊尔》。5 月 8 日，季羡林将此书从平馆取走。①

五月八日

上午十时，先生偕法斯、Roger F. Evans 前往太庙查看此前收缴的日伪图书，随后赴平馆参观。中午，马衡、先生、胡适在故宫博物院设宴招待法斯、Evans，沈兼士、王世襄等人作陪。席间，马衡请法斯考虑资助故宫博物院一套照相复制设备和一台珂罗版印刷机，以复制故宫博物院的藏品(影像)与其他博物馆交换。法斯表示暂时不会考虑该项计划，因为中国局面尚未稳定，现在资助有相当风险。此外，他对王世襄印象非常好，考虑给予他奖学金赴美学习博物馆方法和组织。〔Charles B. Fahs' Diary, Rockefeller Archive Center, Rockefeller Foundation records, Officers' Diaries, RG 12〕

按：法斯认为平馆藏书十分丰富，但尚无读者和研究人员利用，这一问题主要由于北平地区教育机构尚未完全恢复。

晚六时许，南开大学北平校友会假银行公会欢迎张伯苓，梅贻琦、先生、石志仁、李麟玉、郑华炽等八十二人出席。七时半，韩振华致辞，继由严仁英致欢迎词，后由张伯苓致训。会中公布校友会执委选举结果，梅贻琦、韩振华等十一人当选，先生则位列三位候补委员之一。〔《民国日报》(天津)，1947 年 5 月 9 日，第 4 版〕

① 《此心安处是吾乡：季羡林归国日记(1946-1947)》，页 172、205。

按:石志仁(1897—1972),河北乐亭人,铁路机械专家,南开中学毕业,时应任平津区铁路管理局局长。严仁英(1913—2017),女,医学家,严修孙女。

Jessie Lou Tyler 覆函先生,告知史蒂文斯已收到四月十日的信件。

May 8, 1947

Dear Mr. Yuan:

Mr. Stevens has asked me to thank you for your letter of April 10 with the enclosed Plan for Publication of Documents on Sino-Russian Relations and the snapshot of the Rocky Garden in the Winter Palace.

Doubtless you have already talked with Mr. Fahs during his visit in Peiping.

Sincerely yours,

Jessie Lou Tyler

Secretary to Mr. Fahs

〔Rockefeller Foundation. Series 601: China; Subseries 601.R: China-Humanities and Arts. Vol. Box 47. Folder 391〕

按:该函以航空信方式寄送,此件为录副。

五月九日

晚,先生在家设宴款待法斯、Roger F. Evans,何廉、李书华夫妇、康乃尔大学教授 Edwin Arthur Burtt 等人受邀作陪。饭后,先生陪同法斯前往中国政治学会,Edwin Arthur Burtt 在会上作有关印度的演讲。〔Charles B. Fahs' Diary, Rockefeller Archive Center, Rockefeller Foundation records, Officers' Diaries, RG 12〕

按:法斯对先生印象颇佳,认为"Yuan is the nearest to an American promoter I have met in China"。

纳尔逊·洛克菲勒覆函先生,婉拒此前向洛克菲勒基金会申请资助修复北平名胜古迹。

May 9, 1947

Dear Mr. Yuan:

Thank you for your thoughtful letter of April sixteenth. It was a pleasure to have news of you, and to learn that the Library came through the war so well.

I wish that I could send you an encouraging response as to the possibility of Father being helpful in connection with the proposed restorations in Peiping. As I know you will understand, however, with the increasingly heavy demands made on him by the responsibilities he is carrying, he is obliged more than ever to follow certain limiting principles in connection with personal commitments. In view of the extent of the work at Williamsburg, which is not yet finished, he has felt that he must ask to be excused from taking up the many interesting proposals along similar lines which he received, sympathetic though he may be with their objectives, and regrets that he could not make an exception even in this instance.

If I could be of any assistance myself, your own interest in the work would add to my natural sympathy with the values it involves, but the program I have already taken on is so heavy that it would not be possible for me to add to it in this way.

With best wishes for the success of the project, and kindest personal regards in which Mrs. Rockefeller joins me,

Sincerely,

Nelson A. Rockefeller

P. S. Thinking you might like to have them back, I am returning the photographs you enclosed.

〔Rockefeller Foundation, Nelson A. Rockefeller Personal Papers. Box 22 Folder 173〕

按:此件为录副。

五月上旬

齐如山、先生、梅兰芳、王向宸、梁实秋、陈纪滢等提倡设立国剧学会,并函请何思源、杜建时、焦菊隐、萧一山、张道藩、卢冀野、沈兼士、孙楷第等三十二人共同发起。〔《华北日报》,1947 年 5 月 13 日,第 4 版〕

按:先生曾为该会谋划新地,并商故宫博物院借给霞公府南夹道宅院,作为学会及陈列馆址。

五月十日

下午五时许,叶企孙、先生、郑华炽、贺麟、郑昕、冯至、杨业治、张星烺、季羡林等人在板厂胡同中德学会开会，讨论该社团的存续问题。〔《此心安处是吾乡：季羡林归国日记（1946-1947）》，页206〕

五月十二日

先生撰写备忘录，向洛克菲勒基金会申请资助平馆建立缩微胶卷实验室。

With the assistance of the Rockefeller Foundation, a Draeger camera, together with other apparatus, was installed in the P. U. M. C. in 1940-41. Unfortunately, a few days after Pearl Harbour, it was removed by the Japanese Army. Since V-J day much search has been conducted in Peiping and in Tokyo, but without any success. It is generally supposed that it had been destroyed by the Japanese at the time of their surrender.

Since only a small portion of the rare Chinese books in the collection of the National Library of Peiping had been microfilmed at Washington, it is most desirable that other rare items in its collection should also be microfilmed. In addition to these rare books, there are many important manuscript materials of historical value in the possession of the National Library and the National Palace Museum which should be made available to scholars. For this reason, a photoduplication laboratory is urgently needed in Peiping.

The object of the laboratory is not only to assure the protection of valuable and irreparable historical materials, but also to make available to sinological scholars at home and abroad important source materials for research.

The National Library of Peiping has an outstanding collection of western scientific journals. Libraries and research institutions in China, which cannot afford to purchase these journals, depend upon the National Library to supply films for certain articles or for certain issues needed in connection with their research. If the photoduplication laboratory could be set up, it would enable the Library to supply microcopies of research materials wanted by scholars both in China and another country.

A memorandum to this effect was submitted to the Rockefeller Foundation on March 20, 1945. A detailed estimate of the approximate cost for setting up the Laboratory from Mr. Eugene Power of the University Microfilms, Inc. was submitted to the Foundation in May 1946. Since then, the cost of microfilm equipment in the United States has increased considerably. It is estimated that a grant of $ 15,000 would be required for the purchase and shipment of the equipment as listed by Mr. Power. If financial support for this project could be given by the Foundation, the National Library will seek further advice from Mr. Power, who has agreed to come to Peiping, at his own expense, to assist in setting up the Laboratory and in the training of technical personnel.

Respectfully submitted

T. L. Yuan

Director

May 12, 1947

〔Rockefeller Foundation. Series 601: China; Subseries 601.R: China-Humanities and Arts. Vol. Box 47. Folder 393〕

按:此件为打字稿,落款处为先生签名。该备忘录应附在 14 日先生写给法斯的信中。

五月十四日

中午十二时,平津国立院校长谈话会在北海静心斋举行,先生、梅贻琦、郑天挺、金问洙、袁敦礼、黎锦熙、李麟玉、李书华等人出席,先生应为会议主席。会议先就上次会谈所决定之事项进行情形及目前各校一般情况予以报告,交换意见后即午餐。下午一时,继续开会,讨论四项议案。一是各院校每月对公费发给之粮价折款如何确定;二是应请教部普遍提高各级教员待遇;三是各院校经常费不敷甚剧,请教部将各院校经常费最低限度提高六倍;四是下次会议定于六月十一日在大字典编纂处举行谈话会。〔《民国日报》(天津),1947 年 5 月 15 日,第 4 版〕

下午四时,平馆召开复员后第一次馆务会议,先生、王访渔、王重民、赵万里、顾子刚、王祖彝出席。先生作为会议主席,报告以下诸事:

(一)每月第二个星期三下午召开馆务会议,由先生召集各组主任、秘书及文书股长举行;

(二)本日平津院校联合会议情形;

(三)洛克菲勒基金会即将派法斯来平视察,平馆向该会申请两项补助金,共计三万美元。

此后,馆务会议议决以下各案:俸薪调整、职员增加底薪、太庙临时工作职员调整后的待遇、何国贵抚恤、傅增湘捐赠批校本向教部申请奖励、接收各汉奸书籍、洛克菲勒基金会捐赠拍摄设备安置、李耀南薪俸增补。〔《北京图书馆馆史资料汇编(1909-1949)》,页878-882〕

先生覆信于震寰,寄上此前代部索要有关公私函件。

镜宇仁兄大鉴:

五月五日大函,备悉一是。兹将六月十三日朱部长致弟原函寄上,即希台阅,用毕交还为盼。又部长同意资助美图书专家美金三千元一节,弟前接美图书馆协会来函,云此款寄到即可派员来华等语,业已据函转陈,并以附及。专复,即颂时祺。

附原函一件。

袁〇〇拜启

〔国家图书馆档案,档案编号1947-※046-外事5-001001〕

按:此为文书所拟底稿,注明5月14日发,暂系于此。

先生致信法斯,附两份备忘录,并告知中基会和教育部向平馆拨付了相当数量的美金。

May 14, 1947

Dear Mr. Fahs:

It is most gratifying to find that you take so much personal interest in the work of the National Library. I now enclose herewith two memoranda: (1) re the Photoduplication Laboratory, and (2) re the development of our Research Program. I hope you will forward them for us to Dr. Stevens.

In a day or two I shall write to Dr. Stevens stating that for carrying out these projects the National Library is ready to set aside an equal amount of money covered by the Foundation's grant. For instance, the Ministry of Education has given us $10,000 and the China Foundation, $5,000. These two grants will match up the amount of the grant which we hope the Foundation will find it possible to make. At any rate, I hope that our joint efforts will assist us in the realization of our objective.

With many thanks,

Yours sincerely,

T. L. Yuan

P. S. I had a Chinese seal specially made for you as a souvenir of your visit. The inscription was carved by the famous artist, Mr. Chou Hsi-ting, of Peiping.

〔Rockefeller Foundation. Series 601: China; Subseries 601.R: China-Humanities and Arts. Vol. Box 47. Folder 391, Folder 393〕

按:Chou Hsi-ting 即周希丁(1891—1961),原名周家瑞,江西金溪人,传拓专家,亦精于篆刻。此件为打字稿,落款处为先生签名。该信另附 4 页备忘录,涉及苏俄研究中心(Slavic Centre)、日本研究中心(Japanese Centre)、美国研究中心(American Centre)、《图书季刊》英文本四个方面。

Rae Cecilia Kipp 致函先生,寄上美国图书馆协会向战区国家运送成套图书的报告,并告知客岁十二月六日启运书籍的相关信息。

May 14, 1947

Dear Dr. Yuan:

We are enclosing a report on the American Library Association shipment of the Libraries in War Areas set of books which was given to the libraries of China through the generosity of the Rockefeller Foundation. The cartons, numbering 102, were shipped through the auspices of UNRRA and left this country on December 6, 1946 on the boat, S. S. Hopepeak. The material was consigned to UNRRA with an indication that the material was intended for the Chinese Committee on the Distribution of Books.

We hope that this information will enable you to trace the shipment and that the libraries of China will soon have the opportunity of seeing the American publications of the war years. If any further information is needed in order to clarify your position as Chairman of this Committee in regard to the distribution of material, please do not hesitate to call on us for formal authorization.

Yours very sincerely,

Rae Cecilia Kipp

Executive Assistant

〔The American Library Association Archives, China Projects File, Box 2, Books for China, 1944-47, Folder 1〕

按:该函寄送北平,此件为录副。

五月中旬

王芸生至平馆,与先生、赵万里晤谈。〔《大公报》(天津),1947年6月22日,第3版;《大公报》(上海),1947年5月16日,第2版〕

按:5月13日下午2时,王芸生抵达北平,18日前往太庙保存日文图书处参观,21日中午返回天津。

五月十六日

先生致信史蒂文斯,恳请洛克菲勒基金会考虑资助平馆设立日本、苏俄、美国研究中心计划。

May 16, 1947

Dear Dr. Stevens:

We have had a most pleasant visit from Dr. Evans and Dr. Fahs. In the course of our conversations, I have had the opportunity of discussing with them the various phases of our work.

Since this Library has the advantage of having our prewar collection intact, we are now in a better position to develop our research program as outlined in the memorandum which I submitted to the Foundation through Dr. Fahs.

China's close relations with Japan, the Soviet Union and the United States demand the full development of better understanding of one another. I believe that our task in promoting closer cultural interchange through printed materials is an important contribution, although I am rather distressed at the slowness of the development in this country, since it seems so obvious that the distribution of our scholarly effort is so little commensurate with the needs of the second half of the twentieth century.

For the support of our program for 1947 we have received $ 10,000 from the Ministry of Education and $ 5,000 from the China Foundation. With these two grants we are able to have a good start.

I hope that similar support could be given by the Foundation, especially in view of our interest in the Far East. I am happy to say that whatever support the Foundation may be able to extend to us, it will be matched up by grants from the Chinese Government.

With sincere appreciation of your interest and assistance,

Yours sincerely,

T. L. Yuan

Director

〔国立北平图书馆英文信纸。Rockefeller Foundation. Series 601: China; Subseries 601.R: China-Humanities and Arts. Vol. Box 47. Folder 391〕

按:此件为打字稿,落款处为先生签名。

先生致信法斯,告知即将赴上海,期待在沪晤谈。

May 16, 1947

Dear Mr. Fahs:

I enclose my letter to Dr. Stevens. If you have not sent out the two memoranda, will you include this letter also?

I have just had word from the CNAC that reservations have been made for me on the plane leaving for Shanghai tomorrow. I shall look forward to seeing you in Shanghai.

Yours sincerely,

T. L. Yuan

Director

〔国立北平图书馆英文信纸。Rockefeller Foundation. Series 601: China; Subseries 601.R: China-Humanities and Arts. Vol. Box 47. Folder 391〕

按:此件为打字稿,落款处为先生签名。

五月十七日　北平—上海

下午三时,北海公园理事会举行第一次会议,先生、傅增湘、韩振华等十六

人被推选为理事,另有候补理事五名。〔《华北日报》,1947 年 5 月 18 日,第 4 版〕

按:先生被推选极有可能与静心斋属平馆有关。

先生由北平乘飞机南下。〔《益世报》(北平),1947 年 5 月 16 日,第 2 版〕

按:先生对记者称,此行须三周时间,主要是向教育部报告馆务,出席中央研究院评议会、图书分配委员会。

晚,先生致信陈梦家,请其帮忙联系美国出版商并谈钱存训去美事。

梦家吾兄:

故宫博物院拟于秋间将所藏 Jannings 铜器委托美国商店出版(如 R. R. Donnelley & Sons)。兹送上英文说明一份,请与 Kelley 或出版家一商。如能于印成后得到书若干部及版税,尤所企盼。想芝加哥近印之铜器目录其版税等可作援例也。敝处前介绍钱存训君至芝加哥大学主持编目事宜,渠已得到官员护照请转告 Creel 先生,约七月间可以启程。弟今日来沪,两日后北返。匆匆,顺颂大安。

弟袁同礼顿首

五,十七

芝加哥 Graduate Library School 之章程请告其寄弟一份。

〔方继孝藏札〕

按:Jannings 即 Werner Jannings,德国商人,中文名为杨宁史,抗日战争期间,他在河南等地收购大量青铜器,后在王世襄、宋子文、沈兼士等人的多方努力下,该人于 1946 年将所藏铜器“呈献”故宫博物院,但要求专室展出并印行图录,后者由罗樾(Max Loehr)担任编辑、整理工作,本拟由《华裔学志》出版[①],但因为时局因素中断,1956 年由密歇根大学出版社初版,正式题名为 *Chinese Bronze Age Weapons: the Werner Jannings collection in the Chinese National Palace Museum, Peking*。R. R. Donnelley,美国印刷公司,1864 年在芝加哥成立。Kelley 即 Charles F. Kelley(1885-1960),美国艺术史专家,时应任芝加哥艺术博物馆(Art Institute of Chicago)东方部主任,与陈梦家一同编写 *Chinese Bronzes from*

① Tsugio, Mikami. *Monumenta Serica*, Vol. 16, no. 1/2, 1957, pp. 508-512.

the Buckingham Collection。钱存训离沪赴美时间约在9月中旬。

五月十九日

晚六时,徐森玉在来喜设宴,先生、严文郁、黄如今、郑振铎等与席。〔陈福康著《郑振铎年谱(修订本)》,上海:上海外语教育出版社,2017年,页1164〕

按:黄如今,湖南永兴人,时应任长春大学校长。

五月二十二日

英美赠书分配委员会致函各委员,告第二次会议时间地点。

径启者,美国捐赠之图书业已运抵上海,亟待将分配办法予以决定。兹定于本月廿五日(星期日)下午五时半在鸡鸣寺中央研究院举行本会第二次会议,即希准时莅临参加是荷。此致。

国立中央研究院英美赠书分配委员会谨启

五,廿二

〔国家图书馆档案,档案编号1946-※046-外事5-006026〕

按:此件为先生所拟之底稿,实发时间应为23日。

五月二十四日　南京

中华图书馆协会在京理事、监事假中央图书馆举行联席会议。李小缘、蒋复璁(缪镇藩代)、洪有丰、刘国钧、王文山(于震寰代)、汪长炳和徐家麟(陆华深代)、先生,柳诒徵(李恩渥代)、沈学植出席,其中先生为会议主席。首由常务干事于震寰报告会务,后讨论会费、增加收入、理监事任期、中国学术团体联合会年会等议案。〔《中华图书馆协会会报》第21卷第3-4期合刊,页5-6〕

五月二十五日

下午六时,中央研究院英美赠书分配委员会在该院会议室举行第二次会议,翁文灏主席、周鲠生、傅斯年、任鸿隽(先生代)、杭立武、先生、周鸿经出席,顾斗南记录。

先生报告事项:

(一)美国捐赠书籍经美国图书中心寄运到沪者共计一〇四一箱,在途中者共计二二五箱,尚有七五〇箱在美待运。

(二)由美寄沪书箱之运费向由联总担负,近接华盛顿中国物资供应委员会王守竞来电,内称联总结束工作在即,此项运费无法继续承担,在美待运之七五〇箱运费约美金四千六百元,美国图书中心建议由中国物资供应委员会暂行垫付以便继续起运，应否垫付请电覆。本会当即函请教育部核办，现教部已允担负此项运费，由部径电王守竞。

（三）英国捐赠之书共计二九七箱，亦委托联总寄运，因联总结束在即，已函托郑天锡大使转催速寄。

（四）美国图书馆协会捐赠之（1）学术期刊共一四二种，内一百种（每种二份至五份）已与教育部所订购者重复，此外之四十种系医学期刊，均未经教育部订购（每种二份至六份）；（2）一九四四年出版之新书一七八种每种四份，如何分配请公决。

随后，会议讨论事项：

（一）分配原则如何确定案。决议：本会分配各机关之图书以该机关能否充分利用为前提，同时本会应注意区域之分配，公推高等教育司司长周鸿经、先生参照各大学及独立学院现设之科系性质开列清单，并注明特殊需要，由本会委托上海提运清理处分发各院校。

（二）美国图书馆协会捐赠之期刊如何分配案。决议：（1）关于医学期刊分配于国立大学医学院及成绩优良之独立医学院，并有本会征求教育部医学教育委员之意见，以供参考；（2）关于教育部订购重复之期刊一部分分配于成绩优良之私立大学，一部分分配于教会大学，尤应注意其战前所订购之期刊种类，应在可能范围以内使之衔接，关于国际关系之期刊则分配于罗斯福图书馆。

（三）美国图书馆协会捐赠之新书一七八种如何分配案。决议：接受该会之建议，分配于南京、北平、武昌、广州四处之学术机关。

（四）美国图书中心捐赠之图书期刊如何分配案。决议：参照各大学、独立学院及国立研究院所设之科系性质将此批书籍尽先分配，其残缺不全之期刊则俟全部赠书到沪后再行分配，至关于教科书之分配应注意内地各院校之需要平均拨发，关于参考书之分配应调查各国立图书馆实际需要酌予分配。

（五）美方赠书如何致谢案。决议：由翁文灏主任函谢美国图书馆协会、美国图书中心及洛克菲勒基金会。

七时散会。〔国家图书馆档案，档案编号1946-※046-外事5-006028至1946-※046-外事5-006031〕

五月二十七日

平馆向教育部呈文一件,题为《造送本馆三十五年度京沪渝昆部生补费计算表等件请鉴核》,具先生名并钤印。〔中国第二历史档案馆,教育部档案·全卷宗五,国立北平图书馆员工生活补助费名册及俸薪表,案卷号11614(1)〕

按:"生补费"应指生活补助费,下同。

五月

先生向教育部提交呈文一件,题为《呈报点收傅增湘先生捐赠手校各种书籍请转呈行政院优加褒奖并酌给养老医药等费》。〔台北"国史馆",〈北平图书馆总卷〉,数位典藏号019-030402-0003〕

按:此次捐赠共计373种4269册,5月5日平馆派员前往点收,拟专室庋藏、永存纪念。先生认为此批古籍价值极高,特呈教育部请转呈行政院予以褒奖,后又多次与英千里面谈,恳请协助。8月中旬行政院下达指令,由政府颁发匾额并饬财政部拨给奖金四千万元。该件为文书代笔,钤先生名章,关防页不存,附捐赠手校书籍清单一册。

六月初

先生赴上海,协助中央研究院分配英美赠送中国之书刊资料。〔《新星报》(天津),1947年6月22日,第4版〕

六月五日

先生访顾廷龙,告傅增湘以手校本四千余册赠平馆,中有《册府元龟》。〔《顾廷龙日记》,页490〕

六月上旬

先生致信王伯祥,托抄平馆所编清代碑记文史论文索引中收录的笔记目录,并询董作宾《甲骨丛编》书稿能否再印。〔《王伯祥日记》第21册,页261-262〕

按:此信应于6月10日送达,6月12日王伯祥抄录完毕后寄送先生。

六月九日

晚,先生访郑振铎,在其处与马衡、徐森玉、汤安、顾廷龙、钱锺书、李宗侗、钱存训、张珩等人畅谈、饮酒。〔《郑振铎年谱(修订本)》,页1170〕

按:汤安(1887—1967),字临泽,别署临石、邻石,浙江嘉兴人,画家、篆刻家,尤善仿古。

先生致信教育部朱家骅部长，请其根据面谈时所允数目拨付平馆修理、临时等费。

敬陈者，职馆以多年之经营，在战前业已略具规模，内外学者莅平参观者莫不公认为东亚之重要学术机关。屡承惠允宽筹经费、促其发展，俾能使之合于国际之标准。职馆同人莫不感奋。惟年余以来，以库款支绌，勉维现状，而钧部筹得之美金五十万元，职馆迄今未承分配，而本年度扩充改良费亦仅领到壹亿元，指定专作租用北海静心斋之用。此次来京曾将需要迫切情形略予陈述，荷蒙面允于大楼修理费壹亿伍千万外之外，另拨临时费贰亿元，一俟美金外汇及扩充改良费经行政院核准后，当即续拨，并允将原是由请之款列入下次分配预算之内，仰见钧座维护文化之盛意，钦感莫名。微闻主管部分以职原呈首列大楼修理费壹亿伍千万元，认为钧座所批之贰亿元包括此项修理费在内，此种解释与钧座面允者不同，两相差之数为数既钜，不得不重申前请，务恳转嘱主管部份以钧座面允者为根据（修理费一亿五千万元，已于廿二日批准并已汇平，此次增拨之贰亿元则系二十八日批准者），并乞提前电汇至平，以应亟需，不胜迫切待命之至。

六月九日

〔《北京图书馆馆史资料汇编（1909-1949）》，页 895-896〕

按：此件应为先生所抄之副本。

先生致信行政院长张群，请就傅增湘捐书之举拨发奖励费及医药费。大意如下：

敬陈者，江安傅沅叔（增湘）先生，博学硕德，收藏宏富。近以老年多病，乃将其躬自批校之书四千余册，捐赠本馆，每册根据宋元佳椠，朱墨灿然，集毕生之精力悉荟于斯，嘉惠来学，至深且钜。业经本馆报部特呈钧院予以褒奖，并请酌拨医药费，俾资调理。值此紧急经济措施之时，固知军政各费需用浩繁，惟念傅先生以垂暮之年，慨然舍其一生收藏之典籍，捐诸国有，不仅价值钜万，其所风动社会而示范于国民者，意义尤为重大。政府于此，纵或支出一亿二亿，在全年预算中所占甚微，而直接裨益于人民者为功不可胜计。为此仰恳钧座提前批准，不胜感激待命之至。

〔《中国历代国家藏书机构及名家藏读叙传选》，页 148-149〕

陈剑翛致函先生，请在美英捐赠书刊中留意为广西大学分润若干。

守和馆长学兄左右：

上月杪晋京述职，获相逢于道左，车行甚速，未及畅谈，嗣又因各地学潮澎湃，赶回桂林，有疏访候，愧不可言。本校自复员以来，幸得教职员之协助及教育部之扶植，与地方政府之合作渐能循序而进，略复旧观，洵称幸事。惟图书损失甚钜，急待补充，加以外汇结购困难，无法采购或订购。前承贵馆赠配一部份书籍，由香港装箱运送，至当感谢。仍恳费神垂注本校，多多分配。嗣后如联总、英美援华会等机关如有遗馈，无论新旧书物或文法理工农等参考书均所需求，不胜欢迎。至于感激之情，不仅限于弟一人已也。兹托本校法律系教授梁念曾兄顺便面陈一切，毋任依依。匆叩道安。

弟陈剑翛上

卅六，六，九

又，何杰先生在此任教务长，甚得信仰。附及。

〔国立广西大学用笺。南京大学图书馆特藏部〕

按：梁念曾，河北人，北京大学毕业，著有《中国民法总论》，1948年桂林建设印刷所刊行。何杰（1888—1979），字孟绰，广东番禺人，地质学家，1903年入岭南学堂（Canton Christian College），后赴美留学，归国先后在北京大学、北洋大学、中山大学等校任教。时，广西大学应在桂林将军桥附近。

六月十日

先生致信郑振铎，介绍爨汝僖前往面商《域外所藏中国古画集》捐赠、订购事宜。

敬恳者，尊处所印《中国名画集》十四种，以成本较高，未敢根据出版法之规定请发行人按期呈缴。内中有已购预约者，有因上海办事处以款绌关系尚未订购者。兹拟订购全部，务请格外廉价出售，凡能赠送者即请赠送，必须购买者则照价付款，似于公私均能顾到。兹介绍爨君前来面洽，即希赐予指导是荷。顺颂大安。

弟袁同礼顿首

〔《北京图书馆馆史资料汇编(1909-1949)》，页897〕

按：《中国名画集》即《域外所藏中国古画集》，由郑振铎所编，依次分《西域画》《汉晋六朝画》《唐五代画》《宋画》《元画》《明画》

《明遗民画》《明遗民画续集》《清画》8 编，共 24 辑，信中所言 14 种，应指至该年夏已印行者。此为抄件，左侧标注“已出”“待出”各册信息。

六月中旬

先生覆信王重民，同意其在北京大学支全薪。〔《胡适遗稿及秘藏书信》第 24 册，页 92-94〕

按：王重民意欲将此前在平馆所领部分薪水退回。

六月十三日

先生致信联合国经济暨社会理事会亚洲及远东经济委员会中国代表团秘书处，请为平馆征集文献资料。

敝馆搜集我国参加国际会议之资料业已粗具规模、蔚为大观。兹闻联合国经济暨社会理事会亚洲及远东经济委员会定于本月十五日在沪举行会议，商讨远东经济问题，至关重要。内中我国及其他参与各国代表团所印之备忘录与提案及一切文件，莫不为重要史料。敝馆亟愿保存全份以供研究，拟请贵团指定一人代为搜集或代为设法保留一份，一俟奉函示知，当即派员来取。用特专函奉恳，统希查照办理，见复为荷。

〔《北京图书馆馆史资料汇编(1909-1949)》，页 899〕

按：此为抄件。

先生致信朱家骅，申请教育部对平馆增拨经费用以购藏善本古籍。

敬陈者，上海潘明训氏为近代海内藏书家之一，自购得项城袁克文氏旧藏宋刊《礼记正义》（南渡后三山黄唐所刻，海内传为孤本），因颜其斋曰宝礼堂。嗣以袁氏所藏善本旧椠归潘氏者十之六七，藏庋至富。潘氏且有佞宋之癖，苟为善本，重值勿吝，故二十年来所积，几与北杨南瞿相颉颃。其所编《宋本书录》凡四册，内中收入宋版书一百十余种及元版书六种，尤为名贵。而未列入书目者，尚有多种。海盐张菊生元济先生曾为作序，有“余尝登宝礼之堂，纵观所藏琳琅满目，如游群玉之府”，足以知其梗概。潘氏于数年前逝世，上年一月其后人曾欲觅受主，售书还债。经本馆与之接洽，以议价未谐，事遂中止。兹潘氏后人又因需款孔亟，仍愿割爱让诸公家，索价十亿元。价虽过钜，但念时不可失，似宜收归国有，以免散佚。兹特建议由钧部委托张元济、徐鸿宝、郑振铎诸先生与其后人切实商洽，并公同议价，期于有成。

将来如能分藏南北两馆,实为艺林之盛事。惟值此紧急经济措施之时,尤赖钧座特为赞助,俾此批宝贵之收藏归诸国有。全国学术界同深感谢。用特奉陈,敬候钧裁,并盼赐复为感。

袁

六月十三日,上海

〔《北京图书馆馆史资料汇编(1909-1949)》,页 900-901〕

按:此为抄件。

六月二十日

上午,郑振铎、贺昌群至宝庆路平馆上海办事处访问先生,并在此午餐。〔《郑振铎年谱(修订本)》,页 1172〕

六月下旬

先生患气管炎,旋即转为肺炎,问诊于焦湘宗医生。〔《北京图书馆馆史资料汇编(1909-1949)》,页 904〕

按:焦湘宗(1893—1985),字景汉,山东即墨人,1917 年 12 月毕业于同济大学医学院,曾任颜惠庆的私人医生,其诊所时在上海陕西南路 213 号 2 号。

六月二十六日

先生致信法斯,请其考虑资助平馆筹办苏俄研究中心,强调现有文献的珍贵性。

Shanghai, June 26, 1947

Dear Mr. Fahs:

I trust you and Mr. Evans have settled down at your New York office after two months' visit abroad.

While I am in Shanghai, I have gathered together an extremely valuable collection of Russian works on Sinology as well as on Mongolia, Tibet, "Chinese Turkestan", and the Amur Provinces. According to Prof. Gapanovich, many titles may not be duplicated elsewhere, as the Soviets have not given permission to let these books leave their country.

If Dr. Stevens could not recommend a larger grant in view of the political situation in China, I hope he would make a special grant for the development of our Slavic Center. We have really made a good beginning, and I think the project deserves Foundation's support.

When you decide to make us the grant, the quarterly payment of your grant should be sent to the Chase National Bank, Park Avenue Branch, Park Avenue and 60th street, New York City, as the large portion of your possible grant will be used for the acquisition of source materials in Europe and the United States.

Yours sincerely,

T. L. Yuan

Director

〔国立北平图书馆英文信纸。Rockefeller Foundation. Series 601: China; Subseries 601.R: China-Humanities and Arts. Vol. Box 47. Folder 391〕

按:Amur Provinces 即黑龙江省。此件为打字稿,落款处为先生签名。

六月二十九日

先生遵焦湘宗医生之建议,入住中西疗养院,后在此休养一月。〔《北京图书馆馆史资料汇编(1909-1949)》,页 905〕

按:先生似于 7 月 31 日出院。

七月四日

先生致信张全新,请转告噶邦福来馆编纂俄文书目。

日前在沪所购俄文书,经已交邮分批寄上,谅均收到。关于噶邦福先生为馆编订俄文书目一节,拟请尊处代为转告,请噶君利用本年暑假,务将该项目录编订竣事,俾早日付印。并欢迎其夫妇及小孩到静心斋度夏,并自本月份起每月加送研究费二十五万元,在高等司所拨研究费专款内拨付,即希转知会计股予以照拨为荷。近又购得俄文书一批,共用一千二百五十万元,书目容再寄上。

袁

〔《北京图书馆馆史资料汇编(1909-1949)》,页 902〕

按:此为抄件。

七月八日

先生致电王访渔、顾子刚二人,大意如下:

加底薪拟自本月施行,谨拟草案。又生补费余款,请早分配同人。

修绠堂有俄文书,内容甚佳,请派张全新选购。

〔《中国历代国家藏书机构及名家藏读叙传选》,页 149〕

七月九日

先生致信 Dorothy J. Comins,收到其来函及第二份补充清单,为了加快分发已亲赴上海督办,最终报告将会在适当的时候寄出。

July 9, 1947

Dear Miss Comins:

Thank you for your letter of June 10 and a second supplementary list of journals which the ALA has allocated for Chinese libraries.

To expedite the work of distribution of books and journals, I have come down to Shanghai to give the matter my personal supervision. A report will be submitted to your Committee in due course.

I wish to take this opportunity to express once more our grateful appreciation to the American Library Association for the allocation of these scholarly and scientific journals for Chinese libraries. Their presence in China greatly facilitates the scientific research carried on by Chinese scholars.

Sincerely yours,

T. L. Yuan

Director

〔平馆上海办事处英文信纸。The American Library Association Archives, China Projects File, Box 2, Periodicals for Chinese Universities, Correspondence and Lists, 1944–1947〕

按:此件为打字稿,落款处为先生签名,于 7 月 16 日送达。

七月十日

先生致信朱家骅,请教育部为平馆增拨经费。

卧病沪上,荷蒙派员视疾,并承惠允资助医药费用,德意隆情,至为铭感。惟此次致病之由,实以馆中经费拮据,应付维艰,而物质狂涨,巧妇实难为无米之炊。五中焦灼,莫可言宣。此中困难情形,曾经面陈,荷承惠允于政院核准增加经费时,再予增拨。仰见钧座对于职馆关切之殷,全馆同人至为感奋。查职馆本年度预算,经钧部核定者仅有(一)生补费,(二)经常费,(三)临时费三种,而无购书费,以致每购一书,必须在临时费项下撙节开支。今春书估持《明实录》原本三册求售,索价三百万元,检查馆藏目录,正馆中所缺之本,但以无款,竟致失之交臂。此叹之事甚多,实为最伤心之事,而职迄未能忘怀者也。本年四月,曾经申请钧部拨付拾亿元,旋于五、六月间,承拨下三亿五千万元,业已具领,但距实际需要相差尚远。兹闻增加教育经费,业经政院核准,爰奉上概算书一份,请赐量援,务恳将所需余款六亿五千万元提前拨付,以应急需。一俟病体稍愈,再行入京面谢。

〔《北京图书馆馆史资料汇编(1909-1949)》,页903〕

按:此为抄件。

七月十二日

先生致信郑振铎,就其赠送平馆《域外所藏中国古画集》第一辑表示感谢。

承惠赠《唐五代画》、《宋画》及《清画》第一辑,共五册,厚谊隆庆,至深感谢。其余各种自当遵嘱价购,兹于本日汇奉价款捌仟壹百陆拾万元(由上海办事处送上),附购书清单一份,即乞察收给据,以便归账。该书印就并盼就近送交宝庆十七号敝馆办事处。又《中国版画史图录》第六辑,似已预约五部钱存训经手,并希费神一查为荷。

弟袁同礼顿首

七月十二日

〔《北京图书馆馆史资料汇编(1909-1949)》,页898〕

按:此为抄件,结尾处有"《宋画》七月十五日取到"标记。

七月十八日

先生致信中国驻柏林军事代表团缪培基,告知汇寄美金用以将暂存柏林大使馆之书箱运沪。大意如下:

数月前曾上一函,奉恳台端托团中同事闵乃大代敝馆所购之书存于柏林大使馆者(约十箱左右)设法寄沪,谅荷台洽。敝馆同时致伦敦中国银行,以美金300元入贵团账内,作为预备付书箱之运费,想该行已径行函达在案。

〔《中国历代国家藏书机构及名家藏读叙传选》,页150〕

按:缪培基(?—2006),字植根,广东五华人,1930年北京大学毕业,后赴法国留学,在巴黎政治学校学习,归国后历任武汉大学、中山大学教授[1]，时代理中国驻柏林军事代表团团务。

七月

College and Research Libraries 刊登先生文章，题为 The Next Twenty-Five Years in the Development of Chinese Libraries。〔*College and Research Libraries*, Vol. 8, no. 3, 1947, pp. 376-379〕

按：先生文章大致分为综述、Functions of National Libraries、Provincial Libraries、Special Libraries、Salary Situation、Services should be integrated 六部分，该刊由美国图书馆协会下属大学和研究图书馆协会（Association of College & Research Libraries）编辑发行。此篇文章失收于《袁同礼文集》。

八月一日

下午一时，先生搭乘飞机由沪抵平。〔《东南日报》上海，1947 年 8 月 2 日，第 8 版〕

八月三日

上午十时，北平国剧学会假欧美同学会举行成立大会，王瑶卿、王凤卿、李辰冬、金仲仁、尚和玉、胡伯翰、侯喜瑞、郝寿臣、郝遇林、马衡、先生、陈纪滢、梁实秋、张伯谨、张伯驹、齐如山、谭小培等七十余人到场，通过会章并选举理、监事，其中齐如山、王向宸、梁实秋、陈纪滢、先生、胡伯翰、张伯驹、梅兰芳等十一人为理事，马衡、王季高等五人为监事。〔《华北日报》，1947 年 8 月 4 日，第 4 版〕

按：该会本于 1931 年成立，由梅兰芳、余叔岩、齐如山、张伯驹等创办，曾出版画报及戏剧丛刊，会址初设在虎坊桥，1935 年迁至绒线胡同。北平沦陷后，部分文物被日人掠去，会务停顿。本年春，张道藩、何思源、马衡、陈纪莹、王向宸、梁实秋、先生提议恢复国剧学会，由齐如山负责筹备，故宫博物院拨借霞公府南夹道六十八号为会址，用以陈列存留之文物。

八月八日

国剧学会举行理事、监事第一次联席会议，公推齐如山、陈纪滢、王向宸、梁实秋、先生为常务理事，齐如山为理事长，李辰冬为常务监事，又推何思源、张伯谨等十人为名誉理事，并决定近期内举行戏剧讲座，由张伯驹筹备。

---

① 《国立北京大学十八年度学生一览》，1930 年，页 13；《中国留法比瑞同学会同学录》，1943 年，页 198。

〔《华北日报》,1947年8月9日,第4版〕

八月十六日

下午,朱家骅赴故宫博物院,该院举行理事会,胡适、李书华、马衡、先生等出席。会后,马衡陪同朱家骅参观古物、文献、图书三馆。晚六时,马衡设茶点招待。〔《大公报》(天津),1947年8月17日,第2版〕

按:本日上午,朱家骅赴清华、燕京大学考察,两校教授、学生均呼吁改善生活。晚七时,国立北平研究院在中南海四所设宴款待朱家骅。

郝景盛致函先生,请将东北大学农学院补入美英捐赠书刊待分配院校名单之中。

同礼先生道席:

关于美国送给中国各大学书籍,东北大学农学院被遗漏,望便中关照,属人补入,不胜感激。因东大惨遭破坏甚于他校也。专此,敬祝大安。

弟郝景盛敬上

八月十六,1947

〔国立东北大学公用笺。南京大学图书馆特藏部〕

按:郝景盛(1903—1955),河北正定人,林学家、植物学家,毕业于北京大学生物系,后赴德留学,1939年归国,曾任中央大学、东北大学农学院教授。

八月十八日

刘树勋致函先生,请为东北大学留意分配美国捐赠书刊。

同礼馆长勋鉴:

九一八事变后,沈阳本校图书馆内图书悉遭摧毁,以致此次复员后本校特感图书缺乏,不敷师生参考之用,而尤以西文书为甚。闻美国赠送我国西文书籍甚多,由台端会同教育部组织委员会将该项书籍分配于各大学,务希参照东北沦陷后本校遭受特殊损失情况,多予拨给该项西文书籍,无任盼祷。耑此,敬颂勋绥。

国立东北大学代理校长刘树勋敬启

八月十八日

〔国立东北大学公用笺。南京大学图书馆特藏部〕

按:刘树勋(1902—1986),字景异,辽宁昌图人,土木工程学家,毕业于东北大学,后赴美留学,归国后曾任中央大学土木系教授。该函应为文书所撰,落款处钤刘树勋名章。

八月十九日

吴某覆函先生,告知国民政府就傅增湘捐书的褒扬令和奖金已发出。

守和我兄左右:

奉手书敬悉。傅案据查奖金四千万有余,已饬发,褒扬令已呈国府矣,请释注为幸。耑复,敬颂勋绥。

弟吴□顿首

八,十九

〔行政院秘书处用笺。国家图书馆档案,档案编号 1947-※039-采藏 11-003002〕

八月二十二日

先生致信斯文·赫定,请其寄送西北科学考查团完整报告,并略谈平馆现况。

August 22, 1947

Dear Dr. Hedin:

When I was in Europe last year, I tried to come to Sweden to call on you, but owing to various engagements I regret very much that I was not able to do so. Prof. Chen Yuan, who attended the Pen Club conference in Stockholm, told me that you had been enjoying extremely good health, which gave us a great deal of pleasure.

I believe I wrote to you, as well as to the Swedish Legation in China, re our desire to have *The Reports from the Scientific Expedition to the Northwest* which you have edited during the war. It seems that the main difficulty lies in the transportation of these volumes. Now that the mail service has returned to normal, I hope you could give instructions to have these volumes sent to us by registered book-post. We shall be very glad to pay for the postal charges.

I wish to congratulate you and your colleagues for bringing out these reports in such a short time, and I hope that these reports may be made available to Chinese scholars who are keenly interested in the results of your great expedition to the Northwest.

This Library has not had any damage during the war, and we are now continuing the systematic collection of scientific literature. We are hoping that more Swedish publications will be sent to China, especially those printed in English and French, so that closer intercourse will be promoted between scholars of our two countries.

With kindest regards to you and your colleagues,

Very sincerely yours,

T. L. Yuan

Director

〔国立北平图书馆英文信纸。韩琦教授提供〕

按:此件为打字稿,落款处为先生签名。

八月下旬

联合国文教组织中国委员会委员名单公布,共计 120 名人士入选,先生名列其中。〔《申报》,1947 年 8 月 28 日,第 6 版〕

按:该委员会定于 8 月 28 日在南京考试院明志楼召开成立大会。

八月三十一日

晚,金毓黻在墨蝶林设宴,马衡、郑天挺、唐兰、袁敦礼等人受邀与席,先生因病未赴。〔《静晤室日记》第 8 册,页 6396〕

按:墨蝶林为西餐馆,店址应在东单三条。

九月五日

先生致信法斯,告知美国汉学家雷兴等人对北平的访问情况,并请其考虑资助平馆筹建缩微胶卷实验室。

September 5, 1947

Dear Mr. Fahs:

Since you were here, we have made much progress in the acquisition of Slavic materials and in the compilation of the Union Catalogue of Russian Books in Peiping, including those kept at the Russian Orthodox Church. The fathers there are so conservative that they would not let outsiders know the contents of their library until after much negotiation.

We have translated a number of Sino-Russian diplomatic documents issued before the outbreak of the First World War as well as Muraviev's Letter and Correspondence in connection with the occupation of the Amur. These documents are of great interest to history as they throw much light on Sino-Russian diplomacy in the middle of the 19th century.

Over 900 Russian diplomatic documents have been located in Peiping. We shall undertake to have them translated as soon as further financial support is available.

The large amount of scholarly material available in Peiping has greatly impressed Lessing, Bingham and Swisher, who are now here for a visit. They feel keenly the need for a microfilm equipment, as there are many materials which they are anxious to reproduce. In this connection we hope that the Foundation will soon make a decision regarding the setting up of a Laboratory here.

With kindest regards,

Yours very Sincerely,

T. L. Yuan

Director

〔Rockefeller Foundation. Series 601: China; Subseries 601.R: China-Humanities and Arts. Vol. Box 47. Folder 391〕

按:Muraviev 即 Nikolai Muraviev(Никола́й Никола́евич Муравьёв-Аму́рский,1809-1881),通译为尼古拉·尼古拉耶维奇·穆拉维约夫·阿穆尔斯基,俄国将军,19 世纪 50 年代,任东部西伯利亚总督,窃踞黑龙江(Amur),1858 年 5 月他迫使黑龙江将军奕山签订了《瑷珲条约》。Bingham 即 Woodbridge Bingham(1901-1986),美国汉学家,通译作"宾板桥",专攻唐史,长期执教于加州大学伯克利分校。Swisher 即 Earl Swisher(1902-1975),美国记者、汉学家,长期执教于科罗拉多大学,曾担任恒慕义的助手。法斯接到该信后,分别函询了恒慕义、裘开明、Elizabeth Huff 等人对在北平设立缩微文献中心的意见。其中,恒慕义极力支持在平馆设立缩微文献中心,裘开明则认为北平的重要性和安全性都有问题,应该在上海——南京这一地区考虑筹设缩微文献中心。

九月九日

某记者来金鱼胡同宅,先生略谈平馆编纂中美、中英、中印外交史料之进展,并告知教育部虽拨改良费三亿五千万元,但仅敷修缮馆舍之用。〔《经世日报》,1947 年 9 月 10 日,第 4 版〕

九月十日

中午十二时,平津(唐)地区国立院校谈话会假北京大学孑民堂举行新学年第一次会议。胡适、叶企孙、李麟玉、叶正昌(艺专)、钟世铭(北洋大学)、牛文清(大辞典编纂处)、金涛(唐山工学院)、申新柏(铁院)、袁敦礼(北平师范学院)、先生、杨光弼(北平研究院秘书)出席。首由胡适报告赴京向有关部门接洽配发各院校实物以安定教职员生活之经过,并宣读教育部部长朱家骅九日来电,各院校教职员本月起每人每月可先发面粉两袋。经过短暂聚餐,继续讨论各案:教授底薪问题、向政府请拨冬季煤火问题、要求教部将唐山工学院划归平津地区、推定杨光弼为该会秘书、本学年例会轮值及召集办法。三时,散会。〔《大公报》(天津),1947 年 9 月 11 日,第 3 版〕

按:叶正昌(1909—2007),四川铜梁人,画家,时在北平艺术专科学院执教。钟世铭(1879—1965),字蕙生,天津人,北洋大学堂毕业后赴美留学,获哈佛大学博士学位,归国后曾任财政部次长,时任北洋大学校长。金涛、申新柏二人生平待考。下次谈话会拟于 10 月 8 日在师范学院举行。

下午四时许,季羡林至金鱼胡同宅访先生,不值。〔《此心安处是吾乡:季羡林归国日记(1946-1947)》,页 265〕

九月十二日

爨汝僖(上海)覆函先生,谈公私杂事。

守和馆长钧鉴:

昨奉八日手示并现币五万四千元,如数收到。斐云先生到沪后仅见面一次、电话两次,其住居秘密,无从走访。部发医药费仍无消息,曾函请斗南先生催部提早汇沪,所有用费只得暂时停支。郑印西域画集,来薰阁云出书后将卖特价,届时再行订购。闻各轮有征调运兵之说,日前交寄书包,忽得思南路邮局通知取回,何多源君北来能否预定舱位,容再办理。钱先生于昨日返沪,其本月份薪津已由平馆照扣,彼希望每月扣去整数，其零凑汇贵阳，留为缴家之用。另有函呈座右，当蒙批准。耑肃，敬请钧安。

职爨汝僖谨上

九月十二日

〔国立北平图书馆上海办事处信纸。国家图书馆档案，档案编号 1945-※057-综合 5-024003〕

按："钱先生"即钱存训，其夫人许文锦及女儿钱孝岑、钱孝峨、钱孝岳均在贵阳生活，由钱存训四弟钱存造照顾。

九月十五日

下午四时许，季羡林、师觉月赴平馆看书，与先生晤谈。〔《此心安处是吾乡：季羡林归国日记（1946-1947）》，页 267〕

下午四时，联合国教科文组织中国委员会在教育部会议室举行首次执委会，决议推朱家骅为主任委员，胡适、吴贻芳为副主任；推张道藩、瞿世英、程其保为秘书处组织规程草案起草委员；推定各专门委员会委员。其中，李济、先生、蒋复璁、陈桢、凌纯声被推举为图书馆及博物院委员会委员。〔《大公报》（上海），1947 年 9 月 17 日，第 5 版〕

按：另外五个专门委员会为自然科学、社会科学哲学及人文科学、教育、大众传播、艺术及文学等项。

九月十七日

十二时，先生在金鱼胡同寓所设宴款待英千里，后陪同至平馆视察。〔《民国日报》（天津），1947 年 9 月 18 日，第 4 版〕

按：本日，英千里作为教育部社会教育司司长考察北平各文教机构。

九月十九日

晚五时许，远东区基督教会议代表团成员赴平馆参观基本教育资料展览，事毕先生设茶会款待。〔《申报》，1947 年 9 月 20 日，第 7 版〕

按：18 日，远东区基督教会议代表团一行十六人乘飞机抵达北平。是日上午，代表团成员先参观国立北平师范学院及第一附属小学，后游历颐和园，下午先后参观清华大学、燕京大学，至平馆时已颇为疲惫。基本教育资料展览由平馆、北京大学、燕京大学、中国大辞典编纂处供给展品，涉及三个方面，分别为行政与组织、方法与技术、内容与材料。

九月中旬

北京大学公布图书馆学与博物馆学两种专科本年度课程，先生讲授“图书馆学概论”。〔《民国日报》(天津)，1947 年 9 月 21 日，第 4 版〕

按：图书馆学其他科目为“中国目录学”(王重民)、“西洋目录学”(毛子水)、“中国目录学实习”(王重民)，博物馆学课程则多由韩寿萱担任。

九月二十日

中午，胡适、马衡在故宫博物院设宴款待远东区基督教会议代表团成员，并邀袁敦礼、先生、徐悲鸿、陆志韦、李麟玉、王季高、英千里等人作陪，约二时许散，该代表团继续参观故宫博物院。〔《华北日报》，1947 年 9 月 21 日，第 5 版〕

按：上午九时至十二时，王世襄陪同该团参观中西两路，下午参观东路钟表、瓷器、铜器、图书等陈列室。

九月二十四日

朱家骅致电先生。

国立北平图书馆袁馆长守和兄(至密)：

美捐图书亟待处理，务请尽速南来主持。

弟朱家骅。申敬。□印

〔国家图书馆档案，档案编号 1946-※046-外事 5-006043〕

九月二十五日

晚，行政院院长张群在怀仁堂举行茶会，招待北平国立、私立各大、中、小学校长及各级人员百余人，胡适、梅贻琦、袁敦礼、先生、徐悲鸿、徐佩琨、王正廷、李麟玉、石志泉、杨光弼等人到场，何思源、张伯谨、王季高等人到场陪同。会上，胡适等人请求从速提高教员待遇，张群表示返京后即筹划解决。〔《民国日报》(天津)，1947 年 9 月 26 日，第 1 版〕

按：石志泉(1887—1960)，字友儒，湖北孝感人，清末赴日本东京帝国大学攻读法律，并加入同盟会，时应兼任北平朝阳学院院长。

先生覆信朱家骅，婉拒南下主持英美捐赠图书分配之请。

南京教育部朱部长钧鉴：

奉申敬至密电，敬悉壹是。查分配英美捐赠图书事，于七月间曾请翁主任委员另聘洪范五先生为秘书主持其事，并推荐李芳馥、黄维廉两君为常务干事，以便在沪就近处理。日前并函翁主任委员请其面劝洪君从速赴沪，勿再固辞。同礼新病初愈，仍待调养，兼以馆中经费困难，筹措旅费颇属不易，一时不克南下，至深惶悚，敬希亮察是幸。

职袁同礼

申有

〔国家图书馆档案，档案编号 1946-※046-外事 5-006044〕

按：此件为文书所拟之底稿，先生多有修改，并于本日以快邮发出。

先生覆信斯文·赫定，告知居延汉简在美保存情况，并谈平馆所藏西北科学考查团报告的卷期情况，希望其能够协助补齐。

September 25, 1947

Dear Dr. Hedin:

It is a great pleasure to receive your autographic letter of September 5, which shows your hand to be as strong as ever.

I hasten to assure you that Lattimore's report about the wooden MSS discovered by the late Dr. Bergman being safe in Washington, is quite true. When the situation in Hongkong became tense, the MSS were sent to Washington for safe-keeping by the Chinese Committee. They had been photographed, the blurred ones with the latest infra-red photography; but unfortunately, the photographs were lost by the Commercial Press during the Japanese occupation of Hongkong.

Since it will be cheaper to photograph them in the United States, arrangement is now being made to have the work done there before the MSS are returned to China. Dr. Fu Ssu-nien, who is in Washington, is negotiating about the matter. Your proposal to include the volume in the Swedish series of reports is being referred to him.

As to the magnificent reports you are publishing, our Order Department reports to have received only Vol. 8, Pt. 1, which is the first part of Dr. Lessing's monograph on the Lama Temple in Peiping. I hope you will arrange to have the other volumes sent to our library. I assure you many scientists are eager to have the opportunity of reading them.

With my best wishes to you and to Dr. Montell,

Yours sincerely,

T. L. Yuan

Director

〔国立北平图书馆英文信纸。韩琦教授提供〕

按:the magnificent reports 指*Reports from the scientific expedition to the north-western provinces of China under leadership of Dr. Sven Hedin*,实为报告的丛书名,各卷题名不尽相同且卷数并非以出版时间前后为序。Vol.8 似指*Ergebnisse der allgemeinen meteorologischen beobachtungen und der drachenaufstiege an den beiden standlagern bei Ikengüng und am Edsen-gol 1931-32*,1940 年斯德哥尔摩初版。Dr. Lessing's monograph 应指*Yung Ho Kung: an iconography of the Lamaist Cathedral in Peking*,*with notes on Lamaist mythology and cult*, 1942 年瑞典民族学博物馆出版。此件为打字稿,落款处为先生签名。

先生致信史蒂文斯,告知平馆苏俄研究中心进展——北平地区俄文文献联合目录即将完成。

September 25, 1947

Dear Dr. Stevens:

Since Dr. Fahs's visit we have made considerable progress in the development of our Slavic and Japanese Centers. We have greatly strengthened our collection of source materials and we have almost completed the compilation of our union catalogue of Russian books available in various depositories in Peiping.

The availability of the Russian books in our Slavic Centre has stimulated interest in the study of Russian language and literature. Four universities in Peiping have added Russian courses in their curricula. So, there is a large undergraduate enrollment for such courses beginning with the fall term. The demand on the Library for Russian materials and for particular facilities for advanced study have let us to adopt a program of increased buying in the Soviet Union and elsewhere.

When Dr. Fahs was here in May, a memorandum was submitted to him regarding the needs of the Library. I understood from him that the Executive Committee of your Foundation shall meet in the fall when our application for support will be considered. Knowing that you are interested in the promotion of Slavic studies, I trust you will find it possible to support our application and I look forward to hearing from you before long.

With kindest regards,

Yours sincerely,

T. L. Yuan

Director

〔国立北平图书馆英文信纸。Rockefeller Foundation. Series 601: China; Subseries 601.R: China-Humanities and Arts. Vol. Box 47. Folder 391〕

按:此件为打字稿,落款处为先生签名。

先生致信美国图书馆协会援助战区图书馆委员会,告知英美赠书分配委员会已将美方捐赠的图书、期刊发放给中国各图书馆,尤其是私立高校,并表示感谢。

September 25, 1947

Committee on Aid to Libraries in War Areas

American Library Association

Library of Congress Annex, Study 251

Washington, D. C.

U. S. A.

Dear Sirs:

The Chinese Committee on Distribution of Books has completed the distribution among Chinese libraries of the four sets of outstanding American Books published during the war years, which were made available to China by your Committee. The publications were well selected and are meeting the urgent needs of Chinese scholars. They form an exceedingly important contribution toward the replenishment of Chinese libraries.

Among your gifts the most valuable ones are the sets of scholarly, scientific and technical journals published during the war years. They have been distributed among Chinese libraries, especially to those of the private universities as they do not receive the journals purchased by the Ministry of Education, with priority given to those which need the war issues to fill the gaps of their files. These journals are eagerly sought by Chinese scholars and scientists, and their availability greatly facilitates scientific research in China.

I am enclosing herewith the principles governing the distribution of the journals among Chinese libraries as well as lists of these journals indicating to which libraries in China they are being allocated.

Permit me, therefore, to take this opportunity to convey to you our most cordial thanks for your splendid gift. The presence of these books and journals will serve as a token of American friendship toward Chinese scholars.

T. L. Yuan

Secretary

Chinese Committee on the Distribution of Books

〔国立北平图书馆英文信纸。The American Library Association Archives, China Projects File, Box 2, Periodicals for Chinese Universities, Correspondence and Lists, 1944-1947〕

按:此件为打字稿,落款处为先生签名。附1页分配书刊原则,共计8条;美国图书馆协会捐赠各期刊初次分配院校清单(1st Distribution of A. L. A. Journals),共计24页;北平地区各院校分配清单(List of A. L. A. Journals Allocated to the Peiping Area),共计11页。

十月一日

先生致信傅忠谟,告知教育部已将褒奖傅增湘捐书奖金汇平,特派人送上并请撰写收据。

晋生先生惠鉴：

近两月来以病相缠，未得趋教。近维侍祺康吉为祝。顷奉教育部令，拨给尊翁捐书奖金肆仟万元款已汇到，兹派人送上，即请察收，并请掣给收据，以便报部是幸。附钞原令，并希台阅。专此，顺候时祺。

弟袁〇〇

卅六，十，一

附国币肆仟万元钞令一件。

〔国家图书馆档案，档案编号 1947-※039-采藏 11-003001〕

按：傅忠谟（1905—1974），字晋生，同济大学毕业，后随父亲傅增湘学习版本目录学。此件为文书所拟之底稿，先生略加增删。

十月六日

法斯致函先生，告知洛克菲勒基金会不便资助平馆建立苏俄、日本研究中心，缩微胶片实验室则仍待决定。

October 6, 1947

Dear Dr. Yuan:

A reply has long been due you to the various requests which you have made to us both in writing and orally during my visit in Peiping. It has required some time to digest and organize the impressions and information which I obtained in the Far East so that your requests could be considered in their full context.

Under conditions now prevailing in the Far East, we have been forced to conclude that it is not practicable for us to obtain assistance for your centers of Russian or Japanese studies, although you are certainly to be congratulated on the energy which you have shown in preserving for scholarly use the Japanese books left in Peiping and your foresight in trying to provide the necessary foundation in library resources for more widespread study of Russia. Your work should be of great assistance when these subjects come to have a more important share in university education in the Peiping area.

It is still not clear whether your request for assistance in the purchase of a microfilm camera will have to receive the same negative response.

One of the questions which still concerns me is the possibility of your obtaining the necessary film and supplies to make the camera effective if it were installed. When I was in Peiping even the hospitals were unable to obtain urgently needed X-Ray film because of government bans on the importation of photographic supplies. What assurance is there that similar difficulties would not make inoperative any equipment which we helped you to obtain?

I am glad that Lessing, Bingham, and Swisher had good visits at your Library and I shall look forward to hearing their opinions when they return.

Sincerely yours,

Charles B. Fahs

〔Rockefeller Foundation. Series 601: China; Subseries 601.R: China-Humanities and Arts. Vol. Box 47. Folder 391〕

十月[①]上旬

联合国国际博物馆协会中国委员会在北平成立，李济为主席，韩寿萱任秘书，马衡、先生、杨钟健、冯汉骥、郑德坤、曾昭燏、胡肇椿等任委员。〔《马衡年谱长编》，页 980〕

按：10 月 13 日，马衡签发联合国国际博物馆协会中国委员会致教育部代电，将此名单呈请鉴核备案。后，李济辞职，改推杭立武为主席。

十月十四日

下午三时，故宫博物院召开复员后第三次院务会议，马衡、张庭济、先生、赵儒珍、常惠、龚理华、关植耘、黄鹏霄、王孝缙、王世襄、李益华、张德泽、刘鸿逵等出席，马衡为主席，杭承艮记录。报告本院修正组织条例业经立法院通过、接收古物陈列所经过案、接收各项文物案、存素堂丝绣、溥仪留津物品、收购散佚书籍书画案、存渝文物还都经过案、各馆处工作报告等。此外，又讨论议案数项。临时动议中，图书馆提议本院太庙图书馆名称应予

① 《马衡年谱长编》原文有"尚于本年二月间在北平成立中国委员会"之表述，此处似有误，因所有关于该委员会成立的报道，如《科学》（第 29 卷第 12 期）、《外交部周报》（第 44 期）、《申报》、《和平日报》等均记为 10 月间。

改正为“国立北平故宫博物院图书馆太庙分馆”,决议通过。〔《马衡年谱长编》,页 981-983〕

按:太庙一处原名为“国立北平故宫博物院太庙图书分馆”。

傍晚,先生访徐旭生,谈太庙图书馆暂存日伪书籍分配事宜。〔《徐旭生文集》第 10 册,页 1487-1488〕

按:翌日下午,徐旭生偕冯家昇、苏秉琦赴太庙图书馆查看已整理之书籍。

十月十五日

下午,平馆举行英国各出版社之书籍展览会开幕仪式,英议会访华团长亚蒙致辞,先生略作答辞。〔《时事新报》,1947 年 10 月 16 日,第 2 版〕

按:亚蒙即 Charles Ammon(1st Baron Ammon,1873-1960),英国政治家,工党人士。本日上午,该团先赴燕京大学、清华大学参观,中午,北平市政府在颐和园设宴款待。

十月十六日

先生致信史蒂文斯,告知平馆已从美国购买缩微胶片机的部分设备,希望洛克菲勒基金会给予资助《图书季刊》英文本的出版及购买 MicroFile Recordak Model C-2。

16 October, 1947

Dear Dr. Stevens:

With reference to our conversation regarding the need for reproduction of scholarly materials, I am glad to inform you that a 24-inch camera and platemaking equipment which we purchased from American Type Founder, Elizabeth, N. Y., has arrived at Tientsin. The camera and its attached equipment, costing US $ 5,000, were given to us by the Chinese Government. All the films and photographic supplies imported from the United States are tax-free, as we can obtain the import license from the Government without any difficulty.

Since I returned from Europe last November, we have received 300 cases of western books. All of them arrived safely without any damage. Among other things, we are building up a special collection of English poetry, consisting of finely printed editions which I purchased in London and Manchester last summer. We have just had an exhibition of British printing and I now enclose a newspaper clipping which may be of some interest to you.

We are still waiting for your action in regard to a subsidy for continuing the publication of the *Quarterly Bulletin of Chinese Bibliography* and in regard to the equipment for a photo-duplication laboratory in Peiping. With the equipment which we have already purchased from our own funds, we now only need the MicroFile Recordak, Model C-2, which is on sale at the Recordak Corporation, 350 Madison Avenue, costing about US $ 2,950. If you could assist us in obtaining a grant for this camera, we shall be able to set up the laboratory immediately.

I may add that we have purchased the Depue Microfilm Printer, the Recordak Enlarger, Model A1, the Omega D11 Enlarger, the Pako Economy Dryer, with their attached equipment and photographic supplies. We have also purchased four Spencer microfilm readers which are on their way to Peiping from Shanghai. Together with the cost of transportation, they cost us US $ 3,000.

I have just had a letter from Mr. Charles B. Shaw, Librarian at Swarthmore, who is coming to Peiping next week. I am sure he will report to you about our work here.

With kindest regards to you and Messrs. Marshall and Fahs,

Yours Sincerely

T. L. Yuan

Director

〔国立北平图书馆英文信纸。Rockefeller Foundation. Series 601: China; Subseries 601.R: China-Humanities and Arts. Vol. Box 47. Folder 393〕

按:Charles B. Shaw(1894-1962),通译作“沙本生”,1927 年起担任美国斯沃斯莫尔学院(Swarthmore College)图书馆馆长,本年 10 月 24 日抵达北平访问。此件为打字稿,落款处为先生签名,似于 11 月 7 日送达。

十月二十日

先生致信法斯，告知国民政府已拨款购置了照相复制实验室的部分设备，并许诺给予耗材的免税进口许可，希望洛克菲勒基金会能够给予资助，加快该实验室的筹建并为美国国会图书馆等机构复制斯拉夫语馆藏。

October 20th, 1947

Dear Dr. Fahs:

I have pleasure in acknowledging the receipt of your letter of October 6th.

Regarding our centres of Russian and Japanese studies, we are going ahead with our plans, as we have meanwhile received support from the Chinese Government. In our Slavic collection there are a considerable number of titles not represented in the Library of Congress. Requests for microfilm copies of our Slavic material have been received, but we cannot comply with these requests until our photoduplication laboratory is set up.

With regard to the importation of films and photographic supplies for the use of the Library, I can assure you that they will be given tax-free treatment by the Chinese Government and there is no difficulty at all for us to obtain the import license.

Regarding the equipment for a photoduplication laboratory, I may inform you that the Chinese Government has given us $8,000 for the purchase of a 24-inch camera, the Depue Microfilm Printer and other equipment, all of which have been received at Peiping. They represent half of the necessary equipment for the above-mentioned laboratory.

When I was in New York last year, I assured Dr. Stevens that the Chinese Government would assist us in the purchase of some of the more expensive equipment for microphotography, if the Foundation would make a similar grant on a 50-50 basis. Now, with the arrival of the more expensive equipment which were promptly paid by the Chinese Government, we naturally look to your Foundation for some definite action.

Here in Peiping, we have the resources, the academic atmosphere and all the facilities for research. It is only our wish that some of our unique material could be made available to scholars outside of Peiping through microphotography. For this project, we hope the Foundation will lend us its support.

Yours sincerely

T. L. Yuan

Director

〔国立北平图书馆英文信纸。Rockefeller Foundation. Series 601: China; Subseries 601.R: China-Humanities and Arts. Vol. Box 47. Folder 393〕

按:此件为打字稿,落款处为先生签名,应于 11 月 7 日送达。

十月二十四日

下午一时半,美国图书馆专家沙本生由美使馆文化处职员胡绍声陪同乘飞机由沪抵达北平,先生和燕京大学代理校务长窦威廉(William H. Adolph)等人前往机场迎接。〔《华北日报》,1947 年 10 月 25 日,第 5 版〕

按:沙本生来华目的,即考察各大学复员后图书馆设备及美国捐赠图书分配的情形,[①]尤其是教会大学图书馆事业现状。抵平前,沙本生曾发电报与先生。

十月三十日

下午三时许,沙本生赴平馆参观,先生负责陪同并至北海游览,并前往静心斋馆舍视察。〔《华北日报》,1947 年 10 月 31 日,第 5 版〕

十一月初

故宫博物院将影印《唐写本王仁煦刊谬补缺切韵》(明宋濂跋本),先生嘱唐兰写一跋语,附之于后。〔《续修四库全书》经部·小学类第 250 册,页 203〕

按:是年《唐写本王仁煦刊谬补缺切韵》见于书贾,于省吾偕唐兰前往查看,后经马衡主持,由故宫博物院购藏,旋即付印。

十一月二日

下午四时,中华图书馆协会假中国政治学会会所(南池子)举行茶会,欢迎

① 《华北日报》,1947 年 10 月 23 日,第 5 版。

美国图书馆学专家沙本生，六十余人到场，先生为会议主席，先介绍沙本生履历，继由其作演讲，内容涉及联合目录、报纸文献宜用缩微胶片补齐、编目排字法。〔《华北日报》，1947 年 11 月 3 日，第 5 版〕

十一月三日

先生致信朱家骅，就平馆扩充改良费、翌年经常费、购书费提出申请。

骝先部长钧鉴：

此次政院核定社教机关扩充改良费，职曾电请钧座从优分配，谅蒙钧察。诚以职馆年来经费较少，一切设施辄以无款而陷于停顿，以致建设毫无，深资惭疚。此次追加之扩充改良费为数尚丰，拟恳准照职馆所请二十亿零伍千万元之数，特予从优尽数分配，如有余裕并恳酌予增加，俾得少资补救，至为感幸。再三十七年度经常费预算，钧部亦正在核定之中，职馆前送之概算书经常费列四亿六千余万元，已属最低之数，倘今后物价再增，势将仍感不敷应用，敬恳比照中央图书馆之经常费予以同等之分配，俾不致再有匮乏之虞，无任盼祷。又购书费一项，以前各年度未蒙正式列入预算，遇有购书良机，每多失之交臂，此项损失至为重大。前谒张院长、王副院长谈及职馆购书专款，均认为必要允予赞助，但须由钧部先行提出，政院方能核准。务恳于三十七年度预算内将职馆购书费准予一并列入，盼甚感甚。专肃，敬候勋祺。

职袁同礼谨启

十一月三日

〔国立北平图书馆用笺。台北"中央研究院"近代史研究所档案馆，〈朱家骅〉，馆藏号 301-01-09-054，页 64-66〕

按："张院长、王副院长"分指张群、王云五。此次，教育部追加扩充改良费，社会教育机关共计一百亿元，由十八家机构分配，平馆最终仅得六亿元。① 此信应为文书代笔，落款处钤印。

十一月四日

先生致信 Laurence J. Kipp，寄上美国图书中心发送中国书籍的阶段性分配报告、照片，并再次感谢该中心对中国图书馆事业所作出的贡献，希望可以开展新的项目并为中国提供新书和现刊。

---

① 台北"中央研究院"近代史研究所档案馆，〈朱家骅〉，馆藏号 301-01-09-054，页 78。

4 November, 1947

Dear Mr. Kipp:

In reply to your letter of October 3, I take pleasure in sending you an interim report on the distribution of books sent to China by the American Book Centre. Three photographs showing the receipt of an ABC shipment and showing how the books are being used by the public are also enclosed.

The ABC program has materially assisted the rehabilitation of Chinese libraries that no adequate words could be found to express our heartfelt thanks. I am sure that many Chinese librarians would like to join me in conveying to you their sincerest appreciation for your valuable assistance.

We are most happy to learn that a new program is being planned by your Centre and we certainly hope that you will receive the support which such a new program deserves. We hope that it would be possible to include new books and current journals which are especially needed by Chinese institutions.

For your information, I may state that the China Office of the British Council has been subscribing to four sets of about 250 British Scientific and learned journals for distribution to various libraries in China. This arrangement has proved very successful and I hope that something can be done towards the supply of current American journals under the auspices of your Centre.

Thanking you for your interest and assuring you of our ready cooperation at all times,

Yours sincerely,

T. L. Yuan

Director

〔The American Library Association Archives, China Projects File, Box 2, Books for China, 1947〕

按:ABC 即 American Book Centre,该信附四页报告书。

十一月五日

下午四时,西北科学考查团开会,梅贻琦、袁复礼、先生、徐旭生、黄文弼等人出席,商讨改组事宜。〔《徐旭生文集》第10册,页1491〕

按:此次改组应由胡适发起,选出新理事四十人,胡适、马衡、徐佩琨、徐旭生、袁复礼、梅贻琦、先生、傅斯年、杭立武等人当选,其中前五人为常务理事,此外欲向教育部申请预算、重新开展工作。①

先生致信布朗,寄上援助战区图书馆的美国期刊分发的阶段性报告,并告知自己已经从该委员会中辞职,洪有丰接任该会秘书。

5 November, 1947

Dear Mr. Brown:

In addition to the report which we sent in September to the Committee on aid to libraries in war areas, we are sending you herewith an interim report on the distribution of American publications in China, together with a copy of my letter to Mr. L. J. Kipp. Please circulate the report among those of your colleagues who are interested in our work of distribution.

Owing to my other duties, I have resigned as Secretary of the Distribution Committee. Mr. Y. F. Hung, Librarian of the National Central University, is now taking my place as Secretary of the Committee.

Mr. Charles B. Shaw is now touring the country; but his chief interest lies in the development of the 13 Christian Colleges. You will hear from him before very long.

With kindest regards,

Yours sincerely

T. L. Yuan

〔国立北平图书馆英文信纸。The American Library Association Archives, China Projects File, Box 2, Books for China, Correspondence, 1947〕

按:此件为打字稿,落款处为先生签名,于12月5日送达。

---

①《申报》,1947年11月9日,第2版。

十一月六日

先生致信朱家骅，再次申请批准平馆扩建费、来年经常费及购书费之预算。

骝先部长钧鉴：

敬陈者，此次政院核准之追加扩建费，各方来京申请者当不在少数，此中分配之困难当为各方所共谅。职馆经费年来未能大量增加，以致目前经费之拮据较北平任何机关为尤甚。数月以来，虽竭力紧缩、勉力支撑，但一切建设事业莫不陷于停顿。近有东北运来之宋本《说文解字》，为海内孤本，索价四千万元，以无力购买为奸商购去，焦灼之情不堪言状。至盼钧座对于职馆此次应领之扩改费特准从优分配，至少应与中央馆相等，此不得不请特予援助者一也。又明年度经常费，闻职馆经费已定为三亿五千元，而中央馆则定为四亿五千元，但职馆组织设有八组且分散于七处，虽无国际交换处之名义，但实际上与各国交换书报之数量实超出中央馆之上，拟恳钧座将明年度经常费增至四亿五千万元，俾各项事业不致中辍，此不得不请特予援助者又一也。迫切陈词，幸乞垂察。本拟来京面陈，以川资无着，特再函恳。敬候道祺。

职袁同礼敬上

十一月六日

北平图书馆三十六年度所领之经费

一月　扩充改良费　壹亿元

七月　扩充改良费　贰亿元

大楼修理费　壹亿五千万元

迄今尚欠□工人壹亿元，曾请钧部担任向四联总处借款，尚未奉到批示。

〔国立北平图书馆用笺。台北“中央研究院”近代史研究所档案馆，〈朱家骅〉，馆藏号 301-01-09-054，页 67-69〕

按：信中“闻职馆经费已定为三亿五千元，而中央馆则定为四亿五千元”应作“闻职馆经费已定为三亿五千万元，而中央馆则定为四亿五千万元”。此信为先生亲笔。

十一月七日

苏联在平使领馆举办国庆宴会，中方人士吴奇伟、张伯谨副市长、沈履、先

生、马大猷、饶毓泰、雷海宗、张申府等人受邀与席。〔《华北日报》,1947 年 11 月 8 日,第 4 版〕

按:吴奇伟(1891—1953),字晴云,号梧生,广东大埔人,国民革命军陆军中将。

法斯覆函先生,告知洛克菲勒基金会正在考虑给予资助平馆购买 Recordak Model C-2,但需要等到明年,另外暂时不会考虑资助《图书季刊》英文本的编辑出版。

November 7, 1947

Dear Dr. Yuan:

In view of your letter of October 20 and your assurance that you can obtain without difficulty the necessary materials for operation of your laboratory, we are now prepared to recommend a grant in aid to the National Library of Peiping of $3,500 for purchase of the Recordak, Model C-2, Camera which you need to complete your laboratory equipment. However, as our appropriation for this type of grant for the current year is exhausted, it will not be possible to obtain a decision with regard to this recommendation until after January 1, 1948. We shall let you know the result as soon as possible thereafter.

In your letter of October 16 to Mr. Stevens, you raise the question of a subsidy for continuing the publication of the *Quarterly Bulletin of Chinese Bibliography*. I believe that it is not practicable for us to obtain such a subsidy for you at this time. The aid given some years ago was an exception to the general rule that we are unable to obtain subsidies for publications-an exception which we are not able to repeat. I hope that the opportunity which you have had to demonstrate the value of the *Quarterly Bulletin* and to develop both subscriptions and exchanges for it will enable you to continue its publication without subsidy from us.

Sincerely yours,

Charles B. Fahs

〔Rockefeller Foundation. Series 601: China; Subseries 601.R: China-Humanities and Arts. Vol. Box 47. Folder 393〕

按:该函以航空信方式寄送,此件为录副。

十一月上中旬

先生因平馆经费支绌、工作无法继续,向教育部提交辞呈。〔《申报》,1947年11月12日,第7版〕

十一月十一日

先生致信田培林,询问教育部就平津区图书处理委员会中日文图书分配草案之意见。

伯苍次长钧鉴:

敬陈者,查平津区图书处理委员会拟将清理就绪之中日文图书先行分配一事,曾于本年十月十七日拟定分配办法草案,征询尊见,尚未奉到复示。兹以各大学需要较殷,屡来催促,又以天气渐寒,工作不便,似宜及早分配,如此房屋亦可腾出,更便整理。特肃芜缄,即希赐覆为荷。耑此,敬候勋祺。

袁同礼拜启

十一月十一日

〔中国第二历史档案馆,教育部档案·全卷宗五,国立北平图书馆京沪区及昆明办事处工作报告暨庶务方面的文书,案卷号11609〕

按:田培林(1893—1975),字伯苍,河南襄城人,1946年10月到教育部任常务次长。分配办法应为"日伪图书之中文书百分之四十给清华大学,百分之二十给北平研究院"。该信为文书代笔,落款处为先生签名。

平馆向教育部呈文一件,题为《请准转咨外交部将前发给本馆编纂钱存训赴美之官员护照再予延长一年》,具先生名并钤平馆印。

案查三十五年十二月本馆呈派编纂钱存训赴美协助运回善本书籍,并赴英美考察图书馆事业,请转咨外交部发给官员护照一案。奉三十六年二月初一日高字第〇五四四一号训令略开:经函准行政院秘书处转陈核准仰径向外交部洽领护照等因在案。惟该员因事于上月初旬始行抵美,前奉外交部发给之护照仅限一年,至来年二三月间即已期满。该员在美应办事宜尚未完毕,拟请代予转咨外交部,将该员钱存训所领之官员护照再予延长一年,俾资便利,理合具文呈请,伏乞鉴核,令准施行,实为公便。谨呈

教育部

国立北平图书馆馆长袁同礼(北平圕印)

三十六年十一月十一日

〔中国第二历史档案馆,教育部档案·全卷宗5,国立北平图书馆请拨员工学术研究补助费经常费有关文书,案卷号11616〕

十一月十二日

晨七时,美国图书馆专家沙本生乘坐飞机离平赴武汉考察,先生及毛准等赴机场送行。〔《华北日报》,1947年11月13日,第5版〕

下午一时,平津国立院校谈话会假北平研究院会议室举行,郑天挺、黄钰生(南开)、钟世铭(北洋)、殷祖英(师院)、徐佩琨(铁院)、牛文清(大辞典编纂处)、金涛(唐山工学院)、杨光弼(北平研究院)等十余人参加,钟世铭为会议主席,杨光弼记录。首由郑天挺报告向中央信托局及北平行辕商洽各院校教职员冬煤之经过,并转述胡适已接教育部朱家骅来电告知冬煤款项即将汇平。继由殷祖英、黄钰生报告教育部配售各院校学生、职工面粉情况。议决事项分别为,各院校联署电请教育部速拨公用煤款,由郑天挺起草,各院校亦分别电催;行辕核准用煤标准及时间跨度,增聘、转聘教职员分配方法;下次联席会议拟于十二月十日由清华大学主持。四时,会议结束。〔《华北日报》,1947年11月13日,第5版〕

十一月十三日

朱家骅覆函先生,表示平馆追加的扩充改良费不会比央图少,但后者的复员费、经常费因故确实较多。

守和先生大鉴:

接奉本月三日及六日先后手书,忻聆种切。北平图书馆经费困难,弟所深知且极关切,此次分配追加之扩充改良费时,自当特为留意,决不比中央图书馆为少,况平馆规模宏大、成绩卓著,向为弟所重视,年来特拨之款转多,亦为兄所深知,幸纾绮注。去年本部核拨复员费时,中央图书馆由渝回京,一切运输费用与职员川资费,确甚需要,且京馆原有之一切设备大都遗落,迄今尚馆舍未建,更无一安全适当之书库,其所需复员、修建等费,非同其他机关诸尚完好者可比,除第一次复员费之外,亦恐不比尊处为多。至各机关每年度经常费,部中编造核算时,须照预算按照战前旧有预算为标准,此实不合理,亦为本部年来所力争不成者。中央图书馆之正式成立系在战时,一因当时法币贬值,故底数或稍较大,亦不可知。又因一向负部委托兼办国际出版品之交换业务,所费不少,此事列有一数,亦有可能也。因复并及,顺颂台祺。

弟朱家骅拜启

三十六年十一月十三日

〔教育部部长室用笺。国家图书馆档案,档案编号 1945-※057-综合 5-005007 和 1945-※057-综合 5-005008〕

按:此件为打字稿,落款处为朱家骅签名。

十一月十五日

先生致信史密斯森协会,询问平馆尚未收到此前国会图书馆寄送目录卡片的装运日期和邮轮名称,并希望今后可以将每批交换品的信息在运华前告知。

15 November, 1947

Dear Sirs:

The American Library Association informed us in June that the Library of Congress Catalog of Printed Cards consisting of 167 volumes was sent to us through the kindness of your Service. Since we have not received it for so long, we shall be grateful to you if you would inform us of the date of shipment and the name of the steamer on which this Catalog was shipped.

Before the War, we used to receive notices from you in regard to every shipment. This arrangement keeps us informed in advance of your shipments. We hope that in future you will follow the same procedure, so that we shall be notified of every shipment from your Service.

This Library was added to the Depository Library of U. S. Government publications. We hope it will be possible for you to send us the notice of shipment for the cases of these documents.

A number of correspondents in America have been sending us their publications through your Service. If you could include all the packages for this Library in one box, it would save a lot of distribution work by the Chinese Bureau of International Exchanges.

With many thanks for your assistance,

Yours sincerely

T. L. Yuan

Director

〔国立北平图书馆英文信纸。Smithsonian Institution Archives, Records, 1868-1988 (Record Unit 509), Box 1, National Library, Peiping〕

按:此件为打字稿,先生对信文有修改,落款处为其签名,于11月25日送达。

十一月十七日

Frederick Cromwell 覆函先生,告知由洛克菲勒基金会资助购买的援助战区图书馆的一九四六年出版书刊已寄送上海英美捐赠图书期刊分配委员会。

November 17, 1947

Dear Dr. Yuan:

It is our happy privilege to tell you that it is again possible, under our Rockefeller Foundation grant, to send to China a selection of books, this time, titles published in the year 1946. They are being sent directly from the publishers addressed as follows:

Chinese Committee on the Distribution of Books
c/o Academia Sinica
37b Brenan Road
Shanghai, China
GIFT OF AMERICAN LIBRARY ASSOCIATION

Perhaps some of them have already been received. We enclose for your information a list of the titles in this third supplementary shipment.

Allow us to express our gratitude to the Chinese Committee on the Distribution of Books for its courtesy and cooperation in distributing these books, also, to the libraries in China where they will be most useful.

Yours sincerely,

Frederick Cromwell

Director

〔The American Library Association Archives, China Projects File, Box 2, Books for China, 1944-47, Folder 1〕

按:Frederick Cromwell,1947 年 4 月 1 日出任美国图书馆协会国际关系委员会主任。[①] 该函寄送北平,此为抄件,附件书单不存。

十一月十八日

先生致信王云五、陈克文、浦薛凤,请行政院就平馆经常费、购书费格外关注。

云五院长钧鉴、克文、逷生吾兄惠鉴:

前奉瑞电,诸承指示,至以为感。敬陈者,敝馆现有预算,原系按照渝昆分馆暨北平总馆复员后,临时维持费综合核定,为数无多。比年以来,为经费所限,一切设施无法进展,虽经费屡有增加,皆系比例调整,而物价狂涨,依然不敷分配,捉襟见肘,困难滋深。报载三十七年度预算系由贵院主编,拟恳对于敝馆格外垂注,将经常部分锡予增加。此外并恳加入购书专款,俾采购事业不致中断。敝馆在事变前由中华教育文化基会每年拨给中文购书费国币拾万元、西文购书费美金三万元。抗战以来,庚款停付,此项购书费亦即停止,今后购藏新旧图籍不得不仰赖拨给专款,事关文化,谅荷赞助,务希于审核下年预算时,赐予注意。专此奉恳,顺候勋祺,伏维垂察,不具。

弟袁〇〇

卅六,十一,十八

〔国家图书馆档案,档案编号 1945-※057-综合 5-022002 和 1945-※057-综合 5-022003〕

按:浦薛凤(1900—1997),字逷生,江苏常熟人,清华学校毕业后赴美留学,获哈佛大学硕士学位,归国后在东陆大学、浙江大学、清华大学等处执教,后又赴德国留学,抗战期间转入政界,时任行政院副秘书长。此件为底稿。

先生致信法斯,向洛克菲勒基金会申请补助用以购买便携式照相机,并请该基金会资助平馆缩微实验室周转所需耗材的预付款。

---

① Ludington, Flora B., and Frederick Cromwell. "A. L. A. International Activities." *ALA Bulletin*, vol. 41, no. 11, 1947, pp. 353-359.

18 November, 1947

Dear Dr. Fahs:

I acknowledge with many thanks the receipt of your letter of November 7 informing me that you are now prepared to recommend a grant of $ 3,500 to the National Library for the purchase of a Recordak camera for our photoduplication laboratory. As soon as your recommendation is approved, I hope your purchasing department could place the order for us.

Since writing to you last, we have sent the head of our Rare Book Department to Ningpo, Chekiang, to make preliminary arrangements to microfilm the basic historical materials still preserved at that city and its neighborhood. He reported that in the famous Fan family library at Ningpo known as Tien I Ko, there are many rare and unique books and manuscripts of the Ming Dynasty which are not found elsewhere in China.

In addition to the rare items in the Tien I Ko library, there are also important private collections in out-of-the-way places whose owners are unwilling to lend their books and manuscripts, though they could not object to microfilming them at their home. Since there is no electricity in Ningpo and its neighborhood, it will be desirable to have a portable camera which is necessary to enable us to microfilm materials that cannot be sent to Peiping. I shall be exceedingly grateful to you if you could include it in the equipment which the Foundation is prepared to purchase for us out of your grant.

For our photoduplication laboratory a revolving fund is desired to enable us to advance the cost of photographic materials and films, the operating cost of the laboratory will be met out of our own budget for running expenses of the library, but the cost of photographic materials and films cannot be so met, particularly in view of Chinese exchange regulations, for while the Government allots us foreign exchange now and then, it cannot be used to buy materials that are not for our own use. This revolving fund will not be expendable, but only used to pay in advance the cost of materials that will ultimately be paid for by other libraries. In view of the time and the routine involved in importing supplies from abroad, it would be desirable for us to place a large initial order. According to our rough estimate, $3,800 to $4,500 would be necessary depending upon prices and how many American and European libraries would need our films.

A member of our staff is now in Japan making preliminary survey of Chinese historical materials which we would like to microfilm. A portable camera will be especially needed in Japan.

It is therefore our sincere hope that you and Dr. Stevens will see your way to recommending to your Trustees an additional grant for a portable camera and a revolving fund.

Assuring you once more of our sincere appreciation for your interest and assistance, I am

Sincerely yours

T. L. Yuan

Director

〔国立北平图书馆英文信纸。Rockefeller Foundation. Series 601: China; Subseries 601.R: China-Humanities and Arts. Vol. Box 47. Folder 393〕

按:the head of our Rare Book Department 即赵万里,Tien I Ko 即天一阁。此件为打字稿,落款处为先生签名。

十一月十九日

上午,先生给徐旭生打电话,告知本日下午四时图书处理委员会在北京大学孑民堂开会,此前将日伪图书之中文书百分之四十给清华大学,百分之二十给北平研究院(历史研究所)之建议,教育部覆文不赞同。〔《徐旭生文集》第10册,页1494〕

十一月二十日

下午二时,沈兼士的家人在地安门外嘉兴寺[1]举行家祭,胡适、梅贻琦、先

[1] 《徐旭生文集》(第10册,页1495)记作"嘉应寺",有误。

生、袁敦礼、郑天挺、徐旭生等人前往吊唁。〔《民国日报》(天津),1947年11月21日,第4版〕

　　　　按:9月16日,沈兼士去世;11月21日,移榇西郊福田公墓安葬。

十一月二十一日

田培林覆函先生,告日伪图书应以教育部部定办法分配。

　　守和馆长吾兄大鉴:

　　　　接诵十一月十一日惠书,藉谂种切。关于平津区图书处理委员会拟将清理就绪之图书先行分配,以便腾出房屋,更便整理一事,自属切要。业已由部电知处理会依照部定办法办理矣。知关廑注,特以奉闻。专此奉复,并颂勋祺。

　　　　　　　　　　　　　　　　　　　　弟田○○敬启
　　　　　　　　　　　　　　　　　　　　　十一月　　日

　　　　　　　〔中国第二历史档案馆,教育部档案·全卷宗五,国立北平图书
　　　　　　　馆京沪区及昆明办事处工作报告暨庶务方面的文书,案卷号
　　　　　　　11609〕

　　　　按:此件为底稿,该函于21日发出。

十一月二十二日

先生致信朱家骅,请教育部在所拨扩充改良费中考虑增加款项,以便平馆兴建书库。

　　骝先部长钧鉴:

　　　　接奉十一月十三日钧札,敬悉种切。敝馆需款情形,仰蒙垂注,感不去心,自当敬谨遵承。惟敝馆自复员后,增加及接收之书籍为数甚多,原有书库早已不敷应用,故此次追加扩充改良费恳予从优分配,藉资添建书库,非敢过事奢求,此中困难情形谅蒙钧察。拟恳仍本素来爱护敝馆之殷,特予加拨建筑书库用费,俾得早日兴工,至为企盼。肃复,恭候勋祺。

　　　　　　　　　　　　　　　　　　　　职袁同礼谨启
　　　　　　　　　　　　　　　　　　　　十一月二十二日

　　　　　　　〔台北"中央研究院"近代史研究所档案馆,〈朱家骅〉,馆藏号
　　　　　　　301-01-09-054〕

　　　　按:此信为文书代笔,落款处钤先生名章。

十一月二十三日

上午,先生、袁敦礼赴清华大学访袁复礼。午后,在其处遇徐旭生。随后,徐旭生至燕京大学临湖轩听哲学讨论会,会后搭先生汽车返城。〔《徐旭生文集》第10册,页1495〕

按:此次哲学讨论会主讲人为陈康,讲题为“哲学的将来”。

十一月二十五日

史密斯森协会覆函先生,告知此前寄出的四箱书刊及其他六箱美国政府出版物实际发出时间,并表示无法按前请将寄送平馆的书刊单独包装。

November 25, 1947

Dear Dr. Yuan:

Reference is made to your letter of November 15.

The American Library Association has advised the Institution that the four cases received from Brock & Rankin on July 30, 1947 and bearing the address of your library contained the volumes to which you refer. It is understood that it is the practice of the American Library Association to notify the intended recipient that the publications are being sent at the time that the Association places the order with the printer. This would explain the fact that you were notified in June although the publications were not received at this Institution until July 30.

The four cases were numbered 522 to 525, inclusive, and were included in a shipment made to the Chinese Exchange Bureau on August 21. This shipment left New York on the U. S. Lines SS PIONEER WAVE about August 25. Included in this shipment were six cases of official publications numbered 4752, 4794, 4835, 4876, 4917 and 4958, and the Chinese Exchange Bureau was informed that these were for the National Central Library in PEIPING.

The Institution regrets that due to limited working space and other factors, it would be impracticable to comply with your request to pack the individual packages for the National Library of Peiping in separate cases. Of course, the documents comprising the official exchange with the National Library of Peiping are packed in separate cases and the Chinese

Exchange Bureau advised of the numbers of the cases.

Very truly yours,

Acting Chief

International Exchange Service

〔Smithsonian Institution Archives, Records, 1868-1988 (Record Unit 509), Box 1, National Library, Peiping〕

按:Brock & Rankin 应指芝加哥的一家出版社。该件为副本。

十一月二十六日

布朗覆先生两函,其一,告知将与克莱普一同访问日本,协助该国筹建国立图书馆,并可能前往中国,但行程会比较紧凑。

November 26, 1947

Dear Dr. Yuan:

I have wanted to write you for a long time but some matters were pending which could not be discussed until the projects were further along.

In view of the many requests from China to send to China some American technicians in the field of cataloging, etc., we have started some projects which we hope will materialize. So far, they are only in the formative stage.

I have been asked by our War Department to make a short trip to Japan to make recommendations in regard to the organization of a national library in Japan. Mr. Verner W. Clapp, Associate Director of the Library of Congress, and I expect to embark on an Army plane from San Francisco on December 7th. We shall probably be in Japan for thirty days.

I am hoping to make a flying trip from Tokyo to Shanghai, Nanking, and Peiping. I shall probably be in China not over three weeks, but I want to see some university presidents, Miss Bouchard of the American Embassy, some of my library friends, and more especially, you. The trip is not yet definite, but it seems probable that I shall be in China sometime in January. It will be a great pleasure to see you again and my many friends in China. I regret that my trip must be so hurried.

We are mailing this week a number of films and shall send you copies of our letters transmitting the films in a few days.

Yours very truly,

Charles H. Brown

Associate Director

其二，告知已收到汇来的额外一千美元，为中国各大学编制购买书刊目录的工作将于本年底结束，并就此前发送给中国的期刊分配比例表示称赞，对部分书籍糟糕的品相表示歉意。

November 26, 1947

Dear Dr. Yuan:

I have received with much pleasure a note stating that the check for $ 1,000 to pay for the additional work on the compilation of books for Chinese universities has been received. May I thank you for your interest in the matter and for your prompt attention to our request for an additional $ 1,000 in view of the nature of the work. This project will be entirely cleared up, I believe, at the end of this year. The Universal Trading Corporation did report that some of the funds received for the purchase of these books had been used for laboratory equipment, etc. but apparently the decrease in the funds for the purchase of these books was not as serious as we had anticipated.

Furthermore, may I express my pleasure in the allocation of the periodicals from the American Library Association. We figure that about 40% of the periodicals were allocated to private colleges, which is more than we would have thought necessary.

I am sorry about the poor condition of some of the books sent over by the American Book Center, but the shipments from United China Relief were all packed up and were transmitted without opening the boxes. The donations from American libraries were sorted in Washington before shipment, but those from the United China Relief, I understand, were sent as the boxes were received. Books which are in poor condition, of course, should be disposed of in China.

Yours very truly,

Charles H. Brown

Associate Director

〔The American Library Association Archives, China Projects File, Box 2, Chinese Universities, Correspondence, 1946-1947〕

按:1946 年, United China Relief 改组为"援华联合服务会"(United Service to China),1950 年停止运营。

十一月二十七日

朱家骅覆函先生,告知扩充改良费早经核定并通知国库拨发,平馆建设新书库事请将计划呈报,待教育部来年有款时再予考虑。

守和先生大鉴:

顷获本月廿二日手书,忻聆种切。此次追加扩充改良费业经分配完毕,计平馆为六亿元,并早已通知国库速发。承嘱一节,因现年度瞬将届终,再行追加决无希望,部中统筹科目亦早已分配无余,经费支绌万分,即请先送建筑书库计划,俟明年一月后有款时,再行核拨可也。耑此奉复,顺颂台祺。

弟朱家〇顿首

廿七

〔台北"中央研究院"近代史研究所档案馆,〈朱家骅〉,馆藏号 301-01-09-054〕

按:此件为底稿。28 日,该函以航空信方式寄出。

十一月

法国巴黎国际风俗委员会(International Commission on Folk Art)函聘先生为该会副会长之一,并请协助收集中国的风俗资料,以利研究。〔《益世报》(北平),1947 年 11 月 27 日,第 4 版〕

十二月五日

下午,袁复礼、先生访徐旭生,晤谈。〔《徐旭生文集》第 10 册,页 1497〕

十二月十日

中午,平津地区国立各院校长谈话会在清华大学工字厅召开,胡适、袁敦礼、徐佩琨、徐悲鸿、先生及北平研究院、大辞典编纂处、南开、唐山工学

院等处代表出席，梅贻琦为会议主席。〔《华北日报》，1947 年 12 月 10 日，第 5 版〕

十二月十五日

Rae Cecilia Kipp 覆函先生，收到十一月四日的报告并将其录副转发给国际关系委员会成员及其他相关人士，告知布朗将访华。

December 15, 1947

Dear Dr. Yuan:

Your letter and report of November 5 addressed to Mr. Charles H. Brown has been referred to the International Relations Office of the American Library Association for a reply. It gives us great pleasure to acknowledge the receipt of the additional information contained in your report of November 4. We have distributed copies to the Board and other interested persons.

Perhaps, by this time, you have heard from Mr. Brown that he expects to be in China within a month and will have the opportunity of seeing you in person and discussing library problems with you. He is looking forward to his trip to China with great interest and expectation.

In closing, may we say that it was very good of you to supplement our information on the distribution of the American Library Association's sets donated through the generosity of the Rockefeller Foundation. Your report will enable us to complete our records and to inform the Rockefeller Foundation concerning the distribution in China.

With Kindest regards,

Yours very sincerely
Mrs. Rae Cecilia Kipp
Executive Assistant

〔The American Library Association Archives, China Projects File, Box 2, Books for China, Correspondence, 1947〕

十二月二十二日

胡适致函先生，感谢先生捐赠实物与北京大学博物馆筹备处。

守和先生：

承惠赠美国总统威尔逊像片一张、西域人陶甬一件，本馆必慎重保管，公之士林，以副盛意。专函申谢，顺颂台绥。

胡适敬启

十二月二十二日

〔国立北京大学博物馆筹备处用笺。国家图书馆档案，档案编号1945-※057-综合5-002003〕

按：此信为文书代笔，暂系于此。

十二月二十四日

司徒雷登覆函先生，告知无暇赴先生午宴邀请。

Dec. 24, 1947

Dear Dr. Yuan:

I have your letter and appreciate your invitation for lunch with you during our stay in Peiping. Unfortunately, my days are completely filled. Mr. Fu is staying at his house in the city and may be free. His telephone is 20102.

With the season's greetings and my hearty thanks,

Very sincerely yours,

J. Leighton Stuart

〔燕京大学（教务长办公室）信纸。国家图书馆档案，档案编号1945-※057-综合5-017005〕

按：Mr. Fu 应指傅泾波。该函为司徒雷登亲笔。

十二月二十七日

先生致信史密斯森协会，告知香港办事处早已不再使用，请该会将交换品包裹寄送北平。

27 December, 1947

Gentlemen:

We find that you are still using our war-time forwarding address in Hongkong (c/o Fung Ping Shan Library, 94 Bonham Road). As with the end of the war we no longer maintain an office there, please address all documents to us in Peiping.

Yours truly

T. L. Yuan

Director

〔国立北平图书馆英文信纸。Smithsonian Institution Archives, Records, 1868－1988 (Record Unit 509), Box 1, National Library, Peiping〕

按:此件为打字稿,落款处为先生签名。

一九四八年　五十四岁

一月五日

Marybelle Bonchard 女士访胡适，后者招饮，并邀先生、王重民夫妇、韩寿萱等人前来聚谈。〔《胡适日记全集》第 8 册，页 347〕

按：Marybelle Bonchard（1915-2007），幼时曾随父母在天津生活三年，后回美入密歇根大学学习，20 世纪 30 年代入国会图书馆东方部服务，后又在国务院、驻华大使馆等处供职，曾长期担任恒慕义的秘书，与胡适、先生、王重民夫妇皆为旧识，时在北平休假。①

王重民、毛准致函先生，谈北京大学图书馆专科发展的设想。

适之、守和先生道鉴：

美国圕协会远东委员会主席 Brown 就要到中国了。他曾提议由美国圕协会转请罗氏基金会拿五万美金，帮助我们北京大学发展“图书馆博物馆学系”。适之先生因为我们自己还没有根基，婉辞谢绝。他这次来，又想拿 Fulbright Bill 的钱，假借我们北京大学，来举办“西文编目学习班”，我们应该怎样欢迎，或者怎样应付呢？统观他前后这两次善意，我们愿将我们所想到的写在下边：

Brown 想办的图书馆补习班是注重训练西文编目人材，我们现在正办着的“图书馆学专科”，仅教授普通功课，还没有分门训练。可是我们既已举办专科，他若再办一个训练班，未免重复；若从明年暑假，把我们的专科分成“中文编目”和“西文编目”两组，特别请他们来帮忙训练“西文编目组”的人，以其所长，补我所短，似是最好的一种协议方法。我们的图书馆学专科于明春开校后，正想多添两门功课，先作一点准备，叫学生们能有学力来领受他们的训练。

现在“图”、“博”两科开课已经半年了，博物馆的馆址也已奠定，明年就可动工了。而且光阴似箭，一年半以后，我们就有毕业的学生

---

① The Library of Congress, *Information Bulletin*, March 2-8, 1948, p. 9.

了。我们现在正应该为他们开创实习的机会,俾他们到毕业的时候,能有相当的经验。我们想到了“中文编目”和“西文编目”的两大计划若能实现,不但叫在校的学生们可有机会实习,毕业的学生们可继续他们的学业,且于中西学术上,还有大贡献。

美国国会图书馆有一个美国藏书联合目录参考室,英国有一个中央图书馆(National Central Library)全馆仅有一份英国书的联合书目,普林斯敦大学博物馆有一份全世界的耶稣圣画照片,称雄了全世界。北大应该造成中西学术上这类的权威和中心。我们现在有了“图”、“博”两科,正好给这类工作作准备。这类工作看来非常难,可是只要有计划,有恒,有人,有钱,便一定可以成功。

请先就西文说。今年美国给北大圕送到了十六箱国会图书馆印制的图书卡片,希望他永远继续赠送。这份卡片能代表全世界出版的书籍十分之六七,当然以美国英国为最完备,东亚也许就是最不完备的。我们若能源源加入美国印的新卡片,再把我们所能见到的东亚各地出版品随时补入,就能造成一个西洋学术的参考中心。

再说中文书籍,当然以北平所藏为最富,但是北平一共有多少中文书?这些中文书去了重复的共有若干种,有谁能知道呢?清史稿艺文志收了多少?千顷堂书目所著录的,现在尚存多少?又有谁知道呢?也许有人曾经发过野心,要学阮孝绪用一人的力量来编一部现存书目,但事实上是办不到的。只有由一个学术机关,训练了人材,定好了计划,加之以年月,才能作成的。

这件工作,也可以照联合目录的方式来做。并且也还有一些东西作根基。即是北大圕、北平圕、中央圕以及美国的哈佛圕都曾印了些中国书的书目卡片,聚起来也算是一个小小的基础。未作时好像是一座空中楼阁,实地作起来,便有成功的希望,成功之后,才真是一部“中国书目总志”呢!

古今来大工作,大计划,不作便永无成功之日,若冒险开了端,就是成功之始。我们的新博物馆,虽说正在预备向里面装东西,可是经费极感不够。我们图书馆的两大中心的计划,也非有钱不能开始。我们敬请二位先生考虑:这两个大工作是不是应该作?可以作?这次Brown来,我们用什么方法,可以请他重提旧议,转请罗氏基金会津助我们那五万美金?适之先生最初不肯接受,是因为还没有创办我们的

专科。现在专科开始了,极待发展,已经到了可以表示要接受那笔赠款的时期了。总之,我们要研究的是:

1、我们计划的工作,应该不应该作?

2、我们用什么方式,去接受那笔赠款?

因为我们用我们的计划,罗氏基金会未必赞同;可是我们用一种方式接受了那笔款,我们便能照我们的计划去发展了。敬请道安。

毛准、王重民仝上

卅七年一月五日

〔国家图书馆档案,档案编号 1945-※057-综合 5-016009 至 1945-※057-综合 5-016016〕

按:此件为誊抄件,落款处为毛准、王重民签名。

一月八日

John Marshall 致函先生,告知洛克菲勒基金会批准赞助五千美金用以援助平馆重建缩微实验室。

January 8, 1948

Dear Dr. Yuan:

In the absence of Mr. Fahs, I am very glad to be able to report the approval of a grant in aid of $5,000, or as much thereof as may be needed, to the National Library of Peiping toward the purchase of microfilming equipment and materials. This sum is to be available over the period terminating December 31, 1949.

To arrange for payments under the terms of this grant, I suggest that you write Mr. H. M. Gillette, the Assistant Comptroller of the Foundation.

We are happy that the Foundation is able to contribute in this way toward the operation of your microfilm laboratory. Mr. Fahs will return to the office in about a fortnight's time and it may be that he will wish to add some comment then.

Yours sincerely,

John Marshall

〔Rockefeller Foundation. Series 601: China; Subseries 601.R: China-Humanities and Arts. Vol. Box 47. Folder 393〕

按:此件为录副,右上日期被错录为1947年,笔者自行更正,特此说明。

一月十二日

记者来访,先生略谈平馆购书、经常费紧张,难以开展馆务,计划南下向教育部面陈困难。〔《经世日报》(北平),1948年1月13日,第4版〕

一月十四日

中午,平津国立各院校长第五次谈话会在北平艺术专科学校召开,郑天挺、沈履(清华)、鲍觉民(南开)、钟世铭(北洋)、杨光弼(北平研究院)、先生、袁敦礼(北平师院)、徐佩琨(铁院)、徐悲鸿(艺专)、何梅岑(大辞典编纂处)、何砥平(天津艺专)、金涛(唐山工学院)等人出席,徐悲鸿为会议主席,杨光弼记录。会上,先生提议各院校经常费比照去年十二月调整后之数目最少增加三倍发放,议决通过。此外,讨论议案共十件,至一时方结束,会后午餐,二时散。〔《国民日报》(天津),1948年1月15日,第3版〕

先生致信王重民,请其为孙楷第公子谋北京大学图书馆差事联系胡适。

有三吾兄:

子书来信奉上,据余光宗表示,近校中各部门接秘书处通知,凡遇有空额均须举行考试。如能由胡校长下一条子则较易办理,即希速与胡校长一商,径告子书为荷。顺颂大安。

同礼顿首

一,十四

〔国立北平图书馆用笺。中国书店·海淀,四册〕

按:孙楷第之子即孙传芬,曾改名"孙宝明"。[①] 余光宗,江苏丹徒人,北京大学预科毕业,曾任清华学校图书馆职员,时任北京大学图书馆秘书兼总务股长。

一月十五日

美国图书馆界专家布朗、克莱普由南京乘飞机抵达北平,James Dyke van Putten、先生、王重民、韩寿萱等在机场迎接,后 Marybelle Bouchard 女士前来。〔The Library of Congress, *Information Bulletin*, March2-8, 1948, p. 9〕

按:James Dyke van Putten 应为美国新闻处(USIS)驻北平分部主任。

---

① 《胡适遗稿及秘藏书信》第32册,页641-642。

先生致信法斯，询问洛克菲基金会可否给予钱存训奖学金，并再次简述钱存训学术、工作履历。

15th January, 1948

Dear Dr. Fahs:

One of our men, Mr. T. H. Tsien, was invited by the University of Chicago last summer to catalogue Chinese books in its Far Eastern Library, but he is having difficulties with the immigration office and cannot be considered as a member of the staff, because he holds an official passport and cannot receive any honorarium from the University.

It was at first intended that Mr. Tsien should take some library course on the side. Since he cannot be classified as a regular staff member, I wish very much that he may spend his whole time in the Chicago Library School, and also get some practical experience in microphotography, so that when he comes back, he can take charge of our photoduplication laboratory.

Will it be possible for the Rockefeller Foundation to give the National Library of Peiping a fellowship for this purpose? Mr. Tsien, a graduate of the University of Nanking, is one of our best capable men whom I recommended to Dr. Stevens some time ago, and whom you interviewed at Shanghai last May. He was in charge of our Shanghai Office immediately before the war; during the war, he continued to look after our property in Shanghai, and proved to be worthy of the trust placed in him. It is confidently expected that he will be able to contribute much to the working efficiency of the Library on his return. I understand that the Chicago Library School has already agreed to let Mr. Tsien finish the graduate course in one year instead of two. If a fellowship in library science could be given to him, I am sure that he will make the best use of the opportunity thus offered.

In view of the urgency of his case and in view of his accomplishments, I hope that you and Dr. Stevens will give favorable consideration to our request.

With kindest regards,

Your sincerely,

T. L. Yuan

Director

〔国立北平图书馆英文信纸。Rockefeller Foundation. Series 601: China; Subseries 601.R: China-Humanities and Arts. Vol. Box 47. Folder 393〕

按:此件为打字稿,落款处为先生签名,于2月4日送达。

一月十六日

布朗、克莱普参观北京大学,先生设午宴款待,餐后参观协和医学院。〔《中华图书馆协会会报》第21卷第3-4期合刊,1948年5月,页5〕

一月十七日

布朗、克莱普访问平馆,先生、王重民等人负责接待,二人对平馆馆藏备加赞扬。〔《中华图书馆协会会报》第21卷第3-4期合刊,页5〕

按:美国图书馆界欲在平津设立图书馆学讲习会,中美两方共办,经费由美国方面承担,具体实施则请先生主持。①

一月十八日

胡适在平馆设宴,在平中华图书馆协会会员集体欢迎布朗、克莱普。此后,先生和夫人又邀请克莱普观看京剧。〔《中华图书馆协会会报》第21卷第3-4期合刊,1948年5月,页5;The Library of Congress, *Information Bulletin*, March 2-8, 1948, p.10〕

一月中下旬

某日晚,先生陪克莱普赴雍和宫参观。〔The Library of Congress, *Information Bulletin*, March2-8, 1948, p. 10〕

一月十九日

下午一时,布朗、克莱普乘坐飞机离平返沪,先生前往送行。〔《华北日报》,1948年1月20日,第5版〕

按:二人拟将转往广东、武汉等地考察中国图书馆事业。

史密斯森协会覆函先生,该所无法保证所有交寄印刷品都可以订正寄送地址,请平馆联系在美的交换机构。

---

①《申报》,1948年1月28日,第6版;《申报》,1948年2月20日,第6版。

January 19, 1948

Dear Dr. Yuan:

Reference is made to your letter of December 27.

Your letter regarding the use of your war-time forwarding address was referred to the publications division of the Institution and the Exchanges was advised that your present address was being used on Smithsonian publications.

As you know publications sent you from other sources bear your address when received and although the Institution would be glad to comply with your request and change the address on any package that is received for you, the many thousands of packages passing through the Exchanges make it impractical to make corrections in addresses. It is suggested that you notify your individual correspondents direct.

The Institution regrets that it is unable to be of more assistance to you in this matter.

Very truly yours,

Chief Clerk

〔Smithsonian Institution Archives, Records, 1868－1988 (Record Unit 509), Box 1, National Library, Peiping〕

按:此件为录副。

一月二十日

先生致信 John Marshall,感谢洛克菲勒基金会的赞助。

20th January, 1948

Dear Mr. Marshall:

We are happy to learn from your letter of January 8th that a grant-in-aid of $5,000 has been made to the National Library of Peiping towards the purchase of microfilming equipment and materials.

As soon as the Camera is received here, it will be possible for us to set up our photographic laboratory. I am writing to Mr. Gillette about the financial arrangement, with the request that your purchasing department will place the order for us.

We wish to thank the Rockefeller Foundation for the substantial aid it is giving to us, and also to thank the officers of the Foundation for their unfailing interest. It is our hope that our photographic laboratory will be able to render some aid to American scholars after it is set up.

With renewed thanks,

Yours sincerely
T. L. Yuan
Director

Kindly pass on our letter to Mr. Gillett.

〔Rockefeller Foundation. Series 601: China; Subseries 601.R: China-Humanities and Arts. Vol. Box 47. Folder 391〕

按:此件为打字稿,落款和补语则为先生亲笔,该信应于翌日寄出。

一月二十一日

先生致信 H. M. Gillette,请其协助订购缩微胶卷设备并告知预计购买的具体型号。

21st January, 1948

Mr. H. M. Gillette, Assistant Comptroller
Rockefeller Foundation
Dear Mr. Gillette:

Dr. Marshall has informed me that a grant-in-aid of $ 5,000 has been made by the Rockefeller Foundation to the National Library of Peiping toward the purchase of microfilming equipment and materials. The sum is to be available over a period of two years.

As explained in our previous correspondence, the National Library plans to use the grant to buy a Recordak camera, Model C-2, and some other equipment to supplement what we have already bought, besides some films and chemicals.

Will you therefore kindly ask your purchasing department to order for us the following items from the Recordak Corporation, 350 Madison Avenue, New York City:

1 Micro-File Recordak, Model C-2

1 Recordak Enlarger, Model A 1

1 Recordak Library Film Reader, Model C.

(kindly note that our voltage is 220 operating A. C. current.) They should be carefully packed and shipped to this Library via Taku Bar-Tientsin. The invoices and Bill of Lading should be marked "Donation from the Rockefeller Foundation", so that we can arrange for import-license from the Import Control Board in China.

After you have paid the Recordak Corporation for the above items, the balance of the grant may be sent to the Chase National Bank, Park Avenue Branch, Park Avenue at 60th Street, New York City, for the credit of the account of the National Library of Peiping.

Thanking you for your assistance and hoping to hear from you before long,

Yours truly

T. L. Yuan

Director

〔国立北平图书馆英文信纸。Rockefeller Foundation. Series 601: China; Subseries 601.R: China-Humanities and Arts. Vol. Box 47. Folder 393〕

按:此件为打字稿,落款处为先生签名,似于2月9日送达。三款设备处依次标注3500.00、500.00、600.00,应为H. M. Gillette的备注。

一月二十二日

先生致信胡适,就布朗提议由洛克菲勒基金会出资协助北京大学发展图书馆学、博物馆学专业代拟计划书。

适之先生:

关于白郎先生之建议,兹代拟一稿,如荷同意,即希另打复本径寄南京中美教育基金会为荷。此上,顺颂著祺。

同礼敬上

一,廿二

〔国立北平图书馆用笺。台北胡适纪念馆,档案编号HS-JDSHSC-1636-001〕

按:"白郎"即 Charles H. Brown,胡适在其1月16、17日的日记中都提到他和克莱普访华,尤其写道"Brown 已老,今年七十二,颇龙钟,但实甚爱护中国"。"建议"应指1月3日毛准、王重民信中写道的:"他曾提议由美国圕协会转请罗氏基金会拿五万美金,帮助我们北京大学发展'图书馆博物馆学系'",所附拟稿不存。

一月二十六日

先生致信北平市政府,为平馆已故编纂何国贵领取抚恤事。

案查本馆呈请抚恤已故编纂何国贵一案,曾奉教育部上年十二月十八日人字第一五一六七号训令略开:此案经由本部比照教职员抚恤条例规定,核给三十五年十月至十二月年抚恤金叁百肆拾贰元,并按现任待遇比例增给贰拾陆万伍千陆百捌拾元,呈奉核准备案在卷。除分咨财政审计两部查照外,合行填发年抚恤金证书及领据。令仰转发并转知觅保,径向北平市政府具领等因。附发抚恤金证书及领据各一纸,奉此除将证书及收据抄发外,兹派该故编纂之妻江珍(现充本馆职员)携同证件赍函前往贵政府请领,即希查照迅赐核发为荷。此致

北平市政府

中华民国三十七年一月二十六日

馆长袁同礼

〔北京市档案馆档案,档案编号 J001-005-01388〕

一月二十七日

朱家骅致函胡适、先生、毛准,请在平成立教育部收购图书委员会,购买北平书铺所售大宗旧籍。

适之吾兄并转袁守和、毛子水二先生大鉴:

关于北平各书铺顷以存书计重售与造纸厂转作提炼新纸之用一事,确应迅采有效办法以图挽救文献典籍之损失。爰请兄暨守和、子水二先生在平组织教育部收购图书委员会,聘兄为主任委员,毛先生兼秘书,聘书随函附奉,并略举办法要点如次:

一、凡成套具有价值之书刊均在收购之例;

二、为防止重要书刊流入造纸厂所,并顾及避免刺激书价上涨,购时评价宜较废纸价为高;

三、收购之书登记后暂存北大;

四、购书专款之收支由北大会计室负责设置专帐办理；

五、购有成数即造册报部备核，由部分配之；

六、分配对象以1国立中等学校、2国立专科以上学校、3国立社会教育机关。

兹先筹拨购书费拾亿元，俟库款拨部即行汇发。希即查照办理为荷。专此，顺颂时祺。

附聘书三份。

弟朱家骅敬启

一月廿七日

〔教育部部长室用笺。《胡适遗稿及秘藏书信》第25册，页484-485〕

按：此件为打字稿，落款处钤朱家骅印。二月初，北平书业公会已将欲出售旧书会员名册集齐，约六十余家，总售价约为十一点二亿。[1]

一月二十九日

晚，金毓黻在六芳斋设宴，先生、赵万里、王重民三人受邀与席。席间，王重民以唐俊公辑刻《琵琶亭诗》借金毓黻，赵万里谈《千山賸人禅师语录》《续通鉴长编》版本情况。〔《静晤室日记》第9册，页6522〕

按：28日，赵万里访金毓黻，后者请其代邀先生、王重民29日赴宴。

先生致信钱存训，告知收到寄款并谈解决其在美薪酬问题的意见。

存训吾兄：

一月廿一日来函，详悉一切，所附之六十元，亦如数收到（前寄之60、70、70收到后曾函告）。致罗氏基金会之函，俟移民局确定不能支薪时再行发出，亟表同意。届时或须请Creel再写一封信，较吾人更有力也。余容再函，顺颂大安。

同礼顿首

一，廿九

〔钱孝文藏札〕

① 《申报》，1948年2月7日，第6版。

一月三十一日

先生致信钱存训,告知收到寄款并言馆中生活补助费被迫缩减,希望其在美可得足够薪酬。

存训吾兄:

前收到200元后曾经函告,兹又收到60元又70元(一,廿四日寄)共130元均照收,尚余70元,想不久可由尊处寄到矣。

馆中近奉令自二月份起至六月份止,将生补费减少四分之一(每月核减百分之五),故不得不裁员,而尊处之补助费一时亦不易办理,至盼尊处在美薪金可不致有何问题也。顺颂大安。

同礼顿首

一,卅一

〔钱孝文藏札〕

二月四日

法斯致函先生,就钱存训在美困境给予意见。

February 4, 1948

Dear Dr. Yuan:

Your letter of January 15 has just arrived. It leaves me uncertain as to whether Mr. Tsien is already in this country or is still in China. If he is still in China, I should think that it might still be possible to have him enter the United States with a passport and visa which would permit him to take up his work with the University of Chicago as originally planned. If he is already in the United States, perhaps he could talk with me here. I am not at all sure that we can help him but I shall be glad to make any suggestions that seem possible.

Sincerely your

Charles Fahs

〔Rockefeller Foundation. Series 601: China; Subseries 601.R: China-Humanities and Arts. Vol. Box 47. Folder 393〕

按:此函被录副并附于12日致钱存训信中。

二月六日

中午,先生在家设宴款待金毓黻。〔《静晤室日记》第9册,页6542〕

二月九日

下午，先生给徐旭生打电话，后者告知西北科学考查团支绌异常困难，先生遂答应垫付一千万元，帮助度过难关。〔《徐旭生日记》第10册，页1517〕

先生致信钱存训，告知收到寄款并请其查询芝加哥大学图书馆编纂舆图目录卡片的方法和参考资料，另请转寄信件。

存训吾兄：

顷又接到70元前曾接到60+70=130，第二批之贰百元已全数收到，谢谢。罗氏基金会一函知已发出，至以为慰，惟尚须托顾立雅从旁进言。近因Stevens对于东方之事不愿过问，一切由Fahs作主，此人只有祖日之名，对于中国不甚同情也。兹奉还邮票$6.99之支票壹纸，又托代发信二件。此外，请到芝大地图部询问编舆图卡片目录之方法及一切（文献）资料，交邮寄下为感。匆匆，顺颂大安。

弟同礼顿首

二，九

〔钱孝文藏札〕

先生致信王重民，询问刘修业病情并约本周三聚餐。

有三吾弟：

尊夫人患病已大愈否，为念。本星期三（十一日）如无他约，拟请贤伉俪来舍下便餐七时左右为盼。顺颂万安。

同礼顿首

二，九

〔国立北平图书馆便笺。中国书店·海淀，四册〕

George J. Beal致函先生，告知洛克菲勒基金会为平馆采购缩微胶片设备的进展。

February 9, 1948

Dear Dr. Yuan:

We have your letter of January 21st in which you request certain equipment to be purchased by our office under our $5,000 grant to the National Library of Peiping.

Our purchasing department will place the orders for the Recordaks, the Enlarger, and the film reader, through the Recordak Corporation and as soon as the invoices for these have been paid, including shipping charges and insurance, we shall deposit the unused balance of the grant to the Library account with the Chase National Bank, Park Avenue Branch, Park Avenue at 60th Street, New York, in accordance with your request.

Yours very truly,

George J. Beal

〔Rockefeller Foundation. Series 601: China; Subseries 601.R: China-Humanities and Arts. Vol. Box 47. Folder 391〕

二月十一日

柳诒徵致函胡适、先生，请在教部所拨购书专款中协助收购江苏省立国学图书馆散佚旧籍。

适之、守和先生道鉴：

献岁发春，伏维曼福，文化名城，益臻安谧。报载部颁巨款，专托执事收集公家散佚之书，甚盛。盋山旧籍现仅匇合十九万册，尚多阙逸，伏冀分神垂注，遇有坊肆庋售此间藏书，有印记可证者务祈推同舟之谊，一律收购寄递山馆，以昭盛德。省力不足，不得不乞助于中央，谅大贤必矜许其请也。腊尾得裴姓一函，属购旧藏方志，按之馆目，知系廿六、七年敌伪在宁劫迁馆书时散出者，索价甚昂，无可为计。前已函托赵斐云君就近调查。兹谨录原函呈览，如该书尚未他售，即祈以此为嚆矢。涸辙之鱼，仰希河润。临颖愧悚，即颂公绥。

柳诒徵拜启

三七，二，一一

〔江苏省立国学图书馆用笺。台北胡适纪念馆，档案编号 HS-JDSHSC-1561-006〕

按：落款处钤柳诒徵印。

二月十二日

先生致信钱存训，将法斯二月四日函附上并建议其将目前困难告知对方。

存训吾兄：

顷接罗氏基金 Fahs 来函，录副奉上，又致渠一函，即希代为付邮。又能将目前困难情形自写一函，或托 Creel 先生代写，均希尊酌是荷。

匆复，顺颂大安。

弟袁同礼顿首

二，十二

〔钱孝文藏札〕

先生致信法斯，告知钱存训已抵达美国，再次申请资助其在美学习图书馆学。

12th February, 1948

Dear Mr. Fahs:

I wish to thank you for your letter of February 4th with regard to our application for a fellowship on behalf of Mr. Tsien.

Mr. Tsien arrived at Chicago in October, but in view of the fact that he holds an official passport, he cannot receive any pay from the University for the services he renders in connexion with the cataloguing for the Chinese collection. I understand that since October Dr. Creel has been lending him from his private funds. Although the University has written to the Immigration Office several times, no reply has been received.

Since our library is in need of a trained staff to take charge of our photoduplication laboratory, we hope very much that the Foundation will find it possible to give a fellowship to Mr. Tsien on the understanding that he will specialize in microphotography in the graduate Library School of Chicago, so that, on the completion of his studies, he will be appointed to this important post in this Library. In view of the services which he will render to this Library, I sincerely hope that you can assist him in obtaining such a fellowship.

I wish to extend to you our hearty thanks for a grant in aid of $ 5, 000 which the Foundation has given to us toward the purchase of microfilming equipment and materials. At the suggestion of Mr. Marshall, I have written to Mr. Gillette, asking him to request your purchasing Department to order for us the Micro-File Recordak etc., so that we shall be able to receive them in the immediate future.

With renewed thanks,

Yours Sincerely

T. L. Yuan

Director

〔国立北平图书馆英文信纸。Rockefeller Foundation. Series 601: China; Subseries 601.R: China-Humanities and Arts. Vol. Box 47. Folder 393〕

按：此件为打字稿，落款处为先生签名。

二月十三日

先生致信孙楷第，就推荐其子补缺北京大学图书馆职务一事告知进展并请函请胡适或王重民。

子书吾兄：

北大图书馆葛君出缺，嘱推荐令郎一节，已与余君谈过。据称目前北大秘书处通知各单位，如有出缺者一律须经考试。最好请胡校长下一条子，则毛先生较易办理。用特奉闻，即希径函胡校长，或托有三前往代为说项亦可。弟已将尊函交友三，请其从速设法矣。顺颂大安。

弟同礼顿首

二，十三

〔国立北平图书馆便笺。中国书店·海淀，四册〕

按：信中"有三"、"友三"皆指王重民。

二月十五日

先生赠赵钧彤撰《西行日记》（民国排印本）二册予童养年夫妇，以示对后者新婚之祝福。〔上海博古斋2014年季拍第二期艺术品拍卖会〕

按：童养年（1909—2001），江苏睢宁人，原名童寿彭，号养年，时应在国立中央图书馆任职，其妻名"宛文"，姓氏待考。

二月十七日

中午，梅贻琦、先生、袁敦礼、杨光弼等人乘车前往天津。〔《经世日报》（北平），1948年2月18日，第4版〕

按：此次赴津，为平津国立各院校校长本年第二次谈话会，李书华等人则于翌日当天前往。

二月十八日　天津

中午，平津国立各院校长谈话会在南开大学召开，张伯苓、李书华、张含英、梅贻琦、郑华炽、袁敦礼、先生、张长江、李高传、杨光弼等人出席，张伯苓为会议主席，议决九项，主要涉及薪俸、实物配售、经费等案，下月谈话会定于三月十日在铁道学院召开。三时半散会。〔《华北日报》，1948年2月19日，第5版〕

按：张含英（1900—2002），字华甫，山东荷泽人，1918年入北洋大学，后转入北京大学，1921年赴美留学，先后在伊利诺伊大学、康乃尔大学学习，时任北洋大学校长。张长江为天津体育专科学校代表，李高传为北平铁道管理学院代表。

二月十九日

中午，袁敦礼、先生、李书华、牛文清乘车返平。〔《华北日报》，1948年2月22日，第5版〕

二月二十二日

先生致信李泽彰，请商务印书馆将补缴图书送至平馆上海办事处。

伯嘉学长惠鉴：

敝馆为遵照出版法规定，接受出版界呈缴新书，传播文化。荷承赞助，承学之士同深感佩。近查贵公司近年及最近出版新书尚有若干未蒙检送，敢请送本馆上海办事处（宝庆路十七号），以期简□，是为至盼。耑此拜恳，即颂时祺。

弟袁同礼顿首

二，廿二

附书目一份。

〔北京德宝2007年11月艺术品拍卖会〕

按："伯嘉"即李泽彰（1895—?），字伯嘉，湖北蕲春人，曾任商务印书馆经理。此信为文书代笔，落款处为先生签名。3月6日，商务印书馆覆信平馆上海办事处，并呈缴书籍75种。

二月二十四日

中华图书馆协会撰《呈请拨助会报印刷费由》，具先生名并钤印。〔台北"国史馆"，〈中国图书馆协会请补助（教育部）〉，数位典藏号019-030508-0015〕

按：该请附印刷费预算书一纸，申请补助费用一千五百万元。3月初教育部批复补助五百万元，在1947年度扩充改良费保留数项下支付。

先生覆信George J. Beal，申请更换购买设备的型号，并告知寄送注意事项。

24th February, 1948

Dear Mr. Beal:

Thank you for your letter of February 9th and for your kindness in asking your purchasing department to place the orders for us for the Recordaks, the Enlarger and the Reader.

We have just received the following letter from Mr. Eugene Power, University Microfilms, Ann Arbor, Mich.:

> "You asked my opinion as to the equipment which you were getting. I believe if your funds are limited, I would substitute a Model D MicroFile camera for the Model C. This has a maximum reduction ratio of 22 times but for most purposes, especially the type of work which a library such as yours will have, this will be adequate. It has a further advantage, and that is the price is $ 1, 600 as against $ 3, 600 and this additional amount will be just about what you need.
>
> In any event it is not the model C-2 which you want, but the model C-1, for the C-2 does not have a movable cradle, and as such, would not be of much value to you.
>
> I note that you have already ordered a microfile enlarger and a Recordak reader, the price of which, incidentally, has just gone up to $ 600. These are both good. I would advise, however, that you specify very carefully when placing your order, the voltage in use in the location where these cameras will be used. Normally microfile cameras are made for 110 volts and if you have 220, the manufacturer should be notified so that he can make the necessary changes.
>
> You asked for a list of material. I have drawn up such a list and it is enclosed with this letter. The prices are approximate for I am not entirely sure about some of them, but they will be close enough for your purposes, I believe."

May I therefore request your purchasing department to purchase Model D Microfile Camera rather than Model C; and to place order for the equipment as per enclosed list submitted by Mr. Power. Our voltage in use is 220, not 110; the manufacturers should be notified regarding this point.

We wish to express our hearty thanks to your purchasing department for its assistance in placing orders for us. We appreciate very much your cooperation in setting up our Laboratory.

If possible, all equipment should be sent in one shipment. All invoices should be marked "Donation from the Rockefeller Foundation", and should be sent to us well in advance, so that we may ask for tax-free treatment by the Chinese Maritime Customs.

All equipment should be shipped to us via Taku Bar-Tientsin, not via Shanghai, as we advised you in our letter of January 21st.

With renewed thanks,

Yours sincerely

T. L. Yuan

Director

〔国立北平图书馆英文信纸。Rockefeller Foundation. Series 601: China; Subseries 601.R: China-Humanities and Arts. Vol. Box 47. Folder 393〕

按:此件为打字稿,落款处为先生签名。

William A. Heins 致函先生,告知已按要求购买相关设备,并告洛克菲勒基金会资助款在负担运输和保险费用后所剩无几。

February 24, 1948

Dear Dr. Yuan:

Upon receipt of your letter of January 21st, we issued our purchases order No. 421684 for the Model C-2 Recordak, Enlarger and Film Reader.

The total cost of these purchases, including transformers, amount to $ 4,577.87. This will leave a balance of approximately $ 422. The cost of ocean shipping and insurance will consume most of this balance, so there will be very little left for transmission to the Chase National Bank as indicated in your letter.

Upon completion of shipment and payment of all charges concerning these purchases, the balance remaining will be transferred as requested.

Sincerely yours,

William A. Heins

〔Rockefeller Foundation. Series 601: China; Subseries 601.R: China-Humanities and Arts. Vol. Box 47. Folder 393〕

按:William A. Heins 为洛克菲勒基金会采购部(Purchasing Department)负责人。

二月二十六日

先生致信王世杰,请其给予留德学生闵乃大外交官护照以利运送书籍、仪器。

雪艇部长钧鉴:

敬陈者,上年同礼在柏林时,曾为敝馆购到德文科学书籍数百种,连同清华大学所购者,共装十四箱。最近我国驻德军事代表团曾请柏林美军财政组特准放行,未蒙俞允。顷接缪参事来函,谓拟委托留德研究生闵乃大君以私人行李名义,由渠运出德境,再交转运公司寄华。又接闵乃大君来函,内称拟于三月间由德返国,仅有学生护照,如须携带大批图书出境,须有官员护照,美军方面方能放行云云。查闵君已由清华大学聘为教授,将于下月启程来华,拟请大部体念目前德国特殊情形,准予发给闵君官员护照(闵君英文姓名为 Ming Naita),俾此项书籍得以运出德境。敝馆及清华大学同深感谢。倘荷惠允,即希径电我国驻德军事代表团查照,予以科学顾问或咨议名义,以资便利。如何之处,统乞钧裁,赐覆为感。专此,敬颂道祺。

附军事代表团与美军财政组往来信件二件,并乞尊阅。

〔中华图书馆协会笺纸。国家图书馆档案,档案编号 1945-※057-综合 5-008005 和 1945-※057-综合 5-008006〕

按:此件为先生所拟之底稿。

二月下旬

先生与敌伪产业处管理局沟通,为平馆接收汉奸许修直、管冀贤、吴瓯等人藏书作准备。〔《大公报》(天津),1948 年 2 月 25 日,第 3 版〕

按:本月 24 日,该局通知平馆此事。许修直(1881—1954),原名卓然,字西溪,江苏无锡人,曾任汪伪政权的北京市市长;管冀贤,曾任伪华北政务委员会情报局长;吴瓯,曾任伪华北政务委员会内务总署署长,编有《稷香馆丛书》(影印本)。

三月五日

先生致信钱存训，告知自来水笔已收到并询问在美情况。

存训吾兄：

自来水笔昨由沪寄来，奉上美金壹元，归还代垫之修理费，并谢厚意。罗氏基金方面不识有无问题，深盼早日决定办法，俾能安心读书为盼。奉上信四件，请代为转寄为荷。顺颂旅安。

同礼顿首

三，五

〔钱孝文藏札〕

三月七日

中午，胡适、先生、毛准在北京大学召集会议，唐兰、赵万里、刘盼遂、郑天挺、张政烺、徐旭生等人到场。〔《徐旭生日记》第10册，页1522〕

按：3月4日，胡适、先生、毛准向徐旭生等人发出请柬。所谈之事似与教育部在平成立收购图书委员会，购买北平书铺所售大宗旧籍有关。

三月九日

先生致信法斯，请洛克菲勒基金会更换购买设备的型号，并请考虑赞助平馆缩微胶片实验室周转资金。

March 9th, 1948

Dear Dr. Fahs:

Referring to the microfilm laboratory equipment, I wrote to Mr. George J. Beal, on February 24th, that we wanted a cheaper camera, Recordak Model D, together with additional supplies as advised by Mr. Eugene Power of the University Microfilms, Ann Arbor, Mich. I hope that my letter could be received in time to enable your Comptroller to countermand the original order for Model C.

I now enclose my letter to Mr. William A. Heins, and I shall be obliged to you if you will forward it.

When our application for a grant was made, I did not expect that prices in the United States could have gone up so much. When I informed Mr. Eugene Power of the grant, he sent me a list of minimum supplies with rough estimates which I transmitted to Mr. Beal on February 24th, requesting him to place orders for us. They would amount to about $4,500, which with the shipping expenses, would just about use up the grant.

In view of the necessity of purchasing additional films to serve as a revolving stock, I would like to request a supplementary grant to be used as a revolving fund. I shall be most grateful to you if you and Dr. Stevens could make such a recommendation to your trustees.

It may be of interest for you to know that our Library and the National University are cooperating to set up an off-set printing plant in our Library. Most of the equipment has already been received at Peiping.

With many thanks for your assistance,

Yours sincerely

T. L. Yuan

Director

〔国立北平图书馆英文信纸。Rockefeller Foundation. Series 601: China; Subseries 601.R: China-Humanities and Arts. Vol. Box 47. Folder 393〕

按:此件为打字稿,落款处为先生签名,于 3 月 18 日送达。

先生致信 William A. Heins,恳请更换购买设备的型号。

March 9th, 1948.

Dear Mr. Heins:

Thank you so much for your letter of February 24th informing us that you have placed orders for us for Model C-2 Recordak, Enlarger and Film Reader. I hope, by this time, you have received my letter of February 24th, addressed to Mr. Beal, requesting him to substitute a Model D microfile camera for Model C, as advised by Mr. Eugene Power, University Microfilms.

I hope we have not given you too much trouble in ordering these equipments for us, and I look forward to hearing from you upon completion of the shipment.

With many thanks for your assistance,

Yours sincerely

T. L. Yuan

Director

〔国立北平图书馆英文信纸。Rockefeller Foundation. Series 601: China; Subseries 601.R: China-Humanities and Arts. Vol. Box 47. Folder 393〕

按:此件为打字稿,落款处为先生签名,于3月18日送达。

法斯覆函先生,告知芝加哥大学应能解决钱存训的困境,因此洛克菲勒基金会不考虑资助其在美留学。

March 9th, 1948

Dear Dr. Yuan:

In view of your letter of February 12 with regard to Mr. T. H. Tsien I have been in touch with Dr. Herrlee Creel at the University of Chicago. Dr. Creel's reply shows considerable confidence that the University of Chicago will be able to work out with the Immigration authorities the problems involved in employing Mr. Tsien there. They are very pleased with Mr. Tsien's ability and certainly look forward to continuation of his assistance in the library. Under these circumstances, I do not think that we can appropriately consider action here. I think that we must, for the time being at least, continue to assume-as we did when I saw Mr. Tsien and you in China last summer-that he will gain the experience he needs in this country through work at an support by the University of Chicago.

Sincerely yours,

Charles B. Fahs

〔Rockefeller Foundation. Series 601: China; Subseries 601.R: China-Humanities and Arts. Vol. Box 47. Folder 393〕

三月中旬

北平市立图书馆呈请教育局将中山公园分馆改建为“北平市儿童图书馆”,先生表示支持,并拟将平馆现存的儿童阅览书籍寄阅该处。〔《申报》,1948年3月19日,第6版〕

先生致信钱存训,并附法斯九日来函。

存训兄:

Fahs顷来复函,录副奉上,如Creel能设法,即请不必焦虑,想渠必不致使兄有任何困难也。

同礼

外三信请转寄。

〔钱孝文藏札〕

三月十七日

先生密呈教育部，汇报北平某机关盗卖日伪旧书调查情况。〔台北“国史馆”，〈北平图书馆(敌伪图书盗卖)(二)〉，数位典藏号 019-030402-0006〕

按:1948 年 2 月 13 日，南京国民政府以代电令教育部彻查北平某机关盗卖日伪旧书，教育部遂发训令，命先生设法查实。但此事中所谓“某机关”实为国民党北平党部，日伪旧书应为数年前拨交该所暂管，交接人员及相关纸厂均语焉不详，先生作为文化机构人员，并无行政权力彻查，只得将大致情形略陈。4 月 8 日，社会教育司司长英千里签呈教育部，建议派专员北上核查。该件为文书代笔，但钤先生名章、平馆关防印。

三月二十六日[①]

先生、胡适、马衡、谷钟秀、梁思成等人上书李宗仁，恳请维护故都文物建筑，并列举被军政机关占用而被毁坏情形，建议五项办法，希军政机关能迁出、妥加保管爱护。

德邻先生勋鉴:

敬启者，窃维本市昔为国都胜地，文物建筑，伟丽庄严，小至园沼亭台，大至宫殿坛庙，均系历代精心杰构，集建筑之大成，垂华夏之典制，不仅民族精神所寄，且足表现东方艺术特征，即一鳞一爪，亦为国家瑰宝，弥足珍贵。乃近来各机关学校及部队等，恒以种种特殊关系，使用该项古代建筑物，或充办公厅室，或充员工宿舍，自属一时权宜之计，惟部分繁多，往往各徇便利，移挪门窗，敷设电线，添安火炉，轻则污损彩画，重则毁伤架构，对于古建筑罔知爱护，相沿成习，触目惊心。兹谨就切近而显著者略举数例如次:

一、瀛台为南海名迹之一，水木清华，最负盛名。现在翔鸾阁左右延楼所有绿棂白板装修，大部移拆无存，楼成空廊，既碍观瞻，且于建

① 《大公报》(天津)，1948 年 3 月 27 日，第 3 版。

筑保固上亦深有影响。

二、春藕斋为居仁堂内伟丽建筑之一，去岁曾将室内雕刻精美硬木格扇拆除，使古代艺术失散无遗。

三、中南海西八所等各处烟囱，多横出檐下（只图减少烟筒，不接立管及顶帽），致烟火冲薰，额枋彩画失色，且滋危险，又墙外垃圾秽水，随处堆存。

四、大高殿南习礼亭二座，法式精巧（俗称九梁十八柱），系仿紫禁城角楼构造，为国内稀有之古典建筑，现已充作部队眷属宿舍，炊烟四起，日夕薰蒸，损及藻井天花。

五、天安门门楼于三十五年间，甫经修竣，门洞用作仓库，去冬即因军用卡车撞毁东扇大门，以致无法启用。

六、端门内西朝房室内，现已安装锅炉，充作厨房，并毁坏门窗，龌龊不堪。

凡前数例，均隶中枢重地，万目睽睽，尚且如此，则其他散在城郊僻静之古建筑，其外表内容横被毁损者，更不知凡几，似此情形，或轻或重，无不与文物建筑动有关碍，从来祸患忽于未然，戒慎端在细微，故片础犹能移栋，星火尚可燎原。前次延庆楼惨遭回禄，驯使一代文物，沦为废墟，损失之钜，难以数计，衡等抚今思昔，深切隐忧。伏念中央眷顾北平重镇，文化涵濡，特升为陪都，行将恢宏建制，以定百年大计，北平文物整理委员会对于整理既往，筹画将来，职责加重，今有所见，势不容缄默。盖自然之剥蚀广泛诸待培修，人力之摧残损失宁能补救，况且良工不再，覆辙堪寻，与其为事后之绸缪，致伤公帑，曷若作事前之爱护，永保国光。兹为杜渐防微，加强管理使用古建筑起见，拟恳我公惠予分别转令，嗣后凡本市重要古建筑概不准充作机关学校宿舍，如不得已使用古建筑为办公室时，须有适当防火设备，并须经常检查电线火炉烟囱等物以策安全（室内装设烟囱概须伸出檐口以上）。又对于古建筑，不得随意拆改，对于富有艺术价值之装修藻井天花等，尤须妥加爱护，以章文物。倘邀俞允，北平文物建筑前途幸甚。专肃奉达，敬颂勋绥。

袁同礼、胡适、马衡、谷钟秀、梁思成谨启

〔《行政院北平文物整理委员会三十六年度工作概要》，1948 年 5 月，页 5-6〕

三月三十日

先生致信英千里，就北平市市党部盗卖旧书一案，请其在南京就近询问知情人士。

千里司长仁兄尊鉴：

三月二十六日秘函，敬悉种切。所述某机关应系北平市市党部机关，长官系吴铸人先生，其存书是否盗卖，抑另有处理办法，局外人颇难查悉。弟前呈复各节，亦自多方探询，仅得结果如此。现在，吴铸人、胡适之两先生均出席国大会议，胡先生住北极阁中央研究院，似可分别就近一询，或能得到更准确之消息也。专此，顺候勋祺。

弟袁同礼敬启

三，三十

〔台北"国史馆"，〈北平图书馆（敌伪图书盗卖）（二）〉，数位典藏号 019-030402-0006〕

按：吴铸人（1902—1984），名寿金，号梦燕，安徽盱眙人，北京大学毕业，1946 年作为中国国民党中央派系的代表，当选北平市党部主任委员。该信应为文书代笔，但落款处、日期均为先生亲笔。

法斯覆函先生，告知已经更改购买设备的型号，但无法赞助平馆缩微胶片实验室周转资金。

March 30, 1948

Dear Dr. Yuan:

On receipt of your letter of March 9th, I forwarded the enclosed note to Mr. William A. Heins. I understand from him that it is Recordak Model D which they are purchasing for you.

With regard to your further request for money for the purchase of film and the creation of a revolving fund, I can only reply that it does not seem practicable to us to secure such an additional appropriation.

You are to be congratulated on the progress you report in the establishment of an offset printing plant in collaboration with the National University.

Sincerely yours,

Charles B. Fahs

〔Rockefeller Foundation. Series 601: China; Subseries 601.R: China-Humanities and Arts. Vol. Box 47. Folder 393〕

按:此件为录副。

四月十日

上午,台湾省教育参观团赴平馆参观,先生设午宴款待。〔《华北日报》,1948年4月2日,第5版〕

按:本月5日,该团由上海飞平,在北平观摩一周。10日,上午先赴第一民众教育馆参观。

王世杰致函先生,告知驻德军事代表团已协助闵乃大启运书籍。

守和吾兄惠鉴:

上月二日曾复一缄,谅达。关于贵馆存德图书十四箱,嘱为协助闵乃大君携回事,兹已接据柏林驻德军事代表团本月九日复电,略称已遵往协助闵君起运等语。用特转达,敬希察洽为荷。耑布,祗颂时祺。

弟王世杰敬启

四月十日

〔外交部用笺。国家图书馆档案,档案编号1945-※057-综合5-008005至1945-※057-综合5-008007〕

按:此件为打字稿,落款处钤王世杰印。

四月十三日

先生致信美国图书馆协会米来牟,推荐给予在芝加哥大学学习的钱存训奖学金,此函摘录如下:

……

It is extremely kind of you to ask us to submit names of students interested in studying special library methods in the United States. It happens that one of my colleagues, Mr. T. H. Tsien, is now in Chicago and is interested in studying microphotography. If you know of any institution which has facilities for the training of specialists in microphotography, may I ask you to communicate with Mr. Tsien. His address is as follows: Mr. T. H. Tsien, Far Eastern Library, University of Chicago, Chicago, Ill. If a scholarship may be offered in the coming year,

I hope Mr. Tsien may be considered as a suitable candidate.

……

Your sincerely,

T. L. Yuan

Director

〔钱孝文藏札〕

按:此件为录副。

四月十四日

下午一时,平津国立各院校长谈话会在北平研究院召开,郑天挺、叶企孙、温广汉(师院)、杨光弼、徐佩琨(铁院)、张含英(北洋)、张长江(天津体院)、先生、金涛(唐山工学院)、黎锦熙等十余人到场,杨光弼为会议主席。讨论议案六项,涉及冬煤贷款、四联透支、调整拨发生活补助费、经费调整、毕业生就业,下次会议将于五月十二日在平馆召开。二时半,散会。〔《华北日报》,1948年4月15日,第5版〕

四月二十日

Eugene B. Power 致函先生,就购买缩微胶片设备的配件进一步提出建议。

April 20, 1948

Dear Mr. Yuan:

The list which I provided you giving the necessary equipment you will need for your laboratory was, of course, somewhat generalized in that I did not specifically state just what type of winders for example, what type of metal reels, what type of developer, etc. you should have.

My purpose in writing is to suggest that you ask the purchasing agent of the Rockefeller Foundation to communicate with us regarding some of these details, since the wrong type of equipment will not work out satisfactorily.

Sincerely yours,

University Microfilms

Eugene B. Power

〔Rockefeller Foundation. Series 601: China; Subseries 601.R: China-Humanities and Arts. Vol. Box 47. Folder 393〕

按:此件为录副,附于28日先生写给 Beal 的信内,清单不存。

四月二十七日

朱家骅覆函先生,告知前请已函李宗仁。

守和吾兄大鉴:

接诵本月二十一日手书,备聆种切。承示汉奸吴瓯所藏书籍尚未提取一节,已函李德邻先生,请其仍由平馆接收保管矣。希将接收情形与清册报部备案为幸。耑复,顺颂台祺。

弟朱家骅敬启

四月廿七日

按:27日,朱家骅另致信李宗仁,内容如下,

德邻先生勋鉴:

顷接国立北平图书馆馆长袁同礼兄本月二十一日函,谓本馆前奉令接收汉奸吴瓯等十人书籍一案,遵即分别进行。其中惟吴瓯所藏颇多佳本,近闻李德邻先生面嘱北平中央信托局□□接收,因之本馆遂无法提取,拟恳面晤李将军时代予商洽,准予先由该局接收,移交本馆保管以重公物而符功令。如私立华北学院或其他机关需用吴氏藏书时,再由钧部统筹分配,似较合理等语。辄函奉商,敬希□赐主持,仍由该馆接收保管,曷胜企感。耑此,顺颂勋祺。

弟朱家骅敬启

四月廿七日

〔台北“中央研究院”近代史研究所档案馆,〈朱家骅〉,馆藏号301-01-09-054〕

四月二十八日

先生致信 George J. Beal,请其与 Eugene B. Power 联系。

28th April, 1948

Dear Mr. Beal:

With further reference to my letter of 24th February, I beg to enclose herewith copy of a letter of Mr. Eugene B. Power, just received. In this letter you will note that Mr. Power stated that he did not specifically state just what type of equipment we should have. If it is not too late, will you communicate with him regarding some of these details.

With many thanks,

Your truly

T. L. Yuan

Director

〔国立北平图书馆英文信纸。Rockefeller Foundation. Series 601: China; Subseries 601.R: China-Humanities and Arts. Vol. Box 47. Folder 393〕

按:此件为打字稿,落款处为先生签名。

四月

先生向北平历史博物馆捐赠近年来个人收集的汉代瓦鼎、瓦罐,唐代石磨、瓦牛、瓦俑三十三件。〔《民国日报》(天津),1948 年 5 月 1 日,第 3 版〕

五月一日

晚,先生设宴款待翁文灏,并邀资源委员会同仁作陪。〔《大公报》(天津),1948 年 5 月 2 日,第 3 版〕

按:本日上午,翁文灏赴石景山视察炼铁、炼焦各厂及电厂发电情形。下午回城后,傅作义前来拜访,畅谈良久。

五月二日

上午十一时,清华大学举行校友返校节,先生、杨光弼等三百余人到场参加。〔《民国日报》(天津),1948 年 5 月 3 日,第 3 版〕

五月五日

上午,东北文物迁运保管委员会假国史馆北平办事处开会,马衡、先生、毛准、杨振声、于省吾、阎文儒与会,会后金毓黻在鹿鸣春招宴。〔《静晤室日记》第 9 册,页 6589〕

按:于省吾(1896—1984),字思泊,辽宁海城人,古文字学家,1919 年毕业于沈阳高等师范学院,先后执教于辅仁大学、北京大学、燕京大学,时应任故宫博物院专门委员。国史馆北平办事处位于东四牌楼二条五号,时金毓黻兼任该馆北平办事处主任。[1]

① 《静晤室日记》第 8 册,页 6418-6419。

五月六日

洛克菲勒基金会致函先生，告知因生产商问题需更换一种配件。

May 6, 1948

Dear Dr. Yuan:

This is in reference to our purchase order No. 421913 dated March 3, 1948 which covers some of the items requested in your letter of January 21st. Will you kindly cancel the G Filter Series III included on this order as we have just been advised that Recordak Corporation is unable to supply this item. We are issuing our order No. 422970 to Dowling's Inc. as a replacement of this cancellation.

Sincerely yours,

〔Rockefeller Foundation. Series 601: China; Subseries 601.R: China-Humanities and Arts. Vol. Box 47. Folder 393〕

按：此件为底稿。

五月十一日

胡适邀请先生、张政烺、王重民、赵万里一同审阅由其自南京带来的赵一清、厉鄂《菽乳诗》照片，比对天津本全祖望五校《水经注》的底本。〔《胡适日记全集》第8册，页358〕

五月十三日

先生撰证明书一件，事由为《证明范腾端历年所任职务》。〔台北"国史馆"，〈社会教育计划案(二)〉，数字典藏号014-050000-0050〕

按：4月25日，馆员范腾端因病去世。此件为先生向教育部申请抚恤金，为文书代笔，盖平馆关防印。

五月十五日

先生致信朱家骅，询问申请接收汉奸吴瓯旧藏书籍的进展。

骝先部长钧鉴：

敬陈者，敝馆奉令接收汉奸吴瓯等十人书籍，其中吴瓯所藏尚未经提取。曾将详情函达钧座，嗣奉四月二十七日赐书，藉悉已承函恳李德邻先生，请其仍由本馆接收保管，仰维盛意，钦感莫名。未识李先生现有复函否？如有覆函，请饬抄录寄下，以便再向北平中央信托局催其移交，俾资结束，是所祷盼。专此，敬颂钧安。

职袁同礼谨上

五月十五日

〔国立北平图书馆用笺。台北"中央研究院"近代史研究所档案馆,〈朱家骅〉,馆藏号 301-01-09-054,页 85-86〕

按:该信为文书代笔,落款处钤先生名章。

五月中旬

先生向母校哥伦比亚大学捐款。〔《申报》,1948 年 5 月 22 日,第 6 版〕

按:原为法币八百万元,如按官价计算,约为 25 美金。

五月十六日

下午三时,平馆在北海静心斋举办中日战事史料征辑会展览预展,内容分抗战资料、敌伪资料、战时期刊及剪报、战时日报、敌伪期刊、敌伪日报等,展品共计一万五千余件。在茶话会上,先生向记者介绍中日战事史料征辑会的历史、展品重要性和价值,并借此呼吁社会各界积极捐赠相关文物。六时,预展结束。〔《西京日报》,1948 年 5 月 18 日,第 2 版;《大公报》(天津),1948 年 5 月 17 日,第 3 版〕

按:后张全新撰写《中日战事史料会参观记》,分征辑缘起、展品一瞥、余语三部分,刊《大公报·图书周刊》第 52 期。

五月十九日

朱家骅致函先生,告知李宗仁已同意平馆接收、保管吴瓯旧藏书籍。

守和吾兄大鉴:

关于汉奸吴瓯等藏书由平馆接收保管一案,前承台嘱,即经致函李德邻先生关说。顷接复允照办并电饬中央信托局遵照等语,知注转达。顺颂时祺。

弟朱家〇顿首

十九

〔台北"中央研究院"近代史研究所档案馆,〈朱家骅〉,馆藏号 301-01-09-054,页 87〕

按:此件为底稿,该函应于 20 日晚发出。

五月二十二日

平馆与德源营造厂订立合同,营建新闻阅览室七间,先生作为甲方代表签字画押。〔台北"国史馆",〈北平图书馆(敌伪图书盗卖)(一)〉,数位典藏号 019-030402-0005〕

按:该合同造价二十一亿元正,此件为油印,呈教育部备案。

先生致信钱存训，告知已收到两笔美金并言将与法斯晤谈。

存训吾兄：

五月五日所寄之80元及五月八日所寄之70元均先后收到，惟五月三日左右所寄之100元迄今未到，颇为焦急，似可向邮局一询，追其下落，并盼示复为荷。Fahs现在北平，惟因身体不适，尚未得晤。晤时当将内情说明，请其协助，惟此人素有帮助日本之名，对我国文化事业毫不热心，加以国内内战关系，更不易引起他之同情也。顺颂大安。

同礼顿首

五，廿二

〔钱孝文藏札〕

五月二十三日

晚六时许，先生给法斯打电话，对洛克菲勒基金会赞助平馆购买缩微胶卷设备表示感谢，并告知平馆此前存在北海静心斋的俄文文献已移入馆舍，用以为更多读者服务，其中俄国外交大臣穆拉维约夫的文献资料正在翻译。〔Charles B. Fahs' Diary, Rockefeller Archive Center, Rockefeller Foundation records, Officers' Diaries, RG 12〕

按：5月18日，法斯乘飞机从上海抵达北平，宿六国饭店。平馆为翻译、出版稀见俄文史料，曾与哥伦比亚大学俄国研究中心Geroid T. Robinson（1892-1971）教授联系。

五月二十五日

先生致信William A. Heins，请尽快协助将缩微胶卷设备发送北平。

25th May, 1948

Mr. William A. Heins

Dear Sir:

As we are very anxious to set up our photoduplication laboratory, may we request you again to see to it that the microfile cameras and other equipment be shipped to us as soon as you could arrange it.

You may have heard of the proposal of a special committee of the American Historical Association to cooperate with this Library for the microfilming of rare Chinese items. We are therefore most eager to receive the equipments from your Foundation at an early date, so that we shall be able to set up the laboratory as soon as the American technician arrives. Kindly check up whether you have ordered the various equipments per a list submitted by Mr. Eugene Power, which was enclosed in my letter to Mr. George J. Beal, under the date of 24th February.

Hoping to hear from you soon.

Yours truly

T. L. Yuan

〔国立北平图书馆英文信纸。Rockefeller Foundation. Series 601: China; Subseries 601.R: China-Humanities and Arts. Vol. Box 47. Folder 393〕

按:此件为打字稿,落款处为先生签名,于6月11日前送达。

五月二十八日

先生致信钱存训,告知收到所寄美金一百元并请转寄信件。

存训吾兄:

一日所寄之函,内附美钞壹百元,今日始行寄到,用特航函奉达,即希释念为荷。附上数信并希代为转寄。顺颂大安。

同礼顿首

五,廿八

〔国立北平图书馆便笺。钱孝文藏札〕

是年春夏

先生出任北平市立图书馆学讲习班赞助人。〔《北平市立图书馆学讲习班同学录》,1948年〕

按:本年春,该讲习班经北平市教育局核准立案,至六月第一班毕业,共有学员四十七名,大都为北平地区各公共图书馆的职员。

六月初

联合国教科文组织印度籍代表奥勃莱由教育部专员阮康成陪同,访问北平,分别拜访胡适、梅贻琦、李书华、先生。〔《申报》,1948年6月1日,第6版〕

六月六日

中国博物馆协会举行复会第一次筹备会议，先生、韩寿萱、陈梦家、李濂镗、金毓黻、Matthias Eder 等人出席。首由先生开会词，并提议从速办理复会事宜，其他与会人员均有所发言。另，选举执行委员，唐兰、马衡、先生、陈梦家、韩寿萱、Matthias Eder、徐旭生、金毓黻当选。〔《马衡年谱长编》，页1022〕①

按：李濂镗（1896—?），字杏南，河北冀县人，1920 年毕业于北京大学哲学系，后入故宫博物院工作。Matthias Eder（1902-1980），奥地利圣言会神父、辅仁大学教授，中文名叶德礼，1938 年起任《华裔学志》编辑，1940 年起任人类学博物馆主任，并创办《民俗学志》(*Folklore Studies*)。

《大公报》（天津）刊登"中国博物馆协会复会纪念刊"，先生题词。〔《大公报》（天津），1948 年 6 月 6 日，第 4 版〕

按：该报登载马衡、陈梦家、韩寿萱、王重民各一篇文章。

六月九日

中午十二时，平津国立各院校长谈话会在中南海西四所国立北平研究院会议室召开，梅贻琦、李书华、郑天挺、黄国璋（师院代理教务长）、先生、申新柏（铁院秘书）、徐悲鸿、傅恩龄（南开训导长）、徐泽昆（北洋秘书）、刘砥中（天津国立体专教授）、黎锦熙、金涛（唐山工学院教授）出席。议决六项，涉及储蓄冬煤、四联透支、申请增拨外汇、新疆国大代表来平参观、公费生何时截止。下次谈话会拟于七月十四日仍在北平研究院召开。〔《华北日报》，1948 年 6 月 10 日，第 5 版〕

六月十一日

先生致信钱存训，请查阅国外出版日报期刊的简目，并安慰不要过于忧虑，安家之事必可解决。

存训吾兄：

日前托转信数件，匆匆未及附信。兹有十余封并请代为发出，共需邮费若干，亦盼见告，以便奉还。本馆刻正调查国外出版之日报及期刊，兹奉上一简目，并盼补充后示知，以便征求。移民局既久无覆

① 此次会议在北平举行，马衡应未出席，特此说明。

音，或已默许，想学校方面对于尊处之报酬必能解决也。前函述及 Special Library Assin 之奖学金或仍有希望，容再函达。奉上美金支票二百元，请分两次寄下为荷。顺颂大安。

弟同礼顿首

六，十一

U. S. A.

China Tribune. 94–98 Bayard Str., New York 13, N. Y.

Chinese Nationalist Daily. 20 Elizabeth Street, New York City

Chinese Nationalist Daily. 809 Sacramento Street, San Francisco, Calif. 华侨日报

Chinese Daily News. 105 Mott Street, New York City

Chinese Journal. 17 E. Broadway, New York 2, N. Y.

China-American Press: *Chinese-American Daily*, also *Weekly*. 50 Bowery, New York 13, N. Y.

Chinese Times. 117–119 Waverly Place, San Francisco, Calif.

Chinese World. 736 Grant Avenue, San Francisco, Calif.

Young China. Clay Street, San Francisco, Calif.

New China Daily Press. 1124 Smith Street, Honolulu, T. H.

Canada

Chinese Times. 11–B Elizabeth Street, Toronto.

Shing Wah Daily News. 149 Queen Anne Street, Toronto.

Chinese Times. 1 East Pender Street, Vancouver, B. C.

New Republic. P. O. Drawer 548, Victoria, B. C.

Australia

Chinese Times. 75 Ultimo Road, Haymarket, Sydney.

请补充，并将补充之日报报名见示，以便征求。

〔钱孝文藏札〕

按：Special Library Assin 即 Special Library Association。钱存训在此信目录部分补充了两种报纸，分别为 *Chung Sai Yat Po*《中西日报》，716 Sacramento St., San Francisco 8, Calif. *San Min Morning Paper*《三民晨报》，2127 Archer Ave., Chicago 16, Ill.

William A. Heins 覆函先生，告知代平馆订购缩微胶片设备的订单近况。

June 11, 1948

Dear Dr. Yuan:

Your letter of May 25th has been received regarding the microfile camera and equipment. We are enclosing invoices covering our purchase order No. 421913 for the Model D Camera, Model C Reader and Model A Enlarger, and two transformers. The final portion of this equipment had only been received by us a week ago, and will be forwarded to you within the week or ten days. We trust with these invoices you will be in a position to arrange for the import permit.

In reference to the above, we have just received a letter from the Eastman Kodak Company quoting a letter which they had received from you regarding this equipment. Inasmuch as our purchase order was issued to the Recordak Company, a subsidiary of Eastman Kodak Company, they of course were unfamiliar with the transaction. We are writing them today advising that the shipment is being forwarded to you without delay.

In reference to the balance of the material suggested by Mr. Power, this has finally been straightened out, and within the next day or two our purchase order will be issued to cover the materials in question, the major portion of which should go forward to you within a very short time.

Sincerely yours,

William A. Heins

〔Rockefeller Foundation. Series 601: China; Subseries 601.R: China-Humanities and Arts. Vol. Box 47. Folder 393〕

按：此件为录副。

六月二十三日

先生致信钱存训，告知本年洛克菲勒基金会无法赞助其在美留学并请转寄信件。

存训兄：

六月十六日航函收到，敬谢敬谢。Fahs 在平谓本年度名额已满，故须候 1949 年方能考虑，故盼芝校能维持至今冬，想不成问题。惟移民局办事太慢，不知内幕如何，念念。兹附信七件，即希分别转寄为感。顺颂大安。

弟同礼顿首

六，廿三

今日美钞行市每元合国币三百一十万元。

〔钱孝文藏札〕

按：此信中所言“附信”似因疏忽并未附上。

六月二十五日

下午，平馆举行“美国印刷展览”，司徒雷登受邀出席并主持，先生负责接待。〔《传记文学》第94卷第3期，页118〕

六月二十八日

Leonard A. Manuel 致函先生，告知寄送仪器清单和投保等细节。

June 28, 1948

Dear Doctor Yuan:

The enclosed shipping documents as listed cover six cases containing Recordak Apparatus, complete with accessories, consigned to the National Library of Peiping, being forwarded on the S. S. SELMA SALEN, which sailed from New York on June 21, 1948.

A. One original and one non-negotiable copy of Salen-Skaugen Line Bill of Lading No. 130.

B. Chinese Consular Invoice No. 29214, dated June 16, 1948.

C. A copy of our letter to the Chinese Maritime Customs, dated June 28, 1948.

D. The Rockefeller Foundation Packing List and Commercial Invoice, in duplicate, dated June 26, 1948.

E. Duplicate blue copy of order No. 421913.

This shipment has been fully insured against all risks, and in case of loss or damage, kindly communicate with the office. Immediately upon receipt of this material, please sign and return the original copy of the order to this office.

Sincerely yours,

Leonard A. Manuel

〔Rockefeller Foundation. Series 601: China; Subseries 601.R: China-Humanities and Arts. Vol. Box 47. Folder 393〕

按:此件为录副。

是年夏

北平市政府聘先生、韩云峰、韩振华、傅正舜、黎锦熙、张寿龄、王鸿恩、李书华、杨振声、梁思成等二十余人为中南海公园管理委员会委员。〔《华北日报》,1948 年 8 月 15 日,第 4 版〕

按:该委员会议决 8 月 15 日中南海公园开放,但须付费参观。

先生致信美国图书馆协会东方和西南太平洋委员会主席布朗,告知中文资料联合采购计划正式停止。〔《裘开明年谱》,页 307〕

七月一日

晚五时,先生至欧美同学会开会,金毓黻、于省吾、吴千里等七八人到场,并进晚餐。〔《静晤室日记》第 9 册,页 6635〕

按:吴千里,或应为英千里。该会似为东北文物迁运保管委员会会议。

七月三日

先生致信美国图书馆协会国际关系委员会,请考虑给予钱存训奖学金。

July 3, 1948

Dear Madam:

Since receiving your letter of April 27, we have been hoping to hear further from you in regard to a scholarship which your Association plans to offer to a foreign librarian for study of special libraries technique in the United States. We trust your new board has had a chance to discuss this matter at your Conference in June.

You will recall that I recommended Mr. T. H. Tsien as a suitable candidate for such a scholarship. If you have made a decision, may I suggest that you communicate with Mr. Tsien, c/o Far Eastern Library, University of Chicago, Chicago, Ill.

Your truly,

T. L. Yuan

〔钱孝文藏札〕

按:此件为打字稿,落款处为先生签名。该信应寄予钱存训,由其酌情发出。

先生致信史密斯森协会,请寄送1937年以来国际交换服务年报,并请告知已发送的美国政府文件所在邮轮的详细信息。

3rd July, 1948

Dear Sirs:

We shall be much obliged to you if you will kindly send us the available Annual Reports of your Service since 1937. We should like to have a complete file of your reports for our reference.

In order to facilitate checking, will you kindly send us advance notice of each shipment for US Government documents which your Service has been sending to us. We need this information in order to arrange delivery of these cases from Shanghai.

Yours truly

T. L. Yuan

Director

〔国立北平图书馆英文信纸。Smithsonian Institution Archives, Records, 1868–1988 (Record Unit 509), Box 1, National Library, Peiping〕

按:此件为打字稿,先生略作修改,落款处为其签名,于7月19日送达。

七月八日

先生致信钱存训,告知顾立雅已与美移民局达成谅解并同意延长其在美服务期限,此外请其逐批寄送美金。

存训吾兄:

昨接Creel先生来函,内称移民局复函已到,允吾兄在美可延长一年,并谓如今后特别交涉,可为吾兄获到Special Status,但希望服务期限延至五年云云。弟顷复Creel先生,原则同意并谓先定三年之期,期满再延长,当无困难,即希阅后转交。兹奉上支票美金三百元,系弟个人的,请分三次用航邮挂号封口处要严密,信封上写中国字寄至舍下为荷(北平东城金鱼胡同一号旁门袁宅)。匆匆,顺颂旅安。

弟同礼顿首

七，八日

〔钱孝文藏札〕

七月十四日

下午一时，国立平津各院校长谈话会假北平研究院举行，李书华、先生、杨光弼、黎锦熙等十五人参加。会中，首先交换对“七五”事件的态度，决定请胡适邀请地方当局人员商谈办法，再行决议。此后议决四项，分别为（一）学生公费已无法再行垫付，请教育部立刻拨付三个月经费，以资周转；（二）员生配面，请教育部按时发放；（三）催请教育部请行政院拨付冬季煤款；（四）各院校讲师助教提案中不奉准者，再请教育部转呈行政院办理。〔《民国日报》（天津），1948 年 7 月 15 日，第 3 版〕

按：“七五”事件即本年 7 月 5 日，中国东北籍学生游行队伍遭中国青年军枪击的事件。

七月十八日

中南海公园管理委员会召开第一次会议，决定成立设计组，推选先生、黎锦熙、张鹤龄、韩云峰、刘一峰、刘千里、崔云青、王鸿恩、王念根等任设计委员。〔《华北日报》，1948 年 8 月 15 日，第 4 版〕

按：该设计组定于每星期三下午五时开会。

七月十九日

史密斯森协会覆函先生，告知将按前请寄出国际交换服务各年度报告。

July 19, 1948

Dear Dr. Yuan:

Reference is made to your letter of July 3rd.

In compliance with your request the copies of the International Exchange Service Reports will be included in the next shipment.

The institution regrets that it is unable to comply with your request that you be provided with advance notice of each shipment. Notice of each shipment is forwarded by airmail to the Chinese Exchange Bureau at Nanking. Although the Institution would like to comply with this request such a precedent would allow the Institution no alternative than to comply with similar requests from other sources. The probable magnitude of such a task is such as to make it prohibitive.

Very truly yours,

Acting Chief

〔Smithsonian Institution Archives, Records, 1868-1988 (Record Unit 509), Box 1, National Library, Peiping〕

按:此件为录副。

七月二十日

晚,金毓黻、先生在鹿鸣春设宴,英千里、向达、赵万里、韩寿萱、齐如山等人受邀与席。〔《静晤室日记》第9册,页6646〕

七月二十六日

下午四时,中国博物院协会在故宫博物院举行理事选举,由韩寿萱、唐兰主持,采取全国会员函选方式,共选出马衡、先生、徐旭生、韩寿萱、徐森玉、向达、梁思成、李书华、李济、董作宾、唐兰、金毓黼、傅斯年、袁复礼、杭立武、裴文中、庄尚严、张庭济、黄文弼、王世襄、郑振铎等理事二十一人。〔《华北日报》,1948年7月27日,第5版〕

按:因董作宾、傅斯年、王世襄三人身在国外,另增陈梦家、常惠、叶德礼三人为理事。

七月三十日

先生致信李济、夏鼐,请史语所寄赠《殷墟文字》及集刊数册用以对公阅览,平馆馆藏《李朝实录》逾期甚久请归还。

济之、作铭仁兄大鉴:

觉明兄返平,承赐大著,至以为谢。彦堂兄近编《殷墟文字》一种,已由贵所托商务印书馆代为印行,其甲编现已出版,敝馆亟愿入藏。前函该馆,请照出版法呈缴一部,该馆函复谓系代为印行,应向贵所索取;旋函贵所,奉复又嘱径向商务索取。此外,尚有贵所出版之《集刊》自第五本起至最近所出版者,敝馆亦愿入藏。因念两兄对于敝馆夙荷关垂,拟请转托主管人员将上述两项刊物设法赐寄,俾光典藏而供参考,即希察照惠允,无任感荷。又敝馆所藏《李朝实录》,国内仅此一部,前由贵所借阅将逾十载,务请交邮挂号寄下,并妥为包装以免潮湿,不胜企盼。专此,即颂时祺。

弟袁同礼顿首

七，三十

另邮（平邮）奉上杨殿珣著《石刻题跋索引》一部，奉赠贵所，并祈查收。

〔国立北平图书馆用笺。台北“中央研究院”历史语言研究所傅斯年图书馆，“史语所档案”，杂36-67-1〕

按：《殷墟文字》即《中国考古报告集之二——小屯（第二本）：殷墟文字·甲编》，1948年4月初版。该信似为文书代笔，落款处则为先生亲笔。

七月三十一日

先生致信法斯，询问协助在美出版穆拉维耶夫信函的可能性，并请洛克菲勒基金会加快购买缩微胶片拍摄设备。

31th July, 1948

Dear Mr. Fahs:

You will recall that during your visit to Peiping last May, we submitted to you a memorandum regarding the development of our research program. Since then, we have completed a number of projects, including the translation of Muraviev's letters and correspondence which throws much light on the history of the 19th century.

As we are anxious to have this work published in the United States, and knowing your interest in Far Eastern international relations, I am taking the liberty of sending the manuscripts to you in the hope that you will be good enough to send them to a suitable publisher, or to Dr. Mortimer Graves who would also be interested in its publication.

Our Slavic collection has grown considerably since you were here. We are glad to report that we have many items which are not found in American collections. For instance, we have recently sold a number of our duplicates to the University of Washington which is particularly interested in securing our duplicate material.

As we are very anxious to set up our photoduplication laboratory, we have requested Mr. Wm. A. Heins to speed up the shipment of the microfilm equipment ordered through a grant from your Foundation. It seems to have taken a long time for the manufacturers to supply the equipments which are urgently needed here.

T. L. Yuan

Director

〔国立北平图书馆英文信纸。Rockefeller Foundation. Series 601: China; Subseries 601.R: China-Humanities and Arts. Vol. Box 47. Folder 391〕

按:此件为打字稿,落款处为先生签名。

八月一日

夏鼐覆函先生,告知史语所不便赠予书册,请向商务印书馆联络,至于《李朝实录》则须待傅斯年回所后与之洽商。

希和馆长先生赐鉴:

接奉七月卅日大札,敬悉一是。敝所之《殷虚文字》甲编确系由商务出版,敝所仅依著作人所享之权利得赠书数部及优予扣折购买若干,故依出版法应向商务索取(至于乙编,敝所已收回自行出版,仅托商务找人代印,现在印刷中)。至于《集刊》,自第五本起,亦归商务发行,敝所仅得赠书若干部而已,此项赠书皆供给赠送国内外文化机关及交换之用,惟贵馆及中央图书馆依出版法应由发行人呈缴一部,故敝所不另赠送,以免重复。至于商务复函谓系代为印行,应向敝所索取,此乃商人市侩之逃税惯例,君子可欺之以方,贵馆乃为所欺蒙,遽信以真,殊可诧异,尚乞依照出版法严格执行,向商务继续索取,此为出版法之执行问题,尚乞万勿轻易放松、自弃权利。万一其中有数种商务现下确已售罄,而敝所所得赠书尚有剩余者,则请查明开单示知以便补送,此为两全之策,未悉尊意亦以为然否?敝所傅孟真所长已由美国起程返国,八月十六日可抵上海。关于《李朝实录》一事,系傅所长经手,可否请俟傅先生返国再行办理?承惠赐《石刻题跋索引》,至以为谢。专此,敬请道安。

后学夏鼐敬上

八月一日

〔国立中央研究院历史语言研究所信纸。台北"中央研究院"历史语言研究所傅斯年图书馆,"史语所档案",杂36-67-2〕

八月六日

下午四时，中国博物馆协会假故宫博物院会议室召开复会后第一次理事会议，李书华、金毓黻、陈梦家、叶德礼、张庭济、马衡（张庭济代）、韩寿萱、先生、梁思成（陈梦家代）、黄文弼、徐旭生（黄文弼代）、向达（韩寿萱代）、唐兰等出席，其中张庭济为会议主席，杭承艮记录。除报告收支、通讯选举理事结果外，还选举了理事长等职务，结果马衡任理事长，杭立武、先生为副理事长，韩寿萱、李书华、唐兰、金毓黻、黄文弼、张庭济、陈梦家、叶德礼、曾昭燏为常务理事。〔《马衡年谱长编》，页 1028-1029〕

八月十二日

上午九时十五分，北平广播电台暑期讲学节目邀请先生做电台播音，题目为《国际文化合作概况》。〔《华北日报》，1948 年 8 月 12 日，第 5 版〕

按：8 月 9 日，北平广播电台主板的暑期讲学开始第四周，受邀演讲者依次为张效燧、马大猷、沈宝基、先生、徐尊六、郭麟阁。另，先生该演讲稿在本日《华北日报》刊登[①]，失收于《袁同礼文集》。

八月十六日

《报学杂志》刊登先生文章，题为《出版法修正草案意见书》。〔《报学杂志》试刊号，1948 年 8 月 16 日，页 9〕

按：《报学杂志》半月刊，由马星野主编，社址位于南京中山路 39 号，发行者为南京《中央日报》，创刊号于本年 9 月 1 日出版。

八月十七日

法斯致函先生，告知洛克菲勒基金会无法协助出版穆拉维约夫手稿，另为平馆所购器材已陆续寄出。

August 17, 1948

Dear Dr. Yuan:

I have received your manuscript translation of the Muraviev's letters. As there is no possibility of our assisting you directly and finding a publisher, I am forwarding the manuscript to Mr. Graves as suggested in your letter of July 31.

Mr. Heins reports that the Recordak camera was shipped on June 21.

① 《华北日报》，1948 年 8 月 13 日，第 2 版。

The balance of your order has come in slowly. Some four to five hundred dollars' worth of material will be shipped in about two weeks. The remainder has not yet been received and will have to be shipped at a later date.

Sincerely yours,

Charles B. Fahs

〔Rockefeller Foundation. Series 601: China; Subseries 601.R: China-Humanities and Arts. Vol. Box 47. Folder 391〕

九月二日

上午,金毓黻邀请胡适、马衡、先生、赵万里、于省吾、唐兰、毛准、韩寿萱等人为拟购宋版书估价,计有清内府旧藏《集韵》一至五册、《后村居士集》一册、《吕氏家塾读书记》一册,另有明版《玉台新咏》二册,总价为金元一千一百五十四元。赵万里认为其中《集韵》为精椠,值金元千余,故与会诸人均主张购入,几成定议。〔《静晤室日记》第9册,页6669〕

按:1946年,沈阳故宫博物院入藏《集韵》六至十册,如得一至五册,恰好完璧。

九月三日

Leonard A. Manuel致函先生,告知近有缩微胶卷设备从纽约寄出。

September 3, 1948

Dear Dr. Yuan:

The enclosed shipping documents as listed cover four cases of photographic supplies, being forwarded on the S. S. □□□, which sailed from New York recently.

A. One original and one non-negotiable copy of Ivaran Line Bill of Lading No. 92.

B. Chinese Consular Invoice No. 50355, dated September 2, 1948.

C. The Rockefeller Foundation Packing List and Commercial Invoice, dated August 30, 1948.

This shipment has been fully insured against all risks, and in case of loss or damage kindly communicate with this office.

Sincerely yours,

Leonard A. Manuel

〔Rockefeller Foundation. Series 601: China; Subseries 601.R: China-Humanities and Arts. Vol. Box 47. Folder 393〕

按:因此件过于模糊,部份信息无法辨识。

九月六日

先生乘飞机赴沪转京,向教育部交涉经费、各国赠书分配问题。〔《大公报》,1948年9月7日,第3版〕

九月十八日

中午十二时,先生由南京乘飞机返回北平。〔《华北日报》,1948年9月19日,第5版〕

按:某记者来访,先生略谓此次南下,向教部请款略有眉目,世界文教基金委员会亦有可能拨款补助平馆,以解当下困境。此外,全国教育会议本拟今年11月在京举行,但因筹备无措,已展期至明年2月。

九月十九日

下午三时,中国博物馆协会假故宫博物院召开复员后的首次会员大会,马衡、先生、韩寿萱等百余人出席。马衡主持并报告会务情况,唐兰报告今后工作计划。〔《华北日报》,1948年9月20日,第5版〕

下午四时,冯友兰、徐旭生、先生、张东荪等开会筹备孔子二千五百年(1950)诞辰纪念。〔《申报》,1948年9月20日,第7版〕

按:该筹备会定于10月17日假欧美同学会游艺室召开全体大会及干事会,纪念方式包括征集论文或专著、举行演讲和展览会。另外,先生曾有计划由平馆编纂孔子书目。[①]

九月二十七日

唐嗣尧致函先生,介绍高乃欣入职平馆。

守和先生道鉴:

兹有农民银行高副理乃明之弟乃欣,清华大学文学院毕业,沉潜好学,拟在图书馆中任一职务,利用余暇肆力研究学问,请吾兄鉴其向学之诚,于贵馆中酌予位置以助成其志,不胜同感。专牍奉恳,顺颂

① 《大公报》(天津),1948年9月21日,第3版;《华北日报》,1948年10月15日,第5版。

著安。

弟唐嗣尧拜启

九月廿七日

〔国家图书馆档案,档案编号 1945-※057-综合 5-011003〕

按:唐嗣尧(1902—1987),河南南阳人,政、学两界人物,时应任北平参议会副议长,国民政府立法院委员。该函于本日送达,先生即覆信一封,告因名额已满且经费无多,不能延聘。

九月二十八日

晚七时,北京大学在孑民堂设宴款待印度驻华大使 Kavalam Madhava Panikkar,除北大人员外,并邀梅贻琦、先生、马衡等人作陪,席间就中印文化交流,交换意见。九时许散。〔《华北日报》,1948 年 9 月 29 日,第 5 版〕

按:Kavalam Madhava Panikkar(1895-1963),印度学者、记者、历史学家、官员和外交官,通译作"潘尼迦"。本日晚六时,潘尼迦及夫人一行六人赴北京大学,由季羡林陪同参观校图书馆、博物馆。

九月

傅吾康至平馆,与先生晤谈。〔《为中国着迷:一位汉学家的自传》,页 173〕

按:9 月 2 日,傅吾康从重庆白市驿机场出发,途经西安、太原飞赴北平。此次来平,傅吾康将出任北京大学西语系德文教授。

十月十日

北平历史博物馆联合北平市参议会、北平市特种工艺联合会、中央合作金库北平分库、北平工业试验所、中国手工艺协进会北平分会筹备处等团体,在午门楼上该馆第一陈列室举行北平市工艺品特展,为期一周。先生、溥伒、启功等人的收藏亦参展。〔《华北日报》,1948 年 10 月 9 日,第 4 版〕

十月十三日

中午,平津国立院校长谈话会假北平师范学院举行,徐悲鸿、李麟玉、徐佩琨、李书华、张长江、杨光弼、先生、黎锦熙、郑天挺、梅贻琦、袁敦礼等人出席。袁敦礼为会议主席,首由郑天挺报告此前教育部杭立武次长之电文,谓从未停止院校教职员每月配给面粉一袋。后继续开会讨论并通过九案:(一)函教育部转呈政府,请向美政府交涉,准中国学术机关,购放射性元素。(二)物价波动,呈请教育部对员工待遇予以改善。(三)电教育部及粮食部，请照原配给各院校教职员面粉一袋，并通知平津提前办理。（四）冬煤问题请李书华、梅贻琦、袁敦礼、郑天挺往见傅作义司令，请照官价办理。（五）请教育部转中央银行，准平津各院校继续透支，以便周转。（六）电教育部转请行政院，分令平津当局设法对学生所需面、油、盐等必需品，依限价配售，或代为购买。（七）请教育部对研究生津贴加以改善。（八）请教育部对各院校经常费、建筑扩充费等再予增加。（九）下次会议，定于十一月十日假北平研究院办事处举行。〔《民国日报》（天津），1948 年 10 月 14 日，第 3 版〕

十月二十四日

晚八时，蒋介石在北平总统官邸宴请陈垣、胡适、梅贻琦、陆志韦、先生、吴景超、蒋硕杰、赵迺抟、周作仁、刘大中等人，翁文灏、陶希圣作陪。〔陶晋生编《陶希圣日记》上，台北：联经出版事业公司，2014 年，页 177〕

> 按：本日上午，蒋介石、陶希圣等乘军用飞机由南京飞抵北平，六时半降落南屯机场。蒋硕杰（1918—1993），祖籍湖北应城，生于上海，蒋作宾之子，早年赴日、英留学，时应任北京大学经济系教授。赵迺抟（1897—1980），字廉澄，浙江杭州人，1922 年北京大学法科经济门毕业，后赴美留学，获哥伦比亚大学博士学位，归国后长期执教于北京大学经济系。周作仁，字濯生，江苏淮安人，时任北京大学经济系教授。刘大中（1914—1974），祖籍江苏武进，生于北京，交通大学唐山工学院土木工程系毕业，后赴美留学，获康乃尔大学经济学博士学位，时应在清华大学经济系执教。“梅玉涵”当作梅月涵。

十月二十九日

平馆向教育部呈文一件，题为《呈送本馆三十八年度扩充改良费概算书由》，具先生名并钤馆印。

> 窃查本馆明年度应行举办事项以限于经费自当力求紧缩，惟关于购书修缮装订种种费用，均属必不可少者，自应在扩充改良费内列支，复查本馆经常费数额有限，本已不敷应用，胥赖扩充改良费之增拨以资挹注，俾便业务之推行。兹按实际需要情形将三十八年度扩充改良费概算书目拟定为金圆十万元，内中所列均系最低数目且均按目前之购买力计算。敬请鉴核准予照数列入概算案内，俾资支用，将来万一

物价再行波动，仍请准予另具追加概算以便事情。理合造具扩改费概算书七份，备文呈送。伏乞批示遵行，实为公便。谨呈

教育部

即呈送概算书七份。

国立北平图书馆馆长袁同礼（国立北平图书馆印）

三十七年十月二十九日

修缮费一万

购置费二万

购书费三万五（中文一万五、西文二万）

装订费一万五

出版费一万

转运费一万

共计十万

〔中国第二历史档案馆，教育部档案·全卷宗五，国立北平图书馆京沪区及昆明办事处工作报告暨庶务方面的文书，案卷号11609〕

十月三十日

先生致信史蒂文斯，申请洛克菲勒基金会资助个人在美从事研究。

October 30, 1948

Dear Dr. Stevens:

I wish to thank you once more for the grant of $5000 from your Foundation in connection with the completion of our photoduplication laboratory. All equipments have safely arrived and we are waiting for the arrival of an American specialist to assist us in its installation.

Since Dr. Fahs travels so much, I am not sure whether he is in New York just now. I am therefore taking the liberty of writing to you regarding a personal request of mine.

After working strenuously over twenty years, I shall have my sabbatical leave beginning from January, 1949. I hope very much that it would be possible for me to spend it in the United States. Before the War I was engaged in writing a book on Bibliographical Aids to Far Eastern

Studies which, if completed, would be a valuable contribution. But this work was seriously interrupted due to my wartime and postwar services to the Government. I now wish to take advantage of my sabbatical leave to complete this work by consulting the excellent collections of the Library of Congress and other American libraries.

The U. S. Educational Foundation in China has assured me that it would consider to pay my travel expenses between Shanghai and San Francisco, if I could get adequate means of support from other sources while in the United States. As the Foundation has no foreign exchange, it could not meet travel costs in the United States.

Since the Rockefeller Foundation is interested in the promotion of Far Eastern studies, I hope my project may have your support. I would therefore like to apply for a grant in aid for a year to enable me to complete this work. If your Foundation would consider the application favorably, I shall appreciate a cable which would facilitate the securing of my passport and the accommodation on heavily crowded steamers.

Yours sincerely,

Tung-Li Yuan

P. S. Please convey my kindest regards to Dr. Fahs.

〔国立北平图书馆英文信纸。Rockefeller Foundation. Series 601: China; Subseries 601.R: China-Humanities and Arts. Vol. Box 47. Folder 393〕

按:此件为打字稿,先生略作修改,落款处为其签名,于 11 月 8 日送达纽约。

十月三十一日

下午三时,图书馆协会假故宫博物院寿安宫博物院图书馆举行第九次常会,毛准等五十余人出席,先生作为会议主席,报告南京中华图书馆协会要求在平会员对于明春第四次全国教育会议提案委员所提教育问题第十八条"社会教育之制度经费方法等问题,应如何分别解决以谋改进"提出书面意见,以便转呈。后由故宫图书馆主任张允亮讲该馆善本书之特点,至五时半散会。〔《华北日报》,1948 年 11 月 1 日,第 5 版〕

十一月三日

行政院副秘书长浦薛凤覆函先生，谈出版法草案修正条款事。

守和吾兄馆长大鉴：

日前顾斗南先生来院，得读惠书。扩建费系归教部分配，已告顾君径洽。至出版法修正草案第十六条及十九条，院会已改为"分送国立中央图书馆与国立北平图书馆"，送立法院矣。专复，顺颂大祺。

弟浦薛凤复启

十一，三

〔行政院信纸。国家图书馆档案，档案编号 1945-※057-综合 5-022004〕

按：《出版法修正草案》内容可参见先生所写《出版法修正草案意见书》。

十一月四日

平馆向教育部呈文一件，题为《送已故编辑李耀南遗族声请抚恤事实表请予以抚恤》，具先生名并钤印。

案查本馆编辑李耀南于十月十六日患膀胱生毒症，不治身故。兹据该员遗族遵照教职员抚恤条例请求给恤前来。伏查该员在馆自十七年八月起在国民政府统治下任职，实则自民国七年五月即行到馆任事，至今已三十年有奇。该员在职期内，每以馆事为念，劳瘁不辞，抗战时期经派该员押运善本图书到沪，悉心维护，毫无损伤，是其功在国家，厥绩甚懋。此次因病出缺，拟请特予优恤，用酬劳异。当经取据该遗族声请抚恤事实表，连同证件备文呈送，伏乞鉴核施行，实为公便。谨呈

教育部

附事实表三纸，证件一件。

国立北平图书馆馆长袁同礼

中华民国三十七年十一月四日

〔台北"国家发展委员会档案管理局"，〈抚恤总卷机关团体员工案〉，档号 A309000000E/0038/881.06/0001〕

按：1949 年 1 月 8 日，教育部指令平馆，表示虽然符合抚恤原则，但所援引条款有误，请改正后再报。此文全部为文书代笔，落款

处钤“国立北平图书馆馆长”章及关防印。

十一月九日

下午三时，故宫博物院在会议室召开复员后第五次院务会议，马衡、先生、赵儒珍、朱家濂、关植耘、黄鹏霄、王孝缙、常惠、励乃骥、朱家溍、曾广龄、李益华、李仁俊、张德泽、单士魁、唐桢（许协澄代）、刘鸿逵等参加，杭承艮记录。报告、讨论议案甚多。其中，先生提议华北形势紧迫，可否密呈行政院拨紧急措施费存平备用。议决：原则通过，至必要时办理。〔《马衡年谱长编》，页 1053-1056〕

十一月十日

中午十二时，平津国立院校长在中南海北平研究院召开谈话会，胡适、郑天挺、梅贻琦、袁敦礼、张含英、张鸿渐（北洋）、何廉、黄钰生（南开）、李书华、杨光弼、先生、吴作人（艺专）、李麟玉、耿承（唐山工学院）、张长江（天津体院）、黎锦熙等人出席，张含英为会议主席，杨光弼记录。首由主席报告东北大学来函，谓东北各大学院校均愿参加平津院校长谈话会，经全体表决欢迎参加。随后讨论生活类议案九项，如公教人员薪俸亟需调整，增加各校经常、临时各费等。对于迁校问题，各位均认为无考虑必要。〔《华北日报》，1948 年 11 月 11 日，第 5 版〕

十一月十二日

法斯致电先生，告洛克菲勒基金会无法资助先生赴美。

> CANNOT BRING YOU TO U. S. FOR PURPOSE STATED YOUR LETTER.

〔Rockefeller Foundation. Series 601: China; Subseries 601.R: China-Humanities and Arts. Vol. Box 47. Folder 393〕

十一月十八日

先生致信恒慕义，告知北平近况并恳请国会图书馆（东方部）发来访美邀请函。

November 18th, 1948

Dear Dr. Hummel:

Since writing to you last, much has happened in China. With the fall of Jehol and Paoting, a number of American and British nationals have evacuated. Dr. Kennedy and Dr. Rudolph left on Monday, but Dr. Derk

Bodde and his family have decided to remain in Peiping.

Peiping is as calm as ever in spite of these evacuations. Commodity prices have even come down. Both the Government and the people have much confidence in General Fu Tso-yi.

All universities and cultural institutions in Peiping will remain here as there are no transportation facilities for large scale evacuation. But if there is any change of government within the city, the creditable work carried on by various institutions here will again be interrupted.

We have made no plans for the evacuation of our valuable material. All I can report is "business as usual". We have recently taken over the Library and Archive of the former Japanese Embassy in Peiping and I am glad to say that they contain a great deal of valuable material indispensable for research. It would have been dispersed if I had not tried to save it.

From next January I shall have sabbatical leave after the completion of twenty-five years' service. It was my original intention to remain in Peiping in order to continue my researches which were seriously interrupted by the war. But in view of the present situation in North China, I should prefer to spend my sabbatical year in the United States.

Owing to the strict control over foreign exchange, it is difficult for Chinese scholars to obtain passports unless they are invited to visit the States by an educational institution. Since I expect to do my research at the Library of Congress, I wonder whether you could send me a cable which will serve as a cable of appointment and which will state that the Division of Orientalia would be responsible for my expenses while I am in the States. Such a cable would be especially helpful in view of the currency restrictions in China.

If I could come, I shall bring over my family and the trip will be at own expense. So, you may rest assured that you are under no financial obligation whatever.

The U. S. Educational Foundation in China has assured me that they would consider to award me travel grants if I am invited "to visit and associate" myself with the Library of Congress. I have therefore given your name as one of the references in that regard.

With many thanks for your assistance and with kindest regards,

Your sincerely,

Tung-Li Yuan

〔袁同礼家人提供〕

按:Dr. Kennedy 即 George A. Kennedy(1901-1960),美国汉学家,中文名金守拙,1948 年应北京大学之邀担任客座教授。Dr. Rudolph 应指 Richard C. Rudolph(1909-2003),加州大学洛杉矶分校东方语言系创始人,后一直在该校任教。此信附在致吴光清信中,并于本月底前送达恒慕义处。该件应为录副。

翁文灏覆函先生,告平馆上海办事处房产问题已解决,请馆方缴现款购买。

守和吾兄大鉴:

前奉九月二十四日大札,经查案内陈群逆产房屋业已判决没收,确定如无产权纠纷,准依现行加速出售敌伪房地产办法之规定,交贵馆缴现承购。除由院分别行知教育部及苏浙皖区敌伪产业清理处外,特此布复,并颂文祺。

弟翁文灏(印)拜启

十一月廿三日

〔中国第二历史档案馆,教育部档案·全卷宗五,国立北平图书馆京沪区及昆明办事处工作报告暨庶务方面的文书,案卷号11609〕

十一月二十四日

先生致信 C. G. Copley,告知收到首批缩微胶片机的配件,其中大部分完好无损,但因为阅读机的投影灯寿命不长,请求购买六件备用并以空运的方式寄送。

Nov. 24, 1948

Mr. C. G. Copley
The Rockefeller Foundation
1320 Peking Road W., Room 123
Shanghai

Dear Mr. Copley:

We duly received the first shipment of 6 cases of Microfilm camera and related material on the Foundation's grant RF 47141, Humanities, order 421913.

The contents of the cases have been carefully checked. They are in apparent good condition, with the exception of the lamp hood of the enlarger. In this case, the mouth of the metallic hood is now elliptical, through having been knocked about during shipment, but I believe it will not be difficult to repair this locally.

Signed copies of order 421913 and related invoice of June 25, 1948, are enclosed.

We have set up the Microfilm Reader. Since the projection lamp burns out rather easily and there is only one to spare, may I request the Rockefeller Foundation to supply us, on grant RF 47141, six more such 100v 200w projection lamp. They are not available at the electricians here. In view of their relative lightness and the present shipping conditions, I hope that they can be sent by air mail.

With many thanks in advance,

Yours sincerely,

T. L. Yuan

Director

P. S. We are in need of the Foundation's report for 1947. Kindly supply if available.

〔国立北平图书馆英文信纸。Rockefeller Foundation. Series 601: China; Subseries 601.R: China-Humanities and Arts. Vol. Box 47. Folder 393〕

按:此件为打字稿,落款处为先生签名,于 11 月 29 日送达。

十一月二十六日

先生致信平馆南京办事处,请将暂存私立金陵大学之内阁大库舆图各箱编制目录,并估算移运费用。

查存在金陵大学内之内阁大库舆图十余箱,亟须移运安全地点,以防万一。兹已函商北平故宫博物院，将是项地图移存该院南京保存库内，谅荷许可。兹请台端先将详细目录开一清单，以便报部。原箱似应放置潮脑，以策安全。运费若干并盼估计，速为函复，以便筹措是荷。专此，顺候台祺。

弟袁同礼顿首

十一，廿六

〔《北京图书馆馆史资料汇编(1909-1949)》，页 914-915〕

按：此为抄件，未写上款，但据文意可知应寄予平馆南京办事处（顾斗南）。

十一月下旬

教育部督学黄曾樾与北平各国立院校负责谈话，商讨南迁的可能性，胡适、梅贻琦、先生、袁敦礼、李书华、徐悲鸿等前往聚谈，其结论即绝不南迁。〔《申报》，1948 年 11 月 28 日，第 2 版〕

按：黄曾樾（1898—1966），字荫亭，福建永安人，1920 年赴法留学，归国后在交通部、教育部等处任职。

十一月二十七日

下午，先生访金毓黻。〔《静晤室日记》第 9 册，页 6732〕

十一月二十九日

平馆向教育部呈文一件，具先生名并钤印。

案奉钧部本年十一月四日总字第六〇三八六号训令以奉行政院令规定各机关使用敌伪房屋，奉准让售原使用机关者，其应缴使用费之截止期限以行政院核定转账之日为准，转行遵照等因。查上海宝庆路第十七号房屋系汉奸陈群之逆产，胜利后由钧部京沪区特派员拨归本馆使用，以储藏存沪善本书籍。本馆于本年三月十一日呈请钧部照政府机关接收运用敌伪产业处理办法转呈行政院核准拨充本馆使用，嗣奉发追加概算处理办法，内有接收敌伪物资转账之规定。本馆复依据上项规定于本年九月间呈请核转，并于十月间填送各机关部队住用敌伪房屋清册。案内将宝庆路房屋分别填明，请钧部转呈行政院准予办理转账手续各在案。此次奉令，细读文义，自以行政院核定转账为产权确定之标准，上项房屋本馆既经迭次呈请，谅蒙核转，惟迄未奉复，盼切殊深，谨再具文申请，敬乞鉴核，转呈行政院迅赐转账拨交本

馆以资使用，实为公便。谨呈

教育部

国立北平图书馆馆长袁同礼(印)

中华民国三十七年十一月二十九日

〔中国第二历史档案馆，教育部档案·全卷宗五，国立北平图书馆京沪区及昆明办事处工作报告暨庶务方面的文书，案卷号11609〕

先生致信朱家骅，请教部拟定购买平馆驻沪办事处房产的具体办法。

骝先部长钧鉴：

敬陈者，查上海宝庆路十七号民房原系陈群逆产，计楼二层，上下各三间外，有车房及厢房，于三十四年十月由钧部京沪区特派员接收，移交职馆作为庋藏存沪善本书籍之用，节经呈明有案。至三十六年九月因有标卖逆产之讯，当即呈请钧部转呈行政院将该项房产拨交职馆。嗣奉钧部总字第五八八七三号指令，准由部拨款交馆标购等因。遵即与苏浙皖区敌伪产业清理处接洽估价，据云须先得行政院核准后，方可照办。当即呈请钧部依照奉须转帐之规定，恳请转呈行政院予以转帐，旋又在限价期内函请翁院长对于此案提前办理，迄今两月，始奉翁院长十一月二十三日函示，准由职馆缴现承购并以公文分行各方知照。窃念该处房屋现存职馆善本书籍三百余箱，值此时局一时无法迁移，此次承准购留至为感幸。附抄翁院长函，即请察阅，此事或由钧部拨款交馆承购，或由钧部购买交馆使用，拟请迅赐核定以便早日办妥。特函奉陈，敬候钧裁，无任盼祷。专肃，顺颂勋祺，并候赐覆。

职袁同礼(印)谨上

十一月二十九日

〔中国第二历史档案馆，教育部档案·全卷宗五，国立北平图书馆京沪区及昆明办事处工作报告暨庶务方面的文书，案卷号11609〕

按：此件为文书代笔。

十一月三十日

先生致信平馆南京办事处，请该处联系故宫博物院南京保存库商洽移送内阁大库舆图及善本，并估算移运费用。

查本馆在京所存善本、地图十余箱,拟移存故宫博物院首都保存库一节,承北平故宫博物院复函许可,兹致该院南京分院函暨原函各一件,即请速往商洽移运为荷。所须移运费用,请估计需用若干,自当照汇。专此,顺候台祺。

弟袁同礼顿首

十一,三十

又接上海办事处来函,谓本馆之舆图有送台湾之议,请先送至故宫保存库,以便由故宫代运也。

〔《北京图书馆馆史资料汇编(1909-1949)》,页 915〕

按:"谓本馆之舆图有送台湾之议"似指 29 日爨汝僖、李芳馥、王育伊三人合撰之函。[①] 此为抄件,未写上款,但据文意可知应发予平馆南京办事处(顾斗南)。

吴光清覆函先生,告知恒慕义将竭尽全力协助先生及家人赴美,但国会图书馆就发出邀请函(电报)一事十分慎重,现正在评估其合法性和可能的渠道。

Nov. 30, 1948

Dear Mr. Yuan,

I have your letters of Nov. 18 and 22 which arrived together yesterday. I handed your enclosure to Dr. Hummel and he started to make inquiries immediately. Then I had a conference with him about his findings. He said the matter is not as simple as it sounds on paper, but he emphasized that he is very willing to help out and will work very hard on it. After consultation with the authorities-presumably Evans and Clapp-he found out that the main difficulty is the legal complication involved. When a U. S. government agency like the L. C. says that it will pay a certain amount for a certain purpose it is under law to do so-there is no way of getting around it. Because of this they are also thinking of an actual consultantship with a nominal remuneration. Or if this plan does not work out, they thought of several alternate plans including the Fulbright

① 《北京图书馆馆史资料汇编(1909-1949)》,页 913-914。

Plan. Dr. Hummel has in mind the American Library Association. As it is a private organization, may be arrangements like what you suggested might work out whereas in the case of L. C. it cannot be done without violating government regulations. In any case Dr. Hummel said that he will do his very best to see what can be done. He said that in view of your very pleasant association with him and the L. C. for over 20 years, he and the authorities here are glad to do what they can to help. But whoever that issued the cable for the invitation will be held legally responsible if anything should arise in the future. Because of this they have to look into all angles before anything definite is decided upon. Final authority, Dr. Hummel said, will rest with Evans and Clapp. Regardless of the L. C. or other plans, Dr. Hummel emphasized, it will take some time, as it has to go through many proper channels before the plan is approved. From my talk with Dr. Hummel, I am sure that he will do whatever he can to expedite matters. As soon as a concrete plan has been worked out either he or I will cable you.

I have forwarded the other enclosures, and transferred $200 to the Chase National Bank to the credit of the N. L. of Peiping as you instructed. Zunvair Yue has also acknowledged the receipt of your check of $166.25. I hope by this time you have already received my letter of Nov. 18 with 86 enclosed. The bonds which you sent have been safely received. I will take good care of them. About the medicines, they have been sent by the Congressional Drug by registered post. As the cost of sending the packages by air is too high, they went by ordinary mail. The price for each parcel has been marked in the declaration.

With kindest regards, I am

Sincerely,

K. T. Wu

〔袁同礼家人提供〕

按:此件为打字稿,落款处为吴光清签名,该函标记送达时间为“December 7”。

十二月三日

中午，胡适、梅贻琦、袁敦礼、先生等人假北平研究院为黄曾樾饯行。胡适对其北来慰问及协助解决各校困难表示感谢，但迁校之议困难重重，且平津国立各院校长谈话会中已有决议不考虑此事，请黄曾樾南下入京后向朱家骅转达。一时许散会。〔《民国日报》（天津），1948年12月4日，第3版〕

十二月八日

下午，平津唐东北等地国立十七院校长谈话会在清华大学举办。胡适、徐悲鸿、李书华、黎锦熙、先生、袁敦礼、刘曜曦等十余人参加，梅贻琦为召集人。决议各案如下，参加本会以国立专科以上学校为限，欢迎国立蒙藏专科学校参加，再电教部转行政院尽快拨发各校经常、临时各费，前拨冬煤款杯水车薪再电行政院予以增拨应急，再电行政院速令中纺公司发售国立院校员工冬季配布，兼任教授请各校照实际情形按月调整车费，下次会议拟于一月十二日由北平艺术专科学校召集。〔《大公报》（天津），1948年12月9日，第3版〕

先生致信平馆南京办事处，指示移运内阁大库舆图箱件细节。

> 接朱部长来电，谓内阁大库地图将与其他古物一并运往台湾。兹请将各箱重新检查一次，一律加铁皮条并放入潮脑，每箱上加贴本馆封条（另寄），所需各款可在中大退还之壹仟元内报销。附上致杭次长一函，请与接洽是荷。专此，顺颂大安。
>
> 弟袁同礼顿首
>
> 十二，八

〔《北京图书馆馆史资料汇编（1909-1949）》，页916〕

按：此为抄件，未写上款，但据文意可知应发予平馆南京办事处（顾斗南）。

先生覆信杭立武，建议将平馆南京办事处所存内阁大库舆图与古物一并迁移。

> 复杭次长：
>
> 来电错字甚多，但大意已明了。南京所存内阁大库舆图原拟先送故宫保存库与故宫古物一并迁移，如荷同意，即希面告顾斗南照办。

〔国家图书馆档案，档案编号1945-※057-综合5-013003〕

按:此件为先生所拟之底稿,后附文书誊抄一件。

十二月十三日

刘俊卿覆函先生,来信及款项均已收到,但只能随机应变。

守和馆长先生公鉴:

十一日接诵大函,并附启新十万,因值周末办理不及,今则时局又生变化,行情如何,未可逆料,当代相机行事,妥为办理。前嘱之事,详情已函小女面陈矣。专此奉复,顺颂大安。

弟刘俊卿拜启

十二月十三日

〔中兴轮船公司天津办事处用笺。袁同礼家人提供〕

十二月上中旬

某记者来访,先生谓平馆将继续开放,并未考虑南迁,外传迁移广州之说为谣言。〔《大公报》(天津),1948 年 12 月 13 日,第 3 版〕

十二月中下旬①

北京大学文学院古铜兵器漆器特展在松公府西院教务长办公室举行,实物类展品一百八十五种,其中有先生所藏"商周弧援助方□内字戈"。此外,敦煌考古工作展览在松公府蔡元培纪念室举办,其中陈列了相当数量的书籍和巴黎、伦敦两地的照片,均经先生首肯由平馆借出。〔《国立北京大学五十周年纪念:古铜兵器展览会》,1948 年,页 10;《国立北京大学五十周年纪念:敦煌考古工作展览概要》,1948 年,页 15〕

十二月十七日

下午四时半,马衡、梅贻琦、郑天挺、先生、周炳琳等人同访华北"剿总"副秘书长焦蕴华,打听时局消息,但不得要领。〔马思猛整理《马衡日记》,北京:生活·读书·新知三联书店,2018 年,页 23〕

按:焦蕴华(1899—1987),字实斋,河北井陉人,北京高等师范学校毕业,历任天津市教育局局长、北平师范大学总务长等职。

雷兴致函先生,加州大学伯克利分校图书馆馆员 Richard G. Irwin 前往中国购买书籍,请先生给予帮助。

December 17, 1948

① 展览时间应为 12 月 16 日至 19 日,《北京大学五十周年纪念特刊》,1948 年,各种展览会及实验室开放一览,页 1。

Dear Dr. Yuan:

This is to introduce Mr. Richard G. Irwin who is sent by this University to purchase books in order to make our still small holdings of Chinese material somewhat more complete. Needless to say, that any assistance you may be able to give him will be most gratefully acknowledged by the University and by myself personally.

I avail myself of this opportunity to thank you most kindly for your generous cooperation offered to the Library and to myself.

During these trying times my thoughts are often with you and my other Chinese friends. My hope is that none of the cultural values will be destroyed in the accumulation and preservation of which you have had such prominent share.

With my sincerest wishes and warmest personal regards,

as ever yours

F. D. Lessing

〔袁同礼家人提供〕

按：该函为其亲笔。

十二月二十日

先生留致平馆同人函，告知南下述职期间馆务由王重民主持。

同人公鉴：

同礼奉中央来电入京述职，在离平期内，馆务由王重民先生代理，亦经部中核准。王先生与本馆关系最深，在此非常时期得其主持，凡我同人均应共同拥戴、通力合作，俾馆务进行不致停顿，不胜企盼之至。专此，顺候公绥。

袁同礼谨启

十二月廿日

〔《北京图书馆馆史资料汇编(1909-1949)》，页922〕

按：该信后经王重民油印并向馆员公示。

十二月二十一日

下午二时，梅贻琦、李书华、先生、杨武之、张颐等人乘飞机离开北平。晚五时许，专机抵达南京，傅斯年、陈雪屏及蒋经国、彭昭贤等均至机场迎接。

〔《传记文学》第7卷第6期,页44;《马衡日记》,页11;《思忆录》,中文部分页106〕

按:先生与夫人袁慧熙,携袁静、袁澄、袁清三位子女同行。陈雪屏(1901—1999),江苏宜兴人,教育家,1920年入北京大学预科,后在哲学系就读,1926年赴美入哥伦比亚大学,1930年归国,担任东北大学教育心理学系主任,1932年任北京大学理学院心理系教授,抗战胜利后与郑天挺等人奉命前往北平接收伪大学,时任教育部次长,代理部务。

十二月二十二日 南京

中午,李宗仁在传厚岗官邸宴请胡适、梅贻琦、李书华、先生及北方抵南京教授多人。晚,蒋介石在官邸宴请胡适、梅贻琦、李书华、先生,并邀朱家骅、陈雪屏等作陪。〔《申报》,1948年12月23日,第1版〕

十二月二十三日

先生致电马衡,拟请故宫博物院南京分院派梁廷炜押运图书赴台。

北平马院长钧鉴(太密):

图书馆书籍随第二批全部运台,拟请派梁廷炜随同前往。希电知分院。

同礼。(梗)

〔故宫博物院档案,档案图书文书类〕

王重民致函先生,报告平馆情况及北平局势,并请就人事和财务事宜给予指示。

守和吾师道鉴:

阅报知礼拜二即平安抵京,想师母及师兄师姊均已安顿好,此间金鱼胡同住宅已由贾芳兄料理好,大约今天借来大车再拉一次即完。冯家昇愿住,二金不能搬。想详情别有贾芳报告。

吾师此次南行,仅于前晚一晤,因想在巴黎时接吾师离平前所发之信,亦在晚九时以后,两次均使生非常愁怅,都是因以失眠!生礼拜一下午即到馆,曾于礼拜一与礼拜三两次招集各主任各股长开谈话会,到第二次谈话会时,大家隔膜稍稍打开,若再假以时间,不难更趋融洽,则馆务或可无为而治也。即王子访个人,正是他开诚改变作风之秋,他虽跟随转变,旁人对他不一定挟旧恨,也未尝不可安定下来,则不南下亦可。他肯诚心帮忙,亦好也。

大约再经三四天，则一切似可安定下去。生已定出三条规则：

一、职员名额及薪额，一依卅七年十二月份底册。从此不再铨叙，内有二人，俟铨定后，可依部令改薪额。

二、在袁馆长未返馆以前，有因事辞职之职员，不再新聘。必需则从他部分调，否则空之。

三、一律不准预支预借薪水。如有婚丧大故或医药特别费，交由代表会处理之。

今明日可组织成一个职工代表会。则以后馆务、行政方面，由生与王、顾、赵合组行政会议，以行政会与代表会联席会议，为馆中最高机关。

以上对内大计划，本周内可完成。

※　※　※

应变费十五万元，昨日领到，所剩之十二万元，原拟发一月薪水，余数买食粮。而北平正在粮价飞涨，不但飞涨，且有钱都买不到东西。到市面跑了一趟，只有两袋半小米。遂乘昨天开会之便，由大家商议，每职员发一千，每工友发五百，则十二万只余卅五元。遂依此办法发出。出席者皆股长，均可拿千余元者，而肯自己牺牲，只要一千，亦是一好现象。

不过粮是要储，容再设法，生与刘市长瑶章是少时朋友，和高文伯也相熟，拟日内访他们一谈，看官家有无办法？但十之九无法。不论如何，非由部中来一笔特款，不能办此，请吾师特别设法。北大早有准备，不但九月份发出，现在所存，尚够发两个半月连职员眷属在内，实在惊人。想梅校长长部，吾师或将在部内协助，不知有无特别方法？望千万努力！（成不成暂不必让别人知道。）

前晤马叔平先生，知太庙驻兵已搬出。景山亦将搬出，只留数人主瞭望。静心斋早晚在搬出之列。惟庆霄楼驻兵是另一系统，似较难。此事除与校院、故宫联合外，或更托殷祖英伯西找楚总监一商也。

生到馆三日，情形尚佳，并不像最初所想像之难。望能化凶为吉，维持得过去也。（顾子刚好权，但现在想不出主要事付托他。）

※　※　※

贾芳转吾师令生在馆支薪之意，殊为感激，但万万行不得！昨给毅生一信，说明个中情形，今日见他，已说定仍用北大教授维持馆务！因生不辞北大，遇有人捣乱，可拂袖而走，则易解决，若以“馆”为主，生无退身之所，则捣乱者将乘机而起矣！此小事甚明白，望师千万不要向部中建议，发表名义，或支给薪水也。

匆匆，即请道安！

受业王重民上

卅七，十二，廿三。礼拜四

〔袁同礼家人提供〕

按：殷祖英（1895—1966），号伯西，河北房山人，时任河北省政府委员、教育厅厅长。

十二月二十六日

王重民致函先生，告北海静心斋、庆霄楼驻兵隐患，并谈王访渔、顾子刚近况。

守和吾师道鉴：

生到馆已六天，尚未出故事，究竟能否维持，与大家能否相安，非待二三礼拜后，不能看出眉目。然不论如何，生当尽其所能，牺牲一切，来替吾师维护这一项大事业。北海静心斋、庆霄楼两处，最使人担心，也是最不好找办法之事！一二日内，生即着手处理此事，生意静心斋可没有大麻烦，而庆霄楼住的是外兵，无法理喻，到最不得已时，搬出既属不可能（无款，无车），只好请楚总监会同加封，而另委托一个军政机关代为保管。把书目大致开好，看守人便可退出，不知吾师意如何？

在应变时期，庶务处最重要，而负责人只知敷演，在这时候便算不中用。一切大权，多已交给王子访，他这时候不应该再滑头了，究竟他肯否出大气力，现在还看不出。前信说他最好是不走，而事实上在最近他也走不了，若非教部名单有他的名字，很难得到航位，所以现在希望他肯出点气力，向大家替他转圜，便不必再走。此次选举，虽说袁涌进、陆元烈、黄祖勋得票最多，而总务组或与总务有关之人，占了一半，他也算有相当势力，所以正好是他拿真心，出真力的机会。顾子刚无事可做，一天天的和书估作买卖，有点不大好看。拿公家钱，有时还用公家信纸和邮票，更是不好。生不知大同书店与馆方关系如何？即有无股本？可否分一点红利？现在“福利会”即可成立，而分文莫名，能否从大同书店要点钱，即馆方有无可要钱之资格，生一点不知道，请师考虑一下！前信说北大存粮，尚够两个半月之用，我们情形虽不同，然总应有一点，心头上方觉有把握。此事非有一笔特款不可，上信请师设法，不知能否办到？

又教部来一公文，要把代保管之接收来的“伪”书，作价分配，想他现在顾不得，不知部中真意如何？兹将该公事录呈，请作打算，而生则让此间略为分别，列一清单，以便随时可以呈报也。

专此，即请道安！

生重民上

卅七，十二月，廿六日

〔袁同礼家人提供〕

按：转圆，似当作“转圜”。陆元烈，字子如，1937 年入馆；黄祖勋，字秋生，1932 年入馆。

一九四九年　五十五岁

一月三日

顾子刚致函先生,寄上外汇备忘录及支付收据,并询问账户细节。

Jan. 3

Dear Mr. Yuan,

I send you some exchange memos and receipts that concern payments made by you.

Did you keep a separate account for *QB* subscriptions? Was the $4 from Toronto for *QB*? In your statement of the Chase a/c, receipts are classified as (1) Exchange Bought (2) Duplicate Books Sold. How is the China Institute payment of $44.00 to be credited?

Mr. Wang will pay the N.Y. transportation a/c by Chase check. The check will be sent to CF in Shanghai for forwarding, so that everyone concerned will be duly advised.

It is very calm here these few days. The soldiers in my house have been withdrawn and Pei Hai is opened to the public in the first half. The only difficulty is the high prices of necessities.

With best wishes,

Yours Sincerely,

T. K. Koo

〔袁同礼家人提供〕

按:*QB* 即 *Quarterly Bulletin of Chinese Bibliography*,下同;CF 即中基会(China Foundation)。该函为其亲笔,先生在此函第二段三个问号处,分别标注 no,yes,do not know。

一月五日　南京

先生以签呈形式向教育部提出赴美讲学申请。

敬陈者,职从事图书馆事业迄今适满二十五载,美国国会图书馆特邀赴美讲学，一切费用均由该馆担任。窃念我国目前正在争取美援之时，在美工作人员似尚不多，颇愿乘机向美国学术界略事宣传，以期配合，区区微意，谅荷赞许。拟请自本年二月起，准予休假壹年，并请转函外交部发给护照，以便起程，理合具文呈请鉴核批示遵行。谨呈

部长

三十八年一月五日

〔袁同礼家人提供〕

按：1 月 11 日，教育部国际文化教育事业处函告准予。

一月七日

杭立武致函先生，告平馆运台文物进展并曾联署电请李济代为负责一切事务。

守和先生赐鉴：

关于运台文物存放保管等事，李济之兄微电谅邀察阅，谨按关于箱体文物存放已经商准，资源委员会拨借台中糖厂一部分仓库应用。兹拟再请翁咏霓、王雪艇两理事长函请陈辞修主席尽量协助解决各项问题，并拟请傅孟真先生于到台后面商一切，至各机关在台人员自应受李先生之指导，俾能通力合作。经已于四日去一简电，并由各机关联衔公函李先生如下："敬启者，敝所等五机关公物现已陆续运达台湾，因派去之办事人员甚少，而主管者又均须暂时留京，所有公物之收藏以及安全等项，敬请先生惠予照拂，并对敝所等派去之办事人员予以指导督促，无任企感。"除函复李先生外，谨函奉闻。耑此，祗颂新绥。

杭立武拜上

一，七

〔国立中央博物院筹备处用笺。袁同礼家人提供〕

按：该信为文书代笔，落款处钤杭立武印。

一月八日

王重民致函先生，报告北平近况、平馆馆务情况，并请返平。

守和吾师道鉴：

自吾师离平后，尚未奉到亲笔来信，殊为念念。此间情形，尚属平安。馆务、事务方面通交王子访，研究、编目、采访三组通交顾子刚，斐

云仍主善本。如此分配工作,已有一周,一切渐渐安定下去,大概已如吾师离平时之现象矣。生起初最焦急者为太庙、北海驻兵。太庙方面有马叔平先生,解决较早,惟日来又有一极困难之问题,(用作储械)极难处理。数日后,如不能解决,亦只好听之。北海则静心斋早已搬出,庆霄楼几费周转,昨日方腾空。今日即将阅心殿东西迁楼内,予以钉封,或可一劳永逸。再则薪水问题,经北大作保,经"剿总"核准,可先借一月;而吾馆方面,则后得两天,同仁未免稍有损失。好在政府支付书已由南京寄出,大约礼拜一可发三个月。

北平情况,无大变化,想南方报纸上都有。昨日下午,走了两飞机教授,他们到后,可得详细情形。子水及志仁夫人等均在内,想已晤及。

馆中工作,除维持现状外,都在准备总数目,如有书若干,代部接收若干,寄存外人若干及家具若干之类,已有一个大概数目。馆中出版物,亦在总结数目。一切尚称顺利,请勿念。外此有应特别禀请者:

1.会计方面,尚未解决。贾芳在此严重时期,准他辞职,在贾芳方面,如释重负;在生方面,则失掉长城,无可依靠。阮为群虽精明,究少经验,但只要有人,生都不在意。就是他是书记,月薪一百元,而会计员必需有干事以上的资格,生不能提升他,他当然不痛快。此事或挽留贾芳,或提升阮为群,请吾师下手谕,均当遵命。不然快要停顿。

2.年终考绩,不拟举办。因外面攻击王念伦、王子访者尚有人,若再出什么不公平,恐惹麻烦,不如到一时期,再各为设法。工友已一律增薪五元。书记方面,想办一下,正在考虑中,方法决定后再奉闻。

3.教授开始南迁后,惟恐继搬善本书,教部如有此意,则恐出麻烦。昨晤马叔平先生,知南京第二批古物已上船,而北平方面,则十分坚决不迁,不知吾馆如何?

4.议和希望较小,昨日物价又飞涨,吾馆既无钱,又无粮,真是焦虑之至!(北大用学生名义,又已借到面。)日来不断有人借钱,生均一一拒绝。可是必需用品,已花一万余元,买的够用三两个月了!吾师在京沪,不知能否要一笔特别款,来渡此难关。生与陈雪屏尚认识,且有瓜葛之亲,若再请胡适之先生帮忙,未知可一试否?

5.吾师迁沪后,生活情形如何,至以为念。最近作何打算?适之先生西服已运京,是否有意出国?李书华先生有返平消息,盖以京沪无事可作也。生屡与子访、子刚、斐云诸兄商谈,吾师最好早日返平,(师母等无妨留上海)主持馆务。即各方面人等,均赞成此议。时局不论若何变化,吾馆大概没有变化。若环境许可,吾师与其晚来,不如早来也。请详细考虑,是所为祷!生之目的,亦唯在早晚欢迎吾师回来也。

专此,即请道安!

师母师兄师姊同问好!

生重民上

卅八,一月,八日

〔袁同礼家人提供〕

按:"阅心殿"今通称为"悦心殿",位于北海琼岛前山西侧,建于清顺治八年(1651年)。阮为群,平馆馆员,约在1947年入馆。

一月九日

先生赴教育部,与代理部长陈雪屏商谈平馆存沪善本书再次运美计划。〔中国第二历史档案馆,教育部档案·全卷宗5,国立北平图书馆请拨员工学术研究补助费及员工福利费会计纪录的有关文书,案卷号11616(6)〕

一月十日

先生致信赵迺传,附签呈。

述庭吾兄:

昨日与部长商谈运送珍本事。渠嘱备一签呈。兹特奉上,即希转呈,并盼提前办理是感。顺颂□安。

弟同礼顿首

十日

按:赵迺传(1890—1958),字述庭,浙江杭州人,曾任教育部科长,时应任立法委员并兼任教育部事。该信附签呈一件,亦为先生亲笔,内容如下,

敬陈者,职馆存沪宋元善本及敦煌唐人写经,奉令移存美国国会图书馆暂存并影照复本一案,业由司徒大使商得美国政府之同意,由美方代为运送,惟一部分经费须由我方担任。兹以箱件即将起运,需款迫切,拟请钧部呈请行政院特拨专款美金叁千元,

以便支付。在该款未拨到以前并恳函请中华教育文化基金董事会(上海九江路四十五号花旗大楼406号)在该会已核准之职馆购书费项下先行垫付,将来再由钧部担保归还。此外,所需之制箱费约需金圆券贰拾万元,务恳提前汇沪,以资便利。除箱件运抵美京及其影照复本经过另行呈报外,理合备文呈请鉴核批示遵行,实为德便。谨呈

部长陈

国立北平图书馆馆长袁同礼(印)

三十八年一月十日

上海办事处地址:上海宝庆路十七号。

〔中国第二历史档案馆,教育部档案·全卷宗5,国立北平图书馆请拨员工学术研究补助费及员工福利费会计纪录的有关文书,案卷号11616(6)〕

一月十一日

顾子刚致函先生,告知平馆大通银行账户余额,并询问石博鼎捐款用途,另谈北海驻军情况及北平时局。

Jan 11, 1948

Dear Mr. Yuan,

I enclose

(1) A reconciliation of the Chase Bank statement for December. Please note that the net balance of November should be $928.38, not $1,028.38. The other details are to be found in the reconciliation. Two deposits of Dec. 1 and 7 cannot be traced in the file.

Not knowing that you had paid the 6 English accounts out of the Library's own foreign exchange and assuming that you had brought the bills with you, I sent you the 6 Chase memos. By chance I found the bills are in Mr. C. L. Li's hands. Please return the memos.

(2) A letter from Artibus Asiae asking for payment.

(3) Letter from Oxford re Spalding's donation. My suggestion is that Dawson is asked to continue our learned periodical with this 250 pounds. This letter was overlooked by Mr. Chao Yin-hou last time.

(4) Letter from Dr. Miao, Berlin.

There is comparative quiet here, but prices are very high. Flour is 1100; two days ago it was 1600. Cabbage was 24 per □□ yesterday, while meat (pork) was over 400. We got our pay yesterday afternoon.

The soldiers have evacuated the Ch'ing-hisao-lou and Ch'ing-hsin-chai. They also left my house, but we had to give them the Yüeh-hsin-tien. This seems to be a fair bargain.

The papers say very little and often what they say are conflicting. I hope that Peace Rumors will become Facts.

Sincerely,

T. K. Koo

〔袁同礼家人提供〕

按:Mr. C. L. Li 应指李锺履,Chao Yin-hou 待考,Dr. Miao 应指缪培基;Dawson 应指 Dawson Holdings Limited,为图书馆提供期刊、报纸订阅的英国服务公司;Ch'ing-hisao-lou、Ch'ing-hsin-chai、Yüeh-hsin-tien 分别为北海公园中的庆霄楼、静心斋、悦心殿,时都应为平馆馆舍。Jan 11, 1948,由信文及先生回信可知,此处应为 1949 年。该件为其亲笔,后附大通银行平馆账户 1948 年 12 月对账单一纸。

一月十二日

布朗致函先生,愿意协助先生来美,譬如发出邀请。

January 12,1949

My dear Dr. Yuan:

I have no idea whether this letter will ever reach you or not. I was encouraged to write you on account of the fact that Mrs. Fairbank had recently received letters from Peiping.

Dr. Arthur W. Hummel of the Library of Congress has written me of your hope to visit us again in this country some time. I think I could obtain an invitation for you from the American Library Association or possibly from the library of some university. If you receive this letter, I wish you would let me know something about your plans and whether letters addressed to you at Peiping will reach you.

Yours very truly,

Charles H. Brown

Associate Director

〔袁同礼家人提供〕

按：此函似附于1月18日吴光清致先生函中。

一月十四日

王重民致先生两函。其一，劝北返或出国，并谈馆务尤其是会计一职人选问题，另略述北平教育界人士动向。

守和吾师道鉴：

奉一月五日由南京发来手谕，知吾师在京与校院取得联络，为馆筹划甚备。据信中所述，知吾师情绪尚佳，至慰。日来传来胡、梅、李诸公，在京情绪均不佳，并有北返计划，故吾师若无其他有把握计划，亦以早日北返为宜。月前风闻吾师有出国计划，前天晤志仁先生，他推测日内或可成熟，如能出国，亦是无办法中之一办法也。惟出国旅费，必须一次拿到相当数目，即再无接济，亦不至困穷，是为至要！生在此探询各方面意见，佥以吾师最好是即时北返，如不北来，亦不要在南方任职。次，即有机会出国，过一相当短时期，即可从国外欢迎吾师回馆，主持馆务也。这是大家所期望的，不知师之计划如何？

生留此将近一月，馆内外一切尚应付得过去，勿念。际此时期，大家工作仍然不起劲，但亦无法。惟期望大局确定以后，馆中经费能增加，把现有十四个空额都补上，一班少壮派未始不能再振也。可是目前谈不到。

阮为群已就代理会计员职。子访主张把宋琳取消，再调马龙璧帮会计，生均未采纳。现在不应让宋琳辞，正和不应让子访辞，是一个道理。总务权利可加重，但人事方面，总以集中各方面势力，极力避免“党派”的造成为目的。会计若为慎重起见，生或将允多加一个女职员替卢延甲，可于江珍、袁佩如、袁荣礼三人中择一人，如何？

东厂胡同图书，委托北大保管，由梁思永、余逊、汤用彤、张政烺与生五人，合组保管委员会。北大自子水走以前，他希望由朱光潜或杨今甫代理，生则与汤锡予商议，以向觉明为最好。但自子水行后，大家仍要生去作。生又再度与锡老商议,最好请觉明,而毅生、锡予还未决定,还有百分之六十的可能要叫生出来维持。

志仁先生四五日内可南下。叔平先生极镇定,惟为驻兵问题颇难应付。(吾馆能解决,很是万幸!)清华情形不明,似已改变。燕京则陆志韦始终不动,似尚无变化。北平文化界志仁先生行后,将以郑毅生、焦实斋、杨光弼为重镇,生和他们均有相当关系,消息还算灵通!

在央行得立"透支户"最好。现正办理手续,日内可与校院一齐透支一月份及一月内双薪矣(俟"剿总"批准)。

专此,即请道安!

生重民上

一月十四日

〔袁同礼家人提供〕

按:马龙璧,字仲芳,1933 年入馆;江珍,字若伦,1947 年入馆;袁佩如,字锡铮,1937 年入馆;袁荣礼,1947 年入馆。

其二,谈会计人选并请南京办事处将运台文物及相关重要文件录副北寄,另告平馆数位馆员之稿件即将完成,便中请与商务印书馆联系出版事宜。

守和吾师道鉴:

今早上一信,言及会计股加人问题。又于馆中人事通盘计划,如谓俟政局安定,经费有着,便将空额十四人,一齐补上少壮有为的青年们。可是馆内旧人,凡不大习惯编目者,应渐次分派在办事务各股。所以会计股方面,这次拟派一女职员。贾芳辞去,实在是一大损失,所以就各方面情势而论,以袁佩如最为适宜。生已透露此意,而贾芳则坚持不可。生又考虑到江珍、袁荣礼、王佩瑜、关雅诸女职员,江、王有人不欢迎,袁、关已间接表示不愿就。但按诸事实,仍是袁佩如最相宜,可否由吾师来一信劝劝他们。(再说早些占了会计地位,亦较安稳。)

今早又给顾斗南写一信,谈及运台文物及有关此类重要文件,均应有一副本,寄北平保存,以免遗失一份,还有一份作参考。南京办公费,已寄上三千余元,为数虽不多,或可救眉急。俟新调整发下后,再汇上一些。唯南京与北平,一样危险,不知何处先遭不幸。至于联合政府成立以后,国都在南抑在北,恐亦是一大问题。设使将来南京不作国都,则南京办事处要取消,那方面的馆产和职员情形,生一点不知道。故南京所存图书、傢俱、文档，亦应略有一个大概数目，叫北方知道。此事便中请告顾斗南先生。

京沪同仁薪水，能从南京扣发最好，不知进行如何？可否实见？

下午遇向觉明，知汤锡予已访过他，他正在考虑。生与寿萱都十分耸踊他，希望觉明出来整顿一下。

北大下周考试，生所任功课，即作一结束。从此以后，拟每天上午在馆办公，下午便去整理"天主教士译著书目"。从垫款内每月六十元请了北大去年毕业的一个学生王□孝作助手，如此希望仍不至离开书本。所以用垫款者，为不占一个名额；所以另外请人者，用以补偿生为馆所花费光阴也。如再有赴上海之便，见到李伯嘉先生时，请便中一谈吾馆存纸及出版情形。生此目拟三个月编成。杨殿珣之"年谱目录"，张秀民之"安南书录"，梁子涵之"书目目录"，均将脱稿，三四月间，均可付印也。唯纸存南方，而印刷则以在北平较方便，不知可否在北平排版。凡此种种，见李伯嘉时，均请一谈为感。专此，即请道安！

生重民上

一月十四日

〔袁同礼家人提供〕

按：王佩瑜，1944年入馆；关雅，1943年入馆。杨殿珣之"年谱目录"似指《中国历代年谱总录》的底稿，张秀民之"安南书录"应指《安南书目提要》，梁子涵之"书目目录"应指《中国历代书目总录》。

一月十五日

贾芳致函先生，告知平馆人事情况，尤其是会计一职安排，并谈金鱼胡同寓所租金等事。

守公馆长大人尊鉴：

我公离平已三周余，尚未奉候，至歉，乞宥之。近闻府上已移居上海，我公独处首都，想皆平顺。近阅报载首都积极疏散，不审我公及京处同仁如何自处，至念。近和谈忽涨忽弛，总有一日和平可期，届时甚希早日旋旌，以慰同仁之望。馆中诸事大体平顺，且组有"职员福利会"，选委员九人，协助有三先生共谋同仁之安全及福利。委员计：韩永锋、王祖彝、袁涌进、陆元烈、于冠英、黄祖勋、赵荫厚、张我忠及关雅，均能和衷共济，尚希释念。关于会计，职已辞去，刻由阮为群代理，初阮君已接会计,次日传闻王念伦及顾先生谓其为雇员且薪资低,不应骤当此任,故阮君复翻悔,曾上辞呈,有三先生接受后即转呈我公,静候指示,处理延迟数日,阮君复二度接管会计,此事幸告一段落。有三先生对职辞会计兼职事显有不谓然之意,职向王先生详细解释辞职在前,非今日事,故王君略为释然。十五万元每人分得一千元,工役五百元,我公之一千元已由荣礼女士转上,三个月薪及学研费已由馆转拨南京。又办公费一百元及故宫送来十二月份及元月份办公费共三百八十元,均由荣礼女士转上。金鱼胡同房已分由冯家昇及程振宇二先生居住,大厅则用馆中封条暂封,常少亭及刁乐谦仍居外院。经与房东改定合同,除房租与间数外,悉仍旧贯,房间计廿四间(大厅按十五间计),租金月壹佰元,因房捐关系,房东要求三个月调整房租一次,此为暂时规定。余所嘱之事均已一一照办,请释远念。又王君嘱各组股积极办理已编、未编藏书统计,同仁工作大体均佳。北平围城已匝月,市面尚安定,故宫传心殿及太庙后河落弹,幸均未伤人。平市各界组和平促进会连日奔走,尚无端倪,津市已临最后阶段,平市孤城当难苦撑,或可不致遭受破坏。静心斋及庆霄楼驻军已交涉撤出,独悦心殿划为驻军之用,如此则我馆藏书不致遭受破坏,请释念。又近沪上爨、李、王三君致王有三先生函称,平馆将京沪同仁历月薪俸按平区标准自国库支取,改按京沪标准发与同仁,故疑此余款有改作他用或总务会计及出纳有贪黩之虑,请王君澈查。职已将历月帐表点与王君,刻由平馆王、顾二君分函沪上诸公,证明无此事,恰馆中三十七年上半年生补费表册已办妥,径寄顾斗南先生。职已函沪上,如仍不释怀,请至京亲检原册,俾真象大白,并恳我公于晤见沪上诸先生时详为说明,俾释误念,实所深感。余不缕陈,容俟后禀。耑上,谨叩钧安。府上请代致候。

职贾芳谨上

元月十五日

〔袁同礼家人提供〕

按:"金鱼胡同房"即该胡同那家花园,那桐(1856—1925)故居;"房东"应指张寿崇。[1]"常少亭""刁乐谦"二人应为梨园人物。

---

① 《北京文史资料精选:东城卷》,2006年,页305-310。

一月十七日

先生向教育部递交馆藏内阁大库舆图移运呈文,请备案。

敬陈者,奉钧部三十七年十二月十四日社字第六七四九四号代电,内开该馆存京地图由中央博物院代运安全地点等因。奉此,查职馆所藏内阁大库舆图十八箱遵于卅七年十二月二十一日交由中央博物院代运安全地点,理合具文呈请鉴核备案。谨呈

部长、次长

国立北平图书馆馆长袁○○

三十八年一月十七日

〔国家图书馆档案,档案编号 1946-※039-采藏 11-005009 和 1946-※039-采藏 11-005010〕

按:此为抄件,另附"国立北平图书馆存京文物运送联单"1 页,注明庄尚严随古物装车一并赴台。呈送后并未及时获得批复,4 月 5 日再次呈送,教育部于 4 月 20 日指令予以备案。

先生致信顾子刚,告其平馆支出、收入各账户收讫细节,同意用石博鼎捐赠的英镑订购英国学术期刊。

January 17, 1949

Dear Mr. Koo:

I am glad to have your letters of January 3rd and 11. Since all accounts for western books and journals are kept by Mr. C. L. Li, I am returning to you the exchange memos and receipts to be forwarded to him.

All Q. B. subscriptions are entered in our current account and no separate one has been kept. The $4 from Toronto was its payment for the Q. B. The $44 from the China Institute is the payment from Tsing Hua for the duplicate Russian books which we sold to Tsing Hua. It was entered in our account for Duplicate Books Sold, although the actual check was not received by the Chase Bank until December.

The amount of $708.33 which Mr. Wang paid through the China Foundation should be paid out of the Foundation's grant for 1949. Since it was paid from our own funds, it should be refunded as soon as funds from the Foundation is received.

Regarding our deposit of December 7, I cannot recall just now, but you can find out from what source it came from by checking up the advice of credit from the Chase Bank.

I quite agree with you in utilizing the £ 250 from Mr. Spalding's donation for our subscription to British scientific and learned journals. Please wire Dawson to continue our subscription for 1949, but ask the publishers to store the issues for the duration of the present emergency.

With kindest regards,

Your sincerely,

〔袁同礼家人提供〕

按:此件为底稿。

一月十八日

吴光清覆函先生,告知工作申请事不必太急,可等先生到美后再做具体打算,或可申请在大学执教,但请留意移民局的审查。

Washington

Jan. 18, 1949

Dear Mr. Yuan,

I just received your letter of Jan. 7, together with some enclosures which I have already forwarded. On Jan. 10 I cabled you at Nanking, at your request, the following message:

Your and your family passage paid at this end.

Wu, Congressional Library

I hope it will serve the purpose as I am pretty sure the L. C. wouldn't send it. I understand definitely that you will be paid during the period when you serve as Consultant here. At the moment they are not sure what the amount will be, but they are working on that. As to a job after the 6-month period, I think it would be better to look into the matter after you get here. Regarding the U. N. Library, the four top positions-besides Milam's-are all filled and jobs other than these are not very desirable. Since you are coming over very soon, I think it is too early to write Milam about other chances. However, I will be very glad to do so if you want me to. In case no suitable library positions are available after your period here, I think it might be well to look into teaching jobs like the University of Washington and others. After you get here it would be well to make contacts and to look into the matter. In the meantime, Dr. Brown has answered Dr. Hummel's letter-which was written before the L. C. had decided to invite you. In it he enclosed a letter to you which I attach herewith. You will see that he too is interested in seeing you placed. I think coping with the Immigration Office is the hardest problem to solve after you get here. Of course, a job with the U. N. would eliminate that difficulty. A professorship will likewise be most useful as far as staying on is concerned.

The Chase Bank has sent me a check for $ 200 to reimburse me for the amount which I placed in the account of the National Library.

Looking forward to seeing you soon and with best regards, I am

Sincerely,

K. T. Wu

〔袁同礼家人提供〕

按:此件为打字稿,落款处为吴光清签名。

一月中旬

先生及家人移居上海。

一月二十日

顾子刚致函先生,告知平馆在大通银行账户的余额。

Jan. 20, 1949

Dear Mr. Yuan,

I hope you have received my reconciliation of the December Chase a/c. As I have pointed out that you made a mistake of $ 100 in the balance, you might be thinking that there was a shortage. The fact is that there is more money in the Chase Bank than you thought. The following is a break-up of our net balance of $ 1,491.75.

Balance of Library's own Foreign Exchange according to Mr. Yuan's statement	$ 821. 01
Balance of Duplicates and other Sales a/c	203. 81

December deposits not in Mr. Yuan's statement

Dec.1	$ 200. 00		
7	$ 120. 00		
17	4. 00	324. 00	

(Other deposits are in Mr. Yuan's statement of Sales of duplicates)

Unaccounted	142. 93
	$ 1, 491. 75

I should add that payments to 6 English booksellers amounting to $ 126.23 have already been deducted from the net balance in the Chase Bank. Therefore, we should deduct this amount from $ 821.01, making the balance of the library's own foreign exchange $ 694.78, and the total of Unaccounted should be $ 142.93 plus 126.23 = $ 269.16. I wonder where the money could have come from. Maybe there is some error in your various statements now in Mr. Li's hands. Mr. Li says he will go over them as soon as he gets over the duplicates.

If you can remember, please let me know the source of the deposits of $ 200.00 and 120.00 received by Chase in December. They are not in your statement of Sales of duplicates, nor can I trace them in the file. Also, how is Toronto's $ 4 to be credited?

Peace appears to have become more tangible. Air drop of rice was started yesterday. They are dropping the small bags on the ice of Peihai. Some dropped on our small out-houses, including 2 on the bindery, 1 on the power house, 1 on the Yang Feng Chia Tao dormitory, 1 on Hsi Hsiao Shih Chih. There is only slight damage. I hope that with more practice they will be able to drop more accurately.

People are also concerned about strays shells. There have been several casualties, though they were not in this part of the city.

With best wishes.

Your sincerely,

T. K. Koo

〔袁同礼家人提供〕

按：Yang Feng Chia Tao 即养蜂夹道，Hsi Hsiao Shih Chih 待考。此件为打字稿，落款处为其签名。

一月二十一日

闵乃大致函先生，告其前在德国为平馆代购书籍、仪器运输进展并谈在麻省理工大学近况。

守和先生大鉴：

敬复者，接读前函时，适北平危急，常念先生之行动，是否已离北平，兹读十二月卅日来函（今日一月廿一日方收到），得知先生已在申并即将来美为慰。兹赶书若干，或先生仍能读及此函。关于运沪之书籍事，据柏林来函，谓将在一月中可到申，未知先生现已收到否？关于显微照书机头，已由柏林军事代表团交与美旅行社，径寄至晚处，现尚未收到，寄费由晚处于收到时交付。自最后寄至北平之函后，晚又已付美旅行社款项两次，（因先生不久来美，故美旅行社来函，暂不抄写寄上）一为四美元半，一为廿四美金元，深望此项书籍已到申，不然又将付款，所费实太多。承先生代于教育部所谋之事，实深感谢之至，然晚至今未去华盛顿，亦不知其究竟。在此一切，未如晚意，本望能作学术研究，然一为经济所困，不得不工作于他处，二为麻省理工大学门户之见亦深，Prof. Wiener 与 Dr. Lee 亦作此项工作 Dr. Lee 虽曾为晚之教授，然当晚来此初见面时，伊即劝晚返德，故伊当无意助晚，然在另一方向，但在该校权力甚大，与晚来往之教授，既无特殊之贡献（但为人尚好！），又以在该校无力，故经济问题，仍未能在该校解决，以此教授无意与晚共同作研究工作（至今伊未与晚作一次学术之讨论），故晚拟设法转入工业界。现在美无一教授在此范围内（指晚工作，亦德去世教授工作之方向），可称权威，能与晚共同研究。本想与 Prof. Wiener 相接近，虽伊与晚工作方向不同，但伊为算学家，仍可共同工作，但不幸与晚共同工作者，适 Wiener 之姊妹，她故意百方与晚为难，推恐或为排晚之动机，盖她实无学术，反将研究之问题延误，因此之故，欲与 Wiener 相近之动机，亦无形打消，所幸不久，将可面谈。专此，敬请□安！

晚闵乃大顿首

一九四九年一月廿一日

适此函封后，正拟寄出时，接读舍妹来函（一月十日寄出），谓书籍等已到申,晚甚为庆慰,望贵馆将所有收到书籍,详书一名单带来或寄来为盼,俾易于结算。再者,舍妹来函谓,她之工作处,不允她调至沪台,她谓有机会到先生时,拟请先生代为谋事,未知她究否与先生相会,如果□繁先生,晚当后谢。

〔袁同礼家人提供〕

按:Prof. Wiener 即 Norbert Wiener(1894-1964),通译作诺伯特·维纳,美国应用数学家,“控制论”(cybernetics)提出者,1935 年曾应梅贻琦和熊庆来邀请,在清华大学讲学。Dr. Lee 应指李郁荣(Lee Yuk-wing,1904—1989),生于澳门,祖籍广东新会,电机工程学家,1924 年至 1930 年在麻省理工学院学习,并结识诺伯特·维纳,一同开展研究工作,后应顾毓琇邀请回国效力,1934 年担任清华大学电机工程系教授。“舍妹”应指闵乃杰,时应在上海气象台工作。

一月二十五日

先生覆信布朗,略述南下经过,并告知已收到担任国会图书馆顾问的邀请,不久前往华盛顿。

17 Pao Ching Road
Shanghai, China
January 25, 1949

Dear Mr. Brown:

I appreciate very much your letter of January 12 copy of which was forwarded to me here yesterday. Since the occupation of Peiping by the Communists, air services to Peiping have been suspended and your original letter may not get through at all.

When Peiping was surrounded by the Communists, the Government dispatched three planes to Peiping. Dr. Hu Shih took the first plane to Nanking, while Dr. Mei and myself took the second plane.

I have received a cable from the Librarian of Congress offering me an appointment as consultant in the Library of Congress and I am making plans to be at Washington before March 1.

It is a pleasure to learn that you are enjoying good health and are as energetic as ever. I look forward to the pleasure of meeting you before very long.

With warmest regards,

Yours sincerely,

T. L. Yuan

〔Library of Congress, The Central Files, Asiatic 3〕

按:此为抄件。

顾子刚覆函先生,告知财务及账户情况,并谈王重民拟以信件而非电报的方式联系 Dawson Holdings 续订部分杂志,另谈北平时局。

January 25, 1949

Dear Mr. Yuan,

Your letters of January 14 & 17 received. In the meantime, I have sent you two letters re our Chase Bank a/c. There is more money in it than the statement you left here.

(1) The Ministry notifies us that the 物资供应局 which has taken over the Purchasing from the Central Trust will charge 5% on all purchases handled. I do not know whether they will charge us or not.

(2) Another circular from the Ministry informs us that we had a credit of $ 558 at the end of June, 1948 in the grant made from the 4th American Loan. I enclose an excerpt in Chinese, with my notation.

(3) We have written to the China Foundation requesting that the first installment be paid into our A/C regardless of conditions here. I thought of asking for an extending grant to meet the special charges of $ 708.33, but decided that if made at all it would have to be done by you. In view of the financial condition of CF, perhaps there is no hope for that.

(4) Mr. C. M. Wang says we should write and not cable Dawson, because we can't make things very clear in a cablegram, & also because it costs too much. So we have written to renew our periodicals, with some cancellations to assume that the total cost will fall within £ 250, in addition the publishers will hold the issues until mail service to North China should be restored. There appears a good chance that some sort of

agreement about mail will be made.

(5) The local □□□□ arrangement has worked smoothly so far. More soldiers have marched out, but the CP Soldiers have not come yet. Nobody has approached me about taking over, the primary schools, etc., have been approached. But the news about general peace seems rather discouraging.

(6) Enclosed a letter from Dr. Brown.

(7) Enclosed letters for Mr. Li.

(8) The Tibetan Literature Index is being set in type.

Sincerely,

T. K. Koo

〔袁同礼家人提供〕

按:此函为顾子刚亲笔。先生在第四点处标记 It's very difficult to make up a list, as our annual subscriptions total 370 pounds。CP Soldiers 即解放军。a letter from Dr. Brown 即 1 月 12 日布朗函。

一月二十八日(除夕)

夜,先生与妹夫彭昭贤畅谈并互道珍重。〔《思忆录》,中文部分页 106〕

按:翌日,彭昭贤坐船前往奉化。

一月三十一日

先生致信赵元任,告知来美行期并请协助子女在加州大学入学或旁听。

元任吾兄惠鉴:

久未通讯,时以起居为念。近想阖第均吉,至以为祝。弟等于上月由平逃出,在沪已住月余,近应国会图书馆之聘,赴美研究,定于下月四号起程赴美十九日到金山,亟愿将小孩等安顿于加省大学后再赴东美。兹奉上渠等申请书一件、证书二纸,务希吾兄先向当局为之设法,如万一不能作正式生则旁听亦可,但盼能有一住处,统希费神代为筹划,感谢之至。如时间许可,盼来一信,寄下列地址。匆匆,顺颂俪安。

弟袁同礼顿首

一月卅一日

尊夫人同此。

T. L. Yuan, Passenger S/S. Gen. Gordon, American President Lines,

San Francisco, Calif., Arriving Feb. 19

〔University of California, Berkeley, The Bancroft Library, Yuen Ren Chao papers, carton 10, folder 39, Yuan, Tongli and Yuan, Huixi〕

一月下旬

先生与任鸿隽晤谈数次。〔国家图书馆档案，档案编号 1949-&219-013-1-004002〕

按：其中涉及平馆馆务事宜，如请中基会继续拨付购书款。3月30日，任鸿隽致信王重民，表示该款已照发。

二月二日

先生偕家人乘坐戈登将军号邮轮（S. S. General W. H. Gordon）离开上海，前往美国。〔袁同礼家人提供〕

按：同行者有童季龄及其家人。

二月十日

王重民致函先生，禀告平馆接管经过及现状。

守和吾师道鉴：

奉二月三日上海发来手谕，知师四日放洋，若乘飞机，当已平安抵金山，坐船亦已过日本矣！不知师母及师兄师姊都随行否？尤在念念。此间一切照常，大约一二日内，即有文化接管委员会来人接管。所谓"接管"者，是经过一度仪式之后，便于人民政府发生直接关系，并不加派任人来"管"，对旧有人员采取"三原主义"，即所谓"原人"、"原职"、"原薪"也。生接到吾师一月廿四日信后，适报载有古书古物运美之说，即发表一个书面谈话，附带说明吾师赴美，将由欧返平。对一班的人也都发表"以前不得不晋京的苦衷，到了南方，便不好意思一直回来，必须向欧美绕个道儿，几月后一定返回北平"。文化接管委员会对于这件消息，十分高兴。该会主任是钱俊瑞，英国留学生。管图书馆的是王冶秋，北大民19毕业，管博物馆的是刘燿（今名尹达），历语所旧人，曾随梁思永在安阳作过发掘的工作。又有教育部长张宗麟先生，则总管各院校各文化机关。吾馆之事，已接头数次，极为圆满。对于南京教育部之不重视我们，不给经常、购书费，极表示不应该。所以在第一次发维持费时，便格外给了我们一万五千人民券（合十五万金圆）买新书。关于馆务种切，容稍后再写详细报告。吾师南京之行，已获得刘、王二君十分谅解，不论如何，他们都希望吾师能早早回到北平。比方京沪若一二月内能解放，便望师夏秋之间能回来。这次领维持费，据实造册，没有把吾师及生造入，他们便自动的加入，要一样发给薪水。刘、王二君又当面属生为师特别保存吾师应得之薪水和米面。生因顺便说明馆中福利会新成立，没有基金，袁馆长有信来要把薪水捐助。刘、王二君说"反正我们发出，便是袁馆长的私有财产了，只有他本人有处理权，依据他的意志去作，也是对的"。生拟最近一二三月都捐了福利会，在师返抵北平以前的三四个月，便都为师存起来，作为返平以后安家之用。

京沪同仁，于可能范围，当取得联络，并设法接济。请勿念。

生一切都好，就是不能读书了！每念及此，便十分难过。

吾师不论在美在欧，万勿发表任何有关政治之言论，因为处在美洲，差不多算是另一个世界，以不谈为最妙！专此，即请道安！

生重民上

卅八，二月十日

〔袁同礼家人提供〕

按：钱俊瑞（1908—1985），江苏无锡人，经济学家，1931 年加入左翼文化总同盟，时任北平军管会文管委主任。王冶秋（1909—1987），安徽霍邱人，1941 年起担任冯玉祥国文教员与秘书，新中国成立后曾任文化部文物局局长。尹达（1906—1983），原名刘燿，河南滑县人，考古学家、历史学家，1932 年加入中央研究院历史语言研究所考古组，1938 年赴延安。张宗麟（？—1976），祖籍浙江绍兴，生于江苏宿迁，教育学家。该信应邮路不通，耽搁一月有余才寄出。

二月十四日

闵乃大致函先生，因在美谋生不易欲返国，请先生告到美后寓所地址。

守和先生大鉴：

希来美后即告晚先生之寓所，或旅行之计划。以晚忽于一星期前（正晚第二报告结束时）工作处有意外事发生，现似已缩小范围。晚为外国人，头先停止工作，M. I. T.仅给晚之空名，无薪金，故或拟计划三月十八日返国。然自德寄来之显微照书镜头，仍未收到，故拟请美旅行社转寄与先生。斯以急希得知先生之地址为盼，详情如有机会再面谈。专此，即请旅安！

晚闵乃大顿首

二月十四日

他处亦正在接洽中亦在一星期前开始前行，但晚未敢久待，恐款项用了无法返国，加之以护照问题，与各处接洽，较难有望，虽至今尚未确定有答复。

〔袁同礼家人提供〕

二月十五日　檀香山

先生致信何多源。〔University of Chicago Library, Yuan T'ung-li Papers, Box 2〕

二月十六日

先生参观夏威夷大学校园，晚乘坐戈登将军号离开檀香山。〔*Honolulu Star-Bulletin*, February 18, p. 6〕

二月中旬

赵元任覆函先生，告知已致函相关学校联系袁静、袁澄、袁清入学读书，并告萨本栋去世。

守和吾兄：

得悉大驾不日过此为慰，世妹世兄请求入学事已寄信接洽，信底附上备览。弟住 1059 Cragmont Ave, Berkeley 8, Calif，电话为 Landscape 4-1474。吾兄赴华府前盼能多逗留数日，以便畅谈朋友国家好新闻坏新闻（萨本栋一月卅一日在此过去了）一切之一切。此上，即颂旅祉。

弟赵元任上

〔University of Chicago Library, Yuan T'ung-li Papers, Box 2〕

按：1948 年 12 月 30 日，萨本栋抵达加州，旋即入住旧金山某医院，因癌症晚期医治无效，1949 年 1 月 21 日下午去世。该信无落款时间。

二月二十日

李芳馥致函先生，告知国内经济情况及平馆驻沪办事处同仁之窘况。

守和先生赐鉴：

自离国门，瞬经半月，计程日内当可抵华府，沿途一切，谅必平安顺吉。去此乱邦，适彼乐土，昔人所求。故自始，私为公庆，国内军政方面无大变化，但物价直线上涨，速度空前，吾人生存大受威胁，水电及交通工具等自二月十二日起，照一日调整，新价上涨百分之四百，米破万元大关，煤球三千元一担，英文报二百元一份，新闻报七十元一份。私立大学学米定为四石半，国内航空平信起码六十元。十九日交通部宣布，即日起铁路运费邮电价按公式逐旬调整，而政府对公教人员待遇仍依十五倍计算。上海国立院校教授代表，日前进京请愿，得应变费现款一亿。今日教授发表告社会人士书，充满辛酸悲愤，内称“当政衮衮诸公，平日享受程度超过古代帝王……以饕餮之作风养肥自己，以饥饿之政策摧残师儒，措施乖谬，史无前例”，又称“我们的底薪最高每月六百元……就现今最高级而论，一折二扣，依十五倍计算，每月得金元券二千〇七十元，不过市价银洋一元左右…就眼前所得而论，以之买米不足两斗，用之买菜每日不够蔬菜斤半，经年所得不足以付眼前一月水电煤气之需……我们教育别人子女却被迫要让自己子女失学，世间不平之事孰逾于此”，故绝望之下，只祈求早日解放也。行前所支下美钞百元，如数交颂生兄保存，北平方面迄无信来。有三兄之支票亦未寄到。由震旦取来木箱二口，已送回原处，请释念。本期英文季刊已排好三分之一，加入新稿约二十面，约共可得百面，因印刷费过高，以百面为限。又行前蒙介绍往英国文化委员会工作，该会迄无回音，想因时局不定。报载北平且有解放美国新闻处工作人员之呼声，故现存观望态度。因货币贬值直线下行，办事处存在兴业之金圆券只能留作付煤气、水电费之用。沪地同人中因馨有室家之累，最感困厄，子女不能上学，每月所得薪给不足付目下房租、水电费中之任何一项。其次则为朱君义钧，其夫人原在一私立小学教书，本学期因学费过高，大多数学生停学，渠亦因之失业，现在另行谋事中。办事处存有美钞二百六十五元，除留下约半载所须之办公费及海外来书二十一箱所需之提运费外，拟与仝人会商将余款拨作目前救济费之用，以解倒悬，不知公以为然否。肃此，敬请道安。

后学李制馨吾谨上

卅八年二月二十日

阖府统此候安。

〔袁同礼家人提供〕

〔University of Chicago Library, Yuan T'ung-li Papers, Box 2〕

按:朱义钧,字孟衡,约于1946年1月入馆。

二月二十一日

先生及家人抵达旧金山。

二月二十二日　加州

晚,赵元任宴请先生一家。〔赵新那、黄培云编《赵元任年谱》,北京:商务印书馆,1998年,页308〕

二月二十四日

印度政府聘蒋复璁、李济、先生、姚从吾等为印度历史档案委员会名誉撰述员。〔《申报》,1949年2月25日,第2版〕

按:聘期至1952年3月31日止。

二三月间

先生及家人抵达华盛顿。

三月六日

闵乃大覆函先生,告知其决意返国,并谈此前受托所购阅览器材保存近况。

守和先生大鉴:

敬启者,大札奉读,敬谢种种关切。晚现与各处仍在接洽中(指工作),多以护照问题,延迟至今,未能解决。晚之款,适足以返国,深恐工作不能如愿,将来会发生严重问题。普通工作,晚不能被雇,仅有特殊工作,为美人所不能解决或能解决者太少,由移民局之特许者得被雇,或学校之教师亦为例外,不幸晚之英文会话不能胜任,且过去之半年中虽有工作,但仍为经济所困(指医药费等)及无保障之苦,再继续在此,不能忍受,故决意先返国。与各处接洽仍在进行中,将来如能成就,再来美时,至少需有保障。不幸在美未能与先生拜会,深望若干物件,转寄与先生,如代购之照像机、微显读书机、单据等。晚将考虑,必要之单据或将寄至华盛顿先生所指定之地址,照像机或将存于裘开明先生处,显微读书机或带回或亦存于裘开明先生处,最后(如何处理)之报告将在旧金山奉函报告。晚约在三月十三日(或于十二号)或十四日离此,三月十六号离旧金山,同时寄函至美旅行社,请将显微照书机镜头,寄与先生。晚再函柏林,先生将来函柏林查询此事时,望至函缪培基先生,将显微照书机镜头送至美旅行者为汪采雍先生,此系缪培基嘱伊代办者。本言一月中旬即将到美,现已三月上旬,仍未来此。晚先去函至缪及汪,请查问此事,并函告先生。如一月后先生仍未得回音,请先生去函询问为盼。专此,即请大安。

晚闵乃大顿首

三月六日

内附一函系寄与美旅行社。于同一页上特用英文书若干至先生,以免将来交涉时发生问题,盖汪交与美旅行社时谓为 microscope。

按:汪采雍,1931 年入金陵中学高中部,1944 年科隆大学毕业,其博士论文题目应为 Beiträge zum periodischen Randwert Systeme und VollStändigkeitsbeweis。该信所附英文信札如下,

Dear Dr. T. L. Yuan

The microscope sent by Dr. Wang Ysai Jung is actually Microphotographic apparatus for books. Dr. Wang had made a mistake to use this name "microscope".

Very truly yours

Nai-Ta Ming

〔袁同礼家人提供〕

三月七日

何多源覆函先生,告其向教育部催拨外汇之进展。

袁馆长钧鉴:

奉二月十五日由檀岛寄下手谕,敬悉一切。陈雪屏部长随同孙院长飞京,故只能与邓总务司长晤面。当由邓司长饬属员查调案卷,惟久不查到。据邓司长云,最好能将教部核准分配之公文录下,以便办理。因由京迁粤,在此匆忙时间,一切公文均未安置就绪,即教部办公室亦局促于一楼系(在文明路中山大学旧址大钟楼之上),总务司长室仅得属员一人、藤椅二张及办公桌两张而已。现任中等教育司长吴兆棠及前任高教司长唐培经现均兼任敝校教授,源已托吴司长代为催促。据吴司长云,此款系汇往外国者当无问题,只要能调出旧案便可照办。吴司长曾到敝馆借书,现已飞京公干。昨日敝校在南园酒家公宴,邓司长、唐司长均有赴席,源又向其查询,据复一俟查得旧档,当即办理。港津已通航邮,但马季明先生尚未将款寄来。经源函催,截至今日止,仍未汇下,故咭片尚未能代印。兹将马先生来函奉上,请察阅。谨此

奉复，并候旅安。

又中央圕迁台，蒋馆长来穗，但见不到部长，因陈部长已飞京也。

后学何多源上

卅八年三月七日

按：吴兆棠（1905—1964），安徽休宁人，毕业于同济大学，先后留学日本、德国，获博士学位。唐培经（1903—1988），江苏省金坛人，数学家、统计学家、教育家。"咭片"即粤语中的名片，下同。所附马鉴函如下，

多源先生左右：

顷接手书，敬悉北平图书馆尚有余款甚多，存在交通银行。因近事烦虑，以目疾遂致稽延，至深歉仄。兹特先行函告，明日当将此款缮一支票挂号寄上不误。祗颂大安。

弟马鉴谨启

二月廿五日①

〔University of Chicago Library, Yuan T'ung-li Papers, Box 2〕

三月十三日

先生致信赵元任、杨步伟夫妇，告知到华盛顿后住房及儿女入学情况。

元任先生、夫人尊鉴：

伯克莱小留，诸承款待，濒行复蒙走送，厚意隆情，心感无似。到华京后以觅房不易，暂住 apart 式之旅馆，幸有厨房设备，自己烧饭，尚属经济。偶有适当之房，均在 Maryland 一带，以无汽车，颇不方便，现已由友人另觅一房，尚未决定耳。小孩等均已入学补习英文，俟九月间再正式入学。小女静已向 Bryn Mawr 申请奖学金，以竞争者多，恐无何希望，曾在师友栏内"References"写上大名及住址，将来该校或来函询问敝处经济状况，以作参考。日昨交邮寄奉上 Virginia Ham 一包，以作佐餐之用，敬希哂纳。惟弟等未曾尝试，不识口味与中国者是否相同。近接国内友人来函，知情形愈坏，共军如渡江南下，则江南半壁势将不保，沪杭友人或须他迁，则生活更苦矣。匆匆，顺候俪安。

弟袁同礼顿首

① 何多源在此函标注"接此函已十二日之久，但支票尚未见寄下，三月八日源识"。

慧熙附笔致谢

三月十三日

〔University of California, Berkeley, The Bancroft Library, Yuen Ren Chao papers, carton 10, folder 39, Yuan, Tongli and Yuan, Huixi〕

按:“apart 式之旅馆”似指 Castleton Hotel,位于华盛顿北部第 16 街。Maryland 应指华盛顿北的马里兰州地区。Bryn Mawr 应指 Bryn Mawr College(布林莫尔学院),位于宾夕法尼亚州的私立(女子)文理学院,距离费城不远,后袁静顺利拿到该奖学金,并获得最优等荣誉(Summa Cum Laude),毕业后前往哈佛大学攻读博士学位。Virginia Ham 即弗吉尼亚火腿,赵元任覆函中亦有提到。

三月十五日

闵乃大致函先生,告其返国、留美两选皆难,请先生与中国驻美使馆协商再为援助。

守和先生大鉴:

晚在华盛顿承先生之协助,不胜感谢之至。自使馆别后未得再与先生相见,将先生所建议去电教部事再一详商,即按陈先生之嘱先返剑桥待回音。归后转思再三,以去电待复,按国内现处之情形,恐需时太久,不及乘船(指三月卅日)返祖国,待教部允许后,晚手中之款,恐已用尽,又不能订船位返祖国矣,加之船公司已来电话数次,希速决定船位。晚深盼先生能与我国驻美大使相商,暂先借用,晚至国内与梅月涵、顾一樵、潘公展相商,请转请教部追认此款,梅、顾与晚有师生之谊,且梅校长曾嘱晚返母校。潘与晚亦有师生之谊,且伊对晚协助甚多,当在德时曾与潘有函件来往。战中及战后,以与国内隔绝甚久,故不详知潘公展先生之现状,闻在申为上海市议会会长,确否未知。要之确定船位不能迟至本月十七日(公司所云)。晚离此,不能迟至本月廿四以后,加之所租之房必须先告知何时迁出,预告退租,如不能成行,下月将处于何处,不预告退租,如成行又将牺牲下月房租,晚手中款项甚紧,何能牺牲此巨款(当比较而言)。晚现处之情形,非先生所能想□,苟我驻美大使馆能及时与以协助,所费不多,不然则使馆之协助,收费甚巨,即此次三月卅日之船不能赶上,改乘四月十五号之船,则四百美金元之协助,已不敷矣。除晚之长女须付全票外,一月之房租牺牲与生活费用,在□均过预算之外,实以处境不易,故敢再恳请代为协商。显微照书机镜头尚未来,晚将前去询问,此来希无关税之问题。专此,敬请大安。

晚闵乃大顿首

三月十五日

尊夫人及诸公子等统此请安不另!

〔袁同礼家人提供〕

按:先生收到此函后即覆,并援以美金二百元(支票)。

三月十八日

李芳馥覆函先生,禀告平馆驻沪办事处诸事及个人前途、待遇诸困境。

守和先生赐鉴:

来示奉悉,并转示诸同人。兹谨将此间各事报告如下:

(一)日前接有三兄一函,系二月九日所写,内云先生致渠函已收到,"谈到由德国运来的十几箱书的运费问题,我想美金不值钱,航空信未必能寄到,正在委托此间友人带款去,或转托沪上友人去照料那一批书"。"友人"至今未来信,内无一字提及馆中或北平现状。关于北平各文教机关接收、改组情形,除报上曾数次提及辅仁外,其他一无所知。竹幕亦不亚于铁幕也。

(二)柏林运来书箱等十九件,已取到馆,皆系大箱,内有一件,平面积约合二十二平方英尺,想系照像机。闵君乃大私人箱件准闵小姐请暂存办事处,提运费合九万元,照预算者为少。此外,又取到法国交换局运来书一箱,世界贸易公司代购照像机零件一箱,又向 Edwards Michigan 所购书一箱,亦于今日提取到馆。

(三)日昨收到图书清理处通知,由日本追回战时我国被掠图书,内有本馆书籍六十箱(想有图书馆协会书籍),其中一箱属于先生私人,现存该处,拟于下星期内前往提取,送存震旦大学。

(四)2nd Assistant Registrar, University Registry, Oxford 及 Dawson 皆有回信,二百五十英镑已照拨,Dawson 正候本馆订购单,不知子刚兄已寄出否?

(五)前蒙介绍往英国文化委员会工作,顷接 Hedley 来函称有其本国人某，不日抵沪，拟任斯职，故不另聘他人。既如此，似当初不应请人介绍也。

(六)二月份公教人员待遇调整，照七十五倍发放(上海二月份职工人员生活指数为六四三.二六)。自三月份起，薪饷每月到月底依指数计算，本月初照二月份七十五倍增加二倍，预支上海办事处二月份至六月份调整薪饷，总数三十万零一千余元。到三月十四日始收到广州国库寄来支付书，当向国库分署交涉提出二至五月份，照二百廿五倍发给同人。南京办事处收到调整总数为壹百一十一万四千余元，不知国库如何计算支付书，曾见及注明薪饷并无办公费或其他字样，若包括北平在内则又不足数百万元。南京现无国库分署，日前，顾君斗南派董君来沪提取，内拨三十八万五千元归上海办事处。此间各院校向代总统请愿，借到十二亿元，依五百倍计算，发放教职员薪金及学生公费，中央研究院借款二亿薪金，照一千二百五十倍发放。总之，机关各自为政，有钱多发。南京社教机关十五单位向代总统请愿，得款若干。中央博物院分得二百万元，现又进行第二次请款本馆已加入，不知结果如何。另外，顾君斗南直接向代总统府领到二十万元，内十万元拨交上海办事处。本馆所申请之办公费及应变费至今毫无消息。

(七)研究费自一月份起调整为教授二百元、副教授一百五十元、讲师一百元，依指数计算，但只见诸报载。本年度研究费，同人未领到分文，办公费亦同。

(八)近来物价涨风甚烈。大米涨至五万五千元一石，本月十四日大头银元售出最高价为四千二百元，今日涨至七千八百元。本市公教人员月有配米三斗、煤球二担(自一月起，有票无货)、食油三斤(自去年十二月起有票无货)、食盐四斤、食糖二斤，现政府决定自四月份起全部折发代金，不配实物，公教人员又将受打击不小。

(九)英文季刊几经催促，到现在还只排好全稿三分之二，中国科学公司凡事皆好，只有排印工作奇慢。

(十)孙去何来，李蒸有任教长讯(又有朱求回任说，又有梅先生不干改杭立武说)。不过长江形势日紧，京沪有问题只能随机应变耳。

肃此，敬请道安。

后学李馨吾谨上

三月十八日

阖府统此候安。

三月六日上海《大公报·星期论文》载陶孟和撰《搬回古物图书》一文,内有一段如下:"由于日前报纸上披露,北平图书馆将运送其所藏善本图书及唐人写经到美国国会图书馆显微影印的事,(此事曾经该馆正式否认,但仍有人指出,如唐人写经及几部善本书在私人行囊带出,轻而易举,国人对此仍应警觉。)人们便开始揣测这批古物图书运台不过是初步行程,最终目的乃在大西洋的彼岸……"这种深文周纳的揣测,不知先生已见及否?

〔平馆上海办事处英文信纸。University of Chicago Library, Yuan T'ung-li Papers, Box 2〕

按:Hedley 即 George Hedley,时任英国文化协会驻华代表。①

三月二十日

闵乃大覆函先生,感谢寄来美金二百元,但仍恐不敷返国之用,且将来奉还或须一定时日。

守和先生大鉴:

拜读大札并支票一纸(二百美元),除感动至极外,事实上不能烦扰先生过甚,晚正考虑应如何处理此事。我驻外大使既无权决定此事,或为事实之所困,不得已或将落沦在外、更改途径,晚将下函奉告。虽承先生之美意,但仍缺百十余元,此款恐在此易于设法,但问题至国内后,欲奉还先生,至少当需月余。盖晚仅能将饰品与重要用具出卖奉还。或由晚与数处相商,得教部之批准,奉还先生之款。晚回祖国,实非返家,唯赴第二异国而矣,除有权谋事及尚有若干熟人外,与在美或他国无多分别而矣。如万不得已,竟借先生之款。望先生另来一函,俟晚在国内与教部或梅、顾、潘等人相谈时,可示伊等,晚确借款而归。要之,晚正考虑如何能不动用先生之款。得即奉上,兹先奉复,详情待决定后再函告。显微照书机头尚未到,拟星期三将赴(此处)美旅行探问此事。此复,敬请大安!

① *The North-China Daily News*, July 6, 1947, p. 6.

晚闵乃大顿首
三月廿日

尊夫人与诸公子统此请安不另。

前一美人专利律师，伊正欲协助晚，在美京将电话大使馆。晚恐美人不知家国人情，与大使馆谈话中按法而论，故给先生之地址，盖以为我国事多重人情。

船公司请代保存船位至星期一上午十二时，已请延期两次矣。

〔袁同礼家人提供〕

按：将赴（此处）美旅行，似应为"将赴（此处）美旅行社"。先生收到后即覆。

三月二十五日

闵乃大覆函先生，告知其已决定返国，将携带大量书籍、仪器，先生借款须待到上海后设法归还。

守和先生大鉴：

昨晚返寓拜读大札，知教部未准，故晚返国后不必再至教部进行矣。不幸生为中国人，亦无可奈何？昨日晨，方决定计划返国，前奉函时，本拟返欧，以自美至德旅费不多，且德方与晚相适者较多，知晚之能力者亦较夥，然在纽约打听之下，护照签证问题，需若干时日，定船除头等外，需待两三日以后。晚之情形，不能在此多待一月，故不能不放弃此项计划。另有一机会，亦为海军部之工作，（为关于水电等问题）但该定须Clear之问题，且须待两三星期后，方能决定。因亦不能成就，自纽约返此后（昨日晨），始决计返国。先生之款到申后，先与梅校长相商，晚旅费四百美金已领到。例外或不可，但且看情形，但清华大学托晚购书籍仪器。所购之书籍仪器加运费，超过清华大学预付之款（到申后拟详算），且晚有最要在德难购之书籍（电工部），在三百本以上，按平时之价，在八千马克以上（约合美金两千元左右），晚黑买时亦已费去三百美金元以上。另尚送油糖等食物（此多为家岳母所赠），亦约合一百美金左右。万不得已时，或将割爱卖与清华大学，至少在二百美金元以上。且晚亦有一电动计算机，晚黑买时亦在一百美元左右，其价值一百五十至二百美金左右，不得已时亦可卖与清华大学，亦可得（至少）一百美金元，要之一切待至申再说。先生之款务设法整理就绪（但望先生能稍与时日)。再者,寄至上海贵馆之书籍,其价值远过晚前寄上之帐单,内亦有清华大学之一部。晚到申后,当详细整理一次,非贵馆之书籍应书明,暂存贵馆一部书籍,本代贵馆购买。先生在柏林时,本未嘱购买,且有一部重复者,晚计转让清华大学。到申后整理后,函发先生,再相磋商。此本到申后,亦将与梅校长谈及,再者曾奉上之帐目,尚未全,以晚无时清算故也。一小部报纸及书籍仍在柏林,(为数不多)故清算后,方知抑贵馆欠晚或晚欠贵馆一小部分款项。所带之物件将来按美旅行社寄费,按比例计算。今日晚已见裘开明先生,交一保险单,美金四十元零五分,关于帐单晚已交此处之美旅行社,该处另寄帐单至裘先生。匆此,即请旅安!

尊夫人与公子等统此请安不另!

晚闵乃大顿首

三月廿五日

晚全家廿八(明日)午起程赴旧金山,廿九日到卅日午离美。现晚家已无家具,故书写不便,谨后奉告。

〔袁同礼家人提供〕

按:信中"黑买"应为在黑市购买之意。

三月二十六日

钱存训覆函先生,收到支票和《金瓶梅》并谈芝加哥大学中国学生人数及教员变化。

守和先生:

奉到廿二日手示,敬悉一一,承寄支票亦已收照收。华盛顿大学寄回之《金瓶梅》尚未递到,芝大已有一部,一俟收到当代保存。中国学生现无人在此研究哲学,惟有一女士申请奖学金,拟研究中国哲学,尚未核准。芝大现有中国学生约七八十人,另有三四十人在其他各校,西北大学约有二十余人,全体名单正在编印,将来印成当为寄奉一份,学校章程已嘱校中寄奉。邓嗣禹君此间下年已不续聘,改由王伊同君担任,王君今夏在哈佛得博士学位,教现代史及中文。训拟试开一目录学概论,暑假或可抽暇从事准备也。董作宾先生来函表示颇想回芝任课,惟学校方面因无预算(董君在此,原由罗氏基金担任3,000,校方1,500),一时恐不能实现。匆匆,顺候阖府近安。

钱存训顿首

三,廿六

〔University of Chicago Library, Yuan T'ung-li Papers, Box 2〕

按:王伊同(Wang Yi-t'ung,1914—2016),字斯大,江苏江阴人,早年就读于南菁书院、金陵大学、燕京大学。1942 年受聘于金陵大学。1944 年赴哈佛大学东方语文系,获哲学博士学位的博士,其论文题目为 Official relation between China and Japan, 1368-1549,后于 1953 年出版;是年 6 月,邓嗣禹应费正清邀请,回哈佛大学任讲师,讲授"现代中国问题研究"课程。

三月二十八日　纽约

先生拜会史蒂文斯,告中国情况及个人近况。〔David H. Stevens' Diary, Rockefeller Archive Center, Rockefeller Foundation records, Officers' Diaries, RG 12〕

王重民在二月十日函后又补写一节,告平馆馆务尚平稳。

右信写好,因邮件不通,未能寄出。现已隔了一个多月,犹有请师一阅之价值。在此一个多月以内,经过都算良好,且稍有发展。大约四月一日以后,发展更快,下月初再将馆务作详细报告。又及。

三月廿八日

〔袁同礼家人提供〕

三月二十九日

顾子刚致函先生,告知馆务并请在美购买 Dry White Shellac。

Nat. Library, Peiping.

March 29, 1949

Dear Mr. Yuan,

(1) The Municipal Library is asking us for the return of the *华北新报* that we had borrowed. It is said that the *抗战* □ had returned it to you, but no one in the library knows where it is. Do you happen to remember where you had placed it?

(2) Can you buy and mail us 1 lb. of Dry White Shellac? The shellac we can buy here is brightly colored and when dissolved in alcohol is unsatisfactory for use on the books. I am told that there is a contrasting colorless kind to be had in the States. The dry kind is simpler to mail.

(3) Chase Bank February Statement shows they had chased our January check, so Wang's signature is O. K.

(4) The China Foundation has mailed a check for $1350 to the Chase Bank to be deposited to our a/c. Of this 100 must be the special grant for Light & Water. How should we use this money? Mr. F. Y. Wang once said you had already exchanged that money with a lady.

We are doing well here & my health is good too.

Sincerely,

T. K. Koo

〔袁同礼家人提供〕

按:Wang's signature 即指王重民作为代理馆长的签名。该函为其亲笔,寄纽约华美协进社收转。

三月

美国国会图书馆邀请先生出任该馆中文文献顾问。〔*Annual Report of the Librarian of Congress, for the fiscal year ending June 30, 1949*, Washington: United States Government Printing Office, 1950, p. 148〕

按:该职务并非正式馆员,主要工作是对 1947 年以来入藏的中文善本书进行编目、著录,有少许薪水。

四月一日

何多源覆函先生,告知所托印制名片将寄送北平,并谈国民政府教育部长换人。

守和馆长钧鉴:

接寄自檀岛之手谕后,曾上一函,谅蒙察阅。昨马鉴先生已将港币壹佰七十元寄下,咭片亦已代印,迟一二日即可寄往北平王重民先生。现教部经已易人,由杭立武继长,此间中央机关已有一部份迁返南京。谨此奉达,并请大安。

后学何多源上

卅八,四,一

〔广州大学用笺。University of Chicago Library, Yuan T'ung-li Papers, Box 2〕

四月四日

许烺光致函先生,将应邀为联合国教科文组织撰写文章,并告将赴耶鲁大学参加远东学会年会。

April 4, 1949

Dear Dr. Yuan:

Only day before yesterday I learned that you have now come to this country and are serving as advisor to the Library of Congress, and your letter of the 30th of March concerning the UNESCO request for one or two essays came as a very pleasant surprise. I shall indeed, be very glad to write the one or two essays for them. However, the deadline (end of May) seems a little close. However, I shall try my best. I haven't had time to study the details of the directives but shall do so in due time.

We came to Northwestern in 1947 and this is drawing to the close of my second year here. We like it here much better than Columbia or Cornell and hope that before long will have some time to visit the Midwest.

On the 6th and 7th of April there will be an Annual Meeting of the Far Eastern Association at Yale. I am planning to be there on the afternoon of the 6th and the whole of the 7th. If you are going to be there, I shall be very happy to see you indeed.

By the way, is your family here with you in the United States?

With best wishes, I am

Sincerely yours,

Francis L. K. Hsu

P. S. Shall I write to Mr. Mayonx confirming my acceptance of the proposition?

〔University of Chicago Library, Yuan T'ung-li Papers, Box 2〕

按:此件为打字稿,落款及补语为其亲笔。该函寄送先生及家人居所(1725, 21st Street, N. W. Washington, D. C.)。

四月五日

H. M. Gillette 致函先生,告知洛克菲勒基金会资助款余额情况。

April 5, 1949

Dear Dr. Yuan:

In accordance with your recent request, we are enclosing herewith a statement of charges in connection with your $5,000 grant for purchase of microfilming material. This shows a balance available of $697.96 after allowing for the estimated cost of shipping outstanding orders.

We shall hold this balance pending your instructions.

Yours very truly,

H. M. Gillette

〔Rockefeller Foundation. Series 601: China; Subseries 601.R: China-Humanities and Arts. Vol. Box 47. Folder 393〕

按：该函由华美协进社（c/o China Institute 125 East 65th Street New York）转寄。

四月六日　纽黑文市

中午，吴讷孙、李赋宁、李田意在“新中国”餐厅设宴，先生、何永佶、杨联陞等与席。

晚七时，Far Eastern Association 和 American Oriental Society 聚餐，约十时散，先生与杨联陞等人同归。〔《杨联陞日记》（稿本）〕

按：吴讷孙（1919—2002），生于北京，作家，笔名“鹿桥”，西南联合大学毕业，时应在耶鲁大学攻读美术史。李田意（1915—2000），河南汝阳人，1937 年毕业于南开大学，抗战中任西南联大助教，1945 年赴美留学，翌年获耶鲁大学历史学硕士学位，后在该校任教。何永佶（1902—1979），广东番禺人，清华学校毕业，后赴美留学，获哈佛大学政治学博士学位，归国后在北京大学法律系执教，1940 年 4 月在昆明与林同济等人创办《战国策》杂志。4 月 5 日至 7 日，美国东方学会和远东协会在耶鲁大学举办联合年会，先生并不是这两个学术组织的注册会员，但美国图书馆协会在 7 日上午安排了以美国各图书馆东方馆藏编目和图书馆发展为主题的讨论[1]，先生极有可能作为特邀嘉宾参加。

四月八日

H. M. Gillette 致函先生，前信所言余额已汇入平馆在大通银行的帐户，如

① Fairbank, Wilma. “News of the Profession.” *The Far Eastern Quarterly*, vol. 8, no. 4, Association for Asian Studies, 1949, pp. 451-452.

欲返还可随时联系基金会。

April 8, 1949

Dear Dr. Yuan:

Supplementing our letter of April 5th, we wish to advise that the balance of \$697.96 therein mentioned was inadvertently deposited to your account in the Chase Bank.

If you wish to refund any part of this to us for further purchases, no doubt you will so inform us.

Yours very truly,

H. M. Gillette

〔Rockefeller Foundation. Series 601: China; Subseries 601.R: China-Humanities and Arts. Vol. Box 47. Folder 393〕

按:该函由华美协进社转寄。

四月十二日

任鸿隽覆函先生,转告平馆近况并告知中基会已拨付本年度第一期购书款。

守和吾兄左右:

顷奉四月三日手示,敬悉已安抵华都读书憩息,至为忻慰。平馆王重民、顾子刚两君近皆有信来,似平馆虽被接管,尚无其他变动。重民信并云共方当局曾拨大笔款项,令馆中将近今接收书籍全行编目,故度藏书库又感不敷,拟将南长街中基会旧址收回与静生所房屋交换,唯此事能否进行则尚有待于调查矣。报载"中华教育基金委员会"被接收之询,当是"中法……"之误,因本会在平并无任何机关也。平馆购书费第一期一千三百余美金已发,又平馆与美国书肆通信数缄,已由此间代为转寄。知念并闻,专覆,即颂旅祉。

见 Dr. Hummel 及其他友人祈代致意,尊夫人及侄辈并候。

弟鸿隽敬启

内人嘱笔致候

卅八年四月十二日

〔中华教育文化基金董事会用笺。University of Chicago Library, Yuan T'ung-li Papers, Box 2〕

四月十三日

先生致信赵元任,寄上书评文章并告通讯地址。

元任先生:

弟于日前曾到 New Haven 参加美国东方年会,得晤老友甚多,又在美国人类学报见有关于大著之书评,爰附上,即希台阅。前寄上之火腿,不识味道如何?近日报载大批邮包被盗,想该火腿不致为其劫去也。适之先生近日有信否,为念。专此,顺颂俪安。

弟袁同礼顿首

四,十三

最近地址为 1725, 21st. Street, N. W., Washington, D. C.

〔University of California, Berkeley, The Bancroft Library, Yuen Ren Chao papers, carton 10, folder 39, Yuan, Tongli and Yuan, Huixi〕

按:“大著”似指 *Character Text for Mandarin Primer*,通译作《国语入门》或《官话初阶》,1948 年哈佛大学出版社初版,但信中所指书评待考,因并无对应的“美国人类学报”。

四月中上旬

先生向国会图书馆雇用办公室递交职位申请,其属意的岗位为中文编目员(Chinese cataloger)。〔袁同礼家人提供〕

按:4 月 15 日,该办事室负责人 Burnis Walker 致信施永高,请其评价先生的能力和经验是否可以胜任。然而,施永高因前往佛罗里达出差未能及时收到该信,后于 5 月 22 日覆函,对先生的能力和经验给予极高的评价。

四月十七日

赵元任覆函先生,回赠食物及衣物。

Apr. 17, 1949

守和我兄:

前接手书,并承赐赠 Virginia Smithfield 佳肴,多谢多谢!日前寄上食物一包,系寄至 Castleton Hotel 住址,如兄已迁居,希望旅馆对于转寄邮件不擦烂污。又弟有太小之洋服送上,不知世兄合穿否?近年弟之加重,可称谓“Fallacy of the Undistributed Middle”!一笑。此上,即颂俪祉。

弟赵元任

韵卿附笔问候

〔University of Chicago Library, Yuan T'ung-li Papers, Box 2〕

按:“世兄”应指袁澄。Fallacy of the undistributed middle 即逻辑学术语“中词不周延”,是一种形式谬误,指三段论中的中词在大前提或小前提中不周延,而导致论证无效。

四月十八日

先生致信李国钦基金会,递交资助申请,用以研究美国国家档案馆所藏中美外交档案。

April 18,1949

Li Foundation

Woolworth Building

233 Broadway

New York 7, N. Y.

Dear Sirs:

On my previous visit to Washington, my attention was called to the significant collection of Sino-American diplomatic documents preserved in the National Archives. Although they offer a wealth of material for the study of Chinese and American relations, no adequate study has yet been made by scholars, both Chinese and American.

Owing to the occupation of Peiping by the communists, I have therefore obtained two years' leave which I wish to spend at the National Archives in order to have a thorough study of these documents. Although it is primarily a labor of love, I do need a typist and an assistant to assist in typing and copying the huge mass of material. I also need $200 a month for my living expenses, as my own foreign exchange had already been surrendered to the Government at the time of the "New Currency Reform".

I was informed that your Foundation makes occasional grants to scholars engaged in serious research. In view of the importance of the project, I am taking the liberty to apply for a grant-in-aid from your

Foundation. I now enclose herewith a statement for your consideration.

I fully realize that your Foundation will have to meet many obligations and with a limited income it would be impossible to meet with all requests. If the funds available this year have already been allocated, I hope that my request may be taken up for consideration next year. I am sensible of the difficult situation confronting everybody at the present time and I am deeply grateful to your Foundation for whatever consideration you may give to this project.

Yours sincerely,

Tungli

〔袁同礼家人提供〕

按:李国钦(Li Kuo-ching,1887—1961),字炳麟,湖南长沙人,美籍华商领袖,被誉为"钨矿大王",1944 年创办李氏基金会(Li Foundation),该基金会的宗旨是"通过学术交流,促进美中友好关系"。此件为录副。

四月二十日

王毓铨覆函先生,略谈中国古代货币制度。

守和先生道鉴:

示敬悉。当日即奉函于道泉先生,计已到达。因家父母情况不明,拟早日结束此地研究工作,旋里省亲。未知今年能动身否?先晋同行否,尚未定。近两年中国古钱研究、我国古代货币制度,稍有心得。其一、二已见诸拙著短文,其他略举如下,敬请指教。

一、布(镈)之铸造,始于殷末周初,有嫚卣铭文为证。

二、由钱镈不同形而同功之农具发展为不同形制之空首布,钱名甚早,泉名始于王莽。

三、古代东夷之人文化甚高,专用刀货,如即墨、安阳、谭诸东夷之国均如是。齐地原行布钱,"造邦"之后采用刀货,亦东夷之影响。刀货由齐而至燕赵。

四、空首布施行时间极长,晚至周威烈王时,东周仍铸空首布。

五、东夷诸国及齐铸钱之权,国家专有。西方诸国唯秦自惠文王二年始专铸钱。

六、刀之钱名曰化,布曰釿,楚之金饼曰爰是即三种货币之单位,及圜钱出现,仍演用各地不同之货币单位。

七、总观有周一代大势,东方之经济势力远胜西方,东方刀货遍行燕赵,其货币单位日后亦被周地圜钱所采用。圜钱方孔始于东方,周末西方乃仿行之。

略谈如此,语无伦次。敬祈原谅,敬请大安。先晋问好。

晚学毓铨上

四月廿日

〔University of Chicago Library, Yuan T'ung-li Papers, Box 2〕

按:1950 年 3 月,王毓铨、胡先晋夫妇由香港回国。

四月二十五日

裘开明覆函先生,告知寄送所需册页两种并请汇来支票用以取来平馆所购德产照相镜头。

守和吾兄大鉴:

尊示敬悉。所嘱代取哈校来年课程,已于昨日寄上一份,费正清所编共产刊物书目已请其直接寄上二部。前接本地美国转运公司通知,贵馆在德所购照相镜头已抵此,共须运费洋五十六八角二分,前由闵乃大君转来洋四十元零五分,尚欠 $ 16.77,请开一支票 payable to American Express Co.,寄来以便往取该机暂存敝馆。匆复,即请撰安。

弟裘开明谨上

卅八,四,廿五日

嫂夫人请代致意。

〔袁同礼家人提供〕

按:"共产刊物书目"应指 *Chinese Communist Publications: an annotated bibliography of material in the Chinese Library at Harvard University*,费正清、任以都合编,1949 年以油印方式印刷,并未正式出版。

四月二十六日

先生致信 H. M. Gillette,告知洛克菲勒基金会资助款剩余部分拟用来购买摄影耗材。

April 26, 1949

Dear Mr. Gillette:

I beg to acknowledge the receipt of your letters dated April 5 and 8 together with a statement of charges in connection with the purchase of microfilming material for our Library.

The balance of $696.96 which you sent to the Chase Bank has been duly deposited to our account and will be used for the purchase of further photographic supplies for our photoduplication laboratory.

Owing to my absence from Washington, I regret that I have not been able to write to you earlier.

With renewed thanks for your assistance,

Yours sincerely,

T. L. Yuan

Director

〔Rockefeller Foundation. Series 601: China; Subseries 601.R: China-Humanities and Arts. Vol. Box 47. Folder 393〕

按:此件为打字稿,落款处为先生签名。

四月二十八日

费慰梅致函先生,邀请先生加入远东学会,并请将会费寄送该会继任秘书。

April 28, 1949

Dear Dr. Yuan:

It was a satisfaction to the Officers of the Far Eastern Association that you and a number of other non-members of the Association were sufficiently interested in our program and in meeting our nationwide membership to attend our first Annual Meeting in New Haven, April 5-7, 1949.

We hope very much that your attendance at the Meeting has persuaded you of the value of joining us to take a permanent part in our activities. I am enclosing a leaflet which will give you fuller information about the Association. If you decide to become a member, will you kindly fill out the membership blank on the reverse side and mail it with the check for your dues to our new Secretary, Professor Joseph K. Yamagiwa,

Department of Oriental Languages, University of Michigan, Ann Arbor, Mich. The check should be made out to The Far Eastern Association.

Sincerely yours,

Wilma Fairbank

Outgoing Secretary

I do hope you will join us and contribute from your experience to our activities.

〔袁同礼家人提供〕

按:Joseph K. Yamagiwa(1906-1968),日裔美国学者,生于西雅图,后长期担任密歇根大学日语教授、语言文学系主任。此件为打字稿,落款及补语皆为其亲笔。

四月二十九日

布朗致函先生,告知因为邮轮停航无法寄送中国各图书馆订购美方期刊胶片,询问此前订单退款方式,并询问先生谋职进展。

April 29, 1949

My dear Dr. Yuan:

We have been greatly delayed in winding up the orders you sent us for films for various libraries in China. For many months it has been very difficult to get any shipments to Peiping. Now it is impossible to make them to any library in northern China. I am sending you under separate cover a film designated for the Institute of Botany, National Academy of Peiping. I do not know what you want to do with it under the circumstances.

On account of the conditions in China we never made the final transfer of funds to the University of California as I wrote you and Mr. Coney. There is now a balance of $ 137.89 in the deposit made by you as granted by the China Foundation. We would like to clear up this account. Shall we send to you, as Librarian of the National Library of Peiping, a check for this amount or shall we return it to the American office of the China Foundation? If the latter, what is the address of the China Foundation. I see no hope of sending further shipments to China for some months to come. Please let me know what we should do with the balance of $ 137.89. I suppose you are still Librarian of the National Library of Peiping.

I regret we did not have an opportunity for a long personal talk at New Haven. There are so many matters I would like to know about. How did you make out with your conversations at Lake Success? I hope you can find some position in which your experience and admirable qualifications can be used. Of course, you realize that at present most libraries in this country are suffering from the recession and most libraries have reduced budgets for the coming year. However, I am sure that you will eventually find some opening which will give you an opportunity to be of service nationally and internationally.

Yours very truly,
Charles H. Brown
Associate Director

〔袁同礼家人提供〕

按:Lake Success 似指位于纽约的联合国临时总部,待考。此件为打字稿,落款处为其签名,该函寄送国会图书馆。

五月二日

法斯覆函先生,告知其将在本月中下旬前往华盛顿,届时面晤并了解中国、平馆近况,希望暂时停止使用资助款项购买设备和耗材。

May 2. 1949

Dear Dr. Yuan:

Your letter of April 26th to Mr. Gillette has been called to my attention. I expect to be in Washington, D. C. late this month, on May 19th and 20th. I should like, if possible, to see you then and to have from you more information with regard to the present status of purchases and equipment purchased under our grants in aid. I suppose that pending clarification of the situation in China you will wish to hold in abeyance further purchases under the grant in aid.

I wonder whether nine a. m. on May 19th at the Library of Congress would be satisfactory time and place to talk with you.

Sincerely yours,

Charles B. Fahs

〔Rockefeller Foundation. Series 601: China; Subseries 601.R: China-Humanities and Arts. Vol. Box 47. Folder 393〕

按:此件为录副。

五月六日

先生致信法斯,告知在国会图书馆的研究室,欢迎其来华盛顿时晤谈。

May 6, 1949

Dear Dr. Fahs:

Thank you for your letter of May 2nd.

I am delighted to learn that you have returned to New York and I look forward to your forthcoming visit to Washington with much pleasure.

My study at the Library of Congress is No. 237. I shall be glad to meet you there and talk over matters of common interest.

With warmest regards,

Yours sincerely,

T. L. Yuan

〔Rockefeller Foundation. Series 601: China; Subseries 601.R: China-Humanities and Arts. Vol. Box 47. Folder 393〕

按:此件为打字稿,落款处为先生签名。

五月七日

张歆海致函先生,告知其将赴华盛顿并盼藉此晤谈。

守和吾兄赐鉴:

日昨在友人处得悉阖府来美已久,并在华城作居,不胜欣慰。弟多年未去华京,下周拟利用□□假期之便,南来数日,星期二当可到达,住 Wardman Park Hotel。届时造访,藉以畅谭。特先奉告,并请俪安。

弟歆海

五月七日

〔袁同礼家人提供〕

按：张歆海（1900—1972），字叔明，原名张鑫海，生于上海，祖籍浙江海盐，民国外交官，清华学校毕业后赴美留学，归国后曾任教于北京大学、东南大学、光华大学、中央大学，1932 年任国民政府外交部欧美司司长，后又任驻葡萄牙公使、驻波兰公使等，1940 年举家移居美国洛杉矶，1945 年定居纽约长岛。

五月上旬

先生向联合国教科文组织（UNESCO）递交职位申请书。〔袁同礼家人提供〕

按：5 月 18、19 日，该组织覆信先生，告知目前纽约（Lake Success, New York）分部无空闲职位，但已将申请转寄巴黎总部。

五月十四日

陈源（英国）覆函先生，告知联合国教科文组织（巴黎）职员聘任情况。

守和吾兄：

奉手教，敬悉大驾及阖府均已安抵华京，不胜欣慰。缉斋兄仍在巴黎，本月五月聘约期满，本拟返国，以国内情形恶劣，故已应邀受续聘。Unesco 图书馆组人数极有限，高级位置仅有二三个，均已有人。彼等聘约大约均须在明年五月方期满（新任秘书长出来，声明如无特别理由，所有高级职员均一律续聘至明年五月）。届时各方自可推荐适宜人选竞争，但与旧人竞争究非易事。去岁接教后即曾与 Carter 谈过，Carter 谓组织中并无适当地位，可以聘致地位、声望、才力如兄者。Unesco 在巴黎，新秘书长又仅能运用法文（英文可听讲），故法文非常重要。我国同人在此者常有因法文不够，以至不能安于其位。兄近日致力法文，将来如到国际机关任职，可得不少帮助。弟不日去法开会，当再探询有无机缘。国事日恶，弟等在此如坐针毡，亦不知能维持几日。匆匆，顺颂俪祺。

弟陈源顿首

五月十四

〔University of Chicago Library, Yuan T'ung-li Papers, Box 3〕

按："本月五月"当作"本年五月"。Carter 或指 William D. Carter (1909-1989)，该人曾担任联合国教科文组织国际交换部门主任。

五月十九日

法斯至国会图书馆，与先生晤谈。话题涉及洛克菲勒基金会资助款、缩微胶片机、平馆在美账户等方面,先生表示平馆已经由研究图书馆转变为公共、大众图书馆。此外,先生告知法斯来美费用完全由自己负担,虽然作为国会图书馆的荣誉顾问,但薪水只是普通馆员水平。最后,先生表示愿意继续从事研究,希望洛克菲勒基金会可以资助研究计划,但法斯表示这一设想不太可能实现。〔Rockefeller Foundation. Series 601: China; Subseries 601.R: China-Humanities and Arts. Vol. Box 47. Folder 393〕

五月二十一日

先生致信克莱普,请协助向联合国教科文组织申请职务。

May 21, 1949

My dear Mr. Clapp:

I am most grateful to you and Dr. Evans for being able to be associated with the Library of Congress. I should like to stay indefinitely if it were possible for me to do so.

Since my appointment is good for six months, it seems advisable to make some plans now. The Chinese Ambassador suggested that I should join the UNESCO, as he feels that I could be of greater service there.

Since you and Dr. Evans know Director Torres Bodet very well, I wonder whether you could find it possible to make a recommendation. The UNESCO may be fairly well staffed by this time and it may be difficult to find a suitable opening. Nevertheless, I herewith enclose a statement of my academic and professional career which you may perhaps like to have if you have occasion to write to Dr. Bodet on my behalf.

With renewed thanks,

Yours sincerely,

T. L. Yuan

〔Library of Congress, The Central File Macleish-Evans〕

按:Jaime Torres Bodet(1902–1974),墨西哥诗人、作家、教育家,1948年至1952年担任联合国教科文组织主任。6月7日,埃文斯致信Torres Bodet,推荐先生担任联合国教科文组织的相关职务。

六月七日

法斯致函先生,告知洛克菲勒基金会无法资助先生个人研究。

June 7, 1949

Dear Dr. Yuan:

As I promised you at the time of our recent discussion in Washington, D. C., I have explored with my colleagues here the possibility for assistance to your research projects. I regret to say that we do not see any possibility of obtaining such help for you. I can only hope that you will be able to find other ways of continuing your work on Chinese materials.

It was helpful to have from you the clear statement which you gave me with regard to the present status of the grant in aid which The Rockefeller Foundation made to the National Library for microfilm equipment. As you know, this grant in aid expires on December 31 of this year. At that time the balance remaining in the account will revert to the Foundation and should be returned along with the accounting for expenditures made. Of course, this accounting and reversion could be made at an earlier date if in view of disturbed conditions in China it would simplify your own responsibilities to do so.

Sincerely yours,

Charles B. Fahs

〔Rockefeller Foundation. Series 601: China; Subseries 601.R: China-Humanities and Arts. Vol. Box 47. Folder 393〕

按:此件为录副。

六月十一日

先生致信法斯,告知已订购了额外的胶卷设备,其中超出洛克菲勒基金会资助款部分由平馆经费负担。

June 11, 1949

Dear Dr. Fahs:

Referring to the purchase of microfilm equipment as raised in your letter of June 7, I beg to state that I had consulted Mr. Eugene Power and other experts in microphotography. They suggested that an additional Eastman Kodagraph Microfilm Reader and a Stineman reel be purchased out of the balance of the Foundation's grant.

I have accordingly placed the order, but the cost of these items will exceed the balance of your grant. The deficit will be made up from our own funds.

I shall submit to your Foundation a detailed statement of the expenditures together with the invoices as soon as I receive them.

Yours sincerely,

T. L. Yuan

Director

〔Rockefeller Foundation. Series 601: China; Subseries 601.R: China-Humanities and Arts. Vol. Box 47. Folder 393〕

按:此件为打字稿,落款处为先生签名。

六月十五日

洛克菲勒基金会覆函先生,希望平馆的缩微胶片设备能够为外国学者服务。

June 15, 1949

Dear Dr. Yuan:

Thank you for your note of June 11 explaining the use to which you are putting the balance of our grant in aid to the National Library in Peiping. I hope that the microfilm equipment will prove of continuing use not only to Chinese scholarship but to intellectual exchange between China and other countries of the world.

Sincerely yours,

〔Rockefeller Foundation. Series 601: China; Subseries 601.R: China-Humanities and Arts. Vol. Box 47. Folder 393〕

按:写信人应为法斯,落款处印章已无法辨识。

王重民覆函先生,请先生从速回国主持馆务,并谈平馆、个人近况。

守和吾师道鉴:

今日奉到四月十八日手谕,捧读之下,极为欢乐。想师母、师兄、师姊等,必定都好,都快乐。望早早给他们找好学校,即可留在美国读书,而吾师和师母,则应快快返国,不必待到明年也。自上海解放,我们和政府商议,拟即专电吾师快快返国主持馆务。曾与郭沫若、郑振铎、许德珩诸先生商讨,惟恐电文太短,不能说动吾师,遂改由派驻美负责人,专访吾师详谈,一切决定,再由教育界人士联名去电欢迎也。此事曾与希渊先生通信两次,已托他致师一信,详述应早来也。最好是今年秋间离美赴苏联,届时全中国当已解放,则冬初可到北平,而那时正是联合政府已成立,对外邦交恢复,则吾馆对外,当极活跃也。

因邮件不通,最近三个月没有写信,兹再将馆务发展,作一简单报告:①人事:王访渔已撤职查办,王祖彝仅撤职。祖彝还未多说话,子访则屡屡刁难,其意多在攻击顾子刚。子刚已还言,惟恐互奸则出丑也。阮为群、冯宝琳、张我忠等都考入华北大学。新人则招考八人,在中、西两编目股工作。于道泉已返馆,丁濬七月中旬赴英。近因阅览延长,拟再添十人。装订室已决定添四人。②经费:馆员薪给,比早先好多,想已听到。现有办公费每月小米六千余斤(约合四十余万元),购书费每月四千六百斤,事业费每年十五万斤。已支用七万五千斤,买了七十二万张卡片(够用二年或三年),订作七千书套,其余买装订材料。他如买两辆自行车,修葺房屋、宿舍,皆是临时请款。③图书:除每月确定购书经费外,又发来五十万元买新书。那时一斤小米不过九元,故此款至今花不完。收入之书,有贺孔才捐善本八十余种,普通一万二千余册。马某犯罪,抄来藏书八十箱。霍明志达古斋捐出全部藏书,约一万册。华北图书馆交来善本四十余种。华北大学交来赵城金刻藏经四千三百三十卷。其余零星收入,总是源源不绝。自金刻藏经批归吾馆,曾设法亦拟将白云观道藏搬来,但一时未成。而松坡圕已决定并入吾馆,拟将该馆所藏宋刻藏经搬来。此后凡有善本,统归吾馆,盖已成一定例矣。④工作:前接收汉奸图书,已批归吾馆全权支配,连同伦氏、汉奸及新收普通书,已有三十万册未编目,自中文编目增四人后,每月可编五千余册。内因新书太多,拟再聘编旧书三四人,不难每月编两万册,则一年半可编完。太庙日文书四十万册,华北政府允拨费雇临时职工三十人,则半年可分配完,而吾馆除得一正本外,还可得一副本。连旧有可得十二万册至十五万册,唯旧有日文股职员程度不佳,怕需分配之后,方能专心编日文书目,届时需聘二三位精通日文之人。西文编目增两人,一人专编小册子。现西文每月可编五百余种,(500)一年多亦可编完。目前最难者为书库,拟稍稍整理。现已绘图作计划,并专为此加工友二人搬书。对于南京、上海两办事处,尚无具体整顿计划。静生生物研究所已并入北大及北平研究院,那房子想数月内可划归吾馆所有。⑤生个人:现仍以北大教书为主。圕专科今年有毕业生四人,未毕业者尚有八人。自下学年可正式成立,八月招新生时即正式招考第一年级学生。唯因请不到教授,最是困难。现在觉明任北大圕馆长,而汤用彤先生拟调他去作文科研究所所长,命生作北大圕馆长。生则以行政非所长,俟吾师回国后,即仍入书库读书。故与觉明商议,拟请吕叔湘先生来北大圕专科作教授,稍熟习之后,则请他作北大馆长也。生半年以来,不但学无寸进,且忘了许多,故急欲回头读书,再过七八年或十年,方愿作行政职务也。且携回稿子那样多,一点没有整理,实非生所想到者。且教书十年,可多造就一些人才,也是一件极重要的事情。专此,敬请旅安!师母问好!

受业重民上

六月十五日

存香港之币,给马季明写信数封,皆不理。请师调往美国或寄回北平,均可。

〔袁同礼家人提供〕

按:许德珩(1890—1990),原名许础,字楚生,江西德化人,早年入北京大学,后赴法留学,归国后曾任九三学社理事长。冯宝琳(1920—2019),1946年入馆。“马某”即马衡。

是年夏

先生作归国计划。〔《杨联陞日记》(稿本)(本年6月30日)〕

六月二十一日

先生致信克莱普,请其在巴黎就近与联合国教科文组织主任联系,推荐先生前往该处任职。

June 21, 1949

My dear Mr. Clapp:

It was very kind of you to ask Dr. Evans to recommend me to the Director of UNESCO. I am sure that this recommendation will receive due consideration if there is an appropriate opening.

I trust that a further word from you would certainly carry weight. If opportunities occur, perhaps you may like to make some necessary contact on my behalf while you are in Paris. I am particularly interested in the two-year program of technical and economic development for under-developed areas. I understand that that UNESCO will get a special budget of $16,855,500 for elementary, technical and adult education. If the whole project is approved by the Social and Economic Council in July, more technical men will be employed by UNESCO.

I wish you every success in the deliberations of the Conference on Science Abstracting and I am hoping to hear more about it on your return.

Yours sincerely,

T. L. Yuan

〔Library of Congress, The Central File Macleish-Evans〕

按：此时，克莱普应在巴黎参加国际会议。

胡适覆函先生，告知其不会接受“外长”任命，并谈陈寅恪近况，希望先生就“陈垣给胡适的公开信”谈自己的想法。

守和兄：

谢谢你的两封信。

外长事，我事前不知道，直到六月十二早上我在乡间（Ithaca）接到U.P.的电话，才知道有此消息，我还当是流言，不以为真！

此事我决不干，并不是不愿吃苦，实在是因为我自省决无此能力，不可祸国。

寅恪在岭南甚苦，但恐港大更不如岭大。你何不写信给马季明谈谈此事？（程绥楚的话也不可过信。此君是教书匠中的小政客。）

华侨日报（六月十五）登出“陈垣给胡适的公开信”，你看了没有？我盼望你能看见此信，并盼望你能告诉我此信是不是伪造的。此信第一段引我去年十二月十三夜讨论邻苏老人年谱的信末几句话，是完全真的。问题是，此信全部是真的吗？

匆匆问安，并乞问恒先生安。

胡适敬上

卅八，六，廿一

〔University of Chicago Library, Yuan T'ung-li Papers, Box 7〕

按：Ithaca位于纽约州中心，康乃尔大学等高校在此地。程绥楚（1916—1997），字靖宇，湖南衡阳人。“邻苏老人”即杨守敬（1839—1915），湖北宜都人，字鹏云，晚号邻苏老人，年谱为其自编。

七月十九日

王重民致函先生，请购外文刊物并代为联系马鉴。

守和吾师道鉴：

丁濬兄不久赴英，连前信一同到香港付邮，故得再禀数事：

1.寄上美金百元，除订刊物三种，P. M.日报一种及还账外，请从纽约的International Publishers及其他书铺代售莫斯科的Foreign Languages Publishing House各种有关苏联及马列主义的小册子等。

2.丁濬赴英，本来也想托他买一些前进的书报，可是没有外汇。请师给马季明写一信，最好将港币转几十镑到英国，交丁先生买书。生与马先生数信，皆置不答，故请吾师给他写信。

3.L. C.善本书目，又继续印刷，大约二、三月内可印出。五十元不够，如见恒先生，请多准备几百元。又生向他要之编索引用费，亦请早日寄来，或交吾师转，均可。专此，即请钧安！

生重民。

卅八，七，十九

〔袁同礼家人提供〕

按：International Publishers是纽约的一家出版公司，侧重马克思理论著作，涵盖经济学、政治学、历史学等方面，1946年成立，1964年停业。

八月十五日

张印堂覆函先生，告知其本拟返国回清华大学任教但因无船可坐只得推迟，并谈将赴纽约。

守和兄大鉴：

昨奉手教，敬悉一是。关弟下年行址，月前曾致函希渊兄及叶企孙院长，并告于八月间如有去沪轮船，印决返校任教，惟以沪船未通，欲行不能，势将暂请假一年，待明夏海上交通恢复再行返华，除另函清大校当局外，望便中转达希渊兄是荷。

再承询拙著《蒙古问题》一书，该书系《万有文库》之一，商务出版，并不单售，弟未带出，想兄可设法觅得，如能为弟代购一二册，尤所欢迎。

弟去年在密大任教为暂时访问性质，工作待遇均为半时，故未进行继续。近有友人介绍去纽约大学巴芬楼师院任教，系代替该校休假之教授一年，弟决定于九月初启程，将来如有去华府参观机会，当趋前拜访。耑此奉陈，并祝时祺。

弟印堂拜启

八，十五

〔University of Chicago Library, Yuan T'ung-li Papers, Box 2〕

按:《蒙古问题》,《万有文库》第二集七百种,1937 年 3 月初版。

八月二十三日

先生致信联合国人事招聘部门（Recruitment and Examination Section, Personnel Bureau）主管，再次表示愿意申请相关（临时）工作职位。

August 23, 1949

Dear Sir:

I greatly appreciate your kind letter of 18th May (Ref. AFS-228/LV.)

In view of the forthcoming meeting of the General Assembly, it is probable that there might be some opening at the United Nations for positions of temporary nature. I hope your Bureau will kindly contact me if such an opening occurs.

I have followed closely with the outstanding work of the United Nations, and I shall consider it a great privilege if I were able to associate myself with the execution of a small part of the program even for a short period.

I trust that you still keep my papers in connection with my application for employment last spring. I shall be glad to come for an interview if you think it necessary.

Very sincerely yours,

Tung-li Yuan

〔袁同礼家人提供〕

按:此件为录副。

八月二十七日

先生致信罗家伦,询问中华民国政府人员撤离藏区的内情。

志希大使学兄惠鉴:

久未通讯,想起居清豫,阖第安善。年来折冲樽俎,为国宣勤,引企贤劳,益深佩仰。弟于共军入平之前一月奉令撤退,近月以来在美研究我国边疆问题,颇能读书,又恢复学生生活,引以为乐。此次中央驻藏人员被迫撤退,内中情形想必复杂,因念兄处对于中央必有详尽之情报,未识能否抄寄一份,俾明真象,不胜感祷。此间所藏蒙藏新疆之资料为数颇丰,弟得乘机涉历,亦快事也。暑中炎热,新德里尤甚,仍希格外珍摄为荷。专此,顺颂俪安。

弟袁同礼顿首

八,廿七

尊夫人同此问安。

尊处如有关于 Bhutan 及印度最近交涉之资料,亦希惠寄是感。

〔《罗家伦先生文存·附编:师友函札》,页 300-301〕

按:1947 年 2 月 28 日,国民政府任命罗家伦为驻印度特命全权大使。Bhutan 即不丹。

九月二日

何多源覆函先生,告知罗应荣、黄延毓及广州高校近况,并谓平馆欲将存香港大学冯平山图书馆之书北运。

袁先生钧鉴:

八月廿三日手书敬悉。罗应荣先生□所著之《中俄蒙的国际关系》一书尚未出版,渠现在美国但不悉详细地址,渠另有一文名《外蒙古第一次独立的始末》,载在岭南出版之《历史政治学报》第二期,未知曾邀尊览否?黄延毓先生赴英讲学,现住美国(不知其地址),如在美找不到工作则回岭大。教部主要人员全部在广州办公,赴台、渝者均中下□职员,政府决心保卫广州,不欲将主要人员迁渝以动摇人心。敝校因种种困难不拟他迁,岭南亦已开学,学生人数并无减少,有一千一百余人。昨接北平圕七月四日来函,谓香港大学请求将存冯平山之图书他迁,现拟将书运平,嘱源代查存书状况及搬运手续。源已复函请其将运费汇陈君葆先生，如需源赴港代办装运手续亦可，但现尚未获其复函。香港代订杂志之书店有香港德辅道中大公书局一家，但不甚可靠。草此奉复。

何多源

九月二日

〔袁同礼家人提供〕

按：罗应荣（1918—1971），广东兴宁人，法学家、历史学家，1942年毕业于西南联合大学，后考入清华大学法学研究所国际法组研究生，1946年获得硕士学位，论文题目为《中蒙边界问题》，后入岭南大学任讲师，1948年受洛克菲勒基金会资助赴美留学，翌年转入伯克利分校学习国际法，1950年夏归国。黄延毓，广东梅县人，黄遵宪之孙，1932年毕业于岭南大学，1937年赴美留学，1940年获哈佛大学博士学位，毕业后回岭南大学任教，1948年8月13日离港赴英国讲学①，后到美国工作。此件似为吴光清誊抄，与9月13日钱存训函在同一张纸上。

九月十一日

先生自纽约出发前往欧洲。〔袁同礼家人提供〕

九月十三日

钱存训覆函先生，告知芝加哥大学图书馆藏内外蒙古书籍情况，并谈家眷已购得船票来美。大意如下：

久疏函候，敬维起居佳吉。顷奉八月廿七日手谕，因假期未到馆，致稽延奉覆为歉。承询此间所藏内外蒙古书籍，经查阅后，知重要著作均未入藏，另纸录出三种附供一阅。Laufer Collection 有蒙文书若干种，未经编目亦无人能识，并此附闻。敝眷滞港已经三月，幸目下手续均经办妥，定乘二十日开行之 Wilson 号由港启程，下月中可抵此。我公如知有熟人搭乘此船来美者，恳即赐函介绍，俾途中得有照应，特此拜恳。现觅得学校公寓一所，离办事处不远，尚称顺利。匆匆，顺颂阖府近安。

钱存训

九月十三日

① 《南洋商报》，1948年8月14日，第5版。

1)《内外蒙古考察日记》,马鹤天著,民廿一年。

2)《满汉蒙文晰义》,四册。

3)《钦定续纂外藩蒙古回部王公传》十二卷,又表十二卷。

〔University of Chicago Library, Yuan T'ung-li Papers, Box 2〕

按:Laufer Collection 即劳费尔(Berthold Laufer,1874－1934)特藏,芝加哥大学 1947 年购入此批书籍。此件似为吴光清誊抄,信后有补语,似亦吴光清所写,原文为"Orientalia Inc.来明片问 *Russia and the West in Iran, 1918－1948* by George Lenczowski, $ 4.50 □□□□要不要? Book of the Month Club 寄来书三本,其中一 free 其他二者之帐单为 $ 9.00。国会图书馆发薪 $ 132 左右是给您的支票)"。

九月十九日　巴黎

联合国教育科学文化组织(UNESCO)召开第四次大会,中国代表团与会人员为梅贻琦(首席代表)、熊庆来、陈源、李书华、先生。〔《思忆录》,中文部分页 63〕

按:此次会期至 10 月 15 日。

九月中旬

先生致信金问泗。〔《金问泗日记》下册,页 975〕

按:此信于 9 月 21 日送达。

九月二十六日

先生致信联合国教科文组织人事部主管,再次申请应聘相应的岗位,尤其是该组织在日本的工作职位。

September 26, 1949

Dear Sir:

I appreciate very much your kind letter of May 18 with regard to my application for employment with UNESCO.

I am greatly impressed with the immense amount of activities being carried on by the Organization. I should consider it a great privilege if I were able to join the staff of UNESCO and contribute my humble share in the execution of even a small part in its program.

I am much interested in UNESCO activities in Japan. As I am

personally acquainted with many Japanese scholars and as I have a knowledge of the Japanese, I hope very much that opportunities may occur in the future for me to assist UNESCO in carrying out its general program in Japan.

I shall be in Paris until October 6th. If you think it necessary for me to have an interview with officers of the Organization, will you kindly make appointments for me and be good enough to let me know?

Yours truly,

Tung-li Yuan

〔袁同礼家人提供〕

按:此时先生的联系地址为 Elysées Hotel, 100, Rue La Boetie, Paris。该件为录副。

九月二十七日

上午,先生赴联合国教科文组织总部,与人事部助理 Margaret Gorham 女士晤谈。〔袁同礼家人提供〕

按:本日晚些时候,该女士致函先生,请于 9 月 29 日下午 3 时前往该所会见任命与职员关系(Appointments and Staff Relations)主管 Dias,做进一步商谈。

九月

先生卸任国会图书馆中文文献顾问。〔*Annual Report of the Librarian of Congress, for the fiscal year ending June 30, 1949*, Washington: United States Government Printing Office, 1950, p. 148〕

按:此项邀请为期半年左右,似与先生申请联合国教科文组织职务、有意归国等互为因果,彼此影响。

九十月间

先生赴罗马,盘桓一周,曾遇崔道录等。〔袁同礼家人提供〕

按:崔道录,江苏东台人,国立西南大学法律学研究生毕业,随即留校执教,1945 年考取教育部第二届公费留学生,翌年赴罗马大学学习法律。

十月上旬

先生离开巴黎,前往英伦。〔袁同礼家人提供〕

十月十三日

先生致信克莱普,请在国会图书馆代订研究室。

August 13, 1949

Dear Mr. Clapp:

After the UNESCO conference I spent a week in Rome. I was delighted to see that active preparations are being made for the Holy Year in 1950.

I expect to return on the S/S Queen Mary, arriving New York October 27. As I expect to continue my research at the Library of Congress, may I ask you to request Col. Webb to assign me a study room annex beginning from November 1, as I gave up my room before leaving for Paris. I shall greatly appreciate your courtesy in this regard.

I am having a rest here which is so delightful in every way. With kind regards,

Yours sincerely,

T. L. Yuan

〔Library of Congress, The Central File Macleish-Evans〕

按:此件为先生亲笔,时间错写为 August,实应为 October。该信以航空信方式寄送,10 月 17 日送达国会图书馆秘书处。

十月二十日

卜德致函先生,告知其在费城的住址和联系电话,并表示将在该地俱乐部作两场有关中国近况的报告。

October 20, 1949

Dear Dr. Yuan:

It is an unexpected surprise to learn that you are going to be in the Philadelphia area in the near future. When you arrive, you can get in touch with me by phoning Victor 4-8392. My home address is 29 West Phil-Ellena Street, Philadelphia 19. This is in the Germantown section of Philadelphia, some nine miles out from the downtown portion.

On Saturday, Oct. 29, at 9 p. m. (I don't know why it is scheduled so late), I am going to give a talk on what I saw in China before the Chinese

Students Club of Philadelphia. It will be given at the International House, 3905 Spruce Street, West Philadelphia, which is quite near the Univ. of Penn. If you wished to attend this, I am sure you would be quite welcome, and in that case perhaps we could meet for dinner in the vicinity beforehand. I must state frankly, however, that in what I am going to say it will be necessary for me to make remarks which will not be favorable toward the Nationalist Government. Then on Monday, Oct. 31, at 7:15 p. m., I shall be giving a somewhat similar but briefer talk at the Current Events Club, Common Room, Goodhart Hall, Bryn Mawr College. Here again I know you will be more than welcome if you wish to come and are still in Bryn Mawr on that day. I think that Dr. Charles David, Director of the Univ. of Penn. Library, plans to be present.

With cordial greeting,

Sincerely yours,

Derk Bodde

〔University of Chicago Library, Yuan T'ung-li Papers, Box 2〕

按:1949年8月28日,卜德夫妇由塘沽坐船南下,9月9日抵达香港,随后乘飞机回到美国,9月19日回到费城家中。[①] 此件为打字稿,落款处为其签名。

十月二十七日

先生抵达纽约。〔袁同礼家人提供〕

十一月二十一日

Richard G. Irwin 覆函先生,告知加州大学伯克利分校不会购买明版《锦绣万花谷》《金瓶梅》,并谈其东亚馆藏分类上架进度缓慢。

East Asiatic Library,

Nov. 21, 1949

Dr. T. L. Yuan

123 B Street, S. E.,

Washington, D. C.

① Derk Bodde, *Peking Diary, a year of revolution*, New York, 1950, pp. 249, 258.

Dear Dr. Yuan:

Thank you for your letter of the 14th, offering us the chance to secure *Chin-hsiu wan-hua-ku* and *Chin-p'ing-mei* in Ming editions. It so happens that I purchased the former in Shanghai, and we are not interested in the latter, so I shall return the sheet on which they are described to enable you to send it to another library. I wonder whether Chicago University or the University of Pennsylvania have them? We appreciate your thinking of our collection, and would be glad to learn of similar opportunities when they come to your attention, but in this case can only refuse.

We are so badly behind in reclassifying the bulk of our collection, and at the same time so lacking-temporarily-in space, that this year's purchases in China and Japan haven't even been unpacked. I hope that by the time you return to China, we shall have them on the shelves; that will be the best report I could write!

I trust that you are having a profitable time in Washington, and am glad to know of your successful trip to Europe. We shall look forward to seeing you when you do come to the west coast.

Sincerely yours,

Richard G. Irwin

〔University of Chicago Library, Yuan T'ung-li Papers, Box 2〕

按:此件为打字稿,落款处为其签名。

十一月二十四日

先生致信钱存训,谈国内形势并请协助售卖友人熊式一古籍等事。

存训吾兄:

奉到惠书,欣悉宝眷业已安抵芝城,一切顺适,至以为慰。此间食物不昂,想阖家到美以后,均已增加重量,自较在国内为佳也。贵阳近又解放,不识令弟近有信否?筑行人事有无变动?又上月在英闻述尧兄近结婚,又闻英外部言印度主张承认新政府最力,不识渠将来作何计划?令侄令侄女在沪曾有信否?闻沪上失业者较多,似远不如平津也。平馆丁濬君前由弟推荐赴英研究,弟在英伦,渠已往 Glasgow 读书,故未晤面,据其来信北平同事之薪水均未发全,欠伊之薪水颇不少也。英国友人熊式一先生有明活字本《锦绣万花谷》四十八巨册，如芝大尚未入藏，务希设法劝顾立雅先生购入，因活字本书价可略减确不易得也。弟需下列各参考书，而L. C.并未入藏，请将尊处已有者作一标记，以便用互借办法借阅。尊处所选论文题目极有价值，所需之工具书，闻子明兄言，尊处业已采集完全，只有由亚利伯文译成中文者，究有若干，尚无专目。弟正收集此项资料，将来再行奉闻。因L. C.此类藏书不多，尚未获到新资料也。弟在此研究获益匪浅，拟明后年再行返国，沪京两办事处均无信来，大约由沪寄信颇不易也。专此，顺颂时祉。

弟同礼顿首

十一，廿四日

颇需用之书：

《中俄约章会要》　总理衙门印

《中俄约章汇编》　外交部条约司编

《中俄外交史料》　故宫博物院印

《中俄国际约注》　施绍常

《中俄界务沿革记略》　张弢

《中俄边疆形势地图》　中华航空协进会编

《俄程日记》　杨宜治

《陶模之文集》

《使俄日记》　张德彝

《使俄草》　王之春

《小方壶斋舆地丛钞》

《清光绪勘定西北边界俄文译汉图例》　许景澄

《许文肃公遗稿及外集》　许景澄　出使函稿

〔钱孝文藏札〕

按："令弟"即钱存造，时任中国银行贵阳支行经理。[①]"述尧兄"即钱存典（1905—1997），字述尧，毕业于金陵大学，曾任"中华民国驻印度大使馆参事"。[②] 10月6日，钱存训夫人许文锦携三个

①《钱存训文集》第3卷，页321。

② 糜文开《圣雄甘地葬礼记》，《东方杂志》第44卷第5期，页24。

女儿抵达芝加哥。

十一月二十六日

先生致信法斯，告知利用洛克菲勒基金会资助款订购一台缩微阅览器，并谈平馆馆务平稳。

November 26, 1949

Dear Dr. Fahs:

With reference to the balance of your grant ($ 697.96) in connection with the microfilm equipment, I wrote to our Acting Director in Peiping last June and asked whether an additional Microfilm Reader was desired. It took a long time for his reply to reach me and in his letter, it was stated that such a Reader was urgently needed and he would appreciate it if an order for it could be placed at once.

The order was placed with the Eastman Kodak Company and it was only yesterday that I received the following reply dated November 23, 1949:

> "Please pardon our delay in acknowledging receipt of your remittance of $ 697.96. We have received the remittance and have credited it to your account on our books. However, we do not have the Film Reader available for shipment at the present time, and it may be a matter of several months before we can supply it".

I am urging them to arrange early shipment at the early convenient opportunity.

Professor van der Sprenkel and Dr. Bodde have spoken very favorably about conditions in our Library. Everything seems very satisfactory under Mr. C. M. Wang's administration.

Yours sincerely,

T. L. Yuan

Director

〔Rockefeller Foundation. Series 601: China; Subseries 601.R: China-Humanities and Arts. Vol. Box 47. Folder 39〕

按：Professor van der Sprenkel 即 Otto van der Sprenkel（1906－1978），出生于荷兰，后在英国学习经济学，1931 至 1933 年担任多伦多大学政治学讲师，1943 年开始在亚非学院旁听有关中文的课程，1947 作为访问学者赴南开大学，与他人合著*New China: three views*，1950 年伦敦出版。此件为打字稿，落款处为先生签名。

徐家璧覆函先生，告知哥伦比亚大学图书馆或有可能购入《锦绣万花谷》，并谈大陆情况及其有意返国。

守和馆长钧鉴：

敬肃者，顷奉月之二十四日手谕，诵悉种切，无任欣慰。嘱为代查之书单壹纸，兹已查讫，用特奉呈，惜已入藏者无多，恐未能有所裨助，倘似借阅当可由馆际互借寄上不误。至式一先生珍藏之《锦绣万花谷》壹书，已将英文说明转交本部主任（Mr. Howard P. Linton）加以考虑，想日内可得确信，惟现下馆中已有该书，明嘉靖十五年（1536）刊本壹部，且目前购书款项极少，据度情势希望似在可否之间，倘公有意向 Linton 直接推荐此书，请即火速来函可也。又影印明本之《金瓶梅》早经入藏，恐系子刚先生代为搜集，知注特闻。胡绍声君回沪以后，尚未来函，是以不悉其个人印象若何，惟据闻似不如平津安定。《纽约时报》记者 Walter Sullivan 新近离沪，刻在朝鲜汉城报道解放区情形（自十一月二十五日起），内容翔实，似可作为参考，如华府易得该报，不妨检出并按日阅之。刻内子尚留重庆，已数月未得消息，无任焦急。明春如时局稍定，职即有意返国也。匆匆不恭，敬颂道安。

职徐家璧谨上

十一月廿六日夜

阖府统乞代候。

月前寄奉尊处之《哥大中国学生会年刊》壹册，谅已用毕，便中敬恳赐还，以留纪念为感。

〔袁同礼家人提供〕

按：Howard P. Linton（1912－1976），1934 年毕业于达特茅斯学院（Dartmouth College），曾跟随拉铁摩尔学习，1947 年起在哥伦比

亚大学图书馆任职，后负责东亚馆藏。[1] 胡绍声与徐家璧均曾任职于西南联合大学图书馆，且同宿昆明师范学院，彼此十分熟悉。

十一月二十八日

赵万里致函先生，请先生回国重掌平馆馆务。

守和馆长先生：

别后忽已一年，遥想德辉，无任怀念。本馆自解放后，有三兄一秉吾公旧规，多方应付，得以安度难关。现时经常、事业各费及人员，均有增加，各处捐购之书，接踵而至。配合新中国文化建设高潮，此后本馆在全国圕事业中实居领导地位。在新政府文化部部长为沈雁冰。新政府成立前，本馆属于华北人民政府高教会，现时改隶文化部。文物局文化部六局之一。文物局分三处，一、圕处；二、博物馆处；三、文物处。主持下，前途无限光明。文物局负责人郑西谛正局长、王冶秋副局长两先生均以吾公羁居海外，决非长策，拟恳早日回驾新京，共襄建国大业。万里暨本馆多数同人，久随吾公，一旦远离，不胜依恋，望公之来，有如望岁，尚乞俯顺舆情，即日启程赴欧转苏考察返国，固本馆同人之幸，亦全国圕界所殷殷切望也。如何之处，请熟虑后示知为祷为感。赵城金刻藏经四千三百余卷，松坡馆旧藏宋刻大藏，均已移归本馆善本书库。傅沅老本月初婴疾逝世，公子晋生拟遵遗嘱将“双鉴”宋刻《通鉴》、宋抄《洪范政鉴》捐献本馆，以垂永志。谨以附闻。匆上，即请道安。

万里再拜

十一月廿八日

太太前问候，均此。

〔袁同礼家人提供〕

十一月三十日

法斯覆函先生，质疑十一月二十六日来信中表述，因为根据六月十一日来信，洛克菲勒基金会资助已经用尽。

November 30,1949

① Goodrich, L. Carrington. “Obituary: Howard P. Linton (1912 - 1976).” *The Journal of Asian Studies*, vol. 36, no. 2, 1977, p. 329.

Dear Dr. Yuan:

Thank you for your letter of November 26, indicating the present status of our grant in aid to the National Library of Peiping for microfilm equipment. As I understand it, from your earlier letter of June 11, your order to the Eastman Kodak Company constitutes a commitment for more than the balance remaining in our grant in aid, the remainder to be paid out of other funds of the National Library of Peiping under your control.

We shall look forward to a final report from you when this equipment has been shipped.

Sincerely yours,

Charles B. Fahs

〔Rockefeller Foundation. Series 601: China; Subseries 601.R: China-Humanities and Arts. Vol. Box 47. Folder 393〕

按:此件为录副。

十二月八日

先生致信法斯,告知此前洛克菲勒资助款中仍有余款,而六月十一日信中涉及的订单由平馆实际支付。

December 8, 1949

Dear Dr. Fahs:

Thank you so much for your letter of November 30.

I have just received the following letter from the Eastman Kodak Company enclosing a receipt for $697. 96 representing the balance of your grant-in-aid for microfilm equipment for the National Library of Peiping. I am sending this receipt to you, as I think you may like to pass it on to your comptroller so that the account may be closed.

I have also ordered a travelling camera and a Stineman reel which are being paid from our own funds.

When the Reader is shipped by the Eastman Kodak Company, I shall not fail to inform you again.

May I take this opportunity of thanking you once more for your assistance. We are sure that the microfilm equipment will promote greatly the intellectual interchange between China and the Western world.

Sincerely yours,

T. L. Yuan

Director

Letter from Eastman Kodak Co. dated December 7, 1949:

"this refers to your letter of November 28 in which you ask us to send you a receipt for your remittance amounting to $697.96. We are enclosing a statement of your account as it stands on our books as of December 1. This shows receipt of your remittance and the fact that it has been placed to the credit of the National Library of Peiping on an account appearing in our L-Misc. Ledger."

〔Rockefeller Foundation. Series 601: China; Subseries 601. R: China-Humanities and Arts. Vol. Box 47. Folder 393〕

按:此件为打字稿,落款处为先生签名。

十二月九日　华盛顿

崔存璘、高宗武夫妇、先生访胡适,后同进晚餐。〔《胡适日记全集》第8册,页448〕

按:崔存璘(1909—1980),浙江鄞县人,沪江大学毕业,获社会学科学士,1929年入国民政府外交部,时应在台湾驻美机构任职。